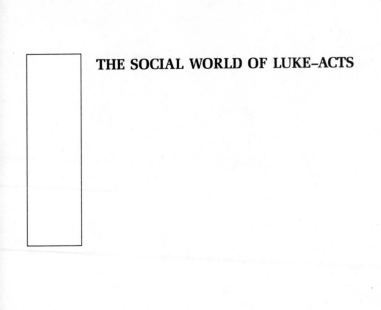

THE SOCIAL WORLD OF LUKE–ACTS

EDITED BY JEROME H. NEYREY

THE

SOCIAL WORLD

OF LUKE–ACTS

MODELS FOR INTERPRETATION

HENDRICKSON PUBLISHERS
PEABODY, MASSACHUSETTS 01961-3473

Copyright © 1991 by Hendrickson Publishers, Inc.
P.O. Box 3473
Peabody, Massachusetts 01961–3473
All rights reserved.
Printed in the United States of America

ISBN 0–943575–48–6

The cover depicts a scene from the frieze of the Dionysiac Mysteries from the Villa of the Mysteries, Pompeii (1st century BC). It appears here courtesy of the Museo Nazionale/National Archaeological Museum in Naples, Italy, and is used with permission.

Library of Congress Cataloging-in-Publication Data

Social world of Luke–Acts: models for interpretation / edited by
    Jerome H. Neyrey
        p. cm.
    Includes bibliographical references and indexes.
    ISBN 0–943575–48–6
    1. Bible. N.T. Luke—Criticism, interpretation, etc. 2. Bible
NT. Acts—Criticism, interpretation, etc. 3. Sociology, Biblical.
4. Ethnology in the Bible. I. Neyrey, Jerome H., 1940–
BS2589.S63 1991
226.4′067—dc20   91-3333
                                                                CIP

TABLE OF CONTENTS

ABBREVIATIONS

ABQ	American Baptist Quarterly
AJS	American Journal of Sociology
ANRW	Aufsteig und Niedergang der Römischen Welt
ARA	Annual Review of Anthropology
ASR	American Sociological Review
ATR	Anglican Theological Review
AUSS	Andrews University Seminary Studies
BJRL	Bulletin of the John Rylands Library
BTB	Biblical Theology Bulletin
CBQ	Catholic Biblical Quarterly
ETL	Ephemerides Theologicae Lovanienses
EvQ	Evangelical Quarterly
EvT	Evangelische Theologie
HR	History of Religion
HTR	Harvard Theological Review
Int	Interpretation
JAAR	Journal of the American Academy of Religion
JBL	Journal of Biblical Literature
JES	Journal of Evangelical Studies
JETS	Journal of the Evangelical Theological Society
JJS	Journal of Jewish Studies
JRelS	Journal of Religious Studies
JRS	Journal of Ritual Studies
JSNT	Journal for the Study of the New Testament
JTS	Journal of Theological Studies

Neot	Neotestamentica
NovT	Novum Testamentum
NRT	Nouvelle Revue Theologique
NTS	New Testament Studies
PRS	Perspective in Religious Studies
RB	Revue Biblique
RelSRev	Religious Studies Review
ResQ	Restoration Quarterly
RevQ	Revue de Qumran
SBLASP	Society of Biblical Literature Abstracts and Seminar Papers
SE	Studia Evangelica
SEA	Svesk Exegetisk Årsbok
SP	Social Problems
TBT	The Bible Today
TDNT	Theological Dictionary of the New Testament
TZ	Theologische Zeitschrift
USQR	Union Seminary Quarterly Review
ZNW	Zeitschrift für die neutestamentliche Wissenschaft

PREFACE

1.0 AUTHORS-COLLABORATORS

In 1986 a group of scholars, who call themselves *The Context Group*, formed a seminar to apply the social sciences for interpretation of biblical texts. Although trained in the contemporary historical-critical method of biblical studies and working with the standard texts, they chose to do something quite different. Far from abandoning the historical-critical method, they enlarged it by calling attention to the use of the social sciences in the task of understanding biblical texts in their full cultural context. This book is the result of that collaboration.

Why this new approach? In the last twenty years we experienced a complexity in the fields of scholarship unforeseen during the years of university training when scholars mastered languages, archeology, texts and the like (see Laszlo 1972; Capra 1983). It seemed that the ideal of scholarship was to learn more and more about less and less. This manner of investigation, which attends to the linear uncovering of the relations between separate facts, has become outmoded with our appreciation of a different dimension, which notes that "wholes" are typical of all groups of interacting parts. Attention must be paid to "wholes" as well as "parts," to "totalities" as well as "facts." Limiting oneself to the atomistic parts of biblical studies leaves the serious reader of the Bible inadequately prepared to deal with more apparent structures, the "wholes," which arise from the interactions of all the parts (see Malina 1981; 1982; 1983; Rohrbaugh 1978; 1987a). Biblical studies requires a restructuring into a larger, more total framework, which is elsewhere called a "systems approach." *The Context Group* was formed to address this need.

In their use of the social sciences for interpretation, the members of this group aimed to produce a comprehensive volume of Luke–Acts studies that might serve as a representative collection of materials and models needed for understanding biblical texts within the cultures of the people who produced them. The members have collectively authored the book and served as its editorial board. Close team work has been the hallmark of the essays by single authors as well as those articles which have been co-authored. The results are individual essays reflecting the many shared conversations that went into the critical review and revision of each draft. As a consequence, this book is not a paste-up of individual essays but a coherent volume born of close collaboration.

2.0 LUKE–ACTS

Luke's two-volume work comprises a third of the New Testament. It ostensibly talks about Jesus and his Palestinian society (the Gospel), as well as about Peter, Paul, and other disciples and their society of Jerusalem, Antioch, Asia Minor, Greece, and Rome (Acts of the Apostles). Furthermore, Luke–Acts itself adopts a perspective on Jesus and the early church explicitly concerned with the social dimensions of the gospel. The scope of Luke's work, both in terms of time periods described and geography covered, offers a complex and diverse world for the investigation of the cultural world of the New Testament. Luke–Acts, moreover, remains a popular text today, one which seems to have particular relevance to our contemporary situation because of, among other things, its concern with rich and poor, roles of women, and inclusiveness of outsiders.

Although the focus in this book is on Luke–Acts, the models and methods presented here can be employed with insight and profit for the interpretation of other New Testament documents. Focussed on Luke–Acts, this volume can serve as a handbook which covers both the interpretation of a specific text and the presentation of an adequately broad historical-critical method of interpretation.

3.0 A DIFFERENT KIND OF BOOK

What is this book? It is not just another collection of exegetical essays on Luke–Acts. Nor is it another attempt at historical reconstruction or social description. The authors aim to discover the meanings implicit in Luke–Acts through attention to the values, social structures and conventions of Luke's society which determine and convey those meanings. Thus *The Social World of Luke–Acts* is a historical-critical reading of a first-century, Mediterranean, biblical document. From start to finish, *The Social World of Luke–Acts* is about the interpretation and meaning of sources from the past. It begins with the assumption that the people of Luke's time, along with their values, attitudes, and behavior, would be extremely strange to modern Western readers (or should be). Because we read Luke's writings in translation, we presume to recognize certain words, such as "mother," "father," "family," and the like. But the meaning of those words in a first-century Mediterranean context is by no means evident. The hands may be the hands of Esau, but the voice is the voice of Jacob—and it should be quite strange to our ears, unless we suffer from anachronism and ethnocentrism.

How do we arrive at such historical-critical understanding and interpretation? First we are required to focus on the particularity of both the people of the past and contemporary readers. For example, a simple awareness of the distance and difference between the people addressed by the text and its modern reader is crucial for any historical-critical interpretation. This involves an awareness of differences in perception, expectation, values, social institutions, and modes of social interaction. We live in two different worlds, as the song goes. The difference is cultural.

How do we begin as modern readers to understand a different cultural world? When we interpret texts, we all work with some model of the way the world works, usually an implicit one drawn from socialization into our own culture. Yet that model, because implicit, is never examined or its adequacy tested. This book is about another set of models, explicit, clear, and tested—scenarios adequate for a different cultural world.

Models make explicit a reader's ways of assessing cultural differences as well as the specific social and cultural properties of Luke's audience. Such explicit awareness of what one is doing in interpretation is the hallmark of the modern historical-critical method. Thus we examine features which include economic relations, basic social patterns such as patron-client relations, institutions, especially the kinship group, first-century personality, peasant society, rituals and ceremonies, conflict, and pivotal values such as honor and shame. We consider these aspects of Luke's society with the aim of understanding how the social dimensions of Luke's texts and context shape the author's perspective, compositional strategy, and message.

For this reason the authors consider this book a type of *handbook*, a desk reference which contains basic social scientific perspectives required by any truly historical-critical method. Hence we chose the models needed for an adequate critical reading of Luke or Paul or any other biblical author. This volume should serve adequately as a basic textbook for historical-critical interpretation of the New Testament and early Christian documents.

4.0 SOCIAL SCIENCES AND HISTORICAL CRITICISM

Historical criticism, the gift of the Enlightenment, has served biblical scholars well as the necessary perspective from which to avoid both allegorical interpretation of the Bible and dogmatic distortion. This volume, while fully "critical," is not limited to historical concerns for presenting biblical meanings of the past as directly relevant for today.

Such historical concerns are usually rooted in a historian's own approach to the sources. Objective history is itself a myth, for the historian's approach is itself controlled by specific questions with a view to locating the information generated by those questions within some theoretical framework of concepts and hypotheses. Our approach seems similar, but in practice differs in two main ways.

> The first is that the historian's conceptualization tends to be implicit, arbitrary, and unsystematic, whereas the social scientist's is explicit and systematic. The second is that the historian's tendency, because his sources usually provide him with some sort of loose narrative pattern to which the facts can be related, is to evade so far as possible the theoretical issues, and also to deal for preference less with the underlying structure than with events and personalities, which are usually far more sharply delineated in historical records than in the materials anthropologists and sociologists commonly use (Barraclough 1978:49–50).

Our concern, then, has been with the examination of the social and cultural patterns and processes, manifest and latent, that were of primary concern to those who first heard the Lukan narrative.

History is about the story line and the sequence of events of the past as relevant to the historian's contemporaries. History is ". . . the study of human societies, with the emphasis on the differences between them and on the changes which have taken place in each over time" (Burke 1980:13). The social sciences, in contrast, look to typical, repeated patterns of social interaction characteristic of a given group of human beings in a specific time and place.

Typical? Particular? The authors of this book are concerned with the historical-critical method of biblical interpretation. Yet, unlike historians, they seek what is *typical* in Luke's society in order to highlight all the better the *particular* and distinctive, for the social sciences focus on general patterns of perception and behavior, not on unique and particular events and persons. Yet without some testable grasp of the general and typical, it is quite impossible to verify whether one's presumed attention to the particular is really about that. As Peter Burke notes, the social sciences are concerned with ". . . the study of human society, with the emphasis on generalizing about its structure" (1980:13).

Hence in their quest for the *particular*, the authors ask about the *typical* institutions of Luke's society: the family, politics, the city, the countryside, patron-client relations, and the health care system. They ask questions from the perspective of social psychology about *typical* viewpoints, values, and behavioral scripts in Luke's society: honor and shame values, conflict, and first-century personality types, etc. They inquire about the prevailing worldview of the people in Luke's historical setting. They examine their births, marriages, coronations, meals, and trials in terms of rituals and ceremonies.

The primary focus here, therefore, is not on the unique, occasional, or particular events in Luke's society, but on common, recurrent patterns of conceptualizing, perceiving, and behaving. Since our task here is one of historical criticism, the common features thus generated will allow the particular to stand out all the more clearly. Our goal, then, is to propose culturally appropriate scenarios for interpreting the Lukan narrative, to see and understand historical particulars within a more encompassing social framework.

5.0 SOCIAL SCIENTIFIC PERSPECTIVE AND LEVELS OF ABSTRACTION

Historical criticism usually examines discrete data, specific actions, times, places, and events. Social scientific criticism looks to the broader, more encompassing social system and the coherence and interrelation of its component parts. This more inclusive perspective, focused on common patterns of perception, organization, and behavior, requires a more comprehensive and therefore higher level of generalization. It necessitates greater abstraction.

This volume pursues such questions as:

— What common values pervade the Mediterranean society of Luke and what characteristic structures result?

— What is the typical economic system in a peasant society? How does it work in general?

— What are the features of patron-client relations, their dynamics?

— What basic institutions organize and regulate social life?

— What is the relationship between city and countryside?

— What characterizes the relation of elites and non-elites in peasant society?

- Who benefits from labelling another person as a deviant, how and why?
- How do ceremonies and rituals of status transformation mark social boundaries and socially situate people?
- What are some of the distinctive features of first-century Mediterranean personality? Of the first-century Mediterranean worldview?
- How are the characteristic aspects of first-century Mediterranean people and their societies reflected implicitly and explicitly in the biblical texts?
- How is Luke–Acts in particular both a reflection of and a reaction to these features of Luke's environment?

The questions are legitimate and urgent. But in asking them, we commit ourselves to working at a higher level of abstraction than is required by contemporary biblical scholarship. Some readers may be uncomfortable with such abstraction, while others may be quite at home with it. This is basically a matter of intellectual aesthetics. Yet it is good for readers to be aware of their biases before they read.

6.0 WHY SUCH A HANDBOOK?

Several years ago *The Ugly American* premiered. Describing the ambassadorial relations of the U.S. with Vietnam, the film made the obvious point that Westerners simply do not understand the countries of the Orient. If such was the case with contemporary U.S. and Oriental cultures, it should be worse with ancient cultures. Readers from the U.S. and other Western cultures generally lack the wide range of adequate scenarios for imagining and understanding the alien culture of a first-century eastern Mediterranean people, most of whom were peasants.

Nurtured on capitalism and individualism, we tend to read our economic conditions and systems back into the society of Jesus and Luke. As individualists, we imagine that the people in Luke and Acts are individualists as well, not group-oriented, dyadic persons. Belonging to nuclear families in which there is increasingly less and less gender differentiation as to status and role, we make a serious mistake when we imagine the family of Luke's society to be like ours or when we neglect to attend to the pervasive gender-based differentiation of roles and status characteristic of that culture. All too often the people in Luke–Acts and their values and behavior are presumed to be the same as that of North Americans and northern Europeans. A conscious attempt to find useful, valid ways of discovering how people in another culture think and act is necessary. The Scylla and Charybdis of biblical scholarship are named anachronism and ethnocentrism. How does one safely avoid these twin dangers?

We need a method for advancing beyond historical eisegesis (ethnocentrism) to historically attuned exegesis informed by social scientific input. A method for understanding the specific meanings imparted by Luke to his first readers requires attention to the social realities shared by the Luke and his fellow Christians. Failure to understand Luke's culture on its own terms imprisons us as "ugly Americans."

7.0 WHAT ARE WE LOOKING AT? THE RIGHT LENSES

It is a commonplace that critical historical reading of the Gospels regularly attends to at least three chronologically successive social settings (*Sitze im Leben*). That is, there are three distinct stages in the history and development of the gospel narratives. First came Jesus himself and his Palestinian society. A second stage involved the early church which remembered his words and interpreted him. Finally, at some time removed from Jesus and his first apostles, the evangelists edited the earlier traditions about Jesus for their later, first-century fellow Christians, producing the Gospels as we now have them. This, of course, is a strictly chronological perspective: it is concerned with proper sequence (Jesus, apostles, evangelists) and with distinctive places (Galilee, Palestine, Syria, Rome, Egypt). Concern for the distinctiveness and particularity bound up with process through time, i.e., with chronology, is characteristic.

While assuming this schema, our concern is not simply with the explicit dimensions of chronology, but equally with the explicit dimensions of meaning that undergird interpretation. We wish to lay bare the matrices of meaning which support our historical-critical conclusions. It will become apparent in the first chapter on reading theory that scholars who use the social sciences do not presume that Western modern readers can easily or accurately understand documents from a foreign culture, much less from a culture two millennia ago. The authors are acutely sensitive to the problems of anachronism and ethnocentrism, or any claim to immaculate perception or "objective study" of historical stones and people and documents.

The authors therefore are aware of the obligation to explain to themselves and their readers the theoretical and methodological lenses through which they are looking as they examine their sources. Hence, each chapter begins with an abstract, general perspective (i.e., a social-science model) appropriate to the subject matter to be investigated. The aim of the model is to explicate at the outset the data to be examined, the set of social properties to be investigated, and the relation of these properties to be analyzed.

With such models, evidence will be gathered, examined, and probed, with a view to the social meaning and significance of the texts under consideration. The models have been derived from anthropologists and sociologists concerned with cross-cultural comparison. Since every historical interpreter approaches the biblical texts with some model of society and social interaction in mind, the advantage of explicitly setting out one's model at the beginning is that it clearly lays bare the presupposed model of social relations and makes it possible for the reader to see how the model organizes and explains the data. This allows for the explicit test of the model in terms of its fit and heuristic power. To proceed otherwise is to proceed with hunches and conclude with guesses. As with a microscope, one needs to know the magnitude of the lens through which one looks. We offer a series of lenses for viewing the cultural world of Luke–Acts.

Within such generalized perspectives, we then consider the specific evidence of Luke–Acts. In most cases, at the end of their respective chapters the authors are careful to set out the meanings conveyed by Luke in terms of the chosen models. This procedure attempts to identify the common perceptions and social patterns that Luke and the Jesus movement groups were seen to reflect or challenge.

8.0 CONTENTS OF THE BOOK

What does one need to know to understand another culture? What areas of social life should one investigate? What points of view should one adopt about self, others, nature, time, space, and the like? A simple answer would be to take the index of chapters from any textbook on cultural anthropology. This list would typically include issues such as self-definition, personality, social institutions, rites and ceremonies, conceptions of sickness and healing, and value dimensions. Inasmuch as we are investigating the Mediterranean society of Luke–Acts, we think it also relevant to examine types of values and social relations characteristic of the Mediterranean region (e.g., honor/shame; patron-client relationships). Furthermore, Luke–Acts invites the reader to examine what a "city" means in that ancient culture, and what "the countryside" involves; these entail economic, political, religious, and other issues.

This social-science approach takes into consideration several of the typical topics and issues found in any basic textbook on sociology and anthropology. The book has three parts: (a) basic societal institutions, (b) social psychology, and (c) mediations of culture.

Institutions. All societies have institutions, i.e., fixed forms of social life. In the society of Luke–Acts, two institutions dominated, the family and politics. Elliott's essay will compare and contrast both. Luke's society was made up of "cities" and countryside. The essays of Rohrbaugh and Oakman examine each respectively. Of great concern in Luke's society were issues of illness and healing, and so Pilch's essay focuses on the health care system and its cultural implications. Finally, since at this time the dominant form of social interaction in the spheres of both kinship and politics was patronage and clientelism, Moxnes' essay addresses these dimensions of social relations.

Social Psychology. From the perspective of social psychology, Malina and Neyrey examine the pivotal value in Luke's culture, the assessment and perception of persons and life in terms of honor and shame. In keeping with this, these authors show how first-century personality types differ from modern, individualistically centered personality. Finally, given the intensely agonistic nature of Luke's society, we must attend to conflict and so to the pervasive way people interact with and label each other in the endless challenges which make up that agonistic society.

Value Clusters. A third group of essays deal with specific forms of behavior that mediate values and worldviews in a highly intensive and focused form. The essays by Neyrey and McVann in this volume look to questions dealing with shared perceptions of the way the society works and of its symbolic universe. Likewise, the values and patterns of Luke's social system are expressed constantly in the many rituals and ceremonies which structure the lives of people, namely, their births, rites of passage, marriages, meals, baptisms, trials, and burials.

9.0 HOW TO READ THIS BOOK

The authors consider it essential that a reader begin with chapter 1, the reading theory on which the whole enterprise rests. Then, the sequence is a matter of preference and interest. The chapters dealing with social psychology were purposely placed early in the book because they are distinctly Western and American concerns, and might serve as a useful entry into the use of social science models for biblical interpretation. Next, the chapters on the institutions of Luke's society provide the reader with information about the social structure and dynamic of Luke's society as well as their symbolic representation. Finally, the reader will find materials which deal with the social behaviors that mediate the basic meanings of Luke's society in symbolic form, that is, its rituals and ceremonies.

The book is equipped with an index of biblical passages as well as with an index of topics and authors. It may be that readers will use these tools for ready access to a complete reading of a specific passage from a variety of perspectives. Such a project would be profitable, for it will give readers a sense of the manner in which the various essays and their specific foci provide a coherent and complementary understanding of common text-segments or issues.

10.0 THE BENEFITS

What advantages are to be gained? First of all, a reader will have a repertoire of scenarios necessary for reading Luke on his own cultural terms. Such readers will truly be able to eavesdrop on Luke and his exotic and foreign society, and to do so with greater accuracy. They will be aided in becoming culturally respectful and perceptive visitors to foreign terrain, not "ugly Americans." The conceptual models employed here encourage the reader to test them personally on his/her own, to "go and do likewise" with other biblical texts. With the models and perspectives of this book a reader will be well equipped to read other New Testament texts and classical documents from the ancient Mediterranean society. By sensitizing themselves to another culture and its social structures, careful readers inevitably learn more about their own society by way of contrast (see Malina and Neyrey 1988:145–51).

This book, moreover, provides a limited introduction to some of the basic issues in cultural anthropology, with bibliography for further reading. Since theology, whether biblical or modern, depends upon analogies that are quite culturally specific, this book will enable the reader concerned with theology to appreciate the theological dimensions in Luke–Acts articulated by Luke with analogies drawn from his social experience.

Jerome H. Neyrey
May 3, 1990

SOCIAL PSYCHOLOGY

1

READING THEORY PERSPECTIVE: READING LUKE–ACTS

Bruce J. Malina

1.0 INTRODUCTION

Suppose for a moment that you are an American visitor to Jerusalem in the Roman Palestine of the mid first-century CE. It is morning during the dry season. The Mediterranean sun shines brightly. You decide it is a good day to go to Gaza to see what is new by way of caravan imports from Egypt. So early in the morning, with sea breezes still cool in the hills, you begin the seaward walk down from Jerusalem on the Gaza–Jerusalem road. Not too far in front of you, you see a person walking, going in the same direction you are. Suddenly you hear a man's voice coming from over a rise in the road. That voice says something that sounds as follows:

נִגַּשׂ וְהוּא נַעֲנֶה וְלֹא יִפְתַּח־פִּיו כַּשֶּׂה לַטֶּבַח יוּבָל

וּכְרָחֵל לִפְנֵי גֹזְזֶיהָ נֶאֱלָמָה וְלֹא יִפְתַּח פִּיו: מֵעֹצֶר וּמִמִּשְׁפָּט לֻקָּח

וְאֶת־דּוֹרוֹ מִי יְשׂוֹחֵחַ כִּי נִגְזַר מֵאֶרֶץ חַיִּים

Obviously what you have just heard are not the squiggles you see written here. Rather what you have heard were sounds, strange sounds, sounds as strange as the squiggles. You notice now that the man in front of you also stops. You go up to him and ask: "What did that mean?" He shrugs his shoulders in response. Obviously he does not understand

English. So you open your arms, shrug your shoulders and throw your head back slightly in that Mediterranean gesture that means: "What is going on, then?" Light dawns in his eyes and he proceeds to tell you:

ὡς πρόβατον ἐπὶ σφαγὴν ἤχθη, καὶ ὡς ἀμνὸς ἐναντίον τοῦ κείραντος αὐτὸν ἄφωνος, οὕτως οὐκ ἀνοίγει τὸ στόμα αὐτοῦ. Ἐν τῇ ταπεινώσει αὐτοῦ ἡ κρίσις αὐτοῦ ἤρθη· τὴν γενεὰν αὐτοῦ τίς διηγήσεται ὅτι αἴρεται ἀπὸ τῆς γῆς ἡ ζωὴ αὐτοῦ.

Again, you get a downpour of strange sounds, indicated here by the strange squiggles used to write down those sounds. By now, you figure out that what the man is telling you in his strange sounds is his version of the sounds you both heard.

It should occur to you by now that you are a foreigner in a foreign land where even a familiar thing like conversing with someone in English is equally alien. Now what would you need to understand your friendly fellow traveller? How would you get to understand his strange sounds? It is probably not unlike the way you would get to understand a contemporary foreigner who does not know English, yet with whom you wish to communicate. Furthermore, I suggest that trying to understand a writing like Luke–Acts involves the same procedure as attempting to understand foreigners speaking to you in their own language. Only in the case of Luke–Acts, as with the example above, you are the foreigner, for, any historically sensitive reading of the New Testament necessarily puts the reader in the role of a stranger in that extremely curious land of the first-century eastern Mediterranean.

The authors of the biblical writings as well as the persons they portray in them all come from this region. They wrote their books in those strange squiggles we call the Hebrew and Greek alphabets. And these strange squiggles all stand for extremely unfamiliar patterns of sounds quite alien to most U.S. ears. How would one get to understand such strange sounds and read the alphabets that represent those sounds? Would it help to transcribe your informant's sounds into our own alphabet?

hōs probaton epi sphagēn ēchthē, kai hōs amnos enantion tou keirantos auton aphōnos, outos ouk anoigei to stoma autou. En tē tapeinōsei autou ē krisis autou ērthē; tēn genean autou tis diēgēsetai hoti airetai apo tēs gēs ē zōē autou.

Even in our own alphabet, not much looks familiar. Does the statement sound any more familiar if you try to read it? Moreover, would a translation of the Greek give you the meaning of what your fellow traveller intended to tell you?

As a sheep led to the slaughter or a lamb before its shearer is dumb, so he opens not his mouth. In his humiliation justice was denied him. Who can describe his generation? For his life is taken up from the earth.

Does this translation tell you what the statement means? If you looked in a biblical concordance, you would find that this passage is from Acts 8:32–33 and is a quote from a Greek translation of Isa 53:7–8. Does that help you now understand what is going on?

If you read the passage in Acts 8, you will find out that the one whose voice you initially heard was a black man, probably a Jew on a pilgrimage to Jerusalem. He is described as a eunuch from the court of Queen Candace in Ethiopia. You will likewise discover that the person from whom you inquired about what was being said was a follower of Jesus of Nazareth named Philip. His Greek name might tell you why he preferred to talk to you in Greek. In Acts, Philip is described as a "deacon." Now that you know his name and social role, and have some minimal information about the words you heard and basic geographical and chronological orientation, can you interpret the passage translated above?

If other people knew only your name, social role, some of your statements, and geographical and chronological information about you, would they now really understand you? If they had some minimal information about an esoteric book you might be reading, would that enable them to understand that book and why you are reading it? What more would they have to know? Would a story of your family history suffice? A story of your life?

Notice that these questions cover the who, what, when, where, and how of the situation. They have not raised the why question, the question of meaning. Why read a passage from Isaiah on the road? Why the need for a Greek translation? Why the social role of Ethiopian official, why the subsequent behavior of Philip? And if we stick to the passage itself, why the mention of lamb and sheep? Why humiliation? And in a Christian writing like Acts, why this passage from the Israelite religious tradition in Isaiah? The answer to all these questions requires historical information of the who, what, when, and where sort. But to find out the why—what it means in the lives of people—requires information from the social system of the time and place of the original audience.

To read Luke–Acts as we propose to do in this book requires familiarity with the social system presupposed by and conveyed through the language patterns of ancient Greek, since Luke–Acts was orginally written in Greek. As we shall have occasion to indicate, the meanings people share are rooted in and derive from a social system. Social system refers to the general ways in which a society provides its members with a socially meaningful way of living. The social system includes: (1) culture, i.e., the accepted ways of interpreting the world and everything in it; (2) social structures, e.g., the accepted ways of marrying, having children, working, governing, worshipping, and understanding God; and the accepted ways of being a person (including self-understanding). People use language to have an effect on others in terms of the meanings of the social system. And people learn those meanings along with the language of their society in the process of growing up.

Incidentally, why do we presume that the strange alphabet of the Greek New Testament can be understood at all? It seems that as a rule human beings continually find patterns everywhere they look, and they invariably find some meaning in those patterns. In the above example, the voice you heard clearly sounded as though it followed some pattern of cadence and articulation. It was not a scream, shriek, moan, groan, or any other sort of unpatterned sound. If it sounded patterned it must be communicating meaning. Or so one would logically conclude. The response to your quizzical gesture produced another shower of sound that surely sounded patterned with cadence and articulation. Again, it seemed clear the man was saying something intelligible. His utterance sounded like it should be conveying meaning because it clearly was patterned (Johnson 1978:3-7).

The case with *squiggles* on a page is quite similar. Look at the Hebrew and Greek passages printed above. While not English, they are surely not the chaotic doodlings of a two-year old claiming to write something. They seem to be patterned and to follow a definite sequencing. The presumption most humans share about patterned soundings and squiggles is that they convey meaning in some way. They are intended to communicate something to another human being. How? Reading is learning how to see patterns in the squiggles. Such patterns are called *wordings*. The wordings, in turn, reveal *meanings*, but only if we share the same social system as the persons who initially wrote the squiggles.

A translation of Luke that simply says his words in terms of our words hardly mediates the *meaning* of the Greek text, the meaning of the Luke and his audience. The reason for this is that *meaning* is not in the *wordings*. Rather *meaning* resides in the social system of individuals that is held together by a shared culture, shared values, and shared meanings along with social institutions and social roles to realize those values and meanings. For example, take a basic New Testament Aramaic word such as *abba* (translated into Greek as *patēr*, and into English as *father*). Would the English "father" fill you with the meanings that a first-century Palestinian Jewish native speaker thought and felt with this word? Frankly, no! Again, I suggest that for a native English speaker who has never lived in a Jewish, Aramaic-speaking community, the word "abba" always means the very same thing as the English "father," since it invariably refers to the roles, behaviors, and meanings ascribed to U.S. fathers. The only way to get "father" to mean what a Jewish, Aramaic speaker like Jesus might have meant by "abba" is to get to know the social system within which the role of "abba" worked (see Elliott 1981:174-80; Malina 1988a; Barr 1988). We insist: *what people say or write conveys and imparts meanings rooted in some so-*

cial system. The purpose of this essay is to explain why this is the case and what that might mean for our understanding of that human skill called reading.

Literate people often take the process of reading for granted. Not a few readers innocent of what the reading process entails share the myth of the "immaculate perception." Because writing is presumed to be an object "out there," it can be observed and handled like other objects, such as rocks or trees. Such a presumption disregards the reality that makes communication with language possible at all, that is, the social system shared by readers and their social groups as well as writers and their social groups.

Put simply, the *squiggles* on the page (regardless of alphabet) have to be deciphered somehow into articulate and distinct patterns by a reader to gain access to the *meanings* communicated by the author of the squiggles. If both reader and writer share the same social system, communication is highly probable. But if either reader or writer come from mutually alien social systems, then non-understanding is the rule, as in the case above where you, the reader, are the stranger in a strange land. Should a translation of the wording (words and sentences) be offered, apart from a comparative explanation of the social systems involved, misunderstanding inevitably follows. In other words, should there be a person available to turn the squiggles into sounds, these sounds too need to be decoded by a hearer to gain access to the sender's meanings — again, provided both share the same social system. This description of hearing and reading a text might sound verbose; however, it is necessary both to dispel the naive objectivism of the "Take up and read!" variety and to facilitate considered analysis.

Reading theory contests two common assumptions among non-critical readers. First, readers of the Bible, professional and non-professional, assume that the categories of their elementary school grammar refer to concrete realities. Letters and words and sentences of spoken language are presumed to be concrete, meaning-bearing, linguistic entities. These concrete words and sentences are presumed to have meanings that are directly accessible to people by the simple process of learning to look at them.

But this is not the case with language. Is not language a flow of patterned soundings articulating wordings and expressing meanings? Are not words and sentences in fact abstractions and ideas treated as concrete things? The sociolinguist Fishman notes that such categories were created by ancient and modern grammarians and lexicographers to facilitate their logical analyses of human thinking (Fishman 1971:91–105). People do not utter *words*; rather, they utter a whole tissue of patterned, articulate, and cadenced sounds which the literate grammarian breaks into smaller repeatable pieces.

Second, the locus of meaning should not be assumed to lie in language systems as such. It is popularly assumed that "biblical thought" is different from our own because of the nature of the languages of the Bible. This is the much quoted Whorfian hypothesis applied to the Bible. It argues that cultural differences including ways of reasoning, perceiving, learning, distinguishing, remembering and the like are directly relatable to the structured differences between languages themselves. But Fishman notes: "Intriguing though this claim may be it is necessary to admit that many years of intensive research have not succeeded in demonstrating it to be tenable" (1971:92). As reading theory indicates, it is not to the structured differences between languages that we have to look, but to the social systems of different peoples.

2.0 READING

Every theory of reading presupposes a set of assumptions concerning the nature of language and the nature of text. How does language work? How does text work? And how does reading work? It is quite apparent that written language does not live in scrolls or books. The markings on a page stand for wordings that represent meanings that can come alive only through the agency of the minds of readers. Before setting out a model of describing what happens when a person reads, I shall begin by setting out some assumptions about language and text.

2.1 On Language

One explanation of the nature of language is rooted in the presupposition that human beings are essentially social beings. Everything anybody does has social motivation and social meaning. From this point of view, the chief purpose of language is to convey meaning to another, and the purpose of this meaning is to have some effect on another. This perspective is often called sociolinguistics.

The approach to sociolinguistics adopted here derives from Michael A.K. Halliday (Halliday 1978; see Cicourel 1985). In this perspective, language is a three–tiered affair consisting of (1) soundings/spellings that (2) realize wordings that (3) realize meanings. And where do the meanings realized in language come from? Given the experience of human beings as essentially social beings, those meanings come from and constitute the social system. This three–tiered model of language would have the Bible reader ask: What social system or social meaning is being expressed in the wordings realized in the spellings of biblical texts?

Everyone who can read the Bible has a rather full understanding of how "the world" works. "The world," however, that we understand so well is the particular world into which the we have been socialized and enculturated. For us this is a twentieth-century, U.S. understanding of how the world and everything and everybody in it works. Without further suspicion and awareness, the untutored reader will necessarily perceive "the world" of Luke (i.e., his social system) as if it were his or her own social system. We call this misreading ethnocentrism, that is, imagining that all people everywhere and at all times think just like I do.

The point is all the more obvious at the level of *words*. As noted previously, words are artificial, arbitrary creations of grammarians cut out of wordings that realize meanings. These words are then said to convey meaning, and this they do as labels, marking off objects of social interest. Yet even in this case, the meanings attached to the labels derive from a social system. Consider the following Greek words written in our equivalent alphabet: Christ, baptism, charism, apocalypse, blasphemy, and chrism. Does writing those words in our alphabet make them any more understandable or meaningful? Take note that for us "Christ" is Jesus of Nazareth's last name; "baptism" is an initiation rite in Christian churches; "charism" is what pop-stars and politicians have when we really like them; "apocalypse" is a story or vision of the end of the world; "blasphemy" is filthy words directed to God; and "chrism" is holy oil used by the Orthodox, Anglo, and Roman Catholic churches. None of these meanings were attached to these words as early Christians used them. Rather, for early Christians "Christ" is a Greek translation of the Jewish social role termed "Messiah" in Hebrew. The word simply cannot be translated adequately since that social role and its job description are unique to ancient Israelite religion. Similarly, "baptism" refers to dipping in a liquid, much as John the Dipper did to people who came to him at the Jordan in the first century; the dipping symbolized a change of one's way of thinking and feeling about life in general and people in particular. "Charism" is the outcome of patronage, what one receives from a patron in the patron-client relationships typical of the Mediterranean. "Apocalypse" means revelation, making known something that was previously not known; "blasphemy" means dishonoring a person by words; and "chrism" means olive oil used for a variety of rubdowns.

Without an awareness of other social forms, other cultures, and other times and places, a person cannot but presume everyone is human in the same way he or she has been taught to be human. So when readers find their Gospel translation telling them what Jesus says about marriage and divorce, the reader will obviously apply those statements to marriage and divorce as the reader experiences them. The same holds true for Jesus' statements about taxes, forgiveness, God as Father, the family, one's "brothers," enemies, and the like. Thus to be fair to the biblical authors and the persons they refer to, one must make some effort to learn about their culture and the social forms realized through their language.

2.2 What Is a Text?

If biblical readers read biblical texts, what in fact is "a text"? What does it mean to interpret a text? Once again, we have the untutored intuition that a text is anything written down. More often than not, a biblical text is a sentence written in the Bible and cited from there. Some people even call such a piece of written wording a "scripture" or a "scriptural text." How such a piece of written wording quoted apart from the rest of the text to which it belongs (its co-text, i.e., accompanying text) is to convey meaning at all is a question most often not considered. But this is crucial since from the perspective of the way people communicate, *a sentence is not a text*. A sentence is simply a sentence. As we all have memorized in elementary school, a sentence is a group of words that expresses a complete thought. In sociolinguistics, however, a text is a "meaningful configuration of language intended to communicate" (De Beaugrande 1980:1).

Just as a sentence is the unit of wording that expresses thought in language, so a "text" is the unit of articulated meaning in language. And since humans use language to convey meaning, "text" is the normal mode of imparting meaning. If interpretation is the process of discerning meaning, then "text" would be the unit of interpretation.

At the same time, texts are formed for the most part by pasting together complete thoughts set forth in the wordings marked off by grammarians as sentences. As a rule it often takes a lengthy set of sentences to realize a simple meaning. As an extreme case, take a philosophical work in several volumes dealing with the meaning of "being" or "time," or any other simple metaphysical idea. To express such meaning may take thousands of sentences.

In this book, Luke–Acts is our "text," our unit of meaning to be interpreted. At times we quote sentences to encapsulate thoughts or ideas. But such sentences are not "texts." Sentences are distinctive in that they can be understood. But texts are distinctive in that they can be interpreted. Very often sentences are well understood, but simply cannot be interpreted. For example, "He does so and continues to do so." The essays presented here are intended not simply to convey some minimal understanding, but to allow for interpretation, for all the contributing authors are quite aware of the need to interpret Luke–Acts. Such a felt need to interpret a text indicates that *some information necessary for a full understanding is lacking*. The interpreter provides this information so that the person or thing being interpreted can be readily and rather fully understood. For adequate communication to take place, then, text needs "context" (literally: *with* + *text*) consisting of the social system within which the linguistic communication originally took place.

2.3 Elements of Reading

Admittedly the foregoing material might seem obscure and esoteric. So it is useful here to summarize the three basic points concerning language, reading and texts.

(1) Language = *squiggles — wordings — meanings*. Obviously, our focus must be on *meaning*, which derives from the social system.

(2) Reading = understanding *squiggles* (*wordings* + *meanings*). Again, we attend to the meaning aspect of language, which can only be known when the social system of the communicator is known.

(3) Text = *unit of meaning*, which needs *interpretation*. Unlike sentences, which are units of wordings, texts refer to the larger unit, such as Luke–Acts; whereas sentences can be understood at some level, texts need interpretation.

To interpret the originally intended meanings in Luke–Acts, the contemporary reader must have access to the social systems of the original audience of those texts. To recover those social systems, we believe it essential to employ adequate, explicit social science models (for classical antiquity, see Carney 1975; Malina 1981). What is lacking for an historical interpretation of the meaning of ancient texts is information about the meanings familiar to the original audience of those texts. But what sort of information? In what form? To clarify this contention, we now turn to reading theory.

2.4 Dimensions of Reading

It is a truism in our society that human beings are simultaneously both individual and social beings. People, therefore, reveal both intrapersonal (individual) as well as interpersonal (social) dimensions in all of their activities. Reading is no exception. It is quite possible that the range of meanings which derive from the reading of a common text derive from individual differences in the reader's knowledge and skills. Readers, however, rarely, if ever, read alone even when they alone read. For example, Harste, Burke, and Woodward (1982) argue that reading is a "socio-psycholinguistic process." The psycholinguistic dimension of the process is the individual, psychological aspect rooted in the way individuals, given their individual, psychological stage of development, perform the activity of reading. The sociolinguistic dimension looks to the group and to the social system to which it belongs. The experts offer the following explanation of these dimensions (emphasis in the original):

> In considering a given text, the *language setting*, which includes where the language is found (home, school, store), in what culture (United States,

Israel, Saudi Arabia), and for and by whom it was produced (peer, superior, subordinate), modifies the *mental setting* in terms of what schema the reader accesses. The accessed schemata direct strategy utilization and, hence, sampling of language setting (Harste, Burke, and Woodward 1982:108).

The language setting and the available strategies of utilization are typically social and best analyzed by *sociolinguistics*. An individual's mental setting is psychological, however, and is best analyzed by *psycholinguistics*. But both dimensions are involved in the process of reading.

The language setting is interpersonal context, while the mental setting is intrapersonal context. Bloome and Green (1984:413–414), for example, suggest that the individual's background knowledge, skills, and general approach to reading can be viewed as the *intrapersonal* context of reading. The intrapersonal context involves an individual's available collection of scenarios or schemes of how the world works, the level of abstraction the individual can master, and his/her usual cognitive style. The intrapersonal is best studied by the methods of experimental psychology and best described in terms of psychological models. Psychological development, however, is always rooted in some primary group, hence in the social dimensions of human being. And this is where the interpersonal context enters the discussion.

The *interpersonal* dimensions of reading involve the language setting within a social system as well as how reading events are organized within a society: how do participants interact? what motivates them to read? what influence do they bring to bear on the reading process and the way the reading process influences their interactions? We shall consider the interpersonal dimensions of reading later.

We can summarize the preceding material conveniently in the following diagram:

DIMENSIONS OF READING Figure 1-1			
(1) Human being	individual	&	social
(2) Reading dimension	*intra*personal	&	*inter*personal
(3) Reading strategy	*psycho*linguistics	&	*socio*linguistics
(4) Reading setting	mental setting	&	language setting

3.0 INTRAPERSONAL DIMENSION: MODELS OF READING

It bears repeating that biblical interpretation is ultimately rooted in the reading of ancient written texts. Since biblical study focuses on texts and entails reading and interpreting texts, we must have some verifiable theory of how reading takes place. This point has been basically overlooked by studies of exegetical method. How does a reader get to understand the meanings through the wordings in the writings? The professional study of the Bible often involves learning about ancient writing systems (orthography) and mastering equally ancient wording systems (lexico-grammar). The outcome of such study set down in dictionaries and grammars has afforded many interesting data.

It is one thing, however, to collect data, and quite another to interpret those data. Are dictionary definitions and grammatical generalizations trustworthy? How can one verify them? Again, we come back to the reading process. Here I will focus upon the meanings that get imparted in the process of reading. While contemporary experimental psychology affords a number of models for understanding the activity of reading, two major models of reading comprehension are currently in vogue.

3.1 Model One: The Propositional Model

I call the first model the *propositional model*. It considers the text as a sort of supersentence. Perhaps this perspective derives from the way we have been taught languages, with the classroom focus on wording, that is, sentence and word level. According to this model, the text evokes mental representations for the reader; these representations consist of a chain or series of propositions which derive directly from the sentences that constitute the text. The text is made up of sentences, which in turn are made up of words. A sort of initial proof of this fact is that we can and often do outline what we read. This outline, when adequate, brings out the chain of propositions latent in the text.

Readers then basically perform two tasks. They parse the text into propositional units and then connect the resulting propositions in some way. This connection is accomplished by means of a superstructure that emerges from the process of outlining. Scholars who adopt this model often call this superstructure a deep structure, story grammar, narrative grammar, or something of the sort. As many will recognize from their "lit" courses, this sort of model undergirds contemporary structural, semiotic, deconstructionist, "Marxist," and aesthetic literary criticism. Such criticism forms the foundation of the biblical exegesis based on these types of criticism (see e.g., Detweiler 1985; Malina 1986a; Moore 1988). They are all rooted in a propositional model of reading.

The drawback to this model is that it cannot be verified experimentally as taking place when a person reads. Nearly all exegetes using such an approach totally disregard research into reading in terms of experimental and social psychology. Yet the psychological research available indicates that the propositional model is far off target since its description of reading is not what goes on in the mind of a reader at all (see Sanford and Garrod 1982, on whom this discussion rests).

This does not mean, however, that texts cannot be parsed in terms of their overall structures (for a full survey of such techniques, see Meyer and Rice 1984:319–51). Indeed, structural exegesis has been done on a number of texts. The question, however, is whether this analysis gets to the *meanings* encoded in the *wordings* expressed in the *squiggles* which one learns to sound out in reading. If the structures mediating meaning are rooted in and derive from the social system in which communication (originally) takes place, propositional models miss the mark. They are rooted in the wording aspect of the text, not its meaning. As such they allow for judgments of aesthetics, of niceness or prettiness in speech. They can also serve as a springboard for ideas derived from a sort of associational flow of ideas. Applied to reading, propositional models of reading comprehension imply a conceptual approach to texts.

Among non-linguists, the validity of propositional models seems to derive from the fact that literate people can and do take notes on what they read. They can outline paragraphs and chapters. Obviously, since the notes are presumed to derive directly from the text, the text must consist of propositional concepts which I, the literate reader, extract as I read. Among linguists, however, these models seem to be rooted in presuppositions about the nature and function of language that derive from treating highly abstract entities like words and sentences as though they were objective things.

But words and sentences are not the end products of language. On the contrary, the end products of language are spoken and/or written texts, that is, meaningful configurations of language intended to communicate. And what texts invariably communicate is information from a social system within specific contexts. But, for not a few exegetes, such models seem to be rooted in the theological enterprise, often articulated in terms of propositions that form a theological system, a set of truths. These theological propositions are actually abstracts or summaries of larger, engrossing stories that form the basic stuff of religion (Barr 1987). And what religious texts, as a rule, set forth are those larger, comprehensive stories. If then a text does not present a chain or series of propositions, what does it evoke in the mind of a reader?

3.2 Model Two: The Scenario Model

A second model of reading comprehension might be called a *scenario model*. By way of contrast, if the *propositional model* attended the *wordings*, then the *scenario model* focuses on *meaning*. Some synonyms for the term "scenario" here include schema, frames, scenes, scripts, gestalts, active structural networks, and memory organization packets (Casson 1983:429). This model considers the text as setting forth a succession of explicit and implicit mental representations of scenes or schemes. These, in turn, evoke corresponding scenes or schemes in the mind of the reader. Such scenes or schemes are composed of a series of settings, episodes, or models. These latter derive directly from the mind of the reader, who carries out appropriate alterations to the settings, episodes, or models as directed by the text.

As in the previous explanation, here too the reader must perform two tasks: (1) call to mind some appropriate scene, scheme, or model as suggested by the text; and (2) then use the identified scene, scheme or model as the larger frame within which to situate the meanings proposed in the text as far as this is possible. In other words, the reader uses the text to identify an appropriate domain or frame of reference and then rearranges that domain according to the arrangements suggested in the text.

Unlike the propositional model, the scenario model of reading does have some validation from contemporary experimental psychology. Meyer and Rice (1984:327) remark that even the structural linguist van Dijk (1977)

> suggests appealing to the content of the topic of discourse, as organized in a "frame," to describe certain macrostructural attributes. For example, a text about a war will derive some of its organization from a war "frame," in which is represented component states and the necessary or probable conditions and consequences of wars in general.

Such frames are the scenarios, scenes, schemata, and the like which the writer evokes in the writing and which the reader brings to the reading.

This model of reading *squiggles* which encode *wordings* which realize *meaning* from a social system is not very different from the social psychology model of how human beings "read" situations. All human beings carry on an interpretative enterprise. As a rule, people carry in their heads one or more models of "society" and "human being" which greatly influence what they look for in their experiences, what they actually see, and what they eventually do with their observations by way of fitting them along with other facts into a larger scheme of explanation. In this respect, every human being, tutored or not, is no different from any trained observer in our society (Garfinkel 1967:262–83). For example, every scientist, like every other human being, holds some general conception of the realm in which he or she is working, that is, some mental picture of how it is put together, how it works, and how one ought to feel about it. Of course, the same is true of the biblical interpreter, professional and non-professional.

The scenario model of reading presupposes that every reader has a full and verifiable grasp of how the world works. As readers, people bring this awareness to a text. In the linguistic interchange that is reading, an author is allowed to present a distinctive set of scenarios of the working world that suggest and motivate readers to rearrange the scenarios which they bring to the reading. Effective communication depends upon the considerateness of the writer or speaker. Considerate authors attempt to understand their readers; they will take up and elaborate the scenarios shared by their readers. And more than this, considerate authors will always strive to develop their scenarios by beginning with what the reader knows and coupling to that the new, unknown features they wish to impart to readers and hearers. Meyer and Rice note:

> Haviland and Clark (1974) have suggested that both the writer and the reader participate in a "given-new contract." Under the contract, the writer is constrained to be relevant (i.e., not confuse the reader with extraneous information), to cooperate, and to consider what the reader knows or doesn't know. Thus the writer constructs his/her sentences so that the "given" or antecedent information (what the reader is expected to know) and the "new" information (what the author is adding to this knowledge) are clearly differentiated . . . Research has shown that readers' comprehension is impaired when this contract is violated by putting "new" information into the topic or "given" position in a sentence (1984:326).

According to these standards the author of Luke–Acts and biblical authors in general "violate the contract" and are all inconsiderate, for they neither begin with what we know about the world nor make any attempt to explain their ancient world in terms of scenarios that contemporary American readers might understand. The author of Luke–Acts presumes we are first-century eastern Mediterraneans, sharing a social system poised on honor and shame, fully aware of what it means to live a city and/or village life, totally immersed in a sick care system concerned with the well being of unfortunates, and believing in limited good assuaged by patrons and brokers. Given that Luke–Acts is a first-century work rooted in a specific time and place, it would be rather silly to expect its author to envision readers thousands of years removed.

Hence if we seek to be fair to biblical authors, we must endeavor to be considerate readers. Considerate readers of documents from the past will obviously make the effort to bring to their reading a set of scenarios proper to the time, place, and culture of the biblical author.

Granted the need to be a considerate reader, the contemporary student of the Luke–Acts will have to learn a set of scenarios comprised of scenes, schemes, or models of varying abstraction that are typical of the first-century eastern Mediterranean. In our own society, the scholarly articulation of such scenes, schemes and models has generally been the métier of social scientists. For this reason, it would seem that the social science approach to biblical interpretation is best suited to the task of reading the biblical books with a view to understanding the meanings communicated by their authors. This scenario model of reading might be called the social context approach.

In summary, of the two models of reading discussed, only the scenario model has any empirical evidence to support it. It attends to meanings, not just wordings. Consequently, only the scenario model can avoid problems of an ethnocentric or inconsiderate reading of texts. It alone fully takes into account the social dimensions of reading: the interpersonal dimension, whose strategy is explained by sociolinguistics.

3.3 Reading and the Interpreter

If the scenario model sketched out above is indeed the way readers comprehend, it would seem that the best contemporary biblical scholars can offer their clientele is a set of scenarios, scenes, models, frames, and domains of reference deriving from and appropriate to the first-century eastern Mediterranean world. All interpretation, it would seem, requires and ultimately rests on such models (see Malina 1982:229–31). Reading and language theory, then, indicate that in this book we concern ourselves with understanding the social system of those who evaluated Jesus, and so come to a set of scenarios adequate for interpreting and understanding Luke–Acts.

4.0 INTERPERSONAL DIMENSIONS

As we noted, psychological perspectives of reading are primarily concerned with the individual reader and how that reader establishes a meaning for a text (i.e., the *intra*personal dimension). Yet readers rarely, if ever, read alone, for reading is anchored in the social or *inter*personal world of the reader and writer. A consideration of reading and social setting will underscore this point.

4.1. Reading and Social Setting

The interpersonal dimension of reading looks to how reading events are organized within a society. It entails understanding the general social system and specific aspects of reading, such as how participants interact, their influence on the reading process, and the way the reading process influences their interactions. How do people use reading to establish a social context? How does the social context then influence reading and the communication of meaning (Bloome and Green 1984:396)?

In Luke–Acts, the initial reading event describes a synagogue reading of Isaiah. "Jesus stood up to read; and there was given to him the book of the prophet Isaiah. He opened the book and found the place where it was written: 'The Spirit of the Lord is upon me . . .'" (Luke 4:16–18). What interpersonal dimensions are involved in this reading event? What information would an interpreter need to understand it? How does such biblical reading establish a social context in the synagogue? And how does the context, the gathering of Galilean Israelites in this case, influence reading and the meanings communicated? Did it matter that many of the people there were illiterate? that they did not understand Hebrew?

Clearly one must know the general cultural and historical features of Luke's world. This includes: (1) the values and structures of the first-century eastern Mediterranean and the Palestinian Jewish context; (2) the common lack of historical sense among the people of the period; (3) the roles of various professional Bible interpreters, that is, the Scribes; (4) their modes of interaction; and (5) the methods of interpreting the texts of the Bible based upon their contemporary needs. In sum, one needs to know the range of scenarios for social interaction actually available in first-century eastern Mediterranean in general and in the area of Bible reading in Jewish Palestine in particular. This is the interpersonal context of reading, and it is the primary concern in sociolinguistic perspectives of reading.

Relative to biblical interpretation, the question here is:

WHO says WHAT to WHOM about WHAT,

in WHAT setting, and for WHAT purpose?

Setting and purpose as well as the persons who interact are determined largely by institutional arrangements, e.g., synagogue, public challenge based on citing the Bible, temple, and public or private teaching. How reading takes place in these environments is determined by the environmental settings which replicate institutional pressures. For example, in synagogue preaching the biblical passage will be explained in terms of contemporary occurrence, while in debate the passage will be used to dishonor opponents; in temple discussions the readings might look to legal precedent.

The situation of biblical interpretation in the U.S., while quite similar in terms of questions to be asked, is quite different in terms of presuppositions to be posited. For Americans reading the Bible, the interpersonal dimension involves general cultural and historical features such as the values and structures of a 1991 United States. This includes the sense of history shared by high school graduates, the various groups of professional Bible interpreters and their modes of interaction, and the methods of interpreting the texts of the Bible based upon previous questions about what to look for. In sum this comprises the range of scenarios for social interaction actually available in the U.S. in general and in the area of Bible reading in particular.

Relative to biblical interpretation, the question still is, who says what to whom about what in what setting for what purpose. Setting, purpose, and the persons who interact in a given setting are determined largely by available institutional affiliations: learned society, university, seminary, church, Sunday school, non-professional Bible study, charismatic prayer group, etc.

The types of readings taking place in these various environments are determined by their environmental settings which replicate institutional pressures. For example, the Bible may be read within the framework of our U.S. educational institution. Thus at a learned society or university, biblical books are viewed in terms of educational concerns determined by the prevailing educational institution in the society. Or we can envision Bible reading within a distinctly religious setting. Seminary, church, Sunday school, and the like persuade the reader to understand what they read in terms of the prevailing religious institution of their socialization. The Bible, moreover, may be read for political purposes, for gaining or applying power: citations of the Bible by politicians, feminist or other activist interpretations with a view to changing institutions. Finally the Bible may equally be used, not read, within the economic institution. Thus it would be conceivable that a Chinese soldier who had never heard of religions of the book to perceive this book as a sheaf of paper and use the fine paper of a Bible to roll a cigarette. He sees the book in terms of utilitarian concerns determined by the prevailing economic institution. Often Bible salespersons and publishers share a similar perception determined by norms of the economic institution. In such an institutional perspective, reading is not at issue.

Thus we are acutely aware of two social settings for reading, that of the author and that of the reader. In the case of Luke–Acts, typical modern readers may be aware of their own social setting, but totally oblivious of Luke's world and his social setting. It is the purpose of the essays in this book to apprise the considerate reader precisely of Luke's social setting by offering adequate scenarios of the way his world worked.

4.2 Reading and Societal Context

While environmental settings do indeed determine types of reading and non-reading, by far the most significant initial cue to the interpersonal dimension of reading derives from what Hall (1976:91–101 and 1983:59–77) has called the prevailing language "context" generally in vogue in a society. Hall refers to *low context* and *high context* societies.

Low context societies produce detailed texts, spell out as much as conceivably possible, and leave little to the imagination. The general norm is that most things must be clearly set out, hence information must be continually added if meaning is to be constant. Such societies are fine-print societies, societies "of law" where every dimension of life must be described by legislators to make things "lawful," even including, for example, detailed legal directions about how much fat is allowed in commercially sold sausage. The *Congressional Record* offers hours of low context reading for those who wish to be entertained in this way. Hall identifies the U.S. and northern European countries as typical examples of low context societies.

High context societies produce sketchy and impressionistic texts, leaving much to the reader's or hearer's imagination. Since people believe few things have to be spelled out, few things are. This is because people have been socialized into shared ways of perceiving and acting. Hence, much can be assumed. People know, for example, that kings go out to war only after the end of the rainy season (2 Sam 11:1), for time in their world is divided into rainy and dry seasons. There simply is no need to explain how time is divided, unlike our calendar which divides time exactly into months, days, hours, and minutes. In high context societies little new information is necessary for meaning to be constant. Hall lists the Mediterranean world as a representative example of high context societies. Clearly the Bible — and Luke–Acts in particular — along with other writings from ancient Mediterranean peoples fit this high context profile. How different, then, it is for low context, Western readers to read a high context document. Attuned to detail, they simply do not know what is assumed in a high context society.

It will help us to understand Hall's observations about high and low context societies if we attend to their respective communication problems. The typical communication problem in low context societies such as the U.S. is giving people information they do not need, hence "talking down" to them by spelling out absolutely everything. Consider the amount of information printed by the U.S. Government Printing Office alone. In contrast, the typical communication problem in high context societies is that of not giving people enough information, hence "mystifying" them. Consider the broad range of mystifications and hidden meanings derived from the Mediterranean, high context Bible in the hands of sincere and honest low context American and northern European readers.

4.3 Contextualized-Decontextualized Reading

Some analysts distinguish between contextualized and decontextualized reading. Contextualized literacy is writing or print which gets meanings from context, (e.g., stop sign, envelope, newspaper ad or article). Thus by being in "a Bible," Luke–Acts is "Scripture" and gets its religious meaning from the location where it is found. And by being bundled along with a collection of first-century eastern Mediterranean writings, Luke–Acts draws its cultural and social meaning from the time and place of its having been collected.

Decontextualized literacy is writing or print which gets its meanings from the print itself, without support from the contextual surrounding. Thus a written work takes on meaning solely because of the reader! Most Americans reading the Rig Veda (Hindu writing) or Tripitaka (Buddhist writing) would find those works sufficiently decontextualized so as to focus on their aesthetic impact alone (Bloome and Green 1984:406).

Similarly, the effort to read the Bible as literature, for its aesthetic majesty and universal ideas, involves an attempt at decontextualization since any aesthetic-literary, ahistorical framework is decontextualized. Much of the reader-response approach to literature is equally decontextualized, totally dismissing the social dimensions of author, original audience and the text in question (e.g., Iser 1972; Moore 1988). But as far as the Bible is concerned, since nearly all Americans have heard of the Bible and have some inkling that it deals with "religion," it would seem that the reading of even snippets of the Bible in the U.S. is always socially contextualized in the realm of "religion." The question for professional interpretation is what context is most appropriate for a fair and just reading of the Bible. Are all of the contexts listed previously amenable to supporting the considerate reader described above?

4.4 Keeping the Intrapersonal and Interpersonal Together

Various analysts of the reading process warn against separating the *intrapersonal* from the *interpersonal* context. Although the two contexts can be theoretically distinguished, difficulties arise in specifying relationships between them (Bloom and Green 1984:414). Part of those difficulties relates to the nature of the phenomena themselves. That is, in order to explore the intrapersonal context, the interpersonal context must be "frozen" or stopped. However in "freezing" the interpersonal context, the nature of the interpersonal context is distorted since it is an evolving, ongoing, dynamic process.

For biblical studies, the question of contexts might be put as follows: what relationship can historical biblical interpretation have for churches? If the scenarios required for a considerate reading of the Gospels are first-century eastern Mediterranean ones, of what relevance can the Gospels be to twentieth-century Americans? One way in which researchers have attempted to capture both the intrapersonal and interpersonal contexts without distorting either has been through juxtaposing research perspectives. For biblical studies, this would require an awareness of our late twentieth century U.S. society and the scenarios it requires for making sense of contemporary writings, as well as an awareness of first-century eastern Mediterranean society and the scenarios it required for making sense of writings from that time and place. Juxtaposing both perspectives would yield the insights of comparative distancing. The people described in biblical writings can be seen in their attempt to make meaning in terms of their own experience, just as we must in terms of our own experience. What ties us and them together is that for believers, they are ancestors in faith being looked at through comparative lenses that are some 2000 or more years thick. Their experiences with the God of Israel, the Father of Jesus of Nazareth, can still resonate for us and allow for appreciative understanding. Yet while the God of Israel might abide forever, the experience of our ancestors will ever remain foreign and alien regardless of how spuriously familiar we might be with it.

5.0. CONCLUSIONS

The essays in this volume take the scenario model of reading for granted. They do not present a new set of ideas from Luke–Acts. Rather each offers at least one scenario with which modern readers might interact with first-century Mediterranean documents and get to understand what the author said and meant to say to his original first-century, eastern Mediterranean audience. Similarly the authors of the essays realize that Luke–Acts is a *high context* document. Much if not most of what is needed for adequate interpretation is simply left unsaid and presumed known from the cultural experience of the first-century eastern Mediterranean reader. This is another reason for providing first-century Mediterranean scenarios taken for granted by "Luke."

Providing such scenarios, and so filling in the context, is intended to facilitate the reader's task of interpreting the text. A fair reading of any document has its intrapersonal and interpersonal dimensions. The intrapersonal is psychologically oriented, requiring an adult reader with a sense of history to be a considerate reader by building the most adequate scenarios possible. In order to be a fair and impartial listener, the considerate reader must be willing to switch levels of abstraction within the scenarios as need arises. The interpersonal dimension looks to the reading process as social event. Thus modern readers of Luke–Acts are presumably contextualized U.S. readers with a sense of history. They read and/or hear these documents in social settings such as church or school, in public or in private. U.S. fairness, therefore, requires that the reader's first step be *to strive to understand what the author says and means to say to his Mediterranean hearers in terms of their culture and within their social setting.* Theirs was a high context society, with much of what they intended to communicate totally absent from the text, yet rather firmly in place in the common social system into which they were socialized. The considerate reader needs to fill in the social system in order not to be mystified.

In the U.S., the reading of New Testament documents such as Luke–Acts takes place in two interpersonal contexts: the educational institution and the religious institution. In the educational institution we are presumably motivated by the value of *knowing the truth*: what did the author actually say and mean? How does this relate to the early Christian movement and its subsequent development? In the religious institution, the value that motivates us is, among others, to *know the basis for the faith* that is in us: what did the author actually say and mean? How does this relate to our faith?

Reading theory indicates that the primary task of the interpreter is building an adequate scenario. Whether our context is education or religion or both, we still are obliged to build adequate scenarios under pain of sticking our words and meanings into the mouths of biblical authors, which is the sin of anachronism and ethnocentrism. Thanks to the common "religious" quality ascribed to biblical books, when we do manage to stick our words into the mouth of biblical authors, we clothe our words with the infallibility and inerrancy ascribed to the Bible. Now this might do for fundamentalist preachers since their own infallibility and inerrancy are crucial to a successful U.S. preaching career, for example, in TV show business.

But for most U.S. readers the requirement of adequate scenario building is simply a question of being fair to biblical authors and the people described in their text. Such adequate scenario building involves the same steps as getting to understand a group of foreigners with whom we are inevitably and necessarily thrown together, for better or worse. On the one hand, we can choose to ignore the foreigners; this would be simply to ignore the Bible. In that way we can never find out what those authors said and meant to say. On the other hand, if we choose to accept and use the Bible as text, we can force those presented in the biblical books to comply with our idea of them much as the Israeli or South African governments have done with their subjected populations. Two thousand years of Western history point up how original biblical meanings have been bloodied and perverted, how the experiences of biblical people have been used to herd people in directions opposed to their own experience, how in reprisal to their having been mishandled in terms of the Bible, many of our contemporaries dismiss biblical experience as totally irrelevant. Nevertheless, we can come to understand our strange and alien biblical ancestors in faith. We can learn to appreciate them and learn to live with their witness even as we must find God in our own contemporary experience. And it is the reading process that both enables and facilitates this task.

2 HONOR AND SHAME IN LUKE–ACTS: PIVOTAL VALUES OF THE MEDITERRANEAN WORLD

Bruce J. Malina and Jerome H. Neyrey

0.0 INTRODUCTION

Visitors to Mediterranean countries are immediately aware of a different social dynamic on the streets and in the marketplaces. People there seem very concerned with appearances. Married women typically dress in black, with kerchiefs concealing their hair. Men congregate in the square to smoke, drink, or play cards. In many places men and women never share the same space at the same time; in fact, the careful observer notices that there are men's places (i.e., the tavern, the animal barn, the wine press) and women's places (i.e., the well, the common ovens). Anthropologists describe these phenomena in terms of a value considered dominant in Mediterranean culture, namely *honor*. To understand the ways such people organize their world and how they structure their social relations we must attend to this paramount value, *honor*. An adequate scenario for understanding the people of the Mediterranean, ancient and modern, must include a firm grasp of the pivotal value of *honor* and its pervasive replication throughout their lives.

1.0 HONOR DEFINED

Honor is the positive value of a person in his or her own eyes plus the positive appreciation of that person in the eyes of his or her social group. In this perspective honor is a claim to positive worth along with the social acknowledgment of that worth by others. Honor is linked with "face" ("saving face") and "respect." At stake is how others see us, and so, how we see ourselves. Unlike Western culture, cultures in which honor is a dominant value depend totally for their sense of worth upon this acknowledgment by others as "honorable." The worst fate is to be called "Fool!" and to be treated as having no value or worth (see Luke 11:40; 12:20; 24:25). Honor, then, serves as a register of social rating which entitles a person to interact in specific ways with equals, superiors, and subordinates, according to the prescribed cultural cues of the society.

From an interpretative point of view, honor indicates a person's social standing and rightful place in society. The particular honor position a person might occupy is located by lines drawn according to one's power, gender, and position on the social scale, that is, one's precedence (Pitt-Rivers 1977:1–17). When a man claims a certain status that is supported by power and gender, he claims honor. For example, as father of a family, his honor is defined in terms of *gender* (male, father) and *position* (head of the household). When he commands his children and they obey him, his *power* is evident. In this situation of command and obedience, his claim to honor as father and head of the household is acknowledged; his children treat him honorably and onlookers acknowledge that he is an honorable father (see 1 Tim 3:4–5). Were his children to disobey him, he would be dishonored or shamed, for his claim would not be acknowledged, either by family or village. He would suffer shame, that is, loss of honor, reputation, and respect.

Yet current anthropology cautions us that such definitions of honor can be too abstract and so empirically empty, for if honor is a claim to worth that is socially acknowledged, *what* is ranked as worthy or unworthy? Similarly if honor refers to a person's social position marked off by power, gender, and precedence, *what* is considered powerful, or proper gender-based behavior, or actual prominence? Honor, then, is an abstract concept that becomes concrete only when a particular society's understanding of power, gender, and precedence is examined. Our abstract definition is based upon lumping together those common qualities that Mediterranean people label as honorable. What is honorable is what people consider valuable and worthy. What, then, do the inhabitants of that culture consider honorable or shameful? Specific instances of valuable, worthy behavior are often quite local, variable, and ad hoc (thus Davis 1987:23).

Consequently, what might be deviant and shameful for one group in one locality may be worthy and honorable for another. Yet all groups are concerned about their honor. "Honor your father and mother" is honorable behavior for most Jews in Jesus' world (Luke 18:20), but in certain circumstances, an offspring might be told that unless he "hates his own father and mother" (14:26) he cannot have honor as a disciple of

Jesus. Honor, then, is the constant; but what constitutes honor might vary from locale to locale, from situation to situation. That the evaluations of moral worth affixed to honor are mutable underscores the possibility of a reversal of values within first-century societies, as Luke 18:20 and 14:26 illustrate.

We must acknowledge that first-century Mediterraneans might consider some behavior as dishonorable or shameful that typical U.S. people do not. For example, in regard to ancient Mediterraneans one observer notes "their predisposition to regard offenses against the social order or conditions that bring about social disorder as being preeminently deviant" (Selby 1974:16). This presupposes that people who upset the social order are acting dishonorably. Naturally, in the time of Luke–Acts the social order in question is that of Roman-controlled Israel, of the aristocratic, Sadducee-controlled temple, of Palestinian towns and villages, and of various associations within these units. In this cultural scenario, it is not surprising that all the Jesus movement groups who tell the story of their origins attest that their central characters clearly behaved as deviants. As we shall see in chapter 10 ("The Symbolic Universe of Luke–Acts"), there is much truth in the charge that "they turn the world upside down," for if we consider Jesus or the Twelve or Paul from the perspective of the social lines of power, gender, and precedence operative in their world, we see that *all acted outside of their inherited social roles and ranks.* Such activity would be clearly dishonorable and shameful if assessed from an elite point of view. But, for group members this activity was worthy of moral affirmation; it was honorable. Honor, then, depends on the vantage point of the actors and perceivers.

A first indication of such "dishonoring" social activity is to be found in the phenomenon of physical mobility, that is, Jesus, his followers, Peter, and Paul travelled in socially unexpected and unusual ways. Such physical mobility replicates the social behavior that rejects ascribed status and implies a willingness to be deviant within the broader context. Yet the willingness to be deviant itself becomes a value worthy of honor within the group (see 1 Cor 1:18–25). Such behaviors that are honor-worthy within early Christian groups can be sketched out by a reading of Luke–Acts from the perspective of honor and shame. Consequently a study of honor and shame in Luke–Acts should yield an array of values preeminently local and/or group-specific. Yet the meaning of honor, its acquisition and loss, its concrete embodiment in persons, and the like are realized in terms of culturally accepted procedures. Some of these procedures include what follows.

1.1 Sources of Honor

Honor can be *ascribed* or *acquired.* First, *ascribed honor* happens to a person passively through birth, family connections, or endowment by notable persons of power. In this, honor is like wealth: *ascribed honor* resembles inherited wealth. Second, *acquired honor* is honor actively sought and achieved, most often at the expense of one's equals in the social contest of challenge and riposte. *Acquired honor* is like wealth obtained through one's efforts, honorable or dishonorable.

1.1.1 Ascribed Honor. Ascribed honor, then, is honor that a person obtains through kinship or endowment, not because of any effort or achievement. When honor is ascribed, it is bestowed on someone by a notable person of power, such as a king or governor. This is so because, if those expected to acknowledge and recognize the new honor demur, the powerful one ascribing the honor has the sanction of power to make the grant of honor stick (see Malina 1986a:82–83). Thus honor can be ascribed by God, a king, aristocrats—in sum, by persons who can claim honor for others and can force acknowledgment of that honor because they have the power and rank to do so. For example, in the story of Jesus, the God of Israel ascribes honor to him: God raised from the dead Jesus, who was utterly shamed and disgraced in his crucifixion, and then enthroned him at his right hand in heaven (Acts 2:34–36), thus indicating God's good pleasure in Jesus. According to Rom 8:17–30, Christians can also expect such ascribed honor from God (on honor and shame in Paul see Corrigan 1986; Forbes 1986; Marshall 1983; Moxnes 1985).

More commonly, ascribed honor derives from kinship, that is, birth into a family. Offspring have the same honor as parents, for honor derives from birth ("like mother, like daughter," Ezek 16:44; "like father, like son," Matt 13:55). Being born into an honorable family makes one honorable, since the family is the repository of the honor of past illustrious ancestors and their accumulated acquired honor. One of the major purposes of genealogies in the Bible is to set out a peoples' honor lines and thus to situate them socially on a scale of prominence (thus Luke 3:23–38). Conversely, hostile questions about Jesus' family and origin look to the same thing: how can Jesus claim special honor as prophet or Son of God, if he is but the son of Joseph the carpenter (Luke 4:22), if his family includes an ordinary mother and brothers in the village (Mark 6:3; Matt 13:54–57), and if his roots are in a peasant village in Galilee (John 7:40–42)?

1.1.2 Acquired Honor. Acquired honor is the socially recognized claim to worth that a person obtains by achievements, such as benefactions (Luke 7:4–5) or prowess (Luke 7:16–17). In Luke's world, honor is particularly acquired by excelling over others in the social interaction that we call challenge and riposte. Challenge-riposte is a type of social interaction in which people hassle each other according to socially defined rules in order to gain the honor of another. An important factor here is the perception by the people in Luke–Acts of the acutely limited nature of all things, honor included. Honor, like all other goods in first-century Mediterranean society, is seen to exist in limited amounts. There is only so much to go around, or at least that is what people learn to perceive. Yet honor, the pivotal concern for Mediterraneans and their kin groups, is greatly desired. It so happens that nearly every interaction with non-family members has undertones of a challenge to honor, either to defend what one has or to gain more.

In the first-century Mediterranean world, every social interaction that takes place outside one's family or outside one's circle of friends is perceived as a challenge to honor, a mutual attempt to acquire honor from one's social equal. Thus gift-giving, invitations to dinner, debates over issues of law, buying and selling, planning marriages, or arranging what we might call cooperative ventures for farming, business, fishing, mutual help — all these sorts of interactions take place according to the patterns of honor called challenge-riposte.

Because of this constant and steady cue in Mediterranean culture, anthropologists call it an *agonistic* culture. What this means, then, is that Mediterraneans tend to consider all social interactions outside the ✓ family, biological or fictive, as potential contests for honor. Furthermore, since honor and reputation, like all goods in life, are limited, every social interaction of this type can turn out to be an affair of honor, a contest or game of honor, in which players are faced with wins, ties, and losses. What do these contests for honor look like?

1.2 Acquiring Honor: Challenge and Riposte

Challenge-riposte describes a constant social tug of war, a game of social push and shove. Challenge-riposte is a type of social communication, since any social interaction is a form of communication. Someone (source) sends a message by means of a culturally recognized channel to a receiving individual, and this produces an effect. The source here is the challenger, while the message is a symbolized thing (e.g., a word, a gift, an invitation) or event (e.g., a slap) or both. The channel of communication is always public, and the publicity of the message guarantees that the receiving individual will react, since even non-action is publicly interpreted, either as a riposte or a loss of honor. Consequently, challenge-riposte within the context of honor is a social interaction with at least three phases:

(a) *challenge* in terms of some action (word, deed, or both) on the part of the challenger;

(b) *perception* of the message by both the individual to whom it is directed and the public at large; and

(c) *reaction* of the receiving individual and the evaluation of the reaction on the part of the public.

The result is a highly stylized interaction which contains the following elements:

Typical Elements in a Challenge-Riposte Exchange

1. Claim (often implied by action or gesture)
2. Challenge
3. Riposte
4. Public Verdict

The challenge-riposte interaction begins with some claim to enter the social space of another (for what follows, see Bourdieu 1966). This claim is always a challenge, and may be positive or negative. A positive reason for entering the social space of another would be to gain a share in that space or to gain a cooperative, mutually beneficial foothold. A negative reason would be to dislodge another from his or her social space, either temporarily or permanently. Thus the source sending the message—always interpreted as a challenge—puts out some behavior, either positive (a word of praise, a gift, a sincere request for help) or negative (a word of insult or threat, a physical affront of varying degrees). These actions constitute the message that has to be perceived and interpreted by the receiving individual as well as the public at large.

Second, the receiver must look upon the action from the viewpoint of its potential to dishonor the receiver's self-respect or self-worth. The receiver has to judge whether and how the challenge falls within the socially acknowledged range of such actions, from a simple questioning of self-esteem to an outright attack on self-esteem to a total denial of self-esteem. Perception of the message is the second step in this interaction.

It is important to note that according to the social patterns of the honor contest, not everyone can engage in the game. According to the rules or code, *only equals can play.* Only an equal can challenge another in such a way that all perceive the interaction as a challenge. Only an equal—who must be recognized as such—can impugn a person's honor or affront another. This is so because the rules of the honor contest require that challengers stand on equal social terms. Thus an inferior on the ladder of social standing, power, and sexual status does not have enough honor to resent the affront of a superior. On the other side, a superior's honor is simply not committed or engaged by an inferior's affront, although the superior has the power to punish impudence. Thus a man can physically affront his children or wife, a high-class person can strike a lower-class person, free men can strike slaves, or the occupying Roman army can make sport of most low-class citizens. Of themselves, these interactions do *not* imply an honor contest. In other words, in the social game of honor, a man is answerable for his honor only to his social equals, namely, to those with whom, in the perceptions of the society, he can compete.

Honor, like all other goods in life, is limited in amount and the fund can neither be created nor destroyed. To win a challenge is to deprive another of his honor and to gain prominence; to lose is to surrender some dimension of one's honor and to lose precedence—but always among equals. The perception of limited good quality in such a society institutionalizes envy even among friends, especially among equals. Challenge-riposte constitutes a zero sum game in which the winner takes all, while the crowds look on and congratulate the winner, all the while hoping that they themselves might be in the winning position and envying the winner's success. Concerning such peer envy and the evil eye rooted in it, see Aalders 1979; Fensham 1967; Ghosh 1983; Johnson 1983; Neyrey 1988a; Walcott 1978.

Because it is a serious matter and honor demands that only equals play, the receiver must judge whether he is equal to the challenger, whether the challenger honors him by regarding him as an equal, or whether the challenger dishonors him by implying equality when there is none, because the receiver is either of a higher level or a lower level. Thus from the perspective of the evangelists, when the various learned groups challenge Jesus, they are implying that he is their equal. But in contrast, the high priest and Pilate do not regard Jesus' activity as a challenge, but rather as an annoyance by an inferior who can be swept aside. Although equal to Pharisees, lawyers and scribes, Jesus is not on the same social footing as the chief priest.

The third step in the interaction concerns the reaction to the message of challenge and so involves the receiver's behavior that enables the public to pass a verdict. The verdict is either a grant of honor taken from the person who received the challenge and awarded to the successful challenger, or a loss of honor by the challenger in favor of the successful recipient of the challenge. Any reaction on the part of the receiver of a challenge comprises his riposte. Such ripostes cover a range of reactions: (a) a positive refusal to act, or (b) acceptance of the message, or (c) a negative refusal to react.

A person receiving the challenge can refuse it positively by a display of scorn, disdain, or contempt (see 2 Sam 16:5–14). Or, the receiver can accept the challenge message and offer a counter-challenge; then the exchange between them will continue. Finally, the receiver can react by offering nothing by way of response; he can fail or neglect to respond, and this will imply dishonor.

The challenge, then, is a threat to usurp the reputation of another, to deprive another of personal reputation. When the person challenged cannot or does not respond to the challenge posed by an equal, personal reputation is lost in the eyes of the public. People will say he cannot or does not know how to defend his honor. Honor is thus lost to the challenger, who correspondingly gains in honor. This set of cultural cues of perception, action, and belief is symbolized in the behavior of conquering kings who take on the titles of the ones they vanquish. It is likewise symbolized in the behavior of the early Christians who applied to the resurrected Jesus all the titles of those who were to overcome evil and death: Messiah, Lord, son of David, Son of God, and the like.

1.3 Replications of Honor

Honor is ultimately the self-respect of dyadic persons who depend constantly on family and kin to affirm their self-worth (see chapter 3, "First-Century Personality"). According to this dependency, honor-conscious people contrast diametrically with U.S. individualism (see Geertz 1976; Malina 1986a). Honor can be replicated by those dimensions of a person that point to the core of dyadic personhood, namely blood and name that bind one to family and kin.

1.3.1 Honor and Blood. Honor, both ascribed and acquired, is often symbolized by blood. Blood means one's own blood, i.e., oneself as a living human being, as well as that of all members of the same biological or fictive family ("Blood is thicker than water"; "Blood will out."). Honor is always presumed to exist within one's own family of blood, i.e., among all of one's blood relatives. A person can always trust blood relatives. Outside that circle, all people are presumed dishonorable, guilty unless proved otherwise, a presumption based on the agonistic quality of competition for the scarce commodity, honor. It is with all these others that one must play the social tug of war, engage in the contest, and put one's own and one's family honor on the line. One instinctively sides with one's blood relatives and family against outsiders.

No one outside the family of blood can be trusted until and unless that trust can be validated and verified. So men of the same village or town who are not blood relatives relate to each other with an implied deep distrust that in practice prevents any effective form of cooperation. Strangers to the village, that is, people of the same cultural group but not resident in the same place, are looked upon as potential enemies, while foreigners, those of other cultural groups just passing through, are considered certain enemies. Consequently, any interaction or conversation between two unrelated men or two unrelated women (the sexes usually do not mix) are engagements in which both sides probe for the least hint of the other's intentions or activities, always presuming hostility. Such interactions are not concerned with sociability, but rather are expressions of opposition and distance. Blood replicates honor; with blood relatives there is no honor contest.

1.3.2 Honor and Name. Sentiments of opposition, distance, and exclusiveness among fellow villagers and their families find a more extended expression in that competition for honor called "a good name."

Since honor is replicated in "blood," the good name of a family signals that honor. Hence, males are known by the name of their fathers and their kinship groups. For example, Peter is "Simon, son of John" (Matt 16:17); James and John are always known as "the sons of Zebedee" (Luke 5:10). To know the family name is to know the honor rating of an individual.

Again, a good name is a central concern of people in every context of public action and gives purpose and meaning to their lives, much as money does in our society. A good name fundamentally means honor adequate to carry on the social interactions necessary for decent human existence, especially for contracting marriages. Oaths are taken on the honor capital stored in family names: "I swear by my father's name." From another point of view, the good name that stands for family honor is equally central because families in the first-century world were not self-sufficient and independent economically. Social life required some degree of interdependence, cooperation, and shared enterprise. In Mediterranean society, extra-familial cooperation took the form of a free association of a contractual kind. In biblical terms, people made implicit or explicit covenants with each other. Persons in the U.S. decline contractual relations with people who have poor credit ratings; similarly, in the Mediterranean world, contractual relations are declined for persons without a good name. No one would freely associate in covenant relationship with another whose honor rating was not good. Thus good name and prestige would be one's most valuable assets.

By metonymy, a name represents the person. That name may be judged honorable or dishonorable by outsiders. One's reputation, then, constitutes one's greatest treasure. But in honor-oriented societies, people experience an ongoing competition for honor and reputation, a continual rivalry, an endless win-tie-or-lose game in which name and honor are always on the line. Attempts to damage reputations are constantly made, although great stress is laid on face-to-face courtesy in terms of formalities. The prestige level of the members of the community is a matter of continual comment. Every quarrel normally leads to imputations of acts and intentions that are dishonorable, which may have nothing to do with the quarrel. Name and reputation, although a person's most precious possession, are one's most vulnerable points. We will clarify this in the chapter on conflict in the discussion of labelling (Malina and Neyrey 1988).

Prestige, or a "good name," derives from the domination of persons rather than from things. Hence, any concern people show for the acquisition of goods stems from their purpose of gaining honor by generously disposing of what one has acquired among equals or socially useful lower-class clients. In other words, an honorable name is acquired through beneficence, not through the fact of possession and/or the keeping of what one has acquired (see Luke 12:16–20). Thus, money, goods, and any sort of wealth are really a means to an honorable name, and any other use of wealth is considered foolish. One must "make friends for yourselves by means of unrighteous mammon" (16:9); there is no honor in simply being called "the richest man in the world."

2.0 HONOR DISPLAYED

The social boundaries which people assimilate through enculturation provide them with a socially shared map that enables and urges them to situate persons, things, and events within a proper context (see chapter 10). Honor-conscious people are dyadic persons who depend on others to instruct them constantly about this shared map and to tell them where persons, things, or events should be situated. The social map, moreover, is usually condensed and expressed in a somewhat compact symbolic form in one's physical person. Consequently, one's physical body symbolizes a sort of personalized map of the social body. The values of the social body are often the values assigned to individual physical bodies writ large, so to speak. For example, the human head is to the physical body what the head of the household is to the social family; the right hand is the body's weapon-bearing member as well as the social body's wielder of power and influence. Honor, then, is displayed especially in certain bodily parts, head, face, and arms. Dishonor is associated with other bodily parts, such as "lick the dirt off my feet" or "kiss my ass."

Honor is also displayed in the place or space where the physical body is located. This concept of honor-as-place is replicated in various ways. A person has a social place on the village map, a specific place where he or she resides (the home), and personal space (one's very person). A person's honor is related to these places. Only certain people have permission to enter either one's familial space, one's home, or one's bodily space to touch, to kiss, to embrace, etc. To enter these spaces without permission must be considered aggressive behavior. And so, one's honor entails maintaining that space.

The honor accorded one space is replicated in the way the other spaces are understood. Replication here means the use of similar and often identical patterns of behavior in different domains. Just as one allows service personnel into one's house for specific purposes, so a person can let service personnel have limited access to one's physical person for specific purposes: a plumber or electrician for the house and a physician or dentist for the physical body. Honor is related, then, to one's place on the map, which means the space one occupies socially and physically. Honor means the maintenance of these spaces, especially bodily space.

2.1 Recognition of Honor

As we suggested above, honor is frequently symbolized by certain bodily features and the treatment given one's physical person. A person's body is normally a symbolized replication of the social value of honor. The head and front of the head (face) play prominent roles. To be seated at the head of the table or to be at the head of the line or to head an organization are so many replications of crowning the head, of males taking off their hats to another, of bowing one's head in the presence of some recognized person. Honor is displayed when the head is crowned, anointed, touched, or covered. Dishonor, however, is symbolized when the head is uncovered or made bare by shaving and when it is cut off, struck, or slapped.

As regards the face, the symbolic nature of the face, a part for the whole, is much like that of the head, with the added dimension of the spatial *front*, the focus of awareness. To *affront* someone is to challenge that person in such a way that the person is and cannot avoid being aware of it. The challenged person is obliged to witness the challenge to his face. In return, the recognition of the challenge takes place on the face. It seems, moreover, that in Semitic culture, this focus of recognition is the center of the face, the nose: the Hebrew word for anger refers to "flared nostrils," and a reference to flared nostrils is most often translated "wrath."

To put it mildly, a physical affront is a challenge to one's honor; unanswered it becomes a dishonor in the judgment of the people who witness the affront. A physical affront symbolizes the breaking of required social and personal boundaries, the entering of a person's bodily space without permission. Because aggressive, it causes resentment. Resentment here means the psychological state of feeling distressed and anxious because the expectations and demands of the ego are not acknowledged by the actual treatment a person receives at the hands of others. It is a sense of moral indignation at the perceived injustice in the behavior of others toward oneself—not in keeping with one's power, sexual status, and social role. In brief, physical affronts refuse to recognize one's honor and prestige, and their physical effrontery symbolizes that refusal. They have crossed into the social space that is the core self.

Concerning physical affronts, any physical boundary-crossing on the part of another in regard to one's space or body presumes and implies the intent to dishonor. In honor societies, actions are more important than words, yet how one speaks is more important than what one says. In physical effrontery, the challenge to honor is presumed to exist unless it is clearly and totally apparent that no challenge is intended (e.g., a child striking an adult). Yet to claim that one did not intend dishonor (e.g., by saying "I didn't mean it" or "Excuse me") is to require a certain indulgence on the part of the one affronted, and this indulgence may or may not be granted. Much would depend upon: (a) the degree of dishonor involved (how, in what circumstance, and where a person struck or touched another); (b) the status of the person challenging (who did the striking); (c) the degree of publicity (what audience witnessed the event). Again, publicity and witnesses are crucial for the acquisition and bestowal of honor. Representatives of public opinion must be present, since honor is all about the court of public opinion and the reputation which that court bestows. Literally, public praise can give life and public ridicule can kill.

2.2 Challenges to Honor

It should be obvious by now that two levels of interpretation are involved in the challenge and riposte of honor: (a) that of the individual challenged—his or her estimation of the intention and status of the challenger; and (b) that of the public witnessing the challenge—its interpretation of the intention and status of the challenger and the challenge in the public forum. It follows that there will be various styles of challenging, ranging from direct affronts through indirect challenges to ambiguous challenges.

Direct affronts include assault on the head or face of another, as well as direct verbal insults, such as "You fool!" (Matt 5:22; see Luke 12:20). Physical affronts are always symbolic affronts that require a riposte. Failure to respond means dishonor and disgrace. The interpretation of direct challenges by the one challenged and by the observing public is obvious.

Indirect and ambiguous challenges are another matter. We identify as an ambiguous affront a challenging word or deed put forth "accidentally, on purpose." For example, a man may "accidentally" bump into another and knock him to the ground. This sort of challenge puts the one challenged in a dilemma. He must decide what the community will judge the challenge to be, for the victim of an affront or challenge is dishonored only when and where he is forced by the public to recognize that he has been challenged and did not respond. As part of this, the victim also has to judge the intentions of the one who seems to be challenging.

At stake is the intention of the would-be challenger. This potential challenger may take defensive, evasive action through certain speech acts. In a variety of ways, he may try publicly to clarify his intentions and thus deflect perceived hostility. This takes the form of swearing, oath making and giving one's "word of honor."

In potential honor challenges, swearing functions to eliminate ambiguity and make explicit one's true intentions (e.g., in business: "I swear to God this is a healthy jackass"). An oath activates a type of implicit curse; for example, if the jackass is sick and dies, God will punish me for calling God to witness to an untruth, hence for dishonoring God. Public opinion, moreover, judges a person dishonored if he or she does not submit to an oath. Swearing oaths, then, should reduce ambiguity, if done truthfully and in good faith. But this is not always the case, for speech may be truthful or false.

Giving a "word of honor" is another speech form which functions to clarify intentions and thus relates to honor challenges. A person can commit personal honor in the contest of life only by sincere intention. To demonstrate sincerity of intention and steadfastness of purpose, a "word of honor" can be given, which functions like an oath or swearing, but which engages only the individual, not God or others. Such a word of honor is only necessary for outsiders who find what a person says or does ambiguous or incredible.

Public speech may put someone's honor on the line. But such public speech remains ambiguous, for it raises the issues of truth and falsehood, which are themselves complicated matters in this society. The giving of a word of honor is rooted in the fact that in honor-conscious cultures, moral commitment to telling the truth unambiguously derives from loyalty to persons to whom such social commitment is due. But who are they? In first-century, limited-good society, there was no such thing as universal, social commitment or loyalty to all people (e.g., the brotherhood of all men). Loyalty was to blood and kin; people were not obligated to tell the truth to everyone, only to kin; nor did everyone have a right to the truth. Rather, the right both to hear the truth and to withhold it belong only to the person of honor, and that in terms of specific situations. To spell this out, the right to the truth exists only where respect is due, that is, to the family and superiors, but not necessarily to equals with whom one competes or to inferiors. Hence, the ambiguity of public speech. Is the right to truth operative in such-and-such a situation?

Furthermore, lying and deception can even be honorable and legitimate (see Matt 6:17–18). It is honorable to lie in order to deceive an "outsider," who has no right to the truth. Yet lying and deception thereby are inherently challenging, for to deceive or lie is to deprive another of respect, to refuse to show honor, and to humiliate. But in the competition for honor, lying is not a dishonorable action for the one who lies, but rather a challenge. To be called a liar by anyone, however, is a great public dishonor.

Therefore, one may risk one's honor by swearing oaths or giving one's word of honor in an attempt, either sincere or calculated, to clarify one's intentions in a potential challenge situation. Yet ambiguity shrouds public speech. In certain circumstances, it is socially acceptable to lie to and deceive those whom one judges not to have a right to the truth. But this is risky business for it constitutes a direct challenge to them. The upshot of this is that we should pay considerable attention to the verbal games being played, who speaks to whom and what forms of speech are used, for honor is displayed in speech.

Continuing our investigation of the ways in which honor is challenged, we note that the boundary lines marking off a person in some way likewise include all that the person holds worthwhile and worthy. This means that along with personal honor, an individual shares in a sort of collective or corporate honor. Included within the bounds of personal honor are all those worthies who control a person's existence, i.e., patrons, kings and God — all whom one holds vertically sacred. Also included is one's family — the horizontally sacred. The reason for this is that like individuals, social groups possess a collective honor.

Just as honor is personal or individual as well as collective or corporate (e.g., family honor, national honor), so other challenges which a person might make can come by what is called a corporate affront. Instead of affronting a given person head on, a challenger may affront someone closely connected with that person's honor. This can happen by dishonoring a man's mother or wife (who is perceived as embedded in her husband) or dishonoring his extended family (his father or blood cousins).

Challenges to honor are life-threatening. To bring things back to normal requires a response, a sort of pushing of the challenger back to his or her own side of the line, along with a fence-mending operation. A dishonored person must attempt to restore his honor. The attempt counts, not the actual restoration of the status previously held. We call this attempt "satisfaction." What is required and suffices for satisfaction in an honor society is that the one dishonored have the opportunity to achieve satisfaction, and that the dishonored follow the rules of the game in doing so. Satisfaction then has the nature of an ordeal, implying a judgment of destiny or fate of God's sanction. Such an attempt signals the person of valor.

3.0 COLLECTIVE HONOR

We noted that honor has both individual and corporate or collective dimensions. Since first-century societies did not consider individualism a pivotal value as we do, collective or corporate honor was one of their major focuses. Social groups, like the family, village, or region, possess a collective honor in which the members participate. For example, "Can anything good come out of Nazareth?" (John 1:46); "Cretans are always liars, evil beasts, lazy gluttons" (Titus 1:12). This perception illustrates what we mean by a dyadic personality (see chapter 3). Depending upon the dimensions of the group, which can range from nuclear family to kingdom or region, the *head* of the group is responsible for the honor of the group with reference to outsiders, and symbolizes its honor as well. Hence members of the group owe loyalty, respect, and obedience of a kind that commits their individual honor without limit and without compromise. This sort of collective honor is to be found in natural and voluntary groupings.

3.1 Honor and the Natural Group

Natural groupings are like ascribed honor in that they depend upon circumstances beyond the individual's control. A person has no control over naturally defining events such as birth, parents' residence, or nationality. In natural groupings, one's intentions to belong count for naught, for the grouping does not result from any free choice, competition, or contract. One is born physically and symbolically into the group, and one is thus obliged to respect, observe, and maintain the boundary lines, the definitions, and the order within the group, that is, its honor code.

Challenges to honor are not all of the same degree or quality, but move along a spectrum from a simple, positive invitation to share a cup of wine to a negative extreme like murder. Just as there are varying degrees of challenge, so also response reactions ought to be at least of the same quality as the challenge, if the challenged person is to maintain honor.

For clarity's sake we distinguish three hypothetical degrees, depending upon whether the challenge to honor is revocable or not, whether the boundaries can be readily repaired or not, and whether the deprivation of honor is slight, significant, or total. The first degree involves extreme and total dishonor of another with no revocation possible. Total dishonor includes murder, adultery, kidnapping, total social degradation of a person by depriving the person of everything needed for status, in sum, all the things listed in the second half of the Ten Commandments. This in fact is what is listed there: outrages against one's fellow Israelite that are irrevocable and require vengeance. The second degree would be a significant deprivation of honor with revocation possible by, for example, restoration of stolen items or monetary compensation for seduction of another's unbetrothed, unmarried daughter. The lowest degree of challenge to honor would be regular interactions that require normal social responses, such as repayment of a gift with one of equal or better value, permission of another to marry my children if he lets my children marry his. In other words, any implicit or explicit dishonor must allow for satisfaction commensurate with the degree of dishonor present.

In regard to natural groupings, we note that any sort of first-degree dishonor done within the group is considered sacrilegious and comprises a category of transgression quite out of the ordinary. Those controlling our existence in natural groups are sacred, religious persons. Thus, murdering a parent is not simply homicide, but parricide; murdering a king is regicide. Crimes against members of one's natural grouping are always felt to be extremely grievous and socially disorienting. Homicide committed on outsiders, however, is not sacrilegious and might even be meritorious, as in defense of the group's honor in war. The Romans called the crime of first-degree transgression in natural groupings *nefas*, and branded the perpetrator *sacer* (literally, "sacred"), meaning the gods would certainly requite him for what he did.

3.2 Honor and the Voluntary Group

Voluntary groupings, like acquired honor, result from calculated choices and are the outcome of contracts or competition. Voluntary groupings in the first century would include trade guilds, municipalities (systems of villages), city-states with republican forms of government, voluntary burial organizations,.Palestinian parties like Pharisees, Sadducees, Essenes, and Zealots. Perhaps the early groups of Christians likewise looked upon their groups as voluntary associations like the Palestinian parties after whom they often modeled themselves.

In voluntary groupings, the members have no sacred qualities as persons because of who they are in relationship to others (kinship). Rather the posts, offices or functions in these groupings bear the qualities otherwise embodied by persons in natural groups. Now it is these posts, offices, and functions which are considered sacred and pure, although many different people can hold them. As for the group in general, the heads of both natural and voluntary groupings set the tone and embody the honor rating of the group, so to speak. While internal opinion as well as public opinion are at work in natural groupings, in voluntary groupings public opinion is sovereign.

From the viewpoint of collective honor, depending on the quality of the grouping, the sacred persons or posts have power over all the dimensions of honor in their respective groups. They arbitrate questions of value; they delimit what can be done or maintained without sacrilege; they define the unconditional allegiance of the members. This is what Jesus and Paul did for the voluntary groupings that formed around them; this is what the rabbis did for the voluntary groupings that adhered to them; and this is what the emperor in Rome or the high priest in Jerusalem did for the natural groupings under their power. Thus these sacred persons or sacred post-holders themselves symbolize both social honor—they have precedence relative to others in their groups—and ethical honor—they are perceived to be implicitly good and noble.

The reason for this is that social honor or precedence (being head of something/someone) is readily convertible into ethical honor or implicit goodness, just as capital or collateral assures credit in our money system. Thus the king of the nation (or the father of the family) simply cannot be dishonored within the group; he is above criticism. What he is guarantees the evaluation of his actions. Any offense against him only stains the offender.

Furthermore, the king in his kingdom (like the father in his family) can do no wrong because he is the arbiter of right and wrong. Criticism tends to be rated as an act of disloyalty, a lack of commitment. No one has a right to question what the king decides to do, just as no individual in the group has any right to follow what he or she might personally think is right or wrong. The king (or father) must be followed and obeyed; he is sufficient conscience for all concerned. This proper attitude is symbolized in rituals of status elevation, all of which accord honor (see Malina and Neyrey 1988). Given such rituals, one must pay honor, even if one does not feel inclined to. For one might assume that if one readily pays honor to persons toward whom honor is felt, then honor paid, especially in public rituals of status elevation, indicates what ought to be felt. Paying honor to those to whom it is owed legitimatizes established power and further integrates societal members in their system of obligatory consent.

4.0 GENDER-BASED HONOR: THE MORAL DIVISION OF LABOR

As mentioned previously, honor refers to the intersection of the societal boundaries of power, gender roles, and respect for those in superior statuses. Up to this point, we have considered basically power, respect, and the male sex. What is the role of the female in the game of honor?

By and large, the honor of the natural group is divided up into either a sexual or a moral division of labor. The sexual division of labor looks mainly to the family and kinship group but can be replicated in other dimensions of life. Thus honor has a male and a female component. When considered from this perspective, the *male* aspect is called *honor*, while the *female* aspect is called *shame*. Shame in this context refers to a woman's sensitivity about what others think, say, and do with regard to her worth.

The modern, Western reader may be confused by the term shame. It can be conveniently summarized as: (a) for males, shame is the loss of honor; shame, then, is a negative experience, as in being shamed; (b) for females, shame is the sensitivity to and defense of honor; female shame (having shame), then is a positive value in a woman; a woman branded as "shameless" means for a female what being shamed means for a male. Concerning shame in comparative perspective, see Abu-Hilal 1982; for the U.S. Kaufman 1974; 1980; Kurtz 1981; Fischer 1985.

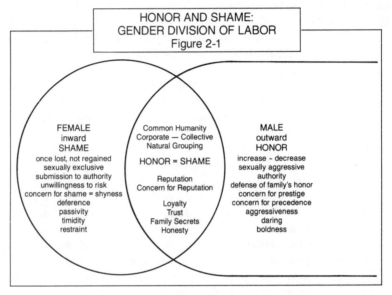

HONOR AND SHAME:
GENDER DIVISION OF LABOR
Figure 2-1

FEMALE
inward
SHAME
once lost, not regained
sexually exclusive
submission to authority
unwillingness to risk
concern for shame = shyness
deference
passivity
timidity
restraint

Common Humanity
Corporate — Collective
Natural Grouping
HONOR = SHAME
Reputation
Concern for Reputation
Loyalty
Trust
Family Secrets
Honesty

MALE
outward
HONOR
increase - decrease
sexually aggressive
authority
defense of family's honor
concern for prestige
concern for precedence
aggressiveness
daring
boldness

In the moral division of labor, honor and shame become sexually specific and sexually embedded. In all societies, it seems, one may make an analytic distinction between the domestic and the public aspects of social organization. And in the Mediterranean, females stand at the center of the domestic, while males are expected to have their primary location in the public sphere. Male honor looks outward to the public sphere, whereas female honor looks inward to the domestic.

To understand this, we must attend to the important symbol of such societies, the sexual organs. First of all, male honor is symbolized by the testicles, which stand for manliness, courage, authority over family, willingness to defend one's reputation, and refusal to submit to humiliation. Female honor is symbolized by the maidenhead (hymen), which stands for female sexual exclusiveness, discretion, shyness, restraint, and timidity. The male clearly lacks the physiological basis for sexual exclusiveness or sexual "purity." He cannot symbolize invasion into his space as the female can. His masculinity, moreover, is in doubt if he maintains sexual purity and does not challenge the boundaries of others through their women. Females, for their part, symbolize their purity by thwarting even the most remote advances to or invasion of their symbolic space. Yet it is the responsible male's duty to protect and defend the purity of his women (wife, sister, daughter), since their dishonor directly implies his own (on the female role, see Delaney 1986; 1987; Giovannini 1987).

The division of honor into male and female corresponds to the division of roles in the family of husband, wife, and children. This sort of division of honor gets replicated in arrangements of space. Recall the distinction that male = public sphere, female = domestic sphere. Let us consider the domestic sphere, that is, female space or female things: the places where females are allowed, the things that females deal with exclusively, like kitchen utensils, drawing water, spinning and sewing, bread baking, or sweeping out the house. All these female spaces and things are centripetal to the family dwelling. They face toward the inside, with a sort of invisible magnet of social pressure turning females inward toward their space in the house or the village. In this arrangement, the wife normally becomes financial administrator with the key to the family chest when and since the husband must go out—to fields, to other villages, on pilgrimage. This is amply illustrated in the description of the ideal good wife in Prov 31:10–31.

If females represent domestic space, an inward direction toward the center, males relate to public space and an outward direction. Hence there are male places and male things, such as farm implements and wine presses and draft animals. If female honor is related to remaining at home and within that sphere, male honor demands that they represent the family outside the home, and so they must be out and abroad. Males, however, who must go out for protracted periods of time without their females, such as traders, traveling merchants, certain types of shepherds, wandering preachers, and the like, necessarily leave their honor in doubt, since their wives are left alone for rather long periods.

To finish off the division of space and labor, all things taken from the inside to the outside are male; all things remaining on the inside are female. The places of contact between the inside and outside (the family courtyard, the village square, or the area by the city gate) are male when males are present, although females when properly chaperoned may sometimes enter when males are present.

4.1 Male Honor

It belongs to the male to defend both corporate honor (i.e., family, clan or village) and any female honor embedded in the corporate honor. Concerns for honor and self-respect are rooted in traditions of masculine personhood, as Gilmore notes:

> One may say confidently, therefore, that a common Mediterranean theme is the elevation of a demonstrated physiological masculinity, an ostentatious, "indomitable virility," to paramountcy in the ascription of male social identity and reputation, whether we gloss this as "honor" or by some other term (1987:10).

Male honor, then, is "libidinized social reputation" (Gilmore 1987:11). For this reason, we should expect all males described in Luke–Acts to reveal traits typical of the Mediterranean male and his concern with his ever-tested virility. When a male loses his honor, he experiences negative shame.

4.2 Female Shame

The female, in contrast, symbolizes the positive shame aspect of corporate honor, that positive sensitivity to the good repute of individuals and groups. Consequently, the honor of the male is involved in the sexual purity of his mother (although his father has the main obligation in this regard), wife, daughters, and sisters, but not in his own sexual purity. According to this pattern, then, *the sexual purity or exclusiveness of the female is embedded within the honor of some male.* The male is responsible for the maintenance of this sexual exclusiveness. When the exclusiveness is lost, the female is negatively labelled "shameless," indicating a loss of "shame," which is female honor. Hence the woman courts disaster by stepping out of socially acceptable boundaries. The honorable woman, however, born with the proper sentiments of shame which she inherits from her mother ("Like mother, like daughter." Ezek 16:44), strives to avoid the human contacts which might expose her to dishonor or "shamelessness."

She cannot be expected to succeed in this endeavor unsupported by male authority and control. This perception underlies public opinion, which makes the deceived husband or father the object of ridicule and dishonor, and entitles them to avenge any outrage committed against them in this way. Furthermore, women not under the tutelage of a male (e.g., notably widows and divorced women) are viewed as stripped of female honor (i.e., "shameless"), hence more like males then females, therefore sexually predatory, aggressive, hence dangerous. Only remarriage would restore their true sexual roles, but often this is not socially possible. This points to the precarious position of the widow and divorcée, as well as to the importance of a bill of divorce enabling and entitling the woman to a new marriage if this can be arranged for her. Such cultural attitudes toward widows are articulated in 1 Tim 5:3–16.

5.0 CONCLUSION: TOWARD DEFINING HONOR AND SHAME

As mentioned previously, honor means a person's (or group's) feeling of self-worth and the public, social acknowledgment of that worth. Honor in this sense applies to both sexes. It is the basis of one's reputation, of one's social standing, regardless of sex. In this common context, where honor is both male and female, the word "shame" is a positive symbol, meaning sensitivity for one's own reputation and sensitivity to the opinion of others. To "have shame" in this sense is an eminently positive value. Any human being worthy of the title "human" or any group worthy of belonging to the family of humankind needs to "have shame," that is, to be sensitive to its honor rating and to be perceptive of the opinion of others. A sense of shame makes the contest of living possible and dignified, since it implies acceptance of and respect for the rules of human interaction.

On the other hand, a "shameless" person is one who does not recognize the rules of human interaction, and hence, social boundaries. The shameless person, who has a dishonorable reputation beyond all social doubt, is outside the boundaries of acceptable moral life. And so, honorable people must deny them the normal social courtesies. To show courtesy to a shameless person makes oneself a fool, since it is foolish to show respect for boundaries when a person acknowledges no boundaries, just as it would be foolish to continue to speak English to a person who does not know the language at all.

One can speak of honor and shame of both males and females only as they pertain to those areas of social life covering common humanity, specifically, natural groupings in which males and females share a common collective honor: the family, village, city, and their collective reputations. Everyday, concrete conduct, which establishes one's reputation and redounds upon one's group, is never independent of the sexual or moral division of labor. It always depends upon gender roles. At this level of perception, when honor is viewed as an exclusive prerogative of one of the sexes, then honor is always male, and shame is always female. Thus in the area of individual, concrete behavior, honor and shame are sex-specific. This represents a lower level of abstraction at which individual males symbolize honor and individual females symbolize shame.

At this level of abstraction, male honor is symbolized in the testicles and expresses itself in typically male behavior: manliness, courage, authority, defense of the family's honor, concern for prestige, and social precedence—all this is honorable behavior for the male. Female shame, on the other hand, is symbolized in the maidenhead and likewise expresses itself in typically female behavior: feelings of shame to reveal nakedness, shyness, blushing, timidity, restraint, sexual exclusiveness—all this is positive shame for the female and makes her honorable.

To move up again to a higher level of assessment in which honor and shame refer to both males and females, people acquire honor by personally aspiring to a certain status and having that status socially validated. On the other hand, people *get shamed* (not *have* shame) when they aspire to a certain status which is denied them by public opinion. When a person realizes he is being denied the status, he is or gets shamed; he is humiliated, and stripped of honor for aspiring to a value not socially his. Honor assessments thus move from the inside (a person's claim) to the outside (public validation). Shame assessments move from the outside (public denial) to the inside (a person's recognition of the denial). To be or get shamed, thus, is to be thwarted or obstructed in one's personal aspiration to worth or status, along with one's recognition of loss of status involved in this attempt.

Again, honor, the common value which is applicable to natural groupings, ranges from internal goodness to social precedence or power. The wicked, powerful king has honor in terms of social precedence, while the good but poor and powerless family has honor in terms of ethical goodness. Conversely, certain families and institutions (e.g., husbands serving as pimps, first-century tavern and inn owners, actors, prostitutes as a class) are considered irretrievably shameless. This is so because they respect no lines of exclusiveness and hence symbolize the chaotic. In this sense, goodness (the female aspect) may lead to a judgment according to which once it is lost, it can never be regained, exactly like female, sexual exclusiveness. On the other hand, emphasis on the aspects as social precedence or power (the male aspect) may lead to a judgment according to which honor can be increased or decreased at the expense of others. Such fluctuating honor will be used as a gauge of social standing.

With the family as repository of natural honor, marriage is always the fusion of the honor of two families. Honor as shame or ethical goodness comes from the mother: she symbolizes it. Honor as social precedence comes from the father: he symbolizes it. The fusion of honor in an honorable marriage thus makes up the social inheritance with which the new family gets set to play the game of life.

6.0 THE MODEL APPLIED

If we scan Luke–Acts in search of the specific words honor and shame, we might be disappointed to find few references (honor: Luke 18:20; shame: Luke 14:9; 16:3). But casting our net wider, we should examine the semantic field of honor and shame:

honor: nouns such as glory, blamelessness, repute, fame, and verbs such as to honor, to glorify, to spread the fame of, to choose, to find acceptable, to be pleased with

shame: nouns such as disgrace, and dishonor, and verbs such as to shame, to be ashamed, to feel ashamed

dishonor: to scorn, to despise, to revile, to reproach, to insult, to blaspheme, to deride, to mock

intention to challenge: nouns such as test and trap, and verbs such as to tempt and to spy on; all questions must be examined in this light

perceptions of being challenged or shamed: nouns such as vengeance, wrath, anger

gestures: to bow down before, to reverence, to bend the knee.

But apart from linguistic frequency, the patterns of honor-shame behavior are everywhere, if the observer knows what to look for. The model developed above can guide our perception of the ever-present phenomenon of concern for honor and shame in the world of Luke–Acts.

6.1 Ascribed and Acquired Honor

6.1.1 Ascribed and Acquired Honor. As the model indicates, honor is either ascribed or acquired. It must be stated immediately that ascribed honor is generally more highly valued in these contexts, for it endures throughout one's life and in every aspect of that life. Achieved honor, however, comes in virtue of performance; and it can and will inevitably be challenged by other performers. Stability (ascribed honor) is preferred to change (achieved honor). Luke's Gospel credits Jesus with both ascribed and acquired honor, but puts greater weight on ascribed honor.

Ascribed honor derives either from kinship and family background or by endowment from an honorable person. It is hardly accidental that Luke begins his Gospel with a detailed portrayal of Jesus' honorable kinship relationships. Recall that Mark and John tell nothing about Jesus' infancy or family relationships; and while Matthew records some material, he pays less attention to Jesus' family background than Luke. From its beginning, then, Luke conditions the reader how to perceive Jesus as an honorable person by carefully noting Jesus' kinship links with royal and priestly stock.

First, Luke tells us about the family of Jesus' mother. Part of her family, at least, belongs to priestly clans. Her kinswoman Elizabeth is a "daughter of Aaron," whose husband is a "priest of the division of Abijah" (1:5). Priestly families enjoyed honorable status (see the portrayal of Jesus as priest in Hebrews). Second, Jesus' father belongs to equally honorable stock, the family of David (1:27; 2:4). Jesus, then, derives great honor by belonging to the two most honorable bloodlines in Israel, priestly and kingly. The genealogy in 3:23–38 only confirms Jesus' honorable kinship relations.

Honor comes from endowment or ascription. The initial part of Luke's narrative emphasizes again and again how Jesus was endowed with maximum honor. By doing this, Luke conditions the reader to perceive Jesus throughout the story as acting from a superior status of endowed honor, God's special agent, i.e., "Christ" and "Son of God." It is God who grants this honor to Jesus. It is both heralded by God's angels or prophets and is directly spoken by God himself. Gabriel tells Mary that God has chosen her son to have exalted honor because of his status as the eternal heir of David:

> He will be great, and will be called the Son of the Most High; and the Lord God will give to him the throne of his father David, and he will reign over the house of Jacob forever; and of his kingdom there will be no end (1:32–33).

These first words about Jesus define him as the most honorable person in Israel who stands at the top of the pyramid as "Son of the Most High" and King of God's people. In a confirming annunciation, God's angels tell shepherds about the honorable status of Jesus: "To you is born this day in the city of David a Savior, who is Christ the Lord" (2:11). The royal Jesus is also the Benefactor ("Savior"), the one anointed by God ("Christ"), who enjoys maximum power ("Lord"). Luke's narrative favors the telling of his story in pairs of episodes and parallel events; he intends the two angelic pronouncements of Jesus' role and status to be taken together as a composite summary of Jesus' honorable status.

Besides angelic pronouncements of God's endowment of great honor to Jesus, Luke records comparable attestations from honorable, prophetic figures. Simeon and Anna, both venerable figures, speak of Jesus as Israel's "salvation" (2:31) or "redemption" (2:38). Simeon in particular delivers a prophetic oracle proclaiming the fulfillment of God's promise that he would live to see "the Lord's Christ," who will be a benefaction to Gentiles ("light") and honor to Israel ("glory"):

> . . . mine eyes have seen thy salvation which thou has prepared in the presence of all peoples, a light for revelation to the Gentiles and for glory to thy people Israel (2:30–32).

This "Christ," moreover, is honorable to all peoples, both Israel and the Gentiles. He is, then, no minor figure in a backwater village, but someone who should command the respect of all peoples.

God himself pronounces Jesus an honorable person, namely, the very "Son of God." Besides Gabriel's attestation that Jesus should be called "the Son of the Most High . . . the Son of God" (1:32, 35), at the Jordan God himself declares Jesus to be "My beloved Son, with thee I am well pleased" (3:22), a declaration repeated at the Transfiguration (9:35). "Son of God," moreover, designates Jesus as God's official, authorized agent (see Psalm 2), implying both his intimacy with God and his sovereign power and authority over God's people.

Inasmuch as the significant rhetorical places in narratives tend to be beginnings and endings, Luke asserts at the beginning of his Gospel that God endowed Jesus with most honorable status. Comparably, at the end of the narrative, Jesus' passion and resurrection, his endowment of honor from God is equally attested. It is indeed ironic that the one who is being dishonored by some is acclaimed to have maximum honor from God, for in his passion Jesus is portrayed as:

Son of God	Luke 22:42, 70; 23:46
Savior	Luke 22:51; 23:43
Prophet	Luke 22:46
Christ	Luke 22:67; 23:35, 39
Chosen One	Luke 23:35
King	Luke 23:2, 37

Jesus' resurrection, moreover, is properly interpreted as God's definitive honoring of him, his "entrance into glory" (24:26, 46; see Malina and Neyrey 1988:129–30). For, as Acts continues, from Jesus' resurrection we should infer: "Let the whole house of Israel know that God has made him both Lord and Christ, this Jesus whom you crucified" (2:36). This Jesus who was crucified God has vindicated and raised up. In regard to ascribed honor, therefore, Jesus is preached to us as a person of singularly honorable bloodlines, who is endowed by the very God of Israel with status and power of the highest sort. Jesus, then, should be acknowledged as the most honorable figure in his world.

6.1.2 *Acquired Honor: Challenge and Riposte.* Acquired honor comes to individuals from their accomplishments, whether it be the building of the city's aqueduct or the slaying of the local dragon. According to Luke 7:4–5, a certain centurion has achieved honor ("worthy") because of his benefaction: "He is worthy to have you do this for him, for he loves our nation, and he has built us our synagogue." Yet in ordinary social interactions in the world of Luke–Acts, honor is typically acquired in the ever-present, public game of push and shove, which we call challenge and riposte. As we appreciate the agonistic quality of the culture in which the Jesus-movement group lived, we know that acquired honor derives from the ceaseless contests in which Jesus and his disciples were endlessly engaged. Those contests may be negative or positive challenges to their honor status.

A quick glance at Luke's Gospel indicates the frequent negative challenges to Jesus' honor, that is, challenges to Jesus' claims to special role or status.

Negative Honor Challenges:
Luke 4:16–30; 5:17–26, 29–32; 6:1–5, 6–11; 10:25–37; 11:14–26, 37–41; 13:10–17; 14:1–6; 15:1–32; 19:1–10, 38–40; 20:1–9, 20–26, 27–40

The challenge-riposte form in which these negative challenges occur typically contains four elements: (a) claim, (b) challenge, (c) riposte, and (d) public verdict. Let us examine one example of this, which can then serve as a model for the reader to examine the other passages just noted.

In Luke 13:10–17, Jesus experiences a severe challenge to his honor. The occasion is the sabbath, when his actions, either that of eating grain or healing, typically draw negative reactions from other claimants for the honor of expounding the correct way of God.

Claim: "Woman, you are freed from your infirmity" (13:12). In our discussion of first-century personalities, we noted how unusual it is for persons to claim a role or status for themselves; given this dyadic situation, one does not personally claim honor and status, but receives this grant of status or honor from others. Nevertheless, it can be noted that Jesus as well as other people act in such a way that a claim is implied. In 13:12, Jesus' pronouncement of healing implies both that he has power from God, presumably as a prophet, and that he is therefore intimate with God (see John 9:31, 33).

Challenge: "The ruler of the synagogue, indignant because Jesus had healed on the sabbath, said: '. . . Come on those days and be healed, and not on the sabbath day' " (13:14). The ruler challenges the implied claim that Jesus is a man of God, a prophet, because he breaks God's law by this anti-sabbath action.

Riposte: "You hypocrites! Does not each of you on the sabbath untie his ox or his ass . . . and lead it away to water it? And ought not this woman, whom Satan bound for eighteen years, be loosed from this bondage on the sabbath day?" (13:15–16). Jesus resorts to name calling ("Hypocrites!"), which is highly effective in ripostes, and he rebuffs the challenge in the best possible manner, by showing that his challengers likewise "break the sabbath."

Verdict: "As he said this, all his adversaries were put to shame; and all the people rejoiced at all the glorious things that were done by him" (13:17). Since challenges to honor do not come from one's family but from those outside, the public nature of the challenge and its riposte demand from the attending public some verdict of winner/loser, that is, who gained honor or lost it. Jesus' challengers were appropriately "shamed"; and so Jesus was acclaimed winner in this particular contest, as the crowds rejoiced in "the glorious things" Jesus did. "Glory" is a cognate of "honor."

Jesus, therefore, both maintained his own honor implied in his claim to be God's prophet and he achieved new honor by his success in shaming his challengers. While Jesus is generally portrayed as the one challenged by rivals, on occasion he issued his own negative challenge to his opponents (Luke 20:41–44). He succeeds, moreover, both in defending his honor and in attacking his rivals.

The challenge-riposte form dramatizes most negative honor challenges in the Gospels. But other negative challenges are noted, which are not told in this form, but which a careful reader will nonetheless perceive as honor challenges. Often challenges come in the form of questions asked of Jesus. The Gospels frequently note that Jesus' religious peers hang on every word of his to try to trap him or to find something with which to accuse him. Part of this strategy manifests itself in questions asked him, which "put him to the test."

The exchange with the lawyer in 10:25–37 illustrates the challenging nature of public questions. The story begins with a challenge to Jesus, "A lawyer stood up to put him to the test saying, 'Teacher, what shall I do to inherit eternal life?' " (10:25). This is no innocent request for information, but a challenge which "put him to the test." In honorable fashion, Jesus' defense consists in answering a question with a question, thus putting the original questioner on the spot, "What is written in the law? how do you read?" (10:26). Questions are challenging, and Jesus answers a challenge with a challenge. The lawyer is forced to answer in traditional fashion (10:27), and so Jesus successfully withstands this honor challenge. The lawyer, however, is shamed by his unsuccessful challenge, and so asks a second question of Jesus to stump him and so recoup his own lost honor: "But he, desiring to justify himself, said to Jesus, 'And who is my neighbor?' " (10:29). Jesus answers directly with the story of the Good Samaritan, a story which is shocking for its elevation of the Samaritan outsider over Jewish priests and levites as examples of covenant compassion. The episode ends with Jesus asking the lawyer a final challenging question, "Which of these three, do you think, proved neighbor to the man who fell among the robbers?" (10:36). The questioning lawyer loses his rematch with Jesus, as he is forced to admit the Samaritan's excellence over his own priests. Jesus has survived the double challenge, answered both questions successfully, and gained immeasurable honor in the process.

Since Jesus' honor consists, in part, of a claim to know God's ways and to teach them truly, he must answer these honor-threatening questions. Silence would imply weakness, and thus shame. For other examples of challenging questions, see 7:18–23; 17:20–21; 20:1–9, 20–26 and 27–40 (see Malina and Neyrey 1988:73–74).

In addition to negative challenges to his honor, Jesus frequently experienced positive challenges as well, as the following list indicates:

Positive Honor Challenges:
Luke 5:12–16; 7:1–10; 8:22–25, 40–56; 9:37–43, 57–62; 12:13–21; 13:1–5; 17:11–19; 18:18–25, 35–43.

As we saw, positive challenges may come in a variety of ways: (a) in a word of praise of Jesus (18:18–19); (b) in a request to Jesus to act as a socially prominent person, e.g., as arbiter of an inheritance (12:13–21); (c) in an offer of discipleship to him by some (9:57–62); and (d) in a request to him for help and benefaction, which comprises the bulk of the miracle stories in Luke's Gospel. A fifth example, a gift (what we call a bribe), is not found in the Gospels.

It may sound strange to Western ears to consider requests for Jesus' help and offerings of discipleship as challenges to his honor. But let us consider them further in terms of Luke's Mediterranean culture. Although

Jesus is gifted with wisdom and power from God, this is not automatically dispensed to any one who stands before him and requests a share of it. In one sense, all of this wealth of wisdom and power belongs to God's covenant family, and outsiders have no particular claim to it, neither Gentiles nor sinners. In fact, it is dishonorable for a parent to give the children's bread to others (see Mark 7:27); charity begins at home. And so, requests for help are challenging and potentially dishonoring, if the family's goods are given to others without something in return. At least such requests must be carefully considered from the perspective of what is honorable behavior.

Every request, question, compliment or offering, then, puts Jesus on the spot. What if he cannot work a healing this day (Luke 9:40)? What if he cannot answer a question, even a friendly question? What if he accepts so-and-so as his disciple? Not every would-be disciple is a credit to him, witness Judas. In this light we might read the triple approach to Jesus of would-be disciples in Luke 9:57–62. The challenging nature of the episode is captured in the way Luke presents Jesus in less than welcoming tones. Jesus tells the first inquirer about the shame of not having an honorable house in which to sleep (9:58). To another, Jesus poses a dilemma, whether to honor one's father by burying him or to dishonor him by leaving him to follow Jesus (9:60). To a third, Jesus poses a comparable choice, one's honorable family or Jesus' band (9:62). The exchanges in 9:57–62, then, indicate that a challenge was put to Jesus by offers of discipleship, offers apparently refused here because of the perceived nature of this challenge.

Even a dinner invitation can be a positive challenge and so is fraught with danger. To accept a dinner invitation is to obligate oneself to reciprocate; the person invited may not have sufficient means for this, and so the dinner invitation is an honor challenge. Moreover, the dinner may become the occasion when Jesus suffers a slight in hospitality, thus dishonoring him (see Luke 7:44–46). In his culture, Jesus must be careful of how social encounters end (see Luke 14:28–32), for they may result in loss of honor for him, which would dishonor the one who sent him. Jesus is beset, therefore, not only by negative challenges to his honor, but by positive ones as well. Social life in the world of Luke–Acts was truly risky business.

6.1.3 *Replications of Honor.* Honor is replicated both by blood and by name. As regards Jesus' blood family, his pedigree, Luke tells the reader that Jesus comes from excellent stock, priestly and royal lines. His mother's family includes Elizabeth, "daughter of Aaron," and Zechariah, "a priest . . . of the division of Abijah." And his father's family is "of the house of David." Furthermore, as his genealogy indicates, Jesus belongs to the noble past of Israel, with blood ties to its kings and patriarchs, which is not quite what one would expect of a carpenter's son from an obscure village in Galilee.

Jesus' blood, moreover, is righteous. Of his cousins Zechariah and Elizabeth, Luke notes that "both were righteous before God, walking in all the commandments and ordinances of the Lord blameless" (1:6). Their son, John, is likewise honorable ("he will be great," 1:15; see 7:28), and he is holy and filled with the Spirit of God (1:15; see 7:26). Jesus' mother is told that "You have found favor with God" (1:30; see 1:28); and for her part, she believes God's word (1:45) and keeps faithfully the rituals of childbirth (2:22–24).

In a special way, Luke has taken pains to indicate that John the Baptizer, who is often considered a rival of Jesus in other documents (John 3:25–30), is a blood relative of Jesus. By asserting that John and Jesus are kinsmen, Luke implies that the great honor of John does not threaten Jesus in any way, but adds to his honor by being part of the same blood family. Hence as Luke tells the story, far from being a competitor with Jesus for honor in Israel, John contributes to Jesus' honor naturally. This sense of noncompetition is expressed in the Gospel by the Lukan device of narrating parallel annunciations (1:5–24, 26–38), parallel canticles (1:46–55, 67–79), and parallel birth notices (1:57–66, 80 and 2:1–12, 15–27, 34–40; on these parallels, see R. Brown 1977:294–95, 297, 409). And so Luke's account of John paints him in noble colors, calling him "great" (1:15) and describing him "in the spirit and power of Elijah" (1:17). If it is permissible to say of John, "among those born of women, none is greater than John" (7:28), then Jesus is all the greater, all the more honorable. The point is, they are not rivals for honor in Israel; but Jesus gains in honor by every tribute paid to John, because they are cousins and blood relatives. Honor is replicated in blood.

Honor is displayed not only in blood but also in one's name. One's honor is never simply that of an individual, but the honor of one's family, clan, village, etc. In this regard, Luke's Gospel tells a divided story. At the key rhetorical points in the narrative, beginning and ending, Jesus is shamed. His own townspeople of Nazareth deny him honor at his inaugural appearance there (4:16–30). Although he had done many signs and wonders, when he claimed to be anointed with the Spirit for liberation of God's people (4:18–19), they thought that he claimed too much honor, which, like all things in a limited-good society, is in short supply at Nazareth. For Jesus to gain this new honor, someone would be perceived as losing it, in this case, the townsfolk of Nazareth. Moreover, given the perception that one's role and status are ascribed at birth, it seems odd for this "son of Joseph," who is but a carpenter, to claim a role and status as the most honorable person in the village. Jesus, who was formerly an equal there, is perceived as claiming the highest status in the village. And so, his claim is rejected by the people at Nazareth and he loses the support of his own. How shameful it is when "his own receive him not"!

Comparably, at the end of his career, his kinsmen in the covenant disown him before their common enemy, the Roman foreigners. Three times during Jesus' trial before Pilate, "the chief priests, the rulers *and the people*" call for his death (23:18, 21, 23). And as he hangs on the cross, the elite of Jerusalem deny him any sympathy or kinship bond with the nation (23:35). If honor rests in family name and clan membership, Jesus is immeasurably shamed by the denial of him by both of these grantors of honor.

Yet honor is bestowed on Jesus from others, who assume kinship roles or represent other voices in the clan. Whereas Jesus' family finds him too much, and so shames him, another person acclaims him "son." God twice called Jesus "Son"—"Beloved Son in whom I am well pleased" (3:22; 9:35). By this God functions as family and ascribes Jesus great honor as a thoroughly pleasing son, which was an unusual compliment in this culture (see Heb 12:5–11). And since the testimony of an honorable person counts for much, God, who is the most honorable of persons, gives witness on Jesus' behalf that must have maximum credibility and exceptional weight.

If a reader were to list all the titles of Jesus in the course of Luke's Gospel, these would be grants of honor as well. The more honorable titles of Jesus in this Gospel would include:

Christ	Luke 2:11; 9:20; 22:67; 23:2, 35, 39; 24:26
King	Luke 1:32–33; 19:38; 23:2, 3, 37, 38
Lord	Luke 1:46; 5:8, 12; 6:5; 7:13; 9:54; 11:1; 24:34
Prophet	Luke 4:24; 7:16, 39; 9:8, 19; 13:33–34; 24:19
Savior	Luke 2:11 (see 7:50; 8:48; 13:23; 17:19; 19:10; 23:39)
Son of God	Luke 1:32, 35; 3:22; 4:3, 9, 41; 8:28; 9:35; 22:70

Whereas many rejected Jesus, both at Nazareth and in Jerusalem, many acclaimed him by these honorable titles, thus balancing the shame from his kinsmen and countrymen. And it would be interesting to note that many of these titles are ascribed to Jesus by people regularly considered honorable themselves, namely, angels (e.g., Gabriel), prophets (e.g., Simeon and Anna), and God (Acts 2:36).

Jesus' honor, then, is replicated in terms of blood, that is, his membership in honorable clans (priestly, royal) and his kinship with honorable people, such as John the Prophet. His honor is replicated in terms of name. Although his townsfolk and indeed many of his nation consider his name worthless, nevertheless others in Israel name him with honorable names.

6.2 Honor Displayed

Honor is displayed in regard to the human body in a variety of ways. Clothing, for example, can signal to the public important information about the wearer. Apart from the fact that certain people in certain roles wear uniforms that identify their roles, a pious Jew might signal his claim to be a covenant observant person by the wearing of phylacteries (Matt 23:5). In the honorable world of conspicuous consumption, which was Jesus' world, wealthy and aristocratic people signal their status by appropriate clothing: "Those who are gorgeously appareled and live in luxury are in kings' courts" (Luke 7:25; see 16:19).

In regard to Jesus, we find only one reference to his clothing, and that an ironic reference. Herod and his court review the claims of Jesus, pretender to the throne of Israel. They find no substance to those claims, which means an honor challenge. Their challenge is narrated in the way they mock the claim and the claimant by "arraying him (Jesus) in gorgeous apparel" (23:11). They shame Jesus, who is judged the false pretender to the throne, by dressing him as if he were that. Clothes make the man and give honor; but overdressing or inappropriate clothing lead to dishonor.

In regard to Jesus' own body, a number of questions can be asked which pertain to honor and shame. (a) What parts of the body are important in Jesus' actions or speech? (b) Who touches Jesus, either with his approval or against his will? (c) Does anyone specifically touch his head or face? (d) Does anyone ever restrict the movement of Jesus' hands and arms?

As noted in the model, certain parts of the physical body denote honor, and certain parts shame (see 1 Cor 12:23–24). The head replicates honor and so it is crowned; Luke apparently omitted the mock crowning of Jesus with a crown of acanthus which is mentioned in Mark 15:16–20. Feet, however, point to a different but related set of implications, and of this bodily member the Gospel makes frequent mention. The honor of Jesus is signalled when other people are at his feet, suggesting that he is "head" to their "feet." People fall on their faces at his feet (8:41; 17:16), either to ask his help or to give thanks, suggesting Jesus' honorable status. Disciples sit at his feet and listen to the words from his mouth (8:35; 10:39), again calling attention to Jesus' high status as teacher. The feet themselves may be treated with respect, thus giving honor to the whole person by a form of metonymy. The sinful woman washed, anointed, and dried Jesus' feet (7:38, 44–46), thus honoring him with singular marks of etiquette which Jesus' host conspicuously denied him. Finally, in the parable in 15:11–24, the dishonored son is honored by his father in terms of the way his son's body is treated. The father commands the servant to put "the best robe" on his shoulders, a ring on his finger and shoes on his feet (15:22).

Another honorable bodily part is the right hand. Like the ancients, we speak of the ruler's "right-hand man," suggesting a position of honor, influence and power. The Synoptic Gospels record how Jesus, after being challenged by priests and Pharisees, challenged them in turn with a conundrum from the scriptures. By honor ranking, "the Christ" is but the latest son of David, and so David should have a title of greater honor because he is the patriarch and founder of the dynasty. But the scriptures say otherwise. David calls his successor, who is "the Christ," by the more honorable title of "Lord." This whole discussion springs from Ps 110:1, where the exalted status of David's successor is couched in terms of bodily parts which denote honor/power and submission (Hay 1973:59–103). The Lord (God) said to my Lord ("the Christ"): "Sit at my right hand, till I make thy enemies a stool for thy feet" (Luke 20:43).

The Christ enjoys maximum honor by virtue of his place seated at God's "right hand" (see Acts 2:34–36). His enemies are correspondingly dishonored by being under his feet, which denotes total lack of status or power (see 1 Cor 15:25–26; Heb 2:6–8).

Christians, moreover, repeatedly used Psalm 110 to speak of the honor of Jesus, especially in regard to his dishonorable death. Luke and other writers perceived Ps 110:1 as a prediction of Jesus' resurrection, when the powerlessness of his arrest and execution would be reversed by God, who would invest him with honor and power (Acts 2:34–36). Honor and power, of course, are symbolized by Jesus' session at God's "right hand." This same idea is communicated by Jesus' own response to the chief priest's question at his Jewish trial. The questioner believes Jesus to be a false Christ and a false prophet, and effectively asks him to confess to this deception: "If you are the Christ, tell us" (22:67). Jesus' response blends two scriptural passages, one from Daniel 7 and the other from Psalm 110. Anticipating rejection, Jesus declares himself the "Son of man," alluding to the noble figure from Daniel who was shamed by men on earth, but honored by God in heaven. This same "Son of man," moreover, will be "seated at the right hand of the power of God" (22:69), that singular place of honor. Of course, this prophecy about Jesus is amply fulfilled by his resurrection and enthronement, as this is narrated in Acts 2:34–36. But Psalm 110 and its reference to Jesus' session at God's "right hand" clearly function as a bodily indicator of Jesus' great honor, especially honor granted after his shameful, powerless death.

As noted above, bodily touching likewise has to do with honor. Some passages record the crowds seeking to touch Jesus for the purpose of connecting with his power (6:19), a touch which we have learned to call a positive honor challenge. The episode of Jesus and the menstruating woman (8:43–48) illustrates this admirably. Four times in the story the point is made that she (or someone) touched Jesus:

(a) A woman . . . came up and touched the fringe of his garment (8:44)
(b) Jesus said, "Who was it that touched me?" (8:45)
(c) But Jesus said, "Some one touched me!" (8:46)
(d) She declared in the presence of all the people why she had touched him and how she had been immediately healed (8:47)

From Luke's concern over this detail we infer that this touching was in some sense surprising, if not unwelcome, to Jesus. All the more so, because the woman who touched him suffered from a malady that in Jesus' culture signifies radical uncleanness, namely, chronic menstruation. Ultimately, the story is resolved in a grant of honor to Jesus, as the woman publicly acclaimed the benefit she received from this touch (8:47). The touch was provocative and Jesus honorably inquired who had touched him and why. A challenge was perceived by the touch and had to be dealt with.

In other situations, Jesus himself initiates the touch, thus signaling a higher status whereby he enters with impunity the space of a person of lower status. Jesus stretched out his hand and touched a leper, "I will; be clean" (5:13). Acting as the superior person in this exchange, Jesus claims honor in his ability to cure and to bestow benefaction. That the leper was healed by this touch adds to Jesus' honor and confirms the appropriateness of his touch. In another situation, some people — presumably women — brought children to Jesus for him to touch. Some rebuked them, but Jesus admitted them (18:15–16). His touch did not diminish his honor but extended acceptance and thus value to those touched.

The passion narrative most dramatically illustrates the grammar of honor and shame in regard to Jesus' body. How dishonoring is the kiss of the traitor (22:48). How dishonoring is the seizure of Jesus and the binding of his arms and hands, which renders him physically impotent in this context (22:54). How shameful is the pinioning of his hands to the cross, not only mutilating his body but rendering him powerless. But inasmuch as honor is particularly associated with head and face, how dishonoring is the fact that Jesus was blindfolded (22:64) and struck, presumably in the face or on the head (22:63–64). As we noted earlier, Luke omits the mock investiture of Jesus, in which it is recorded that his head was crowned with a wreath of acanthus and his face struck with a reed, a shaming of the most honorable part of his body (Mark 15:16–20; Matt 27:27–31).

Continuing our survey of the ways in which honor is displayed, we note now that honor is replicated not just by the names or titles given to the one being honored, but by gifts or invitations bestowed as well. A grant of honor comes to Jesus from a group of women, apparently well-to-do women, who were either aristocrats themselves or were connected to them. For example, among the women who honor Jesus by gifts of material support is Joanna, the wife of Chuza, who was Herod's steward (Luke 8:3). In any event, these are women who enjoy a surplus of money and/or goods in a subsistence society; they are not peasants or people of mean status. Honor, moreover, would be signalled by invitations to Jesus to dine (7:36–50; 11:37); but, as we noted earlier, these invitations could turn into occasions when customary marks of hospitality are denied Jesus, thus shaming him (7:44–46; see 11:37–38 and 14:1). The principle is the same: honorable people bestow grants of honor to others by their gifts to them, their invitations to them, and their association with them.

The honorable person does honorable actions. In the case of Jesus, his benefaction to those who beseech his help would signal the deeds of an honorable leader. It belongs to King and Lord and son of David to make available to God's covenant people the blessings of food, peace, and health.

Jesus' honorable actions are likewise those which illustrate his power, which is itself another synonym of honor. The Gospel emphatically maintains that Jesus has the capability and authority to act powerfully (exousia) and that he exercises that power (dynamis). He has authority unlike that of his peers, which is surely a grant of honor to him but shame to them (4:32–36). Despite slanders to the contrary (11:15), this authorization for powerful acts comes to Jesus from God by his endowment with God's powerful Holy Spirit (4:18–19; 20:2–8) and not through the power of the Evil One (4:6). Jesus' authority is manifested especially in his speech, which is admitted to be powerful (4:36; 5:24; 7:8); his commands immediately issue in powerful results.

Besides acting with legitimate authorization as an honorable figure, Jesus acts with power (dynamis), by which the evangelist means Jesus' miracles, his signs and wonders (4:14). In virtue of this power, Jesus conquers and expels powerful devils (4:36), as well as heals (5:17; see 6:19; 8:46). And the crowds are loud in praise of these honorable acts of power (19:37). Of course, Jesus acts in power not only in his earthly life, but especially when he returns in power and glory (21:27).

6.2.1 Interpretation of a Challenge. As the model noted, speech events allow people engaged in a potential challenge situation to clarify their intentions. The potential challenger can clarify his intentions in the exchange. Luke frequently appeals to God's ancient oaths to clarify the ambiguity of Jesus' situation or that of his followers. The birth of John is interpreted in terms of "the oath which God swore to our father Abraham" (1:73); John's mission, then, bears God's stamp of approval. Any ambiguity attached to him is resolved by appeal to God's own word on his behalf. According to Acts 2:30, "God had sworn with an oath to him that he would set one of his descendants on his throne"; this oath is cited to remove the ambiguity of Jesus' shameful death.

Speech acts, however, can be ambiguous. Witness the address to Jesus in 20:21, "Teacher, we know that you speak and teach rightly, and show no partiality, but truly teach the way of God." This sounds praiseworthy and honorable, for all the right words are used. But it is spoken by spies sent by the scribes and chief priests who seek to trap him in his speech.

The severe challenge to Jesus is masked by these words, but it is present. It matters, then, who speaks, what is said, and on what occasion and to what effect.

Yet, on another occasion, Jesus is asked to testify under oath about his authority and identity, an oath that is intended to remove the perceived ambiguity about him. Although the technical terms of "swearing oaths" are not found here, that is clearly what is happening. On trial, Jesus is asked to give formal testimony, that is, to adjure the truth to this court. And he speaks the truth clearly, without ambiguity or evasion, about his role and status as "the Christ . . . the Son of God" (22:67–69; see 23:3). In this, there is no intention of avoiding an honor challenge on the part of Jesus. His speech, then, appears honorable and defensive of his honor at all times. Lies are told about him and his disciples (Acts 6:11–13), but he always tells the truth.

Although not a trained rabbi, Jesus' teaching gains in credibility and its ambiguity is lessened by his constant giving of his "word of honor." Jesus' characteristic "Amen, Amen, I say to you" seems to function like a word of honor (see Luke 4:24; 12:37; 18:17, 29; 21:32; 23:43).

6.3 Collective Honor

6.3.1 Honor and the Natural Group. The head or leader of the natural grouping symbolizes the honor of that group to outsiders. Except for Acts 12:20–23, no king or father is dishonored. But there is considerable concern for the honor of God, who is the supreme head of Israel, which centers around the charge of "blasphemy" in Luke–Acts. Jesus' opponents think that God is dishonored when Jesus claims to have power to forgive sins (Luke 5:21). Such power belongs exclusively with God; for Jesus to claim it would mean a lessening of God's power, namely, a dishonoring of God. The scribes and the Pharisees perceive a challenge to God's power and honor, hence the charge of "blasphemy" on this occasion. Again Jesus is accused of blasphemy when he claims that he, whom they judge to be a sinful pretender, will be "seated at the right hand of the power of God" (Luke 22:68). In their eyes, God would surely be dishonored by the affront of such a sinful, misguided pretender in the divine presence. Jesus' behavior, then, is classified as first-degree dishonor, that is, sacrilege. In this vein, one might check other references to "blasphemy" in Luke–Acts (Luke 12:10; Acts 6:11; 19:37; 26:11).

From the Christian perspective, however, those who reject Jesus as God's Christ are dishonoring God. The principle of agency is clear in the Gospels: whoever honors Jesus, honors the One who sent him (Luke 9:48); whoever dishonors God's agent, dishonors God. This is illustrated in a variety of ways. In one parable we learn of agents being sent out to collect produce from the owner's vineyard (20:9–16). The agents are systematically dishonored, either "beaten" or "treated shamefully" or "wounded and cast out." By this the owner of the vineyard, who is God, suffers a loss of honor which is extreme and total, with disorienting social consequence. Such dishonor can only be expunged if the owner "comes and destroys those tenants and gives the vineyard to others" (20:16).

In this vein one might examine all the passages in Luke–Acts which talk of the rejection and shaming of God's prophets. Jesus remarks in many places that all of God's prophets suffered rejection and even death, "from Abel to Zechariah" (11:47–51; Acts 7:51–53). Indeed no prophet could suffer except in Jerusalem (13:33–34). Moses was rejected (Acts 7:27, 35, 39), and it is an open question if the "prophet like Moses" will be treated in the same way (Acts 3:22–25). The point is, when God's agents, the prophets, are dishonored, God is dishonored. So it was with Moses, with John the Baptizer (the greatest of prophets, Luke 7:26–28), with Jesus (Luke 4:24), and with Jesus' disciples (Luke 6:23). What must God do to vindicate his honor and that of his agents?

In Acts, we find the constant refrain, "You killed him (the Christ), but God raised him" (2:23–24; 3:14–15; 4:10; 5:30–31; 13:27–30). This refrain is profitably understood in terms of honor and shame, especially the honor of the head of natural groupings. For when Israel rejects God's Christ, it sins and dishonors the God who sent him. But God vindicated his honor by raising Jesus up, both to life and to the throne of grace in heaven. God would truly be dishonored if he failed to act in exalting the Holy One whom he sent as his Christ. This is the thrust of the argument about Psalm 16 in Acts 2:25–28. For, as the Psalm goes, the Holy One of God claimed, "For thou wilt not abandon my soul to Hades, nor let thy Holy One see corruption" (Acts 2:27). God indeed is honor bound to vindicate his Christ, thus restoring the honor of God.

In summary, God, who is the head of the natural grouping, the covenant family of Israel, bears the honor of the group. On the one hand, one part of Israel, the priestly clan, thinks that Jesus dishonors Israel's God by his pretentious claims. On the other hand, Jesus and his disciples claim that the priests dishonor God by rejecting God's prophets and agents. Either way, God's honor is challenged; and Luke is at pains to note God's riposte to this, which is the exaltation of Jesus as Lord and Christ.

6.3.2 *Honor and the Voluntary Group.* In terms of voluntary groups such as the religious parties in Israel, the chiefs and leaders of those groups are always in the public eye defending their honor and that of their party or group. It is here that the game of challenge-riposte is played daily with deadly earnestness. As head of his faction, Jesus bears the honor of the group; hence, even when his disciples are attacked, it is Jesus who defends his and their honor. For example, when Pharisees criticize the lack of piety of Jesus' disciples, who do not fast, it is Jesus who gives the riposte to this honor challenge (Luke 5:30–32). When a man, whose son was suffering from an evil spirit, complained to Jesus that his disciples could not cure the sick boy, it is Jesus whose honor is challenged (Luke 9:37–43). And it is Jesus' words and actions that serve as the riposte to that honor challenge. If Jesus is dishonored, his disciples share that shame. If they are shamed, he is shamed.

Comparably, in Acts we find stories of Peter and Paul on trial before the voluntary grouping of priests and associates. Among them, it is always the chief priest who bears the honor of this group before the public, and so it is he and his associate chief priests who issue the challenge to Peter in the first hearing in 4:6–7 and then in its replay in 5:27–28. Before the chief priest Ananias, Paul claims to be an honorable and observant person, a claim which Ananias challenges by ordering Paul to be struck in the mouth (23:1–2). Paul's riposte is to call down God's judgment on this breach of justice, thus asking God to vindicate his honor (which is God's honor, since Paul is God's agent). Yet some face saving takes place, as Paul pleads ignorance of the public role of Ananias as high priest (23:5), which apparently sufficed for both Paul and the priest to maintain their respective honors. A stalemate ensues. Yet Ananias' honorable role requires him to continue to prosecute Paul, this time before the governor Felix (24:1). As Jesus bears the honor of his faction, so the chief priests in Jesus' trial (Luke 22:66–71) and in Peter's and Paul's trials (Acts 4–5; 23–24) bear and defend the honor of their respective groups before Jews and Gentiles alike.

6.4 Gender-Based Honor

When we noted in the model the moral division of labor between men and women, that understanding of honor and shame suggested binary ways in which men and women relate to this central value. Men direct their attentions outward, away from the home; women look inward, to the home and to places and things germane to it, such as the well or the grinding wheel. Men are aggressive in this type of culture and are concerned with authority and precedence; correspondingly, women are guardians of the family honor. Accordingly, we can begin to imagine scenarios for Luke–Acts based on our understanding of the special way women are understood in an honor-shame society.

Given the fact of dyadic personality in the Mediterranean world, such a phenomenon would suggest that a woman, when she marries, moves to her husband's house and becomes embedded in that new kinship group. She is, then, no longer the daughter of so-and-so, but now the wife of so-and-so. She moves from one male protector, her father, to another, her husband. When we look at how Luke introduces women as characters in the narrative, we observe that they are typically named in relation to their husbands, as the following list indicates:

Zechariah and his wife, Elizabeth—Luke 1:5
Mary, a virgin betrothed to a man named Joseph—Luke 1:27
Herod and Herodias—Luke 3:19
Joanna, the wife of Chuza—Luke 8:3
Ananias and his wife, Sapphira—Acts 5:1
Aquila and his wife, Priscilla—Acts 18:2
Felix and his wife, Drusilla—Acts 24:24
Agrippa and his wife, Bernice—Acts 25:13, 23

The Sadducean problem in Luke 20:28–33 presumes a situation in which the wife and then widow is known in terms of her husband's family and his many brothers. This is evidently the correct cultural pattern. Thus, if a woman appears (e.g., Lydia, Acts 16:13–15) who is not identified as the wife of so-and-so, the reader would be expected to wonder as to her "shame," that is, her defense of feminine sexual exclusivity and family virtue.

According to the grammar of honor and shame, we would expect there to be clear patterns of space that are appropriate to men and to women, patterns which replicate the understanding of male honor and female shame. A simple question can be asked: where does one expect to find the women in the narrative of Luke–Acts? The model suggests "in the home," that is, in private, domestic space relative to the family or to places connected with it, such as wells, ovens, and grain mills (17:35). This is verified by a quick glance at Luke's story:

1. Elizabeth "hid herself" in her home during her confinement (Luke 1:24); when she greeted Mary, her cousin, it was in her house (1:40–43).

2. Peter's mother-in-law, ill and at home, was in the women's quarters of the house; Jesus' appearance in those very quarters needed to be carefully explained (4:38–39). When healed, this woman reassumed her proper role in the household and went to her official space, the kitchen, to prepare food.

3. Jairus' daughter was presumed dead, and she remained in the women's quarters, where Jesus went (8:49–52).

4. Martha and Mary are known only in terms of the interior of their house, where Jesus is their guest (10:38–42). The expected place of Mary, moreover, is with Martha in the women's part of that household, the kitchen; she is not expected in the dining area, and so her presence there requires a special explanation. Jesus' remark to Martha serves to vindicate Mary's exceptional presence in space not expected of her; the story consciously upsets the native perception of how things ought to be.

5. In 15:3–7, the shepherd (a man) is described outside on the hills in search of a lost sheep; balancing that is the woman inside a house sweeping it in search of a lost coin (15:8–10). The parables balance each other in terms of man/outside and female/inside.

The model, then, suggests that we look closely at women appearing in public situations, for this may signal how the reader is to evaluate the persons concerned in terms of honor.

For example, Luke expects us to perceive "the woman of the city" who touches Jesus feet (7:36–38) as a shameless woman, however we interpret the sin implied in the host's remark about "what sort of woman this is who is touching him, for she is a sinner" (7:39). Her very presence in men's space, such as the dining area described, signals a violation of the expectation of where she should be. Likewise, the woman with the flow of blood is doubly dangerous in the narrative: she has a flow of blood, which renders her unclean, and she is abroad in the crowd, even reaching out and touching men (8:42–48).

A reader might test this expectation on the following passages, alert to the clues implied by the place in which women are found (Luke 7:11–17; 8:2–3; 11:27; 13:10–17; 22:54–55; 23:55–56; 24:1–10; Acts 1:13; 21:9). It would matter if the woman is alone or in the company of other women, whether the occasion is a funeral or other business, whether the place is a synagogue or a grove by a river.

The case of widows can confirm the expectations of situations of honor and shame in regard to women. A widow is in a precarious situation in regard to her "shame" because she has no male to defend her and the honor of her children and household. Upon the death of a husband, if he has unmarried brothers, a levirate marriage might be arranged with those brothers, thus guarding the endangered honor of the family (Deut 25:5–10; Luke 20:28–33). It is not surprising, moreover, to find special commands that "widows and orphans" be specially protected (Deut 14:28). The issue at stake is not simply or primarily the financial status of the widow and her children (Luke 20:47), but rather the danger to her reputation, which in this culture is more precious than gold.

Two examples might illustrate this. First, at Nain, Jesus chanced upon a funeral. Healing stories often include details which indicate just how serious the situation is; for example, a person might be ill for twelve years (8:43) or living among graves (8:26). In the case of 7:11–17, the woman is in acute danger. She is a widow, who is now burying her "only son" (7:12), so that she truly has no honor-conscious male to defend her. Jesus' saving action is directed to both mother and son. Of course he revives the dead son; but by this the widow is rid of her "shamelessness" because she now has a male, her son, to defend her and the family's interests.

Second, in 18:1–8 we are told of a widow who is becoming shameless. Evidently there is no male to defend her, no husband and no son; and so she is defenseless and at the mercy of her adversary. So desperate has she become that she publicly badgers the city's "judge" to defend her interests (18:3). Her public reproach to the judge indicates shameless behavior. In both stories, then, Jesus takes the side of these widows, first restoring the son of one widow to life and then narrating how a judge came to the second widow's assistance. Both narratives demand special sympathy for the precarious state of the "shame" of the widow, the value worth more than gold.

In this light, one might examine Acts 1:13. It is presumed by that narrative that Mary is now a widow; she would hardly be living in another man's house if her husband were alive. And since her son Jesus ascended to heaven, Mary is now without the protection of a male, either husband or son. She is, then, in a most precarious situation. But Luke defends the honor of Jesus by guarding the shame of Mary by locating her in a new family, an honorable household, the church. A comparable kind of story is found in John 19:26–27, which may be quite correct culturally as well as historically or theologically.

A final point might be noted. In Acts, Luke repeatedly tells the reader that the Christian preachers enjoyed success with men and women (Acts 8:10; 9:2; 22:4). Of particular interest might be Luke's remark that the women were often "leading women" or "women of high standing" (Acts 13:50; 17:2, 14). Is Luke indicating only that Christianity was attractive to socially prominent women or might he also be suggesting that Christianity was attractive to shame-conscious women, that is, women whose reputations were spotless?

7.0 CONCLUSIONS AND FURTHER PROJECTS

It is truly an understatement to say that the whole of Luke's Gospel, almost every piece of social interaction, should be viewed through the lens of honor and shame. We are familiar with the endless conflicts narrated in the Gospel between Jesus and Satan (4:1–13), his Nazareth neighbors (4:16–30), the Pharisees, and other parties. Jesus' ministry ends in bitter conflict with temple officials and the occupying army of the Romans. It was a career fraught with conflict from start to finish. The perspective of honor and shame helps us to appreciate the agonistic quality of that world, and it offers us a literary and social form (challenge-riposte) to interpret the conflicts.

This perspective, moreover, allows us to examine more accurately the positive aspects of Jesus' life. We are not accustomed to viewing every public action of Jesus as an honor challenge, whether that be requests for Jesus' help, invitations to dinner, offers of discipleship, and the like. But seeing his life through the lens of honor and shame, we begin to view it from the native's perspective and to appreciate the social dynamic as natives see it. Jesus is ever in the public eye, the proper place for an honorable male in his society. Every social interaction in which he is engaged is a potential challenge, both a positive and a negative challenge. His honor, and that of the one who sent him, is ever on the line.

Knowledge of honor and shame, both as value and as behavior, are essential elements of an adequate scenario for interpreting Luke–Acts. If this is the way first-century Mediterraneans perceive their world and act in accord with that perception, then a considerate reader must strive to acquire just such a scenario, for only in this way can a reader begin to appreciate the pervasive social dynamics explained in this chapter as honor and shame, pivotal values of the Mediterranean world.

Thus far we have applied the model of honor and shame to Luke's Gospel. It is our hope that readers and students would be enabled now to take up the task in regard to Acts of the Apostles. And to that end we offer the following suggestions.

Language of Status: one might trace the titles of Jesus in Acts; where is Jesus and what does he do? Note the other actors, whether chief priests, governors, kings, etc. Who has power? Who can imprison, put on trial, and execute?

Sources of Honor: (a) ascribed honor: one might trace the way Jesus' gift of the powerful Spirit serves to give ascribed honor to Peter and the apostles, to Barnabas and Paul, etc. Note the claims to honor in Paul's speeches in Acts 22:4–5; 23:1 and 26:4–5. (b) Achieved honor: examine Simon Magus in Acts 8:4–24.

Challenge-Riposte: (a) one might examine the many passages in Acts, in particular the trials of Peter, Stephen, and Paul. It is a truism that the disciples of Jesus are never out of conflict; they are endlessly challenged. One might examine these conflicts in terms of the honor of the disciples and the honor of God, who is dishonored when they are dishonored.

Gender-based Place and Roles: (a) one might make a list of the men and women in Acts and note where they appear. Are the men always in public space? What do they do in public space? Where are the women who are described (e.g., Acts 12:12)? What roles are they performing in those spaces?

This chapter, moreover, is part of the conversation about the social psychology of the first-century Mediterranean world. And it is expected that its insights be carefully shared with other chapters of this book which treat the same topic from different perspectives. Together honor and shame are an essential component of first-century personality, which simply cannot be understood without it. The symbolic world of Luke–Acts is also a world of honor and shame or gender-based maps; the mapping of Luke's culture begun there can be continued with attention to the way a system is communicated by the classification of all things in this world in terms of honor and shame. And since honor means challenge and riposte, no discussion of conflict would be complete without the consideration of that conflict also in terms of honor challenge and riposte.

3

FIRST-CENTURY PERSONALITY: DYADIC, NOT INDIVIDUAL

Bruce J. Malina and Jerome H. Neyrey

0.0 INTRODUCTION

The fact that many Americans read Luke–Acts and claim to understand what the author means is interesting to say the least, since Luke's discussion of Jesus, Mary, Simeon, Elizabeth, Peter, Paul, or any other person in his story should really be quite difficult for Americans to follow. This is so because whenever Americans start talking about someone, their inevitable frame of reference is psychological and individualistic. If our TV fare (e.g., the nightly news, the soaps and talk shows) is any indication, Americans are totally bent on understanding the individual self, on solving individual problems individualistically, on realizing individual potential. Our common stories point to the individual self pursuing its self-fulfillment in an unfriendly social world (Berman 1987:100–102). When Americans read Luke, they inevitably introject a set of scenarios in which persons are understood individualistically. First-century Mediterraneans are perceived as though they are twentieth-century Americans. Yet this is by no means the way Luke and his world understand persons.

In keeping with the conclusions drawn from the reading theory expressed in chapter 1, we propose an alternative scenario for U.S. and Western readers of the Bible, a scenario in which persons think "sociologically," in terms of gender-based roles, and with constant concern for public awards of respect and honor. This alternative scenario suggests that (a) Luke and his audience perceived human beings differently from Americans, (b) hence they thought differently about who a person might be and what might be the expected range of human behavior.

This suggestion should not be surprising, for readers who use the historical-critical method of biblical interpretation have regularly raised suspicions about the odd personality types described in biblical books. Although we are concerned with Luke and his characters, we can begin this discussion with reference to recent studies of another Mediterranean person, Paul. For example, in his discussion of "Paul's Theological Difficulties with the Law" (1986), Räisänen argues that Paul the theologian is a less coherent and less convincing thinker than is commonly assumed; Paul's conception of the law is inconsistent, unintelligible and unarguable. Granting that Räisänen is correct in his assessment of Paul (and we agree with that assessment), why would first-century eastern Mediterranean people respect and give allegiance to a person who is incoherent, unconvincing, inconsistent, unintelligible and opaque? What sort of scenarios for understanding human beings both as persons and as groups must contemporary Americans bring to the New Testament so that its authors might be understood in a fair and equitable manner?

Some attempts at understanding, usually focused on Paul, include Stendahl's hypothetical intuitions deriving from his history of ideas approach (Stendahl 1963), which resembles Rappaport's approach to Josephus' personality (Rappaport 1976). Such approaches offer little by way of testable explanation. At the same time, Theissen's psychobiology (Theissen 1987) and Callan's rather straightforward psychological assessment (Callan 1987, with excellent overview of previous psychological studies) overlook either the difficulties involved in the psychological assessment of absent, idiosyncratic subjects so well articulated by Stannard (1980) or the problem of selecting an adequate analytic framework from the many that exist (Prochaska 1979).

Given the various constraints involved in dealing with personality in cross-cultural perspective, it seems that at present the best we can attempt is a type of social psychology built upon a circum-Mediterranean *modal personality* that includes the idiosyncrasies of the culture and distinctiveness of social structure in that given time and place. The term *modal personality* refers to a model of the typical qualities expected in a society's ideal, stereotypical, successful person who embodies a culture's definition of the ideal human being. Modal personality, then, embraces a group's "native theory of success":

> A native theory of success thus includes knowledge of the range of available cultural tasks or status positions, their relative importance or value, the competencies essential for attainment or performance, the strategies for attaining the positions or obtaining the cultural tasks, and the expected penalties and rewards for failures and successes. A people's theory of success

develops out of past experiences with cultural tasks, social rewards and relative costs. The theory is either reinforced or altered by contemporary experiences, that is, by perceptions and interpretations of available opportunity structures. . . . Nevertheless to suggest that natives (be they white middle-class Americans, black ghetto residents or African tribesmen) usually have a good knowledge of their status system and of what it takes to make it as behavioral guides is not too far removed from reality (Ogbu 1981:420).

Scenarios for reading Luke–Acts, then, must consist of what first-century native Mediterraneans considered "good knowledge of their status system and of what it takes to make it." On the basis of a configuration consisting of modal personality, the idiosyncrasies of the culture, and the distinctive social structures, we might discuss groups and the types of personalities such groups might allow for. And this will be the approach adopted here.

1.0. PRESUPPOSITIONS

From the outset, we must express as clearly as possible the presuppositions that direct our investigation and exposition. These relate, first of all, to making generalizations about an area as broad as "the Mediterranean." After all, archaeologists continue to traverse the region and delight in distinguishing shard from shard, pebble from pebble. On what basis can one lump all Mediterranean shards and pebbles into a common heap and still have intelligible explanation? Furthermore, not a few persons, given their preferred cognitive styles, have difficulty with retrojecting behavior patterns of contemporary peasants in general, and eastern Mediterranean villagers in particular, to the world of the first century. Is such a procedure an unwarranted anachronism? Finally still others view any high level generalization used in the interpretive enterprise with suspicion and alarm. Can the anxiety of such persons be allayed?

1.1. A Circum-Mediterranean Area as Unit of Analysis

For geographers (and not a few historians) "the Mediterranean region stretches from the northern limit of the olive tree to the northern limit of the palm tree" (Braudel 1972:168). Braudel rejected this climate-based view in favor of a "global" Mediterranean. In the sixteenth century, he writes, the Mediterranean "reached as far as the Azores and the New World, the Red Sea and the Persian Gulf, the Baltic and the loop of the Niger" (ibid.). While the boundaries of this description obviously extend too far for the study of Luke–Acts, there are a number of reasons for considering the Mediterranean region as a single cultural area.

A first indication of this, verifying Braudel's intuition, has been clearly set forth by Murdock in his attempt to categorize illness around the world. In his survey of 186 societies and their theories of illness, Murdock notes:

> Trial and error showed, however, that if North Africa were detached from sub-Saharan Africa and the Near East from Asia, and if both were grouped with Europe to form a composite Circum-Mediterranean region, this would yield three regions reasonably comparable not only to one another but also to each American continent and the Insular Pacific. The experimental tabulation of the incidence of the major theories of illness in these ad hoc regions led to a serendipitous discovery: The theories actually showed some tendency toward segregation by region (1980:42).

Illness theories are replications of the interpretive themes of a culture, and common illness theories would point to common interpretive themes (see Pilch's essay on illness and healing).

There are, however, other reasons for speaking of the unity of the Mediterranean. Jane and Peter Schneider have argued that the different societies of the region have come to resemble each other because they have long been subject to similar social processes: the societies exist on a "pastoral-agrarian continuum" (Schneider and Schneider 1976, cited by Davis 1987:22). Then as Davis observed, "the people of the Mediterranean have been engaged in conquest, commerce, colonialism, connubium and conversation for about five millennia, and it is impossible to imagine that in that period they have not created common institutions (Davis 1987:22–23) For other significant distinctive dimensions of the Mediterranean, see Gilmore 1982 and 1987.

Furthermore, to speak of Mediterraneans or eastern Mediterraneans as if the groups falling under these labels were homogeneous entities requires a level of abstraction and generalization to facilitate comparison. Such abstraction derives from stripping away specific differences and pooling similarities in the populations in question. Patai suggests that we consider the Mediterranean as a culture continent, with specific groups as the culture areas, e.g., Greeks, Jews, and Romans (Patai 1983:278). Such a perspective can be very useful for more focused study. Here we prefer Murdock's circum-Mediterranean area since our task is to describe a typical Mediterranean, and more specifically, a typical eastern Mediterranean person, in comparison with a typical American. Some distinctive regional features may emerge as we proceed. Again, the purpose of developing this sort of description is to provide the twentieth-century American reader of Luke–Acts with a scenario better befitting the times and values of the origin of that work than might ordinarily be available from U.S. experience.

1.2. Presumption of Constancy

There is a truism in the social sciences that most people do what they do because of a lack of awareness of alternative modes of behavior.

Since most people, as a rule, cannot imagine being and doing in any other way, societies tend to be rather stable. The reason why people are and do things in a rather fixed and stable way is that they are bound by hidden rules.

> The idea that man as a cultural being is bound by hidden rules and is not master of his fate may come as a shock to some—it has always been hard to accept. The one thing that is quite clear, however, is that man is bound as long as he remains ignorant of the nature of the hidden pathways culture provides for him. To the traditional questions about free will, determinism, and his unique individuality which the ordinary citizen is apt to bring up when he meets the concept of a world of hidden rules, the anthropologist can give a convincing answer. Of course there are impulses that appear to have independent origins from within, but even these are radically altered by culture so that they are brought into play under controlled circumstances. The man who is attracted to a woman may want to invite her out for a date. The choice as to whether he acts or not is his. What is not his to decide fully is the language he will use, the presents he can give her, the hours he can call, the clothes he can wear, and the fact that in the United States the woman has the ultimate say in the matter (Hall 1959:144).

In traditional societies without literacy and a sense of history indicating things were once different and need not be the way they are, this sort of stability deriving from hidden cultural rules borders on rigidity. And in many, non-technological ways, the Mediterranean world maintains traditional, stable structures and values. How these structures and values might have originated is an interesting question, but not of concern at present. The circum-Mediterranean witnesses distinctive ideological continuity under changing and changed conditions along with the persistence of a significant number of structures and values (gender division of labor, honor and shame, hospitality, patron-client, challenge-riposte, and the like; see the volume edited by Gilmore 1987).

Our contention is that the Mediterranean is peopled by a motley kaleidoscope of highly related societies that have witnessed many meaningful events. Nevertheless, Mediterranean people "over long periods live by essentially the same codes, have the same ideas and beliefs, and handle life crises by established patterns" (Williams 1970:621). The point of our argument here is that unless there is evidence of change in the historical record, there is a presumption of continuity. Mediterranean peasant society and its values may have taken on different forms and shapes during the periods of Roman, Byzantine, Islamic, Latin, Turkish, and Western dominance. Yet these forms and shapes are more of the quality of imported clothing styles and mechanical devices rather than alterations of social structure and values. Modes of interpreting self, others, nature, time, and space based on gender and the gender division of labor in Mediterranean villages would seemingly be more like general Mediterranean antiquity than modern northern European or

American society. We do not argue for equating first-century CE Mediterranean values and meanings with those of twentieth-century Mediterranean villages. Rather our point is that the values and meanings shared by contemporary Mediterranean villagers as described and explained by contemporary anthropologists show qualitatively far greater similarity to the values and meanings communicated in ancient Mediterranean texts than anything the contemporary U.S. or northern Europe can approximate or even imagine. For the building of the scenarios required for reading the New Testament, Mediterranean cultural anthropology is indispensable.

2.0 STRONG GROUP PERSON

To begin with we suggest that Luke and his audience did not comprehend the idea of an individual person in his or her uniqueness. To underscore this aspect of Mediterranean perception we open with a consideration of the strong group individual.

2.1 Not Individual, But Dyadic

Individualism was and still is a way of being a person totally alien to the scenarios of the first-century Mediterranean world. Geertz has attempted a rather precise definition of "individual" in current U.S. usage as "a bounded, unique, more or less integrated motivational and cognitive universe, a dynamic center of awareness, emotion, judgment and action organized into a distinctive whole and set contrastively both against other such wholes and against its social and natural background." And he goes on to note that this way of being human is, "however incorrigible it may seem to us, a rather peculiar idea within the context of the world's cultures" (Geertz 1976:225).

The personal, individualistic, self-centered focus typical of contemporary American experience was simply not of concern to first-century Mediterraneans. Given their cultural experience, such self-concerned individualism would appear quite boring and inconsequential. For group survival it would be dysfunctional. And it would certainly be selectively unattended to. To understand the persons who populate the pages of the New Testament, then, it is important *not* to consider them as individualistic. They did not seek a personal, individualistic savior or anything else of a personal, individualistic sort. If those people were not individualistic, what or how were they?

We submit that what characterized first-century Mediterranean people was not individualistic, but "dyadic" or group-oriented personality. For people of that time and place, the basic, most elementary unit of social analysis is not the individual person but the dyad, a person in relation with and connected to at least one other social unit, in particular, the family. People in this cultural area might be said to share "an undifferentiated family ego mass" (Bowen 1978). They were primarily part of the group in which they found themselves inserted. As they went through the genetically based stages of psychological awareness, they were constantly shown that they exist solely and only because of the group in which they found themselves. Without that group they would cease to be. In essence, a dyadic personality is one that needs another person constantly to know who he or she is (Foster 1961; Selby 1974). Such a person perceives himself as always interrelated to other persons, while occupying a distinct social position both horizontally (with others sharing the same status, ranging from center to periphery) and vertically (with others above and below in social rank).

Group-oriented persons internalize and make their own what others say, do, and think about them because they believe it is necessary, if they are to be human beings, to live out the expectations of others. They need to test this interrelatedness, moving the focus of attention away from their own egos and toward the demands and expectations of others who can grant or withhold reputation or honor.

Mainstream Americans receive little input concerning their personal identity and place in the world. They would be hard pressed to find situations in which they might, as adults, undergo experiences of dyadic information continually fed to them concerning their rank or status in American society. Mainstream American adults do not get their primary self-identity from group-embeddedness. A man born in a log cabin can eventually sleep in the White House; an actor can become president. Students are given preference tests to discern their interests, potentialities, and strengths. All of this would be foreign to dyadic persons, who from the womb would be socialized by the network of social groups to which they belong as to their identity, role, and status. If Americans can be said to define themselves according to their individual decisions so as to know who they are, this would not be the case with a dyadic person. Dyadic persons would expect others to the tell them who they are ("Who do men say that I am?"). And so modern questions of "consciousness" (Did Jesus know he was God?) make no sense in terms of dyadic personalities, who depend on others to tell them who they are, what is expected of them, and where they fit.

In other words, to paraphrase Geertz, "our first-century person would perceive himself as a distinctive whole *set in relation* to other such wholes and *set within* a given social and natural background; every individual is perceived as embedded in some other, in a sequence of embeddedness, so to say" (Malina 1981:55). These persons seem best described as strong group persons. Strong group persons define themselves rather exclusively in terms of the groups in which they are embedded; their total self-awareness emphatically depends upon this group embeddedness. They do not seem to go through the stages of ego formation typical of Western individualistic persons. Although they are single beings, individual persons, and unique in their individual being, their psychological ego reference is primarily to some group. "I" always connotes some "we" (inclusive of the "I"). While the "I" is a single individual, one can presume any communication from an "I" invariably is a communication from a "we." And all strong group persons know what "we's" are involved in their singular interactions.

2.2 Thinking "Socially," Not Psychologically

All strong group persons make sense out of other people by thinking "socially." As we noted previously, this means that the individual person makes sense of everything on the basis of reasons, values, symbols, and modes of assessment typical of the group. By American standards, such "social" thinking entails thinking about persons in terms of stereotypes.

Stereotypical thinking submerges any individuality we might find in another in favor of what is common, general, and presumably shared by the category (such as gender, ethnicity, age) or group to which a person might be assigned. Stereotypical perceptions yield fixed or standard mental pictures which various groups commonly hold of each other. These standard, mental pictures represent their expectations, attitudes, and judgments of others. Since individuals find themselves inserted into various groups by birth, family ties, and the wider ranging ties already forged by their elders, group-oriented personalities take this feature of human experience as primary. Strong group people find it overpoweringly obvious that they are embedded in a group and that they always represent that group. Consequently the common stereotypes of dyadic persons relate to that embeddedness. The following list represents the basic stereotypes whereby first-century Mediterranean people understood themselves and others.

Family and Clan. People are known not individually, but in terms of their families; Simon is "son of Jonah," and James and John are "sons of Zebedee." Knowing the parent or clan, one knows the children ("a chip off the old block").

Place of Origin. Dyadic persons might be known in terms of their place of birth (Jesus of Nazareth; Paul of Tarsus); and depending on the public perception of this place, they are either honorable (Tarsus, no mean city) or dishonorable (what good can come from Nazareth).

Group of Origin. People are known in terms of their *ethnos* (a Jew, a Samaritan), and certain behavior is expected of them in terms of this

("Jews have no dealing with Samaritans," John 4:9; "Cretans are always liars," Titus 1:12). To know one Greek, for example, is to know all Greeks, for it is quite proper to generalize on a sampling of one instance, as Virgil's Trojan says: *Ab uno disce omnes*, "Learn about all (Greeks) from this one Greek" (*Aeneid* II.65).

Inherited Craft-Trade. They might, moreover, be known in terms of trade, craft, or occupation. People have fixed ideas of what it means to be a worker in leather, a landowner, a steward, or a carpenter. Only trouble could arise if that carpenter displayed wisdom, performed great deeds, etc. which do not belong to the role of carpenter.

Parties-Groups. Furthermore, people might be known in terms of their social grouping or faction, as Pharisees or Sadducees and as Stoics or Epicureans. Membership in groups was not a matter of personal, individual choice, but of group-oriented criteria, such as family or clan (Sadducees; often Pharisees), place and/or group of origin (Jesus' faction recruited in and around Capernaum; Pharisee settlements), inherited craft/trade (e.g., scribes). This allowed access to and networking with specific people. And even these groups or *haireses* are known in terms of some stereotypical doctrine (Acts 23:6–8).

Because dyadic persons perceive themselves in terms of qualities specific to their ascribed status, they tend to presume that human character is fixed and unchanging. Every family, village or city would be quite predictable, and so would the individuals who are embedded and share the qualities of a family, village, or nation. Unpredictability, then, derives from something or someone beyond the control of the predictable and unchanging human beings they know. Hence there is no need to look within the human being, that is, to ascribe anything to personal and uniquely individual psychological motives or introspectively generated reasons and motivations.

Moreover, since human beings have no control over their lineage and parentage, dyadic persons tend to perceive the role and status of clans and families as well as of individual members in them as ordained by God. It is important for U.S. readers to realize that the person responsible for the insertion of persons into their specific family, ethnicity, village, region, craft or party, the person responsible for one's gender, is God. Just as a person's insertion into a marriage relation, based on parental selection of marriage partners, is due to God ("What God has joined together . . . ," Matt 19:6), so too of all the other dimensions of human social existence into which individuals are inserted by no choice of their own. Paul, for example, intimates a similar social perspective when he asserts that the body has many parts; it is not all head, not all eye, nor all hand. And this ordering is done by God, for "God arranged the organs in the body, each one of them, as he chose" (1 Cor 12:18); the social body is quite similar, "for there is no authority except from

God, and those that exist have been instituted by God" (Rom 13:1). Since the social order, both theoretically and actually, is God's doing, it follows that there will be a built-in resistance to social mobility and to status and role changing. Thus, if it pleased God to create so-and-so as third son of a farmer in such-and-such a place, this dyadic identity then becomes legitimated as the order of nature: "Only let everyone lead the life which the Lord has assigned to him and in which God has called him" (1 Cor 7:17).

2.3 Honor and Shame

In our estimation, first-century Mediterranean personality cannot be understood without a detailed understanding of the pivotal value of honor and shame. In the previous chapter in this volume, we presented the reader with an in-depth scenario of this value. We expect that information to be supplied here, and so we will not repeat it. Therefore, if a reader is not cognizant of the value of honor and shame and its replication throughout societal life, we urge that the reading of this chapter on first-century personality be interrupted until the essential material on honor and shame is gleaned from chapter two above. We urge the reader not to be deceived by the absence of a full treatment of honor and shame here. It is treated in the previous chapter, and we see no need to duplicate that material here as well.

2.4 Morality and Deviance

2.4.1 (Group) Conscience. In this world, meaningful human existence depends on individuals' full awareness of what others think and feel about them, along with their living up to that awareness. Literally this means "conscience." The Latin word con-scientia and the Greek word syn-eidēsis stand for "with-knowledge," that is, knowledge shared with other, individualized common knowledge, commonly shared meaning, and common sense.

Conscience, then, refers to a person's sensitive attention to his or her public ego-image with the purpose of striving to align personal behavior and self-assessment with that publicly perceived ego-image. Conscience is an internalization of what others say, do, and think about one, since these others play the role of witness and judge. Their verdicts supply the person with grants of honor necessary for meaningful, humane existence.

The dyadic individual is symptomatic and representative of some group. From this perspective, the responsibility for morality and deviance is not on the individual alone, but on the social body in which the individual is embedded. It is because something is amiss in the functioning of the social body that deviance springs up. Thus Paul stigmatizes whole groups, all Jews and Greeks (Rom 1–3) or all Galatians (Gal 3:1), because he sees some socially infecting *hamartia* or sin behind individual sinful actions.

The moral norms we find in the New Testament have relevance for individual behavior. But in all moral listings and descriptions, the individual is not the main concern. They are written from the point of view of the individual-as-embedded-in-something-bigger, the objective horizon of the social body (e.g., the Torah of Israel). Examples of moral descriptions would include the various lists of sins (Mark 7:21–22), the lists of virtues and vices (Gal 5:16–24), and the codes of household duties (Col 3:18–4:1 and 1 Tim 2:8–3:15). The main objective is to keep the family, the village, and the nation sound, both corporately and socially. Among the followers of Jesus, the main problem was to keep the Christian group, the individual church, in harmony and unity, that is, in a sound state (e.g., 1 Cor 12; Rom 12:3–21). In a group, the individual as such was expendable: "It is expedient for you that one man die for the people, and that the whole nation not perish" (John 11:50). For the sake of the group, individuals might be rather ruthlessly ejected from the group as in the Christian excommunication procedures described in 1 Cor 5:5, 13 and Rom 16:17 (see Matt 18:15–18). The soundness of the group, like the behavior of the dyadic personality individually, is heavily determined by its impact on surrounding groups and by the expectations of outsiders (e.g., 1 Thess 4:12; 1 Cor 6:6; 10:32–33; 1 Tim 3:7). Christians had to be at least as good as the outsiders, and in this sense the norms are communicated to insiders by their neighbors.

There is no question but that the essential covenant law, the Ten Commandments, formed the bedrock of basic ethical thinking for Jews and Christians in the first century (see Luke 18:20). But the ethics had little to do with individual consciences. Rather what was of concern was to maintain the rights of God and other males, to not infringe on their prerogatives, to respect the honor of God and other males. Along with the dyadic understanding of one's honor status in family and village, roles carry with them clear perceptions of rights and duties. As we will see, there is a gender-based perception of correct/incorrect behavior. Also typical of this world were the lists of virtues and vices, and the ranking of these as cardinal sins and primary virtues. Good persons, then, internalized the common expectations of them and others, and strived to live up to them. Failure brings not guilt, but public shame (e.g., 2 Sam 12:7; Gal 2:11–14).

2.4.2 Deviance. It is within this framework that we suggest how morality for dyadic persons is seen in relation to "deviance." In the chapter on conflict, we will discuss deviance at considerable length; and to that study we refer readers who seek greater depth on the topic. But for our purposes here, we define deviance as the behavior that violates the sense of order or classification which people construct and maintain so as to make a predictable and intelligent world. Deviance thus is an infraction against socially required law and order. Deviants are people who are caught and labelled for breaking laws or causing social disorders. Now let us see how this might help us understand morality for first-century Mediterranean people.

Contrast, for example, an American and somebody like Luke attempting to explain why they might regard someone as abnormal or as a deviant. In order to explain the breach of the social order that deviance is, the American will look to psychology, to childhood experiences, personality type, to some significant event in the past that affects an adult's dealing with the world. Biography in the U.S. is a description of psychological development in terms of singular events of an individualistic person passing through the psychological stages of life. An abnormal person is assessed as one who is psychologically "retarded," or one who is aberrant, because "neurotic" or "psychotic" due to "having been an abused child," and the like.

In contrast, the Mediterranean person, in the past and present, is anti-introspective. In more direct terms, the Mediterranean is simply not psychologically minded at all. Rather, disturbing or abnormal internal states are blamed on persons, either human ones ("you made me angry") or non-human ones ("for he has a dumb spirit and wherever it seizes him it dashes him down," Mark 9:18). Biography is a description of a person's having fulfilled stereotypical roles that cluster to form a sort of typical prominent or deviant status. For example, Roman elites described their lives in terms of the series of responsible offices they held (cursus honorum). Mediterraneans paid no particular attention to developmental stages apart from raw biology (especially the onset of menses for girls). Thus, a Mediterranean like Luke would describe an abnormal person by saying: "he comes from Crete," "she was a sinner," "he submits to Satan," or "he was possessed." These Lukan designations of abnormality indicate that "the person is in an abnormal position because the matrix of relationships in which he is embedded is abnormal" (Selby 1974:15). The problem is not within a person but outside a person, in faulty interpersonal relations over which a person, usually, has no control. The point is that there really is nothing psychologically unique, personal and idiosyncratic going on within a person at all. All people in a family, neighborhood, or town situated in a distinctive region are presumed to have the same experiences. If any distinctions hold they are regional and gender-based, as we shall see.

What follows from this is the important observation that the honorable man, if he could ever become aware of it, would never expose his distinct individuality, his unique personhood, his inner self with its difficulties, weaknesses, and secret psychological core. He is a person of careful calculation and discretion, normally disavowing any dependence on others. He is adept at keeping his innermost self concealed with a veil of conventionality and formality, ever alert to anything that might lead to his making an exhibition of himself, to anything that would not tally with the socially expected and defined forms of behavior that have entitled him to respect. Jesus is spoken of as a person who does "not regard the face (honor)" (Luke 20:21), but who is intensely concerned about his reputation, "Who do the people say that I am?" (Luke 9:18). Such a person attends acutely to the dyadic impression that others have of him and strives to fulfil their expectations. "Conscience" would have to do with clear perceptions of virtues and vices, not subjective motives. Failure or sin would bring social "shame," not internalized "guilt."

As one might expect, societies featuring dyadic, group-oriented personality provide their members with individual identities that are rather clearly defined. And of course these identities are legitimated by reference to the will of God, as rooted in the order of creation. There is little doubt as to what constitutes male and female behavior, about what mothers and fathers are to do, how sons and daughters are to act at various age levels. This suggests that in the service of maintaining clear identities, certain values will prevail and certain virtues prescribed and certain vices proscribed. The result is a form of exhortation (also called "paraenesis") that is quite commonplace in nature. The New Testament abounds with these forms. As has been pointed out, preachers regularly appealed to what the audience already knows. That is, appeal is made to what is held in common and agreed to in terms of proverbs, maxims, or commonly shared symbols. "Conscience" is largely defined in terms of these commonplace guides to behavior. Specific applications might be made, but rarely are "new" virtues or vices discussed. Even here, moral ideas will be explained in terms of what Greeks called *topoi*, that is, stereotypical ways of understanding the nature of love, justice, anger, and the like.

2.4.3 Social Awareness. We might say, with good reason, that a type of "social" awareness pervades strong group persons. In this they are thoroughly unlike our experience of being psychologically minded, of having introspection a ready companion to self-assessment. For example, the institution of keeping females away from males by means of women's quarters, chaperoning, various gender-based space prohibitions (at the common outdoor oven or common water supply) indicates that behavioral controls exist in the social situation. Thus behavioral controls are "social," deriving from a set of social structures to which all are expected to adhere. Quite definitely, behavioral controls are not in the person. Hence they are not "psychological," inwardly assimilated and under the control of the choice of "conscience." It is situations, not individual persons following internalized norms, that are controlled and that control. The situation is controlled with the full force of custom. There is, then, little concern with controlling the person with the full force of individualistically followed internalized norms (Hall 1959:114). No one would understand something as nonsensical as "Let your own conscience be your guide."

There are, however, social situations in which a person is expected to lose control, while spectators are expected to provide the restraining force, e.g., close women relations are to attempt to jump into the grave of the deceased but also to be held back by others; individuals ready to square off in a fight expect those around them to hold them back; feuds go on escalating yet mediators are to intervene to restrain the feuding parties (see Boehm 1984). It is similarly believed that a male could not possibly suppress the strong urges that surely take possession of him every time he is alone with a woman. And women are considered even more unable to resist males. Both sexes then expect their will power to be provided by other people rather than by personal inhibition (Hall 1959:66–67). Strong group personality involves general lack of personal inhibition in favor of strong social inhibition.

These social-minded, group-oriented, anti-introspective and non-individualistic perspectives have been duly codified in the stories and ethical systems of Judaism, Christianity, and Islam. Those values and lines of behavior which tend to strengthen group cohesion are considered positive values and virtues. But values and lines of behavior that are in any way detrimental to group cohesion are considered negative values, vices or sins. Such codification points to the strong group quality of these ethical systems, to their sanctions in community control rather than individual responsibility.

2.5 Values and Virtues

When one compares U.S. with Mediterranean culture, it becomes immediately clear that a constitutive part of the differences can be identified in terms of values proper to each group. By *value*, we mean the general directionality of behavior, that is, how behavior is supposed to go. We may safely say that a paramount value in U.S. culture is democracy, which is expressed by the right of an individual to vote, own property, make individual decisions, chose a career, marry whomsoever, and be included in Gallup polls. Needless to say, if Mediterraneans are strong group or dyadic persons, this U.S. value would not be operative in their world. Values, then, will differ between cultures. For a more complete sense of contrast between modern Western and ancient Mediterranean values and behavior, see Malina and Neyrey 1988:145–51.

2.5.1 *Differing Cultural Values.* In order to present value contrasts more clearly, we should like to introduce a model developed precisely for discovering diverse values among different ethnic groups. This model was originally constructed by Kluckhohn and Strodtbeck (1961) and subsequently applied by Papajohn and Spiegel (1975) in order to identify variations in values between ethnic groups. It enjoys wide currency today and has proved quite insightful and useful to a variety of people who wish to make comparisons across cultures. The model addresses the following questions: when a crisis or problem arises, how are people expected to react? how are they supposed to behave? to what resource are they expected to turn? Five areas are considered: (a) activity, (b) relations, (c) time orientation, (d) relation of humanity to nature, and (e) human nature. Later in this book John Pilch will develop this model in much greater detail in regard to illness and healing, and to that fuller discussion the reader is directed. Our purpose in mentioning the model here is to indicate that the values of Mediterranean people, Luke's world to be specific, are certainly different from the values of Americans. Any consideration of first-century personality must be acutely aware of these differences. And we have reliable means of uncovering those differences.

In the interest of brevity, we suggest that the differences between the people of Luke's world and that of the contemporary U.S. be identified as follows. Given the question: "What line of behavior are human beings expected to pick as first choice option to face basic human problems?" We get this sort of breakdown:

Behavior Area	Luke's World	U.S. Today
(a) Activity	being	doing
(b) Relations	collateral	individual
(c) Time	present, past	future, present
(d) Man-Nature	subordinate to	mastery over
(e) Human Nature	mixed, evil	neutral

If this model indeed indicates different value orientations, then truly U.S. people will think and act quite different from those in Luke's world.

A. *Activity.* People whose major activity is "being" and surviving, not solving problems or achieving, will tend to express this in terms of a doctrine of divine providence controlling all existence and a view of a role or status given by God which belongs to the order of creation. For example, by having created human beings as he did, God requires children to honor their fathers and mothers by paying for their physical support.

B. *Relations.* People whose relations are basically collateral, that is group oriented and non-individualistic, are dyadic persons whose goals and wishes are subordinate to that of the group. Group well being always comes first.

C. *Time Orientation.* People whose time orientation is to the present, not the future, are interested in today's bread and today's problems; they tend neither to plan for the future nor to delay gratification.

D. *Humanity vis-à-vis Nature.* People who understand humankind as helpless in the face of nature, not its master and subduer, tend not to be technologically progressive or ecologically aware. They are a people used to being put upon by famine, floods, storms, locusts, etc.

E. *Human Nature.* Finally, people who view human nature as a mixture of good and evil, not neutral or therapeutically remediable, readily see the world in dualistic terms as an arena where Evil, Satan, and demons attack God's holy people. This is a world of dishonoring sin and pervasive evil, to which a savior is sent preaching "repentance."

At the very least, modern readers of Luke–Acts should be acutely aware that the people of Luke's world were quite different from themselves. This model of cross-cultural values, then, can be an initial, important step in clarifying the differences and especially in gaining insight to that other world.

2.5.2 Consequent Cultural Virtues. The model of values is quite abstract, but when we put it in conversation with other elements of this analysis of first-century personality, we can begin to suggest specific values and virtues pertinent to the people of Luke's world. For example, "being" as a value correlates with what we described above as a strong group, dyadic person. One's identity is basically given by one's family; one's role and status are understood in terms of group expectations and legitimated in the order of creation (1 Cor 12:24). The consequent moral norm, then, is clear: Be what you are! Born a slave, remain a slave (1 Cor 7:17, 20). The political *cursus honorum* of Romans would be foreign to Luke's audience. One would predict that where the value of "being" is strong, one will find corresponding importance given to obedience, acceptance of suffering, maintaining the status quo, and contentment. Gender identity and roles belong here as well.

"Collateral relations" would suggest that individuals tend to belong to groups, factions, parties or *haireses.* The importance given here to horizontal relationships will express itself in concern for kinship relations, for knowing who is one's neighbor. Loyalty and faithfulness will consequently be valued.

"Present-time Orientation" is the usual value preference of groups and societies in which present survival needs cannot be taken for granted. As such, present time orientation is typical of traditional peasant societies whose proverbs instruct: "Do not be anxious about tomorrow for tomorrow will be anxious for itself," or "Let the day's own trouble be sufficient for the day" (Matt 6:34). People with this orientation are not interested in promises about a remote future, whether it be a utopian transformation of the world or a delayed Messiah. What is important is *today.* If today offers little, then it is to the past that one must look, for the past offers warrants for today. Similarly we are who we are today thanks to our ancestors, as our genealogies indicate (Luke 3:23–38). Tradition, custom, and ancient writings point to elements from the past still present, not unlike one's inherited status, craft, house, and land.

In the Jewish world of Jesus, "the tradition of the elders" was the phrase which described how individuals looked to the past as essentially present. Tradition was the dyadic voice which indicates how people are to think and act in the present. Obviously, the Bible would have pride of place as regards tradition, but there were evidently many schools of interpretation of the Bible, which in time developed into "houses" such as the House of Shammai and the House of Hillel. After the time of Jesus, we hear of "Rabbis" gathering disciples around themselves. Comparable data are readily available for Hellenistic schools and teachers (e.g., Diogenes Laertius). Appeal is generally made to the abiding (that is, present) wisdom of the past: scripture, proverbs, aphorisms, and the like. Herein resides an important aspect of the conscience of the group.

With the foregoing model of value preferences, we have suggested the complex of values which correlate with the people and groups typical of Luke's experience. While these value preferences are fundamental, there are other pivotal values of a more gender-based, personal sort that influence Mediterranean living and orient behavior in a certain direction as well. As we have noted in the chapter on honor and shame, these values were and are of salient importance in the Mediterranean world. Thus for example, in the masculine world of honor, courage and bravery (andreia) are highly valued. One immediately thinks of Jesus' contests in 4:1–13 and 22:39–44 (Neyrey 1985:58–60, 172–79), all of his challenge/riposte scenes, his fearless going to Jerusalem to face his enemies. Honor and self-respect, which are rooted in traditions of masculine personhood, value loyalty, faithfulness, obedience, and respect.

3.0 THE MODEL APPLIED TO LUKE–ACTS

3.1 Not Individual, But Dyadic

At this point we have finished sketching a complicated model of first-century persons. If we have been successful, typical modern American readers must feel perplexed. For if the model is accurate, the people about whom they will read in Luke–Acts seem quite strange, even bizarre by our standards. Such a feeling at this point would be quite appropriate. But that points up the very value of this model: if indeed Luke and the persons he describes are so radically different from us, then an adequate scenario is absolutely essential if we are to understand them at all, much less escape imposing our notions of individualistic personality on them. It remains now for us to take this model of first-century personality and use it as the lens through which to view Luke and his *dramatis personae*.

As the model underscored, strong group persons are dyadic people who understand themselves and others in terms of their embeddedness, primarily their embeddedness in kinship groups. Others as well think of them in terms of parents/kin, clans, ethnicity, party, and craft-trade. And so they are socialized from birth to think of themselves in this way.

Take, for example, the test case of Jesus of Nazareth. From a U.S. perspective, we are inclined to asked about his consciousness, his freedom to shape his life, even his temptation to sin (e.g., *The Last Temptation of Christ*). But perspectives like this would be alien to the people of Luke's world, who are not individualistic, but dyadic. Let us try to illustrate this. Dyadic persons are socialized to understand their role and status by the constant information fed to them by family, neighbors, clan, etc. Turning to Luke's Gospel, we note the following:

Jesus is always told "who he is"; he does not decide his own identity or role as though he were a typical American. God's messengers identify and name him first at the apparition to Mary (Davidic ruler, 1:31–33; Son of God, 1:35), then to the shepherds (Savior, Christ the Lord, 2:11). God's prophets acclaim his role and status at his presentation in the temple (2:31–34, 38). John the Prophet further sharpens his role (3:16– 17). And God himself definitively tells Jesus his identity as Son of God, first at the Jordan theophany (3:22), and again on the mountain (9:35). Of course, what God says about Jesus enjoys precedence in terms of how Jesus and his disciples view him (see Acts 2:22–36). Inspired by God's Spirit, Jesus' disciples continue the dyadic process of naming and identifying Jesus in their sermons and speeches in the Acts of the Apostles.

Other characters likewise feed Jesus information about his role and status. Sometimes demons identify him as the Holy One of God (4:34) or as Son of God (4:41; 8:28). More typically people who have received a blessing from him identify him as God's prophet (7:16; 24:19). In the company of Pharisees, one of them calls him teacher (7:40). And finally, at Caesarea Philippi, the dyadic aspect of first-century personality is illustrated in the exchange between Jesus and his disciples. From the perspective of a first-century audience, he is not playing games with them and he is not being coy when he asks first, "Who do the people say that I am?" (9:19) and then, "But who do you say that I am?" (9:20). A careful examination of Luke–Acts would indicate that all names, titles and indicators of role and status are told *to* Jesus *by* others. And this is hardly accidental.

The point is, dyadic persons need constantly to be told their role, identity and status by those around them. The text of Luke–Acts seems to verify this, as Jesus himself does not individualistically determine his own self but listens to what the significant others around him say about him. Indeed it would be outside the code of honor and shame for Jesus to be promoting himself or seeking honor that did not belong to him. It is no accident that the most serious charge against Jesus is "he *makes himself* such-and-such" (see John 5:18; 10:33; 19:7, 12). As we will show in the chapter on conflict, at his trial the enemies of Jesus argued that he was doing just this: promoting himself, pushing his cause, and falsely claiming honors (22:67; 23:2).

This volume on Luke–Acts cannot tell modern readers all they might wish to know about Jesus in terms of "Christology." We too are vitally interested in such questions. But we think that from a strictly anthropological perspective we can gain much information about Jesus by examining Luke's account of him. A reader would benefit greatly from asking the following questions: what title or names are given to Jesus? by whom? does Jesus ever name himself? Furthermore, the application of labelling theory to this enterprise would seem fruitful and appropriate. We invite the reader to consider the chapter in this volume on conflict, in which such perspectives are further developed (see also Malina and Neyrey 1988).

3.2 Thinking "Socially," Not Psychologically

Dyadic persons think in stereotypes. This may be illustrated by a cursory look at the way people in Luke–Acts tend to be understood in terms of kinship: family and clan; group of origin: ethnicity; place of origin: town, city, region; inherited craft or trade; and, party and group.

Family-Kin. Among the followers of Jesus, James and John are known to us as the "sons of Zebedee" (5:10), James as "the son of Alphaeus" and Judas as the "son of James" (6:15–16). In Acts, Saul is the "son of Kish" (13:21) and David, the "son of Jesse" (13:22). Sopater is the "son of Pyrrhus" (20:4). An unnamed man who helped Paul is sufficiently identified as "the son of Paul's sister" (23:16).

Jesus, too, is always known in Luke in terms of parents and kin. Luke narrates Jesus' genealogy (3:23–38), linking Jesus with the best of Israel's past. Although Luke speaks of Jesus' "mother and father" (2:33, 41, 48), Jesus is primarily known as the "son of God" (1:32, 35; 3:22; 9:35; 10:21–22). It ultimately matters little whether the identification of Jesus as "son of God" comes from heavenly angels or demons (4:3, 9, 34, 41; 8:28), for the testimony is thereby given by all and so its validity is acknowledged. If, then, children are "chips off the old block," Jesus must be holy and honorable indeed; he lives up to the expectation "Be ye holy as I am holy" (Lev 11:44–45).

If knowledge of one's family means knowledge of an individual in the family, one might investigate what seem to be moments of tension in Luke when one's true family are being defined. There may be a conflict over blood ties/natural kinship and fictive kinship. Jesus, for example, insists that he remained in Jerusalem to be about "my Father's business" (2:50), thus indicating allegiance to God-Father over that owed to his biological parents (yet see 18:20). Some passages seem to predict that allegiance to Jesus will mean loss of biological family (12:51–53; 14:25–26; 18:29), but the gaining of a new, fictive family (8:19–21). But the principle is the same: individuals are known in terms of parents, family and kin—biological or fictive.

Clan-Tribe. Although not everyone in Luke is identified in terms of tribe or clan, the important characters are. Mary's kin belong to priestly clans: Zechariah, "of the division of Abijah" and Elizabeth, "a daughter of Aaron" (1:5). This would imply that Mary is of a priestly clan herself. Concerning the heroes in Acts, Barnabas is a Levite (4:36) and Paul is from the tribe of Benjamin (Phil 3:5). Joseph, of course, is of the "house of David" (1:27; 2:4), as is Jesus (1:32–33), who becomes known as the "son of David" (1:32; 18:38–39; 20:41–44). The stature of important persons in Luke–Acts is communicated by special note of their pedigree, both kin and clan, thus extending the honor and identity of the ancestors to the contemporary individual.

Ethnic Group. In the Gospel, all people mentioned are presumed to be Jews, unless specifically identified otherwise. Of course, the most fundamental distinction would then be between Jew and non-Jew. Given the presumption that Israel is a holy people, set apart by God (Acts 10:28), honor accrues from being an offspring of Abraham (3:8). On the contrary, Samaritans are presumed base (9:52), unless a story precisely overturns the stereotype (10:33; 17:16).

Information, then, is communicated by the very naming of a person's ethnos or nation, stereotypical information which Luke presumes a reader to know. Further investigation of this might ask what is signalled by naming Symeon in Acts 13:1 as "Niger" (*Black*); Timothy in Acts 16:1–3 is a complicated figure, whose circumcision no doubt clarifies his ethnic complexity. The problem between the Hellenists and Hebraists in Acts 6 might benefit from further consideration in terms of ethnic/linguistic differences. More importantly, one might ask what new dyadic identity is signalled when the presumption of Israel as a chosen race, set apart, is debated in Acts 10–11. It would not be surprising then, if Jewish Christians took exception to this and other debates which tended to downplay the dyadic distinctiveness of God's covenant people (see Acts 15:1, 5). An interesting test of this perspective might be the claim of Paul to be a Roman citizen (Acts 21:39; 22:28). Or, one might inquire into the phenomenon that Jews were named by multiple names, Jewish names and Hellenistic names (Acts 1:23).

Region, Town, Village. Information about an individual is communicated by identification of one's region, town or village. Peter and companions are from Galilee, which feeds the presumption that they are "uneducated, common men" ('am ha-'aretz, Acts 4:13). One may ask what is presumed by other identifications of people as Galileans (Luke 13:1–2; 22:59). Jerusalem evokes a sense of honor and holiness, as the city of God's temple.

Just as we use expressions like "the sticks," "the boonies," and "a one-horse town," so cities and villages in Luke's world enjoyed reputations which became part of the identity of the individuals from them. In John's Gospel, the common, negative stereotype of Nazareth is sufficient to persuade one character that Jesus cannot be the messiah: "Can anything good come out of Nazareth?" (1:46). Whatever its original or subsequent honor rating, Nazareth is constantly part of Jesus' dyadic identity (Acts 3:6; 4:10; 5:37). In contrast, Paul's hometown, Tarsus, was "no mean city" (Acts 21:39), implying that he is a noble person from a sophisticated place.

It is beyond the scope of this introductory chapter to inform the reader of the honor rating of specific towns and cities, but Luke presumably knows this and it is part of the communication when he identifies specific persons in terms of their region or city:

Barnabas, of Cyprus	Acts 4:36
Nicolaus, of Antioch	Acts 6:5
Apollos, of Alexandria	Acts 18:24
Dionysus the Areopagite, of Athens	Acts 17:34
Sopater, of Beroea	Acts 20:4
Aristarchus and Secundus, of Thessalonica	Acts 20:4
Gaius, of Derbe	Acts 20:4
Tychicus and Trophimus, of Ephesus	Acts 20:4; 21:29
Mnason, of Cyprus	Acts 21:16
Paul, of Tarsus, in Cilicia	Acts 9:11; 21:39; 22:3

After Rome, Antioch and Alexandria were the largest cities in the empire. This is a factor in assessing the reputation of Apollos as an educated, sophisticated person, who satisfied the tastes of the Corinthians beyond what Paul, only from Tarsus, could do. It would be important here to be familiar with the chapters by Rohrbaugh and Oakman on the meaning of city and countryside in Luke's narrative, for they will specify further just who lived in cities and what it meant to live in the countryside.

Party-Group. Besides the identify and honor which come from family and clan, individuals in the Gospels might also belong to voluntary associations (religious parties or haireses), and so be known in terms of them. We are all familiar with Gospel traditions about Pharisees and

Sadducees. Parties in Acts which are called *haireses* include: (a) Sadducees (Acts 5:17), (b) Pharisees (Acts 15:5; 26:5), and (c) Nazarenes, called The Way (Acts 24:5, 14; 28:22). Luke's original readers presumably knew the social and economic inference implied in these labels. Furthermore, although the labels Pharisee and Sadducee are truly complex, readers of the Gospel quickly learn about Pharisees and Sadducees in terms of stereotypical attitudes and actions. Pharisees are "legalists," those concerned with rules and performance, such as fasting and kosher diet, tithing, circumcision, and strict sabbath observance (Luke 5:30; 6:2; 11:38; Acts 11:2; 15:1, 5). They are, moreover, "hypocrites" (Luke 12:1, 56) who practice Torah observance to deceive others (Luke 11:39). It would make an interesting study to examine the stereotypical identification of the Pharisees in Luke 11:37–44, comparing how the Pharisees would describe themselves with how Christians perceive them (see Neyrey 1988b:74–89). Although we know the name of only one Pharisee ("Simon," Luke 7:36, 40), we know him and all other Pharisees by the stereotypical label alone (e.g., Luke 11:38; 14:1–6; 15:1–2; 16:14). Sadducees are known in terms of a stereotype, "those who say there is no resurrection" (Luke 20:27; Acts 23:8). One might legitimately inquire what stereotypical knowledge Luke presumes a reader has to understand his reference to "Stoics and Epicureans" in Paul's Areopagus speech (Acts 17).

Craft-Trade. An important part of the dyadic, stereotypical information about people in Luke's world is their role in society, their craft or trade. Although Christians may interpret their role in an adversarial way, "priests" enjoyed considerable honor by the very fact of being priests. More careful work would have to be done to specify what economic or political benefits would accrue from birth into a priestly clan. What education might be presumed? what duties in the temple? what clothing was worn? whom did they marry?

The world of Luke–Acts is replete with individuals, whose role and status are signalled to us in terms of their craft or trade. In one sense, we learn of people whose jobs would be popularly understood as "unclean." Not only are there tax collectors among Jesus' table companions, but a "chief tax collector," Zacchaeus, becomes Jesus' host (Luke 19:2). In Acts, Peter is thrice noted as a guest of Simon, the tanner (9:43; 10:6, 32), a trade which required the use of urine for processing leather, hence an unclean or mean trade. Lydia is a dyer of purple stuff (Acts 16:14). Aquila, a tentmaker, shares Paul's trade (Acts 18:3). We know of silversmiths (Demetrius, Acts 19:24) and, of course, fishermen (Luke 5:1–11) and carpenters (Mark 6:3; Matt 13:55).

Although we have just identified some of the trades and crafts of the characters of Luke–Acts, there are other people with more honorable roles and jobs, such as the following:

1. *Roman soldiers*: centurions (Luke 7:2; Acts 10:1–43; 27:1–43); tribunes (Acts 21:31–38; 23:17–30)
2. *Roman political appointees*: governors (Luke 23:1–25; Acts 23:24–24:27; 25:1–32); proconsuls (Acts 13:7; 18:12)
3. *Jewish Kings and Roman Emperors*: tetrarchs (Luke 3:1); Herod (Luke 13:31–32; 23:6–12; Acts 12:1–3, 18–23); Agrippa (Acts 25:13–26:32); Caesar (Luke 2:1; 20:22–25; 25:12; 26:32)
4. *Leading men of the city*: Blastus, Herod's chamberlain (Acts 12:20); Chuza, Herod's steward (Luke 8:3); Publius, the chief man of Malta (Acts 28:7–8); Judas and Silas, leading men among the brethren (Acts 15:22); Jairus, ruler of the synagogue (Luke 8:41)

The particular positive or negative evaluation of these figures would depend on the perception of the person describing the scene. Jews in Palestine would hardly think well of the occupying Roman army, even if some of them have important roles and high status. Certainly Luke and others do not think much of Herod (see Acts 12).

In one sense, Luke–Acts was told to peasant and king alike. It stressed that God's power and healing were impartially sent to friend and foe. There is evidently an inclusive sense of a new covenant family, even as it celebrates God's impartiality (Acts 10:34). But in another sense, the significance of this inclusivity and impartiality can only work if there was a prior presumption of honor ranking and rating according to birth and appointment, which manifests itself in social roles, crafts, and trades. Impartiality toward Gentiles makes sense only if there was a prior stereotype of Israel as "God's chosen people," who were set apart from "the nations." And it remains an open question whether according to Luke membership in the Jesus movement devalued or obliterated the dyadic identity communicated by role, craft, or trade. It apparently did not at Corinth.

In summary, although it seems strange and even perverse for Americans to know individuals through stereotypes, this type of understanding one's self and others seems to typify the people in Luke's narratives. When we know a person's father and family (including gender and sibling rank), clan or tribe, ethnos, place of origin (region, village) and trade, according to the canons of Luke's world we truly know them. According to their ways of perceiving and describing, we genuinely know the essential and relevant information about them. In that culture, there simply was not more to know. At least the documents we are studying say no more about them.

One might test this by examining several places in Luke–Acts when characters are introduced or introduce themselves. Philip meets an unnamed person, but one whom we know quite well because we are told he is "an Ethiopian, a eunuch, a minister of Candace the queen of the Ethiopians, in charge of all her treasure" (Acts 8:27). Paul describes himself totally when he states that "I am a Jew, born at Tarsus in Cilicia, but brought up in this city at the feet of Gamaliel, educated according to the strict manner of the law of our fathers" (Acts 22:3). One might compare this with what Paul actually says of himself in one of his own letters: "Circumcised on the eighth day, of the people of Israel, of the tribe of Benjamin, a Hebrew born of Hebrews; as to the law a Pharisee" (Phil 3:4-6; see 2 Cor 11:22-23).

In the world where individuals are known in terms of family, place, party, and role, there would be a corresponding sense of the rights and duties appropriate to each of these classifications. In the sense of "be what you are," a carpenter is a carpenter, not a student of Torah. The reciprocal duties within the household are carefully spelled out in the codes of household duties (see Eph 5:21-6:9). The reader is reminded of the essay in the book on Luke's symbolic universe, in which it is more distinctly spelled out how every thing and person has a specific place in the ordered cosmos of Luke and first-century Jews. There was a clear system of roles and statuses, with corresponding expectations and duties.

What a difference it makes when we read Luke's Gospel if we can tap into the system of duties and expectations. For example, if Jesus is truly "holy," his peers in the synagogue expect him to act as typical holy people act, namely, to separate himself from all that is unclean or evil. It is expected that saints do not eat with sinners (Luke 5:29-32), that observant people fast (5:33), keep the sabbath (6:1-11) and observe customary washing rituals before eating (11:38). An adequate scenario for understanding Jesus' role and status would entail some sense of the social expectations of a prophet (7:38) or holy person. This forms the basis on which people judge Jesus and evaluate him.

3.3 Honor and Shame

Again, we do not wish to convey the impression that honor and shame are not important for understanding both first-century personality and Luke–Acts. We have devoted an entire chapter of this book to the model of honor and shame and its usefulness as a necessary scenario for understanding Luke and his world. We respectfully refer the reader to chapter two of this volume for that detailed study.

3.4 Morality and Deviance

As we pull together threads of the model of a first-century person, we get a fuller sense of the group aspect of morality for the people in the world of Luke–Acts. As strong group persons with dyadic personalities, they are socialized into the rights and duties appropriate to their roles and statuses as group members. Oriented to present-time, they are expected to and do seek contentment in fulfilling such roles. This implies that a virtue like obedience will enjoy pride of place. Obedience naturally includes respect for authority, subordination to superiors within and outside the family as well as complete deference to the traditions of family and group.

Although it is beyond the scope of this essay to examine the complete education and socialization of members of Luke's world, it is worthwhile to survey the ways in which values, customs, and norms which convey traditional moral knowledge are communicated. In other perspectives, this might be called "form criticism," a study of literary forms and their social functions. Such a perspective is greatly enriched when seen precisely in context of a discussion of first-century dyadic persons.

The primary source of moral norms and customs for the Jews of Luke's world was and remained the scriptures. The rights and duties of adult male members of Israel were carefully itemized in the Ten Commandments. And Luke records Jesus enumerating them in response to a question about "inheriting eternal life": "You know the commandments: 'Do not commit adultery, Do not kill, Do not steal, Do not bear false witness, Honor your father and mother'" (18:20). Other customs that define identity for a member of the covenant are also found in scripture, in particular rules concerning circumcision, diet, and sabbath observance. It is surely not accidental that Jesus was himself circumcised on the eighth day (Luke 2:21); his custom was to go to the synagogue for sabbath (4:16). Also, there were customs concerning pilgrimage feasts, consecration of first born, etc. In accord with these, Jesus was dedicated to God as a first-born male (Luke 2:22–24); his family annually went up to Jerusalem to celebrate Passover (2:41). As was noted in the chapter on the symbolic universe of Luke–Acts, from the scriptures was developed a system which sought to order, classify, and structure where every person, thing, place, and time was understood to be "in place" or "out of place." Such an interpretation of scripture needs to be taken into account here, for it represents the immediate and particular appropriation of the sacred tradition by Jesus, his followers, and Luke.

Readers of the New Testament know quite well the constant debates that took place over the meaning of scripture. Although, for example, all are to love God and neighbor (Luke 10:27), there might be considerable discussion about who qualifies as "neighbor" (10:29–37). Scripture, then, remained a vital source of morality for dyadic persons with a past-time orientation.

Yet apart from the scriptures, Luke's Gospel contains an extensive and elaborate repository of traditional morality which is communicated in a variety of formal ways:

Aphorisms	Luke 4:23; 11:17; Acts 14:22; 20:35
Proverbs	Luke 11:33; 12:54–55; 14:34–35; 18:14; 20:25
Parables	Luke 8:4–18; 12:16–21, 35–41; 13:6–9; 15:3–32; 19:11–27; 20:9–18

Prayer Formulae   Luke 11:2–4; 22:42; 23:36
Blessings/Woes   Luke 6:20–26; 11:27–28

Although it might be difficult to classify with precision the various pieces of the Sermon on the Plain (Luke 6:17–49), it illustrates the way in which morality was couched in a variety of traditional forms. The world of Luke–Acts was at home with literary and philosophical conventions, such as the way letters are written (Acts 15:23–29), but especially the *topoi* on issues of theology or morality.

In Acts, Luke frequently speaks about "the Way," meaning the following of Jesus according to certain ways of acting (9:2; 18:25; 19:9, 23; 22:4; 24:14, 22). In this Luke builds on the Jewish tradition of "walking in the way of the Lord." This is concretized in *halakah*, which are specific steps for walking in the way of God. In this regard, scholars commonly point to the special travel narrative of Jesus in Luke's gospel (Luke 9:51–19:27). For as Jesus goes *on his way* to Jerusalem, Luke records a compendium of Christian *halakah* which describe *the Way of Jesus*, that is, discipleship. The point is, customs and moral norms abound in Luke's world; they are the stuff taught in families and readily learned in daily living in villages.

If Christianity is "the Way," what does it mean to be a disciple of Jesus? What specific practices are enjoined? Following Jesus will mean taking up one's cross daily (9:23–27), severing kinship ties (9:57–62), showing therapeutic kindness to the wounded on the way (10:29–37), praying (11:2–4), giving alms (11:41), avoiding covetousness (12:15–21), etc. It would be a valuable project for readers to continue a careful survey of "the Way of Jesus" in Luke 9–19, for herein Luke has provided a compendium of group norms and customs for the disciples of Jesus. Attribution to Jesus and inclusion in the group's foundational document give legitimation to them as *halakah* for Luke's audience. "The Way of Jesus" is now the way of God (Luke 20:21; Acts 18:26).

The reader is reminded of Luke's report that many Jews accused Jesus and his followers of abandoning the customs (*ethos*) of their ancestors, that is changing the *halakah*, or ways of walking in the way of the Lord (see Acts 6:14; 21:21). Some urged an explicit and firm return to the customs of Moses (Acts 15:1). The Jerusalem church was not advocating lawlessness when it rejected "the way of Moses" for the disciples of Jesus, for Luke–Acts contains many indications for upright behavior according to "the way of Jesus."

3.5 Values and Virtues

3.5.1 Cultural Values. In comparing the dominant values of Luke's first-century world with our modern world, we noted that he favors (a) *being* over *doing*, (b) *collateral relations* over *individualism*, (c) *present or past time orientation* over *future*, (d) *subordination to nature* over *mas-*

tery of it, and (e) a view of *human nature as both good and bad*. This complex of values, then, is important to know if we would truly understand the people of Luke's world. For a full discussion of these values and virtues, see Pilch, ch. 7 in this volume.

3.5.2 Consequent Virtues. The values described above are necessarily quite abstract. It might be worthwhile if a specific value typical of Luke and his world were identified and discussed. It comes as no surprise to any reader of the New Testament that "obedience" surfaces as one of the premier virtues which characterize both Jesus and any loyal servant of God. It belongs to the world of a first-century person to value faithful obedience to one who has legitimate authority to command. What is that about and how should one understand it?

The semantic word field for order/command and obedience is quite extensive:

Order:
(a) give orders, command, instruct, tell, enjoin, insist, charge, direct, prescribe-proscribe, appoint

(b) orders, commands, regulations, ordinances, precepts, just demands, decrees, edicts, rules

Obey:
(a) obey, submit to (be disobedient toward), listen to, accept, be subject to, undergo

(b) obedience, submission.

And to this list one might add terms such as faithfulness and loyalty (*pistos, pistis*). Yet readers have not exhausted the range of terminology for obedience because Luke has his own particular ways of expressing just such concepts:

(a) God's will (*thelēma*): Luke 11:2; 22:42; Acts 13:22; 21:14; 22:14

(b) God's plan (*boulē*): Luke 7:20; Acts 2:23; 4:28; 13:26; 20:27

(c) must (*dei*): Luke 2:49; 4:43; 9:22; 11:42; 12:12; 17:25; 18:1; 21:9; 22:7; 24:26, 44; Acts 1:16; 3:21; 4:12; 5:29; 9:6, 16; 14:22; 17:3; 19:21

Jesus, of course, embodies the virtue of obedience best in Luke's narrative. It is hardly incidental that Luke insists that Jesus' family was faithful to the laws of God: Jesus was circumcised on the eighth day (2:21) and dedicated to God according to Exod 13:2, 12 (2:22–24). His parents made annual Passover pilgrimages to the holy city (2:41). When Luke notes that Jesus was in the synagogue on the sabbath, he comments that such "was his custom" (4:16, 33). Anointed by God in his baptism, he is loyal to God when tested (4:1–12). He always seems to know "the will of God" in his regard (9:22; 17:25), and prays in the Garden the prayer of loyalty, "Not my will but thine be done" (22:42). And he dies faithful to God (23:46). There can be no doubt, then, that Luke portrays Jesus as completely and always obedient to God. Given this material, let us try to understand it as representative of a major value of first-century persons.

From the resources of this essay alone, we draw upon notions of honor and shame. It belongs to God to be sovereign, and so to command. How shameful it would be, then, if Jesus were not obedient to God; and God would be dishonored by not being obeyed. Command and obedience, then, belong in the social dynamics of honor and shame values. Related to this, first-century persons are not individualistic in our modern sense, but embedded in relationships. Primarily they are embedded in the institution of kinship and so depend on their parents and elders for clues about what it means to be a good son, an adult male. As everyone knows who has read the proverbial literature in the Bible on how parents raise children, parental discipline was the expected treatment of children. Let us cite an apposite example from a New Testament document:

> It is for discipline that you have to endure. God is treating you as sons; for what son is there whom his father does not discipline? If you are left without discipline, in which all have participated, then you are illegitimate children and not sons. Besides this, we have had earthly fathers to discipline us and we respect them. Shall we not much more be subject to the Father of spirits and live? For they discipline us for a short time at their pleasure, but he disciplines us for our good, that we may share in his holiness. For the moment all discipline seems painful rather than pleasant; later it yields the peaceful fruit of righteousness to those who have been trained by it (Heb 12:7–11).

Adult parents know the code of their society and understand the rights and duties of specific roles and statuses. And they constantly socialize their children to these under the rubric of "discipline." They are bad parents if they do not do this; and their children are bad children if they do not learn this discipline and obey. Furthermore, from our knowledge of the symbolic world of Luke–Acts, we have a sense that every role and status was quite clearly defined in Luke's world. A place for everyone, and everyone in his place. It belongs to adult parents to pass on the code of social relations.

Obedience, then, is a primary value in such a society. As the pattern of society is presented to individuals, they are socialized to accept it. As roles of parent or superior are defined to them, they learn to honor them. Embedded in a world of the Book, they value its traditions and their past. Obedience, then, quite adequately represents the very concept of embeddedness which we are describing in this essay.

4.0 SUMMARY AND FURTHER TASKS

If we have been successful, a modern reader of Luke–Acts will not presume to understand the persons in the New Testament as though they were Americans or modern individualists. We have presented a model which at least approximates a description of the type of persons known to exist in the Mediterranean. They are not individualistic, but dyadic. They think in stereotypes; they act in accord with the gender-based notions of honor and shame as this applies to males and females. As members of a strongly structured society, their symbolic universe is highly systematized and classifies things and persons in great detail. This sense of proper order and place is socialized into children from birth, thus affecting their sense of embeddedness. Internalizing the social codes, they develop a "conscience," not a modern individual evaluation of persons or events, but *cum-scientia*, knowledge of the world given by and shared with the group. It is no wonder, then, that proverbs and aphorisms are crucial communicators of shared values and norms. Nor is it surprising that their literature depends so strongly on formulae or *topoi* for communication of commonly known material. Nor would it be surprising if "paraenesis," the jargon word for moral exhortation in the New Testament, relies so strongly on recalling what is commonly known.

In the section on values, we tried to show how Mediterraneans differ from Americans in the resources they would draw on to solve problems. They perceive the world differently and thus organize their world accordingly. As we noted, they favor being, not doing; their relationships tend to be collateral, not individualistic; theirs is a present time orientation, not a future one; they see themselves as subject to nature, not its master; and they see the world divided into two classes of people, good and bad. And in keeping with these value preferences, certain virtues stand out as intrinsically essential to them, such as obedience and loyalty. An elaborate treatment of the differences between Mediterranean people and modern Americans can be found in Maline and Neyrey 1988:145–51. These insights, then, are the components of a scenario which is necessary and adequate for a modern person to see the world as Luke and his audience did.

Where does a reader go from here? We consider it imperative that this essay be read in close conjunction with the previous one on honor and shame. Furthermore, the worldview of Luke, which is presumed here, will be more carefully unpacked in the essay on the symbolic universe of Luke. And our exposition of the model of value differences in ethnic groups will be further elaborated in Pilch's article on illness and healing. Finally, the embeddedness of individual persons in the major institution of the family will be discussed in detail in the essay by Elliott.

The reader, then, is encouraged to have a conversation between the present essay and other essays in this volume.

Yet it is our hope that, if we have developed an adequate reading scenario for understanding first-century persons, this material might be used more extensively in reading Luke–Acts and other New Testament writings. Obviously, a reader might want to make a list of all the titles attributed to Jesus, noting in particular how they are always said of Jesus by others. In this way one comes to see how a dyadic individual is embedded in some other person or group, dependent on them for basic self-knowledge. This, of course, will be "knowledge with," that is, *cum-scientia* or "conscience." One might also study how people must be asked to join Jesus and his group. No one would presume to offer loyalty and seem to enter into a dyadic relationship like discipleship without first being asked. In this vein, one might turn to Acts and examine how the apostles are portrayed: how they are instructed by Jesus, empowered by Spirit, and how they speak, not on their own, but authorized by Jesus. In particular, the figure of Paul on trial would be a place to test this model of first-century personality, for in many of his trial speeches he gives a brief résumé of his "identity" which is a basic list of stereotypical, dyadic information (Neyrey 1984). We have, moreover, made numerous suggestions for further study and application of this model of first-century personality in the course of its application to Luke–Acts.

4

CONFLICT IN LUKE–ACTS: LABELLING AND DEVIANCE THEORY

Bruce J. Malina and Jerome H. Neyrey

1.0 INTRODUCTION

At every turn, Luke's story of Jesus and his disciples narrates scenes of conflict. On a literary level, Luke conditions his readers at the beginning of his Gospel to expect this conflict; and he provides the correct perspective from which to view it (Giblin 1985:10–18). At Jesus' consecration in the temple, Simeon predicts a conflict-ridden future for the child Jesus: "Behold, this child is set for the fall and rising of many in Israel, and for a sign that is spoken against" (Luke 2:34). In accord with the Lukan motif of prophecy-fulfillment, Simeon's prediction of conflict is abundantly verified in the career of Jesus.

We are all familiar with the forensic trials of Jesus in Luke 22–23, and those of Peter, Stephen, and Paul in Acts. Besides these obvious forms of conflict, Luke frequently notes how the crowds around Jesus are divided into two groups, favorable and hostile. Some examples include: (a) Simon the leper denies Jesus the courtesies of hospitality, while the sinful woman offers them (7:49–50); (b) Zacchaeus repents at Jesus' word, while the bystanders are offended that Jesus eats with this sinner (19:1–10); (c) the Pharisees seek to silence the crowds who acclaim Jesus at his entry into Jerusalem (19:38–40); and (d) the two thieves crucified with Jesus respectively mock and acclaim him (23:39–43). It is hardly an understatement, then, that Luke tells the story of Jesus' career full of conflict, rejection, and hostility.

Inasmuch as Luke is fond of parallels between the Gospel and Acts, we can observe in Acts this same pattern of rejection and acceptance in regard to Jesus' disciples. Like their master, they meet with contrasting reactions. Although the Sadducees reject the apostolic preaching (Acts 4:1–3), 5,000 people believed (4:4); even as the Sanhedrin rejects Peter and his preaching, the crowd reacts positively (5:12–16, 17–32). The success of the mission in Samaria (Acts 8) balances the rejection of Stephen (Acts 6–7). Acts explicitly states on one occasion that "the crowds were divided" (eschisthē, 14:4) at the word of the preacher (Neyrey 1985:121–23). Acts, moreover, ends with a final comment about Paul's preaching in Rome that "Some were convinced . . . while others disbelieved" (28:24). And this quick sketch does not include the forensic trials of Peter, Stephen, and Paul, which are noted at the end of this essay. Both Luke and Acts, then, tell a story of conflict: scenes of rejection and hostility against Jesus and his disciples and their reactions to such encroachment.

The Mediterranean world has traditionally been a conflict-ridden world. Hence it should come as no surprise when Luke's stories of Jesus or early Christian groups emerge as stories of conflict. It is quite significant, however, to note that Mediterranean conflict has always been over practical means to some end, not over the ends themselves. Jesus and the faction he recruited were in conflict with other groups over how best to heed the command of God, not over whether God should be obeyed at all. Such conflict was over practical means; it in no way implied doubts over ends. Conflict over the practical dimensions of realizing a goal or implementing a stage of behavior (for example, how to change residence effectively, from Nazareth to Capernaum; how to start a faction to revitalize Israel; or whom to chose for marriage) in no way means a conflict or even a doubt over the value of the goal or stage of behavior (e.g., to change residence at all; to attempt to revitalize Israel at all; to get married at all). All the conflicts to be noted in Luke–Acts will be conflicts over ways to realize the traditional values of Israel: conflicts over structures, either new ones or revitalized ones, to facilitate proper obedience to the God of Israel.

This chapter concentrates on the record of conflict in Luke–Acts in which Jesus and his disciples are engaged. Besides the literary pattern noted above, other instances of conflict in Luke–Acts include: (a) negative honor challenges against Jesus and his disciples (see chapter on honor and shame) and (b) forensic proceedings against Jesus in the Gospel and against his disciples in Acts. The story of Jesus and his disciples frequently occurs in the context of forensic proceedings. Jesus himself was tried by the Jewish court (22:63–71), by Herod (23:6–12), and by Pilate (23:1–5, 13–25). Our attention lies here on the understanding of this conflict in terms of social science modeling. There are, of course, a number of ways to consider conflict (see Malina 1988b). Here we choose to approach conflict in Luke from the viewpoint of labelling and deviance theory and outfit our model with cross cultural features for interpreting data from Luke, especially the forensic proceedings against Jesus and his disciples (for a similar approach to Matthew see Malina and Neyrey 1988). We shall begin by briefly sketching the field of labelling theory and of the deviance process. We follow this sketch with an application of the resulting model to data presented in Luke.

Of their nature, forensic trials are status degradation rituals, that is, part of a larger scenario of deviance processing. And so, if we would understand in depth the conflict which forensic trials display, we must adopt a scenario which will adequately explain its dynamics. Labelling and deviance theory can give just such an understanding.

2.0 THE MODEL: LABELLING AND DEVIANCE THEORY

2.1 Labelling and Deviance

When people are put on trial, they are necessarily accused of charges which the accuser deems serious. The charges against Jesus are: "We found this man perverting our nation, and forbidding us to give tribute to Caesar, and saying that he himself is Christ a king" (Luke 23:3). Acts 6:13–15; 16:20; 17:6–7; 21:28; and 24:5–6 record comparable charges against Stephen, Paul, and the disciples of Jesus. These charges are the stuff of deviant labels, and it will benefit us to examine what deviance labels are and how they function.

2.1.1 Labelling. People in Luke–Acts frequently call each other various names. Names are social labels by means of which the reader/hearer comes to evaluate and categorize the persons presented in the story both negatively and positively. Concerning positive labels, Jesus calls Peter a "fisher of men" (Luke 5:10), and those who hear the word of God are called "mother" and "brothers" (Luke 8:20). And in a negative vein, John the Baptizer labels some people as "brood of vipers" (Luke 3:7). Jesus, moreover, calls the Pharisees "hypocrites" (Luke 12:1; see 6:42; 13:15). Jesus is himself positively labelled "Christ, King" (Luke 1:35; 2:11), "Prophet" (Luke 7:16, 39), "Teacher" (7:40; 8:49), "Son of God" (1:35; 3:22; 4:3, 9). But some, however, negatively label him "Son of Man" (7:34; 9:26), "demon possessed" (11:15), "polluter" and "revolutionary" (23:5). Labels such as "sinner," "unclean," and "brood of vipers," then, are powerful social weapons. In the mouths of influential persons, they can inflict genuine injury when they succeed in defining a person as radically out of social place. Conflict, then, can be expressed and moni-tored in the ways people hurl derogatory names and epithets against outsiders. This social name-calling is a type of interpersonal behavior technically called *labelling*.

2.1.2 Deviance. As a rule, we consider anyone defined as radically out of social place as a deviant person. Deviants are invariably designated by negative labels: pick-pocket, murderer, rapist, terrorist, squatter, and the like. Negative labels, in fact, are accusations of *deviance*. Behavior is deviant when it violates the sense of order or the set of classification which people perceive to structure their world. In the chapter in this volume on the symbolic universe of Luke, we go into great detail over the precise contours of the system of order and moral meanings into which Jesus, Luke and their readers were socialized. Deviance, then, has to do with violations of that shared social system of meaning and order. Deviance, like the lines what produce it, is a social creation; what is considered "deviant" is what is perceived by members of a social group to violate their shared sense of order. In short, deviance lies in the eyes of the beholders, not the metaphysical nature of things.

Deviance, moreover, is nearly always a matter of moral meanings, of distinguishing the evil and wicked from the good. While socks put in a shirt drawer are "out of place," a deviant is perceived not only as "out of place" but as a mortal threat to the values and structures of society. A deviant, unlike the mislocated socks, threatens the moral universe of the labellers.

A key element in labelling someone a deviant is the understanding of the labellers themselves. Who does this labelling and why? In social science theory, deviance refers to those behaviors and conditions assessed *to jeopardize the interests and social standing of persons who negatively label the behavior or condition.* Whose interests, then, are threatened?

It is important to keep in mind the relationship of deviance to perception. Deviance intrinsically depends on the perceptions and judgments of others: (a) the social system shared by the members of the group is perceived to be violated; and (b) this violation is perceived precisely by those whose interests in that social system are jeopardized. Their reaction to this perceived deviance is the act of social aggression known as negative labelling.

Deviance, therefore, refers to those behaviors and conditions judged to jeopardize the interests and social standing of persons who negatively label the behavior or condition. A deviant person is one who behaves in ways characterized as deviant or who is situated socially in a condition of deviance. A deviant, then, is a person perceived to be out of place to such an extent or in such a way as to be redefined in a new negative place — *the redefinition deriving from the labellers.* People then view this being out of place as a personality trait, an essential quality of personhood. Deviance is a status assumed by persons identified as rule breakers who step out of place in some irrevocable way.

2.1.3 Ascribed/Acquired Status. When people are labelled as deviants, a statement is made about their status in society. Since deviance is a social status, it seems appropriate to define what status entails. In general, the term *status* refers to a person's position within a social system. This is status as social position. At the same time, in such a social system of ranked positions, status is invariably assessed in terms of what others perceive a person's position to be worth. This is status as value. Because status as value depends on the perception and appraisal of others, it is based on two considerations: ascribed characteristics and personal achievements.

Ascribed characteristics include age, sex, birth, physical features, and genealogy. In terms of deviance, then, *ascribed deviant status* is rooted in some quality that befalls a person by no effort of his/her own and which a person continually possesses (= stigma). One thinks of the man born blind (John 9:1) or the man born lame (Acts 3:1). Being born from AIDS infected parents or from parents convicted of treason might result in a person being considered deviant. Here deviance is a matter of being, the very meaning of a person's being.

Achievements are accomplishments deriving from one's personal efforts; these include acquisitions, marriage, occupation, and accomplishments. In terms of deviance, *acquired deviant status* is based on a person's performance of some publicly perceived overt action that is banned. For example, Zacchaeus is a deviant by virtue of his zealous collection of taxes (19:1–10); the woman who anointed Jesus' feet (7:36–39) is a "sinner," who deserves the label because of the group's interpretation of her actions. The younger son who wasted his father's inheritance achieved deviant status by his actions (15:11–16). Here deviance is a matter of doing or saying. In the case of Jesus and his apostles, their enemies will argue that they deserve an *acquired deviant status* because of their actions and words.

2.1.4 Master Status. If the labelling process succeeds, the alleged deviant will be caught up in the role indicated by the label and increasingly live out the demands of the new role. The new label comes to define the person. The *master status* engulfs all other roles and labels. Hence Judas was "the traitor"; the Pharisees were "hypocrites." Closer to our times, Thomas Eagleton became known as a "mental patient"; Gary Hart, a "womanizer"; and some 120 appointees of Ronald Reagan, "white-collar criminals." Any good qualities of the alleged are totally engulfed by the new label which becomes the master status. Thus an action that might take but a few seconds, like shoplifting, might come to define a person for the rest of his or her life.

2.2 The Deviance Process

In general, there are three steps in a typical deviance process:

(a) a group, community or society *interprets* some behavior as deviant,

(b) *defines* the alleged person who so behaves as deviant,

(c) *accords* the *treatment* considered appropriate to such deviants.

This indicates that we should give special attention to the group which interprets and defines. We noted above that deviance derives from the perception of the labellers; it is they who perceive that someone is "out of place" and in violation of the symbolic system of meaning and order of their group. And so, we must focus especially on those who interpret and define deviance in a society. They are formally known as *agents of censure*.

2.2.1 Agents of Censure. In the deviance process, certain people play specific roles in the process of labelling someone a deviant. Although several different roles are involved, we discuss them together, for they all function as agents of censure.

Rule Creators. Certain persons can be identified as likely to initiate a deviance process and to mobilize forces to make it successful. They tend to be people privy to the making and enforcing of societal rules.

Moral Entrepreneurs. Rule creating is the task of *moral entrepreneurs*. Since rule creating is a moral enterprise, a moral entrepreneur is the primary agent in constructing and applying meanings to persons that define them and their behaviors as morally adequate or not. *Rule creators* and *moral entrepreneurs* may turn out to be the same figures, but this is not necessarily so. For example, legislators make laws, but other groups in society may demand that the law be applied in cases where the lawmakers would prefer not to take action.

Interest Groups. Rule creators and moral entrepreneurs form *interest groups*, which are coalitions focusing on shared and distinct interests of group members. Moral entrepreneurs and their followers wish to interpret some behavior as deviant for the purpose of obviating, preventing, or correcting interference *in their interests*. To this end they attempt to change, enforce, or establish rules. They do this by defining certain behaviors or actions and those who engage in them as *inimical to their values and interests*.

By means of new interpretations, rule creators define a state of affairs by drawing or redrawing boundaries around something or someone of social significance, thus situating them as "out of bounds" or as a threat or danger. This step in the deviance process is usually called banning, that is, interpreting some thing or event as bad, evil, wrong and immoral, and imbuing it with negative judgment (guilt/fault).

2.2.2 Dissemination and Broader Respectability. But to succeed, the deviance process usually must *disseminate* its viewpoint and gain *greater respectability.*

Dissemination, which entails consciousness-raising in the target population, involves giving a high degree of visibility to the meanings developed by the moral entrepreneurs and their coalition (e.g., public appearances, challenges, debates).

Broader respectability entails linking the new interpretation with some previously held positive value, while tying the accused to negative values. This attachment is effected: (a) by "borrowing" respectability from existing persons and groups by making alliances with them, (b) by seeking testimonials, and (c) by finding endorsements from prominent persons. Anyone who has ever watched government hearings to confirm cabinet appointments or appointments to the Supreme Court will readily recognize the elements of this process.

2.2.3 Rule Enhancement. Dissemination and respectability are further enhanced by raising awareness concerning the value of the new interpretation or rule itself. To this end, the rule creator has to pursue goals that people are usually reluctant to oppose publicly. Such awareness concerning the value of the new rule is developed and maintained by *rule enhancers,* whose task it is to "convert" others to the interpretation or value being disseminated by the interest group. "Conversion" notably occurs by altering other people's attitudes toward the newly defined deviance.

Attitudes to deviance can be *optimistic* ("It will pass, just a passing phase"); *neutral* ("So what! What else is new?"); *normal* ("It is unusual, but within the range of the normal"); and *pessimistic* ("It is an intolerable evil!"). Rule enhancers must create a *pessimistic* attitude in as many people as possible; they can do this in the following ways: (a) by demonstrating the lack of rules or inadequacy of existing rules; (b) by demonstrating the lack of agencies to enforce existing rules; (c) in sum, by highlighting the lack of means to allay and resolve the stress in question.

All of this can be achieved by converting others to one's point of view, that is, by developing a *counter ideology.* By ideology we mean that set of values, attitudes, and beliefs which group members hold and which hold them, as it were, often unawares, to mark their group off from other, contending groups and to bind group members together. Ideology is related to group interests. The trick is to discover the areas of intolerance in the target population and appeal to them. There are whole areas in which people feel themselves free to be unashamedly intolerant. For example, say "PLO" to an Israeli, "abortion" to a Pro-Lifer, or "socialism" to a Republican and one can watch unashamed intolerance. These areas can be appealed to by moral entrepreneurs who would convert tolerant people to a counter ideology of intolerance. These areas of unashamed intolerance underscore what people really believe in.

A counter ideology points to some alternative values, attitudes, and beliefs, introduced to redirect a group's tolerance or intolerance. Counter ideologies can often be made to ride on the back of existing values. For example, if in first-century Palestine before the destruction of Jerusalem, Galileans are perceived simply as boorish dolts (see John 7:15; Acts 4:13), then a Galilean healer can be made to appear as a harmful boorish dolt in the eyes of sophisticated Jerusalemites.

2.3 Activity of Deviance-Processing Agents

In the case of Jesus and his disciples, the publicly approved deviance-processing agencies are the Jerusalem elites and the local Roman government. These agencies register deviance by defining, classifying, and labelling types of behavior or conditions deemed to be "out of bounds." On the basis of the stereotypes thus created, the agencies subject persons accused of deviance to a ritual of degradation and depersonalization and successfully label them as "outsiders."

The anonymous heads of the factions that actively opposed Jesus took steps from the outset, first to keep track of his activity and then to remove him from the scene. In Galilee the opponents are seen as Pharisees and Herodians, while in Jerusalem the threat to the Jesus movement comes directly from the sources of power: temple priests, elites called elders, and the Roman governor. What all these personages seek to do is to place Jesus firmly in the deviance status. The activity of these deviance-processing agents contains three elements: (a) denunciation, (b) retrospective interpretation, and (c) status degradation ritual.

2.3.1 Denunciation. Successful moral entrepreneurs are effective in getting their potential deviants denounced. Such *denunciation* constitutes a first step in the process of labelling, for it marks a perpetrator as a potential deviant. Garfinkel (1956) developed a model of how denouncers arrange for the successful denunciation of their target victims. His model of four variables highlights a number of questions about the quality of early Christian groups: the denouncer, a perpetrator whose identity is to be transformed; some trait, behavior, or event that serves as reason for the transformation of identity; and witnesses who will denounce the perpetrator in his/her new identity.

The Perpetrator and the Trait. For the denunciation rite to be effective, the following must occur: the perpetrator and the trait must be removed from the ordinary to the "out of the ordinary." An example of this in the Gospel would be the accusation of healing "through Beelzebub" (see also the "signless" prophet). The perpetrator and the trait must be rejected because: (a) the perpetrator and the trait are unique, lethal, and typically symbolic of some negative feature of human existence (e.g., sedition, idolatry, blasphemy, etc.); (b) the symbolic quality of the perpetrator and the trait are seen by witnesses as stark opposites of the counter symbolic figures available (e.g., the respected elites in the gospels, Pharisees, Sadducees, elders), so much so that it only makes sense to condemn the perpetrator. Not to condemn him/her is to reject the opposite. And so, the perpetrator must be made strange, i.e., beyond, above, behind the legitimate order, thus "outside" it.

Denouncer and Witnesses. The denouncer must be so identified with the witnesses (the grantors of shame, individual or moral) that the denouncer is perceived as a publicly known person, not a private individual. After all, deviance labelling, if it is to be successful, must not appear as a vendetta, but as the upholding of the moral order of the universe. Throughout the process the denouncer acts in the capacity of a public figure or head of a faction. The denouncer must underscore the core values of the group in question (here Israel) and deliver the denunciation in the name of those core values (e.g., Jesus disobeys God, flouts Torah). The denouncer must be invested with the right to speak in the name of these core values, which underscores the importance of the stereotypical roles of Jesus' opponents as "chief priests and elders." The denouncer is thus seen as the supporter of the core values of the group at large (i.e., binding and loosing in the community of Israel, official representatives of God-given authority, etc.).

2.3.2 Retrospective Interpretation. When a person is successfully declared a deviant, people who knew the person begin to see connections between the deviant condemnation and all that they know about that deviant's past life, often from infancy. Such a shared understanding of a deviant's life seen through the lenses of his or her newly acquired deviant status is called retrospective interpretation.

Retrospective interpretation often takes place by subjecting alleged deviants to biographical scrutiny and character reconstruction. Analysis begins with the present and looks back for information to clarify the present: some unrecognized character defect present in a person's biography, some events symbolic of a character consistent with the current deviant episode. Or, if nothing of the sort is forthcoming, then psycho-physiological examination may take place, which looks for evidence of duress, brainwashing, evil spirits, etc. Retrospective interpretation then seeks new facts or the interpretation of old ones in an effort to establish consistency between the actor's current deviant behavior and character in order to explain the discreditable conduct and to legitimize the label. The aim is the shaping of a master status for the alleged deviants, a role and status that will engulf everything else known about them.

Official interpretation is the task carried out by *imputational specialists*, whose output is to be found in *case records*. Imputational specialists are found in those places where deviant actors are "served" or "treated": clinics and hospitals, jails and prisons, police stations, welfare agencies, chanceries, and so forth. In these places, imputational specialists assemble information about *selected* aspects of a person's life and aid in assigning a person to the status of a deviant. In compiling the "record," information is chosen selectively, specifically to validate the label, diagnosis, or other attribution. Positive information about the alleged deviant is left open to doubt or simply ignored. Furthermore, data supportive of the label are expressed unequivocally. Consequently, little by way of professional neutrality can be expected. The accumulation and collation of data bolstering judgments of deviance is a matter of partisanship, serving the interests and needs of organizations that process deviants.

Retrospective interpretation seeks to transform publicly the doer of deviance into an "outsider." While almost everyone breaks rules—often of a serious nature—without being caught or labelled, people persist in thinking only of the *publicly identified* rule-breaker as qualitatively different from others. Labelling has as its purpose to cut off the rule-breaker from the rest of society by invoking the socially shared presumption that one thus labelled is essentially and qualitatively different from other members of society, an "outsider," "a special kind of person." The deviance is personified so that the person can be depersonalized.

As we shall see, the gossip reported by the opponents of Jesus in Jerusalem along with the trial scene itself provide a retrospective interpretation of Jesus' career in Galilee and subsequently in Jerusalem. Jesus is seen to be both a pretender and a seducer, hence a deviant worthy of death. Retrospective interpretation, then, is a process by means of which the deviant actor is made into a typical case of the thing the deviant is alleged to have done (Schur 1971:52–56): from being afflicted with inability to see to being "a blind person"; from being afflicted with illness to being "a mental case"; from devious doer to being "a deviant"; from crime perpetrator to "a criminal." Behavior is fused with character, as the devious action and its actor become one in the deviant.

The successful outcome of retrospective interpretation entails the following elements:

1. *Responsibility Affirmed.* The deviant will be duly assigned responsibility for the deviant action. In the process, it will be noted that the deviant freely chose to act in a certain way, hence was fully in control, able to cease and desist when requested to, but freely refused to.

2. *Injury Affirmed.* It will be affirmed that injury or harm did indeed result from the deviant's actions, hence those actions were certainly deviant and immoral. It was not friendly antagonism, mischievousness,

concern for Torah application, but downright viciousness that motivated the deviant's behavior.

3. *Victim(s) Affirmed.* Because of the damage done to so many (parents, friends, the ill, etc.) there is nothing about the deviant's case that might even remotely forgive rule-violating behavior. The victims are morally innocent, the deviant morally vicious.

4. *Condemnation.* The deviant is condemned by all concerned: the populace at large, local officials, and regional officials. This condemnation restores honor to the condemners and brands the one condemned as morally reprehensible. Thus public attention is focused on the shame of the deviant.

5. *Appeal to Authority.* The condemnation and the deviant label will be justified by appeal to some higher order norm: God's will, the good of the people, the honor of the nation.

These successful moves, when they occur, allow the deviance-processing agents to complete their retrospective interpretation. The alleged deviant, however, is not yet completely labelled. A clear ritual process must occur which formally identifies the alleged person as deserving the status of a deviant. Because it is a ritual which describes a change in status from innocent to guilty and from normal to deviant, it is called a status degradation ritual.

2.3.3 Status Degradation Ritual. The activity of retrospective interpretation and the work of imputational specialists culminates in ritual process which we call a status degradation ritual (Garfinkel 1956:420–24). Status degradation rituals publicly categorize, recast, and assign a moral character to deviant actors. This *results in a total change of their identity* to that of "a deviant"; they are engulfed in the *master status* of a deviant.

This transformation takes place in various social settings (trials, hearings, screenings) in which degradation rituals are expressive of moral indignation. Settings are denunciatory; the actor is stigmatized. In the process of this denunciation, the actor's former identity is virtually destroyed and a totally new identity established, a *master status* which engulfs all others. And so, the conflict is resolved by the successful labelling of a deviant: his old identity is destroyed and his old status degraded.

As we shall see, Jesus' arrest and trial should be understood as a status degradation ritual appropriate to his alleged career as a "deviant." The ritual culminates in his public humiliation and crucifixion. According to the classic definition of a ritual, Jesus is set apart for trial, judgment and castigation (*separation*),then crucified (*liminality*), then put in a tomb (*aggregation*). The entombment marks the successful completion of the degradation ritual. Readers are reminded of McVann's chapter in this book on rituals of status transformation.

2.4 Interrupting the Labelling Process

Do all attempts to label someone a deviant succeed? In preparing for a status degradation ritual, those officiating must be firmly in control of the "clarity of moral meaning." This means that an accused person's act must be perceived and assessed to be an *uncommon event* (particularly heinous, terrible, repulsive, etc.). In other words, (a) the act must be judged to be unconstrained; it might have been otherwise; and (b) it must be judged to have violated an important social rule. In this case, clear moral meaning is a requirement for the application of sanctions. Yet try as they might, labellers do not always succeed in labelling someone a deviant.

2.4.1 Neutralization. The persons being labelled deviants are not helpless in the process. They may interrupt the process and so upset the clarity of meaning which the accusers must establish. The jargon word to describe the interruption of the labelling process is *neutralization*, the obfuscation of the clarity of moral meaning. As the existence of the Gospels themselves demonstrates, those opposing Jesus and his faction were not fully successful in maintaining clarity of moral meaning. Early on some of Jesus' followers sought to obfuscate that clarity and provide an *alternative retrospective interpretation*. All the Synoptics offer information about Jesus, hoping to reverse the labelling of him as a deviant. One such example is the report about the Jewish guards at the tomb who were bribed to tell lies: Matt 27:62–66; 28:11–15 (Cadbury 1937). The whole Christian tradition describes the usual neutralization ploys whereby Jesus escapes the negative labelling process.

2.4.2 Alternative Retrospective Interpretation. How do persons simultaneously uphold institutional values in word and sentiment, yet violate them behaviorally? How do they overcome the unfathomable chasm between saying one thing and doing another? The answer is *neutralization*. Use of techniques that neutralize internalized constraints prior to engaging in deviant behavior enables one to deflect self-disapproval that results from internalized proscriptive norms. In regard to neutralizing the attempts at labelling, Pfuhl (1980:65–68) notes five possible techniques which are the obverse of the five elements of successful *retrospective interpretation* just discussed:

1. *Denial of Responsibility.* This refers to the avowal that one has no control over one's actions, that one is driven by external forces to act (compassion, God's will, poverty, insanity, ignorance); thus one is essentially blameless. Comedian Flip Wilson's famous line is appropriate here: "The Devil made me do it." In the case of Jesus, "God made me do it."

2. *Denial of Injury.* This is rooted in the idea that the morality or deviance of one's behavior depends upon injury or harm resulting from

those acts. If unsettling activity caused no harm, it cannot be deviant. In Jesus' case the argument would be mounted that his behavior caused no injury to anybody. As a matter of fact it only proved helpful to many as well as to Israel as a whole.

3. *Denial of the Victim* refers to the procedure of redefining the status and role of the victim of deviant behavior in order to legitimate that behavior. The person whom the alleged deviant injured is not really a victim deserving of sympathy or recompense, but someone who deserved what happened, who had it coming. The victim is thus redefined as moral deviant, with the agent as legitimate moral avenger. Responsibility for rule-violating behavior is accepted and injury admitted, but both are presumed to be fully justified and warranted.

4. *Condemnation of Condemners.* This refers to the rejected person's own moral condemnation of those who disapprove, reject, or condemn the deviant. Jesus' behavior throughout his trial and execution was fully honorable. His condemners, in contrast, proceeded shamefully and underhandedly. In recent celebrated trials, not the accused but the court itself was on trial. By condemning the condemners, it becomes an honor to have been rejected and condemned by such "morally reprehensible" people. The alleged immorality of one's condemners is taken to be far greater than anything done or likely to be done by the one condemned. In this way, as in the actual Gospel story-line, public attention is focused on the condemners rather than on the deviant, and the behavior of the condemners is seen as more reprehensible. This technique redirects the negative sanctions and condemnation from the deviant to the rule enforcers, which seems to be the prevalent apologetic technique underlying the Passion narrative.

5. *Appeal to Higher Loyalties.* This appeal refers to the justification of deviant behavior which explains it as the outcome of a choice in a role conflict which is based upon some higher level norm. In the Gospel narrative, the use of the Hebrew Scriptures is crucial in this appeal (see Luke 24:25–26; Acts 8:32–35). People often find themselves faced with conflicting demands as a consequence of inconsistency in the same role or in contending roles (see Malina 1986b). The choice of one set of values, demands, or expectations entails the violation of another. The violated values, demands or expectations are then defined as being of lesser importance, while the ones followed are defined as being of greater importance for a host of reasons: time constraints, God's will, value to others, etc. Examples include: avoidance of obligations to one's family in order to preach the gospel (Luke 9:59–62; 14:26); association with known deviants (sinners and tax collectors) to facilitate their turning to God (Luke 5:30–32); recruitment of a large following due to healing activity yet denial of any intention to use the power potential of that following.

In summary, the narrative of Luke–Acts is rife with reports of conflict. Yet we now have a model which can provide a necessary and adequate scenario for understanding the social processes at work in dealing with this conflict. Moreover, in addition to the insights we can draw from considering conflict as a negative honor challenge, labelling and deviance theory offers us a second scenario, that is, an in-depth perspective into the complicated dynamics of the conflict between Jesus and his adversaries. We turn now to the Passion narrative in Luke 22–23 as a representative text segment to examine in light of labelling and deviance theory. It remains now for us to use the model for understanding the conflict between Jesus and the elite of Jerusalem.

3.0 THE MODEL APPLIED—THE TRIAL OF JESUS

3.1 Labels Applied to Jesus

Why was Jesus arrested? Because someone labelled him a deviant. But what constituted that deviance in the eyes of his labellers? The forensic charges against him are a starting place to find out what specific labels Luke records as constitutive of the allegation that Jesus was a deviant. "We found this man perverting our nation, forbidding us to pay tribute to Caesar, and saying that he himself is Christ a king" (Luke 23:2).

Since there are effectively two trials of Jesus, a Jewish trial in 22:66–71 and a Roman trial in 23:1–25, we should be more discriminating about the labels/charges ascribed to Jesus in 23:2. From a Jewish point of view, the allegation that Jesus "perverted" God's holy people is the most serious label that could be hurled at him from the perspective of his Jewish labellers. In the LXX "perversion" means to lead into (a) idolatry (Exod 32:7; Ezek 14:5) and (b) "uncleanness" (Deut 32:5; Num 15:39). If John the Baptizer was to "make straight the ways of the Lord" (Luke 3:4), Jesus is accused of "making them crooked." And the law prescribes that perverters be dealt with radically (2 Sam 22:27; Ps 18:26). The full meaning of "pervert," moreover, requires us to recall the materials discussed in the chapter on Luke's symbolic world, where the basic purity system of temple and synagogue were described. Jesus is labelled as one who pollutes the nation, thus subverting its values and structures and so bringing it under God's severe judgment.

"Perversion" summarizes several other labels which are alleged against Jesus by his Jewish opponents. Implicit is the charge that Jesus is a *false* prophet and a *false* christ, for Jesus' alleged perversion would be much less a threat if he were not a public figure who claims authoritatively to teach and to lead God's people. Hence it is at the Jewish trial that Jesus is specifically questioned "If you are the Christ, tell us"

(22:67). And at that trial he is mocked as a "prophet" (22:63–64). These two labels summarize the substance of his role and status in Israel, which his enemies find inconceivable. In sum, the Jews accuse Jesus of *achieved deviance* in that he willfully does and claims things (prophet, Christ) which are of such a heinous nature that he corrupts the nation. The *master status* that they would affix to Jesus, then, is that of a "pretender and perverter": he is but a false prophet and false christ. The perspective of the labellers, moreover, is that of the guardians of the temple system.

The Roman governor, like his counterpart in Acts 18:13, is not interested in the Jewish "purity system," but focuses on the label which belongs to his provenance. He questions Jesus, "Are you the King of the Jews?" (23:3) and finds that label not worth attending to (see Acts 17:7–9). When Jesus is labelled as a revolutionary ("He stirs up the people . . ." 23:5), Pilate pays more attention and sends him to Herod (23:6–12), who ultimately dismissed the charge (23:15). Yet "claimant to Israel's throne" and "insurrectionist" are precisely the labels which, if successfully affixed to Jesus, would ensure his perception by the Romans as a deviant who must be removed. In a Roman context, "royal claimant" and "insurrectionist" would become his *master status*, just as they did for Theudas and Judas the Galilean in Acts 5:36–37 and with the Egyptian revolutionary in Acts 21:38.

Luke narrates that the initial attempt at labelling Jesus was unsuccessful. The Roman judge declared "You brought me this man as one who was perverting the people; and after examining him before you, behold, I did not find this man guilty of any of your charges against him" (23:14). Although the inscription over Jesus' head reads "This is the King of the Jews" (23:38), that is not the label which sums up the deviance for which he was executed. The narrative indicates, then, that Jesus' Jewish accusers must strive further to have Jesus branded as a perverter, a false prophet, and false christ.

3.2 The Deviance Process Against Jesus

3.2.1 *Agents of Censure.* Concerning the *rule creators* in the world described by Luke, the temple elite (priests, Sadducees) functioned in Jerusalem as people most likely to initiate a deviance process against Jesus and mobilize forces to achieve this. They are, of course, the people privy to the making and enforcing of societal rules for Israel, especially in regard to its most important structure and symbol, the temple. The Roman governor, Pilate, is also a *rule creator* in Judea, who attends to Rome's values, interests, and structures.

It so happens that in Luke–Acts the *moral entrepreneurs* are at times identical with the *ruler creators*. There is a brief note that the Pharisees objected to Jesus' being labelled by the crowds as "the King who comes in the name of the Lord" (19:39), but they play no further explicit role in Luke's version of Jesus' trial or the trials of Jesus' disciples in Acts. Although Mark and Matthew portrayed Jesus in conflict with each of the major religious parties during his stay in Jerusalem, Luke telescopes the narrative to indicate that basically the chief priests, scribes, and elders function as *rule creators* and *moral entrepreneurs.*

Jesus' initial actions in Jerusalem, his entry into the holy city (19:37–40), his prediction of the ruin of the holy place (19:41–44), and his judgment on the temple (19:45–46), could hardly fail to come to the attention of "the chief priests, the scribes, and the principal men of the people" who are immediately galvanized against him (19:47–48). It is they who publicly challenge Jesus and demand to know his authority to act as he does (20:1–8). They react to his parable of the tenants (20:9–18) with its explicit attack on them (v 18), and they "tried to lay hands on him at that very hour" (v 19) because "he told this parable against them." As a result, they not only mobilize to keep "watch" on Jesus but send spies "who pretended to be sincere, that they might take hold of what he said, so as to deliver him up to the authority and jurisdiction of the governor" (20:20).

In Luke's version, it is the priests, not the Pharisees, who question him about tribute to Caesar (Luke 20:21–26; cf. Mark 12:13–17). And the Sadducees, the priestly, aristocratic party, take up the hunt by ridiculing any notion of resurrection (20:27–38). Jesus' critical remarks about the temple scribes who "devour widows' houses" (20:45–47) are intensified by the sad spectacle of a poor widow putting two copper coins into the treasury of the temple (21:1–4). The conflict, then, is exclusively between Jesus and the temple elite, who are the *rule creators* of Israel (see Malina-Neyrey 1988:72–81).

The Lukan narrative, then, either has the priests present to challenge Jesus or portrays them as the brunt of Jesus' remarks about a temple in need of reform. There can be no doubt that their interests are directly affected by Jesus' presence and his remarks. As guardians of the values and structures embodied in the temple, they perceive Jesus as inimical to their values and interests. They rise up as the *moral entrepreneurs,* as the group who perceives Jesus as a deviant and who interprets him as such to their world. They proceed to *ban* him. (We direct readers to Elliott's essay in this volume on the institution of the temple, for he will spell out in greater detail the basis for the intense conflict between Jesus and temple.)

3.2.2 Dissemination and Broader Respectability. Yet as Luke repeatedly notes, even the priests, who are the rule creators and the moral entrepreneurs, could not initially succeed in labelling Jesus as a deviant: "They did not find anything they could do, for all the people hung upon his words" (19:48). Irate at his criticism, they would lay hands on him, "but they feared the people" (20:19). Nor could they catch him "in the presence of the people" (20:26). The festival crowd and the extreme diversity of Jewish religious life initially blocked attempts by the chief priests to label Jesus successfully. Having tried to *disseminate* their perceptions, they apparently begin to seek *broader respectability*.

When they instigate a plot against Jesus (22:2), they are immediately able to enlist one of Jesus' own disciples, Judas, to act against him (22:3–6). Furthermore, Luke states that at Jesus' arrest (22:47–53) "a crowd" came against him. This crowd is not synonymous with priests, although they are mentioned indirectly (see "servant of the high priest," 22:50) and directly (22:52–53). Evidently the priests are now able to enlist others, a mob, something they could not do earlier. Jesus is taken to the high priest's house (22:54), where "the assembly" eventually convenes (22:66). This assembly presumably contains Pharisees (see Acts 5:34–39), whom Luke shows on occasion as a group which does not share the point of view of the priestly class (see Acts 23:6–10). Yet the priests eventually persuade the diverse members of the assembly to their point of view, and gain a unanimous judgment that Jesus is a "perverting pretender" (22:71–23:2). Finally the priests win broader respectability for their deviance labelling of Jesus by winning the crowds to their cause (23:18, 20, 23). They are able, then, to label Jesus as a "perverting pretender" in the minds of diverse peoples, thus winning broader respectability for their cause, which allows them to succeed in declaring Jesus to be a deviant.

In Acts of the Apostles, Luke consistently portrays the chief priests as the *rule creators* and *moral entrepreneurs* of the labelling process against Jesus' disciples. It is always the chief priests who arrest Peter and John (Acts 4:1–4; 5:17); they enlist Paul to their cause (Acts 9:1–2; 22:5); they vow to fast until Paul is killed (23:14–25); and they attempt to label Paul a deviant before the governor Felix (24:1ff.). In Acts, however, the priests succeed neither in *disseminating* their negative judgment of Jesus' disciples nor in winning *broader respectability* against them. They cannot again persuade their earlier allies, the Pharisees, in an alliance against Peter (Acts 5:34–38) or against Paul (Acts 23:6–10). Luke even reports a defection in their own priestly ranks (Acts 6:7). According to the narrative in Acts, the priests appear to have lost the necessary *clarity of moral meaning* to take effective action against Jesus' disciples.

3.2.3 Activity of Deviance Process Agency. Because the chief priests are the sole custodians of the temple and the exclusive interpreters of the structures necessary for its proper maintenance, they function in the trial of Jesus as the "agency" skilled at interpreting what is clean and unclean. Their role is prescribed in scripture as the agency whose official task it is:

(a) to examine persons suspected of uncleanness (see Lev 13:6, 10),

(b) to declare people "unclean" (Lev 13:8, 14–15) or "clean" (Lev 13:6, 13, 17),

(c) to process people by means of appropriate public sacrifices and offerings which certify their cleanness (Lev 14:10–20), that is, status elevation rituals, and

(d) to "value" persons, livestock, and objects (Lev 27).

Even in Luke, the legitimacy of this role of the temple priests is affirmed (Luke 5:14). Furthermore, in the chapter of this book where the Jewish symbolic universe is discussed, we examine the role of the priests vis-à-vis Israel's central symbol. The present notice of the priests as the official agency which processes "clean and unclean" builds on that fuller discussion.

3.2.4 *Denunciation*. The priests are charged with an official interpretation of Jesus because they are the *imputational specialists* who function in the labelling process to assemble information about selected aspects of a person's life and to aid in assigning the alleged the status of a deviant. Theirs is the task of assembling a *case record* and of creating a selective reading of Jesus' history to illustrate their claims that he is and always was a deviant. Of course, we do not have their actual record, only Luke's report of the trial. But if the two charges against Jesus were his claim to be a false prophet (22:63–65) and a false Christ (22:67), the Gospel narrative provides considerable evidence that Jesus always was discussed in these terms. The priests could claim that Jesus has always acted as a false prophet and a false christ. It could be argued, then, that the (false) claim to be a prophet and the Christ is a *master status*, so that everything else one knows about Jesus would be engulfed by this one behavior.

3.2.5 *Retrospective Interpretation*. As we noted, we do not have the priest's case record. But by studying the apologetic explanations provided by Luke throughout the Gospel for Jesus' actions and words, we can gain a sense of how Luke imagines his enemies would perceive Jesus. Let us, then, play the devil's advocate and itemize the data from the Gospel which Jesus' accusers could marshall to show that he always was a pretending deceiver.

False Prophet. At his inaugural synagogue appearance, he spoke like a prophet (Luke 4:18–19//Isa 61:1–2; 58:6), expected rejection like a prophet (4:24) and compared himself with two prophets (4:25–27). He performed deeds to elicit this label of prophet from others (7:16). He linked himself with the Baptizer, "a prophet and greater than a prophet" (7:26). In the company of others, he would be taken for a prophet, either by Simon (7:39) or by the crowds (9:19). In the face of criticism, he rebuked his opponents as those who kill prophets (11:47); he made light of threats to his life by comparing himself with prophets, all of whom were rejected as well (13:31–35). His demeanor, activity and claims in Jerusalem are but the latest instances of his pretentious presentation of himself as a prophet. He always was a (false) prophet.

False christs. Jesus described himself in his inaugural public appearance as one "anointed" with God's Spirit (4:18). And he cajoled his disciples into acclaiming him as "Christ of God" (9:20), just as he deceived the crowds coming into Jerusalem to acclaim him as "King, who comes in the name of the Lord" (19:38). He promoted the title "Christ" so that it grew larger than life, greater than David (20:41–44). He always was passing himself off as Christ and king.

Those in charge of Israel's temple served as experts in matters of purity and pollution, and they judged that the pretenses of Jesus in Jerusalem during that fateful week were neither of minor importance nor a passing phenomenon which could be excused or ignored. Unquestionably Jesus behaved and presented himself in ways which threatened the divinely ordained temple system and thus endangered the whole nation. And his pretensions were longstanding, even personality traits. Jesus is perceived as having an *achieved deviant status.*

The retrospective interpretation of Jesus succeeded in creating a most pessimistic evaluation of his behavior.

1. *Responsibility Affirmed.* When confronted, Jesus openly admitted in their hearing to be "the Christ" and "Son of God" (22:67–70).

2. *Injury Affirmed.* By claiming to be what he could not possibly be, Jesus had definitively transgressed the values and system of the temple. His was no minor pretense, but a threat to the divine will embodied in the temple.

3. *Victim(s) Affirmed.* All suffer because of Jesus' behavior, and the whole nation would be adversely affected if Jesus' maverick actions and claims did not cease.

4. *Condemnation.* It is important to note that all present at the trial agreed that Jesus was a deviant (22:71) and all condemned him.

5. *Appeal to Higher Loyalty.* In the charges against Jesus before Pilate, the moral entrepreneurs appealed to several higher loyalties. Jesus perverted the nation, and so God's sovereign will was being corrupted. Purification of the nation was demanded. Jesus was cited as a threat to the empire, and so Caesar's rule needed to be strengthened and the miscreant punished. God and Caesar, then, both required that this deviant be dealt with definitively.

3.2.6 *Status Degradation Ritual.* The Passion narrative is itself the record of a complex status degradation ritual whereby Jesus was ritually redefined. His status was most decidedly changed:

(a) from free person to convicted criminal

(b) from honored citizen to dishonored outsider

(c) from the respected "King of the Jews" at his entrance into Jerusalem to the mocked "King of the Jews" on the cross, and

(d) from alive to dead

Trials by their nature are status degradation rituals in which moral entrepreneurs urge rule creators to declare the accused to be a deviant and to process the deviant in appropriate ways. Jesus experienced a complicated series of trials. First, he was subjected to a Jewish trial (22:63–71) where he was declared a pretentious false prophet and false christ. The Sanhedrin then functioned as moral entrepreneurs to the Roman governor, Pilate, who was the ultimate rule creator in Roman Palestine. The Sanhedrin demanded another trial (23:1–4), charging that Jesus was a deviant even in Roman terms. A third trial occurred when Herod heard the case against Jesus, for he was the rule creator in Galilee (23:6–12). The case was eventually brought back to Pilate, where in a final trial the "whole crowd" of Jerusalem elites and non-elites were unanimous in their verdict that Jesus was a deviant of the worst sort and should be removed from their midst permanently (23:13–25). These trials, then, constitute the status degradation rituals whereby Jesus was declared to be in the ranks of achieved deviants. He suffered a dramatic loss of status, as he was degraded and labelled a deviant.

At each level of the trial, Jesus was treated in a shameful way, which ritually served to degrade his status. As the Jewish trial began, he was "mocked": (a) they dishonored his head by blindfolding him; (b) they "beat him," presumably on the face and about the head; (c) they challenged his status as a prophet by testing him "Prophecy! Who is it that struck you?"; and (d) they heaped verbal abuse on him: "And they spoke many other words against him, reviling him" (22:63–64). All of these details indicate that Jesus' status has been publicly and ritually changed to that of a dishonorable, impotent person.

In the trial before Herod, not only was Jesus shamefully accused by leading citizens (23:10), but Luke describes a ritual whereby Jesus was degraded. The judge and his entourage discredited Jesus' status: "Herod with his soldiers treated him with contempt and mocked him" (23:11a). Their contempt denied Jesus the labels of prophet and Christ; and this contempt was dramatized by the ironic investiture of Jesus in the robe of an honorable, prominent person ("arraying him in gorgeous apparel," 23:11b). It is interesting to note that Luke did not record the scene where Jesus was mocked and degraded by the Roman soldiers prior to his death (see Matt 27:27–31), which is an exceptional example of a status degradation ritual (see Malina and Neyrey 1988:89–90).

At the final hearing before Pilate, Jesus' status as an honored member of his society was completely shattered. His countrymen, who should defend him against the foreign oppressor, unanimously demanded that he be killed. Pilate proposed only to "chastise him and release him" (23:22), itself a degradation ritual. But that was not radical enough for the crowds who demanded nothing less than the ultimate destruction of Jesus' person, his death, and especially his death in the most shameful manner: "Crucify him! Crucify him!" (23:21).

The degradation of Jesus culminated in his crucifixion. Here Jesus is reaggregated, not among the upstanding in Israel, but among discarded deviants. The rulers explicitly rejected his alleged status as Christ and mocked him as a statusless figure: "The rulers scoffed at him, saying, 'He saved others; let him save himself, if he is the Christ of God, his Chosen One' " (23:35). They were joined by Jesus' executioners, who rejected Jesus' status as King, "If you are the King of the Jews, save yourself" (23:37). Even a criminal crucified with him taunted him, "Are you not the Christ? Save yourself and us" (23:39). Finally, the complete and irrevocable loss of status occurred when Jesus died. His final degradation was dramatized when his body was punctured and disfigured (see the mention of wounds in his hands and feet in 24:38) and when his physical life was painfully denied him. In the canons of his culture, he suffered irreparable loss of honor and status (see Gal 3:13//Deut 21:22–23). Apart from denial of an honorable burial, Jesus had been degraded to the limits his culture can imagine.

In terms of the three stages of ritual process, Jesus has been *separated* from his peers and his original status. By his arrest, he was put in a *liminal* state where he experienced a stripping of his former identity: gone are the favorable acclamations of him, gone too are the elements of power and honor, gone also are his acclaimers. In this liminal stage, he learned the role of a deviant by the rejection he experienced, by the physical dishonor he endured and by the company he was forced to keep. He was treated as a deviant among other deviants. Finally he was *reaggregated* into his world, but now with a new status affixed him. He was a criminal who was condemned, mocked and executed. His world is now that of "transgressors" (22:37) and the dead, no longer the world of those who may enter the temple and who are alive and whole.

3.3 Interrupting the Labelling Process

The deviant labelling of Jesus, however, was contested—witness the Gospel of Luke which argues just the opposite. Jesus' opponents were not fully successful in maintaining the clarity of their moral interpretation. It is the reactions by Jesus and his followers to the attempt to label him a deviant that now interest us. They engaged in defensive strategy which has two aspects, *neutralization* and *alternative interpretation*.

3.3.1 Neutralization. Many strategies have been noted in the sociology of deviance how alleged deviants struggle to avoid that label. They do not all apply to the case of Jesus or his disciples, but some do. Jesus did not *acquiesce* in deviant label, nor *repudiate* his status as prophet and Christ, nor *flee* from his enemies, nor *modify* and re-name himself. Rather, he and his followers *redefined* him. He and they continued to affirm his status and role as God's prophet and Christ, thus never accepting the allegations that he was a pretender, a false prophet. What needed most redefinition was the fact of a shameful death generally accorded a sinful, dishonorable person. Jesus and his disciples, then, attempted to *neutralize* the deviance label.

3.3.2 Alternative Retrospective Interpretation. First and foremost, a correct *retrospective interpretation* of Jesus was necessary which would set the record straight that not only was Jesus *not* a deviant, but he was actually a prominent person deserving higher status than he was accorded. As we noted earlier, this is typically done by reversing the assertions made by his labellers who attempted to construct a deviant retrospective interpretation. In the case of Jesus, the correct retrospective interpretation argued the following five points.

1. *Denial of Responsibility.* Jesus claimed again and again that it was God's will that he go to Jerusalem to be rejected and killed (9:22; 18:31). As he prayed in the Garden, he explicitly tried to evade this divine necessity, but eventually acceded obediently. This will of God was clearly expressed in God's scriptures, which prophesy "that the Christ must suffer and so enter into his glory" (24:25–26, 44–45). This motif of "according to the scriptures," then, functioned apologetically in the Passion narrative to illustrate that Jesus' arrest, trial, and execution were the responsibility of God himself. In their fulfillment, Jesus was *not* disowned by God or humiliated or dishonored by him, because like the righteous sufferer in the Psalms or the prophets of old, his trial and death were precisely acts of obedience to God. The responsibility, then, is God's. By responding in obedience and faithfulness, Jesus assumed the most virtuous posture possible in Israel, that of the obedient son (see Phil 2:9; Heb 3:2, 6).

2. *Denial of Injury.* Although Jesus himself died, his behavior, which led some to label him a deviant, caused no harm. In fact it was a benefaction to many! He was declared a "Savior" at his birth (2:11); prophets looking for Israel's redemption or Jerusalem's consolation rejoiced at his coming (2:25, 38). He was acclaimed as Israel's "horn of salvation" (1:69). His so-called deviant behavior was truly benefaction: "to preach the good news to the poor . . . to proclaim release to captives . . . recovering of sight to the blind . . . to set at liberty those oppressed" (4:18). If one carefully examines his behavior, he was a constant source of healing, forgiveness, mercy, and liberation to many. And

if one examines his status degradation ritual, one finds that he continued to be a benefactor even as he himself was degraded. He healed the wounded ear of one of his captors (22:51); he looked mercifully into the face of the disciple who had just disowned him (22:61–62). And to a genuine deviant crucified with him he promised nothing less than "Paradise" (23:43). His followers would expand on this data from his life and acclaim him the "Author of life" (Acts 3:15), "the head of the corner" where salvation alone is found (Acts 4:11–12), and the "leader and savior" who is to give repentance to Israel and forgiveness of its sins (Acts 5:31). Jesus, then, caused no injury, only benefaction and salvation (see Danker 1982).

3. *Denial of Victims.* No one could come forward who had been harmed by Jesus. On the contrary a legion of people helped by him could be brought forth to testify to his benefaction.

4. *Condemning the Condemners.* An important defensive maneuver for an accused person is to cast doubts on the legality of the proceedings, namely, to judge one's judges and to put the court itself on trial. It is quite possible that the judges and courts were *not* pursuing justice, but acting unjustly. In the case of Jesus' trials and judges, the narrative condemned his condemners.

> (a) The narrator indicates that the Jewish trial of Jesus was illegal in many respects (Lohse 1971:867–68). The prisoner was physically intimidated before the hearing began (22:63–65). The trial presumably took place in an unauthorized place, the high priest's house (22:54), not the impartial place of justice. The witness was asked to incriminate himself (22:67, 70).

> (b) The Roman judge three times dismissed the charges against Jesus, and declared him innocent (23:4, 14, 22); even Jesus' executioner declared him innocent (23:47). So when Jesus was condemned to be crucified, an innocent person was being unjustly judged.

> (c) In the Barabbas episode, injustice was formally dramatized: the crowds demanded the release of a known murderer (23:19, 25) who was truly guilty, and they condemned a person declared innocent (23:18, 21, 23, 25). Justice was clearly perverted: the guilty were set free and the innocent condemned.

> (d) It could be argued, moreover, that Jesus' arrest and trial were not the results of a pursuit of justice, but the actions of evil, even demonic people. Jesus' trusted disciple, Judas, was dishonorably bribed to betray his leader (22:5). More importantly, he was also described as an evil person possessed of Satan and so acting against Jesus under Satan's influence (22:3). When arrested, Jesus described that event as the work of "the power of darkness" (22:53). Evil, then, attacked good.

The reader, therefore, should draw the conclusion that the judges of Jesus acted unjustly and for evil motives (see Mark 15:10); they were even under the influence of Satan. The condemners are thereby condemned.

5. *Appeal to Higher Loyalty.* Jesus never denied that he was God's prophet and Christ, nor did he ever disavow the behavior attendant upon

these titles. The actions which his enemies condemned were fully justified because Jesus acted in accord with a higher loyalty, namely, God's personal authorization. His death especially was portrayed as obedience to God, and so did not belong in the realm of just punishment for sin but in the realm of basic faithfulness to God.

The narrative, moreover, goes to great lengths to portray the arrested and dying Jesus as a person righteous according to the perception of piety in Israel. First, he kept the sacred ceremony of Passover in all its ritual detail (22:7ff.), thus showing himself observant of the customs respected by pious people. After this, he retired to the Mount of Olives "as was his custom" to pray (22:39) a prayer of obedience to God: "Father, if thou art willing, remove this cup from me; nevertheless not my will, but thine, be done" (22:42). At the moment of his death, when he might be expected to curse his executioners or finally confess his guilt, he prayed again, this time from the Psalms: "Father, into your hands I commit my spirit" (23:46//Ps 31:5). All of the Gospels portray Jesus praying the Psalms on the cross, but Luke most clearly indicates Jesus' dying words as a prayer of ultimate faithfulness to God. In this Jesus continued to demonstrates his knowledge of God's will (9:22, 44; 18:31–33); he continued his life-long practice of prayer (3:21; 6:12; 9:28), and he steadfastly maintained faithfulness and obedience to the God of Israel (4:1–12).

The dying words of Jesus, which are a formal prayer of faithfulness in God, are a typical prayer of a suffering righteous person. Just as all of his actions were necessitated by God's commission (4:18), so especially his death is best seen as an act of faithful obedience. According to Luke's narrative, then, the labelling process has been successfully interrupted. The evangelist has been able to construct an alternative and correct *retrospective interpretation* of Jesus which negates the negative labelling process and even exonerates and elevates him.

4.0 FURTHER EXAMINATION OF CONFLICT IN LUKE–ACTS

In this essay, we focused on the Passion narrative as a text which would benefit from being perceived according to the scenario of labelling and deviance theory. Clearly there are many other places in Luke's Gospel where Jesus and others are negatively labelled, especially incidents such as 7:39; 11:14–23, 37–41; and 16:14. These and other passages may profitably be analyzed from the perspective of labelling and deviance theory.

In Acts, moreover, a host of forensic charges are made against Jesus' disciples, charges which could become deviant labels if the deviance process against the disciples succeeded:

Peter:
1. (false) expounder of the resurrection (4:2)

2. disobedient to legitimate authority (5:27–28)

Stephen:
3. "he speaks against this holy place and the Law; he says that Jesus will destroy this place and change the customs which Moses delivered to us" (6:13–14)

4. blasphemy (7:57)

Paul:
5. "disturbing the city; he advocates customs not lawful for Romans to accept and practice" (16:20–21)

6. "they turn the world upside down; they act against the decrees of Caesar, saying that there is another king, Jesus" (17:6)

7. "This man is persuading men to worship God contrary to the law" (18:13)

8. sacrilege and blasphemy (19:37)

9. "This is the man who is teaching people everywhere against the people and the law and this place . . . and he has defiled this holy place" (21:28)

10. "a pestilent fellow, an agitator among all the Jews throughout the world, and a ringleader of the sect of the Nazarenes" (24:5).

And these charges occur during the numerous forensic trials to which Peter, Stephen and Paul are subjected.

Text of Acts	Person	Place
4:3–23	Peter et al.	Jerusalem
5:17–40	Peter et al.	Jerusalem
6:9–7:60	Stephen	Jerusalem
16:19–36	Paul and Silas	Philippi
17:5–9	Paul et al.	Thessalonica
18:12–17	Paul	Corinth
21:27–22:30	Paul	Jerusalem
22:30–23:10	Paul	Caesarea
24:1–26	Paul	Caesarea
25:5–12	Paul	Caesarea
25:24–26:32	Paul	Caesarea
28	Paul	Rome

The model of labelling and deviance which was presented in the earlier part of this chapter can serve as a valuable scenario for examining both the deviant labels alleged against Jesus' disciples and the forensic trials, or *status degradation rituals*, to which they are subjected. The model would allow us to understand why certain people raised the cry against the disciples, why they expressed their indignation in certain charges, and what they hoped to accomplish by establishing the disciples as deviants. The model would also suggest the strategies by which the disciples avoided the deviant labels and upset the degradation rituals.

And so we hope that we have presented the reader with a valuable tool for understanding the conflict so pervasive in Luke–Acts. If we have succeeded in presenting the scenario which is necessary and adequate for understanding these scenes of conflict, then the reader has greatly benefited and possesses a model which can be employed in reading more of Luke–Acts, as well as other New Testament documents.

Yet this chapter invites the reader to enter into conversation with other essays in this volume. If one would understand more clearly the temple system and its place in the symbolic universe of Luke–Acts, then the essay by Elliott on the temple as institution and the study by Neyrey on temple and symbolic universe would deepen the reader's appreciation of the role of temple and temple functionaries in the conflict of Jesus. And since conflict may also be understood in terms of the pivotal value of honor and shame, a complete reading of conflict scenes in Luke–Acts would entail an examination of them as negative honor challenges. And in this regard, since Jesus' trial should be understood as a status degradation ritual, a fuller appreciation of the dishonor Jesus suffered would bring the reader back to the chapter on honor and shame. In particular, a reader would greatly benefit by taking the modeling of status transformation rituals in the chapter by McVann and applying that material in greater detail to the trial and execution of Jesus. Finally, in terms of the presentation of Jesus as a pious victim of injustice who maintained faithfulness and obedience to God to the end, the study on honor and shame indicated why and how that virtue was perceived as a preeminent value in Mediterranean culture.

SOCIAL INSTITUTIONS

5 | THE PRE-INDUSTRIAL CITY IN LUKE–ACTS: URBAN SOCIAL RELATIONS

Richard L. Rohrbaugh

0.0 INTRODUCTION

Fully one half of the references to the "city" in the New Testament are in the Lukan writings, equally divided between the Gospel and the book of Acts. Whether any significance should be attached to this has not been altogether clear to New Testament scholars. Neither has the possibility been explored that Luke uses the characteristics of the urban setting in order to articulate his understanding of the Good News. Initial inquiries into Luke's use of the term "city" have lacked a sociological model of the urban system and pre-industrial city. Using such a fresh approach would go a long way toward providing an adequate scenario for understanding the writings of Luke in which the city plays a key role.

1.0 USING THE TERM "CITY"

Before beginning a discussion of our model, it seems helpful to think about the way that the term "city" has been used in the Bible.

1.1 Ancient Understandings of the Concept

In the New Testament, ninety different places are named that may have been cities, although not all of them can be identified today. The chart below lists those named in Luke–Acts that are in direct or implied association with the word "city" (polis):

Luke	Acts	
Arimathea	Azotus (Ashdod)	Joppa
Bethlehem	Antioch (Pisidia)	Lasea
Bethsaida	Athens	Lystra
Capernaum	Caesarea	Philippi
Chorazin	Corinth	Tarsus
Jerusalem	Damascus	Thessalonica
Nain	Derbe	Thyatira
Nazareth	Ephesus	Tyre
Sidon	Iconium	
Tyre	Jerusalem	

Obviously other cities such as Rome and Antioch in Syria are mentioned, but our list above shows all of the sites which Luke specifically designates by the term "city."

Several items on the list are worthy of comment. Note that Luke (2:4) calls Bethlehem a "city" (polis), while John (7:42) calls it a "village" (kōmē). Similarly, Bethsaida is called a city in Luke (9:10) and a village in Mark (8:23). This kind of inconsistency is also reflected in the writings of Josephus who calls Jotapata both city and village and labels Hebron and Gischala both city and small hamlet (polichnē). Capernaum, which Luke consistently calls a city, etymologically means "village of Nahum." In Jesus' day Nazareth, another location Luke exclusively designates a city, was off the main roads of lower Galilee and was no more than a hamlet of a few hundred people. It is usually assumed that by calling Nazareth a city Luke betrays his lack of familiarity with Palestine, but it may also be that like many ancient authors he simply uses the term "city" in a non-technical sense. For readers of the English New Testament the problem is compounded because translators frequently translate the same Greek word, polis, both "city" and "town" (cf. Luke 8:1 and 8:4 in the RSV), words that can have different connotations for the modern reader.

In antiquity a city was nearly always linked to a group of surrounding villages, which the Old Testament sometimes called its "daughters" (bnwt; see Judg 1:17). This is evident in references such as 1 Macc 5:65, "He struck Hebron and its villages" and Mark 8:27, "the villages of Caesarea Philippi." The exceptions were the cities of the Levites which were given pasture land rather than villages (Num 35:1–8). Josephus indicates that Julia was the capital of a toparchy that had fourteen villages associated with it (Ant. 20.159). These villages often provided the city with a major portion of its income. Nazareth may have been such a village belonging to the nearby city of Sepphoris.

In the Old Testament the city is distinguished from the village by having surrounding walls (Lev 25:31). Moreover, legal distinctions in the disposition of property were drawn on the basis of this definition. A village house could never be sold in perpetuity and could always be redeemed; yet after the sale of a house in the city, a buyer had only one year to reconsider (Lev 25:13–17, 25–31). In the New Testament this distinction between cities and villages is maintained (Matt 9:35; 10:11; Mark 6:56; Luke 8:1; 13:22), although no criteria for the distinction are provided. In the period after the New Testament, rabbis came to designate a village as a place lacking a synagogue.

Writing late in the second century of the common era, Pausanias reveals something of the Greco-Roman understanding of a city. In a kind of travel-guide to the Greek cities of Phocis, a region opposite the Peloponnesus near Delphi, Pausanias first calls Panopeus a "city," but then raises doubts by wondering

> if indeed one can give the name of city to those who possess no public buildings (archeia), no gymnasium, no theatre, no market-place, no water descending to a fountain, but live in bare shelters just like mountain huts on the edges of ravines (X.iv.1).

Obviously he expects cities to be more than containers for large numbers of people. Exactly how the term city should be used, however, is something even contemporary social theorists have been unable to decide.

1.2 Anachronistic Understandings of the Concept

In the same way that our understanding of the term "city" can cause confusion, so also can projection of the patterns and dynamics of modern cities back onto those of antiquity. For example, Wayne Meeks, in his book *First Urban Christians*, tries to imagine what led the city-dwellers of the Greco-Roman world to join Christian communities like those described in the book of Acts. He imagines a harried city life not unlike that in the fast-paced cities of today:

> Urban life in the early Roman Empire was scarcely less complicated than our own, in proportion to the scale of knowledge available to an individual and the demands made upon him. Its complexity-its untidiness to the mind-may well have been felt with special acuteness by people who were marginal or transient, either physically or socially or both, as so many of the identifiable members of Pauline churches seem to have been (1983:104).

It does not take too much thought, however, to realize that the city described here is from the twentieth century rather than the first. Incredible complexity, physical and social mobility, and information overload are things we deal with today all the time. They produce in us strong feelings of loneliness, anxiety, and alienation. "Finding" such feelings in the ancient city, Meeks uses them to explain why these ancient city-dwellers joined the Christian movement (1983:191). But as one reviewer has pointed out, what Meeks is really doing is resorting to "modern popular psychology to explain why first-century Mediterraneans might join and adhere to the Pauline type of church" (Malina 1985:349).

In part Meeks is led into this by uncritically applying a theoretical concept, the notion of "status inconsistency," to the societies of the ancient Mediterranean. "Status inconsistency" (e.g., poor but honored, rich but despised) is a modern concept designed to study the social tensions of modern societies. Meeks thereby imagined in ancient cities the rising social aspirations and accompanying emotional stresses typical of socially mobile groups in America. Jerome Murphy-O'Connor takes a similar tack in his otherwise excellent descriptions of the ancient city of Corinth. Citing status inconsistencies in Corinth, he writes, "A feeling of frustration was inevitable; what was the point of a life in which the full exploitation of one's talents was blocked by circumstances outside one's control" (1984:153). Modern notions of self-actualization are not hard to spot here.

But equally problematical are the assumptions made about the ancient city itself. Information overload was not much of a problem in ancient cities and social mobility was nearly non-existent. It was not a conceivable expectation for most people any more than was the idea of "full exploitation of one's talents." It is highly unlikely that these things were prime causes of alienation and social isolation for ancient city inhabitants. Social mobility, when it did occur, was usually downward. Ancient people therefore imagined the struggle to be hanging on to what they had, not gaining more. Fear of loss or depression over having lost out already was more likely a motive than rising aspirations. Meeks and Murphy O'Connor, then, do not provide us with adequate scenarios for understanding urban life in antiquity. Their observations drawn from the industrial world simply do not hold true for ancient societies.

A more adequate scenario can be found in a description of the artisans who inhabited pre-industrial cities. As Gerhard Lenski has shown, "In most agrarian societies, the artisan class was originally recruited from the ranks of the dispossessed peasantry and their non-inheriting sons and was continually replenished from these sources" (1966:278). He adds that they were lower on the status scale than peasants and had lower incomes. Having lost their connection to the land and to their extended families when they migrated to the cities, they had consequently lost the status and protection of their previous connections. Getting reconnected to a group would therefore have had little to do with the psychology of harried and overly complicated city life or rising social expectations. It would have had much to do with fear for the next meal.

What is needed, then, is a picture of ancient cities which avoids anachronisms. For this purpose we propose a model of cities and the broader urban system of which they were a part that is appropriate to the pre-industrial world rather than our modern industrial era. Our primary purpose in what follows will be to sort out the confusion introduced into comment on Luke's use of urban settings by inappropriate projection of the patterns of industrial cities onto those of antiquity. As a case in point, our model of the urban system will be used as a heuristic device in looking at the parable of the Great Supper in Luke 14:15–24, a story that not only takes place in the city, but does so in a uniquely knowing way. Finally, in the process of looking at the text in Luke 14, it may also be possible to comment about recent discussion of the audience, setting, and purpose of Luke–Acts.

2.0 A MODEL OF THE URBAN SYSTEM

We begin our investigation of the "city" in Luke's writings with a discussion of current theory of urban "systems." We focus particularly on what Anthony Leeds (1979) has called "social urbanization," that is, the integration/interaction of component parts of urbanized societies. For reasons that will become obvious, we have chosen deliberately to avoid treating the city as an isolated construct that can be understood apart from a regional system. Instead we shall follow the basic thesis set out by Leeds

> . . . that in human settlement patterns in general all aggregations or nucleations ('localities'), from "tribal villages" to "megalopolises," can only be fully understood if looked at as nodal points within societal systems or between hierarchic levels of such systems. Explicit in the model is the argument that nucleations (villages, towns, or cities) can never be looked at in isolation, as closed systems, as tightly bounded entities (1980:6, 11).

It is thus the urban society, not simply the city within it, that must first be understood.

This also means that we shall not try to define the term "city" as an isolated phenomenon. Modern attempts to do so have produced little agreement in the anthropological literature to date. Among the widely followed (if now abandoned) attempts at doing so was that of Louis Wirth, who believed on the basis of three variables — number, density and heterogeneity of population — that it would be possible to "explain the characteristics of urban life and to account for the differences between cities of various sizes and types" (1951:44). Gideon Sjoberg expanded Wirth's list of criteria slightly by adding that essential to the city is "a wide range of non-agricultural specialists, most significant of whom are the literati" (1960:11). It was on the basis of such a definition that Sjoberg formulated his now classic cross-cultural typology of the pre-industrial city.

More recent theorists, however, have not seen Wirth's definition (or the numerous variations thereof) as adequate, not only because the variables chosen demonstrably lack the explanatory power claimed for them, but also because this approach isolates the city from the system of which it is a part. That is particularly true of those definitions assuming the now widely discredited notion of a rural-urban contrast (Sorokin) or continuum (Redfield) that treats the urban and rural as closed or even opposed social systems.

2.1 Model One: The Urban System as a Whole

Our approach thus begins not with an allegedly universal definition of the city as such, but with a regional model of the urban system as a whole. We begin with the idea that within a regional system, at least at a very general level, all human "nucleations," including villages, towns, and cities, in all types of societies, have the same function: to facilitate various forms of exchange, transfer, and communication, while linking any one locality with other localities and with the society at large. Such localizations may vary in size and complexity (family, village, town, megalopolis), but at the most general level their function is the same.

2.1.1 Horizontal Differentiation. Among these nucleations, however, specializations begin to occur which create what we might call "horizontal" differentiation within a total system. This means that at a less general level the same things are not done at all nodes in the system and that some localities take on specialized roles. Moreover, one specialization necessarily requires another—specialties usually come in sets. "A *structure* of interrelated differentiations" is thus created in which the city and village take on different, although frequently overlapping, roles (Leeds 1979:231). What distinguishes them is not that particular functions are typical of the city and others of the village. Instead it is simply that some localities become collecting points for more of these specialties and end up with a greater diversity of function. What distinguishes cities therefore is an accumulation of specializations, not the presence of any particular one. As Eric Lampard puts it, "The city is, in this sense, *a multifaceted central place*, a focus of generalized nodality" (1965:540).

A major implication of all this is that the terms "urban" and "rural" do not describe polar opposites or closed systems. Cities and hinterland are inherently linked and the specialties present in them are intrinsically parts of a *single* system. As Leeds sums up the model:

> ... all people, all action, all culture, all social organization, all technology become specialized. Hence, insofar as such systems display those properties conventionally designated as "urban," we are *obliged* to regard the *entire* society as urban and cities merely as concentrations of more or less large ranges and arrays of certain types of specialties (1980:7).

Or to put the matter another way, a peasant is an urban man. The peasant has a native understanding of the complexity of urban systems. He knows how the system works, in whose interests (the urban elite) it is organized, and that his special struggle is to hang on to what place he has in it. Likewise, peasantry cannot be seen as a "stage" of evolution somewhere between the tribal and the urban. It is rather one specialization within the whole system of specializations that includes the city.

2.1.2 Vertical differentiation. A system functionally differentiated into rural and urban components nonetheless remains an integrated whole. The pattern that links the parts of the system, however, can vary substantially from one society to the next. Leeds argues that what determines the organizational pattern in a particular society, including the pattern within the cities themselves, is above all else the character of social class relations (1979:234).

To illustrate what this means, several organizational aspects of the pre-industrial urban system deserve comment. They will suggest that not only is there a horizontal differentiation — certain nodes becoming collecting points for specialized functions — but that a vertical differentiation, a hierarchy, between city and hinterland typifies the system as well.

This can be seen in the fact that the urbanization of antiquity was the result, at least in part, of the organization and appropriation by cities of an agricultural surplus produced in the hinterlands (Lenski 1966:190– 297). Villages had the capacity neither to store nor protect a social product of substantial variety or size. Thus cities accumulated what was produced beyond the subsistence needs of the peasants. By bureaucratic, military, commercial, or fiduciary means, they became centers of control — primarily over land use and raw materials — and thereby determined the conditions under which all other parts of the system operated. The diagram below illustrates the way the system worked.

We may further illustrate how all this worked by comparing the labor needs of the industrial and pre-industrial city. In contrast to agrarian societies in which the primary economic unit was the family, in the industrial city of today the labor unit is of necessity the individual worker. Capital concentration, cost efficiency, and exploding specialization of the labor process (as opposed to specialization of product in antiquity) all require a large, mobile labor force composed of persons who can be detached from their geographical and social place of origin. These people thus constitute a flexible work-force for employers seeking to adapt to changing market conditions at minimum cost.

Such a pattern within our cities is directly related to the pattern linking city and hinterlands. That relationship is a tightly knit one ensuring the flow of capital and labor toward the cities. Marketplace and channels of communication/transportation come to include the hinterlands along with the city. What is created is a system, an urbanized system, in which the necessary roles and exchanges are structured and enhanced.

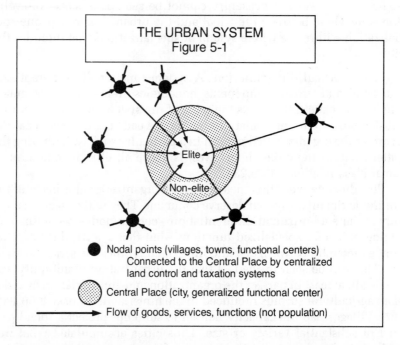

THE URBAN SYSTEM
Figure 5-1

Elite

Non-elite

● Nodal points (villages, towns, functional centers)
   Connected to the Central Place by centralized
   land control and taxation systems

⬭ Central Place (city, generalized functional center)

⟶ Flow of goods, services, functions (not population)

By contrast, pre-industrial cities existed in a system which required a socially and geographically fixed labor force. Specialists in the city primarily produced the goods and services needed by the urban elite, who were the only existing consumer market. Since that market was small, the labor force needed to supply it was correspondingly small and, as Leeds notes, it thus became a "major interest to keep others than these out of the towns, fixed in their own agrarian, mining or extractive areas" (1979:238). In fact most agrarian societies established legal restrictions on city residence that kept the peasants out.

Pre-industrial city and agricultural hinterlands were thus linked neither through the flow of labor and capital, nor by their mutual participation in a common marketplace, but through centralized land control and the religious/political systems of taxation. The need for a socially or geographically detached labor force was small and sporadic. Contact between persons in the two areas was minimized and usually mediated by a politically or religiously defined group of persons. The hinterlands were not a general source of labor, and efficient means of transportation and communication were not necessary to link the system. As Lampard concludes:

Justified by the liturgical authority of priestcraft, enlarged and defended by the combative force of captains and kings, the mobilization of a net social product at the center constituted an unprecedented concentration of energy potential on a minute territorial base. This *implosion* of energies, to adopt Lewis Mumford's term, was henceforth subject only to the limits of control techniques at the disposal of decision-making groups lodged at the node. Their demands gradually shaped the composition of the social product and their purposes governed the allocation and utilization of the crucial net (1965:542).

In sum, the pattern in antiquity was far different than what we see today. The system depended on "the geographical as well as the social distancing of classes and separation physically of their functions in the productive and sociopolitical processes" (Leeds 1979:240). Horizontal differentiation of a center from its surrounding territory is thus only part of the urbanizing process. It is matched by a concurrent vertical differentiation—what Lampard calls "social-structural stratification"— that permeates the system. It begins in the hierarchical relation of city and country and extends to the well-known two-class stratification cited by Sjoberg and others as an internal characteristic of all pre-industrial cities (Sjoberg 1960:108–144).

2.2 Model Two: The Pre-industrial City

In order to see how all this worked it is necessary to flesh out a model of the pre-industrial city itself. Our goal will be to see the ways it differed from the industrial cities with which we are familiar today.

2.2.1 Demography and Ecology. The cities of antiquity were small, and in most areas no more than 5–7% of the population lived in cities. Earlier estimates that Rome and other major cities had populations in excess of one million are almost certainly wrong. Recent studies suggest 200,000 for Rome, though very few ancient cities exceeded 100,000. Douglas Oakman has argued that in Roman Palestine no city exceeded 35,000 and that perhaps no more than two or three cities there exceeded 10,000. Because density was extremely high by modern standards, the area occupied by urban sites was small. The Jericho and Megiddo of the Old Testament period covered about twelve acres. Debir was about eight. The Jerusalem of Jesus' day was about forty-six.

In general, pre-industrial cities housed two different populations: the elite, who occupied the center of the city, and the non-elite, who occupied the outlying areas. The elite, though usually no more than 5–10% of the total population, dominated both city and country. Being the only group with disposable income, they formed the only real market population in antiquity. Their control of the political and economic systems was usually legitimated by a religious and educational bureaucracy that became the keeper of the so-called great tradition. This is the "official" version, usually written, of a culture's religion, values and world view. It articulates the values and mores the elite manifest.

Physically and socially isolated from the elite was the bulk of the city population, the non-elite, whose presence in the city was required to serve the needs of those in control. Although birth rates were high in all segments of the city population, survival rates meant that large extended families were characteristic only of the elite. Non-elite city populations were continually replenished by the dispossessed of the countryside whose lack of skills often relegated them to menial tasks as day laborers.

2.2.2 Function. In our model of the urban system we learned that cities became collecting points for a wide variety of functions. Chief among these were political and economic functions, although apart from centralized political power the economic control which enabled the elite to expropriate the economic surplus of the hinterlands would have been impossible. Few cities became prominent by virtue of religious importance alone; yet the religious, educational, and cultural systems of the city acted powerfully to integrate and legitimate the network of other functions the city performed. Since control of these by the elite was essential to their dominance, temple and palace became the twin foci of most pre-industrial cities.

Manual labor, and all but the largest-scale trade, was engaged in only by non-elite and outcast groups within the city. Production was on a small scale, limited mostly to homes and small shops. Few businesses had employees who were not members of the family. The collection of taxes and tribute from the villages and hinterland controlled by the city were the major source of income for the elite. On the phenomenon of the absentee landlord, see the essays of Oakman and Moxnes in this volume.

2.2.3 Spatial Organization. As Sjoberg and others have pointed out, both the internal social stratification of the city and its peculiar functions in the system were mirrored in the physical configuration of nearly all pre-industrial cities. The central area contained the palace, the temple, and the residences of both the political and religious elite. Such centers often were surrounded by internal walls of their own and were tightly bunched to facilitate both communication and protection. The temple centers of Mesopotamian cities are a well-known example. So also would be the acropolis areas of many cities in the Greco-Roman world. Jeremias' description of Jerusalem in the time of Jesus is another, though in Jerusalem's case the palace of Herod and the temple dominated the upper and lower areas of the city respectively (1969:18–21). Market areas were usually alongside the religious center, as were those in Jerusalem clustered in the Tyropoeon Valley near the temple.

Elsewhere in the city internal walls divided sections populated by those needed there to serve the elite. Such sections frequently separated ethnic or occupational groups. The internal walls, moreover, were usually arranged so that watchmen could control traffic and communication between sections or so that guards be advantageously positioned in times of military emergency. Most streets were unpaved, narrow, badly crowded and would not have allowed passage of wheeled vehicles. Many would have been choked with refuse and frequented by scavenging dogs, pigs, birds, and other animals. Shallow depressions in the streets allowed some drainage, but also acted as open sewers. Large open spaces were few in most cities and those that did exist were often at intersections of the few paved thoroughfares. Such open squares often served as gathering places for ceremonies or public announcements.

Particular families or occupational groups, frequently organized into guilds, might control an entire street or city sector. Many guilds had their own internal hierarchical social structure. As Sjoberg has suggested, the non-elite usually fanned out toward the periphery of the city with outcast groups including ethnic groups, small-time merchants, and those practicing despised occupations (e.g., tanners), living at the very edge or outside the city walls (1960:97–100). Gates in the internal city walls controlled interaction between these various groups and were closed at night, thereby cutting off inter-group communication.

The following diagram will help to visualize the spatial organization we have been describing.

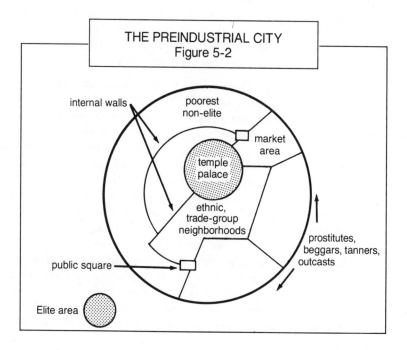

THE PREINDUSTRIAL CITY
Figure 5-2

internal walls

poorest
non-elite

market
area

temple
palace

ethnic,
trade-group
neighborhoods

prostitutes,
beggars, tanners,
outcasts

public square

Elite area

Pre-industrial cities were thus clear examples of what has been called "human territoriality." By this is meant "the attempt by an individual or group to affect, influence or control people, phenomena, and relationships, by delimiting and asserting control over a geographical area" (Sack 1986:19). Because territoriality is a social construct, it is by its very nature a means of social control. In addition, however, by regulating access it can also be a way of controlling both land and the flow of resources, especially when land and resources are in short supply. And as Sack points out, geographic territoriality is an effective means of communicating as well as creating both the classification of people and the reification of power. It can make relationships across boundaries impersonal at the same time that relationships within boundaries are personalized and solidified (Sack 1986:32–34).

2.2.4 Patterns of Interaction. Coming from the perspective of urban studies, Lenski and Lampard have also shown how systems of hierarchical control tended to produce strong feelings of solidarity among people or groups which were differentiated by the system in similar ways. Thus people of the same occupation, age, sex, ethnic group, or social class often saw in their categoric identification a set of interests at odds with the larger system. For the same reason, marriage, as well as most other types of social intercourse, that cut across such lines was nearly nonexistent. A member of the urban elite took significant steps to avoid contact with other groups except to obtain needed goods and services. Such a person would experience a serious loss of status if found to be socializing with groups other than his own. Thus social and geographical distancing, enforced and communicated by interior walls, characterized both internal city relations and those between city and country.

2.2.5 Communication. The means of communication were not well developed nor did they need to be. Proximity facilitated communication among the elite as did their near monopoly on writing. Town criers, street singers, story-tellers, actors, priests, astrologers, and magicians all kept up a flow of information among the majority, though word-of-mouth was the primary means of communication. Record-keeping, another important tool of control, was inconsistent but largely in the hands of the elite.

In sum, the patterns of pre-industrial cities were very much the consequence of the role played by the city in the larger urban system. As the center of control, the city gathered to itself those non-elite necessary to serve its needs as it carried out the specialized functions it had collected. It was a system characterized by the dominance of a small center, by sharp social stratification, and by a physical and social distancing of component populations that were linked by carefully controlled hierarchical relations. The city was a ready example of human territoriality in which the elite occupied a fortified center, ethnic, socio-economic and occupational groups the periphery, and outcasts the area immediately outside the city walls.

3.0 TESTING THE MODEL: THE GREAT SUPPER IN LUKE 14:15–24

Analysis of Luke 14:15–24 provides a ready test case for the heuristic value of our model of the urban system. In applying the model our thesis is that Luke's version of this parable knowingly uses features of the urban system in order to make its point and that these features would have been readily apparent to Luke's intended audience. Along the way we may also comment on anachronistic assumptions about the text introduced by modern scholars who have drawn their perceptions from the modern city rather than the pre-industrial one. The main purpose of using the model is to develop a reading scenario that allows us to understand Luke on his own terms.

3.1 The Text Unit

Luke 14:15–24 has occasioned extensive comment. We can thus begin our analysis by summarizing certain aspects of the work of other interpreters. To begin with, it has frequently been noted that 14:1–24 appears to be a unified section, though disagreement exists about whether the unity is to be attributed to Luke or to a hypothetical source. A chiastic pattern may or may not be there, although there can be little doubt that the arrangement of the traditions within the unit is intentional. The entire unit is set at a sabbath dinner in the home of a leading Pharisee. It begins in 14:1–6 with the healing of a man with dropsy and a comment by Jesus about healing on a sabbath day. In 14:7–11 Luke tells a parable about those who choose places of honor at a marriage feast. Luke 14:12–14 is a saying about inviting the "poor, the maimed, the lame and the blind" to dinners or banquets, to which has been added (by Luke?) the eschatological comment in 14:15, "Blessed is he who shall eat bread in the kingdom of God," which then introduces the parable of the Great Supper. The presence of the saying has led many, following Jeremias, to assert the eschatological character of what follows.

It may be, however, that 14:1–24 is not the unit at which we should be looking. James Resseguie suggests that the whole of 14:1–33 should be viewed together as a narrative in which conflicting ideological points of view are juxtaposed and contrasted. One view is "exaltation-oriented," seeking to gain recognition before others, the other "humiliation-oriented," avoiding the self-promotion of the first outlook (1982:46). In the first half of the unit (14:1–24) the audience of Pharisees and lawyers is hostile to Jesus. The latter half (14:25–33) is addressed to a crowd which includes potential disciples. Karris agrees that 14:1–33 belong together, noting that 14:25–33 presses the issues raised in 14:1–24, making them a matter of discipleship for those following Jesus. That is especially true for those with possessions (Karris 1978:121). Pointedly, the section concludes: "So therefore, whoever of you does not renounce *all that he has* cannot be my disciple" (14:33).

We might also add that the parables in chapter 15 follow up this train of thought, suggesting that the kingdom will include unexpected or overlooked people who epitomize the humiliation-oriented point of view. Moreover, Luke introduces chapter 15 with the comment that "tax collectors and sinners were all drawing near"; he then describes the murmuring of the Pharisees that Jesus not only receives such people, he "eats with them." The point is that the parable of the Great Supper is placed in the context of a larger discussion of eating and associating with the unexpected people whom the kingdom includes. The question to which we must return then is one about the reason meals, rich hosts and unexpected guests are of such obvious concern to Luke.

3.2 The Origin and Form of the Parable

The much-discussed origin and form of the parable are not altogether clear. Three versions exist: one in Luke, a near parallel in the Gospel of Thomas (64:1–2), and a heavily edited version in Matthew (22:1–13). Some scholars have argued that Luke's is the most primitive version (Plummer, Manson, Ellis), others that it is the one in Thomas (Jeremias, Perrin, Crossan, Fitzmyer). Still others have seen a common source behind all three texts. A few have argued for the independent origin of the synoptic and Thomas versions (Perrin), with some suggesting "Q" as the source behind the parable in Luke and Matthew (Fitzmyer). Many would agree with F. W. Beare that the parable is now sufficiently "mangled" so that if the parable does go back to Jesus, "it is no longer possible to tell in what form it was first uttered, or in what context" (1981:432).

3.3 Luke's Version of the Story

For our purposes, however, it is less the original version of the story than that which appears in Luke that is of interest. That is so because only Luke appears to knowingly use the features of the urban system described above. In order to make this clear, however, it is necessary to draw attention to certain features of the Lukan story that are unique among the three accounts.

The Host. In Matthew the host of the meal is a "king." In Luke, as in Thomas, the host is designated simply as "a certain man." In spite of the indefinite pronoun, however, the Lukan setting of the text in the home of a leader (*archōn*) of the Pharisees suggests that we should assume Luke has in mind someone like this person hosting Jesus (see 14:1).

The *Occasion.* In Matthew the occasion is a "wedding feast," while in Thomas it is simply a "dinner," and in Luke, a "great supper." One gets the impression that Luke is talking about a host with the means to hold festive dinners of considerable size. Some see in the adjective "great" a reference to the messianic banquet (Jeremias 1955:69), thus allegorizing the setting in line with allegorical features usually held to exist elsewhere in the story. Yet no textual warrant for this exists whatsoever and, as we shall argue below, the heavy-handed allegorization of the story in Matthew need not be imported here.

The *Original Invitation.* Contrary to Thomas, Matthew and Luke state that the original guests are invited twice. Crossan thinks the Thomas version more likely original because the refusal of the second invitation by the original guests is inexplicable to him (1973:72). He also argues that the double invitation fits the allegorizing needs of both Matthew and Luke, a point with which we shall again take issue in the case of Luke. We may note, however, that evidence of just such double invitations exists in papyrus texts (Kim 1975:397), and, as we shall see, the double invitation serves a clear purpose in the urban system of pre-industrial cities.

The *Excuses.* Both synoptic versions of the story contain three excuses by those initially invited. The four excuses in Thomas appear to have been adapted to the appended logion (64:2) excluding businessmen and merchants from the places of the Father. Two of those in Matthew are similar to the first two in Luke, while the third is adapted to fit the fact that feast being held in Matthew is itself a wedding.

The *Reaction of the Host.* Only Matthew and Luke recount the anger of the rejected host. Although this item is also taken by some as evidence of allegorization (the occasion for rejection of the Jews and evangelization of the Gentiles), we shall again propose that it is so only in Matthew. Our model will suggest that we follow Karris and a number of others in treating the refusal of the supper invitation as a problem *within* Luke's community rather than one between Luke and recalcitrant Jews. The anger of the host must then be seen in that context as well.

The *Final Invitations.* Since all extant versions of the story describe the servant(s) going out onto the city streets to obtain the needed guests, Scott suggests that this is part of the "originating structure" of the parable (1986:26). In Matthew the newly invited guests are "the good and the bad." In Thomas they are whomever the servant should "happen to meet." Only in Luke are there two groups: (a) the "poor and maimed and blind and lame" from the city streets, and (b) those from the "highways and hedges" outside the city walls. This double invitation to the new guests is thus Luke's alone and, as we shall see, it is significant.

The Banquet Hall. In Matthew and Luke, although not in Thomas
the banquet hall is filled. The fact is simply noted in Matthew, but has
been heightened considerably in Luke by the addition of the second
invitation. The significance we should attach to this will remain unclear, however, until we arrive at a better understanding of the second
invitation.

The Conclusion. Finally, we note the different conclusion of each
version of the story. Matthew's king spots a wedding guest with no wedding garment, which leads to a conclusion required by his allegorical
reworking of the tradition to fit salvation history. The concluding logion in Thomas is a clear addition, perhaps to be seen as a "warning
not to let material cares distract one from the invitation to true gnosis"
(Crossan 1973:73) or, more broadly, as an "otherworldly ethic" (King
1987:21). Luke's conclusion is quite different. He adds a saying that
Crossan somewhat disdainfully characterizes as "moralizing" about a
"rather doubtful ethical greatness." It can be more appropriately treated
as a simple warning to those the parable addresses, though it will of
course be important to understand exactly who that is.

3.4 Luke's Use of the System and City

It is time now to turn to our primary task: using the model of the
pre-industrial urban system as a reading scenario for understanding
Luke's version of the parable and its purpose in his community. In doing
so we shall focus on the special Lukan features of the story which, as
listed above, can serve as a convenient outline for our study.

The Host. Note that the host of the great supper is simply "a certain man," not a "king." The fact that he can hold a banquet of such
proportions clearly places him among the urban elite. Unless the response to the second set of invitations was extremely spotty, we are talking about a very large banquet indeed. The adjective "great" simply
underscores this and need not be seen as cryptically eschatological. Hearers of the story would immediately catch the idea that we are talking
about a host with considerable means, making the contrast between him
and the final guests as stark as possible.

The person being talked about is therefore a leading member of that
elite urban group which both sets the terms for and controls access to
social interaction between itself and others in the society. This host's
social obligations to his peers would thus have been considerable, and
maintaining his position among them depended on how well he carried these out. As in all honor-shame societies, social approval of the
way these obligations were met was critical for the host and his family.

The Occasion. That the story is told while Jesus sits at a dinner in
the home of a leading Pharisee would, as we noted above, lead the hearer
to assume that the host of the story was not unlike the host listening

across the table. Later readers in the time of Luke, however, would obviously be thinking less about the hosts of Jesus' time than of their own.

The Original Invitation. As we noted above, in Luke (and Matthew) the servant of the host is sent out to summon those who had been previously invited. As the papyrus evidence indicates, this kind of double invitation was not uncommon among the upper classes of the city (see also Esth 5:8; 6:14; Philo, *Opif.* 78). In fact, it fits well with the dynamics of the pre-industrial urban system and is a common pattern in Middle Eastern village life today.

It is not, as many have anachronistically suggested, simply a matter of giving the guests ample notice. J. D. Crossan takes that approach, assuming that "A man decides on a sudden dinner that very day and sends out his servant to his friends as the dinner is being prepared. Because of a lack of warning each one finds a perfectly reasonable excuse" (1973:73). Crossan suggests that it is the "untimeliness" of this first invitation in the story that has led Luke to construct a second one, a view that we suggest is a simple but obvious anachronism on the part of a modern interpreter with a busy schedule.

In the pre-industrial city a double invitation would have several purposes. Initially the potential guest would have to decide if this was a social obligation he could afford to return in kind. Reciprocity in regard to meals was expected in the culture of Luke. But more importantly, the time between invitations would allow opportunity for potential guests to find out what the festive occasion might be, who is coming, and whether all had been done appropriately in arranging the dinner. Only then would the discerning guest be comfortable showing up. The nearly complete social stratification of pre-industrial cities required keeping social contacts across class lines to a minimum and elaborate networks of informal communication monitored such contacts to enforce rigidly the social code.

The point is nicely illustrated by a rabbinic commentary on the Old Testament book of Lamentations. When arguing that the sons of Zion are "precious," the midrash asserts that "None of them would attend a banquet unless he was invited twice" (*Lam. R.* 4:2). The meaning is clarified by the following text where we read a story about a Jerusalemite who mistakenly invited the wrong person to his banquet with tragic results.

Thus in the Lukan parable, the host has properly offered this courtesy of a double invitation to his intended guests. Peer approval, however, is not forthcoming as the excuses being offered by the invitees clearly show. Their excuses, seemingly irrelevant to the Western, industrialized mind, are standard fare in the dynamics of honor-shame societies. The point is not the excuses at hand, but social disapproval of the arrangement being made, a point to which their seeming irrelevance contributes.

Something is wrong with the supper being offered or the guests would not only appear, social opinion would demand that they do so.

The question then is, what is wrong with the supper? In suggesting what might have been wrong, Jeremias cites the well-known rabbinic story (j. *Sanh.* 6.23c) of Bar Ma 'jan in which a tax collector who had become wealthy attempted to provide a splendid banquet for the city fathers. But they uniformly declined his invitation on the flimsiest of excuses. In light of this story, Jeremias argues that we can understand the odd behavior of the guests in Luke 14:18–20. "The host is to be understood as a tax-collector who has become wealthy and has sent out invitations in the hope that this will enable him to be fully accepted in the highest circles" (1955:141). Like the guests in the story of Bar Ma 'jan, these guests also refuse to show.

The parallel illustrates the dynamics of dinner invitations in pre-industrial societies. Either all the guests come or none do, because none would risk coming to a banquet shunned by important others. What does not follow is that the host in Luke 14:15–24 is a wealthy tax collector. If he were, the story would lose its point (see Luke 19:1–10). In a story told in the home of a leading Pharisee, identifying the host as an aspiring tax collector would elicit a nod of understanding approval toward the guests who refused to come and a condemnation of the host who invited such a person—clearly not the intention of the story. The story depends for its point on the reader being forced to face the possibility that it approves the host and contains serious criticism of the guests who do not show. The double invitation to the original guests thus plays on the pattern of social interaction common in pre-industrial cities by setting up a situation in which the invited guests must decide whether the meal is one they should attend. Likewise, it leads the reader to anticipate acceptance or refusal on the part of the invitees as an important clue to the possibilities the story holds.

The Excuses. As the story unfolds, then, the double invitation leads to a considered judgment on the part of the invited persons that something is wrong. They signal this with excuses that are clearly beside the point, although nowhere is the reader given a clue as to what really caused the trouble. Why did the original guests stay away? This critical question is itself the means by which the parable functions as parable. If, as we shall argue, Luke is using the parable to confront the rich of his own community who are avoiding association with poor Christians, the question about why guests stay away is exactly the question that the parable intends to force upon the reader. The typical diversionary answers of Middle Eastern, honor-shame social interaction thus function perfectly to assert a challenge readers must answer for themselves.

Given their diversionary nature, the excuses nonetheless give us additional information about the guests and the proposed supper. In the exploitative urban system of the pre-industrial world, much of the land outside the city was owned by the urban elite. The first of the three excusees has bought a field outside the city and is thus in this group of absentee landlords. As Kenneth Bailey has pointed out, no one in the Middle East would buy a field without having walked every square inch of it and investigated both its past ownership and profit record (1980:96).

The second excuse is from a man who has bought five yoke of oxen. L. Schottroff and W. Stegemann estimate that ten oxen could plow about 45 hectares, or something over 100 acres (1986:101). Douglas Oakman cites evidence of some families owning as much as 3 to 6 acres per adult, although a subsistence plot in Palestine in the first century was about 1.5 acres per adult (1986:61). Since half of the land would have been left fallow each year, the owner needing five oxen is obviously the owner of a very large piece of property. The third person making excuses has recently married. Some have seen in this the Old Testament provision that a newly married man was excused from both business and military obligation for one year (Deut 24:5). While this is possible, it may also be that the newlywed claims that he has burdensome social obligations of his own and cannot take on the new reciprocal obligations that accepting this dinner invitation would entail.

These three guests are thus much a part of the urban elite, perhaps even among its leading members who could be expected to signal for the remaining guests (since clearly the banquet was intended for more than a host and three guests) whether attendance was socially appropriate. It is also clear that these elite guests play according to the rules: their excuses conceal the real reason for the social disapproval as the system demands. Nor do they break ranks. If one does not show, none do. None will risk cutting himself off from his peers.

The Reaction of the Host. Both Matthew and Luke record the anger of the refused host. In Matthew this becomes the occasion for his allegorical account of the burning of the city belonging to those who refused the invitation. Our thesis is that in Luke the problem is different. It is not one of the Jews refusing Jesus, but one of elite Christians within Luke's own community refusing table fellowship with the poor. Since we shall be in a position to spell that out more fully later, it is enough for now to say that we see little warrant for treating the host or his anger allegorically in Luke's version of the story.

The Final Invitations. Thus far the story has raised a series of unanswered questions to challenge the perceptive reader. Now it takes its most surprising turn. The angered host sends a servant to the streets and lanes of the city to invite "the poor and maimed and blind and lame." Unlike his peers who are unwilling to break ranks, the host does so both physically and socially by inviting this sort of people to his home.

It will be recalled from our description of pre-industrial cities that the central areas in which the elite lived were walled off from the outlying precincts in which the non-elite dwelt. Furthermore, outlying areas of the cities often had walls separating ethnic, occupational and income groups from each other. Without regard for the distinctions the walls imply, the servant goes out to all and all are invited. Moreover, they are asked to come into a part of the city in which they do not belong. To have them there serving the commercial or domestic needs of the elite is one thing, but to invite them there for a social occasion is a physical breach of socially loaded space. It would have been bad enough had the host gone to a dinner in a non-elite area of the city; deliberately bringing the non-elite into the sanctuary of the elite after dark would have struck the readers of Luke's parable as beyond comprehension.

But Luke presses the issue even further. In describing how the servants went out into the city streets, Matthew had used the somewhat general term, "thoroughfare" (*tas diexodous tōn hodōn*, literally: the passing of the road), probably referring to the place where the main street exited the city gate. Luke, however, deeply conscious of the pattern of the city, is far more specific. He tells how the servant went to both the wider streets or squares which served as the normal locations for communication with the non-elite (*tas plateias*) and also to the narrow streets and alleys along which the poorest of the non-elite people lived (*rhymas*). Often these lanes were little more than open sewers, so narrow that donkeys could not pass along them. In other words, the host has gone far beyond the normal mode of communication in seeking out guests totally unlike those first invited. These are not the aspiring poor of the city, as anachronistic capitalist readings would have it, nor are they those who might have been expected to jump at the chance for social advancement. Rather, they are persons whom the walls and gates of the central precincts of pre-industrial cities were designed to shield from view. They are the very ones the walls were meant to keep in their proper place.

The Banquet Hall. Luke is then the only one who tells us that the banquet hall was not yet filled. This allows Luke to describe an invitation to yet another group of people, those outside the city walls along the roads and hedges (*tas hodous kai phragmous*). *Hodos* is of course the usual term for road, while *phragmos* describes the fences or hedges built to enclose fields or other property. Once again, therefore, Luke is specific in pointing to a location in the urban system that housed a particular population: the area immediately outside the city was inhabited by both outcasts and those requiring access to the city but not permitted to live within it.

These final guests are not, as is frequently assumed, country people. The peasant population lived in villages, not along the roads just outside the city. An already prepared banquet, moreover, would not allow travel to neighboring villages to seek participants. Instead, those just outside the walls usually included ethnic groups, tanners, and traders (along with the more commonly noted beggars and prostitutes), many of whom would have had business in the city (serving the needs of the elite) that required proximity to it. But they were not allowed to live inside the city walls.

What becomes clear is Luke's curious statement that these final guests should be "compelled" (anankason) to come in. Strong were the sanctions preventing those living immediately outside the walls from coming into the city for reasons other than business. Such people would have immediately understood the invitation as an inexplicable breach of the system. Considerable compulsion would be required to induce them to attend the supper. They are hardly people who "need a free meal" (Tannehill 1986:129); they are wary outsiders who are rightly suspicious of those who break the system.

These were a group of people who were neither of the city nor of the country. They were afforded neither the protection of city walls nor attachment to a village. Socially they were isolated from city elite, city non-elite, and villagers alike. Thus Luke's second invitation, like the first, pointedly specifies a particular group in the urban system.

The Conclusion. If our understanding of the parable has been correct to this point, Luke's conclusion for the parable may also have to be seen in a new light. It is usually construed as an eschatological statement and it may well be that in some measure. But at a more basic level it may also be a rather blunt statement about participation in the Christian community. Those who reject the community by shunning association with its less reputable members will no longer be invited to participate.

In sum, our analysis of the urban system shows that Luke understands those finally invited to be (1) the urban non-elite and (2) those dependent on the city who live just outside it. Moreover, these new invitations are broadcast by word of mouth to any and all comers. The original invitations would have gone only to known persons whose social rank could be carefully scrutinized. The elite did not socialize with people they did not know. Those among them who did would be immediately and permanently ostracized because they could not be trusted to protect the system. We come then to what this story is really all about: a member of the elite, a host, making a break with the "system" in the most public and radical sort of way.

How far will the host go in making the break? The second invitation removes all doubt. The sight of the master's servant inviting and even compelling outsiders to breach the bounds of the system by entering the precincts of the elite would have been enough to sever whatever shaky (as shown by the refusal of the original invitation) ties the host may have

[handwritten marginalia: no indication of repentance for calling the 1st group]

had with his own kind of people. We hear of a host who prepared to go all the way.

[handwritten marginalia: But how does the host provoke the steward — a conversion... in that he experiences a... (and why do the first invited not come?)]

4.0 LUKE'S USE OF THE PARABLE

This brings us squarely to the question of Luke's use of the parable in his own situation. H. J. Cadbury saw that the Jesus of Luke spoke to "possessors, not to the dispossessed" and that his rebuke of wealth "betokens a concern for the oppressor rather than simply pity for the oppressed" (1958:262–63). More recently, in attempting to explore the *Sitz im Leben* of Luke, R. J. Karris has collected the evidence that "Luke is primarily taken up with the rich members, their concerns, and the problems which they pose for the community" (1978:124). As he puts it, "Their concerns . . . revolve around the question: do our possessions prevent us from being genuine Christians?" In the same vein, Schottroff and Stegemann offer a cogent and perceptive portrayal of Luke as the "evangelist to the rich" who uses the tradition about Jesus and the poor (of whose lives he knows little other than what he has learned from the tradition) to confront the rich of his own congregation with the meaning of the gospel.

Do possessions prevent the rich from being genuine Christians? In light of our study of Luke 14:15–24, we can construe that question a bit more broadly: Does remaining part of the social network with one's fellow elite prevent one from being part of the Christian community which includes the non-elite? Using the parable of the Great Supper, Luke has given an unequivocal and uncompromising answer.

Table fellowship *within* the Christian community is thus the issue Luke addresses by the parable. Elite Christians who participated in the socially inclusive Christian community risked being cut off from the prior social networks on which their positions depended. It is not simply "worldly cares" or "excessive materialism" that holds them back. It is nothing less than the network in which they have been embedded since birth. It is their friendships, their place of residence, their economic survival (and probably health as well), the well-being of their extended families and even the "system" of the elite that is at stake. If becoming part of the Christian community provided a social haven for the poor, it occasioned a social disaster for the rich. For many rich Christians their social position in elite circles was no doubt shaky enough that preparing a banquet for their peers might seem like a good way to solidify it. As a way of reassuring their friends that they had not broken faith with the system, they would invite only the right people, which is exactly what Jesus criticizes in 14:12–14. They would choose the best seats at whatever dinners they attended to signal the same thing. But in 14:15–24 Luke shows them that in so doing they not only face rejection by peers, they face rejection by God. Theirs is an excruciating bind which Luke sees with startling clarity: a decision must be made that might cost them everything in their former world. Just such is made explicit in 14:26–33, the section immediately following the parable of the Great Supper. Luke inserts the words of Jesus: "If anyone comes to me and does not hate his own father and mother and wife and children and brothers and sisters, and even his own life, he cannot be my disciple." The point is then driven home: "He who does not renounce *all that he has* cannot be my disciple" (14:33).

Therefore, by using the patterns of the urban system with knowing effect Luke shows just how far it is necessary to go to maintain one's place in the inclusive urban congregations that are his world. As a man of the city, he knows the costs peculiar to the elite. He also knows that table fellowship is the litmus test the elite will watch. The story of the Great Supper thus stands alongside the heavy emphasis Luke places on Jesus' table fellowship with tax collectors and sinners. That tradition and the parable both provide positive examples which the rich Christians must confront and warn them of the consequences that result from trying to hang on to an old way of life.

5.0 BEYOND LUKE 14

Our study of the "city" in Luke–Acts has focused exclusively on Luke 14:15–24, because it is the clearest place to see in full detail how "city" was perceived by Luke. It was the prime place where our models of the urban system and pre-industrial city could be tested and prove themselves necessary for an adequate understanding of Luke and his world. The following remarks are suggestions about how the models developed and the insights gained from Luke 14 might equip a person for further reading in Luke–Acts.

In applying the models of the urban system and pre-industrial city to other texts in Luke–Acts, we must think again about the term "city." As we have seen, Luke himself is not very precise in using it. Jerusalem, for example, was undoubtedly a city by any technical definition available. Nazareth and Bethlehem certainly were not. It is also interesting to see the places Luke adds the term city where other Gospel writers do not have it (4:31, 43; 5:12; 7:37; 8:4, 27, 39; 9:10; 10:1; 14:21; 19:17, 19; 23:19). One might compare these Lukan texts with the parallel ones in Matthew and Mark to get a sense of the environment Luke imagines for Jesus.

In spite of this editorial feature of Luke, much of Jesus' ministry takes place outside cities. In fact most of the largest cities in the region

(Sepphoris, Scythopolis, Samaria, Caesarea) are never mentioned in the Gospel. Why? Compare this with Acts. How many incidents in Acts take place in the countryside?

It will also be recalled that we refrained from defining the term "city" using specific characteristics such as size of population. We decided instead that the name could be given to "central places" that collect a variety of functions. What might be interesting, therefore, is to see the way certain locations in Luke–Acts function as central places. One might go through Luke–Acts, for example, and list the reasons people or groups enter "cities" or other places named by Luke. Are they coming for political reasons? Economic reasons? Religious reasons? Remember that not all central places have the same function. Equally important to note is where these people entering cities come from. Does this tell us anything about who they are and where in the city they might stay?

Special note should also be taken of the reasons people come to Jerusalem (2:22, 41–42; 4:9; 9:51–53, 13:33; 24:33; Acts 8:27; 9:2, 26; 11:2; 12:25; 13:31; 15:2; 18:21; 19:21; 20:16, 22; 21:12, 13; 22:5, 17; 24:11; 25:1, 20). Many scholars have noted the special role Jerusalem seems to play in Luke. He refers to it twice as often as any other Gospel writer. Jesus' final pilgrimage to Jerusalem (see 9:51, 53; 13:22; 17:11; 19:11) plays a central role in Luke's story. What kind of central place is it? Note that only Luke portrays Jesus weeping over Jerusalem as he enters the city (19:41). Of course Jerusalem is also the city from which the mission in Acts begins. Yet Luke ends his story of the early mission in Rome. Is this a shift of "central place"? How and why does it occur?

It is also instructive to use the model of the urban system to reflect on the reactions of city people to events that occur. What is implied in Luke 8:34–37; 9:5; 10:10–15; Acts 13:50–51; 16:19–39; 19:23–41? What would be the effect of the "great crowd" approaching the city in Luke 7:11? Why does Luke note the crowd in 7:12? Why does Jesus withdraw from the city so frequently (cf. Luke 21:37; 22:39)? What is the city afraid of in Luke 8:26–39?

One should also think about the model of the city itself. In light of the size of ancient cities, what are we to make of the numbers in Luke 9:14; 12:1; Acts 2:41; 4:4? Note also the frequent references to the presence of ethnically mixed populations (Acts 2:5; 6:6–8; 9:22; 11:19; 13:1, 5, 44; 14:1; 17:1, 10, 17, 21; 18:3, 4, 19; 21:17. Where would they have lived? What status would they have had? Why is Arimathea pointedly called a "Jewish" city (Luke 23:50)? What is implied by the designation of a city as one's "own" (Luke 2:3, 39)? Why are people designated by the name of their city (e.g., Luke 4:34)?

At the beginning of the chapter we provided a list of the places Luke specifically designates cities, though obviously cities are in view at many other points in the text. As one goes through the Gospel or the book of

Acts, every time an event takes place in an urban environment, make a list of all the people mentioned. What kind of people are they? What roles do they play in the story? With whom do they interact? In what space? What is implied about internal city dynamics in Luke 20:45–47; Acts 13:50; 15:5; 16:19–20; 19:23–40?

Special attention should be given to indications of status. What dynamics are involved? Are they typical of the pre-industrial city? What occupations are mentioned? Although there are not a large number of them designated in the text, those that are should be seen in light of our comments about both guilds and occupational areas and about those who do and do not belong in the city (e.g., Acts 10:5, 34; 18:3; 19:23). Why is Simon's house by the sea? The point is that the model examined above should prove a useful tool in reading Luke–Acts. If it has providing an appropriate reading scenario for Luke 14, it should have a bearing on how we read and interpret other Lukan narratives.

6.0 CONCLUSION

In using the model of either the urban system or the pre-industrial city, we are trying to imagine the situation that would have been evoked in the minds of early readers of Luke–Acts. It would have been a scenario quite different from what we might imagine for a city environment since we do not live in or know pre-industrial cities. Cities were neither commercial centers, nor loci of public agencies providing services to residents, nor marketplaces for the surrounding countryside. There were no suburbs for the upwardly mobile. Nor can we imagine harried commuters, or the home as a private retreat at the end of the day (for any but the small number of elite), or weekend flights to the beach.

The cities of antiquity simply did not look, smell or sound like cities of today. People were not in them for the same reasons we are, nor did life in them match what urban life has come to be today. Ethnocentric and socially anachronistic readings of the New Testament seem inevitable in whatever degree we fail to recognize that this is so. Models drawn from cross-cultural study of pre-industrial cities can be a tool to help us imagine the environment Luke presumed his ancient readers would know. They can also help us as modern readers let the Bible speak to our world on its terms rather our own.

6

THE COUNTRYSIDE IN LUKE–ACTS

Douglas E. Oakman

". . . and a report concerning him went out
through all the surrounding country" (Luke 4:14)

1.0 THE PROJECT

Richard Rohrbaugh's essay in this volume provided a scenario for understanding the meaning of "the city" in Luke's world. Yet as also needs to be recognized, Luke devotes no little space to the countryside in his two-volume work. This is especially apparent in the Gospel, where Luke includes much material not encountered in the other Gospels. The neighborly hospitality and conviviality that suggest village locales (Luke 11:5–8 and 15:9) or the country estates of the Rich Fool (12:16–21) and the rich man who has a dishonest steward (16:1–8) provide windows directly into the milieu of first-century followers of Jesus. Luke also provides scenes like that of Mary's journey to her rural cousin's home (1:39–40) or of the shepherds tending their flocks in the fields at the time of Jesus' birth (2:8).

Luke's vocabulary further suggests countryside as an area for investigation. Of the twenty-eight occurrences of the Greek word for "country" or "rural precinct" (chōra) in the New Testament, seventeen occurrences (60%) are in Luke–Acts. Admittedly, some of these are generic references to "country," as, "A nobleman went into a far country" (Luke 19:12). Other references are to agricultural locales (12:16). Luke uses a nuanced variety of Greek words for rural areas: "Field" (*agros*) appears eleven times in Luke–Acts, sixteen times in Matthew, and once in Mark. "Surrounding countryside" (*perichōros*) appears six times in Luke–Acts, twice in Matthew, and once in Mark. "Piece of land" (*chōrion*) occurs six times in Acts, once each in Matthew, Mark, and John. An exploration of this theme, therefore, seems fully warranted. Yet what is the appropriate scenario for understanding "the countryside" in Luke–Acts?

In our quest to find an adequate scenario for understanding "the countryside," two sets of questions will initially guide this essay:

(1) Is Luke familiar at first hand with the realities of the Palestinian countryside or the countryside elsewhere in the Roman Empire? Or does Luke betray evidence of idealized or romanticized conceptions of the essentially rural milieu of nascent Christianity? How also does Luke stand with respect to important political-economic questions affecting the interests of the countryside? In other words, what is the sociology of Luke's knowledge of the countryside? To some extent, these sociological questions are a part of the traditional question regarding the life-setting (*Sitz im Leben*) of the Lukan Gospel: Where in the Roman Empire did Luke write?

(2) How has Luke handled the rural Jesus traditions that form a part of his narrative world? Is there a discernable literary and thematic role for the countryside here? Or has Luke simply embraced the countryside out of necessity, because it is in the tradition? These questions are more focused upon Luke's literary conception.

Neither of these sets of questions can be adequately addressed without the broader perspectives developed in the next section of the study. To construct an adequate scenario for understanding "the countryside" in Luke–Acts, we will draw upon the results of modern studies of rural and peasant societies.

2.0 CONCEPTUALIZING THE COUNTRYSIDE OF MEDITERRANEAN ANTIQUITY

2.1 A General Sociological Model for the Ancient Countryside

Modern historians of the ancient world (Rostovtzeff, Ste. Croix, and MacMullen) have noted a fundamental polarity between country and city. This conceptual polarity traces its roots back to the classical writers. Thus as early as the eighth century BCE, the Greek poet Hesiod contrasts the goodness of the village engaged in agricultural work with the evil of the city-state occupied by war and the shipping trade (*Works and Days*, 225–247). Writing in the first century BCE, Horace sums up the Roman agrarian ideal of the late Republic when he says:

A man is happy when, far from the business world, like the earliest tribe of men he cultivates the family farm with his team, and is free from usury's ties . . . when he keeps away from the Forum and the proud doorways of influential men (*Epodes* 11).

While an absolute dichotomy between city and countryside in antiquity is hardly tenable, a number of sociological indicators point to significant differences between the two realms. The accumulating results of economic anthropology, modern rural sociology, and peasant studies can help to bring out these differences quite precisely.

To start with, the construction of conceptual models for the countryside in antiquity might employ either a broadly *functionalist* or a broadly *conflict* approach, in view of two of the dominant paradigms in sociological theory. Functionalist sociological theory, otherwise known as structural-functionalism or equilibrium theory, envisions societies as systems with needs, in the service of which social behaviors are "functional." Functional theory often focuses on why societies remain stable over time. The alternative, conflict theory, looks at societies as the arena for competing groups and interests. Conflict theory frequently attempts to understand why and how societies change. Figure 6-1 illustrates some of the implications of this choice:

CONFLICT AND FUNCTIONAL THEORIES Figure 6-1		
	Functionalist	*Conflict*
(1) Interests as	Uniting	Dividing
(2) Social relations as	Mutually advantageous	Exploitative advantageous
(3) Social unity by	Consensus	Coercion
(4) Definition of society	System with needs	Stage for class struggle
(5) Nature of humanity	Requires restraining institutions	Institutions distort human nature
(6) Inequality as	Social necessity	Unnecessary, promotes conflict
(7) The state	Promotes common good	Instrument of oppression
(8) Social class	Heuristic concept	Objective social groups with different interests
Source: Sanders, 1977:9 based on work of A. E. Havens.		

The *functionalist* approach will be congenial to the guardians of society, who tend to think of social order as "an organic system" and the best of all social possibilities. In terms of the countryside of antiquity, the functionalist approach will talk about the symbiosis or mutual dependence of city and country folk and will assume a stance like the following: Augustus and the armies of Rome provided order, and the country people supplied the bread of empire (*mutual advantage* [2]). The empire was in the best *interests* (1) of agricultural producers. The country people as a rule were happy, well-adjusted, and supportive of the status quo (*consensus* [3]). The empire required a few to govern and the many to work on the farm (*system with needs* [4]). A functionalist reading of antiquity might stress, "For rulers are not a terror to good conduct, but to bad" (Rom 13:3; cf. 1 Pet 2:14: *Human nature requires restraining institutions* [5]; *the state promotes the common good* [7]). As for *social classes* (8) in the Roman Empire, MacMullen epitomizes the functionalist views of many modern historians of classical antiquity when he writes, "The very number [of legislative and cultural social classifications] seems to have worked against class feeling" (1966:198). MacMullen effectively denies with this statement the objective reality of social class; at most "class" can be a term of conceptual convenience.

The *conflict* approach will tend to focus on the discontent of the subjugated and expose the harmful effects of the "system," as well as indicate its chief beneficiaries. In this view, Augustus and the ruling groups of the empire *exploited* (2) the majority of agricultural producers (*state an instrument of oppression* [7]). The empire was not in the best material *interests* (1) of the producer and injected deep-seated hostility and bitterness into the *social relations* (2, 4) of its members—especially between city and country. At times, this hostility broke out into open conflict. Military operations by the state against insurgents, bandits, or rebels were more often necessary than history produced from an elite perspective might lead us to believe (*coercion* [3, 7]). The rural populace in such a distorted social situation looked upon human nature as basically good when liberated from the burden of empire (5). *Inequality and oppression* (6) were not in the original nature of things (see Hesiod, *Works and Days*, 109–20). From this perspective, *social class* (8) is delineated clearly between those who have and those who have not, between those who do not toil for what they eat and those who do, between those who rob and extort and those who are never adequately compensated for their labor.

Objectively speaking, though, the choice of one or the other perspectives might be made with a concern for appropriateness to the specific sociological situation. A conflict approach is assumed in the development of the model that follows, in view of the political situation of agrarian (peasant) societies in general and of early Roman Palestine in particular. Important terms in the discussion are italicized and defined as they occur.

2.1.1 *The General Nature of Agrarian/Peasant Society.* An *agrarian society*, typical of the majority of those in Mediterranean antiquity, is one built predominantly upon the plow and agricultural production (Lenski and Lenski 1974:207; Lenski 1966:192). The chief productive factor in agrarian economies is land. Control of land is one of the central political questions of agrarian societies. Furthermore, human and animal energies supply the dominant energies of such societies. Ability to mobilize these energies for useful social ends is also an important agrarian political question. Given the generally low level of technology and the meager energy resources of these types of societies, agriculture is generally of a low-yield sort. This means that as a rule there is a very narrow margin between what can be harvested and what is needed by the majority of agriculturalists for food, seed, or animal fodder. There might be just enough, but not much more. As we shall see in a moment, the social and political condition of country folk compounds this basic productive problem.

Agrarian societies can also be considered *peasant societies*, "a set of villages socially bound up with preindustrial cities" (Malina 1981:71). These types of societies are stratified into essentially two *social classes* — a small ruling elite in the cities and a mass of toiling agriculturalists in the villages whose labor and product supports that elite. Another way to delineate "social class" within peasant/agrarian societies is to look at who controls the land and the distribution of its products. Elites will control more or most and be advantaged in the distribution. A more sophisticated analysis will discern at least two further classes in these types of societies, a service class to the political elite (priests, soldiers, merchants, craftsmen) and a service class to the village (traveling or local craftsmen, village elders, local religious leaders). Lenski (1966:284) has estimated that only 2% of the agrarian population belongs to the ruling elite, about 8% comprises the service class in the cities, and the remaining 90% or so tills the soil or services the village.

2.1.2 Agrarian Economics. The economic aspect of agrarian/peasant societies has been described or interpreted in detail by social scientists and historians such as Weber, Heichelheim, Polanyi, Wolf, Braudel, Lenski, and Sorokin. Rural economic realities do not comprise a separate social institution (as our notion of the family farm "business" in the Midwest might lead us to imagine). Rather, ancient economic life was normally conducted within kinship or political institutions. Put in the technical jargon of cultural anthropology, what moderns think of as economic realities are in agrarian/peasant societies embedded in political or kinship contexts (Polanyi 1957; Malina 1981 and 1986a). An example will clarify this: in modern America, family members leave home and go to work somewhere else. During leisure time, family members may spend money in a stranger's place of business. All members know what "the economy" is, because it impersonally affects and organizes their personal lives in many particular ways. By contrast, the ancient family tilled the soil or worked together to produce some specialized product. The home was the place of work. In fact, the Greek word "economy" (*oikonomia*) means "management of the household." In the rural village money transactions were rare. The usual course was bartering something of mutual value for something else, and then only with someone who was known by the family and trusted (like family). Otherwise, the landlord or the state agent (political institutions) would compel the family to give up produce or product for rent or taxes. "The economy" as an overarching social institution did not exist for the ancient person.

Hence, agrarian *exchange* frequently takes place through non-market means. "Exchange" means the transferring of control over material or cultural goods between persons. Village exchanges are more or less rigorously accounted for. Economic anthropology, the social science subdiscipline that concerns itself with non-industrial economic systems, thus speaks of either *balanced* or *general reciprocity* as characteristic of village barter. Exchanges are balanced if done on a quid pro quo basis and when the debt is liquidated fairly quickly. A balanced exchange might be one family's receipt of three loaves of bread on Monday (consider Luke 11:5) and the repayment to the other family on Wednesday of a basket of figs. The debt is not left outstanding for very long. The valuables exchanged are of roughly equal value (in the eyes of the parties involved).

Close kin in a peasant village, however, might operate on a different basis, on the basis of general reciprocity. This means that the exchange is essentially unilateral — a gift from one party to another — and that the "debt" may go uncollected for a long time if at all (Luke 11:11). The dominant form of exchange toward those distant from the kinship group or toward strangers will be *negative reciprocity*, the attempt to acquire something of value for something of less or no value (on "reciprocity," see further the essays in this volume by Moxnes, Elliott).

In contrast, the basic economic structure of ancient societies from the elites' point of view was that of a *redistributive* network. This means that taxes and rents flowed relentlessly away from the rural producers to the storehouses of cities (especially Rome), private estates, and temples. This *surplus*, which might have gone to feed extra mouths in the village, ended up being redistributed for other ends by the ruling groups. (Note: Social scientists argue as to whether surplus is the right word under these circumstances, since "surplus" is at the expense of peasant subsistence: See Wolf, 1966:110–11.) All ancient societies were, therefore, *political economies*, because the powerful could compel rents and taxes to support their cultured lifestyle.

In Greco-Roman antiquity, the ruling elites lived in cities. Hence, the world empire of the Romans was governed through the city-state of Rome. Cities, in addition to being centers of higher culture, were economically parasitic upon the countryside, and urbanites spent significant amounts of time engaged in activities other than agriculture. Cities could function as administrative centers or tax collection points. They could also function as commercial centers. Trade and commerce in antiquity primarily benefited cities and local or state oligarchies, but not the peasants in country villages.

"Industry" and "finance," terms which must be viewed as modern economic anachronisms, require careful nuance when applied to the ancient agrarian world. In antiquity there was no mass production based upon systematic division of labor, no broad-based free market, no credit institutions analogous to modern industrial capitalist institutions. Pottery, weapons, and other specialized goods were produced in households, not factories. The family remained the basic unit of production in antiquity, whether on the farm or in the city. Loans and credit were available, but debt routinely functioned to create dependencies rather than to capitalize profit-making enterprises. Interest-free loans might be made between friends or near kin; otherwise, interest rates in antiquity were exorbitant and usurious (sometimes as high as 50%). Elites conducted their political affairs in cities, but also adhered to the peasant ideal of self-sufficiency (see 2.1.3) and household economy (so as not to be politically dependent upon others) by concentrating lands into great estates. War and conquest sometimes made this task easier, as in the case of the growth of Roman magnates and latifundia, the large Italian agricultural estates, during the late Republic, which occurred about a century before Luke. During normal times, peasant debt secured by land and foreclosure enforced by courts (controlled by elites) played a much larger role in land concentration in the hands of the few. Figure 6-2 indicates how this process worked. Elites had access to "capital" through trade, taxation, and interest on money loans. With the narrow margin between subsistence and famine, peasants did not accumulate capital and once in debt found it difficult to get out.

Although Jewish law prohibited loans at interest, there is evidence that certain kinds of subtle usury were practiced in early Roman Palestine. Rabbi Hillel's *prozbul*, for instance, discussed in m. *Shebiith* 10, was a legal fiction designed to avoid the debt release in the seventh year mandated by Old Testament law (Deut 15:1–3). Ostensibly to help debtors by making credit more readily available, the *prozbul* institution worked against the long-term interests of peasant-debtors. The creditor, by turning debt contracts over to a court, could thereby sidestep the literal meaning of Deut 15:3, "your hand shall release" (i.e., in the seventh year). Furthermore, the *prozbul* debt was secured upon immovable property (houses, land). Thus eventually, the first-century creditor wrested away control of the peasant's plot by enforcing foreclosure through the courts. The peasant became the new landlord's *tenant*, liable to pay rent in the future. Unequal distribution of wealth and poor harvests for the peasant made this practice feasible, but the need for economic security and social status on the part of the elites undoubtedly fueled the escalation of indebtedness and concentration of land in early first-century Palestine (see further Kautsky 1982). Figure 6-2 represents a dynamic model of the general process, envisioned over an indefinite period of time.

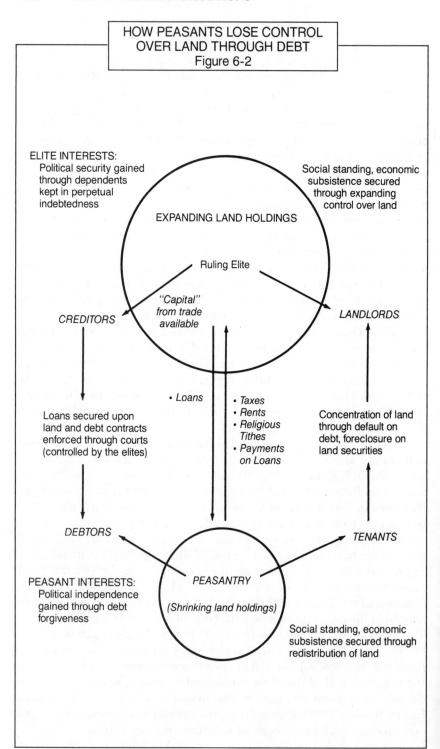

HOW PEASANTS LOSE CONTROL
OVER LAND THROUGH DEBT
Figure 6-2

ELITE INTERESTS:
Political security gained
through dependents
kept in perpetual
indebtedness

Social standing, economic
subsistence secured
through expanding
control over land

EXPANDING LAND HOLDINGS

Ruling Elite

"Capital"
from trade
available

CREDITORS

LANDLORDS

• Loans

• Taxes
• Rents
• Religious
  Tithes
• Payments
  on Loans

Loans secured upon
land and debt contracts
enforced through courts
(controlled by the elites)

Concentration of land
through default on
debt, foreclosure on
land securities

DEBTORS

TENANTS

PEASANTRY

(Shrinking land holdings)

PEASANT INTERESTS:
Political independence
gained through debt
forgiveness

Social standing, economic
subsistence secured through
redistribution of land

2.1.3 Typical Peasant Values. The chronic, politically induced poverty of peasant existence produces characteristic attitudes and values in peasant communities. Peasants generally consider the goods of life to exist in limited supply. This view accords with the *zero-sum nature of* peasant economics: if someone gets ahead, someone else is sure to have lost (Foster 1967:304–5). A corollary of this perception is the *institutionalized envy* of the village. No one can get too far ahead of his neighbors without bringing into play village envy and inimical gossip. This gossip and envy may shame the offender into sharing; hence, gossip and envy function as a pressure toward redistribution of wealth. Peasants themselves come to expect very little out of life; any gain is traditionally carried off by the landlord. This peasant *wantlessness* coalesces with a stress in peasant life upon *self-sufficiency.* This means not only household self-sufficiency, having everything necessary for life within the productive realm of the peasant family and depending for nothing upon outsiders, but also being content with the little there is. The peasantry knows all too well what indebtedness to outsiders does to the subsistence margin (again consider Figure 6-2).

On the other hand, peasants will not endure exploitation beyond a certain point:

> The right to subsistence—to the preservation of one's status in all the dimensions of the ideal man's role—is the active moral principle in peasant societies. In other words, the only time our first-century villager or non-elite urbanite will rebel is when his subsistence is taken away. (Malina 1981:77; see Scott 1976).

Given the role that debt plays in the loss of peasant control over land, it is not surprising that the two chief themes of ancient peasant rebellions were "abolition of debt" and "redistribution of land" (Ste. Croix 1981). Peasant or rural radicalism does not aim at collectivization of property, as does modern industrial urban radicalism, but rather the maximum distribution of landed property possible (Sanders 1977).

2.1.4 Elite Control Mechanisms. Understandably then, ancient elites had to develop strategies to deal with the simmering anger of the peasantry. *Patronage*—the development of interpersonal bonds between social unequals—was a social institution that evolved in various forms throughout the ancient Mediterranean world in order to alleviate the otherwise harsh exploitation by the landlord and redistributive state (see the chapter by Moxnes). Through the practice of patronage by the elites, for instance through occasional remissions of overdue rent or through the sponsorship of a village festival, potentially explosive relations with peasant households might be headed off by actions designed to suggest solicitude and good will. Bonds of loyalty and gratefulness can sometimes avert the anger generated by naked exploitation. There were periods in antiquity, however, when exploitative pressures became too great and peasant banditry or revolt resulted. At such times, as during the Jewish War 66–70 CE, the ruling groups were forced to take *military action* against insurgency.

2.1.5 Peasant Religion. Like rural economics, the rural religion of antiquity was normally embedded within kinship and political contexts. Peasant religion tends to be magical and geared to assuring the success of the agricultural work. While most peasant religion is informal and conducted within the everyday routines of the family and village, peasant "superstition" encourages a strong bond to form between peasant and religious specialist ("priest"), the latter insuring that the correct ritual actions are taken at the right times. The arrangement tends to work against the peasant economically when a priesthood becomes centralized outside the village and a strong temple organization demands frequent religious dues (another form of redistributive economy). When religious and/or political taxation pressures became too great, peasant religion can be linked with protest against exploitative temple, city, or state (e.g., as in Hesiod or the Old Testament prophet Micah). The Jesus tradition originally had strong overtones of rural protest (Theissen 1976 and 1978).

2.2 A Specific Model for the Countryside in the Traditions of Luke

A model of agrarian social stratification to suit Luke's traditions about Jesus can be developed out of the foregoing general concepts as in Figure 6-3. The chief question the model answers is, Who controlled the land? The primary variables in the model are (a) the amount of land held or controlled (only in very general terms, see 2.3.1 and 2.3.2) and (b) the social identities of the controlling parties. As the figure indicates, the model contains nine components that go into a full picture of the countryside in Luke–Acts.

A. Social Stratification	F. Sayings and Proverbs and
B. Land Controlled by	Rural Realities
Gentile Cities	G. Economic Realities: Taxes
C. Land Controlled by	Debt, Oppression
Jewish Elites or Roman Agents	H. Hunger, Robbery, Violence
D. Large Estates and Patronage	and General Insecurity
E. Village Relations/	I. Oppressed and Economically
Realities	Marginated Groups

Thus, the model delineates the general pattern of social stratification as a function of land control or land tenure. It represents a static model and supplies a convenient map to selective social features of the ancient countryside. Yet, this model can provide an adequate scenario of what Luke understands by "the countryside."

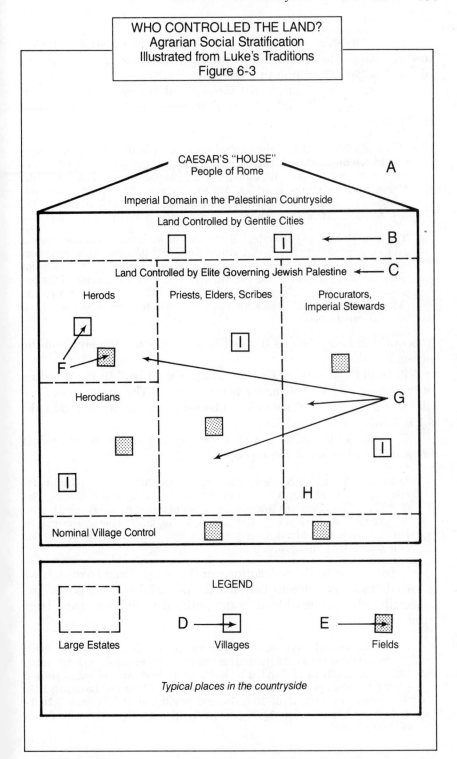

WHO CONTROLLED THE LAND?
Agrarian Social Stratification
Illustrated from Luke's Traditions
Figure 6-3

CAESAR'S "HOUSE"
People of Rome
A

Imperial Domain in the Palestinian Countryside

Land Controlled by Gentile Cities

B

Land Controlled by Elite Governing Jewish Palestine ⟵ C

Herods | Priests, Elders, Scribes | Procurators, Imperial Stewards

F

Herodians

G

H

Nominal Village Control

LEGEND

Large Estates | D ⟶ | Villages | E ⟶ | Fields

Typical places in the countryside

The letters shown in Figure 6-3 are keyed to the material in the following listing. The model can be overlaid, like a mosaic, with pieces of the rural Jesus tradition in Luke–Acts.

A. *Social Stratification.* All through Luke's writings there is evidence of the great disparities in wealth, power, and privilege present in the Roman Empire.

> The powerful and those who control large amounts of land appear prominently. A representative listing of this in Luke–Acts includes: Luke 1:5 (Herod the Great); 2:1 (Caesar Augustus); 3:1–2 (Tiberias Caesar, Pontius Pilate, Herod Antipas, Philip, Lysanias, Annas, Caiaphas); 12:16 (unnamed landlord); 16:1 (rich man with an estate); Barnabas, who owns land (Acts 4:36–37); and 13:1 (Manean, member of Herod Antipas' court).

> The conditions of the powerless, destitute, and dishonored are also shown, even contrasted with the former group: Luke 3:11 (sharing coats, food necessary); 6:20–25 (Beatitudes for the poor, hungry, sorrowing, but woes for the rich); 16:19–31 (Dives and Lazarus). The bitterness and anger of the oppressed sometimes shines through: Luke 1:52–53 (Mary's song, the "Magnificat"); 6:24–25 (woes for the rich); 8:18 (to him who has . . .); 16:23 (Dives in hell).

The world of Luke, then, is divided into two classes: the elite and the non-elite.

B. *Land Controlled by Gentile Cities.* Not all land in the Palestine of the Jesus tradition was under Jewish control. The presence of Gentiles and foreigners injected cultural issues into agrarian conflict: Luke 8:26, 34 (Gerasene Demoniac).

C. *Land Controlled by Jewish Elites or Roman Agents.* Luke–Acts gives information about these people in passing:

> Luke 1:5 and Acts 23:35 (Herod the Great) ; Luke 3:1 and 23:1 (Pontius Pilate); Luke 3:1, 19; 8:3; 9:7, 9; 13:31; 23:7, 8, 11, 12, 15 and Acts 4:27; 13:1 (Herod Antipas); Acts 13:1 (Manean, member of Herod Antipas's court); Luke 3:1 (Annas); 3:1 (Caiaphas); Acts 12:1, 6, 11, 19, 20–21 (Herod Agrippa I); Luke 7:3; Acts 4:5 (elders); Luke 9:22; Acts 6:12 (scribes); Luke 20:1; 22:52; Acts 4:18; 23:2 (chief priests).

D. *Large Estates, Estate Relations, or Patronage.* From Luke–Acts we get a glimpse into relations between the powerful and the powerless, especially relations embedded in the political institution of the large rural estate:

> Luke 8:18 (more will be given to the rich and powerful); 12:16–21 (Rich fool); 12:33–34 (alms); 12:42–46 (faithful servant); 12:47f (discipline of servants); 13:6–9 (fig tree); 14:18 (buying a field); 14:19 (five! yoke of oxen); 16:1–8 (unjust steward); 16:10–13 (loyal service); 16:19–31 (Dives and Lazarus); 17:7–10 (servant's reward); 18:18–30 (ruler and wealth); 19:11–26 (minas); 20:9–19 (wicked tenants); Acts 12:20 (Herod Agrippa deprives Tyre and Sidon of "king's grain").

E. *Village Relations/Realities.* Likewise, Luke–Acts gives us a glimpse of those who lives in villages, some of their physical surroundings, and social conditions:

Luke 1:58 (neighbors and kinsfolk); 4:16–30 (Nazareth); 6:1–4 (gleaning); 7:11–15 (Nain); 7:32 (children in the market); 8:4–8 (sower); 9:1–6 (disciples' mission in villages); 9:52–56 (xenophobia of villagers); 10:38–42 (hospitality of Martha and Mary); 11:5–8 (importunate friend); 12:6 (price of sparrows); 12:13f (dividing inheritance); 12:22–30 (on anxiety); 12:39 (thief at midnight); 12:52–53 (household orientation); 13:19 (mustard plant in fields); 13:21 (leaven); 14:28–29 (building a tower); 15:3–6 (lost sheep); 15:8–10 (lost coin); 15:11–32 (prodigal son); 17:12 (lepers in a Samaritan village); 19:31 (reality of eminent domain); 24:13–31 (village hospitality); Acts 8:25 (gospel proclaimed to Samaritan villages); 11:28–29 (famine under Claudius).

F. *Sayings and Proverbs Reflecting Rural Realities.* This agrarian oral wisdom can directly or indirectly give us information about realities in the countryside:

Luke 3:8 (bear fruits reflecting repentance); 3:9 (axe); 3:17 (winnowing fork); 5:36 (old garment patched); 5:37 (old wineskins); 6:34–35 (lending without expecting in return); 6:38 (giving full measure); 6:41–42 (speck and log); 6:43 (good and bad trees); 6:44 (figs not gathered from thorns); 6:48–49 (building house on a rock); 7:32 (children in market); 8:16 (light and lampstand); 8:18 (to him who has . . .); 9:25 (gaining the whole world); 10:2 (harvest is plentiful); 10:7 (laborer deserves wages); 11:11–13 (father and gifts); 14:28 (cost of tower building); 14:34–35 (salt and dunghill); 16:13 (you cannot serve God and Mammon); 20:47–21:4 (widows' houses devoured); 21:29–31 (fig tree as a sign of the times).

G. *Economic Realities—Debt, Taxation, Oppression.* The political character of ancient economics, redistribution, and debt all come to expression in Lukan traditions:

Luke 2:2 (census of Quirinius); 3:13 (overcollection of taxes); 3:14 (extortion); 4:19 (hope for Jubilee release?); 5:27 (tax office); 6:34 (lending and usurious return); 7:41–42 (two debtors); 8:18 ("the rich keep getting richer"); 11:4 (forgiveness petition); 12:58f (debt bondage); 19:1–10 (Zacchaeus); 19:11–27 (minas and lending at interest); 19:45–48 (temple cleansing); 20:9–16 ("wicked" tenants); 20:20–26 (tribute to Caesar); 20:47–21:4 (widows' houses devoured).

H. *Hunger, Robbery, Violence, and General Insecurity.* Luke–Acts reveals the general conditions of political insecurity and subsistence anxiety in the ancient countryside:

Luke 1:53 (feeding the hungry); 3:10–14 (John's words to tax collectors and soldiers); 3:19–20 (Herod imprisons John the Baptist); 4:29 (villagers at Nazareth try to kill Jesus); 6:1 (plucking grain on the sabbath); 6:20f, 24–25 (Beatitudes and woes); 9:12–17 (feeding of the 5000); 9:52–56; 10:5–8, 10–12 (xenophobia of villagers); 10:29–37 (good Samaritan); 11:34–36 (sound eye); 12:22–31 (anxiety); 12:46–48 (beating of servants); 12:51–53 (division in households); 12:58–59 (threat of prison); 13:1, 4 (building accidents? police actions?); 20:9–16 (violence of tenants); 20:47–21:4 (widows' houses devoured); 21:5–6 (temple will be violently destroyed); 22:36, 38, 49–52; 23:19, 32, 39–43 (robber allusions); 23:26 (Simon of Cyrene-forced labor); Acts 5:36–37 (mention of the revolutionaries Theudas and Judas the Galilean); 11:28–29 (famine under Claudius).

I. *Oppressed and Economically Marginated Groups.* Many marginalized and landless people appear in the pages of Luke–Acts:

Luke 2:8 (shepherds); 2:36–38 (widows); 4:25 (Elijah and widows); 5:12–16 (leper); 6:20–21 (hungry and poor); 7:11–12 (widow at Nain); 7:41–42 (debtors); 8:18 (powerless, have-nots); 12:58–59 (debtors); 17:11–19 (lepers); 20:9–16 (tenants); 21:1–4 (widows); Acts 3:2 (lame man).

The model indicated by Figure 6-3 provides, then, a comprehensive and adequate scenario for understanding the countryside. This Lukan material, along with the various dimensions of Figure 6-3, are now discussed in detail.

2.3 Imaging the Countryside Through the Model and Luke's Traditions

2.3.1 Who Controlled the Land? The land of early first-century Palestine was directly or indirectly under the political control of Caesar or the people of Rome. Caesar thought of his rich empire as a large "household," but imperial taxation (through control of land) amounted in fact to a gigantic redistributive economy. Caesar had "inherited" lucrative estates from the Hasmoneans in the Esdraelon Plain and the Jericho area. The rest of the land was nominally under the ownership of the people of Rome, but in practice it was controlled by the local elites of Palestine who acted as Roman agents of subjugation (even if unwillingly).

With reference back to Figure 6-3, the major classes of these elites are indicated: Gentile cities (B) controlled land along the Mediterranean coast, in Samaria, and in the Transjordan (Luke 8:26). The Jewish areas (C) were controlled for the most part by the Herods, with oversight from imperial agents like Pontius Pilate (Luke 23:1). Smaller shares went to political subordinates — stewards of Caesar's estates and to other "secular" landowners (Herodians, Elders of the Jews, Scribes, etc.). Luke–Acts speaks of several Herods: (a) Herod the Great is mentioned as a chronological reference point in Luke 1:5. (b) Herod Antipas, the first Herod's son as well as governor of Galilee when Jesus was alive, appears numerous times in the Gospel of Luke (3:1, 19; 8:3; 9:7, 9; 13:31; 23:7, 8, 11, 12, 15). (c) Grandson Herod Agrippa I makes an entrance in the pages of Acts (12:1, 6, 11, 19, 20–21; 13:1). The Herodians, large landholders who were political partisans of the family of Herod, are known to us from Matthew (22:16) and Mark (3:6; 12:13), but Luke remains silent about them (unless Manean was one, Acts 13:1).

Elders ("leading men" of the Jewish people in the first century, possibly in part Herodians) are mentioned in both Luke (e.g., 7:3) and Acts (e.g., 4:5). In the same breath, Luke includes the scribes (e.g., Luke 9:22; Acts 6:12). The high priestly families held land also, passed down from generation to generation in the Second Temple period and perhaps increasingly augmented by land acquired through default on debts or temple dedications. These "chief priests" appear in Luke–Acts as leading opponents of Jesus or his followers (Luke 20:1; 22:52; Acts 4:18; 23:2). Most land tended to be under the control, therefore, of indigenous or foreign elites. It was subject at all times to rents and taxes of various sorts. Little, if any, land was under indigenous village control during the first century ("Nominal village control" in Figure 6-3; see further below).

As we have seen, the landlords of Jesus' Palestine were accumulating land at the expense of the peasantry through debt manipulation. The concentration of land control in the hands of the elite few resulted in marked social stratification [A]. Although he is called "Fool," the rich man who builds greater barns was undoubtedly familiar throughout the first-century Mediterranean world (12:16–21; a useful comparison can be made to the famous character of Trimalchio in the *Satyricon* of Petronius). There were those who owned vineyards (13:6–9), who could buy more fields (14:18), who had many oxen (14:19).

By contrast, there were those in material want who needed charity (3:11). Some in both Jesus' and Luke's audience needed to contemplate giving alms and benefactions: Luke 12:33–34; 18:22; and 19:11–26. Distribution of goods was not always done equitably (8:18); and characteristically there was a political aspect to distribution. The strong and powerful could take what they needed or desired (3:14). Herod Agrippa could turn food into a political weapon (Acts 12:20). Eminent domain was a fact of life (Luke 19:31). The reality of *slavery*—unfree, coerced labor—is everywhere attested: Luke 12:42–46; 16:10–13; 17:7–10. Sharp social stratification is the manifest background for the Lukan beatitudes and woes (6:20–25). A most graphic picture of social division is offered, moreover, in the story of Dives and Lazarus (16:19–31). In general, wealth, land, and the subsistence security that control of land represents were not within peasant grasp.

2.3.2 Who Worked the Land? The estate lands of these ruling elites were worked by peasants. Most of this rural populace, which in Palestine was predominantly Jewish, dwelt in villages. Village lands without question were subject to taxation. The level of taxation may have been as high as 50% of the total crop in some cases (Oakman, 1986:71). As a result, relations between elites and peasants were frequently not cordial (Luke 20:9–19). Undoubtedly only a few village parcels were free of rent to a local landlord. These were the lands of "middle peasants," a group whose size is difficult to determine from the historical sources.

The percentage of land under direct village control by "small peasants" is also uncertain from the historical record. It will have been very small.

Most village lands were estate lands of the Herods and their agents or of the Jewish elders and priestly families. Jewish villagers, moreover, needed to set aside produce or land to meet temple obligations. This was at minimum a tenth of the harvest, a tithe (Deut 14:22). Certainly some Jewish villages were the homes of rural priests such as Zechariah (Luke 1:5, 39–40), who received a portion of the village harvest. The reality of rural priests might explain why a priest and Levite were going down from Jerusalem to Jericho in 10:31–32. Other Jewish village lands may have comprised part of the temple "estate" proper under the conviction that "the land belongs to Yahweh" (Lev 25:23 – a Priestly tradition).

2.3.3 Character of First-Century Village Life. Besides the large estate, village [B] and field [C] (Luke 6:1–4) are envisioned in Luke's Gospel as the primary social settings of the ancient Palestinian countryside. The wilderness areas stand over against the sown fields and the cities as the refuge of demons and social rebels (Luke 4:2; 8:29; 11:24; Acts 21:38).

The villages of ancient Palestine seem to have been organized along kinship or quasi-kinship lines (Luke 1:58). Many villages will have been comprised of members of a single extended family. Mutual help was expected within the village community (11:5–8). Generosity in line with general reciprocity was the village ideal (6:38; 11:11–13). Frugality was a way of life, but did not preclude common celebration (15:6, 8–9, 22–23). Economic exchange within familial or quasi-familial context is evident.

Hospitality might perhaps be extended to outsiders (Luke 10:8, 38; and 24:13–31). Peasant villagers as a rule, however, tend to be suspicious and mistrustful of strangers, because outsiders so often violate the interests of the village community. This defensiveness can be seen behind Luke 9:5, 52–56; and 10:10. Recall the tendency of peasant villagers to behave toward outsiders in terms of negative reciprocity. Perceived betrayal of peasant family or village interests means ostracism or worse: Luke 4:23–29 (Jesus nearly killed by angry residents of Nazareth) and 15:19 (Prodigal Son not worthy to be called a son).

2.3.4 Typical Economic Experience in the Village. For the most part, peasant villagers of the first century CE were *labor generalists*, that is, proficient at a number of agricultural and domestic tasks. The peasant family normally produced and consumed most of what it needed "in-house." Simple technology and life-needs permitted most things to be built or constructed by family members, such as houses (Luke 6:48–49) or towers (14:28–29). All villages were primarily agricultural production centers, but since agriculture normally did not keep villagers occupied year around, there was opportunity for its members to adopt other economic pursuits. This incentive was increased by any surplus village children. Surplus village labor power could easily be absorbed into the labor needs of the large estates (10:2). These workers were paid wages by the day (10:7).

There is evidence outside the New Testament that Palestinian villages tended to specialize in certain much-needed crafts—notably crafts related to clothes, building, special foods, fishing, medicine, metal working, tools, etc. (Klausner 1925:177–78). Handicraft and small craft production was absorbed in intra- and inter-village barter, probably by the temple economy as well (Luke 13:4). Many products of craftsmen, however, were only available to the elites. Any such economic activity was purely supplemental for the village economy. The predominant activity at all times remained agriculture.

Broad agricultural experience is attested in sayings and proverbs of the Lukan Jesus tradition [F]. First, familiarity with a variety of Palestinian flora and crops is indicated: grain (Luke 6:1; 8:5–8), weeds (6:44), grapes and wine (5:37–39; 6:44), figs (6:44; 21:29–31), orchards (6:43), condiments (11:42; 13:19). Second, farm animals—both of Jews and of Gentiles—are sometimes mentioned: sheep or lambs (2:8; 10:3; 15:3–6), swine (8:32; 15:16), a colt (19:30). The tradition is quite familiar with village or agricultural operations and tools: axe (3:9), winnowing fork (3:17), new woven cloth (5:36), broadcast sowing (8:5), oil lamp (8:16), plow (9:62), women serving guests (10:40), baking, and providing hospitality to strangers (11:5–6), care of fig trees (13:6–9), use of leaven (13:21), salt and dunghills (14:35), servant plowing (17:7).

The basic economic problem of all ancient village life, as has been already stressed, was the narrow margin between subsistence and famine. Mutual help (Luke 11:5) and liberal gleaning rights (6:1–4) were normal institutions that carried villagers through lean periods of the year. Since peasant villagers and urban poor had little food reserves, the chief economic effects of any serious famine invariably fell upon them (Luke 15:13–16; Acts 11:28–29). Heavy rents and taxations only strained this narrow margin. Understandably, many peasants lived under constant anxiety over subsistence. Words of the Lukan Jesus tradition address this anxiety, admonishing disciples to trust in a providential God (Luke 12:22, 24, 29–31).

There is good reason to believe that chronic overtaxation and debts played a significant role in the unrest in Palestine preceding the Jewish War and earlier in the genesis of the Jesus movement [G]. Luke knows the paraphernalia of Roman taxation: The census (2:2), the toll collector's office (5:27), and tribute to Caesar (20:20–26). Oppressive taxation can be inferred from the tradition (3:13–14; 20:22; 23:2). Accumulated wealth, or "Mammon" (from an Aramaic word meaning "wealth"), was adjudged evil from an agrarian perspective because it was perceived as gained unjustly (16:9, 11). Moreover, Mammon represented an eternal threat to one's life (9:25; 12:20). While Luke's story of the minas (19:12–27) differs in a number of details from the parallel version in Matthew 25:14–30, the general picture of loans at interest (usury) and their social consequences becomes clear. Interest violated the zero-sum sensibilities of peasant villagers. The typical peasant response to wealth — hiding it in the ground — is shamed by the story. The rewards of unjust gain in reality mean the control of villages' agricultural increase. Insolvent debtors faced prison (Luke 12:58–59).

Concerning debt, Luke's version of the Lord's Prayer contains the significant fourth petition (fifth petition in Matthew's Gospel, Matt 6:12): "Forgive us our sins, for we ourselves forgive every one who is in debt to us" (11:4). Luke also expands the saying at Luke 6:32–33 (= Matt 5:46–47) with the significant statement, "lend, expecting nothing in return" (6:35). This remarkable Lukan special tradition clearly forbids usury. Elsewhere, Lukan tradition places a definite stress upon debt forgiveness and its beneficial effects (7:41–42; 16:1–8). Forgiveness or restitution can also be contemplated in the case of overtaxation (19:8).

2.3.5 Peasant Disaffection. Violence became a regular part of village experience and rural consciousness (Luke 1:51–52; 9:54) [H]. Violence might include extortion (Luke 3:14); forceful removal of rent from the threshing floor (see 20:10); fraud (3:13; 19:8); robbery, by those who had left the normal courses of society (10:30; 12:39); police actions (13:1) or forceful imprisonment (3:19–20; 12:58–59). Estate slaves were often beaten (12:46–48). Forced labor was possible (23:26). Intra-village conflict might originate because of inheritance disputes (12:13–14; 15:28,30); or it might be provoked through an external cause (4:29; 12:51–53).

Robbers were a fact of life (Luke 10:30; 22:36, 38, 49–52; 23:19, 32, 39–43; Acts 5:36–37). These were often painted by ancient aristocrats like Josephus as self-serving and self-aggrandizing, but many were undoubtedly "Robin Hoods" — the type of peasant leaders whom Hobsbawm has called social bandits — who effected forceful redistribution of goods they believed had been robbed from the countryside by the powerful (see implied popular support for the brigand Eleazar, Josephus, *War* 2.253).

2.3.6 Peasant Victims. Luke's tradition knows of a host of social misfits and down-and-outers [I]. These are the victims of the Roman agrarian order. Their individual life-courses are never recounted, but their plight makes sense from the perspective of typical agrarian disorder. Given the narrow margin between subsistence and starvation, the presence of the hungry and poor is not surprising (6:20–21). The pressure toward debt has already been indicated (7:41–42; 12:58–59). Many widows appear in Luke's pages (2:36–38; 4:25; 7:11–12; 18:3; 20:47; 21:1–4). Without a husband, widows were particularly vulnerable to exploitation and abandonment within agrarian societies; many Old Testament passages attest to their perennial vulnerability (Exod 22:22–24; Isa 1:17; Mal 3:5). Their goods and household were prey for legal disputes (Luke 18:3; 20:47). In a highly politicized, redistributive economy, the powerless were the standard victims. Loss of adequate means of subsistence meant loss of honor or status within the community (see Malina, 1981:85).

Another group of people fit within this category: Those whose lack of physical health meant exclusion from the normal affairs of society. Lepers epitomize this ostracized group (Luke 17:12). For them, physical healing must also mean restoration of status within the community. Ill health implies undignified dependence upon others' generosity (Luke 18:35; Acts 3:2). So in Luke, Jesus restores numerous people to health and reinvigorates their social standing (e.g., Luke 4:39; 5:14; 7:15; 18:43). The disciples duplicate this work in Acts (e.g., 3:8; 9:40; 19:11). We suspect a significant connection between Jesus' feeding work (9:17), advocacy for the hungry (6:21), and Jesus' healing work.

Luke's Jesus makes this kind of liberation and healing a hallmark of his ministry (4:18–19). Jesus' inaugural sermon recalls the Jubilee tradition of the Old Testament (Lev 25; Deut 15; Isa 61), wherein the covenant community is kept healthy by periodic redistribution of land, redemption of slaves, and abolition of indebtedness (see Hollenbach 1985). If Luke has not made this an overt program in the Gospel and Acts, his allusion to the issue of religiously mandated agrarian reform prompts the final part of this investigation.

This concludes the presentation of a general model for understanding the countryside. Taking a conflict approach (vs functionalist approach), we have examined a typical peasant agrarian world. This model has provided a complex but rich scenario for understanding the constant references to the countryside and things pertaining to it in Luke–Acts. But this does not exhaust the project, for it remains a question whether Luke simply reports things the way they are or whether he envisions a different way of living on the land. In asking this question, we are shifting from an abstract investigation of how peasant agrarian societies work.

3.0 TENSIONS WITHIN THE LUKAN CONCEPTION: HOW DOES LUKE REPRESENT THE COUNTRYSIDE?

3.1 Preliminary Considerations

As we have seen in the foregoing, Luke apportions a good deal of space to the countryside. He has received and chosen to leave the countryside somewhat unexpurgated in the tradition. We now turn to consider how Luke represents the countryside in his two-volume work. This venture both utilizes and goes somewhat beyond the traditional redaction-critical method; it might better be termed *interest criticism*, in accord with our adoption of a conflict framework for analysis. Using the foregoing sociological concepts and models as a backdrop, we propose to see how Luke's conception embraces the standard interests of the countryside. Does Luke come out clearly in favor of rural interests, or does his presentation militate against those interests, or is the situation somewhat in between these two extremes? A few preliminary observations are in order.

As Rohrbaugh's essay indicated, the word commonly translated as "city" in Luke–Acts (*polis*), combined with information from Palestinian archaeology, Josephus, and the Talmud, shows that apparently Luke applies the word indiscriminately to places that were patently villages in Jesus' own day. This is certainly true of Nazareth (Luke 1:26) and Nain (7:11), possibly true of Bethlehem (2:4, because the appellation "city of David" was traditional). On the other hand, Luke can utilize the Greek word for village, *kōmē*, quite appropriately (5:17; 8:1 in coordination with "city," 9:6, etc.). This phenomenon may simply indicate Luke's unfamiliarity with Palestine, as is sometimes suggested. Luke, however, may have in mind a distinction for *polis* and *kōmē* that we are as yet unaware of—he may, for instance, use *polis* at times in the technical sense of "town," where a population settlement serves as an agricultural market center or tax collection point or simply as a granary for the surrounding fields. (On the use of *polis* for a chief city of a rural district, see examples from the Egyptian papyri in Moulton-Milligan 1980:525). "Villages" (*kōmai*) would then be smaller satellite settlements of "cities" (*poleis*). It is not possible to settle at this point whether Luke is ignorant of Palestinian settlement patterns or really better informed about such distinctions at a certain point of time than we are. Luke's use of terminology would not seem to be an easy indicator of his interests.

Perhaps more significant than terminology, Luke emphasizes again and again that the message of Jesus in the Gospel and of the various evangelists in Acts consistently reached peasants and the rural precincts. Consider the following passages:

> Pharisees from every village in Galilee come to hear Jesus (Luke 5:17); Jesus passes through "city and village" in his preaching tours (8:1; see 13:22); Jesus thoroughly covers Galilean villages (9:6; 10:38); Jesus visits Samaritan villages (9:52, 56; 17:12). In Acts 8:25 the disciples evangelize many villages of the Samaritans.

Even more important than these references are Luke's summaries regarding "surrounding country":

> Jesus' fame spreads through all the surrounding country of Galilee (Luke 4:14, 37); Luke believes Jesus' fame also reached everywhere in Judea (7:17,

but Nain is not in Judea); the Hellenists are dispersed throughout the Judean and Samaritan countryside (Acts 8:1); even Paul preaches to the Judean countryside (26:20); in Acts 14:6–7 Paul and Barnabas preach to Lystra and Derbe and all the surrounding country; the Word of God spreads through the whole countryside of Pisidian Antioch (13:49); the Galatian and Phrygian countrysides receive the good news (16:6; 18:23).

Most of these countryside references occur in Lukan summaries of the gospel's progress. What the list seems to imply, then, is that Luke has at least a passing interest in the countryside as an object of evangelization. It remains to explore whether Luke's Gospel authentically represents rural interests.

3.2 The Politics of the Countryside: Violent Realism or Irenic Idealism?

Ramsay MacMullen begins his study *Roman Social Relations* by noting an encounter on the road between the party of young Marcus Aurelius and two shepherds. The encounter was a brief but violent one, which MacMullen observes was rather typical in rural areas during the period of emergent Christianity. According to Josephus (*War* 2.60), a Judaean shepherd named Athronges declared himself king and engaged in violent brigandage at the turn of the eras. Conflict between shepherd and settled folk became a commonplace in the Tannaitic traditions of the second century CE (Goodman 1983:24; Baron 1952:254). Shepherds invariably kept flocks belonging to others; the enmity between them and settled villagers arose because mobile flocks were a grave danger to the sown fields and shepherds were careless of others' fields. MacMullen sums up the general character of the ancient countryside and wilderness areas in this way: "The less populated countryside throughout the empire approached a state of endemic warfare, from which only a stout cudgel, a fast horse, or a well-built little fortress gave protection" (1974:4).

It is significant for our theme, then, that Luke tell at the beginning of his gospel the (to us) quaint story about the shepherds at the birth of Jesus. Does Luke intend that one of the more violence-prone groups of rural antiquity is the first to hear of "peace on earth," or is the countryside in Luke the place where peace is assumed to be prevalent, or where peace may get a receptive or sympathetic hearing? If so, then Luke has idealized the countryside into a region of peacefulness. Of course, this would militate against what is known of the authentic ancient countryside from historians like MacMullen and what could be predicted about the countryside by conflict theory. A genuine restoration of peace between shepherds and peasant villagers of antiquity would have been the resettlement of shepherds upon land and the incorporation of their flocks into the rural economy. We suspect Luke of irenic idealism here.

Consideration of some other of Luke's material seems to bear out the idealizing tendency of Luke's conception. Both John and Jesus are born in the countryside proper (Luke 1:57, 65; 2:7); both John and Jesus are reared away from major cities (Luke 1:80; 2:51). John's ministry takes place in the wilderness (3:3). Jesus' testings begin in the wilderness, but end in Jerusalem. Often Jesus escapes to a lonely place for refuge (4:42). By contrast, cities (even if some of Luke's "cities" are patently villages) are frequently the place of confrontation and conflict over the message of peace and salvation (Nazareth: 4:29; "One of the cities": 5:21; Capernaum[?]: 6:11; Jerusalem: 13:34; 19:42; etc.). Significant intracity conflict surrounding the message continues in Acts (5:18; 6:12; but see 7:58; 12:1–3; 13:45; 14:5, 19). Of course, the tradition compels Luke to acknowledge conflict in the countryside and wilderness as well (Luke 6:1–5; 10:30–35). But the narrative of Luke–Acts seems to suggest that John and Jesus flourish in "villages," but experience conflict in "cities."

The issue, then, is how Luke understands or interprets the nature of that conflict. What does it signify? Luke has, as we have seen, several allusions to robbers and swords. The relationship between this conflict and rural oppression is not clarified by the evangelist. Luke also knows of conflict within rural households (10:40; 12:52–53), but this conflict is over Jesus rather than explicitly rural concerns. Only if Luke understands Jesus as representing rural interests, can this conflict be understood as pro-countryside.

As Figures 6-2 and 6-3 have made clear, one significant measuring stick of rural interests and the cause of rural unrest in antiquity was the issue of land control. Luke's narrative gives a mixed perspective on this important rural preoccupation. Luke 4:19 might allude to the ancient Jubilee traditions of Leviticus 25 and Isaiah 61:1–4 that promised redemption of family land. However, a consideration of the one tradition in the Synoptic Gospels that seems to address radical peasant demands for land redistribution, namely Mark 10:28–30 and parallels, shows that the crucial part is omitted by Luke. Mark 10:29 and Matt 19:29 expressly state that Jesus' disciples have left *fields* for the gospel's sake. Luke omits the reference to fields. Furthermore, Mark 10:30 promises the disciples *fields* in the age to come. Both Matthew and Luke delete this reference in their versions. Luke also lacks the Matthean beatitude, "The meek shall inherit the land" (Matt 5:5), which might resonate with peasant radicalism.

In the same vein, the so-called Wicked Tenants parable (Luke 20:9–16) vividly shows the tenor of landlord-tenant relationships in the early empire and indicates that a frequent bone of rural contention was who got the fruits of the land. As Luke has used this tradition, however, the point has been allegorized into a condemnation of the "tenants' " stewardship (i.e., Israel's present leadership) of the vineyard (God's people). This point becomes clear from Luke 20:19. Luke does not utilize the story in any manifest way as a critique of landed relations, nor is Luke sympathetic with the tenants. Similarly, Luke 13:6–9 plays upon such tensions, but Luke places the story in a context emphasizing accountability to God and repentance (12:47–48, 56, 58; 13:3, 5). Finally, in Acts 2:44–45; 4:32–37; 5:1–11, Luke stresses the collective holding of the early Jerusalem church's land. Such collective property would militate against peasant radicalism's demand for land redistribution. From this, Luke does not seem to take a pro-countryside stance.

In one critical area, therefore, Luke apparently fails to represent adequately the interests of the ancient countryside. Collective control of land, as advocated in Acts, would not be acceptable to peasant villagers. For them, redistribution of land implies redistribution of inheritable plots that will sustain the honor and political independence of individual families. Collective control simply substitutes one landlord for another. Luke holds up a rather idealized countryside in his narrative, a view which does not mesh with this one crucial peasant interest, but where Jesus' and the apostles' message takes root and where a more or less peaceful refuge from the violence waiting the message in the cities is possible. An investigation of Luke's handling of political economy will bear out this impression in another way.

3.3 The Economics of the Countryside: Place of Generosity or Stinginess?

Just as control of land was a crucial question for peasants in antiquity, so also was the harsh experience of political economy in the form of debt. Luke has a significant amount of material dealing with debt, as the analysis of 2.3.4 above has indicated. However, a careful consideration of that material will also reveal that Luke has not focused on the connection between debt and loss of land or between debt forgiveness and restoration of control over land. These are the accents one would expect if Luke were overtly concerned with the interests of countryfolk. Luke's Jubilary allusion in 4:18–19 does not specifically mention debt remission or land redemption. Yet Luke has much to say about creditors, to whom peasants are indebted. For example, Luke's version of the Lord's Prayer has the significant, "for we ourselves also forgive every one who is in debt to us" (11:4). Taken by itself, this petition might appeal to rural folk. But they are usually in debt and themselves in need of debt remission. In its present form, the petition makes more sense on the lips of creditors—the first part "Forgive us our sins" even suggests the Publican of Luke 18:13. A creditor-moral is explicitly drawn from Luke 7:41–42. And surely Luke 6:35 has in mind the behavior of creditors. Since this saying explicitly advocates loans without expecting interest or even return of principle, the passage envisions pure general reciprocity or gift. Moreover, Luke's Jesus does not limit this loan to kin or near-kin in the village; apparently such reciprocity is to be practiced even toward strangers. Similarly, the actions of the Good Samaritan (10:33–35) represent the practice of general reciprocity toward strangers. The restitution of Zacchaeus (19:8) and the debt forgiveness of the Unjust Steward (16:6–7) also fit this picture. Only in a partial and incomplete way can Luke's debt material be said to serve the interests of the countryside related to debt. Luke uses the material to draw morals for creditors.

Giving and sharing are unmistakably prominent emphases in Luke–Acts, as a series of sayings at Luke 6:34–38; 16:9–13; and Acts 20:35 suggest. Luke seems to have urged reciprocity exchanges as a mark of the Jesus/Christian movement. This is in line with the tradition about Jesus, to judge from Luke's use of his sources, both Mark and Q: Mark 6:38 (sharing among 5000), Mark 10:21 (rich are to give to the poor), Matt 5:42 (giving to whomever asks), and many other Gospel passages would suggest. For Luke, however, reciprocity does not seem to change the political structure of social intercourse, nor does it mark the disappearance of social hierarchy per se within the Christian community (see Luke 22:26 with its parallels). Luke 12:48 is a central text for understanding the Lukan conception of material and political stewardship.

There are, of course, criticisms of the rich and powerful (1:52–53; 6:24–26) balanced with utopian passages like 12:33 or Acts 2:44–46. Yet Luke also acknowledges that some people in the early Christian movement (and in Luke's community) possessed more than others. So he mentions the wealthy women who supported Jesus during the ministry (Luke 8:3); he notes the special ministration of Joseph of Arimathea (23:53); and he acknowledges that some early Christians had special means (Acts 4:37; 12:12). Luke is impressed with their example of sharing, but he never clearly states that the whole politico-economic order of the Roman agrarian state will be dramatically altered by Jesus or the kingdom of God. Patronage and the redistributive function of the community will still be necessary.

Leaders of the Christian community are not to be called "benefactors." Nonetheless, they are to be benefactors (22:25–26; see chapter by Moxnes). That Luke has an ideology based upon the practice of Hellenistic benefaction seems clear (Danker 1987:28–46). General reciprocity is normally practiced within close kin relationships (11:11–12) That the country mores of antiquity could easily sympathize with this standard when generalized to those beyond the kin group is questionable. The Prodigal Son story depicts a generous father who gives despite being wronged. Would a peasant patriarch act in this way? Perhaps.

Yet recall that most peasant households strive for self-sufficiency, face narrow margins between subsistence and famine, often account for barter exchanges on the basis of balanced reciprocity, and have an oversupply of children to care for. Under the typical circumstances of first-century Palestine, most peasant fathers would not have been so generous. Children who acted in a dishonorable way could be disowned. Ac-

cording to peasant norms, the Prodigal's brother would be the one re-
warded with the fatted calf. Peasants would feel the injustice of the
father's endangering the family subsistence for the younger son's fri-
volity (see the similar reading of Bailey, 1980). And to give on this basis
to complete strangers, as the Good Samaritan does, would be difficult
to expect from a village patriarch or any normal peasant.

Most villagers in Jesus' rural environment would have been stingy,
as are most peasants under the pressure of subsistence and village envy.
Peasants at the time of the early empire were probably forced by heavy
taxation to account carefully for everything and call in debts on a strict
quid pro quo basis. If Jesus told stories like the Prodigal Son or Good
Samaritan, it was to subvert traditional village morality and open up the
countryside to other possibilities. In them is urged the practice of general reciprocity as characteristic of the kingdom of God and as radical
protest against the agrarian situation in early Roman Palestine (Oakman
1986:215–216). In Luke's narrative, the stories of the Prodigal Son and
Good Samaritan undoubtedly function to shame those who have amassed
goods into sharing them. The story of Dives and Lazarus serves a similar purpose (16:19–31).

From the tradition, Jesus appears to have envisioned the destruction of the temple as a prelude to a general socio-economic arrangement devoid of redistributive political economy (see Mark 13:2; 14:58).
Yet Luke plays down this element in the Jesus tradition compared to the
other evangelists (Luke 19:45–46), and he "historicizes" the allusion to
the temple destruction (Luke 21:6,20). Mark 13:2 and 14 imply the
temple's destruction will accompany the final apocalyptic events of the
establishment of God's reign (Mark 13:26), but Luke's parallel passages
look back to the historical destruction of the temple in the Jewish War.
The redistributive political economy of the temple is defunct in Luke's
view as a divine mechanism for social justice, probably to be replaced
by a redistributive Christian community (Acts 2:44–45; 4:32–37). Redistribution by its nature involves unequal status and a "division of labor"
(Luke 22:25–26; Acts 6:1–4). There must be faithful overseers of the distribution and guardians of the store (Luke 12:41–48). All of Luke's incorporation of reciprocity exchanges and debt remissions do not change
this social fact.

Luke gives the general impression that a reciprocity motif is operative within a social setting still marked by unequal status and redistributive economic mechanisms. Hence, it is still a hierarchical benefaction
or patronage motif. It is not a strategy for a general restructuring of society in the direction of primitive village exchange without redistributive institutions or patrons/landlords/creditors, as seemed to be the
direction of the tradition of Jesus' exclusive emphasis upon general reciprocity toward all. Yet since Luke clearly keeps the reciprocity motif ap-

plicable to all, so as to violate normal peasant sensitivities, he has preserved an authentic theme of the Jesus tradition in his own limited way.

3.4 Conclusion: Luke's Elite-Directed Moralism

The political implication of Luke–Acts is a hotly debated topic today (Cassidy and Scharper 1984). The foregoing analysis has shown that this debate needs to be broadened and deepened in its scope. Ancient politics invariably encompassed broad social and economic questions. For the countryside, ancient politics were invariably bad news. Redistributive economy worked against the interests of rural agriculturalists. Has the Lukan Gospel addressed good news to that situation? Only partially.

Luke followed superficially the traditions about Jesus in urging the remission of literal debts and in retaining the necessity of the destruction of the Jewish temple (which for Luke was an accomplished fact). Yet in my view, for Jesus, debt remission and temple destruction were bound up with an ideology of God's kingdom that envisioned the abolishment of social stratification per se (Oakman 1986:213–216). So according to Mark 10:22 and Matt 19:22, Jesus can send the rich young man away sorrowing; this seems close to the historical meaning of Jesus' ministry. Luke's rich ruler, however, does not go away (Luke 18:23), though he is sad. Luke, therefore, must reckon with wealth and privilege in his community (Karris, 1978:120, 122–24), and he is strenuously trying to turn the hearts of the powerful to the powerless and dishonored poor by his discriminating use of the radical Jesus tradition (Luke 12:48; 19:8–9; 22:26).

In wrestling with this persuasive task, Luke does not simply endorse the demands of peasant radicalism, as Jesus very nearly did in the name of God's kingdom. The debt petition in Luke's version of the Lord's Prayer indicates how Luke redacts material that might originally have addressed peasant hopes for debt abolition. It becomes, so to speak, a challenge now thrown in the creditor's court. The Dishonest Steward gives some debt relief, to be sure, but he is not the landlord. Zacchaeus promises restitution for fraudulent exactions, but he is not the imperial procurator. Likewise, Luke's silence on redistribution of land control, except when land tenure is firmly vested in the Christian community as in Acts, does not provide a satisfying solution to the plight of the ancient peasantry. Luke may envision "Rich Fools" in his own community, who are more interested in stored grain than in helping the disadvantaged of the community. Luke never says that the kingdom of God is incompatible with large estates whose (Christian) landlords open their hands to "make friends" by means of unrighteous Mammon. Lazaruses may expect to become part of the estate, but not to be rid of estates altogether. Thus, Luke's "peasant moral economy" is limited in scope to domestic concerns. The political dimensions of rural oppression are left alone.

What was originally a radical social critique by Jesus and his followers of the violent and oppressive political-economic order in the countryside under the early empire becomes in Luke's conception a rather innocuous sharing-ethic ambiguous in its import for rural dwellers. The countryside is apparently idealized by Luke as a place particularly receptive to this message. Cities resist God's purposes and violently kill his agents, but nonetheless (in Luke's view) primarily urban hearts need change, and then peace (as Luke understands it) will prevail. No dramatic social reconstruction—such as the elimination of the preindustrial city or Roman imperium—is to be expected or is necessary.

Thus, while Luke has preserved much of the countryside in the early Jesus tradition for us, he has to some extent revised the original intention of the Jesus movement. For Jesus, the kingdom of God was world reconstruction, especially beneficial for a rural populace oppressed by debt and without secure subsistence. For Luke, political expediency demands that the world restructuring be limited to alleviating the harshest aspects of political economy within the local Christian community by benefaction and generalized reciprocity. According to Luke, by no means was the Jesus group "turning the world upside down" (Acts 17:6) by envisioning a different political-economic order.

We may finally hazard an hypothesis as to Luke's "place" between city and country. As Luke addresses his patron Theophilus (and others like him), he stands sociologically somewhere between preindustrial city and peasant village, without endorsing unambiguously the interests and values of either one. Luke does not look to the countryside as one who labors on the land. He does not share some of the core rural interests of antiquity. He does not seem "native" to the country, at least on the evidence of his narrative. Yet Luke cannot ignore the countryside either, because of its prominence in the early Jesus traditions. Luke sees in certain aspects of the peasant moral economy a solution to difficulties within his own community.

Luke's community probably resides in a large town or city somewhere in the Roman Empire. Early tradition traces Luke's origins to Antioch in Syria (Jackson and Lake 1930:2:233, 235; Fitzmyer 1981:1:42; see also the essays of Rohrbaugh and Robbins in this volume). Luke's community undoubtedly includes landlords who control parts of Luke's immediate countryside, and whose "estate people" may be part of the community. The landlords control Luke's community as well. Perhaps the country members are numerous. Their normal environment is field and village outside of the city/town. They are regularly seen, but rarely heard. One can envision frequent interaction in Luke's community between city/town dwellers and country peasants, but along the predictable political lines of the Roman Empire. On just this point, Rohrbaugh's treatment of Luke 14:15–24 in this volume is crucial. This mixed social constitution explains the preservation of rural Jesus traditions and their continuing significance for the community. Luke's literary work, however, addresses primarily the landlords and creditors in the interests of the well-being of the whole community. It is the behavior of the powerful and the rich that affects the quality of communal life for all.

4.0 CONCLUSIONS REGARDING THIS SOCIOLOGICAL METHOD

The sociological models developed in this essay, whatever their imperfections, have proven useful for developing an adequate scenario to understand rural interests and values and for seeing how Luke handles them. Other essays in this volume argue that Luke developed through his reading of the Jesus tradition a "moral economy of the peasant," and that he shifted the focus of early Christian life away from redistributive temple religion toward household reciprocity.

Our labors have corroborated these suggestions from a different angle, but with questions as to their meaning and value for rural folk. A conflict approach has allowed us to probe the basic interests of the countryside and to reflect persistently upon Luke's representation of those interests. While Luke views the countryside in a positive way in his two-volume work, his rural traditions have not spoken so much for rural interests as for Luke's argument to the powerful and wealthy of his own community (like Theophilus?) for benefaction and generalized reciprocity toward the non-elites in the group. We see this when explicit models clarifying rural interests are held up to Luke's rural themes and those themes "fit" the model-template rather imperfectly.

Our efforts have also highlighted the importance and interrelationship of politics, religion, economics, and kinship in Luke's ancient context. Malina (1981 and 1986a) are especially illuminating here. Politics and kinship have priority in antiquity, structuring economy and religion in definable ways (village and family = reciprocity; state, temple, and large estate = redistribution).

Much more along this road can and needs to be done. The models in this essay have served their purpose, but they can undoubtedly be refined or improved upon. Similar studies need to be undertaken with respect to other early Christian literature. Only in this way can a comprehensive picture of the impact of the Jesus movement upon country and city in the Roman Empire be developed and evaluated. For the present, the reader has gained a greater sensitivity to the values and interests at stake within early Christianity and to the importance of the countryside as the home of the original Jesus movement.

This essay, furthermore, should be read in conversation with other essays in this volume which deal with matters of land, food, institutions, patronage and the like. Since "the city" and the "countryside" reflect two sides of the same coin, Rohrbaugh's analysis of the city and in particular Luke 14:14–25 illustrates further what we have asserted here. Since meals entail distribution of food and reciprocity, Neyrey's essay on meals as ceremony rounds out aspects of this study. Moxnes' material on patronage and benefaction has a direct bearing on how elites are supposed to treat peasants. And Elliott's essay on the institutions of temple and household give further salience to the arguments advanced here.

7 SICKNESS AND HEALING IN LUKE–ACTS

John J. Pilch

1.0 INTRODUCTION

Sickness and healing, while common features in Luke–Acts, are by no means easy to understand. Let us take, for example, the number of instances of blindness and its healing in Luke's two volumes. The evangelist narrates the traditional story of how Jesus healed a blind man (18:35–43//Matt 9:27–51//Matt 20:29–34//Mark 10:46–52). In Acts, however, we have the curious phenomenon of the temporary blindness of Paul from which he is quickly healed (9:18; 22:13). Along with this, we find the story of Paul cursing Elymas the magician with blindness; this blindness, says Paul, is due to "the hand of the Lord" and will last "for a time" (13:6–11). Blindness, then, may be (a) longstanding, signaling a genuine disease, or (b) temporary as in the case of Paul and Elymas. Blindness befell Paul, who was a sinner (Gal 1:13; 1 Cor 15:9), and Elymas, who withstood the gospel, thus suggesting a symbolic dimension to it. Yet how are we to understand these varying examples of sickness and healing? How do we understand these accounts? What is an adequate scenario for understanding this and similar material in Luke–Acts?

Readers are too often misled by the assumption that the author of Luke–Acts is the same "Luke the physician" whom Paul greets in Col 4:14. Thus they explore the nature of physical blindness, contrasting "real" blindness with "metaphorical" blindness and investigating spontaneous healing and other similar avenues of interpretation. This is the result of our modern, scientific perspective, which has been called "medical materialism." This is an inadequate scenario for understanding Luke–Acts.

"Medical materialism" is an anthropological term for the tendency to utilize modern, Western, scientific medical concepts and models to interpret apparent health concerns in all cultures of all times without regard for cultural differences. Scholars who search a biblical document for its vocabulary of sickness and/or healing are often unwittingly guilty of such medical materialism or medical ethnocentrism. The problem arises because many modern readers tend to interpret the language of sickness and healing in the Gospels in a way that shows little concern for the meaning of this language in Luke's own world.

Even modern attempts to respect the meanings of the Greek and Hebrew vocabulary of the Bible that describe these sickness and healing events present a formidable problem. One scholar correctly cautions:

> It is important to see words in terms of usage, not to argue from theoretical studies of etymologies, and so to realize the inherent flexibility of language, whose nuances are not to be hardened into subtly rigid distinctions of general application (Hemer 1986:52).

Thus on the basis of Luke's varied Greek vocabulary alone (*nosoi, mastigoi, astheneia,* etc.) little if anything can be safely deduced about his understanding of sickness and healing. A new perspective is needed. It is important to name the obstacles that a modern reader faces, but naming the problems is not enough.

If the problem of interpretation lies in our perception, how can we begin to perceive like Luke? What is needed is a way to imagine Luke's language of sickness and healing in terms of his own culture, that is, a new scenario. Sensitivity to cultural differences and the requirements of cross-cultural investigations and comparisons call for the reader to utilize appropriate social science methods and concepts. How different, but how necessary it is for us to understand that health or well-being is but an example of *good fortune* (Worsley 1982:330). Alternately, sickness is but one example of a wide range of *misfortunes*. The key lies in understanding the relation of sickness and healing to *fortune* and *misfortune*, not a modern idea, but one quite frequent in and more appropriate to other cultures.

To understand why a specific sickness is considered a misfortune in a given society, one needs also to know the cultural values and social norms of that society. Let us try, then, to see sickness and healing from the cultural perspective of Luke, who was certainly not a modern scientific physician and very likely not a physician in antiquity either.

Social science methods and concepts are tools of retrieval as well as aids to interpretation (Pilch 1986). This chapter, then, constructs several social-science models for reading the stories about illness and healing in Luke–Acts: (a) cross-cultural concepts of sickness and healing, (b) the health care system in Luke–Acts, and (c) a taxonomy of illnesses. In the light of cross-culturally appropriate methods, models, and concepts, many hitherto ignored data in the Luke–Acts emerge as significant.

The application of cross-culturally developed methods, models, and concepts regarding health-care systems helps cast Jesus' and his followers' healing activity in a new light. This approach, moreover, serves as a useful check against the ethnocentric bias or theological creativity of an investigator. Furthermore, the taxonomy or way of clustering the healings of Jesus reported in Luke–Acts should reflect the values which guide a *Mediterranean* way of perceiving and interpreting "health" realities.

2.0 DEFINING HEALTH AND HEALING IN LUKE–ACTS

2.1 Theory of Cultural Variations in Values

How hard but how necessary it is for us to learn that "It is no longer possible to assume that generalizations based on observations of one culture have a universal applicability" (Papajohn and Spiegel 1975:19). Bible interpreters need to be wary of imposing observations drawn from Western culture upon Mediterranean culture. Scientifically based Western understandings of health and sickness and healing and curing cannot be imposed upon information from the biblical period. Medical anthropology identifies this erroneous methodology as "medicocentrism," which is a belief that scientific Western medicine is the only truth relative to health and sickness questions. Outside this framework there is no truth and no authentic cures take place. "Apparent" cures can be explained by subsequent advances in scientific knowledge or perhaps as a form of "mind over matter." The appropriate scenario rejects medicocentrism for understanding sickness and healing, however, and must deal dramatically with the issue of culture foreign to ours.

2.2 The Model

In order validly to generalize from culture to culture, an interpreter needs a systematic theory of cultural variations in values such as that proposed by F. R. Kluckhohn and F. L. Strodtbeck (1961) and applied by clinical practitioners as reported in Papajohn and Spiegel (1975) and McGoldrick et al. (1982).

Values determine the identification of human misfortunes like illness, the appropriate and inappropriate responses to it, as well as the expected outcomes of treatment if indeed treatment is available.

All theories have assumptions that are best put in the open.

(a) there are only a very limited number of common human problems for which all peoples in all places must find a solution;

(b) the range of possible solutions is neither limitless nor random;

(c) all variants or alternatives of all solutions are in varying degrees present in the total cultural structure of every society. One solution, however, dominates.

In regard to the first point, the common problems and the range of solutions are these:

Problems	Solution A	Solution B	Solution C
(1) Activity	Being	Being-in-becoming	Doing
(2) Relationships	Lineal	Collateral	Individualistic
(3) Time	Past	Present	Future
(4) Humanity and Nature	Subjugated to	Harmony with	Mastery over
(5) Human Nature	Evil	Neutral or mixture of good and evil	Good

Second, we evidently find in columns A, B, and C a range of solutions to the problems listed in the left column. And third, while each culture will select one of the three solutions as primary, the other two are also available either for different circumstances or for different subgroups. Let us now go through this list of problems and solutions, identifying our Western perspective and then suggesting how Luke and his world would see the matter.

2.2.1 The Model Applied to the United States. Generally speaking, the solutions in column C in the diagram above represent the primary choices of United States mainstream citizens.

(1) *Activity:* mainstream Americans emphasize *doing* over being or becoming; we are an activist people, a people on the move. Yet in the United States, increasing numbers of people—even if still a minority—elect *being-in-becoming* as their primary choice, that is, they prefer that kind of activity which has as its goal the development of all aspects of the self as an integrated whole. This is evident in the multitudinous and variously defined "holistic" groups, whether they specialize in health, spirituality, or even skiing!

Being-in-becoming also describes an assumption that human beings develop through stages. This perspective has become very popular in recent Western developmental psychology represented by Lawrence Kohlberg and James Fowler; it offers a "second" order choice to solving problems uncommon among mainstream U.S. citizens but popular among subgroups.

(2) *Relationships:* mainstream U.S. citizens also prefer to be highly *individualistic.* Anthropologist Clifford Geertz notes that U.S. citizens

form the most highly individualistic society in recorded history. He goes on to observe that this way of being human is, "however incorrigible it may seem to us, a rather peculiar idea within the context of the world's cultures" (Geertz 1976:225). In this perspective individual goals have primacy over the goals of either the collateral group (equals, other citizens, friends, or kin) or the lineal group (superiors, leaders, the government).

(3) *Time:* mainstream U.S. citizens are definitely future-oriented. The future will always be bigger and better, and no one wants to be considered "old fashioned" by holding on to old things. Futurism is a popular enterprise, and future planning (from ten to twenty-five years hence) is essential to the success of any American corporate venture. Often the present is not thoroughly enjoyed, because the future is felt to impinge. "Only two more days till vacation ends and school/work begins again."

The insignificance of the past to Americans is demonstrated by a widespread ignorance of (anybody's) history except for one's personal life-span. It is only the steady increase of elderly (85 years old and older, the fastest growing age-cohort at the present time) in the United States population that begins to challenge the belief that the "youth [alone] are the future of America." This fact forces Americans to deal with the past.

(4) *Humanity and Nature:* mainstream U.S. citizens are nearly unanimously convinced nature exists to be mastered and put at the service of human beings. We bridge rivers and bays, make lakes where none existed before, blast holes through mountains, etc. Americans have difficulty understanding other cultures who want to live in harmony with nature (e.g., native Americans) or worse, those who yield to it.

(5) *Human Nature:* mainstream U.S. citizens believe that human nature is either good or a mixture of good and evil which requires control and effort but which also can excuse some occasional human lapses. Few Americans continue the Puritan belief that humans are basically evil but perfectible.

The configuration, then, of the primary value orientations peculiar to mainstream U.S. culture emphasizes: *doing, individualism, future-orientation, mastery over nature, human nature as good or mixed.* It is not surprising that a typical and representative definition of health from this perspective would be:

> [Health is] the ability to perform (*doing*) those functions which allow the organism to maintain itself (*individualism*), all other things being equal, in the range of activity (*doing*) open to most other members of the species (e.g., within two standard deviations from the norm) and which are conducive toward the maintenance of the species (Engelhardt 1981:32).

Presupposed in this definition is strong faith in scientific Western medicine's current and continued *mastery over nature* (e.g., the ability to eradicate disease, to improve upon nature with artificial limbs and organ transplants, to develop wonder drugs, etc.) as well as the conviction that human beings who do get sick or disabled are of "good *nature*" and will try to regain normal function as soon a possible by seeking out the appropriate healer and complying with the prescribed therapy.

2.2.2 *The Model Applied to Luke–Acts.* Turning to the New Testament world, we find a totally different perception of problems and solutions. Different values suggest different perspectives. New Testament society in general might be considered to be similar to Greek rural society, whose primary value orientation preferences tend to emphasize a blend of the perspectives under columns A and B of the figure in 2.2: *being, collateral relationships, the present, subjugation to nature, and a view of human nature as a mixture of good and bad* (Papajohn & Spiegel 1975:180).

(1) *Activity: Being* as a primary value orientation is manifested in the spontaneous expression of impulses and desires. We note this in the natural, spontaneous reaction of the townsfolk in Nazareth when they absorbed Jesus' statement that no prophet is without honor except in his own country: "When they heard this all in the synagogue were filled with wrath. And they rose up and put him out of the city . . ." (Luke 4:28). Or we note the refusal to act spontaneously, which is criticized as deviating from social expectations: "They (this generation)," said Jesus, "are like children sitting in the market place and calling to one another, 'we piped to you, and you did not dance; we wailed, and you did not weep' " (Luke 7:31–35). Failure to respond with spontaneity to the cue spoiled the children's game.

Yet another dimension of this value orientation of *being* is the sentiment voiced in Qoheleth: "A living dog is better than a dead lion" (9:4). The dog might have no owner, suffer with mange, be malnourished, lack a limb, be sightless, yet it would be better off than the dead lion because it would still be alive, that is, still *be*. Life (i.e., *being*) is obviously preferable to death. For example, a centurion pleads for his dying slave (Luke 7:1–10); and Jesus restores a widow's only son to life (7:11–17). Life, moreover, in a good state of being (e.g., clean, pure, whole) is preferable to life in an undesirable state (e.g., unclean with leprosy, blind, deaf, mute). Hence in 5:12–16 and 17:11–19, Jesus restores lepers to a clean state of being.

(2) *Relationships:* When *collateral relationships* constitute the primary value orientations, group goals are preferable to individual goals. In this kind of situation, people relate to each other on the basis of the goals of the laterally extended group. When Peter's mother-in-law is healed Luke notes that "immediately she rose and served them" (4:38–39). The woman's cultural role is to serve at table, a group-oriented task

or goal. Had she desired to run about and broadcast her good fortune, her individual purpose would have superseded the group goals. But she "served them" instead; this is what a dutiful woman/wife ought to do. As is illustrated in the chapter on first-century personality, this value preference characterizes first-century Mediterranean groups like the Jewish peasantry and Jesus himself both with the Twelve and in his preaching.

Another example of *collateral relationships* is the report: "All those who had any that were sick with various diseases brought them to Jesus" (Luke 4:40) and he healed them. It is evident that the extended family brings its sick members to Jesus for healing, demonstrating their lateral or horizontal relationships with kin and neighbors. Similarly, elders appeal to Jesus to heal a centurion's sick servant (Luke 7:1–10), indicating how local Jewish elders serve as collateral mediators with Jesus. Emphasis on *collateral relationships* or cooperation with others (rather than competition) is also revealed in passages which reflect aspects of dyadic contract as well as patron-client relationships. When Jesus occasions an unexpected large catch of fish for Simon, James, and John, they reciprocate by leaving everything and following him (Luke 5:1–11), according to the principles of dyadic contract in which a favor received (fish) entails a favor owed (discipleship). Recall also what Luke said of the women who followed Jesus: "They had been healed of evil spirits and infirmities" (Luke 8:2). They reciprocate Jesus' healing with donations of money. While some people who are healed repay their debt directly to Jesus by following him, Jesus himself advises the Seventy of an alternative acceptable form of reciprocity in terms of collateral relationships: "Whenever you enter a town and they receive you, eat what is set before you." As laborers, they deserve support for preaching a word of "peace." And he implies that on the basis of the demands of dyadic contracts, they should reciprocate this hospitality by healing the sick in that town (Luke 10:8). Healing, then, can be an integral part of collateral relationships.

Other groups in the Mediterranean world of the New Testament would select lineal relationships as a primary value orientation, that is they would order their behavior in terms of some hierarchical perspective or some vertical dimension. Thus his audience is startled to observe that Jesus commands unclean spirits with authority and power and they come out (Luke 4:36). In their perspective, this power over spirits puts Jesus in a position higher than them. Similarly, the centurion whose slave is ill (Luke 7:1–10) recognizes that Jesus' superior position to the forces of sickness and death parallels his own superior position to the soldiers under his command. Jesus has but to say a word and his will is done (7:7–8).

Jesus' relationships, however, are a matter of considerable controversy in Luke–Acts. When Peter is asked, "By what power or name do you do this (i.e., heal a lame person)?" he responds: "By the name of Jesus Christ of Nazareth this man is standing before you well" (Acts 4:7). In a reverse kind of judgment, Jesus' enemies believe that he is subservient to Beelzebul, prince of demons, by whose power he can cast out demons (Luke 11:15). A society that attends to hierarchical ordering is always interested in learning "who's in charge." In matters of health and healing, this is a fundamental concern.

(c) Time: Regarding time values, peasant societies are primarily oriented toward the present time. Peasants worry about the crop or the flock today, day to day. Hence, it is not surprising to find in the Our Father a petition for "daily" bread each day (11:3). Indeed, literally the text reads: give us today tomorrow's bread! In that world, tomorrow is part of the rather widely perceived present. Luke moreover, emphasizes how God's salvation in Jesus is found "today" (Luke 2:11; 4:21; 19:9; 23:43). The future, moreover, is unknowable and unpredictable. In response to the question: "Lord, will you at this time restore the kingdom to Israel?" Jesus answers: "It is not for you to know times or seasons which the Father has fixed by his own authority" (Acts 1:7; compare Mark 13:32). Jesus' exhortation not to worry about food, drink, or clothing—so unrealistic to Americans who plan their future in meticulous details—is another illustration of a peasant's focus on present time (Luke 12:22–34//Matt 6:25–34).

At the same time, focus on the present results in a concern about people's present hunger. Rather than accept the disciples' suggestion that he dismiss the crowd of 5,000 and let them fend for themselves, Jesus is concerned that they be fed now (Luke 9:10–17).

Unlike peasants, however, other first-century Mediterranean people affirm the past as a primary time value orientation. Elites, such as Levites, certainly needed to know their priestly pedigree. Genealogies are important for priests, as well as throne claimants. At times, even ordinary folk saw a value to the past which could validate a claim to and secure present membership and benefits in God's covenant. John challenged his listeners' excessive reliance on the past: "Do not begin to say to yourselves 'We have Abraham as our father'; for I tell you God is able from these stones to raise up children to Abraham" (Luke 3:8). The past legitimates important status in the present.

Jesus' penchant for healing people on the sabbath may also reflect his preference for the needs of the present moment (e.g., the man in synagogue with an unclean spirit, Luke 4:31–37; Simon's mother-in-law, 4:48–49; the man in synagogue with a withered right hand, 6:6–11; the bent woman, 13:10–17; and the man with dropsy, 14:1–6). In this regard, he stands in contrast with the scribes' and Pharisees' primary value orientation toward the past, namely, to "Keep holy the sabbath" (Luke 6:7). Sabbath observance is a tribute to God's resting on the sabbath after creation, a past focus.

(d) *Humanity and Nature*: With regard to *nature* it seems quite clear that first-century Palestinians felt there was little a human being could do to counteract the forces of nature. So, Jesus' healings and miracles stand out as exceptional events in a world where humankind had no power over nature. When Jesus casts out a demon, the crowd is genuinely amazed: "With authority and power he commands the unclean spirits, and they come out" (Luke 5:36). When Jesus calms the storm, his disciples marvel: "Who then is this, that he commands even wind and water, and they obey him?" (Luke 8:24–25).

This sense of marvel in a world where no power over nature was expected continues in Acts. For example, Peter's success in healing the lame man is attributed to the name or person of Jesus, who has demonstrated his unusual power over nature (Acts 2:11–26). When Paul manages to survive the natural course of a snake bite, the people judge him to be "god" (Acts 28:6). That a human being in this culture could take command of nature or be immune to its effects is wondrous and awesome. Paul and his fellow travelers are pounded by a terrible storm, over which mortals could have no control, but over which God was surely in charge (Acts 26:21–25).

(e) *Human Nature*: Finally, relative to *human nature*, first-century Palestinian belief is reflected in Jesus' retort to the magistrate who addresses him as "Good Teacher." Jesus answers: "No one is good but God alone" (Luke 18:19). Does this imply that humankind is evil? Not at all. On the one hand, this response manifests the cultural humility expected from anyone who is paid a compliment. After all, given the pivotal belief in the evil eye in this culture, a malevolent spirit might hear this compliment and do something to cause a good person like Jesus to become or do something evil. Evil is expected in this world. So the common and predictable strategy is to deny the compliment.

Jesus' statement actually reflects the first-century belief that *human nature is a mixture of good and evil propensities*. Each case must be judged accordingly. Notice then how Jesus continues his sentence; he rehearses the commandments which prescribe good behavior (Luke 18:20). They who have kept them can be called "good." Indeed, in the Great Sermon in 6:26–49, Jesus urges followers to "do good"; and he acknowledges that good people will be able to do good, while bad people will not (6:43–45).

From the perspective of these collective insights, a definition of health that would match such a preference of value orientations might be patterned after that offered by the World Health Organization. Health is: "a state of complete well-being and not merely the absence of disease or infirmity." The emphasis here is on a *state of being* rather than on the ability to function as in Western culture. Such a definition makes a significant difference in interpreting the healing activities reported in the New Testament documents.

2.3 Summary

Not only must modern observers and interpreters clarify their own viewpoint and articulate their own values, they must strive as well to imagine a new scenario and learn the viewpoint and values of another culture whom they would study. This first model on viewpoint and value, then, has gone far toward equipping a reader of Luke–Acts with the tools for understanding sickness and healing in that different culture. The diagram on page 184 not only describes a typical Western viewpoint and value (column C), but indicates the viewpoint and value of Luke and his New Testament world.

In general, the emphasis one would expect in Luke–Acts would be as follows:

(a) on *being and/or becoming* (that is, on *states*), not on *doing* (activity);
(b) on *collateral* and *lineal relationships*, not on *individualism*;
(c) on *present* and *past* time orientation, not on the *future*;
(d) on the *uncontrollable* factor of *nature*, not on its *manipulation* or *mastery*;
(e) on *human nature*, which can be both *good and bad*, not *neutral* or *correctable*.

This viewpoint and the values it embodies would yield a definition of *health* as a *state of complete well-being*, not the restoration of individual activity or performance. Sickness and healing, then, would be perceived quite differently in this matrix than in our Western, scientific perspective. Different values are at stake.

This first model has given us a general viewpoint and a broad horizon against which to read Luke's two-volume work. The generality of this first step requires that we move closer to the documents and examine them in greater detail to learn the specific ways in which Luke speaks of sickness and healing, that is, a Lukan taxonomy of illness. But to put that into proper context, we next need to present some basic definitions and to present the health care system that is reflected in Luke–Acts.

3.0 THE HEALTH CARE SYSTEM IN LUKE–ACTS

3.1 Defining Terms

As we begin to examine specific passages in Luke–Acts, we must be as clear as possible on the terms we use to describe and classify the sickness mentioned there. Fortunately, we are not the first readers to grapple with this problem, and we can borrow from the field of medical anthropology the standard terms used there. In this way, we can tap into the valuable work done there, even as we gain necessary precision in our professional language.

In medical anthropology, the word "sickness" is a blanket term describing a reality, while the words "disease" and "illness" are explanatory concepts and terms useful in exploring different facets of that single reality. Think of "sickness" as genus, and "disease" and "illness" as species. It is important to note that these English words have been so designated in modern times by medical anthropologists to describe more accurately the human experience of *misfortune* in the realm of health and well-being. These words do not seem to have any one-to-one counterpart in classical or New Testament Greek. In other words, Greek or Hebrew words that are translated "disease" or "illness" or even "sickness" in the Bible reflect the interpretation of the translator and should not be interpreted with the medical anthropological precision just indicated. In this regard Hemer's caution about drawing conclusions based on the "uncertain terminology of literary sources" such as New Testament Greek vocabulary is quite appropriate. The modern interpreter needs to ask of each instance in the biblical literature: can this *emic* (native) report be fairly interpreted by the *etic* (outsider, in this case medical anthropological) term "disease" or "illness?"

Disease: The concept and word "disease" reflect a biomedical perspective that sees abnormalities in the structure or function of organ systems. Whether or not they are culturally recognized, these pathological states do exist (Kleinman 1980:72). As such, a disease affects individuals and only individuals are treated. To think in terms of individuals and individual disease is a perspective quite foreign to Luke's first-century world, which was, as we noted above, radically group oriented. There persons were dyadic individuals rather than rugged individualists. Considering that this kind of knowledge of disease hinges on the identification of pathogens, germs, viruses, and other microscopic entities, it is clear that biblical people would be entirely ignorant of a disease. They might be experiencing one but would not have the necessary concepts or terminology to know and express it, much less the microscope to view it. Evidently, if we are interested in Luke's narrative and his cultural world, we will *not* use the term "disease" very much if at all, for it is a term foreign to Luke' culture. Instead, we will employ the term "illness."

Illness: The concept and word "illness" reflect a sociocultural perspective that depends entirely upon social and personal perception of certain socially disvalued states including but not necessarily restricted to what modern Western science would recognize as a disease. Let us cite a classic example. Leprosy as described in the Lev 13–14 is simply not the modern Hansen's Disease (*mycobacterium leprae*), but rather some kind of repulsive skin condition. Yet the sociocultural concern over it and consequences of this condition are very real. In other words, biblical leprosy is definitely not a "disease" but it is an "illness" (Pilch 1981).

Curing and Healing: Technically speaking, when therapy can affect a disease so as to check or remove it, that activity is called "curing." As a matter of actual fact, cures are relatively rare even in modern, Western scientific medicine. When an intervention affects an illness, that activity is called "healing." The rule of thumb is: curing :: disease, as healing :: illness. Since healing essentially involves the provision of personal and social meaning for the life problems that accompany human health misfortunes, all illnesses are healed, always and infallibly since all human beings ultimately find some meaning in a life-situation including disvalued states.

In biblical reports evidence for the incidence, identification, and management of "disease" is difficult, if not impossible to discover with certitude. Thus it cannot be known with certainty whether in modern terms anyone ever "cured" an afflicted person. Consequently, modern readers of the Gospels might be taking a hopeless and even misguided approach if they concentrate on issues of "disease" and "curing." On the other hand, in modern terminology the obvious social concern that accompanies the reports of human health-related misfortunes in the New Testament is evidence that the discussion of them in the Gospels centers on "illness" and these are almost always "healed." This suggests that all of Jesus' dealings with the sick in Luke's Gospel are truly *healings*, although they may not be *cures* in the technical sense.

3.2 The Health Care System

Although no one is quite sure whether health care now or ever was delivered in a "systematic" fashion (Mackintosh 1978), the health care system is a conceptual model with three overlapping parts: a professional sector, a popular sector, and a folk sector. It would actually be more accurate to call this a *sickness* care system since that is the primary focus, but *health* care system is the recognized and acceptable term. And it serves well as an effective heuristic tool for analyzing the way sickness is identified and labelled (that is, place into a "taxonomy" or proper category) and managed in all cultures.

3.2.1 *The Professional Sector.* The professional sector of a health care system includes the professional, trained and credentialed healers. If the Greek word *hiatros* ("physician") can be assumed to identify a professional healer, there are two (possibly three) relevant passages to review: Luke 4:23; 5:31; and 8:43.

(a) The proverb Jesus cites in 4:23 " 'Physician, heal yourself'; what we have heard you did at Capernaum, do here also in your own country" is common to the Synoptics and common in antiquity (Nolland 1979). It always depends on context for its meaning, and the word "physician" is almost always applied figuratively. An analogous contemporary proverb, "every dog has its day" almost never refers to dogs; but humans are never offended when this proverb is applied to situations of human misfortune or bad luck.

The Lukan context of this proverb (4:21–44) is larger than that found in the other evangelists. It suggests that Jesus identifies himself as a prophet (4:24) who exorcizes and heals. The identity is repeated and confirmed in 13:33: "I cast out demons and perform cures . . . it cannot be that a prophet should perish away from Jerusalem." Others too acknowledge and reinforce the identity (Luke 7:16; 9:8, 19; 24:19). Being a prophet who exorcizes and heals is very likely part of Jesus' specific identity as a folk-healer.

(b) In 5:31, Luke's Jesus once more quotes a proverb: "Those who are well have no need of a physician, but those who are sick." It is cited as an explanation for his socializing with tax collectors and sinners. Only in Luke does Jesus specify that he has come to call sinners "to repentance" (eis metanoian).

Once again the context of the word "physician" adds a further piece of information useful for understanding the kind of illness a healer in Luke's community would be expected to address. Tax collecting and the condition of a sinner entailed a distortion of social life as it should properly be lived in Israel. To refocus one's personal meaning in life, repentance/metanoia is required. That, in fact, is a consistent subject of preaching (see Luke 3:3, 8; 5:2; 10:13; 11:32; 13:3, 5; 15:7, 10; 16:30; 17:3, 4; 24:27; Acts 2:38; 3:19; 8:22; 11:18; 13:24; 17:30; 19:4; 20:21; 26:20).

(c) Though omitted in important manuscripts (P[75], B, D), Luke 8:43 (//Mk 6:26) is found with a variant lection in others (ℵ, A, C, K, L, P, W): "and (the woman who suffered from a flow of blood for twelve years) had spent all her living upon physicians." On the basis of manuscript evidence and customary Lukan style, it makes sense to omit the phrase. That Luke the alleged physician deliberately struck it from his source to spare "his own" from criticism is an unwarranted anachronistic interpretation.

From a medical anthropological perspective, Mark, who scores the failure of physicians to heal the woman, highlights the failure of the professional sector of the health care system in this instance. Luke, whether or not he has willfully expunged the criticism of physicians, quite clearly points to the failure of all sectors of the health care system in the phrase he does use: she "could not be healed by anyone."

Furthermore, by mentioning physicians explicitly, Mark (and perhaps also Luke?) would be specifying the sector in which the woman might have placed the most confidence considering that that is where she exhausted her resources. Folk healers, after all, are not entirely "free" either (Press 1982:192–93). In the biblical world, a person involved in a healing transaction with anyone would be involved in a dyadic contract and would definitely owe the healer something (see 2.2.2 above). In the Gospels, rather than pay Jesus directly people give glory to God (e.g., 7:16; Malina 1981).

In summary, neither in the Gospel nor Acts is there any direct and explicit information about the professional sector of the health care sector. Yet the key word that belongs to that sector offers insight into the community's understanding of the role of a healer and the nature of illness.

In the Gospel, Jesus adopts the image of a healing prophet, or prophet-healer. A central function of his healing ministry is to lead those whose lives have lost cultural meaning back to the proper purpose and direction in life. That is, the prophet-healer preaches repentance, change of heart, transformation of horizons, broadening of perspectives.

3.2.2 *The Popular Sector.* The principal concern of the lay, non-professional, non-specialist popular culture is health and health maintenance, not sickness and cure. But obviously this focus on health sensitizes people to notice deviance from the culturally defined norm known as "health." Therefore, it is in this, the popular sector, that the deviant condition known as "sickness" is first observed, defined, and treated. There are several levels in the popular sector of the health care system: the individual, family, social network, and community beliefs and activities. Each level yields additional information about the entire system.

(a) At the level of *individual persons,* Luke–Acts reports twenty-three cases involving men and eight involving women. In the Gospel, *men* are afflicted in three symbolic body-zones (Malina 1979; 1981, more on the meaning of this in a subsequent section): mouth-ears (1:20, 64; 11:14–23; 22:47–54a); hands-feet (5:17–26; 6:6–11); heart-eyes (7:21; 18:35–43). People with skin problems (lepers, Pilch 1981) are cleansed (5:12–16; 17:11–19). Possessed individuals are freed (4:31–37; 8:26–34; 9:37–43a; 11:14–23). And dead or near dead are raised (7:1–10; 7:11–16).

The cases in Acts involving *men* reflect only two of the symbolic three body-zones: hands-feet (3:1–10; 9:32–35; 14:8–18; 28:1–6) and heart-eyes (9:18 //22:13; 13:1–12). Spirit-induced ills afflict Herod (12:13, stricken by an angel of the Lord, eaten by worms) and the sons of Sceva (19:14–16). There is one raising from the dead: 20:7–12.

Women in the Gospel reflect some distinctively feminine experiences such as difficulty in conception (1:24, 35) and menstrual irregularity (8:42b–48). One is raised from the dead (8:40–42a, 49–56); one cured of a fever (4:38–39); one is freed from a spirit of infirmity (13:10–17) and others from evil spirits (8:2). In Acts only two cases involving *women* are reported: Tabitha is raised from the dead (9:36–43) and a slave girl is released from bondage to an evil spirit (16:16–24).

At this point what does the health care system model reveal? Men and women are reported to suffer a variety of ills, some of which are experienced by both groups (death; possession of a spirit) and others which are experienced by each group singly (only men are reported with skin problems/leprosy), only women obviously suffer from distinctively feminine problems (difficulty in conception; menstruation).

Further, only men's ills seem to fit into one of the three identified symbolic body-zones. Curiously in the Gospel all three zones are affected while in Acts only two are affected. We shall need another model to interpret the significance of this observation and it will be presented and explained in section 4.0, discussing a taxonomy of illness. For women, what emerges from a bird's-eye view of Luke–Acts at this level of the health care system model is that specifically feminine ailments no longer plague women in Acts. As with the men, however, evil/unclean spirits still pose problems as also does Sister Death.

(b) Kinship is one of the two formal institutions in the biblical world, so it is no surprise that the *family—including fictive kin—* is involved and affected in many of the instances of illness reported in Luke–Acts. For example, the death of a son is tragic enough, but for a widow it is double jeopardy (7:11–16), since she relies on that male next-of-kin for her livelihood. Jesus effectively saved her life too by restoring her son to his life. Conversely, when Paul healed the slave girl with the spirit of divination (Acts 16:24), her masters felt adversely affected by her change of fortune. In all cultures, no sick person suffers alone; kin are always affected and involved in all the stages of the illness.

This level of the health care system model reminds the investigator to keep in mind that in the Mediterranean world ever more so than in the modern western world, illness affects and involves everyone in the kinship group. The consequences of healings therefore affect this wider group as well.

(c) Still another pathway for seeking help in an illness episode is the *social network*, that is, the set of contacts with relatives, friends, neighbors, etc., through which individuals maintain a social identity and receive emotional support, material aid, services and information, and develop new social contacts (Mitchell 1969; Weidman 1982).

One way in which "health" status is maintained and continually "checked" among the personalities who populate the pages of the Bible follows the normal pattern of dyadic relationships. Malina (1979) notes that in the Middle East persons are not viewed as individuals but rather as dyadic personalities; the same is true in the Far East (Ohnuki-Tierney 1984:67; Dumont 1970). Such a person lives in a continual dependence upon the opinions of others, including the judgment of whether or not one is ill.

According to Berkman (1981) networks can be classified into two major categories: (1) according to structure or morphology or (2) according to the type or quality of interaction. For example, consider Peter's and John's healing of the paralytic in Acts 3:1–4:22. The paralytic, who was more than 40 years old, was carried to the temple gate daily by "them," probably family, friends, or neighbors. This cripple from birth who begged here was known by many, some of whom may have been daily benefactors. Thus, in the crippled man's network, those who carried him maintained one kind of interaction probably rooted in *ḥesed* (a kinship virtue), whereas those who saw him begging and gave alms had another quality of interaction with him probably rooted in *zedekah* (Isa 56:1; Sir 3:29–4:10).

(d) Finally, the popular sector of the health care system is characterized by a distinctive set of *community beliefs and practices* (Gaines 1982:243–44). For example, belief in spirits and spirit-aggression including possession is found in all the Gospels but seems especially prominent in Luke. Murdock (1980:73) observes that such a belief is virtually universal and shows no tendency to cluster in a particular ideational region as do, for example, witchcraft theories. Evidence indicates that every society which depends primarily on animal husbandry for its economic livelihood regards spirit aggression as either the predominant or definitely an important secondary cause of illness. This is especially true where large domestic animals are the focus: camels, sheep, and goats.

Murdock conjectures that this phenomenon might possibly derive from the aleatory dimension of life because shepherd-types appear to be at greater risk than land-owner types. Shepherd-types deal with aggression all the time: they must protect themselves and their animals from aggression of other people and/or animals, and they must always be prepared to use aggression to ward off aggression. Of course, shepherd-types can also suffer from nature, and so they have to depend upon the protection and support of supernatural beings who hold mastery over nature.

As mentioned above, Luke's worldview lies heavily under the influences of spirits, demons, and the like. Jesus is conceived by the power of the Holy Spirit (1:35) and at his Baptism the Holy Spirit descends upon him in the form of a dove (3:21). Still full of the Holy Spirit and under his impulse, Jesus goes to the desert to do battle with the devil, a malicious spirit whom be bests (4:1–13). Then Jesus returns in the power of the Spirit to Galilee, teaches in synagogues, and one day reads the text of Isaiah that says: "The Spirit of the Lord is upon me . . ." (4:18). In the very next episodes, while teaching in the Capernaum synagogue Jesus frees a man from the unclean spirit that had possessed him (4:31–37) and then, following the interpretation of Hull (1974), Jesus frees Simon's mother-in-law from the demon "Fever" that had possessed her (4:38–39). The section ends with a summary statement that Jesus healed people sick with a variety of diseases and "demons also came out of many" (4:40–41). Finally, in a passage found only in Luke, Jesus asserts: "Behold I cast out demons and perform cures today and tomorrow" (13:32). He thus proclaims his identity as an exorcist. Recall the evidence from the professional sector above where Jesus is presented as a prophet who heals and exorcizes.

In addition to spirit-related illness episodes reported by other evangelists (4:33–37; 8:26–39; 9:37–43a, 49; 11:14–15, 24–26) Luke adds these reports: 10:17 (disciples against demons); 22:3 (Satan entered Judas); 22:31–34 (Satan wants to sift Simon); Acts 8:7 (Deacon Philip casts out unclean spirits); 12:23 (Herod afflicted by an angel of the Lord); 19:12 (Paul's power through handkerchiefs and cloths against evil spirits); 19:14–16 (sons of Sceva).

And in his descriptions of ailments afflicting women, the spirits are given a very prominent place in Luke's reports: Peter's mother-in-law is afflicted by a spirit named fever (4:38); among the women who follow Jesus, some were freed from evil spirits and infirmities (8:2–3); in the raising of Jairus' daughter, Luke notes: "her spirit returned and she got up at once" (8:58); the stooped-over woman had a spirit of infirmity (13:10) and was bound by Satan for 18 years (13:16); Paul liberates a woman possessed by a spirit of divination (Acts 16:16).

In summary, it should be obvious that in Luke's understanding and reports spirit-possession looms very large, and healers such as Jesus, Peter, Philip the Deacon, and Paul must be able to address this human ailment with some measure of success. Furthermore, the four levels operative in the popular sector of the health care system surface much information about illness (including the results of spirit-aggression) in the world of Luke–Acts as well as those who are afflicted by and involved with the illness (men and women; families; and social networks). The heuristic value of this part of the model seems apparent. But its inability to interpret all the information surfaced makes the investigator impatient to move on to another model, taxonomies of illness. Yet one more sector of the health care system model, the folk sector, awaits exploration before we can make that move.

3.2.3 The Folk Sector. In Luke's Gospel Jesus identifies himself as an authorized, spirit-filled prophet who vanquishes unclean spirits and illnesses associated with them. His constituency accepts and affirms this identity (Luke 7:16; 9:8, 19; 14:19). In addition, Jesus heals illnesses not associated with any spirit. As such, then, Luke's Jesus is a folk-healer, and his "license to practice" is tacitly granted and acknowledged by each individual sick person and the local community. Luke's report that some of the crowd doubted his abilities as a folk healer and questioned the source of his power (Luke 11:15; Matt 9:34) only highlights the limitations of a folk-healer's abilities. Indeed, some communities prefer that the folk-healer not practice in their midst (see Luke 8:37).

The power of Jesus relative to evil-spirits and demons, however, is noteworthy. Except for exorcisms, Jesus generally has no power at all in his social world (Malina 1986a:83). Power is the capacity to produce conformity based on what's necessary for the good of the group. And politics deals in part with how members of a group achieve and use power to implement public goals (Lewellen 1983:89).

Jesus' exorcisms, the instances in which he does have access to power, can from the definition of politics just given be identified as political actions performed for the purpose of restoring correct order to society. Since kinship and politics were the only two formal, that is, distinct and free-standing, social institutions that existed in the first-century Mediterranean world, the political dimensions of Jesus' healing activity would be self-evident to all witnesses, friendly and hostile alike.

Contemporary medical anthropology supports this insight. It views a theory of disease as a sign or emblem that marks what a group values, disvalues, and preoccupies itself with (Fabrega 1974:274). In Jesus' world, spirit-possession was a disvalued state, while the relationship of spirits to this world preoccupied him and his contemporaries.

Within this scheme, the healing enterprise is concerned with diagnosing the problem, prognosing outcomes, and applying suitable therapies. Another way of viewing this process is that the healing enterprise seeks to explain, predict, and control reality. In the Beelzebul episode (Luke 11:14–26), the problem diagnosed is a case of spirit-possession. The prognosis is that the cast-out spirit might return with seven more powerful demons to repossess the person. The therapy Jesus applied or the reality Jesus seeks to control is "he who is not with me is against me, who does not gather with me scatters" (11:23). Since Jesus has effective power against demons, he has the power to maintain order in society as it should be. By keeping demons in their place, Jesus maintains good order in society. He also controls reality as he and his contemporaries understood it. Anyone who would stand in the way of that power, challenge it, or obstruct it, stands in the way of the order that belongs in society.

Though folk healers in general vary widely from culture to culture and even within a culture from one another, some common characteristics can be observed across cultures (Press 1982).

(a) The folk healer shares significant elements of the constituency's world view and health concepts. All the Mediterranean contemporaries of Jesus and his followers believed in the reality of a spirit world that regularly meddled in human affairs. The reason why the spirit world might appear more evident or active in Luke than in the other evangelists is that his readers were probably more inclined to this way of perceiving and understanding.

(b) Folk healers accept *everything* that is presented (technically described as behavioral and somatic symptoms) as *naturally co-occurring elements of a syndrome.* The story of the gerasene demoniac (8:26–33) is a good example. That he wore no clothes and lived not in a house but among tombs are some of the behaviors which a modern Western diagnostician (other than a psychiatrist) would put aside to focus on the "real" problem, the "alleged" possession. The folk healer views everything as of equal importance. When Luke reports that the healed demoniac was now "clothed," it is not improbable to suspect that Jesus encouraged him to dress or at least made it possible for him to acknowledge what he ought to do about his appearance. Likewise, Jesus' final instruction "Return home" and tell what God did may also be part of the therapy instructing him on his proper residence: home and not among tombs.

(c) The majority of folk healers treat their *clients as "outpatients."* Amusing or silly as this self-evident statement might sound to the modern reader concerned with rising health care costs involved in episodes of hospitalization, it is a key element in the folk-healing process especially among Mediterranean peasants who are very public people (Hall 1983). Jesus and his healing disciples in Acts always have a crowd or an audience. It was difficult for Jesus to find an isolated place to rest and pray. The publicity involved in healing episodes is very likely bound up with the core values of Mediterranean culture, honor and shame. The folk healer is an honorable person but needs to enjoy continuing success to maintain honor. A crowd will always assure this honor because it witnesses the successful venture.

(d) Folk curers take *the patient's view of illness at face value.* In no instance did Jesus ever ignore or correct the "presenting symptoms" as communicated by the sick person or surrogate. Different cultures tend to emphasize one area of symptoms more than others. Modern Italians favor visceral symptoms in their reports, Irish favor throat-area symptoms (Press 1982:190). The pan-Mediterranean emphasis on visual dimensions of existence (Gilmore 1982:197) may explain the prevalence of a blindness and seeing concern in Luke–Acts.

(e) The *vocabulary* folk healers use to describe an illness is *invariably associated with the sick person's everyday experience and belief system.* The varied terms for malevolent spirits (unclean spirits, evil spirits, demons, etc.) quite likely reflect the lay perspective on this kind of illness which is rooted in the Mediterranean belief in spirits. Contemporary Western exegetes who seek to tally and distinguish the various kinds of spirits mentioned are likely expecting too much precision from first-century Mediterranean vocabulary.

(f) Since folk curers are native to the community and know well its mores, history, and scandals, they *make special use of the historical and social context of each illness.* Jesus taught in the synagogues (4:15) and many of his healings took place in that context or bore some relationship to the synagogue (4:33; 6:6; 7:1—centurion built the synagogue for us; 8:40 Jairus—chief of the synagogue; and 13:10). Through the social network of the synagogue and its informal communication system, the personal lives of those who attend would be known and disseminated. While the Gospel narratives often sound as if petitioners meet Jesus for the first time, it is highly probable that his visits and teaching activity in the various synagogues provided him with more than a passing acquaintance with many people in the area. They may even have been members of a far-flung personal kinship network involving actual and fictive kin of Jesus himself.

In conclusion, Luke's portrayal of Jesus as an anointed, spirit-filled, exorcising-and-healing prophet and the community's general acknowledgement and acceptance of him as such sets Jesus clearly in the folk-sector of the health care system reflected in Luke–Acts. The summary statements in Luke's Gospel repeatedly tell of the people who come to hear him teach, to be healed of ills, and purged of unclean spirits.

The health care system model, thus, with its three intersecting sectors not only helps us mine more information from the text than a cursory reading, but it also describes the context in which healers would function. Insights from the professional and the popular sectors flesh out the picture of Jesus' activity which is properly situated in the folk sector of that system. It is now time to focus more specifically on the misfortunes Jesus healed and try to build a taxonomy that would best account for those reported in Luke–Acts.

4.0 THE TAXONOMY OF ILLNESSES IN LUKE–ACTS

The identification, classification, and clustering of illnesses into culturally meaningful categories is called a taxonomy. In the modern, scientific, Western practice of medicine, a complete taxonomy of physical and mental health problems can be found in manuals of differential diagnosis. Your physician may have consulted such a book after listening to your report of a recent physical experience or set of experiences. The modern physician's challenge is to translate your "lay" report into appropriate professional jargon and then seek to locate your "real" problem on a grid or map of respiratory, circulatory, or other-system problems.

Historians of ancient medicine classify the works of some ancient writers as comparable to these modern manuals since they list, describe, and discuss the "health" problems known to them in their own culture.

Some writings of Hippocrates and Galen are often categorized in this way. Critics of this approach believe it to be medico-centric, that is, contemporary historians of medicine too often unwittingly impose modern scientific Western interpretations on these ancient texts.

Furthermore, some interpreters of biblical literature occasionally utilize such ancient Latin or Greek resources in analyzing biblical texts. This strategy produces mixed results precisely because of the potential interpretative hazards just mentioned. Biblical authors themselves do not appear to have had at hand any of these ancient resources, nor do they use the terminology utilized by those ancient authors. In fact, such ancient volumes may represent an elite understanding of human health misfortunes.

Biblical interpreters, therefore, fare better by taking seriously the reports of biblical authors and then resorting to both Mediterranean and medical anthropology for fresh insights to make sense of the admittedly meager data in biblical literature. Utilizing the tools of Mediterranean and medical anthropology, a biblical interpreter can construct a few different illness taxonomies from the data in Luke–Acts.

4.1 A Taxonomy Based on Spirit Involvement

The first taxonomy would embrace illnesses in which a spirit is involved. Modern readers of the Bible are struck by the frequent reports of spirit possession and illness associated with spirits. Recall the report above that Murdock (1980:73) noted that belief in spirits is practically universal and shows no tendency to emerge in a particular ideational region as do witchcraft theories. Recall also all the instances or spirit involvement in human affairs listed there (see 3.2.2.d above).

George Foster (1976) proposes a twofold taxonomy for illnesses in non-Western medical systems that would be based on whether or not spirits are involved. The insights of Murdock and Foster suggest that a spirit-focused taxonomy would fittingly address the New Testament data but with a major modification for "believers."

The New Testament associates some misfortunes with malevolent (unclean, evil, etc.) spirits. Presumably the other misfortunes are ascribed to God, as in the case of Elymas the magician (Acts 13:9–11). Thus Foster's taxonomy could be more appropriately modified to: (a) illnesses in which a malevolent spirit is involved and (b) illness in which no malevolent spirit is involved (though God is or might be so perceived).

Several times earlier, we have noted that illness is understood in terms of "misfortune." This concept is important here, because "fortune or "mis-fortune" in the world of Luke–Acts comes not from personal human activity but from the operation on humans by gods or spirits. This is a world in which the first question to be asked in the case of fortune or misfortune is "Who did this to me?" Hence, when we investigate a taxonomy of illness based on spirit involvement, we are tapping into a basic conception of the way the world works, namely, that a "spirit" (or god) has acted upon a mortal.

4.2 The Taxonomy Applied to Luke–Acts

As was observed above, Luke's world view is heavily influenced by the perception of the activity of good and bad spirits, demons, and the like. In fact, this feature is more prominent in Luke–Acts than in the other Gospels. The activity of the spirits and demons is especially linked to sickness and, moreover, Jesus "cures" those who are ill by means of the powerful, healing Spirit of God.

To grasp the importance of this for our study of illness and healing in Luke, we turn to a passage found only in Luke. Jesus asserts: "Behold I cast out demons and perform cures today and tomorrow" (13:32). Casting out demons is itself, not just another cure, but a way of describing the illness itself. By this association of the relationship of evil spirits and healing, Luke thus proclaims Jesus' identity as an exorcist. But "exorcist" is our term; Luke considers Jesus' exorcisms as the healing of illnesses.

Let us not understate the amount or importance of spirit-related illness in Luke–Acts. Luke, of course, received many stories from other Gospel traditions. For example, the other evangelists also report episodes of spirit-related illness:

(1) Luke 4:33–37 = Mark 1:21–28   (2) Luke 8:26–39 = Mark 5:1–20
(3) Luke 9:37–43a = Mark 9:33–37   (4) Luke 9:49 = Mark 9:38–41
(5) Luke 11:14–15 = Matt 9:32–34   (6) Luke 11:24–26 = Matt 12:43–45

In addition to these, Luke adds his own reports of the presence and activity of spirits, demons and Satan:

(1) in the Gospel of Luke: 10:17 (disciples against demons); 22:3 (Satan entered Judas); 22:31–34 (Satan wants to sift Simon)

(2) in Acts of the Apostles: 8:7 (Deacon Philip casts out unclean spirits); 12:23 (Herod afflicted by an angel of the Lord); 19:12 (Paul's power exerted through handkerchiefs and cloths against evil spirits); 19:14–16 (seven sons of Sceva try to exorcize in Jesus' name).

The malevolent presence of demons and unclean spirits in Luke–Acts is truly considerable.

In Luke's descriptions of ailments afflicting women, the spirit is given a very prominent place in Luke's reports. As noted above, Peter's mother-in-law is afflicted by a spirit named "Fever" (4:38); among the women who follow Jesus, some were freed from evil spirits and infirmities (8:2–3); in the raising of Jairus' daughter, Luke notes: "Her spirit returned and she got up at once" (8:58); the stooped-over woman had a spirit of infirmity (13:10) and was bound by Satan for 18 years (13:16).

And in Acts, Paul liberates a woman possessed by a spirit of divination (Acts 16:16). It should be obvious that in Luke's understanding and reports, spirit-possession looms very large, and healers such as Jesus, Peter, Philip the Deacon, and Paul are able to address this human ailment with some measure of success.

A review of the summary statements in Luke–Acts detailing illnesses and summarizing healings does indeed reveal that possessions or spirit-caused maladies are one category of illness: 4:40–41; 5:17; 6:18; 7:21, 22–23; 8:2–3; 9:1, 2, 10–11; 10:9, 17–20; 13:32; Acts 5:15–16 (Peter); 8:6–7 (Philip); 10:38 (Peter about Jesus); 19:11–12 (Paul). It is important to keep in mind that even though spirit-related ailments form one category of illness, that is, one taxonomy, each episode must be interpreted on its own merit, for each will be distinctively different (Good 1981).

4.3 A Taxonomy Based on Symbolic Body Zones Affected

In our quest to learn how Luke and other inhabitants of his world perceived illnesses, we inquired (see p. 194 above) about the parts of the body which tend to be afflicted with illness. Again, let us not impose our scientific, Western viewpoint of how the body is perceived, but strive to learn how ancients understand and describe the body.

Malina (1979; 1981:60–64) formulated and developed a pattern of personality perception quite easily discernible among the largely Semitic biblical authors. Human beings are perceived as socially embedded and interacting personalities reacting to persons and things outside them; in other words, they are not Western individualists. Biblical personalities, moreover, are not introspective and find it very difficult, if not impossible, to know what goes on inside themselves and others (1 Sam 16:7 "for the Lord sees not as human beings see; human beings look on the outward appearance, but the Lord looks on the heart").

This is a world where "hypocrisy" is considered a constant plague, with the consequence that people are actually deceiving others by hiding their inner, evil thoughts behind a facade of orthopraxis (Luke 6:42; 12:1, 56; 13:15). They are like actors (the literal meaning of the Greek word *hypokritēs*) who refuse to be their authentic selves but rather play another role. Yet some powerful, prophetic figures, such as Jesus, penetrate this facade. Consider the significance of Jesus' comment in Luke 5:22, "Why do you question in your hearts?" He could read human hearts; he was not deceived by appearances. This has implications for Jesus' healings, for he can discern what illness is within, and he can read hearts to know what spirit is present. Healing, then, may require a "physician" who can discern spirits and inner states, as well as apply correct healing technique.

More to the point, however, people in the Semitic world simply did not perceive human activity related to the same bodily organs which we do. In that culture, the individual person and the outside world with which that person interacts are described metaphorically by using parts of the human body as metaphors. In fact, this body is divided into three zones of organs and behavior.

> *Zone One*: Westerners associate thought with the brain, not so the people in Luke's world. Human beings have hearts for thinking together with eyes that collect data for the heart.

> *Zone Two*: Humans have mouths for communicating along with ears that collect the communications of others. This activity is very important in biblical culture and receives a considerable amount of attention (see Jas 3:1–12).

> *Zone Three*: They have hands and feet for acting or behaving.

To state this in another way, human beings consist of three mutually interpenetrating yet distinguishable symbolic zones for interacting with various environments: (1) the zone of emotion-fused thought (*heart-eyes*); (2) the zone of self-expressive speech (*mouth-ears*); and (3) the zone of purposeful action (*hands-feet*).

	Bodily parts	Functions
Zone One:	heart/eyes	emotion-fused thought
Zone Two:	mouth/ears	self-expressive speech
Zone Three:	hands/feet	purposeful action

According to Malina, these three zones describe human behavior throughout the Bible from Genesis to Revelation. He presents a rather comprehensive list of the vocabulary that pertains to or reflects each zone. It will be of considerable importance to us as we read the narrative of illness and healing in Luke–Acts to attend to what bodily parts are ill, whether eyes, ears or hands. For correct understanding of the symbolic significance of eyes, ears or hands may signal misfortune in regard to thought, speech or action. For a comprehensive list of this vocabulary, see Malina 1981:61–62.

This second taxonomy of illness based on symbolic body zones is able to cluster those reports in which specific parts of the body or their distinct activities are mentioned. Interpretation of the reports then hinges on noticing which zones are omitted, or which are healed, etc. Let us now apply this taxonomy to Luke's narrative.

4.4. The Taxonomy Applied to Luke–Acts

Our author reports thirty-one episodes of sick individuals involving twenty-three men and eight women, who are afflicted differently in terms of bodily zones. In the Gospel, men are afflicted in all three symbolic body-zones:

> 1. *Heart-eyes*: Of Jesus it is reported that "on many that were blind he bestowed sight" (7:21); a blind man near Jericho regains sight (18:35–43).

2. *Mouth-ears*: Zechariah, father of John the Baptist is stricken dumb then regains his speech (1:20, 64); Jesus casts out a demon who was dumb (11:14–23); the ear of the high priest's slave is amputated and then healed (22:47–54a).

3. *Hands-feet*: A paralytic is able to walk away healed in his feet and legs (5:17–26); a man in a synagogue with withered right hand is restored to wholeness (6:6–11); the dead or near dead are restored to life; they who could do no activity whatever are given back that potential (7:1–10, 11–16).

Affected in all three zones, men are totally unhealthy.

The cases in Acts involving men reflect only two of the three symbolic zones: (1) *Heart-eyes*: Ananias heals Paul's temporary blindness (9:18//22:13); Bar-Jesus, known also as Elymas, is made temporarily blind by Paul (13:1–12). (2) *Hands-feet*: Peter heals the man lame from birth at Beautiful Gate of the temple (3:1–10); Peter heals the eight-year bed-ridden paralytic Aeneas (9:32–35); Paul heals the born-paralytic at Lystra (14:8–18); Paul survives a lethal snake bite on the hand (28:1–6; see Luke 10:19).

Women in the Gospel reflect some distinctively feminine experiences such as difficulty in conception (1:24, Elizabeth; 1:34, Mary) and menstrual irregularity (8:42b-48). This would pertain to the *hand-feet* zone, the zone of purposeful activity, since child-bearing and child-rearing are activities (a hands-feet function in this schema) committed to women in this culture. One woman, Jairus' daughter, is raised from the dead (8:40–42a, 49–56) which also pertains to the hands-feet zone. The dead can perform no purposeful activity, only the living can do that. Peter's mother-in-law is freed from a demon named "Fever" (4:38–39) and immediately begins to serve them; this suggests that she, too, was affected in the hands-feet zone: lying in bed is to be deprived of foot and hand activity, being up and around as a woman ought. The bent women is freed from a spirit of infirmity (13:10–17) and is able to stand up straight again, suggesting yet another healing in the hands-feet zone. All of the women healed in Luke's Gospel, then, were healed in the symbolic bodily zone of *hands-feet*, the zone of purposeful activity.

There are but two healings of women in Acts, and they give no significantly different picture. First, Tabitha is raised from the dead (9:36–43, the hands-feet zone), and a slave girl who was a soothsayer is purged of the evil spirit who prompts her to speak in this way (16:16–24, the mouth-ears zone).

From this taxonomic description, we might draw some conclusions. The overall picture for men is that whereas in the Gospel they are ailing in all three symbolic zones, in Acts the mouth-ears (consider all those speeches!) are problem-free, but heart-eyes (understanding) and hands-feet (actually doing, missionizing) are still in the process of being healed.

For women, what emerges is that specifically feminine ailments no longer plague women in Acts as they did in the Gospel. But the symbolic zone of purposeful activity (hands-feet) continues to require healing or empowering. Recall how in the Gospel Elizabeth and Mary composed canticles of praise and gratitude, and other women in search of healing were able to approach and dialogue with Jesus. The mouth-ears zone which appeared "healthy" in the Gospel needs healing in Acts 16 because it has fallen under the domination of an evil spirit and is being exploited by men.

This latter observation suggests something known from studies on pain (see Pilch 1988a). Our biblical ancestors did not expect pain to be eliminated; it could only be alleviated. In a similar vein, healing was quite likely not expected to be "lasting." It is very possible that the ailment could return later. Certainly this is obvious in the story of the spirit cast out who would return with seven more at a later time. So it should not be surprising that Gospel women are quite wholesome in the mouth-ears zone, but at least one woman in Acts is presented as stricken in that very same zone and in need of healing. A reader needs to be constantly aware of the shifting context of each instance.

In the light of the reflections immediately preceding relative to the symbolic body-zones, there were instances where a spirit-related illness was interpreted by means of the symbolic body-zone taxonomy. This suggests that both taxonomies: the spirit-related taxonomy and the symbolic body-zone taxonomy could be collapsed into one. Then the unified taxonomy would have two sections which occasionally overlap. In this way, the dead could be considered as suffering from a hand-feet misfortune (as well as a mouth-ears and heart-eyes misfortune, since nothing works in death!).

Further, lepers or those afflicted with skin problems could also be considered as afflicted with a hands-feet illness since their malady excludes them from participating in the holy community, particularly at worship. Their "purposeful activity" which is what the hands-feet symbolic body zone highlights is severely limited. Indeed, the skin problem condition they called "leprosy" prevented them from performing the most purposeful activity known in their culture: joining the group in publicly acknowledging the One who has control over their existence.

In the final analysis, this holistic perspective on the illness category of human misfortunes in Luke–Acts prompts the observation that in the ministry of Jesus, all human beings are totally in need of God's redemption (all three zones), which redemption Jesus provides. When all zones are affected, this totality of zones correlates with the complete need of redemption. Persons totally dominated by Satan experience total powerlessness, and like people affected in all three zones are also in need of redemption or empowerment. In Acts, since redemption is at hand in the preaching of the gospel, zone two (mouth-ears) is trouble free, but the problems that remain are: (a) correct thought/understanding (heart-eyes, recall, Peter excuses the killing of Jesus as "ignorance," and

Paul explains the scriptures to people who don't understand (Acts 13); and (b) what a believer should do (hands-feet, i.e., one should walk like a Christian, be a follower of "the Way"). Even Acts 15 is a matter of doing. One important conclusion to be drawn from these efforts to "heal" the hands-feet symbolic body zone is to suggest that Christianity is now a halakah that replaced earlier halakah.

4.5 A Taxonomy Based on Purity and Impurity

Considering the difficulty which accompanies imagining skin problems (leprosy) as part of a taxonomy based on symbolic body zones, it is alternatively possible to construct a taxonomy of illnesses based on degrees of impurity (Malina 1981; Neyrey 1986b; Pilch 1981). Skin problems called "leprosy" affect the body's boundary and thus symbolize threats to purity or wholeness. People with skins problems are considered impure (Lev 13–14) because their body's boundary has been invaded and their presence in the community obviously violates the community's boundary. The presence of people with skin problems in the community makes it unclean, impure, and lacking in wholeness and holiness.

Men and women with uncontrolled or uncontrollable bodily effluvia (Lev 15) are also impure, as are people who come into contact with them. The woman with the uncontrollable hemorrhage (Luke 8:42b-48) who touched Jesus' garment in hope of healing was herself considered impure and by touching Jesus rendered him impure as well. Jesus remedied her condition and restored her to purity, wholeness, and holiness, but he obviously didn't consider himself adversely affected by her touch.

Similarly, people afflicted in one or another of the symbolic body zones can also be considered unwhole or impure because of their perceived lack of symbolic bodily integrity which also points to a deficiency in purity, wholeness, holiness. The same could be said for those possessed or affected in some way by a malevolent spirit. Thus, a taxonomy based on impurity could be another all-encompassing category for explaining the illnesses listed in the Gospels.

In each instance Jesus' therapeutic activity restores afflicted individuals to purity, to wholeness. The practical outcome is that such healed individuals are also restored to full and active membership in the holy community, the people of God. This taxonomy can be developed in greater detail in another article.

To summarize, at least three different taxonomies can be constructed that would facilitate the understanding of health-misfortunes reported in the Gospels to guide the interpretation of healings narrated. George Foster's taxonomy of illnesses based on the influence of a spirit or lack of such influence can be refined for interpreting biblical texts to include illness associated with a malevolent spirit and illnesses presumably attributable to God's will since God is ultimately responsible for everything that happens.

Another taxonomy can rightfully be based on the first-century Mediterranean tripartite understanding of symbolic body zones (hands-feet, heart-eyes, mouth-ears) that permeates the Bible from beginning to end. Many of the illness reported fit into such a taxonomy and significant interpretations emerge by observing which zones remain unaffected and which zones seem amenable to therapeutic activity.

Finally, perhaps the most comprehensive taxonomy is one based on different kinds of impurity. This one could easily subsume the other taxonomies. Given the penchant for first-century Mediterranean people to judge one another on the basis of externals, a pure or whole person is one quite visibly clean, pure, whole. Anyone with a skin lesion ("leprosy") is visibly unclean, unwhole, impure. An individual possessed or affected by a malevolent spirit is similarly impure, unclean, unwhole. Deficiencies in one or another of the three symbolic body zones are somewhat more difficult to judge hence impurity based on the alleged malfunctioning of these zones could be a matter of dispute. A more detailed analysis would have to be pursued.

4.6 Illness Taxonomies in Luke–Acts and the Cultural Value Preference for Being and Being-in-Becoming

Whatever taxonomy the investigator finally decides to construct, it will be important to remember that biblical people hold *being* as a primary value orientation (see above 2.2.2) and *being-in-becoming* as a close second choice. Being-in-becoming favors the development of all aspects of the self as an integrated whole. Integral harmony of the three symbolic body zones makes for a healthy and whole person. Ill people suffer a deficiency or malfunction in one or another of these zones. Ultimately, a sick person is restored to a proper state of being not to an ability to function.

But what of the hands-feet zone? Does it not bespeak activity, or *doing*? Certainly to some extent, but that is not the primary focus among first century-Mediterranean peasants. Healed paralytics in the Bible did not go job hunting the very next day. Healing was viewed as restoration to integrity and wholeness, not necessarily to function. The healed paralytic was a whole person again. (On the importance of "wholeness" as a major value in Luke's world, see Neyrey 1986a:142, 156–58). Restoring the dead to life was the restoration to a preferable state of *being* not a second chance at *doing*. A review of all the instances which are traditionally viewed as a restoration to *doing* can be better interpreted as the healing of the hands-feet zone and a restoration to a desirable state of *being* or *being-in-becoming*.

This important observation indicates that many of the healings or health concerns in the Bible refer to a state rather than a function. In this, Luke and his Mediterranean world are quite different from modern, individualistic Westerners. Only if one knows the cultural clues will a considerate reader understand that the lengthy discussion of "leprosy" in Lev 13–14 concerns not activities or the ability to function but rather a state of being. At stake there is a description of who is unworthy to be part of the holy community, to approach the Lord in the holy place (Lev 21:18). In this regard, the concerns are with states of being rather than functions. Persons who have a blemish, who are blind or lame, have a mutilated face or a limb too long, an injured foot or hand, a hunchback, a dwarf, a sight defect, an itching disease or scabs, or crushed testicles are certainly capable of "doing." But their specific condition describes a state of unwholeness, and thus they are not permitted to join in the social behavior of group worship of God. Again, the issue is one of a state of unworthiness not the loss of bodily activities. A Western observer whose culture favors *doing* over *being* would tend to interpret some of these handicaps as functional deficiencies. Such allegedly "disabled" individuals vigorously reject this judgment because in many instances they are able to function. Biblical people prefer to view these same conditions as deficiencies in *being* or *being-in-becoming*.

5.0 CONCLUSION

Drawing upon models and concepts from Mediterranean and medical anthropology helps an interpreter to be a respectful reader of biblical material like Luke–Acts. The Mediterranean cultural preference for being or being-in-becoming recommends a definition of health which emphasizes a state of wholesomeness. The biblical culture's acceptance of spirits as operative and interfering in human affairs validates a division of human ailments into those involving malevolent spirits and those attributable to the spirit known as God.

Biblical culture's view of the healthy and wholesome human being as composed of three balanced symbolic body zones helps identify and categorize the ailments suffered which were presented for healing. Another look at the same material from the perspective of purity, wholeness, cleanness and its opposites: impurity, uncleanness and unwholeness suggests perhaps the most comprehensive taxonomy of all: one based on purity concerns.

From the perspective of symbolic body zones, Luke appears to have singled out the heart-eyes zone as a leit-motif in Luke–Acts though the other dimensions also remain present. To my knowledge, these insights are unique contributions from the application of social-science models and concepts to the interpretation of biblical texts.

8 TEMPLE VERSUS HOUSEHOLD IN LUKE–ACTS: A CONTRAST IN SOCIAL INSTITUTIONS

John H. Elliott

0.0 INTRODUCTION

One of the most remarkable characteristics of Luke–Acts is the elaborate historical, geographical, and social concretization it gives to the good news concerning Jesus as savior of the last and the lowly, the emergent church, and the saving acts of God in human history. More detail on the persons, groups, institutions, places, dates, and events surrounding Jesus and the early Christian movement is contained here than in any other writing of the New Testament. The function of this detail, however, is not simply to provide a "realistic" background to an essentially independent message, but rather to give that message concrete content and shape in space and time and human interaction, for Luke writes both as historiographer and theologian. His theological aim is to convince his Christian audience of the certainty of the things they have been taught (Luke 1:1–4) so as to strengthen faith and commitment. His method for doing so is that of a historical and geographical profile, because for Luke the theologian God saves in and through human history and for Luke the historian the ultimate arbiter of truth is the historical and social record.

Among the means by which Luke has chosen to concretize the message and meaning of the good news is his depiction of the two basic institutions of Judaism and early Christianity, namely, the Jerusalem *temple* and the private *household* (*oikos, oikia*). Quantitatively, the Lukan references to these institutions outnumber those of any other New Testament writing. Qualitatively, as the use of common and special tradition, structural arrangement, and coordination of themes demonstrate, temple and household constitute key elements in Luke's Gospel of the reign of God in human history. Although this focus of Luke's work is generally recognized (Baltzer 1965; Bachmann 1980; Weinert 1981, 1982; Cassidy and Scharper 1983; Casalengo 1984; Koenig 1985; Esler 1987), far less attention has been given to what appears to be a deliberate contrast drawn between temple and household and the social and ideological ramifications of this contrast in the narrative of Luke–Acts. This essay, therefore, aims to investigate the contrast of two major institutions in Luke–Acts, the temple and the household. It seeks to determine the roles these contrasting institutions played in Luke's social concretization of the gospel.

1.0 INSTITUTIONS

The term "institution," of course, is not part of Luke's vocabulary or even of his thought-world. Like his ancient contemporaries, he spoke not of schematized wholes but rather of related parts: *temple* as a holy place of prayer and sacrifice, priests, rulers, law and lawyers, purity observance; and *household* as homes, family members, servants, friends, meals, hospitality, and domestic life. Luke the first-century historiographer, in other words, tells his story from a "native's" point of view or what is termed in anthropology the "emic" perspective. From an analytical, social-scientific point of view, or "etic" perspective, however, what Luke portrays are aspects of the two major institutions of first-century Palestinian society, the Jerusalem temple and the private household.

Institutions comprise social associations or processes which are highly organized, systematized in terms of roles, relationships, and responsibilities, and stable over time. As "institutions" in the formal sociological sense, the temple and the household entail not simply different spaces for worship or residence, respectively, but differently organized sectors and systems of social life. Therefore our investigation of the main Lukan material pertaining to the institutions of temple and household will include not only explicit terminological references to "temple" (*naos, oikos [tou theou], to hieron*) and "household" (*oikos, oikia*) but also their semantic fields and social domains. This comprises:

(a) all the connected groups, roles, structures, and patterns of behavior;

(b) norms, values and cultural symbols;

(c) economic, political, and ideological features which comprise their respective institutional character.

Such an inclusive body of data will provide a comprehensive basis for relating and analyzing the distinctive features of each institution and the implications of their contrast in Luke–Acts. The thesis advanced in this chapter is that in the Lukan economy of salvation, the temple system and the household represent opposed types of social institutions. Only one of them, the household, is capable of embodying socially and ideologically the structures, values, and goals of an inclusive gospel of universal salvation. By combining an analysis of the Lukan temple/ household contrast with aspects of previous exegetical research, and by filtering this data through the lens of an anthropological model of alternate types of ancient social relations, I intend to show its general function in the narrative: how this contrast coheres with dominant Lukan themes, how it advances Luke's conception of the gospel and depiction of Christian community, and why it made compelling sense in Luke's social context.

This study is a follow-up on some brief comments I made concerning the significance of the household in Luke–Acts in my earlier work, *A Home for the Homeless*. There, in a sketch of "the significance and function of the *household* in the Old and New Testaments" (1981:182–200), I observed that

> In Luke–Acts the household is prominently contrasted to the temple, the bankrupt seat of Jewish power and piety, and to the city, the area of "Caesar's network" and locus of social control . . . . For the Christians [of Luke–Acts] the *oikos* constitutes not simply an additional form of social identity and religious allegiance alongside others such as the temple, the synagogue or the city. The Christian oikos is rather a decisive alternative according to Luke. Membership in the former involves constant conflict with and critique of the latter (1981:193–94).

Expanding on these brief observations, I shall now turn to an examination of the complete Lukan narrative and the role of the temple/household contrast in particular.

2.0 TEMPLE AND HOUSEHOLD: ASPECTS OF CONTRAST

2.1 Temple and Household in Luke 18:9–14

The contrast between temple and household in the critical parable of the Pharisee and the Tax Collector (Luke 18:9–14) may serve as our point of departure. In this parable, intended by Luke as an indictment of those persuaded of their righteousness and despising of others (18:9), three contrasts are drawn between (a) the actors and their actions, (b) the content of their prayers, and (c) locale. *Actors:* The actors are key figures of the Lukan narrative; they represent throughout the Gospel those at the center and those on the periphery of Judaism's social and religious life. *Prayers:* The Pharisee, certain of his favor with God and his superiority over others like the tax collector, plies God in prayer with his punctilious piety (18:11–12). By contrast, the self-deprecating tax collector throws himself as a sinner fully on God's mercy (18:13). *Locale:* The upshot of the story (18:14) involves not only a contrast in Jesus' verdict between the tax collector who was justified by God and the Pharisee who was not, but also a shift in locale. "This man *went down to his house* (*oikos*) justified rather than the other" (18:14a). The story begins in the temple, the "Holy Place" (*to hieron*), which is the conventional place for demarcating social and religious differences; it concludes in the house (*oikos*) as the locus of the justified. The parable, then, functions in terms of three basic contrasts.

In the parable itself the contrast in locales at first glance appears of minor importance. The framing function, however, of *hieron* ("holy place," "temple") and *oikos* ("house") gives cause to pause. One commentator, in fact, maintains that:

> These descriptions of the "where" of human living, pointing to two different loci and thus to a spatial contradiction between "temple" and "house," *hieron* and *oikos*, seem to me to represent the primary dialectical contradiction in the story (Mottu 1974:199).

For Mottu, temple and household denote contrasting social spaces and contrasting forms of social life; the temple, an alienating form of collective, institutional life; the *house*, a creative form of integrative group life. He goes on to observe that:

> As long as the two antagonists look at the temple as their locus of reference, they stay in an alienated organization of space that makes human reality inhuman. The *skopos* (goal) of the story seems to me to be located in an invitation to change the rules of the common spatial game, to transform collectives into groups and to give a "house" to displaced persons. No conversion, no morals, no opposition of two "characters" is the *skopos*; but a shift of space, a structural change, a transformation of *where* people live is what we are invited to accomplish. The opposition between the Pharisee and the tax collector is only the secondary aspect of the dominant contradiction which is the spatial contradiction between temple and house, collective and group, alienated and human space (Mottu 1974:201–2).

Mottu expands on these observations from a phenomenological point of view informed by the work of John-Paul Sartre. He is expressly not concerned with correlating this text with the Lukan project as a whole (1974:197). Consequently, his thoroughly negative reading of the significance of temple in this parable lacks balance with the positive portrayal of the temple found earlier in Luke 1–2. He fails to capture "Luke's ambivalent attitude to the temple" (Esler 1987:133–35). Nevertheless, the dramatic contrast he notes between temple and household in this parable of special Lukan material appears to me worthy of further analysis in light of Luke's entire composition. Is more implied here than first meets the eye? Are temple and household contrasted elsewhere in the Lukan narrative? Does it appear that this contrast involves opposing forms of social organization, relations, and values? Do temple and household and their respective networks of relations depict in Luke–Acts contrasted styles of piety and behavior? A sustained examination of Luke–Acts indicates that such, indeed, appears to be the case.

2.2 Temple and Household in the General Structure of Luke–Acts

Two structural features of Luke–Acts indicate that the contrast between temple and household in Luke 18:9–14 is neither accidental nor singular. First, as has long been recognized, it is with scenes in the temple that the first half of the Lukan two-volume work begins and ends. Commencing with the story of Zechariah's priestly service in the temple and the angelic announcement of his son's birth (1:5–23), the Gospel concludes with the disciples' parting with the risen Lord and return to Jerusalem where they were "continually in the temple blessing God" (24:50–53). Temple scenes thus provide a grand framework or *inclusio* for the first half of Luke–Acts.

It is likewise the case, moreover, that as temple scenes frame the first half of the Luke–Acts, scenes in the household frame the second half. Commencing with the gathering of the faithful in the house with the upper room after the Lord's ascension (Acts 1:12–14), Acts concludes with Paul's house confinement in Rome and his unhindered proclamation of the gospel (28:30–31). Once again, but on a grander scale, the scene shifts from temple to household.

A second structural indication of this contrast is evident in the early narrative of Acts. Within the first eight chapters the scene shifts with regularity between the *household*, where the believers assemble, pray, receive the Spirit, break bread and generously share all things in common, and the *temple* as the center of political and religious control, a place for seeking alms, and the scene and object of conflict (arrest and imprisonment, critique of temple rulers, mob violence, beating, and death):

Consistent Shifts of Locale:
House – Acts 1:13–2:45; 4:23–5:11; 6:1–7; 8:4ff.
Temple – Acts 3:1–4:22; 5:12–40; 6:8–8:3

This pattern of alternating scenes clearly demarcates two areas of action and two differentiated communities, their variant forms of social and economic organization, and their ultimately contrasting loyalties. The one represents temple rule, norms and allegiance; the other, a new community of witnesses to the resurrected Christ based in the household, inspired by the divine Spirit and loyal to the God who does not dwell in man-made houses or temples (Casalengo 1984:146–47, 196–97).

In these early chapters of Acts, the temple is both the scene and the subject of conflict. An instance of almseeking and healing at the temple (3:1–4:22) becomes an occasion for distinguishing between those who take and those who give life, those who killed the "Author of life" (3:15) and those who heal in his name (3:16). Temple authorities (priests, temple captain, and Sadducees, 4:1; rulers, elders, scribes, high priests and family, 4:5–6, 5:17; Sanhedrin, 4:5–6, 15; 5:21, 27; 6:12–15) in their jealousy (5:17) and opposition to the apostles' teaching (4:2; 5:18, 27–28; 6:57), and their actions of arrest, imprisonment, beating, and killing (4:3; 5:18, 40; 6:57–58), defend monopolistic temple interests by seeking to suppress the joyous community which gives health (3:1–10; 5:16), celebrates the covenant of Abraham given through God's resurrected servant to "all the families of the earth" (3:25–26), praises God (4:24–30), and is filled with the Spirit (4:8; 5:21; 7:55).

For Stephen, who was charged with speaking "words against this holy place and the law" (6:13–14), death is the result of his verdict both on the temple as the house of Solomon but not the dwelling place of God and on its functionaries as the murderers of the Righteous One (7:46–58). In the only other set of references to the Jerusalem temple in Acts, Paul's temple visit and the plot against his life (21:26–36 and Paul's defense in Acts 22–26), the temple is portrayed similarly as the scene of assassination conspiracy, conflict over purity, and political collusion (temple authorities and Romans). After Stephen's death, the persecution of the Jerusalem church, and the church's dispersion (8:1ff), it is the household, on the other hand, which becomes the basis of the church's life and the focus of its mission.

Throughout Luke–Acts a transition thus becomes apparent in regard to temple and household. In Luke the Jerusalem temple marks a structural frame (Luke 1–2; 24:52–53) and focus (9:51: "he set his face to go to Jerusalem"; cf. 13:22; 17:11; 18:31; 19:28) to Jesus' life's journey. Household visits and instruction (7:1–10, 36–50; 8:40–56; 10:38–42; 12:13–53; 13:18–30; 14:1–24; 16:1–17:10; 18:18–34; 19:1–10) frequently provide the positive contrast to the negative climax of confrontation and death in Jerusalem.

In Acts the household becomes increasingly prominent as the scene and focus of the Christian movement which gradually shifts from Jerusalem and the temple to the households of the diaspora. At first the messianic community gathers both at the temple and in households (2:43–47; 5:42). But the attempt at peaceful coexistence fails. Agents of the temple become the hunters and followers of Jesus, the hunted. Stephen's speech and his stoning in connection with remarks concerning the temple form a turning point between the earliest phase of the church's life and its connection with the temple (Acts 1:1–8:1a) and its full-scale mission to the households of the diaspora (8:1b–28:31). In the remainder of Luke's account, the temple plays no positive role as a place of Christian assembly or symbol of Christian identity. Along with the synagogue, which represents the extension of temple authority and values, the temple reckons only negatively as a locale of Jewish-Christian conflict over purity and its implications for the course of universal salvation. By contrast, the story of the Jesus movement concentrates positively on the household as the focus of the movement's recruitment, the locus of its assembly, worship, and mutual support, and the basis for the social embodiment of its evangelical message.

In sum, the juxtaposition of scenes in Acts 1–8 and the inclusive framework of Luke (temple) compared with its counterpart in Acts (household) suggest a purposeful contrast of locales, groups, and institutions within a historical and theological movement commencing with the temple and concluding with the household.

These larger patterns of contrast in the Lukan narrative appear consistent with the contrast drawn between temple and household in Luke 18:9–14. The temple and the household constitute not simply different sites of activity but bases of different and conflicting groups of actors with differing and conflicting sets of interests and allegiances. From commencement to close of the Lukan narrative, moreover, it is the household which gradually replaces the temple as the actual sphere of God's saving presence. The temple, at first the locale of hoped for salvation and symbol of Israel's holy union with God, eventually is unmasked as the political concentration of power opposed to God's people and the truly righteous. The household, on the other hand, once the gathering place of the powerless and the marginalized, eventually emerges as the institution where God's spirit is truly active and where familial relations, shared resources, and communal values concretize the vision of a salvation available to all the families of the earth.

This general picture gained from initial structural observations now needs filling in with more specific detail. How are both the temple and the household depicted in Luke–Acts? By what terms and semantic fields (i.e., related terms encompassing a specific area of cultural experience; Nida 1975) are they identified and evaluated? What domains of social (economic, political, religious-ideological) experience do they represent? What agents, interest groups, activities, attitudes, expectations, norms, goals, and values do they embrace? What, in other words, are their specific institutional features as presented in Luke–Acts, and how does their contrast serve to concretize Luke's particular conception of the good news? A survey of the more salient features of both temple and household in the Lukan narrative will indicate both the major importance ascribed to each and the chief aspects of their contrast as alternative forms of social organization, identity, and commitment.

3.0 THE TEMPLE IN LUKE-ACTS

3.1 Temple Terminology, Semantic Field, and Scenes

In Luke-Acts three Greek expressions are used to designate the Jerusalem temple: *naos* ("temple"), *oikos* (*tou theou*) ("house [of God]"), and *to hieron* ("the holy place").

(a) *Naos* ("temple") occurs four times in Luke, thrice identifying the scene of Zechariah's priestly activity (1:9, 21, 22), and once in a reference to the rending of the temple curtain at Jesus' death (23:45; cf. Matt 27:51 and Mark 15:38). In Acts the term designates pagan "temples" (17:24) or miniature silver replicas of the Artemis temple of Ephesus (19:24).

(b) *Oikos [tou Theou]* ("house [of God]") is a second term for the Jerusalem temple. It appears four times in Luke and once in Acts, all in contexts of conflict or censure. In conflict with the Pharisees over the sanctity of the sabbath rest, Jesus defends his disciples' plucking and eating grain with an appeal to David's entering the house of God and eating the bread of the Presence, a privilege reserved only to priests (Luke 6:4). In censure of the lawyers (and Pharisees) for burdening people with the law but not aiding their entrance into the kingdom (11:45-52) and for consenting with the murderous deeds of their fathers, Jesus refers to the shed blood of the prophets, including that of Zechariah who perished between the altar and the "sanctuary" (RSV; *oikos*, 11:51). In 13:35, Jesus' word of judgment, "Behold, your house (*oikos*) is forsaken," is ambiguous, referring either to the temple in particular or to Jerusalem (cf. 13:34 and Weinert, 1982). Both are interchangeable as symbols of a condemned Israel. Finally, Jesus condemns the temple merchants with the words: "It is written, 'My house (*oikos*) shall be a house (*oikos*) of prayer;' but you have made it a den of robbers" (19:45-46). In Acts, Stephen affirms that God "does not dwell in houses made with hands" (Isa 66:1-2). He contests God's dwelling in the house (*oikos*) built by Solomon (7:47-50).

(c) The substantive *to hieron* ("the holy place"), however, is used fourteen times in Luke and twenty-four times in Acts. This constitutes more citations than in the rest of the New Testament writings combined. It is, moreover, the predominant Lukan term for designating the Jerusalem temple, including its buildings, precincts, and courts, as "the sanctuary" or "holy place." For Judaism, the temple as Israel's central holy place represented the chief visible symbol of its identity as God's holy people. The holiness of its space, its personnel (priests [*hiereis*] = "holy functionaries"; chief priests [*archiereis*]; Levites), its sacrifices, and the laws of holiness it enforced symbolized a holy people's union with the Holy One of Israel. This link between the holy place and the holy people and their demarcation from all that was unholy was derived from the Torah; and it was elaborated, maintained, and legitimated in an ideology and system of holiness which defined Jewish identity and regulated all aspects of Jewish life. Where temple and Torah are involved in Luke's narrative, therefore, crucial issues regarding norms of holy behavior and social interaction, and the boundaries of God's holy people are at stake.

From surveying temple terminology, we turn to scenes which take place in the temple. In Luke, the temple as holy place is first the scene of the initial events of the Gospel narrative: Jesus' presentation, Mary's purification (in accord with Torah), Simeon's and Anna's blessing of the child, and, years later, of Jesus' discussion with teachers after the occasion of a Passover pilgrimage (2:22–51). Initially, the temple is the place where Jesus' fidelity to the Law, his role as agent of divine salvation, redemption and mercy, and his wisdom are manifested.

With the commencement of his public ministry, however, the temple scenes in Luke–Acts take on a more ominous hue. In Luke's redaction of the temptation account, it is Jesus' confrontation with devil at the temple which forms the climactic conclusion of the episode (4:9–13; cf. Matt 4:5–7). In the parable of the Pharisee and the tax collector (18:9–14), the holy place as a scene of alienation between the holy Pharisee and the unholy tax collector is contrasted to the household of the justified sinner. Upon his arrival in Jerusalem, that ominous moment long anticipated in the narrative (9:30–31, 51; 13:22; 17:11; 18:31–34), it is the holy place and the holy city which form the combined object of Jesus' passionate condemnation (19:41–44, 45–46; cf. 13:33–35). Thereafter, the temple reckons primarily as the arena of Jesus' conflict with the temple's chief and related legal authorities (e.g., chief priests, Sadducees, scribes, elders; Sanhedrin) and their conspiracy with the Roman governor to take his life (19:45–47; 20:1–22:6; 22:47–23:25).

At the conclusion of Luke (24:52–53), as at the outset of Acts (2:46; 3:1; 5:12, 20, 42), the disciples worship or teach in the temple. But the holy place continues as an arena of conflict (Acts 3:1–4:22; 5:12–42). For Paul, as for Jesus, despite his conformity to the law (Acts 21:17–26) the holy place and the holy city remain the locale of hostility, political collusion, and conspiracy against innocent life (21:27–26:32).

This review of explicit temple scenes also exposes elements of the semantic field associated with temple in Luke–Acts. This wider semantic field reflects a set of terms related to a specific area of cultural life (Nida 1975:22), in this case the social domain of the Jerusalem temple. It provides a broader picture of the features associated with the temple in the Lukan narrative. Sacrifice, prayer, praise, revelation, hope of salvation, tithing, and legal observance are all activities associated with the temple. But so is priestly political power, economic disparities, scribal arrogance, exploitation of the poor, conflict of Jesus and his followers with temple authority, their critique of the temple establishment, death plots, and unjust executions. The temple and Jerusalem, the Holy Place and the Holy City, constitute for Luke the dominating public center of Jewish society and a web of social relations within which the Jesus movement was born but with which it also came into irremediable conflict. The Holy Place and the holiness ideology it embodies eventually emerge in Luke–Acts as an entire system at odds with the will of God and the realization of salvation.

3.2 The Temple Network in Luke–Acts

In Luke–Acts various interrelated groups of the temple network are depicted as playing key roles in the opposition to Jesus and his followers: chief priests and minor clergy, scribes, elders, Sanhedrin, Sadducees and Pharisees.

(a) At the pinnacle of the temple hierarchy were the *chief priests* (*archiereis*). Allied with the *Sadducean* faction (Acts 5:17), and controlled by the Roman governor, this priestly aristocracy represented the power of the temple over all aspects of Jewish political, economic, social, and cultural life. With the *scribes-lawyers* and *elders* (the landed, lay aristocracy), they also constituted the *Sanhedrin*, the "supreme court" of the Jews. In Luke–Acts, as in the other Gospels, it is these wielders of Judaism's unified political, economic, legal, and religious power who play the decisive role in the conflict involving the Jesus movement. The *temple police* (*strategoi*, only in Luke–Acts) exercise the coercive power of the holy place (Luke 22:4, 52; Acts 4:1; 5:2, 24, 26). The chief priests, together with the scribes and elders and in collusion with Rome (Luke 23:1–25; Acts 24–26), conspire with an agent of Satan (Judas Iscariot, Luke 22:3) to kill Jesus (Luke 9:22; 19:27; 20:1, 19; 22:2, 4, 52, 66; 23:10, 13; 24:20) and suppress his movement (Acts 4:5, 23; 5:27; 6:12–15; 9:1, 14; 22:30–26:32).

(b) *Scribes* are not cultic officials but rather official interpreters of the Mosaic law (Torah). They constituted a further arm of the temple apparatus described by Luke. As noted, they held a key position in the Sanhedrin and, like the faction of the Pharisees, represented the link between temple authority and Torah observance. In Luke's account, it is these scribal temple and Torah authorities who embodied the injustice and oppression of the temple as an economic institution. The *Pharisees* were condemned by Jesus as "lovers of money" (16:14) and "extortionists" (11:42; cf. also 11:37–44; 12:1; 15:1–31; 16:14–15; 18:9–14); likewise the *temple merchants* were accused of making the house of God "a den of thieves" (19:45–47). Similarly, the scribes are censured for seeking public honor in the synagogues, while they secretly "devour widows' houses" (20:47). Jesus' exposure of their machinations (cf. also 20:1–26) attacks the economic as well as religious corruption of temple politics. He condemns a system organized not for prayer, justice, and mercy but for self-aggrandizement and exploitation. Accordingly, in Luke–Acts, the scribes also play a major role in the plot against Jesus and his followers (Luke 11:54; 19:47; 20:19; 22:2, 66; 23:10; Acts 4:5; 6:12; 22:30–23:15).

(c) Other temple personnel, ordinary priests (hiereis: Luke 1:5; 5:14; 6:4; 10:31; 17:14; Acts 4:1; 6:7) and a Levite (Luke 10:31) represent, with the lay faction of the Pharisees, a further key aspect of the temple network as seen in Luke–Acts. This concerns the fundamental conception of the temple as the "holy place" where holy priestly personnel served (e.g., Luke 1:8). Here also purification was effected (Luke 2:22) and certified in accord with Torah (Luke 5:14; 17:14; Lev. 13–14), and all matters regarding the "holiness" = "purity" = "cleanness" of the Jewish people were regulated. The Pharisees, who enforced temple purity regulations still more rigorously, had extended the norms of temple and priestly holiness to the bed and board of every observant Jewish home. In Luke–Acts this purity system, symbolized by the temple and controlled by the temple establishment, becomes a major point of controversy and contrast concerning the praxis of the temple guardians and that of Jesus and his followers. In order to grasp the implications of this conflict over purity, it is necessary to see how Judaism's purity system functioned from a social scientific point of view.

3.3 The Temple Purity System

As Malina (1981:122–52) and Neyrey (1986b:91–128; cf. Neusner 1973) have shown, the temple purity system established and controlled the social identity, social classifications, and social boundaries of the Jewish people as the holy people of God. As Neyrey noted in his essay in this volume on the symbolic universe of Israel, Israel's land and places (m. Kelim 1.6–9), classes of persons (t. Megillah 2.7), holy times (m. Moed), and unholy physical "uncleannesses" (m. Kelim 1.3) were all classified and ranked according to degrees of purity or impurity. This system established the structure and social stratification of the Jewish community (Jeremias 1969:271–358), the norms of public and private behavior, and the lines of demarcation between holy Israelites and those at or beyond the margins of God's holy people (i.e., physical or social deviants, Samaritans, and Gentiles).

This organization of society along purity lines called for a careful avoidance of contact with all that was judged impure or unholy (sinners, lepers, blind, lame, menstruants, corpses, toll collectors, Samaritans, Gentiles) and proper respect for holy places (temple, synagogue), holy persons (temple personnel), acts of purification (hand washing before meals) and holy times (sabbath, festivals). According to this system of economic and social stratification legitimated by purity classifications, the rich were ranked above the poor, the clergy above the laity, urban dwellers (especially in Jerusalem) above the rural peasantry (especially in distant Galilee), men above women, married above unmarried, healthy above the ill, conformists above deviants.

According to Luke, as well as the other Evangelists, it was this system of purity and the exclusivity and injustice that it fostered which Jesus challenged (Borg 1984). This challenge, so wide-reaching in its political and social ramifications, inevitably led to conflict, death, and social division.

The picture Luke paints of Jesus' attitude toward purity norms is a complex one. On the one hand, Jesus, his family, and followers respected the holiness of the temple as a house of prayer (Luke 19:46; Acts 3:1), a place of purification (Luke 2:22; 5:14; 17:14), pilgrimage (Luke 2:41; 9:51), and festivals (Luke 22:7; Acts 2:1; 20:16). Likewise, the synagogue is acknowledged as a place of teaching and hearing (Luke 4:16–30; Acts 13:5 etc.). On the other hand, the ministry of Jesus and his movement also is marked by what is perceived to be a flagrant disregard of the purity norms concerning persons, behavior, times and places.

If a catalogue were made of the perceived violations by Jesus of the purity system of his day, it would include the following:

A. Jesus and his followers regularly associate with and frequently "cleanse"/"sanctify" unholy persons:

—the physically unclean (lepers: Luke 5:12–15; 7:22; 17:11–19, cf. 4:27; cripples: Luke 5:17–26; Acts 3:1–10; 9:32–34; menstruants: Luke 8:42–48; the blind: Luke 7:21, cf. 4:18; the sick: Luke 4:38–40; Acts 5:15–16; a eunuch: Acts 8:26–39; the demon possessed: Luke 4:31–37; 8:26–39; Acts 16:16–18; the dead: Luke 7:11–17; 8:49–56; Acts 9:36–41; 20:9–10.

—"sinners": Luke 5:8–10, 30; 7:34, 37–39; 15:1–2.

—tax/toll collectors: Luke 5:27–32; 7:29, 34; 15:1–2; 18:9–14; 19:1–10; cf. 18:9–14.

—Samaritans: 9:52; 17:11–19; Acts 8; cf. Luke 10:29–37.

—Gentiles: Luke 4:26–27; 7:1–10; 8:26; 24:27; Acts 1:8; 10:1–11:18; cf. 15:6–20; 28:28.

B. They also disregard the purity lines drawn around holy behavior:

—by eating common food with common people (Luke 9:10–17) and specifically unclean persons: Luke 5:27–31; 7:34; 15:1–2; 19:7; Acts 10–11.

—by neglecting cleansing rituals: Luke 11:37

—by disregarding dietary regulations: Luke 10:7–8; Acts 10–11.

—by touching unclean bodies: corpses (Luke 7:14, 8:54; Acts 9:40–41; 20:10); lepers (Luke 5:13); menstruants (Luke 8:44); and the tears, hair, and lips of a sinful woman (Luke 7:38).

C. *Holy times* are also violated:

- no strict sabbath observance (Luke 6:1–5, 6–11; 13:10–16)
- no fasting days (Luke 5:33–34; see criticism of fasting in Luke 18:12).

D. Finally, *holy places and personnel* are criticized and disrespected:

- critical remarks against the temple and its network: the temple (Luke 19:45–47; 21:6; Acts 6:14; 7:48–50); the chief priests, scribes, and elders (Luke 9:22; 20:9–20; 22:50–53, 67–71; Acts 4:8–12; 5:29–32; 7:51–53); priest and Levite (Luke 10:29–37); scribes (Luke 11:45–52; 15:1–32; 20:45–47); Sadducees (Acts 4:8–12; 23:6–9; cf. Luke 20:27–40); Pharisees (Luke 7:36–50; 11:37–44; 12:1–3; 14:1–24; 15:1–32; 16:14–15; 18:9–14; cf. 5:17–26; 6:1–5, 6–11, 39–42; 12:56; 13:10–17).

- critical remarks against the Holy City of Jerusalem: Luke 13:33–35; 19:41–44; 21:20–24.

- disregard for the limits of the Holy Land and the Holy People of Judaism: Jesus' commission to his followers to leave the Land "for the ends of the world" (Acts 1:8) and "to preach in his name to all nations (Gentiles)" (Luke 24:47; cf. Acts 28:29).

Consequently, the incriminating charge of defilement levelled against Jesus and his company becomes a global one. Jesus is accused of "perverting our nation" (Luke 23:2, 14); Stephen is charged with speaking "blasphemous words against Moses and God, . . . this Holy Place and the Law . . . claiming that this Jesus of Nazareth will destroy this place and will change the customs which Moses delivered to us" (Acts 6:11–14). And Paul is denounced as "teaching men everywhere against the people and the law and this place" and by, bringing Greeks into the temple, "defiling this Holy Place" (Acts 21:28). This process of labelling Jesus and his followers as anti-temple and anti-system agitators has been dealt with at greater length in the essay in this book by Malina and Neyrey (see also Malina and Neyrey 1988:86–88).

3.4 The Temple Institution in Luke–Acts: A Summary

In the Lukan narrative the temple gradually emerges as an institution whose managers, interests, and ideology stand diametrically opposed to the ministry and mission of Jesus and his community. The temple was no mere building but a structure symbolic of Jewish national identity, constituted by Torah and an elaborate purity system. Yet the temple was for Luke a holy place which had lost its power to make holy, that is, to bring all who were unholy into communion with the Holy One. Through its collusion with Rome and its oppression and exploitation of its own people, this center of Jewish political, economic, and social power was once, but is no longer the place where the hope of the world's salvation and the universal experience of God's mercy could be realized.

Temple functionaries and other agencies of the temple network appear guided by their own self-interests in preserving an exploitative regime in which the mighty remain in their seats, and nothing but disdain and neglect are shown those of low degree. For all those outside the holy boundaries of Israel, the physical limits of the Holy Place and the social restrictions of its purity system effectively prohibited the access of all to sanctification, health, and salvation. Within the borders of Israel demarcated by the purity system, the economic power of the temple from taxes, tithes, sacrifices, and offerings was used to promote the programs of the powerful at the expense of the powerless. Priest and Levite protected their purity rather than extended mercy (Luke 10:31–32). Scribes devoured widows' houses (20:46–47), Pharisees paid tithes but neglected justice and mercy (11:42); chief priests and Sanhedrin conspired to condemn the critics and eradicate the agents of change (Luke 22:2; Acts 4:1–22; 5:17–18).

According to Luke–Acts, the call to repentance was met with the plot to remove the heralds and prophets of repentance. Efforts to redefine the purity which God requires and consequently the behavioral norms and social identity of God's holy people were denounced as plots to pervert the nation and its sacred customs. Reform program was countered by death plot, critique by condemnation.

We have considered all the related aspects of the temple as a comprehensive social institution, its political, economic, social, and cultural dimensions, and its accompanying purity ideology. This has provided us with a full picture of the temple system as portrayed and evaluated by Luke. Such a scenario is indispensable for an adequate and considerate reading of Luke–Acts. Failure to take into account this full range of data can lead only to unbalanced and inaccurate conclusions. Thus Weinert's contention (1981) that "Luke avoids any polemic against the temple" appears wide of the mark. Weinert isolates references to the temple from those concerning temple authorities and their unjust programs (see Cassidy 1983 and Tannehill 1986:169–99); he understates Jesus' and Stephen's critique of the Holy Place and its management, and ignores the negative implications of the temple's purity system altogether. This survey, moreover, has revealed what for Luke are those key issues over which the Jesus movement and temple establishment collided. Finally, this analysis has highlighted salient features of a political institution, the temple, with which another form of institution based on kinship, namely the household, can profitably be compared.

4.0 THE HOUSEHOLD IN LUKE–ACTS

As we have seen, Luke negatively portrays a society demarcated by these bonds and boundaries of social identity and a temple administration intent on the elimination of temple critics and purity violators. Over against this, Luke sees a community in solidarity with Jesus and the righteous victims of temple "justice." This community is organized not around the temple but around the household. It is bound by an ethos of mercy and justice and a vision of universal salvation.

4.1 Household Terminology, Semantic Field and Significance

In Luke–Acts the "house" (*oikia*) and "household" (*oikos*) comprise family and kin, personnel and property. They play a prominent, if not dominant, role in the narrative. The term *oikia* appears twenty-five times in Luke and twelve times in Acts; *oikos*, thirty-four times in Luke and twenty-five times in Acts. These references to domestic residences and communities are joined by numerous related terms of the *oik*-root.

(a) One stem refers to household managers and management: *oikodomos* = builder; *oikodomein* = to build; *oikonomein* = to manage; *oikonomia* = management; *oikonomos* = manager; *oiketēs* = household servants.

(b) Another stem of the *oik*- root refers to further aspects and conditions of habitation: *katoikein* = to dwell; *katoikia* = dwelling place; *metoikizein* = to removed to another place of habitation; *oikema* = room, apartment; *panoikia* = whole household; *paroikein* = to inhabit as an alien; *paroikos* = alien; *perioikein* = to live in the neighborhood of; *perioikos* = neighborhood.

The range of this terminology alone already gives a strong impression of the importance which domestic conditions and relations play in Luke's social concretization of the gospel.

More than any other writing of the New Testament, Luke–Acts makes clear the fundamental role which private houses and households played in the spread of the Jesus movement, the domestic form of organization it assumed, and the social relations and values it fostered. In contrast to the temple, which is the place of hostility and the focus of critique, the household represents in Luke–Acts the favored setting of the teaching and healing ministry of Jesus and his followers. It is the typical location of the gospel's reception and the church's growth. Moreover, characteristic features of domestic life illustrate in the Lukan narrative notable aspects of Christian values and social relations rooted in the institution of kinship: solidarity, loyalty, trust, mutuality of obligations, generosity, sharing, and the like.

4.2 Household Settings

Houses, homes, and households provide in Luke–Acts the setting for a wide range of events in the life of Jesus and his followers:

—the proclamation of the gospel, the experience of forgiveness of sins, salvation and the presence of the Spirit: Luke 1:39–56; 5:17–26; 7:36–50; 8:38–

39, 49–56; 9:4; 10:5–7; 12:3; 15:11–32; 18:14; 19:1–10; Acts 2:1–42; 5:42; 10:1–48; 11:14–15; 16:25–34; 18:7–8; 22:16

— teaching: Luke 7:36–50; 10:38–42; 11:37–52; 14:1–24; 22:24–38; Acts 2:42; 5:42; 18:11; 20:7–12, 20; 28:30–31.

— healing: Luke 4:38–41; 5:18–26; 7:1–10; 8:4–56; Acts 9:10–19, 32–35, 36–43; 20:7–12; 28:7–10.

— prophecy: Acts 2:1–21; 21:8–14.

— revelations and visions: Luke 1:26–38; 24:28–35; Acts 1:13–26; 9:10–19; 10:1–8, 9–23; 11:13–14; 13:2; 18:7–10.

— recognition of the resurrected Christ: Luke 24:28–32.

— redefining the family of Jesus: Luke 8:19–21.

— hospitality and lodging: Luke 19:1–10; Acts 9:10–19, 43; 10:6; 12:12–17; 16:15, 34; 17:5; 18:7; 21:8, 16; (27:3); 28:7–10, 13–14.

— hospitality of meals and table fellowship: Luke 5:29–39; 7:36–50; 10:38–42; 11:37–52; 14:1–24, cf. 15:2; 22:7–38; 24:28–32, 36–49; Acts 9:19; 10:1–11:18; 16:34.

— worship (prayer, praise, fasting, passover meal, baptism, Lord's Supper): Luke 1:39–56; 22:7–38; 24:28–35; Acts 1:14; 2:46–47; 4:23–31; 9:10–19; 10:1–8; 12:12; 13:2; 16:33; 20:7–10.

— sharing property and distribution of goods to the needy: Luke 19:1–10; Acts 2:44–45; 4:34–37; 6:1–6; 9:36–42; 10:1–2; cf. 20:34–35.

4.3 House Churches: Basic Social Organization

Houses and households constitute not only the settings for the reception of the good news in Luke–Acts. As house churches, they also represent the basic social organization through which the gospel advances from Palestine to Rome. Literally, the church spread "*from house to house*" (Acts 20:20): from the households of Galilee, Jerusalem and Jericho to those of Damascus (Acts 9:10–19), Joppa (9:43; 10:6, 17–18, 32), Caesarea (10:1–11:18; 21:8), Tyre (21:3–6), Philippi (16:15, 34, 40), Thessalonica (17:5–7), Ephesus (20:20), Troas (20:7–12), Corinth (18:3, 7–8), and Rome (28:16, 23, 30–31). The hospitality, fellowship, and mutual support typical of these house church communities united itinerant prophets and residential believers in a cooperative effort which, for Luke, was essential to the success of the church's missionary enterprise (Koenig 1985:85–123).

4.4 Domestic Life in the Teaching of Jesus

Scenes of domestic life likewise play a major role in the Lukan presentation of the teaching of Jesus. Of the thirty-one parables which Luke relates, no less than eighteen involve aspects of domestic activity and household management (i.e., *oikonomia*). Some few of these come to Luke from the tradition, such as Luke 8:5–8; 12:35–40; 12:42–46; 13:18–19; 14:15–24; 15:3–7; 20:9–18; and many others are unique to Luke: 7:41–43; 11:5–8; 12:16–21; 13:24–30; 14:7–11; 14:28–30; 15:8–10; 15:11–32; 16:1–8; 16:19–31; 17:7–10. Furthermore, familial relations, domestic crises, and responsibilities of household management figure also in briefer sayings of Jesus as Luke's preferred basis for illuminating major features of life in the kingdom of God: 9:46–48; 11:14–23; 12:22–34, 35–48; 13:20–21; 18:15–17. Children of the household are contrasted to temple and Torah authorities to exemplify humility, dependence on God, and discipleship (Kodell 1987). In Luke's perspective, to hear the words of Jesus and do them may be compared to building one's house on a firm foundation (Luke 6:46–49/Matt 7:24–27).

4.5 Household Blocks of Teaching

At points in the Lukan composition, moreover, blocks of teaching concerning discipleship appear organized around related household concerns. Let us consider 12:1–53 and 14:1–17:10.

(a) *Luke 12:1–53:* Verses 1–3 = no household secrets; 4–12 = no anxiety over survival; 13–21, 22–31, 32–34 = inheritance, covetousness, possessions, almsgiving, trust in a divine Father's care; 35–40 = household vigilance; 41–48 = domestic steward's faithfulness; 49–53 = divisions in the household.

(b) Luke 14:1–17:10: 14:1–6, 7–11, 12–14, 15–24 = dining, healing, inclusive hospitality; 14:25–35 = renunciation of family to follow Jesus; 15:1–32 = eating with and embracing the "lost"; 16:1–9, 10–12 = prudent and faithful household management; 16:13, 14–15 = household loyalties and priorities; 16:16–17 = household [kingdom] entrance; 16:18 = marital unity; 16:19–31 = domestic inhospitality and unrepentance; 17:1–4, 5–6 = offense to children ["little ones"], forgiveness of brothers, faith; 17:7–10 = the duty and status of household servants.

It is not accidental that as Jesus is "on the way" to Jerusalem, Luke portrays him as talking about "the Way" of discipleship. And Luke 12:1–53 and 14:1–17:10 both embody basic teachings on the right and wrong way of living in the household of God.

4.6 Household as Symbol of the Kingdom of God

Throughout all this teaching of the Lukan Jesus, the household serves as the most apposite sphere and symbol of social life for illustrating features of life under the reign of God. In this connection the institution of kinship and family based on consanguinity and affinity provides a model for a community of fictive kin united by the bonds of mercy, faith, and filial obedience. The boundaries of this symbolical family or household of God are expanded to include the marginalized, the outcasts, Samaritans, and Gentiles.

In this kingdom/household, God is experienced as a merciful, generous, and forgiving "father" (Luke 2:49; 6:36; 9:36; 10:21–22; 11:1, 13; 12:30, 32; 22:29, 42; 23:34, 46; 24:49; Acts 1:4, 7; 2:33). Jesus is recognized as "Son of God" (Luke 1:35; 3:22; 4:3, 9, 41; 8:28; 9:35; 10:22; 20:13; 22:70; Acts 8:37; 9:20; 13:53). In contrast to the "children of Jerusalem" (13:34), believers who hear and do Jesus' words form his new family (8:19–21) and become the true "children" of the heavenly Father (11:13; 24:49), "brothers and sisters," one with another (Luke 6:41–42; 8:19–21; 17:3–4; 22:32; Acts 1:15–16; 2:29, 37; 6:3; 9:17, 30; 10:23; 11:1, 12, 29; 12:17; 14:2; 15:1, 3, 7, 12, 22–23, 32–33, 36, 40; 16:2, 40; 17:6, 10, 14; 18:18, 27; 21:7, 17, 20, 22; 22:13; 28:14, 15).

In this kingdom/household, Jesus is the generous lord and "householder" (oikodespotēs): 12:35–40; 13:22–30; 14:7–11, 12–14, 15–24; 19:11–27). The meals of which he speaks (14:7–24; 15:3–32), over which he presides (22:7–38; 24:28–31, 36–49) and at which he serves (12:37; 22:27) are all signs of the inclusiveness, fellowship, status reversal, reciprocal service, and joy typical of life in the kingdom/household of God.

Those who share in the fellowship of this household are those who hear the householder's words and do them: "household stewards" (oikonomos, 12:42; 16:1–9) and "servants" (oiketēs, 16:13). They are responsible for the things entrusted to them. Their master's humble service in the household is the model for their own (17:7–10; 22:24–27). In the household of God they are united with their Lord and one another in new, inclusive bonds of kinship (8:19–21), generosity, and friendship (11:5–13; 12:4; 14:7–11,12–14; 16:9). As Jesus was "the friend of tax collectors and sinners" (7:34, cf. 7:36–50; 15:2; 19:1–10), so Acts makes clear that the friendship of his followers likewise knew no social or ethnic limits (Acts 10:24; 19:31; 27:3).

4.7 Household and Mercy

Showing mercy (eleos, eleeō) and performing merciful acts of lovingkindness (eleēmosynē) are, for Luke, actions especially typical of the kingdom/household of God (12:33). The Lukan Gospel begins with rejoicing over the divine mercy linked with Jesus (1:76–79) and manifested to lowly women, Mary (1:50, 54) and Elizabeth (1:58), as representatives of expectant Israel. Mercy, moreover, is exercised concretely in the healing of sinners and the unclean: lepers (17:11–19); a blind man (18:35–43); one near death (10:29–37); a lame man (Acts 3:1–10). Beyond the mere gift of alms, works of mercy involve deeds of lovingkindness: hospitality, the rearing of orphans, assistance at weddings, redemption of prisoners, care for the sick, burial of the dead, comfort of mourners (Strack-Billerbeck 1961:536–610) — actions noted by Luke as typical of Jesus and his community.

This mercy knows no limits set by purity regulations but is available to and practiced by all who do the Father's will (10:25–37; 11:37–41; 17:11, 19; 18:35–43; Acts 3:1–10; 9:36–43; 10:2, 4, 31; 24:17). To love one's enemies, do good, lend with no expectation of return is to be a child of the Most High. As God the father is merciful (*oiktirmōn*), so his children are to be merciful (6:35–36).

4.8 The Household Institution in Luke–Acts: A Summary

In Luke–Acts the household plays a paramount role in the ministry, teaching, and mission of Jesus and his followers. Historically and geographically, households of believers marked the way-stations of the spread of the gospel from Galilee to Rome. Economically and socially, they constituted independent, self-sufficient communities organized on the basis of kinship and household management. Politically, they played no part in Palestine's power structure except as the supplier of its economic resources and the object of its devouring policies. The gospel, then, spread through the institution of the family, not through politics. Only by the time of Constantine did "the Way" play any role whatsoever in the other major institution of the day, politics.

Here among the households of the holy and the unholy, the wealthy and the poor, Jews and Gentiles of high and low degree, the good news of a holiness and wholeness available to all made its initial and sustained advance. Household organization was determined by the structure and roles of the family and regulated by the traditional customs and codes of family life and kinship relations. These domestic structures and codes, in turn, supplied Jesus and his company with the basic models and metaphors for illustrating the relations and conditions of life in the kingdom of God. Biological kinship and its attendant roles, relations, and responsibilities served as the model for conceptualizing relations with God as father and fellow believers as brothers and sisters in the family of God. Qualities of both the honorable human father and the divine parent— generosity, mercy, hospitality, loyalty, friendship—were those qualities to be emulated by the family as a whole.

The household thus serves in Luke–Acts as both a historical and a metaphorical reality. The church which grows through household conversions becomes at the same time a worldwide household of faith. The contrast of household to the temple as historical institution and erstwhile sacred symbol is clear:

— political institution vs. kinship institution; centralization of power and coercion vs. diffusion of the powerless households and familial commitment;

— economic exploitation vs. material sharing;

— stratification by purity vs. integration via kinship and fictive kinship bonds;

— exclusion and alienation based on purity lines vs. inclusion based on mercy and faith.

For Luke, the temple is the object of critique and the arena of rejection, Satan-inspired conflict and death. In contrast, the household is the object of praise and the sphere of repentance, concord, and divinely conferred life. Thus, in Luke's account, the Spirit of God and its sanctifying power moves from temple to household, from the chief symbol of Jewish national identity to the principal symbol of a community united with a heavenly Father. In Luke–Acts the household emerges as the preeminent sphere and symbol of the reception of the gospel, Christian identity, and solidarity in the Spirit.

5.0 TEMPLE AND HOUSEHOLD CONTRASTED

The evidence indeed supports the thesis we urged earlier that throughout Luke–Acts, temple and household represent distinctly different and contrasted types of social institutions with conflicting sets of structures, interests, values, beliefs, and behaviors. The table on page 231 summarizes the salient contrasts.

6.0 TEMPLE, HOUSEHOLD, AND CONTRASTING SETS OF SOCIAL RELATIONS

Thus far it has become clear that in Luke–Acts temple and household symbolize different and opposed forms of social organization, identity, and allegiance. Now it is appropriate to inquire as to the reason for this particular choice of symbols. It goes without saying, of course, that both the temple and the household played major roles in the actual history of Jesus and the Jesus movement. Neither are fictions of Luke's narrative world. But what explains their particular elaboration, accentuation, and contrast in Luke's narrative? Why are temple and household poles around which Luke has woven his story? How does Luke's depiction and contrast of temple and household institutions resonate with the societal structures familiar to his audience? Why did Luke have reason to expect that a contrast of these two institutions and the social relations they involve would strike his hearers/readers as plausible and persuasive? Recent studies by Halvor Moxnes and Bruce Malina describe a useful social-scientific model for pursuing these questions.

Halvor Moxnes notes (1987, 1988) that the significance of particular institutions and groups in Luke–Acts and their function in the narrative can best be determined by examining them in relation to the social

CONTRASTING FEATURES OF
TEMPLE AND HOUSEHOLD
Figure 8-1

TEMPLE	HOUSEHOLD

1. SPACE

National sanctuary located in Jerusalem, the Holy City	Communal profane space located in villages and cities
One single temple	Many households
Spatial demarcation of degrees of holiness	Spatial demarcation of degrees of intimacy
Central locus and symbol of political power	Diffused, distant from political power

2. PERSONNEL

Chief priests and families; priests and levites; moneychangers; temple police	Families, fictive kin; householders, stewards, servants, friends
Sanhedrin (chief priests, scribes, elders)	Neighbors, guests
Pharisees and Sadducees	

3. POLITICAL RELATIONS

Central base of political, economic, social, and cultural (religious) power	Periphery, no public power; base of kinship
Temple and administration under direct Roman control	Indirect Roman control
Bureaucratic authority (offices and qualifications)	Traditional authority ascribed roles and statuses

4. ECONOMIC RELATIONS

Treasury, Temple tax, sacrifices offerings, tithes to priests	Reciprocal generosity; property in common
Accumulation of debts	Forgiveness of debts
Expropriation of property; "greed"; "den of thieves"	Sharing of property
Oppression of the poor and powerless	Care for poor and powerless
No justice or mercy	Justice (rightly ordered relations and resources and mercy)
Redistribution of resources according to interests of wielders of power	Sharing of resources according to availability and need

5. SOCIAL RELATIONS

Stratified society according to degrees of purity (Torah)	Solidary kin and fictive kin group ("brothers and sisters, children of God" by faith and mercy)
Rank according to bureaucratic roles	Rank according to traditional familial roles
Exclusive space and society according to purity (Torah); zone of alienation and self-justification	Inclusive groups according to faith and mercy; zone of integration and divine justification
Sphere of unrepentance, conflict, death plotting	Sphere of acceptance, repentance, concord, life
Temple system object of Jesus' critique	Domestic relations object of Jesus' teaching and praise

6. SYMBOLIC FEATURES

Perversion of God's dwelling place; sphere of Satan's activity	The dwelling place of the Spirit; sphere of God's activity
Chief public symbol of Jewish identity and purity	Chief social symbol of the kingdom of God and Christian holiness

relations typical of the society within which and for which Luke writes. Following the work of Marshall Sahlins (1965), Moxnes demonstrates that the underlying economic and social modes of interaction and conflict described in Luke–Acts were broader contrasting patterns of relations based on ancient systems of either *reciprocity* or *redistribution*.

(a) *Reciprocal* (direct, person-to-person, give-and-take) forms of interaction were characteristic of the household and local village life in first-century Palestine.

(b) Centralized accumulation of agricultural surplus and *redistribution* were typical of the general temple-based economy.

According to Moxnes, these contrasting modes of social exchange played a key role in shaping social dimensions of the conflict between the Jesus movement and the temple establishment as described in Luke–Acts. Before considering this role in more detail, however, let us first examine the analytical model and its operative terms in light of the clarifying remarks of Bruce Malina.

6.1 A Comparative Model of Ancient Social Relations

In his pioneering study, *Christian Origins and Cultural Anthropology*, Bruce Malina (1986a:98–111) proposed a schema for analyzing differing forms of social relations and interactions characteristic of the societies and groups described in the biblical writings. This schema coordinates research by social and economic anthropologists on primitive and peasant societies analogous to those of the biblical period (Sahlins 1965; Carney 1975:137–234; Sack 1986:52–91).

Malina notes that forms of social relations (including economic exchanges) in pre-industrial societies fall along a spectrum marked by types of *reciprocity* at one pole of the spectrum to types of *redistribution* or centricity at the other. (a) *Reciprocal* relations, which involve personal, back-and-forth exchanges of goods and services, are typical of small-scale societies, tribal organizations, village, and household life. At this level of direct, personal, and local interaction, food, clothing, shelter, hospitality and other basic necessities of social life are either:

(1) shared freely according to generosity or need (*generalized reciprocity*),

(2) exchanged symmetrically according to the interests of both parties (*balanced reciprocity*), or

(3) obtained with no concern for the other's self-interest (*negative reciprocity*).

The types of reciprocity will vary according to prevailing social conditions: the proximity (personal and geographical) of the agents, and the purpose, mode, place, and time of the interactions. Households, kin and fictive kin groups regularly practice generalized reciprocity among themselves, evidencing the closeness of social bonds and the concern for freely given mutual support. Balanced and negative forms of exchange are typical where social ties and trust between groups are weaker and interactions are more infrequent.

(b) Forms of *redistribution*, on the other hand, are typical of large-scale societies with central storehouse economies such as the temple-based societies of Mesopotamia, Egypt, Palestine, and Rome (Carney 1975:172–75). While these political economies include reciprocal forms of exchange on local levels, their differentiating feature is the pooling of goods and services in a central storehouse, generally linked to a temple, and their centralized political control and redistribution by a powerful elite or temple hierarchy. In this form of social organization, based on the political rather than the kinship institution, the management of the entire collectivity is of paramount concern and redistribution occurs according to the interests of those in power.

> Centricity with its pooling and redistribution generates the perception of social unity . . . replicates the social structure with its rank order, and presupposes centralized organization of social order and social action (Malina 1986a:110).

Economic and social relations are asymmetrical and stratified according to norms favoring the elites. In place of the consensus and commitment typical of kinship-based reciprocal relations, submission and allegiance are marshalled through a consolidation of political, legal, and military power, enforcement of social stratification and boundaries, and control of the cultural (including religious) tradition. See Sack (1986:61, 68, 71) for diagrammatic summaries of reciprocity and redistribution patterns, and Scott (1977) for their relevance to the issue of justice in particular. Contrasting features of these orderings of social and economic relations are summarized in Figure 8-2.

This model summarizes and compares differing forms of social organization and interaction typical of pre-industrial societies including those of Jesus' and Luke's time. In particular it clarifies in abstract terms differences in the ways that small-scale, kinship-based groups and large-scale, national populations with a centralized political base were socially organized to manage the exchange of goods and services and all forms of social interchange.

For our purposes the model is useful in three important ways. First, it provides a schema for conceptualizing differing forms of social organization prevalent in the Mediterranean world of the first century and known to Luke and his audience. This was a world rife with competing systems of *redistribution* (Palestine, local monarchies, Rome) and *reciprocity* (families, villages, urban enclaves). Second, the contrasting features of redistribution and reciprocity arrangements which the model

---

CONTRASTS IN REDISTRIBUTION AND RECIPROCITY
Figure 8-2

REDISTRIBUTION	GENERALIZED RECIPROCITY

1. SCALE

Large-scale national populations	Small-scale village populations, urban groups

2. POLITICAL RELATIONS

Centralized political, economic, social, and ideological control	Power sharing, consensus
Coerced pooling of agricultural surplus; corvée; imposition of debts, taxes, tithes; redistribution according to interests of elites	Voluntary, back-and-forth sharing of "gifts"; food, shelter, clothing, tools, etc.; giving without expectation of immediate return

3. ECONOMIC RELATIONS

Central storehouse economy with temple depot	Diffused, local "household" management
Centralized control of production, distribution, consumption of resources and services	Household control of production etc.
Redistribution of available surplus according to interests of power wielders	Reciprocal exchange of goods and services according to their availability and need
Economic and social imbalance of "haves/have nots," elites and sub-elites according to control of resources means, and relations of production	Balanced relations through mutual sharing of goods at common disposal

4. SOCIAL RELATIONS

Indirect interaction of classes through mediating agencies; maintenance of allegiance to system through socialization and norm enforcement	Direct, face-to-face interaction of agents; fidelity in obligations as a matter of familial loyalty and group honor
Social roles and status according to political and economic power, proximity/distance from power center, law, military	Traditional domestic roles and status; honor and prestige according to exercise of generosity and commitment to traditional norms of mutual sharing

5. CULTURAL TRADITION

Centralized control of cultural tradition, ideology shaped by interests of elites and temple hierarchies	Cultural tradition shared through domestic networks and interest of kin and fictive kin solidarity

6. LIMITATIONS

Centralization prone to agglomeration of power and resources, totalitarianism; land expropriation;	Reciprocal relations constrained by absence of centralized authority and group pressure
Redistribution inadequate in times of crisis (crop failure; plagues) resulting in sub-subsistence conditions, banditry, and at times revolt	Obligations of reciprocity especially stressed in crises involving personal survival

makes evident provide categories for organizing and analyzing Luke's description and assessment of economic-social conditions. This in turn will help clarify implications of the choice of temple and household as contrasting foci of the Lukan narrative. Finally, the fit between the social arrangements of Luke's world and the material and accents of his composition will allow us then to assess the plausibility and persuasive power of Luke's story concerning temple and household for his contemporary audience.

6.2 The Model Applied to Luke–Acts

The social arrangements typical of Luke's world find echoes in the material and patterns of his two-volume work. When this model of contrasting forms of social relations is used as a lens through which to analyze the social data of Luke–Acts, it becomes apparent that in his contrast of temple and household Luke is describing and evaluating two different types of social organization known to his audience:

temple : *redistribution* :: household : *reciprocity*.

In the language of our model, one type is a centralized, politically controlled *redistributive* system with the Jerusalem temple as its center, and the other, a movement organized around households and kin/fictive kin relations, which is united by bonds and obligations of *generalized reciprocity*.

Temple and Redistribution. The Jerusalem temple is the base of first-century Palestine's redistribution economy; the destabilizing impact of the management of this system in all areas of Palestinian life has been described by Oakman (1986:37–91) and others (Hamilton 1964; Brown 1976; Fennelly 1978; Houtart 1980:218–60; Belo 1981:60–86; Füssel 1987:29–50). This system is controlled politically by an alliance of large landholders (chief priestly families, lay elders, Herodians) in collaboration with Rome's colonialist policy, through an excessive burden of tribute, temple taxes and offerings, tithes, and other debts. It was seriously altering ancient land-holding patterns and eroding traditional forms of social relations. An ever-increasing amount of the peasant population, incapable of meeting the enormous demands of Rome and the temple, was being forced to sell its lands and its family members into debt slavery. Impoverishment of the masses, imprisonment, destitution, and social unrest were on the rise. The gap between the landed "haves" and the landless "have-nots" was growing, village patterns of cooperative labor and reciprocal social relations were being destroyed, and the poor and the powerless, once protected by the norms of Torah, were now the objects of exploitation and abandonment.

From Luke's perspective, this was a system which had grown morally bankrupt. The temple, once a holy house of prayer had become a "den of thieves" (Luke 19:46). The guardians of temple law, purity, and power had become preoccupied with status and class differentiation (Luke 11:43, 52; 15:2; 16:15; 18:11). They imposed heavy burdens (Luke 11:46), ignored the needy (Luke 10:29–37), neglected justice and the love of God (Luke 11:42), were full of extortion and wickedness (Luke 11:39), and devoured widow's houses (Luke 20:47). Jesus is credited with judging their interpretation of Torah and the cultural tradition as oppressive and self-serving (Luke 11:37–52; 16:14–15; 18:11–12; 20:9–19). Their response to criticism was violent and murderous (Luke 11:53–54; 19:47; 20:19; 21:12; 22:2, 47–23:5; Acts 3:13–15; 4:1–3 etc.). Precisely because it had failed in the *redistribution* of not only material resources but also justice, mercy, and peace, the entire system and its chief symbol, the temple, was destined by God for destruction (Luke 11:34–35; 19:41–44; 21:5–6, 20–24).

Household and Reciprocity. In contrast, however, to this bankrupt system of temple and redistribution was an organization of communal life marked by the *reciprocities* of kinship, friendship, and domestic relations. As our model makes clear, the features of domestic life which Luke has accented are relations characterized by forms of *generalized reciprocity.*

Within the Christian network of households and the community of "brothers and sisters in the faith," social relations were intimate, inclusive, and governed by the reciprocity characteristic of family and friends. In this private sphere social (including religious) life was self-contained and economically self-supporting. Resources were not directed under compulsion to a distant center and redistributed according to the interests of those in power, but were shared directly according to availability and need (Luke 6:3–36; 11:5–13; 12:33; 15:3–32; 18:22; 19:1–10; Acts 2:44–47; 5:32–37; 6:1–6). No holy place or hierarchy set standards for social differentiation because in the brotherhood of the faithful all was holy (Luke 11:4–41; Acts 10:1–11:18; 15:9). Especially leaders were told to be servants (Luke 17:7–10; 22:24–27). *Humility* (Luke 14:7–11; 18:14) rather than elitism, *inclusivity* (Luke 14:12–24; Acts 10:1–11:18) rather than exclusivity, *consensus* (Acts 2:42; 4:32) rather than constraint, *personal commitment* (Acts 3:11–16; 4:8–12; 5:23–31) rather abstract allegiance was the rule here, as typical of reciprocal relations.

The private space of house and home was the scene of hospitality, generosity, friendship, deeds of mercy, acts of mutual aid and comfort, and familial love and fraternal support, unmeasured and unlimited. These household actions welded bonds of intimacy and solidarity. Here the honorable person was the generous one who had given all away, and so was wealthy beyond measure in social prestige and honor before God (Luke 12:33–34; 18:22; 21:1–4). Here in relations marked by reciprocity, giving (Luke 14:12–24) and forgiving (Luke 7:37–50; 11:4; 15:1–32; 19:1–10) were never once-for-all but ongoing activities which bound partners in an open-ended and continuous relationship.

These contrasts in the structures, norms, and values associated with *redistributive* or *reciprocal* forms of social relations represented by temple and household make it clear how and why the household rather than the temple served Luke as the most apposite image for concretizing both the good news of the kingdom and the social features of a Christian community faithful to a God of mercy and justice. The ethos of the kingdom, according to Luke, is shaped by the logic of generalized reciprocity typical of the household and the bonds and obligation of kin and fictive kinship. Given the economic and social cleavages within the missionary communities addressed in Luke–Acts (Karris 1978; Esler 1987:164–200), it was precisely this ethos of sharing which was essential for the continued viability, solidarity, and growth of the fledgling movement.

Luke's interest in the reciprocities of the household is especially evident in his stress on giving/forgiving/lending without expectation of return (Luke 6:30, 35; 7:41–42; 10:29–37; 11:4; 14:12–14, 15–24; Acts 20:35) other than a future heavenly reward (Luke 6:37–38; 12:32–34; 14:12–14, 15–24; 18:22). This benevolence (mercy/alms) is intended especially for "the poor, the maimed, the lame, the blind" (Luke 14:13), those lost and lowly ones (Luke 19:10), social deviants and ethnic outsiders (Samaritans, Gentiles) to whom the gospel of Jesus was particularly directed (Luke 4:16–30; 12:33; 18:22; 19:8–9).

Such deeds of mercy and justice/righteousness (Karris 1985:23–78) are explicitly identified as the true purity (11:41). They unite benefactors with both beneficiaries and their benefactor God (6:35–36; 12:29–34) and Lord (Acts 10:38). Thus mercy rather than cultic purity is the essential bond between the people of God and their heavenly Father (Luke 6:36; Borg 1984:73–195).

This benevolence is exemplified by the centurion at Capernaum (Luke 7:1–10), the good Samaritan (10:29–37), Zacchaeus (19:1–10), Barnabas (Acts 4:36–37), and Cornelius (Acts 10:2). It typifies the mutual sharing of the Christian community in general (Acts 2:43–47; 4:32–37); and it embodies the generosity of its divine Benefactor (Danker 1987, 1988). Such benevolence thereby establishes its honor in a benefaction-conscious society (Danker 1982).

Therefore, we draw the following conclusions about Luke's model of the household as the ideal type of social relations. Giving without expectation of return, hospitality and the sharing of food and shelter, care for the ill, generous support of those in need, forgiveness of debts and redemption of those in debt are all actions characteristic of kin groups and the ethos of the household. The model of social relations is one of generalized reciprocity. In Luke–Acts this pattern of domestic relations, and the intimacy and solidarity it presumes, serves as the decisive model for the identity and ethos of the Christian community as a whole. This form of community ordered around the roles, relationships, and responsibilities of the household stands in stark contrast to the exploitative redistributive system of the temple and embodies an alternate vision of salvation based not on cultic purity but on the gift of divine mercy and its imitation in the family of faith.

In the search for the necessary and adequate scenario for understanding social relations in Luke, we have learned much about the institutions of temple and household. What we now have is a rather precise portrait of temple and household, whose highlights and hues are conformed to the artist-author's perspective and the contours of his work as a whole. Luke's portrait, moreover, will have been plausible and persuasive to his contemporary audience because it presumed and conformed to facts of social and economic life known from personal experience. Though by the time of Luke's writing the Jerusalem temple lay in ruins for decades or more, his audience was well acquainted with the opposing types of social organization represented by a temple state on the one hand and a network of households on the other. This audience could hardly miss the implications of Luke's pointed contrast between a Holy Place which had become an exploitative den of thieves and a widespread community of brothers and sisters who in faith and deeds of lovingkindness shared all things in common.

7.0 CONCLUSION

Temple and household and the contrasting realities which they embody assume a fundamental significance in Luke–Acts, both structurally and thematically. As the temple frames and provides the central focus for the first segment of Luke's narrative (the Gospel), the household frames and marks the chief focus of the second part of the narrative (Acts). In the structure of Luke–Acts, this shift in focus embraces and replicates a major plot device pervading the entire narrative. At the same time, this transition in venue and focus from temple to household charts for Luke the actual historical and geographical movement of the gospel from its inception in the Holy Land, the Holy City and the Holy Place to its dissemination through the households of the diaspora, "from Jerusalem, Judaea and Samaria to the end of the earth" (Acts 1:8).

Thematically, moreover, temple and household are linked with basic Lukan emphases and contrasts. The social and economic system centered in temple, Torah, and purity failed in terms of just redistribution.

It became for Luke a negative foil with which to compare the social and economic relations of the household as the arena of justice, mercy, and koinonia and as the sphere of the Spirit's presence. Thus a typical dualistic scene is presented in Luke–Acts.

Temple. On one side is a system dominated by a central holy place, an exclusivist holiness ideology, a hierarchically stratified social order, and exploitative economic interests. This system proved incapable of mediating the inclusive salvation envisioned by the prophets.

Household. Over against it, Luke contrasts the domestic associations of the movement initiated by Jesus. Here the gospel of a universal salvation is socially embodied in a community of "brothers and sisters" where repentance, faith, forgiveness, generosity, mercy and justice, familial loyalty and friendship unite the faithful with a God of mercy and a Servant-Lord.

Household scenarios and domestic imagery disclose distinctively Lukan christological, soteriological, and ecclesiological themes: Jesus Christ as exalted Servant and Benefactor; salvation for the lost and the lowly, women and outcasts, Gentiles and sinners; repentance and forgiveness; almsgiving and mercy; hospitality and table-fellowship. The household, in fact, functions as Luke's prime metaphor for depicting social life in the kingdom of God.

The themes of promise and fulfillment and Christianity's continuity with Israel likewise are linked with temple and household. For Luke the hope of Israel's salvation, initially linked with the temple, is finally realized in the reciprocities of the household. The role of the temple has been superseded and there is no reason for regret over its destruction. His critique, however, is specific, not general. It is directed not against the Jews as a people but against a bankrupt political system of temple-Torah-purity in particular. In his economy of salvation, the new household of Jesus Messiah, not the temple, constitutes the continuing dwelling place of the Spirit. It is Christianity's enduring bond with the house of Abraham in whose posterity "all the families of the earth will be blessed."

The contrast and developing conflict of temple-based and household-based communities also epitomizes historically, geographically, socially, and ideologically Luke's view of the cleavage between the worlds and allegiances of Judaism and Christianity. It is the latter, he maintains, which alone constitutes the fulfillment of the prophetic hopes and the divine promise of a universal salvation offered by a God of mercy who in Jesus Christ has made all things clean and all persons children of one universal family.

Returning to where we began, we can conclude that the "dominant contradiction" between alienated and human space which Mottu saw expressed in the temple/household contrast of Luke 18:9–14 is part of a larger Lukan pattern in which the temple and the household point to contradictory definitions of social and religious life. Our comparative model of social relations has enabled us to see that this contradiction involves not simply differing locales but differing structures of economic and social organization. It contains opposing forms of social relations, alternative sets of values and loyalties, and contrasting symbols of social and religious identity. By identifying the salient areas of contrast between these two dominant institutions, the model explicates features of temple and household which are presumed but implicit in the predominantly theological narrative of Luke–Acts. In Luke's predominantly theological vocabulary, the temple was a house of prayer and hope perverted into a den of thieves. It became the dominant symbol of a holiness ethic opposed to the inclusive holiness of God. The household, in turn, was the zone of the Spirit and the home of the children of God, the prime metaphor of life in the kingdom. Translated into social terms, from Luke's perspective the temple, its authorities, its law, and its controlling purity ideology represented an exclusivist, exploitative, and alienating system incapable of providing access to or symbolizing the ultimate sources of personal and communal sustenance. It opposed but failed to contain a reforming movement seeking justice and support for the powerless and intent on extending the boundaries of Israel to include all seeking a place of belonging, acceptance, and succor. This new movement was shaped in its ethos and ethic by the reciprocities of kinship and friendship, and united by a sense of common brotherhood/ sisterhood under one divine Father. It freed itself from the restraints of temple purity, allegiance, and national boundaries as it embraced "all the families of the earth" in its worldwide mission.

This essay, then, provides a necessary and adequate scenario for understanding the basic institutions of Luke's world. The careful reader might take the basic modeling and examine in closer detail one or another of the many passages mentioned in the essay which exemplify the institutions of temple and/or household, especially in terms of their implied system of social relations. It is our hope to open doors with this modeling, and invite students and readers to explore more broadly and deeply the Lukan text.

This essay, moreover, should be read in conjunction with other studies in this volume, for it contributes to them at times and depends on them in turn. In particular, the whole discussion of reciprocity would take a reader to the study by Moxnes on patron-client relations. And in regard to issues of debt, land and the elite class, the essays by Rohrbaugh and Oakman necessarily fill in the picture. The discussion of the purity system of the temple is more specifically developed in Neyrey's essay on the symbolic universe of Luke–Acts. Likewise the conflict represented between Jesus and the temple system is described more fully in the chapter on conflict and deviance by Malina and Neyrey.

9

PATRON-CLIENT RELATIONS AND THE NEW COMMUNITY IN LUKE–ACTS

Halvor Moxnes

0.0 INTRODUCTION

We are all familiar with the story of the Roman centurion who asks Jesus to heal his slave and who then becomes a model of faith. The best known version of this story is the one given by Matthew (Matt 8:5–13) in which there is a direct dialogue between the centurion and Jesus. In Luke, however, the centurion addresses Jesus through mediators, and the pattern of social relations becomes more complex:

> Now a centurion had a slave *who was dear to him*, who was sick and at the point of death. When he heard of Jesus, he sent to him *elders of the Jews*, asking him to come and heal his slave. And when they came to *Jesus*, they besought him earnestly, saying, "He is worthy to have you do this for him, for he loves our nation and he built us a synagogue." And Jesus went with them. When he was not far from the house, the centurion sent *friends* to him, saying to him: "Lord, do not trouble your-self, for I am not worthy to have you come under my roof; therefore I did not presume to come to you. But say the word, and let my servant be healed. For I am a man set under authority, with soldiers under me: and I say to one, "Go," and he goes, and to another, "Come," and he comes; and to my slave, "Do this," and he does it." When Jesus heard this he marveled at him, and turned and said to the multitude that fol-lowed him, "I tell you, not even in Israel have I found such faith." And when those who had been sent returned to the house, they found the slave well (Luke 7:2–10).

Why has Luke phrased the story so differently? Instead of Matthew's personal, direct encounter between Jesus and the centurion, their contact is carefully mediated by two delegations, one of "elders of the Jews," the other consisting of "friends." What is the social and cultural context presupposed by Luke? Why is the contact mediated in this way? What type of relationship between the Roman centurion and the Jewish elders makes them act as mediators? And who are the centurion's "friends"? The polite phrases in 7:4–6 make us realize that we are observing the giving of favors and that there is a web of reciprocities spun between the various actors of the story. The story presupposes an intricate set of social relations between various actors: the centurion, his slave, Jesus, and the two groups of "elders" and "friends," who, although primarily related to the centurion, are in a position to contact with Jesus.

To Luke and his audience the narrative made perfect sense. We, however, live in a different culture and therefore require special scenarios to make these social relations and interactions intelligible. In order to understand this story we must know the social institution of "patronage," the relationship of patron and client. It is the purpose of this chapter to present a model of patronage and to show how it offers a necessary and enlightening scenario for comprehending this and other Lukan narratives.

1.0 PATRONAGE DEFINED

Patronage is a model or analytical construct which the social scientist applies in order to understand and explain a range of apparent different social relationships: father-son, God-man, saint-devotee, godfather-godchild, lord-vassal, landlord-tenant, politician-voter, professor-assistant, and so forth. All these different sets of social relationships can thus be considered from one particular point of view which may render them comprehensible (Blok 1969:366).

Patron-client relations are social relationships between individuals based on a strong element of inequality and difference in power. The basic structure of the relationship is an exchange of different and very unequal resources. A patron has social, economic, and political resources that are needed by a client. In return, a client can give expressions of loyalty and honor that are useful for the patron.

2.0 "UNIVERSALIST SOCIETIES" vs PATRON-CLIENT RELATIONS

In his Gospel, Luke places heavy emphasis upon economic exchange and social relations. In order to understand the social structure of the communities described by Luke, we need models which combine both social and economic relations (see Moxnes 1988). Patron-client relations is just such a model which is broad enough to cover various types of relations and at the same time distinct enough to be of analytical use. But can a model that is useful to analyze personal relations be applied to larger social structures like the Palestinian society Luke describes? To answer that question some observations on differences between ancient and modern societies are in order. These differences apply not only to organization and structure, but also to ideas about social order.

2.1 "Universalist Societies": Modern, Western-Style Democracies

The political and social system with which citizens of North American and Northern European countries are best acquainted is a universalist society with a central government and bureaucracy (Eisenstadt and Roniger 1984:169–71, 184–200). In this type of society citizens expect to have access on an equal basis to goods and services provided by the state. Access to goods is based on universal criteria, e.g., being a citizen and taxpayer or a member of a certain age group. Thus, these goods and services are regarded as a right, not as a favor provided by the state. To emphasize this point many states have passed laws to ensure that these rights are not made dependent upon race, gender, or religion.

From this perspective there is little room for patron-client relationships. This is so because patronage is a relationship in which, as a special favor, a patron provides for his client access to scarce resources that are not universally accessible. Consequently, in many modern societies such relations are often looked upon as unfair. For many, "patronage" is a bad word, associated with, for example, organized crime. Some scholars who study patronage primarily within modern societies hold this view. They argue that patronage stands "outside the officially proclaimed formal morality of the society," (Gellner 1977:4) and that "patronage networks . . . promote privileged, discriminatory access to scarce goods at the expense of universalistic criteria." Consequently, they also lack "official legitimacy" (Waterbury 1977:334).

Thus, we may say that patronage is alien not only to a socialist analysis of class structures (Gilsenan 1977), but to most modern ideologies of government as well, since they are based on the idea of equal rights for all citizens. One student of patronage has pointed out that even the term itself may be absent from some languages. He takes this as an indication that patronage is a system totally foreign to the national ideologies of these language groups: "The historical example closest to the ideal type of fully centralized authority is probably modern Scandinavia. It has been pointed out to me that the word "patronage" cannot be translated into the Swedish or Norwegian language" (Saller 1982:4).

This does not mean that modern societies in fact do provide equal rights for everybody. We, too, know something about "old boy networks" or about having "the right connections," and we depend on individuals who have more resources than others. But there is a strong reluctance to speak of "patronage." Patronage therefore is something which may exist, but which is not willingly spoken of or conceptualized. It connotes a set of social relations which are in conflict with some of the most sacred societal values of Western democratic culture.

Consequently, we find it difficult to envisage societies in which patronage does not only openly exist, but where it is regarded as a natural way of structuring social and political relations. There is a basic difference between a patronage worldview and the way in which we think of society and the world as a whole. Northern Europeans and North Americans often think of society and state as organizations in which citizens are members with equal rights. In ancient societies people thought of society much more in personal terms, as relations within a body. And members were regarded as basically unequal in terms of gender and status.

Social relations in ancient societies were linked to symbolic images that differ from those common to our societies. Most clearly related to patron-client relations were images focusing upon honor (see the chapter on honor and shame by Malina-Neyrey). Moreover, social relations were put within a framework of ideas about the social and cosmic order. It was generally held that economic and social order were given or ordained by God (1 Cor 12:18, 24). Ancient societies, therefore, are very different from modern societies. There were no strong beliefs, such as we hold, that society could even be changed. Access to resources or positions was not even in principle free and equal to everybody as it is to us. Access was mediated and channelled through special groups or individuals. Consequently, the system was dominated by the elites and their values, and it was set up to preserve their privileged positions.

2.2 The Roman Empire: A System of Personal Relations

Patronage cannot easily exist within a democratic state with a central government and an efficient bureaucracy. This modern type of centralized government based on universalistic principles stands at one end of a spectrum of various forms of state structures. The feudal system, in which there is almost no bureaucracy and all relations are personal, stands at the other end. Intermediate types of state organizations are often combined with brokerage and friendship (Blok 1969).

Brokerage and friendship are the two most relevant types of patron-client relationships for a study of Mediterranean society in the time of the Roman Empire (Saller 1982:3–38). As regards brokerage, a broker serves as a mediator between two parties. Brokerage is often found in societies in which the central government does not control all of its territory and where the population does not have direct contact with or access to the government. This was true of relations between Rome and many foreign territories dominated by the Romans. On a smaller scale relations between a city and its dependent rural areas showed the same structure.

Concerning *friendship*, in states with a strong central organization patronage might take the form of "friendship." Friendship was not so much an emotional attachment as a form of social and even political contract based on reciprocity. Well-placed members of the elite in the center could provide their "friends" or "clients" in the provinces with access to the central administration. In modern, universalist societies we regard this structure as a corrupt interference with the system of government. Why then was this perceived as perfectly legitimate within the governing structure of the Roman Empire?

2.2.1 A fusion of the private and the public. In Roman models of society the relations between public, professional life and personal, family life were different from those of most modern societies. We make a clear distinction between the role of individuals as parents, spouses, or friends on the one hand and their role as public officials on the other. Within one set of relations we might expect them to show preferential treatment (parents, friends), but in others we expect strict impartiality (public officials). In Roman ideology, however, there were no such distinctions. In a study of Roman social relations, R. P. Saller says that ". . . in the Roman Weltanschauung there was no strong differentiation between Roman aristocrats' public and private social roles, with the idea that the exchange of favors was appropriate only in the latter. . . . What sets Rome and other pre-modern societies apart from modern bureaucracies is that according to the ideology in Roman society public figures, from municipal administrators to the emperors, were not only expected, but were supposed to use their position to bestow beneficia on friends" (Saller 1982:30).

Even the emperor played a patronal role. He was looked upon more as a powerful father figure than as an imperial administrator: "The crucial quality which gave the emperor his patronal character was the expectation that he would distribute beneficia in accordance with particularistic rather than universal criteria. That is, the distribution depended upon individual approaches to and relationships with the emperor who was supposed to be generous to family, friends and those who could approach him in person" (Saller 1982:33).

2.2.2 The Emperor and His "Friends": Dio Chrysostom. A vivid illustration of this attitude is found in several of the speeches of Dio Chrysostom, a famous rhetor and philosopher who is of particular interest to us since he was almost a contemporary of Luke. Dio belonged to a rich family from the town Prusa in Asia Minor and served both as a benefactor within that town and as a broker between it and various emperors. Therefore, he provides an excellent illustration of social relations within the Roman Empire, seen from the point of view of the rich elite (Jones 1978). In several of his speeches he portrays the ideal king, believed to be the emperor Trajan. He gives a picture of the emperor as a patron who acted on the basis of "friendship," not impartiality.

A major portion of one of his speeches (Or. 3:86–122) discusses how dependent a good king is upon his "friends." The military and administrative structure of the empire was not an impersonal bureaucracy, but bound to the emperor out of personal loyalty. However, Roman history often proved that this fidelity could not be taken for granted. Therefore the emperor needed faithful friends in charge: "I presume that our greatest necessities, arms, walls, troops, and cities, without friends to control them are neither useful nor profitable, nay, they are exceedingly precarious; while friends, even without these are helpful" (Or. 3:94).

A king, Dio argues, needs many "friends." It is shameful for him to have fewer friends than a private citizen. And a king can make friends from the very best men, "since all the means for making friends are his. . . ." Dio unhesitatingly speaks of "making friends," that is, creating personal alliances, as part of the emperor's policy for appointing officials: "Now, who is more able to appoint governors? Who needs more executives? Who has it in his power to give a part in a greater enterprise? Who is in a better position to put a man in charge of military operations? Who can confer more illustrious honors? Whose table lends greater distinction? And if friendship could be bought, who has greater means to forestall every possible rival" (Or. 3:131–32). As a consequence, officials and military commanders were not "public officials" in a modern sense; rather, they were servants and representatives of the emperor. They shared in his power and similarly related in a personal way to the people whom they administered. In Oratio 44 Dio shows how the emperor ruled the empire and the cities in Asia Minor that were in "alliance" with Rome by personal benefactions. These benefactions were secured through brokers and mediators, one of whom was Dio Chrysostom himself (Jones 1978:105–14).

Thus, within the Roman Empire in the first century, political and personal relations were fused. Patron-client relationship, therefore, is a central concept needed for understanding the way in which this type of society functioned, both on the level of the administration of Rome and its provinces, and on the level of relations in small scale communities. The time has now come to take a closer look at the structure and characteristics of patron-client relationships.

3.0 PATRONAGE AS A MODEL

In the previous section we dealt with patronage as a dominant part of the political system in the Roman Empire, using as an example the role of the emperor. In this section we will look more at the various elements of patron-client relations, that is, those aspects that makes patronage useful as a model in a study of social relations. Moreover, we will focus particularly on patronage within local communities or between local communities and cities. Some of the most important theoretical studies have been made by S. Eisenstadt and L. Roniger, and we shall follow their analysis (Eisenstadt and Roniger 1984:1–42).

3.1 Usefulness of Patron-Client Studies

Where do Eisenstadt and Roniger situate their model within differing approaches to the study of societies and groups? They distance themselves from the school of structural-functionalism represented by, for instance, Talcott Parsons, Edward Shils, and Robert K. Merton. This school assumed that within a society or a group there was a basic social consensus based on values and goals. Therefore it did not focus on conflicts and the use of power within groups, and it had difficulty in explaining social changes (Eisenstadt and Roniger 1984:21–28).

There was one common theme in the various forms of criticism of the structural-functionalist approach: no institutional arrangement (i.e., the formal structure of school, factory, family, behavior, or ritual) is to be taken for granted. Eisenstadt and Roniger outline the alternative to structural-functionalism in this way:

> Instead, the very setting up of institutional arrangements was viewed as constituting a problem for analysis, and many of these approaches stressed that every institutional structure or order develops, is maintained and is changed through a process of continuous interaction, negotiation and struggle among those who participate in it (1984:25).

The focus on interaction, negotiation and conflict in sociology and social anthropology has come together in the study of patron-client relations. Instead of starting with a preexisting notion of group structure, studies of patron-client relations ask: What are the different relationships within a group? How is power divided among the actors in these relationships? Is there equality or asymmetry? What forms of exchange take place? What symbolic meaning do these relationships have; in particular, what meaning is attached to the unequal status of actors? How are these relations linked to concepts of honor, status, and the social order? Moreover, how do these relations — and consequently also the structure of the group — change?

3.2 Characteristics of Patron-Client Relations

Among the characteristics of patron-client relationships the following are of particular interest for our study (Eisenstadt and Roniger 1984, 48–49):

(a) Interaction between patron and client is based on *simultaneous exchange of different types of resources*. A patron has instrumental, economic, and political resources and can therefore give support and protection; a client, in return, can give promises and expressions of solidarity and loyalty.

(b) There is a strong element of *solidarity* in these relations, linked to personal honor and *obligations*.

(c) There may be a *spiritual attachment*, however ambivalent, between patrons and clients.

(d) Patron-client relations are seemingly *binding* and *long range*, ideally of life-long endurance. However, such relations between individuals are in principle entered into voluntarily, and can be abandoned voluntarily.

(e) Patron-client relations are based on a very strong element of *inequality* and *difference in power*. A patron has a monopoly on certain positions and resources that are of vital importance for his client.

What results is a relationship with a paradoxical combination of elements. Inequality and asymmetry in power are combined with expressions of mutual solidarity. Potential coercion and exploitation from the patron is combined with apparently voluntary relations and mutual obligations.

3.3 Brokerage

The form of patronage discussed thus far is that of a patron who gives to his client from his own resources. However, patronage can take other forms, one of which is brokerage (Blok 1969). In brokerage the broker-patron functions as a mediator who gives a client access to the resources of a more powerful patron. We have already mentioned that this form was dominant in the Roman Empire. Well-connected members of the Roman elite served as brokers between the central government (the emperor) and local cities. Members of the provincial elite had the same function between a local administrative center and the surrounding rural districts.

Brokerage involves a relationship between several actors. The same person may simultaneously be a broker (mediator) between higher and lower-ranking people or groups, and a patron to clients below him. In traditional societies brokerage serves multiple purposes. Relations between center and periphery cover a wide range of areas: economic and administrative as well as religious and cultural. Since brokerage can deal with multiple aspects of relations between the center and periphery, different persons can act as brokers. A broker can be a representative for the central power, for instance a military commander, or a wealthy land-owner in the village, or even a "holy man" (Brown 1971). In a wider sense certain groups or professions can serve as brokers, such as teachers, priests, and artists. Thus brokers form a channel of communication be-tween the power and the culture of the urban elite ("the great tradition") and the traditional norms and values of village peasants ("the little tra-dition" Malina 1981:73–75).

3.4 The Benefactor-Patron

Another, predominant form of patronage in antiquity was the "benefactor" or "patron" to a city or local community (Danker 1982). On a smaller scale it is an institution similar to that of the emperor, who was praised as a benefactor to the empire (Millar 1977). Benefaction to a city was frequently expressed through the erection of public buildings such as temples, basilicas, and aqueducts. It could also take the form of the instigation and payment for public festivals and sacrifices, or pub-lic distribution of food.

The reward for these services was public honor expressed in dif-ferent ways. Often, however, these demonstrations of benefaction were not primarily spontaneous expressions of public spirit, but part of a fierce competition for public office. If elected, moreover, public officials were expected and even required to continue to show generosity in a similar manner. Thus, public office could be a heavy financial burden. Demands for patronage could actually pressure the rich to share their wealth, a traditional way of preventing economic differences from becoming too great. In this way wealth spent for the common good was "translated" into status and honor; but because of the fierce competition for public office, the power which the benefactor held over the city population was very tenuous. Thus, the clients could exert pressure upon their patrons. There were strong expectations as to how a patron ought to behave.

3.5 An Example from Dio Chrysostom

Dio Chrysostom is an example of a "public patron," that is, a per-son who shows patronage towards a larger community (Jones 1978:104–14). In *Oratio* 46 he describes how he was mobbed during a grain short-age and accused of holding back his own wealth rather than using it for the public good. This illustrates the typical pressure upon elites from below to share during a period of need. Dio's answer is the elite response from above, and shows his sense of distinction between the elite and the poor. He refutes the accusation and asserts that he has behaved honor-ably. He proceeds to give examples of what was regarded as honorable behavior by the rich toward the poor: although he was a rich landowner, he did not deprive his poor neighbors of their possessions or evict them from their small holdings (Or. 46:7–8).

Likewise, Dio gives insights into the various motives for public bene-factions on the part of the rich. One such motif was concern for general welfare. Desire for repute (doxa) and honor (timē) was a very important motive for patronage, so much so that the term "love of honor" (philotimia) developed the meaning of public munificence. The impor-tance of public opinion and estimation similarly explains a third motif, fear of dislike or envy (phthonos) toward those whose prosperity was conspicuous.

Honor was granted in the form of public recognition. Dio gives a large number of examples of how benefactors were honored (Or. 31; 44; Jones 1978:26–35, 105–14). Statues constitute the highest honor, the word for "honor" (timē) becoming synonymous with "statue." Statues had sanctity: to erase the names of citizens carved on them meant to inflict shame upon them (Or. 31). Other honors included portraits and inscrip-tions, proclamations, public burials, and burial games to be celebrated in their memory, presents or a generous reception, invitations to the pub-lic table of the city or front seats at the theater. This list shows how pa-tronage was transformed into public status.

4.0 THE MODEL APPLIED TO LUKE–ACTS

The world described in Luke's Gospel is complex and contains a large number of social relations. Before we can study these relations, we must reflect on the levels of Luke's narrative. On its surface level it is a narrative about Jesus' travels with his disciples through Palestine. Thus, it deals with Jewish society at large, with its institutions and groups. Within this larger context the main focus is upon Jesus and his group of followers and sympathizers. Consequently, it is possible to study both internal relations within each of these two main groupings and re-lations between the two.

What complicates matters, however, is that Luke does not write "pure" history. In line with the tradition of history writing of his time, there was no conflict between the ideal of a true historical rendering of the past and of telling the story with the purpose of influencing one's readers (Aune 1987:77–115). In this way Luke's narrative is made trans-parent, so that it becomes relevant for his readers. Thus, his description of groups and actors in Palestine at the time of Jesus is not "neutral," but colored by his evaluations. Similarly in his description of Jesus and his followers, particularly in the speeches of Jesus, Luke addresses his audience with a view to influencing their relations. Consequently, we shall try to distinguish between the patron-client relations as they can be observed in Luke's narrative, the evaluations which he makes and the ideals of patron-client relations which he puts forth.

S. Silverman discusses a similar problem in his study "Patronage as Myth" (1977:7–19). He emphasizes that we should "set forth our concepts in such a way that we can investigate the interplay between values and behavior, between belief and action (1977:19). And so he distinguishes between an etic analysis which deals with how people actually behave, and an emic analysis which is concerned with the cognitive patterning of what is supposed to happen and of what does happen.

Concerning this last area, Silverman says that "the more relevant questions would be: What does it mean to be a 'patron' and how is it appropriate for one to behave?" (1977:10). In his own studies of an Italian village he became interested in the apparent discrepancy between the small quantities actually exchanged within a patron-client relationship and the importance attributed to these relationships by the village population. This made him raise the question of the relation between myth and reality. He found that myths were not mirrors of social reality or direct guidelines for behavior. Nevertheless these myths had a function. The myth of generous patronage had been used by the local elites to back up their claims to autonomy for their community. However, the myth could be used by the poor to express a different picture of patronage than that put forth by the elite:

> Ideas about appropriateness might well include the expectation that patrons will often not do what they are supposed to. It may be expected, for instance, that they will abuse their positions or exploit their clients while adopting the manners and language of paternalism. Such expectations cannot be taken as descriptions of real behavior any more than can statements of ideals (Silverman 1977:10).

Silverman pointed out how the patronage myth had been used by the local elite for their own purposes. From a similar perspective J. Waterbury observed: "It is not difficult to conclude that patronage is not only a manifestation of class domination, but crucial to its continued maintenance" (Waterbury 1977:354). In Dio we found an example of patronage discussed from the point of view of the rich. However, the myth of beneficial patronage could also be perpetuated by clients and used as a means of pressure upon the wealthy (Saller 1982:37–38). In some instances this pressure might be effective within the severe limitations that the patron-client relations allowed. But as Silverman pointed out, even if the myth was being perpetuated, it might actually include negative expectations to the patron.

On the basis of Silverman's discussion, a number of questions can be addressed to Luke's Gospel. From what perspective does Luke speak of patron-client relations? What is myth or ideal, and what is reality? How does he conceptualize this relationship? Moreover, does he himself speak as a patron or as a client?

We shall first apply Silverman's distinction between etic analysis (analysis of how people actually behave) and emic analysis (analysis of their cognitive patterns) to patron-client relations in Jewish society in Palestine at large. In the next section, focusing more specifically upon the Jesus movement, the emic analysis becomes predominant. This perspective is chosen since the Lukan narratives and speeches are mostly concerned with conceptualizations of patron-client relations in the "new community." Finally, an attempt will be made to draw inferences from the study of Luke–Acts about social relations and social processes within Luke's historical community.

4.1 Patron-Client Relations in Luke's Palestine

At the basis of the description of social structures in Luke lies the difference between center and periphery, between city and rural villages, and between Jerusalem and outlying regions. This contrast affects all areas of power: political, economic, and religious. Center-periphery contrast is not just a "background" to a "religious" main theme of the book. Rather, these two themes are totally integrated in the narrative about Jesus.

The main perspective of this section, therefore, is patron-client relations within the center-periphery contrast. What form does patronage take in this context? In parable and narrative Luke describes the world of the villages (the periphery), while the world of the elite (the center) is seen from afar. Periphery and center are culturally miles apart. The rich, who are luxuriously dressed, live away at Herod's court (7:25). Herod interferes in the periphery at irregular intervals, as a bad omen of the outside power that will destroy Jesus (3:19–20; 9:7–9; 13:31–33). Although distant, the outside world and the central power had their representatives in the village.

4.1.1 *Patrons, Clients, and Brokers.* We are now in a better position to understand the narrative about the centurion in Capernaum who made contact with Jesus through "elders of the Jews" and a group of "friends" (7:1–10). The key to his relationships with these groups lies in his position as a patron. He represents the outside military and administrative power, and he is himself a non-Jew. But he had apparently established himself in a trusted position in the town, for he had taken upon himself the role of patron to the town. One example of his benefaction was standing the expense for a synagogue building. Since he was a military commander and therefore had his power from the outside, it is probable that he served also as a mediator between this peripheral town and central authorities. In short, he was a broker. In return for his favors to the town, the town elders, who were his clients ("he sent them"), established contact with Jesus. In customary fashion they praise the centurion and recommend him to Jesus as an honorable person: "He is worthy to have you do this for him, for he loves our nation, and he built us our synagogue" (7:4–5).

This delegation of elders also indicates the respect shown to Jesus, the potential patron. He is addressed "Lord" (7:6) and is considered more powerful than the centurion. This is indicated in the second message to Jesus by the centurion's "friends," his associates. Through them the centurion declares his own unworthiness by means of traditional phrases and thus allows the power of Jesus to shine forth even more clearly. In Luke's narrative this is a positive honor challenge, in which the powerful centurion, an important patron in the area, concedes larger honor to Jesus and addresses him as benefactor and patron (see chapter on honor and shame by Malina and Neyrey).

Beyond Luke 7:1–10, there are three parables in particular which illustrate patron-client relations. The Lukan narratives of Jesus' travels and his encounters with people focus mostly on administrative and military powers from the outside. Certain parables in Luke confirm and complement this picture with their focus on ownership and control of land. In the parable of the "nobleman" who went abroad to establish a kingdom for himself, the "servants" (*douloi*) who served him well were given as reward authority over five or ten "cities" (Luke 19:11–27). Whether or not this parable alludes to the princes of the Herod family who obtained the status of vassal kings from the Roman emperor, the situation is typical of patron-client relations between central power and peripheral vassals. The "servants" were trusted associates or agents of the prince, and they should be regarded as clients, not as slaves. Their reward may have been that of command of a toparchy, an administrative unit comprising several villages.

On a smaller scale, the parable of the dishonest steward (Luke 16:1–9) tells about an absentee landlord. He lived in the city, but had tenants on his large estates on the periphery who owed him considerable sums. Thus there exists a patron-client relationship between landowner and tenant. This landowner had a steward (*oikonomos*) who served as his agent. Apparently he had considerable authority to conduct business on his master's behalf. There is an element of trust between them which adds to the master-servant relationship the more kinship-like character of patron-client relations (Malina 1988a). The steward himself serves as a broker between his master and his master's tenants. But his mastery of a difficult situation shows itself in the way in which he uses his position as a broker to create patron-client links between himself and his master's tenants (16:4–7). By reducing their debts, they become indebted to him, and thus obliged to receive him as a guest in time of need.

A third parable also speaks of a steward (*oikonomos*) who is a house manager with responsibility for his master's house slaves (12:42–46). A comparison with Matthew's version of the same story (24:45–51) shows that only Luke employs the technical vocabulary which indicates the trusted position of the steward, *oikonomos* (Luke 12:42), and emphasizes his position as a middleman or broker vis-à-vis the servants. They are addressed as "boys" and "maids" (*paides, paidiskai*). In Matthew's version, the steward is called *doulos* together with the other servants, and the others are spoken of as his "fellow servants" (*syndouloi*, Matt 24:49).

These narratives and parables clearly show the dependent relationship of the villagers in relation to a central ruler and/or rich absentee landlords in the cities. The village population stands in a client relationship to a patron, be it an ethnarch, an absentee landlord, or a local big landowner. But the distance between the village and the center is so great that there can be no immediate and direct contact. Therefore the middleman becomes such an important figure. The central patron acts through an intermediary who functions as a broker in this relationship.

We found middlemen or brokers in the story of the centurion (7:1–10), the dishonest steward (16:1–9) and the parable of watchfulness (12:42–46). In particular the parable of the house manager is important in that his role is directly compared to that of the apostles (12:41). Thus, the image of the broker is linked to the picture of the Twelve as they serve as "delegate benefactors" (Danker 1987:42–43), assisting Jesus in his benefactions. Thus, it is clear from the way that Luke tells his story that the position of the mediator or broker is of particular importance. Luke employs this role to give a picture of society in which the broker has an important function within the system of social stratification and social relations. Moreover, it is significant that this role is also used as a model for the leadership within the Jesus community.

What is the dynamic of this patronage structure in Luke's Gospel? There can be no doubt that it is a top-heavy structure with pressure on the villagers. This is indicated by the large number of instances in which Luke speaks of debts and loans (6:34, 7:41–42; 12:58–59; 16:1–9). The import of this becomes clear when we realize that loans were not granted by banking institutions. A peasant had to go the a rich landowner to borrow money, grain for seed, etc. Consequently, to receive a loan meant to enter into a personal relationship with this landowner, to become his client. A situation of large debts is well known and taken as a fact of life by Luke, in the same manner as he frequently speaks of hunger and going hungry. Pressure by taxes and outright robbery by soldiers (3:14) add to the picture of village communities under stress. The essay by Oakman in this volume should be consulted on this point.

4.1.2 *Expectations of the Rich as Patrons.* It is not easy to distinguish between historical information and judgment in Luke, but what we have noticed so far corresponds well to what we know about the economic situation in first-century Palestine from other sources. Our next step is to ask the emic question: how did Luke conceptualize patronage? what were his views of the expectations which people had of patrons, not only how patrons ought to behave, but also how they were expected to behave?

Luke portrays "the rich" in negative terms. They are easily recognized: they dress in luxurious clothes (7:25; 16:19) and feast and drink sumptuously (12:19; 16:19). "Rich" is not just an economic category, but rather a name for members of the elite. Notice, for instance, the statement by Jesus that "those who are gorgeously apparelled and live in luxury are in kings' courts" (7:25). Moreover, it is expected that the rich will show a selfish and ungenerous attitude. "The rich fool" in the parable in 12:16–21 clearly belongs to the ungenerous rich. There was nothing morally wrong in the way he got his fortune; it was through a good harvest. But his behavior shows that he is selfish, for his invitation to "eat, drink and be merry" (12:19) is directed solely to himself. His plans to build bigger barns to store his grain shows that he does not want to act as a patron.

Dio Chrysostom's speech during a grain shortage in Prusa (see 3.5 above) illuminates this parable. When accused of hoarding grain to raise prices, Dio defended himself against accusations that he held back his own wealth rather than using it for the common good (Or. 46:8). Thus, in the eyes of common folks in the village, the rich man in Luke's parable was not only selfish at the moment. By building larger barns he wanted to secure his position and store grain for periods of scarcity and hunger. Thus, he would make the villagers more dependant of him when in needy times they would have to buy grain at a high price.

Another "rich man" in the parable in Luke 16:19–31 belongs to the same category. The beggar Lazarus lies outside his gate while the rich man, elegantly dressed, feasts inside. Through Luke's description of his dress and behavior, he rendered a judgment of the moral character of the rich man. The reader is led to understand that from this person the poor can have no expectation of generosity. From these parables, then, "the rich" as an elite group are effectively dismissed as benefactors in the world of Luke's Gospel; they are portrayed as unwilling to show such generosity as one should rightly expect from them.

Luke gives only one example of a rich man's generosity, the story of Zacchaeus, chief tax collector in Jericho (Luke 19:1–10). He was rich, but because of his status as an outsider he did not belong to the elite; he is never portrayed as a patron. Instead, he serves as an example of how tax-collectors and non-elite followed the will of God, while the leaders of the Jewish people did not (7:29–30).

4.1.3 Community Leaders Who Block Access to God. The rich elite were patrons in their own right who could give from their own resources. The priestly elite in Jerusalem were also part of the social elite and had access to wealth. Apart from them, Jewish community leaders functioned more as brokers. They were above all connected with the temple and with Torah, as priests, scribes and Pharisees. In Jewish society, moreover, power was intimately linked to God, and access to God was granted through temple and Torah.

In the major part of Luke's narrative, community leaders are represented by heads of the synagogue, Pharisees and scribes. According to Luke, however, in almost every instance they do not facilitate access to God, but instead block it. This becomes the theme of several of the conflict scenes between them and Jesus. People who are in need of healing or salvation come to Jesus, but the community leaders try to use the Torah to stop them by means of arguments based on legality, sabbath observance etc. (5:21; 6:2, 7; 13:14). Thus, these leaders who are supposed to be "brokers" (or "friends") do not fulfill their function. This suggests that Jesus will fill that needed role of friend, patron, and broker.

In a way peculiar to Luke some of these community leaders, namely the Pharisees, are identified with the rich elite. Historically, it may be more correct to speak of the Pharisees as a faction within Palestine. In the Gospel narratives, however, they clearly play the role of leaders in virtue of their function as overseers of Torah observance. Moreover, they are obviously competing with Jesus for leadership of the people. In 14:1–14 we meet a rich Pharisee, who was a leader of the people; he invited for dinner his rich neighbors together with relatives and friends (14:12). It was a dinner comparable to that of the rich man in Luke 16:19, an exchange of carefully balanced reciprocity among the rich. Jesus' exhortation (14:12–14) shows that the poor and the outcasts of the village were excluded from such dinners. Thus, the Pharisees, too, were exclusively sharing among themselves, not with others. They were failing as brokers.

They are accused, moreover, of exploiting the poor. Instead of showing generosity through almsgiving (11:41), they are extortioners (11:39). They claim the honors of patrons and benefactors to a community (11:43), but without justification. Their oppression of the poor discredits them as community leaders and takes away their legitimation. But the situation as Luke describes it is even worse than that. The Pharisees are accused of being "lovers of money" (16:14), that is, of serving Mammon, not God (16:13). No wonder that they could not act as brokers between God and the village people. They were themselves not in the service of God, but of the enemy (see 7:30). "Mammon" in Luke does not just mean "money," but implies a system of unjust structures of exploitation and oppression. Thus, the accusation against the Pharisees that they were "lovers of money" is the total delegitimation of them as brokers.

With this, Luke has described, not the historical situation and the real expectations of patrons and brokers in first-century Palestine, but his own social system. In this picture, the people of Israel suffer "negative patronage": they expect nothing either from the rich elites or from their community leaders. Not only is there very little positive contact between the elites in the urban centers and the periphery, but even their own community leaders have joined forces with the "negative patrons." The village communities are thus left to themselves.

5.0 GOD AS PATRON AND JESUS AS BROKER

As the thesis of this section, I suggest that there is a transformation of the concept of patronage and of patron-client relations in Luke's Gospel. We started the last section with two observation. First, patron-client relations deal with power in two spheres: the center-periphery (city-village, Jerusalem-Galilee) and God-human beings; second, these two spheres are interrelated. Jesus moves in both spheres; and more than that, he combines them both in his own person.

The story of Jesus begins in Galilee in the north. The middle section of Luke's Gospel, the Travel Narrative in Luke 9–19, takes Jesus from the periphery to Jerusalem, the national center of power and cult. A new fellowship is formed around Jesus in Galilee, which follows him on his journey and into Jerusalem, the center. This is also a fellowship of patronage and patron-client relations. But what is the concept of patronage and the ideals of patrons in this new fellowship (the emic question)? From what perspective does Luke view this new patron-client relationship? How is Jesus' "conquest" of the center reflected in the transformation of the conceptions of patronage?

5.1 God as Benefactor and Patron

It is axiomatic for Luke and others that God is the ultimate benefactor and patron of all. Luke significantly heralds this main theme in the two hymns at the beginning of his Gospel, 1:46–55 and 1:68–79. In Judaism, moreover, the world was viewed in terms of personal relations. God is an exclusive patron: God expected an exclusive relationship between himself as patron and the Jews as clients. Therefore, Luke can take it for granted that it was impossible to be a client of God and Mammon at the same time (16:13). The conflict was one of claims to undivided loyalty. This is also the underlying problem in the controversy over paying taxes to Caesar (20:19–26). Did the emperor make claims to status as patron in the same way as God, so that taxpaying became a matter of being the client of Caesar rather than of God? This was a problem which would continue to trouble Christians through the centuries.

It is a characteristic motif of Luke that God's benefactions are directed towards the poor and the lowly, while he sends the rich and mighty away (1:51–53). Thus, God performs a reversal of existing situations (6:20–26). This picture of God brings him directly into the other relationships described by Luke, between center and periphery, patrons and clients. Moreover, God is portrayed in such a way that he takes sides in these conflicts, for he uses his benefactions to the benefit of the lowly and powerless.

5.2 Jesus as Broker

The central theme of the Gospel is that God acts as a benefactor-patron through Jesus. Jesus is not a patron in his own right, distributing his own resources, but a broker who gives access to the benefactions of God. He mediates between the people of Israel and God (Malina 1988a). And so his conflict with the old leadership of Israel becomes understandable, for it is a conflict over the right and the power to give access to God.

Jesus gives access to God through proclaiming the kingdom (4:16–19), through healing the sick and delivering those afflicted by evil spirits. The healing narratives variously illustrate the following points. (a) Jesus is a broker; his healings or other powerful acts are performed in the name of God or with the power of God. (b) God is the ultimate source of the healings. This is indicated by the response of the people giving praise to God (5:25–26; 7:16; 13:13; 18:43). By honoring God the people accept their status as clients. (c) Jesus has access to power, but the fundamental question always was, "Who has the power?" and "Is that power legitimate or illegitimate?" Jesus shares legitimately in the power of God (4:32; 6:19), thus he puts his opponents to shame, and creates a group of followers, his disciples.

In the perspective of relation between center and periphery (city and village) Jesus as mediator clearly identifies with the periphery, the rural and the lowly. It is to them that he gives direct access to God. The controversial point, however, is that in doing this, Jesus is not a mediator along the center-periphery axis. He does not have access to the traditional channels to God, via temple and Torah, which are localized in Jerusalem, the center. Instead, he comes from Galilee, from the periphery. The conflict with Jewish leaders presented in Jesus' travels through Galilee and Judea intensifies when he enters Jerusalem. Thus, he does not conform to the model of "mediation" or brokerage imposed from the center upon the periphery. Therefore, Jesus as a broker has a problem within Israel in that he does not represent the center. As a mediator from the outside he is rejected by the elites and the establishment.

Jesus is discredited by the company which he keeps. He is accused of being "a friend" of tax-collectors and sinners (6:34; 15:1–2; 19:1–10). As we noted above, "friend" is a word which belongs to the terminology of patronage and local alliances. It has wider implications than our modern types of friendship understood primarily as emotional relationships (Eisenstadt and Roniger 1984:61–62). Thus, the accusation implies that he makes tax-collectors and sinners his clients and that he enters into an unholy alliance with them and all that they represent.

Given the competitive character of an honor-shame society, the question "Who is the greatest?" would frequently arise. Such a question has to do with brokerage and patronage. On one occasion, Jesus sets up as a model and identifies with a child, totally without power and prestige (9:46–48), with nothing to exchange for honor and status. Finally, at the Last Supper the question "Who is the greatest?" comes up again. Jesus refers as a matter of fact to the established order of status and honor in his society when he says: "Which is the greater, one who sits at table, or one who serves? Is it not the one who sits at table?" (22:27). But then Jesus himself enters the picture in a surprising way: "But I am among you as one who serves (ho diakonōn)." This statement represents a new concept of leadership and patronage.

The import of this event is brought out by a comparison with the parable of the servants awaiting their master home from a wedding feast (Luke 12:35–40). For those who stay awake, there is an unexpected reward: "Blessed are those servants whom the master finds awake when he comes; truly, I say to you, he will gird himself and have them sit at the table, and he will come and serve (diakonēsei) them" (12:37). The word "to serve" was linked to food; it was the task of nurturing, associated with women and servants. Thus, it was the task of providing life, but it had low status compared to that of free men. Both in the parable and in the narrative of the Last Supper there is a paradoxical contrast between the master and the lowly task that he is performing. Jesus is the master and benefactor, but now he appears in a totally unexpected role. He identifies greatness with the act of serving rather than being served. Brokerage, then, is central to Luke's agenda, but not as a means to honor and status. The result is a transformation of the traditional concept of patronage.

Luke's criticism of the Jewish leadership is scathing, and Jesus is clearly presented as an alternative to them. But Luke's alternative could not be couched in modern terms that would come naturally to our minds. We would speak of democracy instead of patron-client relations and of universal rights instead of favors based on patronage. But Luke could only express his alternative within his own world view and the social universe of his time. The very concept of patronage and the understanding of community and cosmos in terms of personal relations were perceived by Luke as part of nature. Luke's alternative had to be expressed in terms of Jesus as benefactor and broker-patron, and of personal relations between Jesus and his followers.

In summary, Luke's description of Jesus as broker and benefactor combines the terminology of power identified with the center, and the terminology of serving and of the lowly, associated with the periphery. Jesus comes from the periphery to the center, to Jerusalem, to the temple, but he is not recognized as a broker between the two spheres. As Elliott shows in his essay, Luke discredits the temple as an institution when Jesus cleanses it of its economic power as center (19:45–46). Thus, he displaces the illegitimate power of the city, of the center, and highlights in his person the legitimate power: "prayer to God" (19:46). Consequently, a new form of leadership is necessary. And this leadership is not based on extraction from people, such as the temple economy, but on "serving," the simple and life-giving activity of the household, associated with women and servants. There is a strange transformation of the very concept of patronage. The institution is preserved, but the greatness traditionally associated with the role of the patron is now intimately linked with the act of serving. This transformation of roles is not confined to Jesus; it also becomes visible in Luke's description of the disciples of Jesus.

5.3 Apostles as Brokers

It is clear from Luke's description of the Twelve that they also should be defined as brokers. They were called by Jesus (6:12–16), given shares of his power and authority to heal and to preach the kingdom of God (9:1–6), and became his followers and clients. In their dealings with new followers they in turn became patrons in the form of brokers. More than the other evangelists Luke compares the role of the Twelve to well-known social roles of his milieu. Thus we noticed that the role of the steward (middleman) in the parable of watchfulness (12:41–48) is directly applied to the apostles. The main role of the steward in this parable is to provide food for the household servants (12:42). All the while he remains responsible to his master to perform that task faithfully.

Similarly, in Jesus' farewell speech (22:29–30), Luke's picture of the Twelve as leaders of Israel emphasizes the element of serving food. At the farewell meal a discussion of "who is the greatest?" arose. Jesus compares the apostles to contemporary leaders: "The kings of the Gentiles exercise lordship over them; and those in authority over them are called benefactors. But not so with you; rather, let the greatest among you become as the youngest, and the leader as one who serves" (22:25–26). A comparison with the parallel passages in Mark 10:43–44 and Matt 20:26–27 provides perspective on Luke's special emphasis in his version. Mark and Matthew speak of those who "want to become greatest/ first" and the behavior that will bring them to that goal. Luke, on the other hand, addresses those who *are* the greatest or who *are* leaders, and give rules for their behavior. Thus, it is a matter of the behavior expected of leaders. The question is not how to obtain greatness, but how the great should behave. It is possible, therefore, to read Luke at this point as accepting structures of leadership, but emphasizing a transformation of their role and their status. The greatest and the leaders will have no different status from the young and those who serve at tables, that is, they will have no power and no special honor.

Again there is the same transformation of patronage role as in the case of Jesus himself. The disciples are not to replace traditional leaders. Luke does not even seem to argue that instead of being "bad leaders," they shall be "good leaders" who use their power for the benefit of their clients. If that were so, they could rightly claim the title benefactor and expect honor and respect. But there is even a break with "the good leader" model. D. Lull (1986) argues that "benefactor" in 22:25 serves as a positive model for the role of the apostles. He rightly criticizes a traditional interpretation which holds that the point of v. 25 is that kings make false claims to be benefactors. However, he misses the element of contrast between the description of kings and benefactors in v. 25 and the imagery of "servant" and "young" in v. 26, a contrast which is obvious also in the parallel passage 9:46–48. The Twelve are installed as judges of Israel (22:29–30), but at the same time they are to imitate Jesus "as one who serves" (22:27). There is, then, a break with the patron-client relationship at its most crucial point: a service performed or a favor done shall *not* be transformed into status and honor.

A benefactor could rightly claim power and authority (Danker 1982:436–85). The apostles, however, are to be different. There is a discrepancy between their power as brokers and their status. As "judges," that is, central authorities, they are at the same time to "serve." Thus, they are to combine male leadership roles with the role of providing food, a function within the confines of the home, performed by women and servants, at the periphery of a society dominated by free men.

The ambiguity of the role of leadership is emphasized also in the commissioning of the Twelve and the Seventy as missionaries (9:1–6; 10:1–12). They are to go without property and possessions or means to defend themselves, that is, they are to be total outsiders in society. But they bring with them the full powers of God to heal and to preach the kingdom. They come as brokers who give access to the power of God. Their reception by supporters means the establishment of a patronage bond, but of a new kind. Therefore, some of the same confusing broker terminology used of Jesus is also used of the apostles. They are mediators between God and people, commissioned by Jesus and sharing in his power. Moreover, they must also share his identity. They must be both rulers on the thrones of Israel and servants and bearers of the cross (9:23–27; 14:27).

5.4 Women as Clients and Benefactors

When we turn to other types of relations within the community of followers of Jesus, those which involve women are of particular interest.

For the following I am especially indebted to a major study in progress by my colleague Turid Karlsen Seim of the Faculty of Theology at the University of Oslo. Women in Luke–Acts are primarily described in their relations to Jesus and to his disciples or early Christian missionaries. They use their resources to care for Jesus or male leaders in terms of hospitality, providing food and a place to stay.

An example from Acts 16 can be a starting point for reviewing the roles of women in Luke's writings. In the description of Paul's travels, a women named Lydia played an important role as his benefactor in Philippi (Acts 16:14–15). Luke explains how Paul spoke to a group of women at the riverside:

> One who heard us was a woman named Lydia, from the city of Thyatira, a seller of purple goods, who was a worshipper of God. The Lord opened her heart to give heed to what was said by Paul. And when she was baptized, with her household, she besought us, saying, "If you have judged me to be faithful to the Lord, come to my house and stay." And she prevailed upon us (Acts 16:14–15).

Luke here described the relationship between Paul and Lydia as a complex patron-client relationship. Lydia was a seller of purple goods, and thus probably belonged to a number of active working women of relatively low status, but who had the opportunity to enhance their status through their own work and initiative (Kampen 1981:20–32). One of the ways they could do that was by being patrons. She had her own house and household, which was baptized together with her. She was an independent women of a type found in many communities, who gave room to a house church. In this she performs the function a patron.

But in Luke's story it is Paul who is the superior, since he is on a special mission from God (Acts 16:9) and thus serves as a broker between God and Lydia and her household. Moreover, the situation reflects a pattern of reciprocity in which Paul gives the greatest gift and Lydia reciprocates. Lydia has her heart opened by God when she hears the words preached by Paul and she is baptized. In response, she implores Paul to come to her house and stay there, as a sign of recognition that she is faithful to the Lord. This pattern is identical with the reception of the seventy disciples in Luke 10:7–9. And so, hosting the apostle is a reciprocity for the favor which he provided. But Lydia as the host/patron is inferior in role and status to the apostle/broker. Paul's acceptance of her insistent invitation means a recognition of her loyalty and a granting of honor.

Luke describes Lydia as a patron who considers her benefactions as an act of reciprocity for the far greater spiritual benefits that she has received. Moreover, her patronage is offered very humbly; if her gift is accepted, she in fact receives the larger gift of recognition of her faith. In this way patronage is accepted, but always at the discretion of the apostle. In contrast to Acts 16, the apocryphal Acts of Peter narrates that the privilege of patronage in reciprocity for healing is denied by the apostle (Stoops 1986:94).

Beyond the example of Lydia, we can study the role of women patrons in Luke's narrative in their function vis-à-vis Jesus and the disciples, especially the "wandering charismatics." Its relationship begins with Jesus' initiative in the form of healing; and reciprocally the women who have been healed "serve" him (diakonein, 4:38–39; 8:1–3). At least one of them belonged to the elite, Joanna, the wife of Chuza, who was Herod's steward (8:3). But even she, who on the basis of her status could act as patron, actually "served." Luke's terminology implies that these women do not merely "provide," but that what they do is an act of "service." If "service" is understood for Jesus and the Twelve in terms of patronage and benefaction, the same would seem to apply to Luke's women. Some of the women mentioned by name had a longstanding relationship of "service" to Jesus: They were healed by him (8:1–3); they followed him and served him in Galilee (8:3); they followed him to his crucifixion, and prepared his body for the funeral (23:49, 55–24:2). Having service as their main task, many of the women in Luke–Acts exemplify in their lives the model of Jesus as "the patron who serves" (22:27).

In this section of our study of patronage we have been primarily concerned with the emic question, that is, Luke's concept of patronage. We may consider Luke's description of women patrons as an effort to integrate traditional social patterns into the structure of the "new community" of believers. In this new community Christ or the apostle/missionary is the patron-broker representing the ultimate benefactor, God himself. Through miracles, preaching and baptism they make converts and "clients" of these, even if they are of high social status. Thus, it becomes a privilege to act as host and benefactor to Christ, to the apostle or to the missionary. The usual pattern of patronage with its unequal relationship between patron and client is now put within the structure of the new community and transformed.

5.5 Patrons Without Clients: A Community of Equals

So far we have primarily discussed patron-client relations between Jesus and the disciples or between the apostles and other followers. Now the time has come to look at relations between members of the community, especially concerning the way in which scarce resources were shared.

The issue of "rich and poor" and of the "communism" of the first Christian community in Acts has always created much interest and caused much discussion. Communism, however, is a modern ideology and social system based on the idea of egalitarian relations, and far from Luke's conceptions of the world. The model of patronage provides a better perspective on Luke's advice for social relations between believers. How were those who had something to share and behave towards those who were in need? Within the different types of patronage that we have discussed, this relationship is not that of the broker model (which explained the role of Jesus and of the disciples) or that of the client-reciprocity model (which explained the role of women vis-à-vis Jesus and wandering preachers). Rather, this relationship is that of a patron who shares his or her own resources with a person or a group with less resources within the Jesus group.

We found that Luke spoke plainly of the negative expectations of the poor towards the rich elites (see 4.1.2 above). Although the rich ought to behave like generous patrons, the poor expect them to be selfish and non-generous. But what positive image does Luke paint of patronage? The narrative of Jesus at dinner in the house of the rich Pharisee serves as an illustration. Jesus accuses the Pharisee of engaging in a reciprocal exchange only among his equals, and therefore says: "When you give a dinner or a banquet, do not invite your friends or your brothers or your kinsmen or your rich neighbors, lest they also invite you in return, and you be repaid" (14:12). The alternative is: "But when you give a feast, invite the poor, the maimed, the blind, and you will be blessed, because they cannot repay you. You will be repaid at the resurrection of the just" (14:13-14). Jesus here urges a break with the system of reciprocities in which a gift is always repaid by the recipient (Mauss 1967).

This statement represents an important transformation of the very basis for patronage. First, one is urged to give to the poor who cannot repay in kind. The second and main point is that one shall not expect any return from them, not even in terms of gratitude or glorification. "Giving" shall no longer be used to create clients, and thus the very basis for patronage is taken away.

According to the model, patron-client relationships are held together by reciprocity within a structure of great inequality between patron and client when it comes to resources and power. If one is to act as a patron but without any expectations of reciprocity in terms of gratitude and loyalty from one's client, the power aspect is removed from the relationship. Then social relations are supposed to function on the basis of an equal status as fictive kin in God's household, differences in resources notwithstanding. It is a radical departure from a situation in which wealth, status, and power determine social relations.

Luke's descriptions of relations in the first community in Jerusalem have elements of this transformation of the patron concept (Acts 2:43–47; 4:32–37). One part of the description (2:44; 4:32) emphasizes that they had everything in common, in line with the Greek idea that "friends have everything in common." Those, however, who possessed land or houses are singled out: "For as many as were possessors of lands or houses sold them, and brought the proceeds of what was sold and laid it at the apostles' feet; and distribution was made to each as any had need" (4:34–35). The ideal, dramatically contrasted with the story of Ananias and Sapphira (5:1–11), shows acts of benefactions to the needy, in particular, by disciples who can act as patrons of the community. But the distribution of goods is made by the apostles. As leaders of the community they function as brokers. Thus, the donor-patrons do not receive any special honor or reward. Their gift is an act of service towards those in need, but it is not to be transformed into status for the benefactors. It does not give them a special honor, but it is a sign of the spirit of unity within the community.

The model for this behavior within Luke–Acts is Israel's very God who reverses the fortunes of poor and rich (1:53–55; 6:20–26). Since God is the great patron of all this, transformation of the concept of patronage is possible and legitimate. The human patron who is asked to give without expecting any return is promised a return from God "at the resurrection of the just" (14:14). Thus, there are three parties involved, the patron, the client, and God. The human patron is urged to give to needy clients without expecting any return (6:34–35; 14:13–14). The human patron will be repaid, however, by the third party, God, who is the great benefactor of all, even of the wealthy. He invites everybody to his great banquet (14:15–24); he is the giver of life and can also take it back (12:20–21). In the admonitions to give to the poor, the promise of a reward from God serves as a motivation (14:14). In this way God acts as the patron of the poor and the needy through human patrons. In a similar manner the needy are urged to trust in God, not in human patrons (11:9–11; 12:29–31; 18:29–30). Consequently, Luke is arguing for a transformation of patron-client relations.

6.0 SUMMARY, CONCLUSIONS, AND FURTHER PROJECTS

6.1 Paradoxical Patronage

What picture emerges from this survey of conceptions of patron-client relations in the new community? We found two basic patterns, that of the patron-broker-client type, and that of the simpler patron-client type.

The broker-client model deals with the most fundamental aspect of the Jesus group: its claim to give access to the power of God. Jesus and his disciples as "delegate" brokers bypass the traditional urban and legal central power of temple and Torah by proclaiming the immediacy of the kingdom of God (17:20–21) and by performing miracles of healing. Jesus' brokerage, moreover, is both exclusive (Acts 4:10–12) and necessary (Acts 13:38–39). Thus Luke shows that the source of Jesus' power is God himself and that his power is legitimate. Jesus, however, retains an identification with the lowly, for he is not a broker from the traditional source of power who bestows favors upon the poor for the purpose of thereby gaining clients.

The model of the "patron-servant" was closely linked to Jesus' role as broker between center and periphery, but as one who came from the wrong sector, identified with the lowly and the outsiders. Gradually local Christian communities became more stable and socially integrated, and the element of dislocation that is present in the paradoxical combination of "patron" and "servant" in the words of Jesus was lost from their own experience. However, the concept of the charismatic as mediator between God and human beings, and even between city and village, was a powerful image. It resurfaced after some generations in "holy men" who lived in deserts and remote areas, and who also combined spiritual and social brokerage (P. Brown 1971).

This radical transformation of the concept of patronage serves as well as a model for the apostles, leaders, and disciples of the community. The context of leadership, however, signals that this transformation is controversial: it comes as a rebuke to one of the strongest impetuses for patronage in Luke's cultural environment, namely the competition for honor so as to be "the greatest" (9:46–48; 22:24–27). Thus, it appears that the question of authority has been answered with a paradox which leaves the roles of patron and servant in tension. The "greatest" is to provide food, but not as a patron who distributes his resources. Rather "the greatest" actually waits on tables and thus performs the task of women and servants. This tension has largely been resolved in the role of the women as "client-patrons." They are clients of Jesus, his disciples and travelling missionaries. They "serve" with their possessions in return for the gifts of healing and the word of the kingdom. They are the ideal imitators of Jesus as servant. Relations between individual members of the community are discussed in terms of economic and social exchange. Yet they are presented more in terms of a transformation of patron-client relations than of brokerage. The point of transformation lies in the pressure upon patrons to give without expecting any returns in the form of clients or heightened status in the community. For clients this resulted in freedom from the binds of patronage. Thus, this transformation of a traditional concept of patronage is central to the system of social relations in the community: they are not to be determined on the basis of existing social and economic inequality or on mutuality in exchange within these relations. Likewise, to give generously to the needy meant to identify with God in his compassion and love (6:31–36; 7:42; 11:4).

More than the other evangelists Luke has used the terminology of the patron-client relationship to describe the relations between Jesus and his disciples as well as relations within the community of believers. He must have found the structures and images of this relationship useful vis-à-vis his readers. The dedication of his books to Theophilus (Luke 1:3; Acts 1:1) may indicate that he was Luke's patron, and that Luke was addressing a Hellenistic milieu well acquainted with the categories of patron-client relationships. But at the same time Luke presents a radical transformation of the patronage system as a model for social relations within the Christian community.

6.2 The Social Setting of Luke's Community

Is it possible to move from these concepts of patronage to the social situation of Luke's community? This can only be done with great caution. There is still no scholarly consensus on the geographical or social location of Luke's community. It has been argued that Luke's criticism of the rich indicates that his Gospel was addressed to a group with many rich members (Karris 1978). But the negative expectations towards the "rich elites" appear to point to them as outsiders to the Lukan community. Therefore, it is more likely that the community was a non-elite group that looked with suspicion upon the rich elites in their surroundings. This does not, however, exclude the possibility of social and economic differences within the community, and even people of some wealth among its members. The non-elites in Hellenistic cities consisted of many diverse groups: slaves of different categories, freedmen, foreign merchants and craftsmen, free, but poor citizens, etc. The first Christian communities probably were made up of members from these groups, maybe with some women of higher status.

Within these non-elite groups there was some social mobility. Patronage and generosity could be used by freedmen to buy status and honor, and were some of the few means available to gain respect and to advance socially. Thus, it is only to be expected that these same mechanisms were at work within Christian communities as well, for instance, in the form of wealthy members serving as patrons by opening their houses as meeting places, "house churches." The admonitions, then, not to use benefactions to make clients may be indicative of tensions within the community. If this is so, these statements are expressions of a patronage ideology viewed "from below." It is the positive counterpart to the negative expectations of the rich elite voiced in the Gospel, a pressure on behalf of those with least resources upon the more resourceful not to use their benefactions to make the needy into clients.

6.3 Further Study: Patronage in Luke–Acts

If this essay has offered an adequate scenario for social relations in Luke's community, what might a reader do now with this information? Of course, more detailed study of specific passages might be undertaken from this perspective. One might branch out in a totally different direction and examine the many references to prayer to God in light of patronage (Malina 1980). In the same vein, one might examine terms such as "grace" and "mercy" and "election" in terms of God's patronage. Even the gift of the Holy Spirit in Acts might be profitably studied in this light.

Yet more importantly, a conversation might ensue between this essay and other essays in this volume, a conversation which would add an important element or clarification to other studies. Clearly the study by Richard Rohrbaugh on the parable of the great supper in Luke 14:14–24 depends on a model of patronage as well as the pre-industrial city; our findings are mutually reinforcing. Likewise, with the essay by John Elliott on the institutions of temple and household. Our argument that Jesus is a broker, but not like the temple and priestly brokers in Jerusalem, takes strength from Elliott's insights and adds to them as well. Neyrey's essay on meals and social relations alluded to the patronage model, which is fully developed here. Meals and food distribution, moreover, are dominant forms of patronage in Luke–Acts. With a full understanding of patron-client relations, then, a reader is all the more equipped with an adequate scenario for understanding Luke and his world.

SOCIAL DYNAMICS

10

THE SYMBOLIC UNIVERSE OF LUKE–ACTS: "THEY TURN THE WORLD UPSIDE DOWN"

Jerome H. Neyrey

1.0 THE STARTING POINT AND THE PROJECT

1.1 A Question of Perceptions

When hostile Jews hailed Jason and the brethren before the magistrates in Thessalonica, they accused them of a serious charge: "They turn the world upside down" (Acts 17:6). In their eyes, the Christian missionaries were trying to destroy the order and structure of the world. This charge is made before a Roman court, but according to Luke–Acts it represents a widespread Jewish perception of the Jesus movement. Earlier in Acts, other Jews perceived Stephen advocating the same thing, namely, the total destruction of the orderly world of Judaism, "We heard him speak blasphemous words against Moses and God" (6:11); and "This man never ceases to speak against this holy place and the law; we heard him say that this Jesus of Nazareth will destroy this place, and will change the customs which Moses delivered to us" (Acts 6:13–14). Later on, the Jerusalem church was concerned over the way Paul was perceived by certain of his countrymen who were zealous for the law. They reported a rumor to Paul, "That you teach all the Jews who are among the Gentiles to forsake Moses, telling them not to circumcise their children or observe the customs" (Acts 21:21). Finally, crowds in the temple gathered around Paul to accuse him, "This is the man who is teaching men everywhere against the people and the Law and this place" (21:28). Many Jews, then, perceived Jesus, Stephen, Paul, and other Christians as subverting the Jewish "world." They were accused of attacking the major institution of the day, the temple, by rejecting the major symbol of Israel's faith ("this holy place"); they were perceived as dismissing the prerogatives of Israel as a chosen collective ("the people"). They were thought to abrogate the principles by which the faith of this chosen people was structured ("Moses," "the law," "the customs"), and the rituals which symbolize that faith ("circumcision"). They were perceived as rejecting "God" and even upsetting the system of nature by "turning the world upside down." In the eyes of some, then, the Christians appeared to urge a revolution against the traditional values and structures of Israelite faith.

Christian apology to these charges, however, would give a different interpretation of their behavior. Christians would argue that they were not revolting against the system, but only reforming it (Theissen; Malina 1984:61–62). But this is just the point: there was a clear perception by Jews in the first century of what it means to be an observant Israelite, which was symbolized in the social importance of certain customs, rituals, places, and persons. Some were perceived as maintaining the status quo of that system (e.g., priests and Sadducees), others were perceived as attempting to reform it (Pharisees), and still others were perceived as overthrowing it (Jesus and his disciples). It was a question of perception and point of view.

As we learned in the earlier chapter on reading theory, Luke and his contemporaries shared common scenarios about the way the world was structured and operated. As Luke tells his story, the participants in his narrative and indeed in his social world share a common understanding of the symbols of their "world," even if some are said to reject them. They, at least, have a shared perception of that world. Yet we modern readers of Luke–Acts must struggle to discover an adequate scenario of the world of Luke to make sense of the charges against the Jesus movement and his corresponding apology. It is the aim of this chapter to develop a model to recover in detail the symbolic universe of first-century Jews, and so to gain a sense of how that universe was perceived. In this we would begin to sketch for ourselves one of the many scenarios necessary for reading a document from another time and culture.

Several issues emerge. We are first interested in developing a model which can allow us to map out the way Jews in the first-century perceived their world, that is, their symbolic universe. Second, we must examine whether and to what extent Luke's story of Jesus and his early disciples indicates that they disagree with that clear perception of a symbolic universe. On this point, there might be conflicting perspectives, that of the Jews which are noted above, and that of Luke. Let us, however, attempt first to explore the what and how of the symbolic universe of first-century Jews.

1.2 Defining Oneself

At an abstract level, we note that human beings are always attempting to find or impose order on the world in which they live, which means that they have a symbolic view of the way the universe should be structured and ordered (Berger and Luckmann). This perception is generally quite implicit and comes with being socialized as a child into the ways and workings of a family and clan. By imposing order, people are attempting to define themselves. Chaos, the complete absence of any order, was and is a terrifying concept, for it implies that there are no patterns, no identifications, no rules, no structures in the universe. A cosmos is fundamentally preferable to chaos. People, then, seek to find order or to impose it on their world so as to give it intelligibility and to define themselves in relation to it. In this they are seeking and producing socially shared meanings. By erecting imaginary and/or real lines, people define "my" or "ours" in relation to what is "yours" and "theirs," which is the function of city walls, fences, boundaries, and the like.

People can be observed to draw lines which define and give meaning to their world in terms of six basic areas: self, others, nature, time, space, and God (Malina 1981:25). Let us take a few examples. *Self:* it is important to know whose son one is (Luke 3:23; 5:10), to what family one belongs, of what clan one is a member, and from what nation one holds citizenship (Acts 22:26–28). *Others:* those who are not siblings or members of my family or clan do not have the same claims on my loyalty. They do not have the same rights or duties which come with such membership (Luke 10:29–37). They are "outsiders." *Time:* we distinguish seasons of person's life (childhood, adolescence, adulthood, old age), as well as seasons of the year, months, and days. Our calendar not only divides work days from rest days, but tells us when special holidays occur, which might be birthdays and anniversaries in the basic institution of the family or feasts and holy days in the other institution of the temple. *Place:* not only do we distinguish the public village square from the private family house, we distinguish common rooms in the house (kitchen) from private rooms (bedrooms) and special rooms (living room). There are places particular to men and to women. All of these distinctions and classifications are evidence of our need to give shape and definition to our world or to bring order out of chaos. From birth people are socialized into perceiving the world in this way. Such is the stuff of a symbolic universe.

2.0 THE BASIC MODEL: PURITY AND ORDER IN ISRAEL

2.1 What is "Purity"?

It is the business of anthropologists to discover the system of lines, definitions and classifications which makes up the symbolic universe of a given culture. In this chapter, we are adapting the works of British anthropologist Mary Douglas in developing the following model for perceiving the lines of a cultural system or symbolic universe. Douglas calls the orderly system of lines and classifications "purity," a term which brings out the sense of correctness when the system is known and observed. "Purity" is an abstract terms which stands for the order of a social system, that is, the pattern of perceptions and the system of classifications. All people have a sense of what is "pure" and what is "polluted," although just what constitutes "purity" and "pollution" changes from culture to culture.

In trying to find out the "purity" or order which structures a symbolic universe, it is useful to begin with an analysis of it opposite, "pollution" or "dirt." The key observation is that "dirt" is what people consider to be "matter out of place," that is, disorder. This implies that there is first a set of ordered relations and then a contravention of that order.

> The idea of dirt implies a structure of idea. For us dirt is a kind of compendium category for all events which blur, smudge, contradict, or otherwise confuse accepted classifications. The underlying feeling is that a system of values which is habitually expressed in a given arrangement of things has been violated (Douglas 1975:51).

The labelling of something as "dirty" or polluted, then, implies that there is a system whereby people classify, situate, or organize their world. "Purity" and "pollution" are but the abstract code names for system or order and its contravention.

"Purity" and "pollution" can exist on a grand or small scale. For example, during the day out on the farm a farmer is covered with dust and chaff, while his shoes are caked with dung and mud. This is not "dirt," for mud, dung, etc. are "in place" in the fields outside. But should the farmer enter his house, prop his boots on the coffee table or sit at supper in his dirty clothes, that mud, dung, and chaff now become "dirt." Inside they are "out of place." For "dirt" denotes the wrong thing, at the wrong time, and in the wrong place. On a larger scale, in certain cultures there are specific places where women are "in place," such as the village well and oven or the kitchen; accordingly women are "pure" in these places. There are, however, places where women should not be, such as near the farm implements, in the village square when men are present, the local tavern, or the wine cellar. In this perspective, these are men's places and a woman would be "out of place" by entering them. Such systems exist; and the natives know them because of constant socialization. We, on the other hand, must learn these systems of order or "purity."

"Purity," then, is the orderly system whereby people perceive that certain things belong in certain places at certain times. "Purity" is the abstract way of indicating what fits, what is appropriate, and what is in place. "Purity" refers to a system, a coherent and detailed drawing of lines in the world to peg, classify, and structure that world. "Purity" is a cultural map which indicates "a place for everything and everything in its place."

What is a symbolic system? Cultures embody and express core values. These values are structured in the cultural life of group. A core value in the U.S. is democracy, which is structured in terms of elections, opinion polls, etc. The core value influences how things are classified and where they are located. It is the overarching rationale for behavior, the principal justification for the shape of the system. The core value, moreover, is replicated throughout the system, giving it direction, clarity, and consistency. Abstractly, what accords with this value and its structural expressions is "pure"; what contravenes it in any way is "polluted."

Thus far we have discoursed on an abstract level to expose a way of thinking that can apply to many concrete instances both ancient and modern. When we turn to first-century Judaism, the abstract notions of "pure" and "polluted" take on dramatic specificity. "Pure" and "polluted" are the precise words commonly used to label specific persons, places, and things; and their meaning derives from specific symbols and structures.

Semantic Word Field for "Purity" and "Pollution"

A. *Terms for "Purity":*

1. clean, to cleanse, cleanness (*katharos, katharizō, katharismos*): Luke 2:22; 5:12; 11:41; Acts 10:15; 15:9

2. sweep (*saroō*): Luke 11:25//Matt 12:44

3. pure, to purify, purity (*hagnos, hagnizō, hagnotēs*): Acts 21:24, 26; 24:18

4. holy, to make holy, holiness (*hagios, hagiazō, hagiotēs, hagiasmos*): Luke 1:35, 49; 4:34; 11:2; Acts 20;32; 2 Cor 1:12; 1 Thess 4:3–7

5. pure (*pistikos*): Mark 14:3; Jn 12:3

6. innocent (*akeraios*): Matt 10:16; Rom 16:19

7. spotless (*amiantos*): Heb 7:26; 13:4; Jas 1:27; 1 Pet 1:4

8. unstained (*aspilos*): Jas 1:27; 1 Pet 1:19; 2 Pet 3:14

9. blameless (*amōmos*): Eph 1:4; 5:27; Phil 2:15; Col 1:22; 1 Pet 1:19

10. blameless (*anenklētos*): 1 Cor 1:8; Col 1:22; Titus 1:6–7

11. faultless (anepilemptos): 1 Tim 3:2; 5:7; 6:14

12. innocent (amemtos): Luke 1:6; Phil 3:6

13. innocent (athōos): Matt 27:4, 24

14. innocent (akakos): Heb 7:26

B. Terms for "Pollution":

1. defilement, to defile (miasmos, miainō, miasma): John 18:28; Titus 1:15; 2 Pet 2:10, 20

2. defilement, to defile (molysmos, molynō): 1 Cor 8:7; 2 Cor 7:1; Rev 3:4

3. unclean (akathartos): Luke 4:33, 36; 6:18; 8:29; 9:42; Acts 5:16; 8:7

4. impure (akathartos, akatharsia): Luke 4:33; 9:42; Acts 5:16; 10:14, 28; Rom 1:24; 6:14

5. spot (spilos, spiloō): Eph 5:27; 2 Pet 2:13; Jas 3:6; Jude 23

6. stain, (mōmos): 2 Pet 2:13

7. common, profane (koinos, koinoō): Acts 10:14–15,28; 11:8–9; 21:28

8. defilement (halisgēma): Acts 15:20

And so when we turn to first-century Judaism, "purity" and "pollution" are no longer just abstract terms for discussion purposes; they are no longer words about the general ordering of some world. Rather they are terms pertinent to a specific ordering of this world. They refer with precision to specific persons, things, times, etc. that are perceived as "pure" or "polluted." It is just this specificity that we hope to uncover by asking sensitively about the maps operative in the perceptions of first-century Jews.

"Purity," then, is used in two senses in this chapter. "Purity" is the abstract term which describes the system whereby persons, places, things, etc. are "in place." It is also the concrete term used in first-century Judaism to describe persons, places, things, etc. in relation to specific values and structures relative to Israel's temple.

2.2 Order in Creation and Temple

One of the core values of first-century Judaism was God's "holiness": "Ye shall be holy, for I the Lord your God am holy" (Lev 19:2). This phrase, "for I am holy," became a refrain echoing throughout the Bible (Lev 11:44, 45; 19:2; 20:7, 26; 21:28; see 1 Pet. 1:16; Matt 5:48). God's "holiness" was understood as divine power to bless and to curse, that is, to order the world: "God's work through the blessing is essentially to create order, through which men's affairs prosper" (Douglas 1966:50). When the blessing was withdrawn, confusion occurred, along with barrenness and pestilence (see Deut 28:15–24). God's prime act of blessing occurred in the ordering of the world at its creation.

Creation. The creation story in Gen 1, which is generally known as the "Priestly Account," fully expresses the divine order of the world. It encoded various "maps" or configurations of lines which God made for Israel to perceive and follow (Soler 1976). If we would understand the world as first-century Jews did, Gen 1 is an excellent window into that world-as-it-was-perceived.

When analyzed, the creation story in Gen 1 yields many maps. According to it, God did not make things helter skelter, but arranged them orderly in a proper cosmos. By constantly "separating" things (Gen 1:4, 7, 14), God created a series of maps which order, classify, and define the world as Jews came to see it:

Time: at creation time was separated into day and night, and the week was then separated into work days and sabbath rest; sun, moon and stars serve to mark that time precisely. The fundamentals of a calendar are thus established.

Things: at creation animals, birds, and fish were created in their pure form (no hybrids, no unclean creatures); each class was separated in terms of its proper place, food, and means of locomotion.

Place: at creation dry land was separated from the waters above and below; with the creation of animals, birds, and fish, each creature was separated into its proper place: animals roam the earth, birds fly in the air, and fish swim in the sea.

Diet: at creation a proper diet was assigned each creature.

Role/Status: at creation the hierarchy of creation was established; the heavens "rule" over the night and the sun "rules" the day; among the creatures on the dry land, Adam was given dominion over them all (1:26, 28).

Creation, the premier act of ordering and classifying the world, constitutes the original map of "purity" or holiness for Israel. The holy God expressed holiness through this order. And so subsequent holiness among God's creatures involves "keeping distinct the categories of creation." Holiness, then, expresses God's act of definition, discrimination, and order (Soler 1976:24–30).

Temple. "Be ye holy, as I am holy" became the norm which indicated how things in Israel's world should replicate and express the divine order established in God's initial, programmatic action of creation. This "holiness" came to be embodied especially in the central symbol of Israel's culture, the temple system, where specific maps, replicating the patterns of Gen 1, regulated that focal symbol of the Jewish world, which was often thought to be the center of the universe.

Things: what animals may be offered on the altar? Only "holy" animals, that is, those which are in accord with the definition of a clean animal and which are physically perfect (unblemished).

Persons: who may offer them? Only a "holy" priest, who has the right blood lines, enjoys an unblemished physical condition, and is in a state of ritual purity. Who may participate in the sacrifice? Only Israelites and only those with whole bodies (Fennelly 1983:274-75).

Place: where should the offering be made? Only in Jerusalem's temple, which is a microcosm of creation. Even within the temple, there are specific places for priests, for Israelites, for women, and for Gentiles.

Time: when should the offering be made? What offering is appropriate for what occasion? All of this is specified in the liturgical calendar.

The temple and its sacrificial system became the concrete structural expression of the ordering encoded in Gen 1 and thus of God's holiness. After the monarchy was abolished, it became the central and dominant symbol of Israel's culture, religion, and politics. John Elliott's chapter in this book examines "temple" as a political-economic institution; but for our purposes here, we treat it as a concrete expression of certain core values and therefore as the chief symbol of Israel's symbolic universe.

The order of creation served as a blueprint for the shape of the temple system. But it also yielded maps for structuring aspects of Jewish life apart from the temple. Our task as foreign observers is to search out the structural expressions of this core value in the maps which first-century Jews made to give shape and clarity to their daily world, maps which replicate the order of creation and temple. By "map" we mean the concrete and systematic patterns of organizing, locating, and classifying persons, places, times, actions, etc. according to some abstract notion of "purity" or order. Turning to first-century Judaism, we are aided in our task of investigating its maps by Douglas's discussion of the map of dietary rules (1966:41-57) and by Malina's description of "purity" in the Judaism of Jesus' time (1981:131-37).

2.3 Order and Other Maps

We can recover other specific maps which illustrate how first-century Jews had "a place for everything and everything in its place."

Maps of Places: As Matt 23:16-22 indicates, Jews could order space in terms of progressive degrees of holiness. The clearest examples of this is the map of places from m. *Kelim*:

There are ten degrees of holiness:

1. The *Land of Israel* is holier than any other land . . .

2. The *walled cities* (of the land of Israel) are still more holy . . .

3. *Within the walls* (of Jerusalem) is still more holy . . .

4. The *Temple Mount* is still more holy . . .

5. The *Rampart* is still more holy . . .

6. The *Court of the Women* is still more holy . . .

7. The *Court of the Israelites* is still more holy . . .

8. The *Court of the Priests* is still more holy . . .

9. *Between the Porch and the Altar* is still more holy . . .

10. The *Sanctuary* is still more holy . . .

The *Holy of Holies* is still more holy . . . (m. *Kelim* 1.6–9).

Since Gentiles are not God's people, they are not on the map at all (Acts 10:28). Yet Israel is "holy," separated from the nations as God's own people. This map of places, moreover, contains an important principle of classification. There are ten progressive degrees of "holiness": one moves upward and inward to the center, from non-temple to temple, from outer courts to the Holy of Holies where God is enthroned on the cherubim. The principle of classification (and hence, of "holiness") is proximity to the heart of the temple.

Map of People. People likewise can be mapped. The following passage lists people who may be present for the reading of the scroll of Esther; like the map of places in m. *Kelim*, it ranks them in a specific sequence according to a discernible hierarchical principle:

1. Priests
2. Levites
3. Israelites
4. Converts
5. Freed Slaves
6. Disqualified priests
7. Netzins (temple slaves)
8. Mamzers (bastards)
9. Those with damaged testicles
10. Those without a penis (t. *Meg.* 2.7).

Two principles of classification are operative here. (a) "Holiness" means wholeness, and so people with damaged bodies are ranked last, and people with damaged family lines (slaves, bastards) are ranked next to last. (b) The ranking of people on this map replicates the map of places, for one's rank corresponds to one's proximity to the center of the temple. Priests are first because they enter the Holy of Holies, Levites next because they enter the Sanctuary, Israelites next because they stand in the Courts, etc. This map of people and the previous map of places contain a hierarchical ranking of one's place on the social map. It is possible and necessary to know exactly where people should stand.

Map of Uncleannesses. If holiness can be classified, certain maps of uncleanness likewise indicate a corresponding hierarchical classification even of pollution.

1. "There are things which convey uncleanness by contact (e.g., a dead creeping thing, male semen).

2. They are exceeded by carrion . . .

3. They are exceeded by him that has connexion with a menstruant . . .

4. They are exceeded by the issue of him that has a flux, by his spittle, his semen, and his urine . . .

5. They are exceeded by [the uncleanness of] what is ridden upon [by him that has a flux] . . .

6. [The uncleanness of] what is ridden upon [by him that has a flux] is exceeded by what he lies upon . . .

7. [The uncleanness of] what he lies upon is exceeded by the uncleanness of him that has a flux . . . " (m. Kelim 1.3).

Such a map indicates the degree of uncleanness of some person or thing, suggesting a proportional, corresponding strategy for dealing with it. Roman Catholics will be reminded of their own classification of sins in terms of imperfections, venial, and mortal sins.

Map of Times. Times may be mapped as well, for Jews certainly had both a lunar and a solar calendar to differentiate days and seasons, by means of which they identified days of pilgrimage, sacrifice, fasting, and feasting. The very structure of the Mishnah tractate, *Moed,* is an index of special, classified times, with lists of appropriate rules for observing these times:

m. Moed	Special Times
1. Shabbat and Erubin	Sabbath
2. Pesahim	Feast of Passover
3. Yoma	Day of Atonement
4. Sukkoth	Feast of Tabernacles
5. Yom Tob	Festival Days
6. Rosh ha-Shana	Feast of New Year
7. Taanith	Days of Fasting
8. Megillah	Feast of Purim
9. Moed Katan	Mid-Festival Days

Where "purity" concerns are strong, one needs to classify more and more things to know precisely where they belong. In such a situation one comes to expect a proliferation of maps or more precision about the lines of maps. And this seems to be the case in the Judaism of Jesus' time. A text dated later than New Testament times, m. Aboth, urges a series of "fences" around the law. We include it here because it illustrates so well the classifying mentality and the urge to make maps common among first-century Jews.

The tradition is a fence around the law;
tithes are a fence around riches;
vows are a fence around abstinence;
a fence around wisdom is silence (m. Aboth 3.14).

"Fences" might be called "the tradition of the elders" (Mark 7:4, 5), for they are the continued mapping of life, the extended impulse to order, classify, and define (see the "Antitheses" in Matt 5:21–48). New "fences" are either new maps or further refinement of old maps.

2.4 Maps and Boundary Lines

These specific maps, moreover, make concrete the principle of "a place for everything and everything in its place." An anthropologist like Douglas, moreover, predicts that there will be considerable attention paid by a purity-conscious group to patterns of ordering, that is, the lines, boundaries, and structure which indicate just where each person, place, thing, etc. belongs. "The image of society," Douglas says," has form; it has external boundaries, margins, internal lines" (Douglas 1966:114). This prediction, we quickly learn, is amply verified by first-century Judaism.

Boundaries. Boundary lines basically indicate who's "in" and who's "out," or what belongs and what does not. For example, there are clear and specific boundary lines separating members and non-members of God's covenant people (Lev 20:26; John 4:8; Acts 10:28). The practice of circumcision, kosher diet, and sabbath observance indicate that one is an insider to the covenant.

Structure. The very maps we studied earlier are Jewish attempts to classify and locate all times, places, persons, etc. As they classify, they indicate the hierarchical, internal structure of Jewish culture, just as bishops, priests, and deacons structure some churches, and generals, colonels and lieutenants structure an army, and doctors, nurses and orderlies structure a hospital.

Margins. Since "purity" means the exact classification of persons, places, things, etc., there is great concern over things which either do not fit a given definition or do not find an exact place on the map. Something out of place is inherently suspect. Things, persons, places, etc. are "pure" when fully within their allotted category or location; but when they straddle a line or blur a definition, they are moving out of place and begin to be thought of as "impure." Such things are perceived as dangerous and threatening, precisely because the perceivers are unsure of just how to classify them.

These general ideas can be illustrated by reference to specific instances of this type of thinking in the first-century world. We find considerable concern where to fix lines and boundaries. We find people using not only the general category of order and disorder, but the specific terminology of "clean"/ "unclean," or "pure"/"polluted" in reference to what is "in place" or "out of place." As we shall see, first-century Jews focused their attention more on boundaries and margins, than on internal structure. Examples of this abound:

1. Consecrated covenant people belong in the realm of God's holy land. Gentiles, Romans especially, are not covenant members and so are out of place in the holy land of Israel, especially in its sacred city and more so in its temple (see Acts 21:28).

2. The dead do not belong in the realm of the living but in their own realm of tombs and graveyards. The worst aspect of the possessed man in Mark 5:5 was that he left the realm of the living to dwell among tombs; his cure then permitted him to leave the realm of the dead and to be properly dressed and seated again among the living (5:15).

3. The sick do not belong in the realm of the healthy; lepers should dwell apart and cry "Unclean!" (Luke 5:12–16). To a certain extent, so should paralytics, the blind, the deaf etc. What a surprise, then, to hear of a paralytic being lowered through the roof into Jesus' "home" (Luke 5:17–19).

4. Inasmuch as holiness is related to wholeness (one must be completely what one is), people with defective bodies (e.g., eunuchs) are unclean; a man with crushed testicles, for example, may not enter the temple area to offer sacrifice (Lev 21:20); defective animals are not fit offerings for the holy God.

5. Sinners, likewise, do not belong in the same space as observant Jews, which occasions criticism when Jesus eats at the table of a tax collector (Luke 5:27; 15:1; 19:5).

6. Certain foods do not fit the full definition of what it means to be a sky, earth, or sea creature (Douglas 1966:51–57), and so they are marginal, unclean, and polluting. Until a heavenly voice told him otherwise, Peter would never think of eating such (Acts 10:11–14).

7. Since there is a specific time for everything, especially a time for "work" and a time for "rest," if "work" is done at the wrong time, that is, on the sabbath, it is out of place (Luke 6:1–5).

8. Finally, apropos of wholeness, there is a general prohibition against mixing kinds: *clothing*: wool and linen should never be mixed; *agriculture*: plowing should be done by either ox or ass, but never by the two yolked together; *crops*: only one kind of seed should be sown in a given field at any one time; *husbandry*: cattle of one kind should not be bred with that of another kind (Lev 19:19; Deut 22:9–11).

Since each thing has its proper place, the mixing of two kinds blurs distinctions and creates hybrids, which are perceived as unclean. All of these examples have to do with concern for boundary lines and margins.

"Purity," then, has to do with system, order, and classification. It attends to correct labels and accurate definitions; it assigns appropriate physical space to things and people as well as their proper social location; it is concerned with completeness and wholeness. The prerequisite of such a system is clarity, the ability to know exactly *what* something is and *where* it belongs. This need for clarity requires precise criteria which can be easily observed, and thus expresses itself in a concern for external and observable phenomena.

2.5 The Map of the Body

The human body constitutes one of the most important maps, for it is a microcosm of the larger social macrocosm. Classical literature contains many examples of the physical body as a symbol of the social body-politic (1 Cor 12:12–26). From an anthropologist's point of view, Mary Douglas develops this theme of the body as symbol in ways that are important for our investigation. She argues that the physical body is a replica of the social body, a symbol of it:

> The body is a model which can stand for any bounded system. Its boundaries can represent any boundaries which are threatened or precarious (Douglas 1966:115).

We are invited, then, to consider a map of the body which replicates the map of society.

Douglas predicts that the same norms which govern the "purity" of the social body will tend to be replicated in terms of the physical body as well. Just as the social body draws boundary lines around itself, restricts admission (e.g., passports), expels foreign or unclean objects, guards its gates and entrances, so this tendency to order, classify, and locate is replicated in the physical body. "Body control is an expression of social control," says Douglas; conversely, "abandonment of bodily control in ritual responds to the requirements of a social experience which is being expressed" (Douglas 1982a:70–71). "The physical experience of body . . . sustains a particular view of society" (Douglas 1982a:65). Douglas predicts that in an orderly culture with a strong classification system and with vigorous "purity" concerns, we would expect there to be clear rules for the map of the body concerning: (1) boundaries, (2) structure, and (3) margins.

2.5.1 Bodily Boundaries. (bodily surfaces, orifices of the body). As society is ordered and guards its boundaries, so too the physical body. The boundary of the physical body is its skin, and by synecdoche clothing, which replicates that boundary. Since clothing signals gender classification, women should wear women's clothing and men men's (Deut 22:5). Certain clothing, moreover, indicates social location, such as priestly garments (Exod 28), which must be made of one kind of material, not a mixture of wool and linen (Lev 19:19). Observant people, moreover, might wear clothing which tells of this concern for observance, namely, phylacteries (Matt 23:5). Nudity—the absence of clothing—removes the classification system and blurs the map and all lines on it. Nudity, then, is at least dangerous and threatening, and often polluting and shameful (see Gen 3:10–11; Ezek 16:39).

The true boundary of the body, its skin, has orifices which are gateways to the interior of the body, just as walled cities have gates, and countries have ports of entry or customs crosspoints. These orifices are the object of great scrutiny. As gates to the interior, they must screen out what does not belong and guard against a pollutant entering within. The guarded orifices tend to be the eyes, mouth, ears, genitals.

1. The eye is the "lamp of the body." If the eye is sound, the whole body will be sound; if it is not, the whole body will be filled with darkness (Luke 11:34–36).

2. The mouth is guarded against unkosher foods entering into the body; for unclean foods will pollute a pure body (Acts 10:14). The mouth, by virtue of the speech which it utters, can corrupt the whole body, if the "tongue is a fire" (Jas 3:6).

3. Concerning the sexual orifices, we find rules for intermarriage which prescribe who may cross the sexual orifice and marry whom. There are rules prohibiting exogamus marriages (Neh 13:23–28; 1 Cor 7:39; 2 Cor 6:14). And there are even rules for Israelites which regulate who may marry whom: "The priestly, levitic, and Israelitish stocks may intermarry; impaired priestly stocks, proselytes, and freedman stocks may intermarry; the proselyte, freedman, bastard, Nathin, sketuki, and asufi stocks may intermarry" (m. Kid. 4.1). People with defective sex organs, such as eunuchs, cannot marry anyone; their line is literally cut off from Israel (Malina 1981:105–12).

From this perspective, one would expect that where classification systems are strong and purity concerns are high, there will be considerably more attention given to bodily surfaces and orifices than to bodily interior; attention is given to boundaries and margins, not structure. The reader is reminded of the earlier remark about "fences" around the law. The bodily equivalent of "fences" is the guarding of the surface of the body and its orifices. If one can defend them adequately, there will be little danger of pollutants entering the body.

2.5.2 Bodily Structure. In a well-regulated society, where roles and classifications are clear, there will be a corresponding replication of this in the physical body. A hierarchy of social roles is mirrored in the hierarchy of bodily organs: eyes over hands, head over feet (1 Cor 12); right is preferred to left; higher is preferred to lower. As well as there is a structural hierarchy of bodily parts, there is a corresponding concern to supervise the parts of the body which are in dangerous contact with the outside world. Hands, feet, eyes, which are the external provinces of the body, are singled out for special scrutiny (Mark 9:42–48).

2.5.3 Bodily Margins. Since lines should be clear and things, persons, places, and times should be fully in their right place, there should not be too much or too little. "Too much" means that something spills over into other areas where it does not belong; "too little" suggests that something is incompletely in its place or unsettled in it. As regards the body, "too much" is polluting, as in the case of a hermaphrodite which is both male and female. In this vein effeminate males and masculine females are "too much," being both male and female (Murphy-O'Connor 1980:482–500).

Bodies might have "too little" and so be defective and unclean. Eunuchs, those with damaged testicles, and those without a penis lack adequate sexual organs; they are deficient in what it means to be male (see *map of people, t. Meg.* 2:7 above). Those with bodily defects such as the lame, the blind, and the deaf are lacking wholeness according to Lev 21:16–20. Lacking bodily wholeness, they lack holiness. Such may not be priests nor may they bring offerings into the holy temple.

Thus we finish elaborating the model which can help us understand the symbolic universe of Jews, Jesus, and Luke. We have come to learn about "purity," the system of the way the world is perceived. Persons, places, things, and times can be ordered, classified and ranked in some systematic way. A person, place, thing, or time is "pure" or "holy" insofar as it has a specific place and stays in that place. We have examined the theoretical system of Gen 1 and the more concrete replication of that in the temple. From these we learn of corresponding patterns for perceiving and ordering social relations and even the physical body. These considerations yielded a variety of specific maps which structured Jewish life in Jesus' time. They suffice to illustrate the basic workings of a system of "purity" or order. From them, we can begin to sense the symbolic world of first-century Israel, gaining a general sense of a world carefully ordered and a perception of the precise forms of that ordering.

If the model is correct, it should enable us to begin to perceive the universe as they did. In particular, it should enable us to have quite specific and concrete images of what they meant by "holy" and "unclean," "blemished," "polluted" and the like. These concrete expressions of the abstract model are valuable clues into the native's point of view. Given both our abstract model and its specific realization in first-century Judaism, we now inquire how Jews would perceive the Jesus movement and how Jesus and his disciples interpret themselves in terms of this shared symbolic world.

3.0 THE MODEL APPLIED: JESUS AND JEWISH MAPS

Jesus, Stephen, and Paul were charged with "perverting our nation" (Luke 23:2, 14), with speaking "against the law of Moses and God" (Acts 6:11–13), and with "teaching against 'the people' and 'the law' and 'this place' " (Acts 21:28). These charges presume that Jesus and his followers shared the same symbolic universe as their accusers, although they are perceived as rejecting the ordering of the world according to traditional perceptions. According to that symbolic universe, some Jews accuse Jesus and followers of violating the purity system of Israel both in practice and in principle. Christians, it is charged, do not respect the clear maps of their religious/political culture; they cross all the lines that should be respected. Within certain parameters, *this is so.* According to Luke, Jesus and his disciples show flagrant disregard both in principle and in practice for maps of places, persons, times, and the physical body.

3.1 Maps of Places

For example, it is easy to cull from the Gospel instances where Jesus and his followers disregard the map of places, whether that place is the holy temple, the holy city, or the holy land. Regarding the temple, Luke narrates that Jesus once entered it and disturbed its system as he "began to drive out those who sold" (Luke 19:45–46). Jesus, moreover, foretold the temple's ruin: "There will not be left one stone upon another that will not be thrown down" (Luke 21:6). On a narrative level, at least, there is substance to the claims of some irate Jews: "We heard him (Stephen) say that this Jesus of Nazareth will destroy this place" (Acts 6:14). Stephen himself is said to have spoken "against this holy place." And this charge is true, for as has been shown in regard to Stephen's speech, the prophecy that Israel "will come out and worship me *in this place*" (Acts 7:7) was incorrectly interpreted as a reference to the Jerusalem temple (Dahl 1976:74–75). The temple, Stephen said, was *not* God's designated place of worship (see Acts 7:48–50). Finally, Paul is perceived as defiling the holy place by "bringing Greeks into the temple" (21:28).

Concerning the holy city, Luke narrates that Jesus regularly spoke against Jerusalem, proclaiming its desolation (Luke 13:34–35; 19:41–44; 21:20–24). Concerning the holy land of Israel, Jesus himself left it and entered that of the unclean Samaritans (Luke 9:51–56). He commanded his apostles to leave it as well and go not only to Samaria but "to the ends of the earth" (Acts 1:8). He thereby showed supreme disregard for the holiness of the land of Israel.

Luke–Acts, then, recorded statements that imply that neither Jesus nor his followers respected the holy places of Israel; they disregarded the map of places. And in doing so, they were perceived as rejecting a major symbol of God's holiness-as-order in Israel.

3.2 Maps of Persons

Nor did they respect the map of people, that is, the people with whom it is appropriate for an observant Jew to live and eat. For example, when Jesus traveled outside of the holy land of Israel, he crossed into Gentile territory and had dealings with Gentiles (Luke 8:26–37); and even in Galilee he had dealings with Gentiles (7:1–10). He boasted that this contact was expected of God's prophets, inasmuch as Elijah lived with the widow of Zarephtha in the land of Sidon (4:26) and Elisha healed Namaan the Syrian (4:27). Samaritans, with whom no observant Jew should have any dealings (John 4:9), were objects of Jesus' healing attention (Luke 17:11–19) and his praise (Luke 10:29–37); Samaritans were welcome in Jesus' circle of covenant followers (Acts 8). Jesus, moreover, commanded his disciples to leave the holy land and to proselytize unclean Gentiles "in all Judea, Samaria, and to the ends of the earth" (Acts 1:8). Luke and his readers knew quite well what this signified, for Peter enunciated the relevant principle to a Gentile: "You yourselves know how unlawful it is for a Jew to associate with and to visit anyone of another nation" (Acts 10:28).

The dead, who rank among the most unclean of all people, were objects of Jesus' touch and that of his disciples:

—the son of the widow of Nain (Luke 7:11–17)

—Jairus's daughter (Luke 8:49–56)

—Tabitha (Acts 9:36–41)

—Eutychus (Acts 20:9–10)

Whereas a priest and a Levite would not stop and touch the man left "half dead" by robbers, a Samaritan did; and Jesus praised this (Luke 10:30–33).

The morally unclean were the objects of Jesus's attention. He regularly ate with tax collectors and sinners (Luke 5:27–32; 7:29, 31–34; 15:1–2; 18:4–14; 19:1–10). He was not offended, as he should be, by the approach of a public sinful woman (Luke 7:37–39). His chief apostle, Peter, admitted that he too was a sinful man and that Jesus should avoid his company (Luke 5:8–10), yet Jesus made him his right-hand man.

The physically unclean seemed to get Jesus' full attention. He was regularly in contact with lepers (Luke 5:12–16; 17:11–19) and menstruants (Luke 8:42–48). And the bodily unwhole were also objects of Jesus' ministry:

—cripples (Luke 5:17–26; Acts 3:1–10; 9:32–34)

—the blind (Luke 7:21)

—the sick (Luke 4:38–40; Acts 5:15–16)

—the possessed (Luke 4:31–37; 8:26–39; Acts 16:16–18).

He declared, moreover, that these people who are physically unwhole/unclean should be invited to table as honored guests (Luke 14:13, 21), a gesture which violated a deep sense of holiness-as-wholeness which is expressed in Lev 21:17–20. Included here are people from unclean trades. Peter lodges with Simon, a tanner (Acts 9:43; 10:6), whose profession was unclean. Shepherds were the first to hear of the birth of

God's Holy One (Luke 2:8–18); in one of Jesus' parables a swineherder was received back into the family with no particular ado (Luke 15:15–16). Far from maintaining a defensive posture in regard to the unclean of Jewish society, Jesus and his disciples disregarded the map of people entirely. These contacts, moreover, were not accidental but intentional on their part.

3.3 Maps of Times

Jesus does not seem to have regarded the map of sacred times because of his perceived violation of the sabbath observance (Luke 6:1–5, 6–11; 13:10–17). Nor did he observe days of fasting (Luke 5:33–35).

3.4 Maps of the Body

Nor did Jesus observe the expectations encoded in the map of the body to defend its holiness.

1. *Bodily Surface.* Jesus was in bodily contact with persons, the surface of whose bodies was unclean, such as lepers (Luke 5:13). A woman with disheveled hair, a disorderly surface, wiped Jesus' feet with her hair (Luke 7:38).

2. *Bodily Orifices.* Jesus showed no concern to guard against anything coming from his or another's orifices:

— the *mouth for eating*: he ate common bread with common people (Luke 9:10–17); he regularly ate with unclean people, tax collectors and sinners (5:27–31; 7:34; 15:1–2; 19:7). In an analogous way, he did not wash his hands, the required ritual which made them clean so as to safeguard the purity of the mouth (9:10–17). He and his disciples totally disregarded the dietary laws (Luke 10:7–8; Acts 10–11);

— the *mouth for kissing*: he allowed himself to be kissed by a sinful woman (Luke 7:38; see 22:48);

— the *sexual orifice*: he was touched by a menstruating woman (Luke 8:43–48). His disciples did not require circumcision, the ritual concern of Jews for the male sexual orifice (Acts 15:1, 5 and 21:21).

3. *Bodily Defect.* Philip the deacon catechized and baptized the Ethiopian eunuch, whose sexual deficiency would render him cultically unclean because of bodily unwholeness (Acts 8:26–39).

4. *Unclean Bodies.* Jesus touched unclean corpses (8:54; see 7:14) and so did his disciples (Acts 9:40–41; 20:10).

The issue of diet and circumcision were no small matters, for they were the specific rituals which tended to define a Jew. Hence, when Jesus and his followers abrogated dietary laws or rejected circumcision, they rejected the distinctive practices of "the people Israel," thus implying that there is no such thing as a holy people, a people set apart for God. In this they imply that bodily orifices need not be guarded.

Neither Jesus nor his disciples seemed to practice any defensive strategy, but trampled on the lines of the maps of their symbolic world and rationalized their behavior as well. They themselves did not respect the meanings encoded in the maps which make up Israel's life and faith and they taught others to disregard them as well. Moreover, *they knew what they were doing.* And so, from the perspective of temple and synagogue Jews, Jesus and his followers were a "pollution" in Israel. It is no wonder then, that Jesus and his followers were said to "turn the world upside down," for they ostensibly disregarded the fundamental lines which express the value and structures of first-century Judaism.

4.0 LUKE'S DEFENSE OF JESUS' PURITY

Although we have just surveyed data indicating that Jesus and his disciples disregarded in principle and practice the system of Jewish order and holiness, that is not the whole story. Luke–Acts also narrates that Jesus and his followers respected and observed many of the maps which define membership in the covenant of Israel.

4.1 Aspects of Jesus' Purity

According to Luke, Jesus and his followers knew the symbolic universe which we have taken pains to recover. Although they indeed crossed the lines of certain maps and challenged the validity of other maps, Luke's perspective considers them neither unclean nor unconcerned about matters of purity, either in general or in specific instances. Nothing could be further from the truth. There is a strong apologetic strain in Luke–Acts which argues that despite Jesus' crossing of lines, he was a *holy* figure, whose holiness is asserted in many ways, directly and indirectly.

4.1.1 *Pedigree.* Since people can be mapped, it matters where Jesus is situated. His mother was related to priestly stock; Zechariah was "of the division of Abijah" (Luke 1:5) and Elizabeth "of the daughters of Aaron" (1:5). Both were "righteous before God, walking in all commandments and ordinances of the Lord blameless" (1:6). They were kin of Mary, the mother of Jesus, which meant that she had blood ties to the priestly clan. His father was "of the house of David" (1:27; 2:4; 3:23, 31–32). Jesus, then, belonged to the two most sacred family lines in Israel, priestly and royal. By this, Luke indicates his high rating on the map of people.

4.1.2 *Observances.* Jesus was no stranger to the rules which denote full covenant membership. He himself was circumcised on the eighth day (2:21) and dedicated to God according to Ex 13:2, 12 (2:22–24). He was, then, no stranger to the *map of the body* which applied to Jewish males. Nor was he stranger to the *map of (Jewish) time*: he made the annual Passover pilgrimage to the holy city (2:41). And, "as was his custom, on the sabbath day" (4:16), Jesus went to the synagogue and read from the Torah. Later, he traveled to Jerusalem to celebrate the Passover, just as his parents regularly did (2:41). As regards the *map of places,* he appeared in the temple for his dedication when an infant (2:22); and when twelve years old he remained there teaching (2:46–49). He was said to be a regular worshipper in the synagogue on the sabbath (4:16, 33). When he finally arrived in Jerusalem, he was zealous for God's temple (19:45–46), and even came there daily to teach (19:47). Luke, then, goes out of his way to indicate that Jesus was no 'am ha-'aretz, a person uneducated in the ways of Israel and its organizing maps (see Acts 4:13). Nor was he always and everywhere in revolt against those maps.

4.1.3 *Evaluation.* In a culture where public testimony about individuals was important for their honor rating, Luke took considerable pains to record the many attestations of Jesus' exceptional holiness. Most important were the witnesses about Jesus from heaven itself.

1. God's holy angels announced his birth as "the Holy One, Son of God" (1:35) and as "the Savior, Christ the Lord" (2:11).

2. Then God's prophets acclaimed his importance to the people, first in the temple (2:25–32, 38), and then at the Jordan (3:16–17). Simeon, "devout and righteous and looking for the consolation of Israel" (2:25) blessed him; Anna, who "did not depart from the temple, worshipping with fasting and prayer night and day" (2:37), acclaimed him.

3. Finally, Israel's holy God twice appeared to Jesus in theophanies, each time acclaiming him as a holy figure: "Thou art my beloved Son; with thee I am well pleased" (3:22; 9:35). As Jesus went about in his ministry, "God was with him" (Acts 10:38). And God acted swiftly and vigorously in Jesus' resurrection, so that God's "Holy One may not see corruption" (Acts 2:27; 13:35). God even seated this Jesus at his right hand in his holy presence (Acts 2:34–36; 7:55).

People with impeccable credentials, then, attested to Jesus' superior holiness. It all depends on one's perspective.

4.1.4 *Sinlessness.* In diverse ways, Luke proclaimed Jesus' radical holiness according to the canons of his culture. Jesus was explicitly confessed as "the Holy One" by angels (1:35), by prophets (Acts 2:27/Ps 16:10), and by men (Acts 3:14; 4:27, 30). His judges acquitted him of the charges against him (23:4, 14–15, 22), thus affirming his radical innocence. Crucified with him, the good thief proclaimed his innocence (23:41), as did his executioner (23:47). He was "the Righteous One," whom God raised from the shame of death (Acts 3:15; 7:52; 22:14).

Again, Jesus was no *'am ha-'aretz*, no maverick, no rebel against God and Israel. On the contrary, Luke showed him complying with many of the criteria of his culture which define holiness. He fits and fits highly on all the maps that structure the Jewish system of "purity" or order. According to Luke, then, Jesus' holiness must be rated as very high indeed. If Jesus ultimately perceives the world differently than temple and synagogue Jews, it is not because he was ignorant of their symbolic universe. He was an insider, but a reforming insider.

In keeping with his gospel presentation of Jesus in terms of Jewish perceptions of "purity," Luke made comparable observations about Jesus' disciples in Acts. Peter and the early disciples regularly attended the temple to pray (Acts 2:46; 3:1; 5:20; 21:26). Prayers, moreover, might be made in private homes (4:24–31; 20:7–12), as well as in the temple, but pray they did. In regard to the disciples' holiness, God lavished the Holy Spirit upon them, thus purifying and consecrating them (2:1–4; 9:17). Frequently Luke recorded that God gave the Holy Spirit to Gentile outsiders, thus purifying them and making them members of God's holy people (8:14–18). After this phenomenon happened in regard to Cornelius (10:44–48; 11:15–18), Peter explained its programmatic significance, "And God who knows the heart bore witness to them, giving them the Holy Spirit just as he did to us; and he made no distinction between us and them, but *cleansed* their hearts by faith" (15:8–9). And Luke took special pains in his description of the ex-Pharisee Paul to insist on his "cleanness" both in his former life as one "zealous for the law" (22:3; 26:4–5) and in his present life as a disciple of Jesus (18:6; 20:26). Jesus' disciples, then, knew and observed many of the prescriptions which denote holiness; they deserved to enjoy a good reputation as "holy" people, even if not fully observant of all the maps of Israel's system. This, moreover, was no minor matter to Luke as he told his story.

4.2 Jesus Untouched by Uncleanness

Luke emphasized that Jesus was in constant contact with the dead, lepers, menstruants, the blind, those with defective bodies, as well as with tax collectors and public sinners. All of these people rank low on the map of persons because of their lack of bodily wholeness. Yet far from being polluted by these contacts, Jesus gave life, purity, and wholeness to the unclean. In this way, Luke defused any accusation that Jesus was himself unclean.

1. The dead were raised up (Luke 7:11–17; 8:54–55).

2. Lepers were "made clean" (Luke 5:13).

3. Menstruants were healed (Luke 8:44).

4. The blind were made to see (Luke 7:21).

5. Those with bodily defects were made whole (Luke 4:40; 5:17–25).

6. Those possessed by demons were freed (Luke 4:31–37; 8:26–35).

7. Sinners were forgiven (Luke 5:24; 7:47; 15:1–32; 19:1–10).

According to Luke's story, in no case and at no time was Jesus ever compromised by his contact with the unclean of Israel, despite the judgment of the Pharisees to the contrary: "If this man were a prophet, he would know who and what sort of woman this is who is touching him, for she is a sinner" (7:39).

In fact, Luke stresses that Jesus' God-given role was that of physician to sinners (5:31), shepherd to the lost (15:3–6; see also 24:13–35), and savior from sin and pollution (Acts 5:30; 13:38–39; Acts 4:10–12; 5:31). Luke described many of Jesus' actions as "making clean" those who are unclean (5:12–13; 7:22; 17:14–17), just as he describes how God "cleansed" both foods (Acts 10:15; 11:9) and peoples (15:9). Only holiness and cleanness, then, resulted from the actions of Jesus and his followers.

In all societies, there are special people authorized to cross lines and deal with the "unclean" of that society: police engage criminals, doctors treat disease, ministers deal with sinners, etc. While they themselves do not belong to the realm of criminals, diseased or sinners, police, doctors and ministers cross into that world. Not everyone is permitted to cross those lines, but only special people authorized to do so, who might be called "limit breakers" (Malina 1986a:143–154). Jesus was officially designated by God as just such an agent. He did not cross those lines because he belonged to the world of the unclean, but because he was commissioned as "physician" to the sick (Luke 5:30–32; see 4:23).

4.3 Jesus and New Maps of Purity

Although in Luke 1–4 Jesus was said to be observant of the maps of Israel's holiness system, from ch 5 onward he is reported as constantly crossing the lines of the maps of that system. This in itself is evidence that in Luke's perception, Jesus shared the same symbolic universe as the rest of the Jews in his time. In the eyes of many Jews, moreover, Jesus refused to abide by the ordered system which was expressed by the maps of his culture. Luke, however, did not see Jesus abrogating Jewish concern for holiness but rather redrawing the maps according to new lines and boundaries. In fact, Luke portrayed Jesus and his disciples drawing new maps of a reformed purity system. Reform, not revolt describes the Lukan viewpoint.

New Map of Holy Places. The prophet Stephen asserted that God prophesied that "after they shall come out, they shall worship me in *this place*" (Acts 7:7; Exod 3:12). As Stephen argued, the true fulfill-ment of "in this place" was *not* the temple in Jerusalem, as the Jews mistakenly thought: "The most high does not dwell in houses made with hands" (7:48). Rather, "in this place" refers to Jesus, who is the stone rejected by the builders but whom God has raised up and "which has become the head of the corner" (Acts 4:10–12). Jesus as the cornerstone of the true temple becomes the new center of the map and all holiness is measured in proximity to him. A temple of the God of Israel still ex-ists in Luke's symbolic universe, but a new map of holy space has been made.

Although Acts recorded that Peter, Paul, and other disciples went to the temple, they were never said to offer sacrifices for sin there. Jesus is the unique savior (Acts 4:11–12; 5:31), and all sins are forgiven in his name, not by the old rites performed in the old sacred space. So if Chris-tians continued to go to the traditional holy place, it was nevertheless clear that they no longer relied on it and its ritual for forgiveness of sins (Acts 13:38–39).

New Map of People. To a Jew, the only people on the map were God's holy people, who had been "set apart." In many ways the map of people was redrawn by Jesus in Luke–Acts in ways that were radically inclu-sive. For example, at Pentecost Jesus poured the Holy Spirit on the apostles who could then speak to people from all over the world in their native languages (Acts 2:9–11). "What does it mean?" but that the new and true map of God's chosen people was not restricted to Israelites liv-ing in Judea and speaking Aramaic, but included peoples from all coun-tries (see Acts 10:44–48; 15:8–9). Jesus, of course, commanded a mission to "Jerusalem, all Judea, Samaria, and the ends of the earth" (Acts 1:8). In an interesting test case, an Ethiopian eunuch (a foreigner with a bodily defect) was evangelized (Acts 8:26–39). In another test case, Peter had a vision of "*all kinds* of animals and reptiles and birds of the air" de-scending from heaven (Acts 10:12). The issue was not just foods, but people. A heavenly voice proclaimed "what God has cleansed, you must not call common" (10:15), which Peter interpreted vis-à-vis people: "You yourselves know how unlawful it is for a Jew to associate with or to visit any one of another nation; but God has shown me that I should *not call any person common or unclean*" (10:28). In keeping with this, we re-call Jesus' instructions concerning whom to invite to one's banquet table. Those whom Lev 21:17–20 declared "unclean" are precisely the people to be invited: "the poor, the maimed, the lame, the blind" (Luke 14:13).

Unlike the Jewish map of persons, this new Christian map was con-sciously inclusive in scope. Peter twice proclaimed God's "impartiality" to the Gentile Cornelius, "Truly I perceive that God shows no partial-ity; but in every nation any one who fears him and does what is right is acceptable to him" (Acts 10:34). And at the Jerusalem council, Peter again affirmed God's inclusive choice, "God made no distinction between us and them, but cleansed their hearts by faith" (15:9). Luke, then, was conscious of a new map of persons; he acknowledged its novelty, its divine source, and its implication for the church.

New Map of the Body. Luke's conscious reporting of the abrogation of the old map of the body indicates his knowledge of it in principle and practice. We focus on two specific customs, circumcision and diet. On the one hand, Jesus himself was circumcised (2:21), yet by the middle of Acts we read learn that *circumcision* was no longer required (Acts 15:1, 5). Likewise Peter boasts in Acts 10 that he could not eat of the animals in the sheet descending from heaven; he perceives things differently when told, "What God has cleansed, you must not call common" (Acts 10:15; 11:9; see Luke 10:7–8). The two most important rules of the old map of the body are set aside.

According to Luke, then, "purity" was no longer measured according to the old map of the body. Peter declared that those who were not circumcised and who did not keep a kosher diet were not "unclean"; "God who knows the heart bore witness to them, giving them the Holy Spirit . . . he cleansed their hearts by faith" (Acts 15:8–9). There was evidently a new perception of the body among the followers of Jesus. As one who shared the general symbolic universe, Luke understood how these two particularistic rules for the body functioned to separate Israel from its gentile neighbors and to define its "holy" character. By the abolition of these distinguishing body rules characteristic of first-century Jews, the new map of the body conformed to the new map of people, which was inclusive in character, not exclusive.

The issue for Luke is not whether there should be maps at all, but which maps and upon which values should they be based. Luke does not present Jesus and his followers as repudiating all values, and so advocating lawlessness. Rather, they are reformers proposing a new value and a new way of structuring the faith of Israel. Yet it is clear that Luke understood the Jesus movement to be repudiating the temple, both as a symbol and as an institution.

5.0 JUSTIFICATION FOR JESUS' NEW HOLINESS SYSTEM

Luke showed that even on certain Jewish terms Jesus himself was holy and "in place." Yet this same Jesus disregarded parts of the traditional Jewish holiness system and created new maps. But *by what right?* After all, was not God's will clear? Were not the scriptures, the law of Moses, clear on issues such as sabbath, circumcision, and diet? By what right did Jesus disagree with God and God's word? The answer to this is a major issue in Luke–Acts and an important further refinement of

Luke's symbolic world. In two basic ways Luke supplied the basis for Christian theory and praxis in regard to a new holiness system and to new maps. When we ask this question, we inquire about the values and structures which shaped Luke's particular symbolic world, namely, how he differed from first-century Judaism.

5.1. Christian View of the Scriptures

Undoubtedly the scriptures have something to say about values and maps, both for Jews and the followers of Jesus. But how to understand the scriptures? One distinctive strand of the Lukan interpretation of the scriptures was to see them as prophecy, not law. It is a commonplace now to speak about the Lukan theme of prophecy-fulfillment, or proof from prophecy (Talbert 1984b). For Luke, the core of the scriptures lay in the prophecy to David and to Abraham (Luke 1:32–33, 54–55, 69–73), the promise of a horn of salvation, a descendant to sit on David's throne. The correct reading of "the Law, the Prophets and the Writings" was to see them as prophetically referring to Jesus (Luke 24:25–27, 44–47). Conversely, then, the legal basis for the holiness system which the Pharisees et al. found in the scriptures was not correct, for the scriptures are prophecy, not law. Luke perceived Jesus and his followers reforming the way the scriptures should be read, not rejecting them. They were still valid, but only when read according to a new perspective. Such a hermeneutical perspective formed the basis for Luke's new maps.

Moreover, Luke argued that in some key instances the core of the scriptures was not understood correctly by the Jews. Stephen's whole speech in Acts 7 constitutes an extended argument that "in this place" (Acts 7:7) was never correctly understood by the Jews, who established a temple and a holiness system based on it. "In this place" is a prophecy of Jesus, not of a physical building.

Another way that Christians revised the reading of the scriptures was to argue that the legal prescriptions of the law of Moses were just that, *from Moses*, not from God. Peter branded the law of Moses as a "yoke which neither our fathers nor we have been able to bear" (Acts 15:10). And Paul spoke of the inadequacy of the law of Moses to make holy: "By Jesus every one is freed from everything from which you could not be freed by the law of Moses" (Acts 13:39). Luke implied that the problem lay not with God, but with Moses. Clearly a difference of opinion existed: followers of Moses perceived Christians as rejecting the ancestral traditions, while followers of Jesus saw them in need of reform. Nevertheless, we sense here that Jesus and his followers still structure their world according to God's scriptures, but under a different rubric than the temple and its adherents.

5.2 The God of Jesus Christ in Luke–Acts

The essential apologetic for the new maps which characterize the Jesus movement group ultimately resided in Luke's doctrine of God. Some claimed that the Christians "spoke against God" (Acts 6:11), and it is true that Christians described God differently from the way the Pharisees and the chief priests did. Yet they claimed to "worship the God of our fathers, believing everything laid down by the law or written in the prophets" (Acts 24:14). Herein lay their legitimation.

If Israel's maps were drawn on the basis of God's "holiness," which meant order and separateness, then the maps drawn by Jesus and his followers realized a different value. While not rejecting "holiness" as an important attribute of God, they articulated other values, like "mercy," as essential characteristics of God and values for God's people. "Mercy" is the code word for the three aspects of the Christian God to be discussed next (Luke 1:50, 54, 58, 72, 78; see Matt 9:13; 12:7).

God's Impartiality. Peter's vision in Acts 10 and the oracle which interpreted it both affirmed the new principle of God's mercy-as-impartiality: "What God has cleansed, you must not call common." This applied not only to foods, but especially to people. Peter said to Cornelius: "Truly I perceive that God shows no partiality" (Acts 10:34). And in the Jerusalem council's discussion of the Gentiles, Peter spoke again: "God made no distinction between them and us, giving them the Holy Spirit just as God did us" (15:8–9). Taking a perspective different from Gen 1, where God acted to separate, make distinctions, and show partiality, Luke argued that correct theology proclaims just the opposite (Dahl 1976:178–191; Bassler 1979). God's chief attribute, which is mercy, not holiness, implies a strategy of mission, hospitality and inclusiveness (Neyrey 1986b:118).

God and Abraham-David. Luke's view of the salvation history of God's people was not particularistic in that it did not begin with the exodus and the shaping of a people set apart by Torah on Sinai (Acts 13:17). Rather, Luke perceived God's history with humankind beginning with his merciful promises, first to Abraham (Acts 7:2–8) and then to David (Acts 13:22–23). On these two promises, not the Torah at Sinai, rests the identity of God's covenant people.

Biblical literature distinguishes two types of covenant, the covenant with Moses and that with Abraham and David (Clements 1967). The difference between the two types rests on the way God is perceived as acting. With Moses, God acted in "holiness" to gather a special people as his own, which he separated from the nations and made holy by the Law. This tends to be an exclusive covenant. With Abraham and David, God acted in "mercy" to elect unlikely people to receive blessings and promises by grace; this covenant was perceived as being inclusive in nature

(Gal 3:7–8; Rom 4:11–12, 17). First-century Christians argued that the type of covenant which God made with Abraham and David stands permanently as the authentic way God works. This was, moreover, an ideological statement about God's inclusivity and impartiality, which contradicted what the temple and synagogue said about Israel's separateness and exclusivity.

God's Reversals: If God's basic principle was mercy-as-impartiality, it was also characteristic of Lukan theology that God "reversed" former situations which celebrated distinctions and partiality. In a rhetorically significant place at the beginning of Luke's Gospel, Mary explained the basis of God's new action—reversal, a principle which holds true for the rest of Luke–Acts (Dupont:1980).

> God has scattered the proud in the imagination of their hearts, God has put down the mighty from their thrones and exalted those of low degree; God has filled the hungry with good things, and the rich God has sent away empty (Luke 1:51–53).

It is generally acknowledged that in this canticle Luke borrowed heavily from Old Testament materials, such as Hannah's canticle in 1 Sam 2. In this and other scriptures we learn of God's "reversals:"

> 1. God chooses the younger over the elder: Abel over Cain, Isaac over Ishmael, Jacob over Esau, Joseph over his 11 brothers, David over his siblings, and Solomon over his brothers (see Rom 9:9–13).

> 2. God abases the proud but saves the lowly (Job 22:29; Sir 11:4–6; see 1 Cor 1:19; 3:19).

> 3. God makes the fruitful barren and the barren fruitful (Isa 54:1; 1 Sam 2:5; Gal 4:27).

Such a theological perspective, then, is rooted in God's Word and legitimated as a major way in which God wishes to be perceived (see also Luke 10:21 and Acts 4:10–11).

Luke did not say in 1:51–53 that God hates the mighty or the rich, but that God himself upset the perceived map which indicated who enjoyed God's favor and who was in the inner circle of God's elect. That former map of people, based on the old maps of honor and holiness, was not the only indicator of God's favor, for God surprised the world by including the dishonored and the unclean in the covenant and by showering blessings on them too. "Reversal," therefore, may be too strong a word for this principle; inclusivity and impartiality better describe what is intended by this in Luke–Acts. Hence, God was reversing the status of unclean Gentiles when the Holy Spirit was poured on them, as in the case of Cornelius (Acts 10:44–47; 11:17), the Samaritans (Acts 8:14–17), and the Ephesians (Acts 19:2–7).

In Jesus' own actions and teaching, Luke indicated many more reversals, based on the principle of how God works in the world. Examples might include the following.

1. The child Jesus sits among the learned, "listening to them and asking them questions" (Luke 2:46): the unschooled teaches the teachers.

2. Jesus acclaims the poor, the hungry, and the sorrowful "Happy!" but he pronounces "Woe" upon the rich, the well-fed, and those laughing.

3. Followers of Jesus who lose their lives save them, but those who save their lives lose them (9:24).

4. Jesus proclaims that the last will be first and the first last (13:30). Again he states that those who exalt themselves will be humbled; but those who humble themselves will be exalted (14:7; 18:14).

5. The greatest among Jesus' followers must become as the youngest, and the leader as one who serves (22:26).

6. The preferred guests at a special banquet table should be the unclean of Israel, rather than its elite and pure folk (14:12–14).

7. A Pharisee, who observed all the traditional holiness maps ("I am not like other men . . . I fast twice a week, I give tithes of all that I get"), is supplanted by the sinful but repentant tax collector (Luke 18:9–14).

Again, Luke did not say that Jesus condemned those whose lives were happy, who enjoyed honor in society, who were learned, or who had status. He did not banish them from the map of God's covenant members. Rather he rearranged the lines of the map so that those formerly excluded from the map were included and those on the outer circles of the map were now closer to the center.

Yet to a devout, first-century Jew, this sounds as though the world has been turned upside down. For according to the perception of those who espouse more traditional maps, that is, Jews with strong holiness concerns, Christians seemed to reverse the world:

low is high / and high is low
empty is full / and full is empty
dead is alive / and alive is dead
last is first / and first is least
sad is happy / and happy is sad
losing is saving / and saving is losing
rejection is exaltation / and exaltation is rejection
unclean is clean / and clean is unclean
sinner is favored / unfavored is the righteous

In this perception the world has been turned upside down. But to an insider, Jesus and his followers were not destroying the system or rejecting traditional values, but rather restructuring the system and redrawing the lines of the maps according to the principle of God's "mercy." It is ever a question of perception.

Nevertheless, two radically different perspectives existed on the way the universe was ordered. The impulse to order was strong in both cases. It should be noted that Luke and the early Christians in one sense affirmed the basic elements of Israel's system of order and purity, namely, faith in the God of Israel and belief in God's scriptures. The different perceptions both of God and the scriptures account for the different configuration of lines, boundaries, and classifications. Observant Jews labelled them as revolutionaries, while Christians claimed to be authentic reformers. The decisive conflict centered around the "correct" interpretation of the tradition.

6.0 JESUS: MAKER AND GUARDIAN OF BOUNDARIES

Although observant Jews perceive Jesus and his followers as "turning the world upside down," Luke does not present them as lawless or mapless people. They do not advocate chaos in place of cosmos. On the contrary, Luke portrayed Jesus drawing new maps and reforming old ones, not destroying the system. Maps mean lines and boundaries. Although Luke indicates that Jesus pursued an inclusive agenda, he nevertheless created and defended boundaries which clearly indicate where people stand in relation to God and who is "in" or "out" of the covenant.

6.1 Jesus Builds Boundaries

"Purity" is the abstract word we have used for the system of boundaries, lines, and fences which classify persons, places, and times. Jesus' preaching and that of his followers built boundaries, for people must judge the message preached by these new prophets and decide where they stand in relation to it. And so, faith in Jesus as God's prophet and covenant leader became a genuine boundary line separating true members of God's covenant from all others, Jews and Gentiles alike. John described this in terms of Jesus winnowing grain, separating wheat from chaff (Luke 3:17); in other places, it takes the form of "woes" against unbelievers who will be cast down (10:13–15). Some unbelievers are compared to chicks who refuse the shelter of the hen (13:34).

Jesus and "Schism." In his programmatic prophecy, Simeon called Jesus a dividing line: "This child is set for the fall and rise of many in Israel" (Luke 2:34). Throughout Luke–Acts Luke presents us with a recurring "division" over Jesus' preaching (Acts 14:4). Jesus and his message occasion the building of distinct lines and boundaries (Jervell 1972:41–74). Examples of this division or schism in Luke–Acts include:

1. Failure and success attend the sowing of the word-seed (Luke 8:4–8).

2. Simon treats Jesus with little courtesy, while the sinful woman washes, kisses, and anoints his feet (Luke 7:49–50).

3. The rich young man rejects Jesus' teaching on wealth, while the apostles respond favorably (Luke 18:18–30).

4. Zacchaeus repents at Jesus' word, while crowds criticize Jesus for dealing with sinners (Luke 19:1–10).

5. Crowds acclaim Jesus at his entry into Jerusalem, while the Pharisees seek to silence them (Luke 19:38–40).

6. At the cross, one thief mocks Jesus, while the second asks for a share in his kingdom (Luke 23:39–43).

7. The Sadducees reject the apostolic preaching, while 5,000 others become believers (Acts 4:1–4).

8. Many people accept Peter's preaching, while the Sanhedrin tries to silence him (Acts 5:12–16/17–32).

9. The rejection of Stephen (Acts 6–7) is juxtaposed with the success of the mission among the Samaritans and an Ethiopian eunuch (Acts 8).

10. Paul's preaching at Antioch in Pisidia leads to acceptance (13:42–43, 48–49) and rejection (13:44–47, 50–51).

11. Contrasting results are recorded of the Christian preaching at Thessalonica (Acts 17:2–4/5–9), Beroea (17:12/13), Athens (17:18, 32), and Corinth (18:5–11).

12. Sadducees and Pharisees divide over the issue of the resurrection (Acts 23:6–9).

13. Finally at Rome, it is noted that "some were convinced . . . while others disbelieved" (Acts 28:24).

Jesus' rise and fall is based on faith or its lack in hearers of the word. A clear, absolute boundary, then, is established on the basis of Christian preaching about who is in/out of God's covenant community.

Reaction to God's Prophets. Faith-as-loyalty became a boundary marker; it found expression in the Lukan theme of the acceptance/rejection of God's prophets. When he sent out the Seventy, Jesus states the principle: "Who rejects you rejects me, and who rejects me rejects him who sent me" (Luke 10:16). In another place, Luke argued that Israel had always tended to be disloyal to God by rejecting the prophets sent to it (Luke 13:34–35; Acts 7:52). Jesus is the latest of God's prophets; he, of course, was rejected by many in Israel but accepted by others, who became his disciples and then members of "The Way." And so, reaction to God's prophets became a boundary line, which discriminated between those who accepted God and those who did not (Luke 10:16).

The Prophet Like Moses. Particular attention is given to Israel's reaction both to Moses himself and then to the prophet like Moses.

As Stephen's speech shows, Moses was the prophet "whom they refused": "Our fathers refused to obey him, but thrust him aside" (Acts
7:39; see vv 27–28, 35). Then God raised up a prophet like Moses (Acts
3:22; 7:37), and with the coming of this new prophet also came a new
warning: "And it shall be that every soul that does not listen to that
prophet shall be destroyed from the people" (Acts 3:23). Reaction to
Moses or his prophetic successor, then, functions as a boundary line
determining whether one is in or out of God's covenant people.

In summary, Jesus' word and the word about him constitute a boundary which separates God's authentic covenant people from all others.
The division is radical indeed; for according to Luke–Acts, only in Jesus
can one find salvation. Only in his name is there salvation (Acts 4:12);
only in Jesus can one be saved from what the law of Moses could not
save (Acts 13:39). In short, there is no salvation outside the community
gathered around Jesus. As Jesus said in the Gospel: "Who is not with
me is against me; who does not gather with me scatters" (Luke 11:23).

6.2 Church vs. Synagogue: Clear Boundaries

Boundary lines which define Jesus and his group were drawn by
the very abolition of certain purity traditions. As we noted above, Jews
separated themselves from the rest of the world by observing three particularistic customs: circumcision, diet, and strict sabbath observance.
Christians, however, began to distinguish themselves from such Jews as
the people who *do not keep* these exclusive customs. They separated
themselves from the synagogue by the *non-keeping* of scripture-based,
distinguishing Jewish customs. By redrawing these lines, Jesus and his
followers were engaged in a process of self-definition. And so a new map
was drawn, indicating that the followers of Jesus are radically independent from the synagogue:

Synagogue	Church
dietary laws	no dietary laws (Acts 10:15)
circumcision	no circumcision (Acts 15:1, 5 and 19)
strict sabbath	no strict sabbath observance (Luke 6:1–11)
washing rites	no washing rites (Luke 11:37)
temple & sacrifices	no temple, no sacrifices Luke 21:6; Acts 7:48–50)

There can be no mistaking the boundary between church and synagogue.
The abrogation of these customs indicates that new maps have been
drawn and that new boundaries exist.

6.3 Jesus the Judge — Guardian of Boundaries

If boundaries, lines, and fences are erected, they should be defended.
By portraying Jesus as judge, Luke shows that Jesus vigorously guards

the boundaries he has erected. For Luke, Jesus is unquestionably heralded as the Judge of the World, that is, the ultimate guardian of the gate to God's holy presence. The formula in Acts 10:42 and 17:31 may be quite traditional, but it nevertheless proclaims Jesus as "judge of the living and the dead." He ultimately determines who enters into and who stays outside of God's presence (see Luke 23:43).

The confession of Jesus as "judge of the living and the dead" in Acts completes the presentation of Jesus' comparable role in the Gospel. In the Gospel aspects of Jesus' prophetic judgment abound (Neyrey 1985:115–26). For example, it is Jesus who will separate wheat from chaff (Luke 3:17); he pronounces woes on unbelieving cities (Luke 10:13–15), declaring them outsiders. Jesus shuts the door against those who refuse his invitation (13:25). In essence, prophetic judgment separates the good from the bad, as wheat is separated from chaff, sheep from goats, and wise from foolish (Neyrey 1987:538).

The principle of Jesus' judgment is clear. Those who acknowledge Jesus openly, the Son of Man will acknowledge before God and his holy angels; but those who deny Jesus will be denied before the angels of God (Luke 12:8–9). In another place it is just as bluntly stated: "Whoever is ashamed of me and my word, of him will the Son of Man be ashamed when he comes in his glory and the glory of his father and of the holy angels" (Luke 9:26; see par. Matt 10:33; Mark 8:38; 2 Tim 2:12).

To complete the picture, we note other acts of judgment in Luke's second volume. Jesus proclaimed that the Twelve would sit on thrones, judging the tribes of Israel (Luke 22:29–30). This prophecy is fulfilled in Acts when Peter judges Ananias and Sapphira for their "lie against the Holy Spirit" (Acts 5:3). Judged and sentenced, they die and are "carried out" of the group, crossing not only the boundary of membership/non-membership but also that of life/death and holiness/sin.

7.0 CONCLUSION

This chapter aimed at developing a model by which we could gain some sense of the symbolic world of Luke–Acts. Evidently it has functioned at a rather abstract level in that it aimed at developing ways to detect the basic patterns of order and classification with which Luke and his audience perceive the world. The model was concerned with "purity," the basic sense of order and proper placement, which is a feature of every culture, but in varying degrees. The model was first illustrated in terms of first-century Judaism, which perceived "purity" in terms of God's holiness, a value orientation conceptually expressed in creation (Gen 1) and structurally realized in the temple. This served as a foil for investigating the way Luke and his circle perceived a different system. According to Luke, Jesus and his followers indeed maintained strong "purity" concerns, but took issue with the Judaism of that day in terms not only of specific boundaries and classifications, but also values. While not rejecting "holiness," they celebrated God's "mercy" and the strategy of inclusion and hospitality it implies.

To their observant Jewish neighbors, they indeed "turned the world upside down," for they did not respect or observe the value orientation (God's holiness-as-separation) or its major symbolic and structural expressions. Thus were they perceived. But according to them, they were not antinomians or revolutionaries. Concerned with "purity," they perceived and articulated a different value (God's mercy-as-inclusivity/impartiality). Maintaining their rootedness in Israel's scriptures and in worship of Israel's God, they disputed with observant Jews over where to draw the lines and how to classify persons, places, things and times. They offered a reformed system, but a concern for "purity" nonetheless.

The model developed here, then, is flexible enough to explain both Jewish and Christian perceptions of the world. It should be adequate to deal with other variations, such as Greek, Egyptian, and Roman perceptions of the cosmos. The development here has focused on Jewish and Christian symbolic perceptions of the cosmos because they appear to be the most basic orientations of Jesus and his followers in the first century, which is the world of Luke–Acts.

In focusing on the exposition of patterns of order, structure, and classification, we have by no means exhausted the investigation of other elements of a symbolic universe. Readers of Luke–Acts might well supplement this material with a more particular examination of the "cultural cosmology" of that world through the further use of the models of Mary Douglas. Her book, *Natural Symbols*, investigates many aspects of a symbolic universe, which book has been synthesized and adapted specifically for use of New Testament students by Isenberg (1977) and Malina (1986a). This particular chapter, however, summarizes the thrust of Douglas's work and can serve as a useful introduction to more elaborate models for discerning cultural perceptions and symbolic universes.

This chapter, while abstract at times, will gain in specificity in relation to other chapters in this volume. The persistent quest to know the exact "place" where every person or thing or place belongs is made quite particular in the study of honor and shame (Malina-Neyrey). Issues of clean and unclean become quite specific when seen in relation to sickness and healing (Pilch). The socialization of individuals to know the cultural codes of their world is treated in the chapter on first-century personality (Malina-Neyrey). The importance of the temple, treated here as symbol, is dealt with more extensively in the chapter on embedded religion and institutions (Elliott). Understanding how rituals deal with crossing lines and boundaries (McVann) gains clarity when seen in conjunction with the cultural perception of lines as described here. And the discussion of the meal-as-ceremony makes explicit many of the elements of this model of purity. The truth of any model is its ability adequately to explain data and to generate fresh insights. We find the model of purity trustworthy in regard to Luke's world, both the Jewish and Christian perceptions of it. Our assessment remains that this model can account for most of the conflictual dynamics in Luke–Acts, because it can explain from the native's point of view just where the conflicts lie and why certain issues were contested. A student might want to take the semantic word field noted early in the chapter and pursue it, or examine the many controversies in Luke–Acts in light of "purity." It is our contention that individual episodes in the text will be greatly enlightened by examination from this perspective.

THE SOCIAL LOCATION OF THE IMPLIED AUTHOR OF LUKE–ACTS

Vernon K. Robbins

1.0 INTRODUCTION: SOCIAL LOCATION

In the tradition of literary-historical interpretation, the social setting of Luke–Acts is highly debated. Susan Garrett recently asserted:

> Interpreters of biblical texts cannot question their authors. Further, because very little is known about the social setting in which some of the biblical documents were produced, interpreters often do not even know for certain which culture or cultures are relevant to a given text. Was "Luke" a second-generation Christian, or third-? What was his ethnic origin? Was he an inhabitant of country, town, or city, and in what part of the empire? What was the character of his and his community's relationship to Jews and to pagans in that locale? (Garrett 1989:12)

Despite debate about such questions, explicit inquiry about the context in which we interpret Luke–Acts contributes to our understanding of it in the milieu of first-century Mediterranean Christianity.

Yet it would not be enough to know the social context in which an author produced Luke–Acts. We often assume that once we know this, it would then be a simple task to trace correlations between that context and an author's thought. For example, if the author of Luke–Acts was urban, we assume that he might think like other urbanites we know about from the first century. If Gentile, he probably shares a way of thinking typical of that world.

Tracing correlations between thought and social context, however, is a notoriously difficult task in the sociology of knowledge. We can never assume that all persons in a given context thought alike. Nor is there any necessary causality linking context and ideas. It is much more likely that a range of ideas will appear as plausible alternatives to people who share a given social location. In a positive sense, therefore, our task is to show that Luke's ideas are within the range that would seem plausible in a particular context. Negatively we can show that the ideas are unlikely in the context we imagine for the author. Identifying such a range of ideas is never an easy task. Hence, our search for the context of Luke–Acts will have to be both indirect and hypothetical.

1.1 Defining Social Location

We use the term "social location" because "context" is too broad for our purposes. A "social location" is a position in a social system which reflects a world view, or what Peter Berger calls "a socially constructed province of meaning": a perception of how things work, what is real, where things belong, and how they fit together (Berger and Luckmann 1966:24–25; Rohrbaugh 1987a:109).

Of course, understanding a social location assumes that there is a relation between thought and the social conditions under which it occurs. There is a so-called social base—what Karl Mannheim first termed an "existential base" (Mannheim 1968)—underlying any particular way of thinking, as if a substructure of social conditions were the foundation on which the superstructure of thought can be said to rest. We must also ask of what this social base for knowledge or belief consists and how it is to be identified. What characteristics qualify a group or process as a social location of thought?

1.2 Social Base of Knowledge

Marxist theorists see social class as the key social location of thought. Important as class may be, other locations are important as well. R. K. Merton, for example, notes that not only groups, but also social processes, such as social position, class, ethnicity, and mobility, can themselves provide a social base for certain types of thinking (Merton 1968:514).

Obviously some social locations are easier to specify than others. For example, groups designated by gender tend to have clear and identifiable boundaries. Similarly sharp boundaries can be found in distinctions such as citizen/non-citizen, Jew/Gentile, and slave/free.

As New Testament scholars think about additional social groups and social locations, however, particularly those which do not fall as neatly together as do gender or race, how are we to know what counts as a group? How do we handle the complexities created by the overlapping character of group participation? We need criteria to designate a social location of thought in a clear and distinct way. In laying these out, we recognize what a social location is and what it is not. It is what Peter Berger calls a "plausibility structure," a socially constructed province of meaning (Berger and Luckmann 1966:24–25). It is not reducible to the material conditions of life because it is itself a mental construct, a socially produced and maintained picture of the world.

This means that the social base is not the cause of other ideas, but the context in which other ideas are interpreted and understood as realistic possibilities. Social locations are heuristic constructs, not explanatory ones.

To begin to say what social locations are, it is necessary to sharpen the way we use the terms "group" and "social location," particularly insofar as the term group is commonly used in a non-technical sense. A generation, for example, may be a social location of thought, but it is not a group. It is not an organization or association. Members of a generation, class, or any other social location may never get to know each other, may have no physical association whatsoever, but nonetheless live, so to speak, at the same location and hence share similar experience. Thus a generation lives through the same historical period. A class shares the same relation to the means of production. Common position or structural location in a social system thus provides the key.

It is not that certain experiences produce certain beliefs, but given certain experiences, a limited range of beliefs should be plausible options for most of those who share the social location (see Abercrombie 1980:38). And for our purposes, description of such limited ranges of experience should help us understand the way a set of ideas were taken by those who adopted them.

In sum, then, the common structural position occupied by a number of individuals in relation to a larger social whole entails a social location. Specification of a social location would ideally designate the limited range of experience a position implies (showing how it is distinctive), together with the process by which that position comes to be occupied. If we could reach some agreement about the social location of the thought in Luke–Acts, it might be possible to correlate the ideas with plausible social contexts in the Mediterranean world.

2.0 LANGUAGE AND SOCIO-RHETORICAL CRITICISM

We must now reckon with the nature of language in the documents we are analyzing, and for this we draw on insights from sociolinguistics discussed by Malina in this volume (see Halliday 1978; Fowler 1981). We use them, however, in the context of a method called socio-rhetorical criticism (Robbins 1984, 1987). Some of its presuppositions are as follows:

(a) Language is constitutive of social communication.

(b) Language signifies social functions.

(c) Statements in a document are intratextual functions that presuppose extratextual systems of social interaction.

(d) Some of the major issues of socio-rhetorical criticism concern the relation of information to patterns of activity in various arenas of the social system presupposed by the intratextual phenomena. For example, what is the relation of the information and functions in the social arena of beliefs and ideologies to information and functions in other social arenas, such as culture, technology, and population structure?

At the beginning, the interpreter must be aware that language signifies social functions. Any understanding of the signs in a document presupposes social arenas that provide meanings for human beings. Since understanding is a present activity, all knowledge is contemporary knowledge, even what we call knowledge of the past. This means that every person, at whatever time, reads a document through envisioned social arenas. What differs considerably are the conceptual frameworks and technologies people develop to investigate documents from the past.

If a reader wishes to interpret ancient Mediterranean literature through techniques that contextualize literature in pre-industrial society during the time of the Roman Empire, then it is necessary to find conceptual frameworks and scenarios designed to position our modern knowledge in pre-industrial social contexts. Malina's essay on reading theory in this volume indicates that because language is constitutive of social communication, we use social scenarios to contextualize what we read, and this contextualization produces the meanings we perceive in the text. If we can identify the arenas of the social system presupposed by various phenomena in the text, and if we can delineate the location, role, and competencies certain phenomena exhibit within different arenas of the social system, then we can make some progress toward identifying the social location of the thought within the entire document.

3.0 A MODEL OF THE SOCIAL LOCATION
OF NARRATIVE DISCOURSE

Previous discussions of the social context of Luke–Acts have lacked a systematic framework for the investigation. One of the contributions from the social sciences is its use of carefully constructed and empirically tested conceptual models to provide a framework which orients modern readers toward arenas within pre-industrial social systems (Carney 1975:xiii–ix, 1–43).

3.1 Social Science Model of Social Location

The present study uses a conceptual model for analyzing the social location of Luke–Acts. A comprehensive framework for investigating phenomena in Mediterranean society during the time of the Roman Empire is available in the works of T. F. Carney (1975:246) and J. H. Elliott (1986:14). In Figure 11-1 the nine basic arenas of a social system are listed in the column on the left of the model: previous events, natural environment and resources, population structure, technology, socialization and personality, culture, foreign affairs, belief systems and ideologies, and the political-military-legal system. Our model can help us to identify the social framework for documents written in Mediterranean society during the Roman Empire. Once we have itemized this social framework, our next challenge is to determine the intratextual phenomena that should be placed in the narrative function column. What can be said about these nine categories from the document Luke–Acts?

3.2 Narrative Discourse Model

Since Luke–Acts is narrative discourse, we must develop a second part of our model, namely, a comprehensive list of four intratextual functions from narrative communication. This study uses intratextual categories from Seymour Chatman's narrative-communication model as modified by Jeff Staley (1988:21–49). Accordingly, we give special attention to four aspects of intratextual functions in Luke–Acts:

(1) characters and their audiences
(2) narrator and narratee
(3) inscribed author and inscribed reader
(4) implied author and implied reader

By analyzing intratextual functions in Luke–Acts in light of the social systems in Mediterranean society during the Roman Empire, we hope to be able to identify aspects of the social location of thought within Luke's two volumes.

3.2.1 Characters and Audiences. A "character" is "a category of existents which inhabit the story world of a narrative and mimic human beings. . . . These characters . . . can . . . tell stories, becoming narrators . . . " (Staley 1988:47). Characters have an audience or a sequence of audiences as they speak and act. Because these audiences signify socially perceived contexts for speech and action, consideration of them contributes to our analysis. A full study of the characters in Luke–Acts observes both the presence (and absence) of certain characters and their limited range of knowledge. We select here those characters in Luke–Acts who appear to function prominently in one or another social arena in the Mediterranean world.

THE SOCIAL LOCATION OF LUKE-ACTS:
A TWO-PART MODEL
Figure 11-1

2. NARRATIVE FUNCTIONS

Characters/Audiences

Narrator/Narratee

Inscribed Author/Inscribed Reader

Implied Author/Implied Reader

1. ARENAS OF THE
SOCIAL SYSTEM

1. Previous Events
2. Natural Environment
   and Resources
3. Population Structure
4. Technology
5. Socialization and
   Personality
6. Culture
7. Foreign Affairs
8. Belief Systems
   and Ideologies
9. Political-Military-
   Legal System

3.2.2 Narrator. Since Luke–Acts is by internal definition a narrative (Luke 1:1), the discourse has a narrator. The narrator, or "the teller of a story" (Staley 1988:37), presents the characters and the situations in which they speak and act. Although it is tempting to think that the narrator speaks directly to us the readers, we must be on our guard. Since we are self-reflective readers, we see both ourselves reading the text and the narrator speaking intratextually to an imagined counterpart. This imagined counterpart is called the narratee, the figure "to whom narrators address comments; and like narrators, they are always intratextual" (Staley 1988:43).

3.2.3 Inscribed Author and Inscribed Reader. In Luke–Acts, a narrator speaking in third person presents the characters in their situations. But in the prefaces and sea voyages of Luke–Acts the narrator speaks in a first person mode. We will call this narrator the inscribed author, whose counterpart is the inscribed reader. The narrator in Luke–Acts never gives the inscribed author a name. Since Christian tradition attributes the two volumes to Luke, the associate of Paul, readers regularly perceive this inscribed author to be a male named Luke.

The inscribed author addresses an inscribed reader named Theophilus. From what the inscribed author says to Theophilus, we see that an inscribed reader may have prior knowledge of some of the characters and events in the story. In Luke–Acts the inscribed author wants to give more accurate information concerning the things of which Theophilus has already "been informed" (Luke 1:4). The inscribed author reappears in the sea-voyages in Acts through the medium of first person plural narration, but here the inscribed reader Theophilus is only implied.

3.2.4 Implied Author and Implied Reader. Of all the intratextual functions, the most pervasive and important is that of the implied author, whose counterpart is the implied reader. The implied author is "that singular consciousness which the reader constructs from the words of a text; a consciousness which knows the story backward and forward . . . the static, overarching view of a text that a reader might develop from multiple readings" (Staley 1988:29). Since "the implied author in the text . . . operates within a closed medium (print) whose linguistic signifiers (Koine Greek) open up into the much broader social world of the first century CE" (Staley 1988:30), our primary goal is to identify the social location of the implied author as constituted in the language, ideology, and social relations in the text (see Wolff 1981:136).

The implied author has the competencies of all the characters plus the competencies of the narrator and inscribed author. Thus the implied author transcends the limitations of any one of the characters or other actants in the text by also possessing the competencies of the forms, styles, strategies, and manipulative ploys of the narrative discourse (see Staley 1988:29). Thus, the social location of the implied author lies in all the competencies that signify certain kinds of relations to and activities within processes at work in various arenas of Mediterranean society.

Implied authors address implied readers. A text's implied reader is

> the affective quality of a text. It is an entity evoked and continually nurtured by the text . . . the "moving toward the gradual revelation," the text's "linearity." . . . The implied reader only has knowledge of what has been read up to the given moment . . . is limited by its temporal status. An implied reader must also gain all its knowledge of the story from the narrative medium itself, even if the general outline of the story is known in a culture (Staley 1988:33–35).

Let us recall that we, the real readers, provide the meanings that the characters, narrator, inscribed author, and implied author communicate to their intratextual counterparts. We supply these meanings by means of the scenarios we envision for their interaction. If our scenarios are twentieth-century situations and contexts in industrialized society, then we will supply these meanings to their interaction. But if we use scenarios introduced in other chapters in this volume to envision the meanings, we may take some steps toward an interpretation of Luke–Acts in a social location of thought in pre-industrialized Mediterranean society.

4.0 THE MODEL APPLIED TO LUKE–ACTS

We simply cannot explore all aspects of the social location of the implied author of Luke–Acts. Our strategy, then, is to make sorties through the text according to the basic arenas of a social system (see Figure 11-1).

4.1 Previous Events

A common social location may arise from a common relation to previous events. For example, today a generation of people in the United States has a relation to the Vietnam War. People born after it may have a relation to the war through discourse of one kind or another about it. Narrative accounts of previous events are one kind of discourse about it, and a particular selection and way of telling the stories evokes a common social location.

Luke–Acts is narrative discourse about previous events. Throughout Luke–Acts a particular selection of characters from Israel's heritage and Roman history appears in the narrative. On the one hand, the narrator selects events associated with Abraham, Joseph, Moses, David, Solomon, Elijah, and Elisha from previous biblical history (Acts 7:2–47; Luke 4:25–27). In other words, characters from biblical history come from the "great traditions" of Israel located in the Torah and the Prophets. From the perspective of the narrator, events from the great traditions of Israel lead to Christian events in an environment of Jewish-Roman rule.

On the other hand, we do not find events associated with great moments in Greco-Roman culture and history prior to Caesar Augustus. For example, no reference is made to Homeric literature, Alexander the Great, or the Punic Wars. There is a reference to Zeus and Hermes in Acts 14:12–13, but otherwise Luke–Acts is generally silent about Greco-Roman history.

Beginning with Caesar Augustus and Herod the Great, the events in Luke–Acts occur in an environment of Jewish-Roman history through the reign of Tiberius Caesar (14–37 CE; Luke 3:1), Gaius Caligula (37–41 CE), and Claudius (41–54 CE; Acts 11:28; 18:2), ending during the reign of the emperor Nero (54–68 CE), which overlaps the reign of Herod Agrippa II (53–ca. 100 CE; Acts 25:13–26:32). Luke–Acts contains no reference to Nero by name, but various people refer to him either as Caesar (Acts 25:8, 10–12, 21; 26:32; 27:24; 28:19) or Sebastos [Augustus] (Acts 25:21, 25).

Within this framework, Luke–Acts selects events that begin with Zechariah the priest, of the division of Abijah (1 Chron 24:10), and his wife Elizabeth (Luke 1:5–67); Joseph, of the house of King David, and his wife Mary (Luke 1:26–56; 2:1–51); John the Baptizer (Luke 1:57–66); the righteous and devout Simeon (Luke 2:22–35); the prophetess Anna (Luke 2:36–38); and Jesus of Nazareth (Luke 2:4–52). Then major additional people appear through twelve disciples who become apostles (Luke 6:13–16); seventy (or seventy-two) additional people who go into mission; seven Hellenists who serve their widows (Acts 6:1–6). Saul/Paul, who appears at the death of Stephen (Acts 8:1), becomes a member of the Christian movement after being encountered by the risen Lord (Acts 9:1–19) and begins to preach in the name of Jesus (Acts 9:27). Events surrounding Paul's activities occupy Acts from chapter 13 to the end of the narrative. All of these events occur as previous events in Luke–Acts. As a result, the social location evoked by previous events is complex but limited in striking ways to biblical heritage and to Jewish-Roman history from the time of Caesar Augustus and Herod to Nero and Herod Agrippa II. The special events within this Jewish-Roman environment concern John the Baptizer, Jesus, and their followers.

But the events recounted in Luke–Acts do not simply have the nature of events that lay outside the text. Rather, the implied author has produced previous events in the form of a social product, a product to be read.

As a beginning point, a number of characters in Luke–Acts recall previous events for particular social reasons. Jesus presents events associated with Elijah and Elisha to show healings of Gentiles (Luke 4:25–27), and Stephen recounts actions of Abraham, Joseph, Moses, David, and Solomon to criticize the "temple made with hands" (Acts 7:2–47). The Pharisee Gamaliel, in the presence of the Jerusalem council, refers to earlier revolutionary activity by Theudas and Judas the Galilean to recall their deaths and the scattering of their followers (Acts 5:36–37); and Paul recounts to the inhabitants of Jerusalem (Acts 22:4–21) and to King Agrippa (Acts 26:9–20) previous events in his life to try and change their perceptions and allegiances.

Not only do certain characters recount previous events, but at one point the narrator intrudes to refer to Herod Agrippa I's killing of James the brother of John (Acts 12:2) and to Agrippa I's death shortly thereafter (12:20–22). In Luke–Acts, therefore, both the narrator and the characters produce previous events for audiences in a manner that shows special interest in biblical heritage, healing of Gentiles, criticism of the Jerusalem temple, recruitment into activities and beliefs associated with Jesus, persecution of people whom public authorities consider to be dangerous, and death administered to specific people for various reasons.

Beyond the narrator and the characters, the inscribed author refers to previous events where eyewitnesses and ministers of the account (or "word") have transmitted information, and "many" have compiled a narrative of the things he himself is narrating (Luke 1:1–2). The inscribed author, then, performs a specialized function of finding accounts of previous events from both oral and written discourse and producing previous events as a social product. The inscribed author refers to his own writing of the document (Luke 1:4), then refers to the writing of the first volume as a previous event (Acts 1:1). The "ordered" fashion (Luke 1:3) in which the inscribed author produces the events indicates that special goals and values are at stake. Moreover, the inscribed author's presentation of the previous events to an inscribed reader with the Roman name Theophilus evokes a social location similar to Josephus, who also exhibits a knowledge of events in biblical heritage and post-biblical Jewish history, and addresses an inscribed reader with a Roman name.

4.2 Natural Environment and Resources

The arena of natural environment, which concerns geographical space, can take us a step further in defining social location. The resources perceived as really or potentially present within a geographical space depend on the perspective of the person viewing that space.

The implied author of Luke–Acts envisions a geographical space that extends from Ethiopia (Acts 8:26–39) and Cyrenaica (Acts 2:10) at the southern and southwesternmost point around the eastern Mediterranean to Rome at the northwesternmost point. Yet the primary geographical space lies between Jerusalem and Rome. From the point of view of Luke–Acts, this space contains land, the Great Sea, one river called the Jordan, and one lake called Gennesareth (Luke 5:1), which the other Gospel writers call the Sea of Galilee. The implied author of Luke–Acts will not call any inland body of water a sea; this terminology is reserved for the great Mediterranean Sea (Robbins 1978).

For the implied author, the major resource on land are ports (Acts 27:2), cities, and towns. And the major resource in ports, cities, and towns are houses where people receive hospitality. Alternative social locations of thought could perceive major resources on land to be wild animals to be hunted, gold, copper, or iron to be mined, or pyramids to be plundered; not so in Luke–Acts.

The perception of houses within cities locates the thought within human-made culture rather than undeveloped natural environment. This presupposes, therefore, the amassing of material goods that support the hospitality that occurs in houses. The implied author has in view barns full of grain, flocks of sheep, and vineyards, but these are simply presupposed as sources for the presence of the resources in the ports, cities, and towns. Also, the thought of the implied author is located at points of receiving hospitality rather than giving hospitality. There is never any criticism of a person who accepts hospitality. But the thought in the document criticizes or commends ways in which people offer hospitality to those who, it is presupposed, should receive it. The implied author also has in view houses in which people are kept under guard. In some instances, people who experience this kind of imprisoned hospitality may invite others to visit them in these houses (Acts 28:16–29).

Where, then, is the social location of the implied author? The implied author both produces previous events as a social product among persons who live in cities and towns and implies that the natural environment of land and sea is a place of travel, and thus of hospitability to the traveler. Accordingly, one of the highest values of the implied author is hospitality. In the geographical space between Jerusalem and Rome, the implied author evokes a social location seeking hospitality in the midst of a heritage that merges biblical, Jewish, Roman, and Christian events in a particular way.

4.3 Population Structure

Population structure opens the issues of age, gender, level of health and resources, and location in country, village, town, or city (Carney 1975:88–89). Our analysis already points to a social location within cities, and Rohrbaugh, Oakman, and Moxnes have chapters in this volume which analyze aspects of city/country and poverty/wealth. Therefore, we will not discuss location in country, village, town, or city, or repeat previous materials on poverty and wealth here. In addition, with Pilch's chapter on illness, we need not pursue levels of health. This section, then, will focus on age, gender, and the mixed population in view in Luke–Acts.

With respect to young people in Luke, John the Baptizer and Jesus appear at birth (Luke 1:57; 2:7), then Jesus amazes the teachers in the Jerusalem temple when he is twelve years old. The adult Jesus uses a child to illustrate greatness (Luke 9:47–8) and insists that small children be allowed to come to him (Luke 18:16–17). Jesus heals a demonized boy (Luke 9:38–42) and a girl who is about twelve years old (Luke 8:41–42, 49–56). There are but a few old people in Luke. Zechariah and Elizabeth, the parents of John the Baptizer, are advanced in years (Luke 1:7). The righteous and devout Simeon is approaching death (Luke 1:25–35), and the prophetess Anna is more than eighty-four years old. Beyond this, however, there is little emphasis on advanced age in Luke.

In contrast to Luke, there are no young children in sight in Acts. A slave girl (Acts 16:16–18) and four unmarried daughters (Acts 21:9) appear, but they are engaged in adult, not children's activity. The implied author views the world in which Christianity spreads from Jerusalem to Rome as an adult domain.

We are told of a large number of females in the adult world of Luke–Acts (Finley 1969). Elizabeth and Mary have prominent roles in the setting of the birth and infancy of John and Jesus (Luke 1:24–2:35). The prophetess Anna, sees Jesus and praises God for the redemption of Israel (Luke 2:36–38). Then throughout Luke, the narrator either refers to or presents a significant number of named and unnamed women: Herodias (3:19); a widow of Zarephath (4:26); Simon's mother-in-law (4:38); a widow (7:13); a woman of the city (7:37–50); Mary Magdalene, Joanna, and Susanna (8:3); Jesus' mother (8:19–20); Martha and her sister Mary (10:38–42); an unnamed woman (11:27–28); the queen of the South (11:31); a woman with an eighteen-year infirmity (13:11–13); Lot's wife (17:32); a widow (18:1–8); a poor widow (21:1–4); a maid (22:56–57); a great multitude of women (23:27–31); and women from Galilee (23:49, 55; 24:10).

Also throughout Acts the narrator either refers to or presents a significant number of women: Sapphira (5:1–11); widows (6:1); Candace, queen of the Ethiopians (8:27); widows (9:39, 41); Dorcas [Tabitha] (9:36–41); Mary, mother of John Mark (12:12); a maid named Rhoda (12:13); Lydia, a seller of purple goods (16:14, 40); a slave girl with a spirit of divination (16:16–18); leading women (17:4); Greek women of high standing (17:12); Damaris (17:34); Priscilla, a tentmaker (18:2–3, 18, 26); four unmarried daughters who prophesied (21:9); Drusilla, wife of Felix (24:24); and Bernice, wife of King Agrippa (25:13, 23; 26:30).

Perhaps the most remarkable feature of population structure, however, is the ethnic variety the narrator of Acts presents among members of the Christian movement. The variety comes into view in Acts through three related motifs: (1) gathering in cities; (2) scattering as a result of persecution; and (3) traveling. Through these motifs, people with different native languages and identities programmatically join the Christian movement sanctioned by God.

On the one hand, a representative mixture of all peoples and areas join the Christian movement as a result of their presence in cities. In the narrative sequence of Acts, this motif begins with Pentecost. From the narrator's point of view, the people gathered in Jerusalem were "Jews from every nation under heaven" (Acts 2:5). The narrator identifies Galileans (2:7), Parthians, Medes, Elamites (2:9), Cretans, Arabs, and Romans (2:11) in a manner that appears to be based on race, language, or dialect. The narrator identifies others on the basis of geography: those who dwell in Mesopotamia, Judea, Cappadocia, Pontus, Asia, Phrygia, Pamphylia, Egypt, and the parts of Libya belonging to Cyrene (2:9). In addition, the narrator identifies both Jews and proselytes among the Romans staying in Jerusalem (2:10–11). From the narrator's perspective, when Peter preached to this mixed population of Jews in Jerusalem, three thousand of them joined the Christian movement, and additional ones joined day by day after this (2:41, 47). At the end of this episode, then, more than three thousand Jews or proselytes representing a wide mixture of native languages and identities joined the Christian movement in its initial stages. A few chapters later, an Ethiopian eunuch who had come to Jerusalem to pray becomes a member of the Christian movement. Thus, the view of the narrator is that "Jews from every nation under heaven" gather in Jerusalem, and since the Christian movement begins with a large number of people from this group, Christianity is constituted by a wide mixture of people with different native languages, locations, and identities.

Through the related motif of scattering (van Unnik 1980:242–47), people of still different varieties join Christianity. Among the Christians in Jerusalem were Hellenists and Hebrews (6:1). The stoning of Stephen (7:58), one of the Hellenist deacons, led to the scattering of Christians from Jerusalem (8:1, 4; 11:19). As a result, Samaritans (8:12), a Gentile centurion Cornelius with his kinsmen and close friends (10:1–8, 44–48), Jews from Phoenicia, Cyprus, and Antioch (11:19), and Greeks at Antioch (11:20) joined the Christian movement. The acceptance of Gentiles is a shock to Peter and other leaders from Jewish heritage (Acts 10), but the presence of wide diversity within Judaism itself prepares the implied reader for this move. As a result of the gathering and the scattering that occurs in the first eleven chapters of Acts, Christianity begins as a highly mixed population.

Once the Christian movement has become a highly mixed population, additional varieties of people join the movement as a result of traveling. Programmatically, people respond throughout Cyprus (13:4–12), Asia Minor, Macedonia (Acts 16:9–17:14), and Greece (Acts 17:15–18:17).

In sum, the implied author has in view people from as far south and west as Ethiopia and Cyrenaica, as far east as Arabia, Elam, Media, and Parthia, as far north as the southern coast of the Euxine Sea and the northern coastal region of the Aegean Sea, and as far west as Rome. Every kind of person living in this area, including many women, become fully-constituted members of Christianity. Yet, the implied reader observes the implied author's lack of vision west beyond Italy, north above the Euxine Sea, and east into India. Indeed, the social location of thought appears to lie among a cosmopolitan population mixture somewhere between the western coast of Asia Minor and Syria.

Thus, a look at the mixture of population in Luke–Acts suggests a social location of thought among the kind of mixed population found in cosmopolitan cities in the eastern Mediterranean. The limited boundaries of the implied author's vision suggest that the social location of thought in Luke–Acts does not lie in elite groups that have access to Gaul, Spain, and India, nor in ethnic groups that refuse to associate with a mixed population. Rather, the thought is located among networks of people in eastern Mediterranean cities representing a wide variety of native languages and geographical areas.

4.4 Technology

Technology is identifiable by the application of knowledge for practical ends. In our experience, a wide variety of technological phenomena signify vigorous activity in the spheres of written, spoken, and visual communication, medicine, agriculture, fabrics, travel, and many other areas. We live in a technological age, and the spheres where technology is present appear through the objects and procedures that come into view as we go from one situation to another.

According to T. F. Carney, "a lack of technological development is one of the most striking characteristics of the traditional societies of antiquity" (1975:106, 132–33). Since the dominant values of the ruling elite are anti-economic, expertise is built up in the areas of literature, the military, and administration, not in the areas of commerce and industry (Carney 1975:107).

Our search through Luke–Acts reveals technological activity in four spheres: administration, sea travel, writing, and crafts.

In the sphere of administration, we know of census taking, as well as tax collection. Also, geographical space has been divided into districts over which specific people have jurisdiction. In addition, the administrative aspects of the military are in view, though the major technology of warfare like stone-throwing machines or machines for shooting spears or arrows are not in view. The reader sees only whips, swords, and crosses on which people are hung.

There is a surprising amount of technology of sea travel. Not only does the implied author exhibit knowledge of the storms and winds on the Great Sea but harbors, lees, and depths of the water at various places. In addition, the reader encounters data about kinds of anchors and techniques for sailing in rough weather (Acts 27:1–20).

The technological sphere of writing includes literary skills and rhetoric. Loveday Alexander (1986) recently made a breakthrough in analysis of this sphere in Luke–Acts. Her extensive search through Mediterranean literature for comparative analysis of the prefaces to Luke and Acts reveals a social location that is perhaps best described as "technical writer." The Lukan preface, which she identifies as "label + address," exhibits writing practices in a social location of technical or professional prose, which she calls "the scientific tradition." Writing within this social location reveals an appreciation for work of people in the artisan class, in contrast to the disdain elite writers hold for work performed by artisans. Using a detailed scheme for the syntactical structure of the prefaces, Alexander discovers the closest analogy to the Lukan prefaces in "middlebrow," technical literature, and the closest individual analogy to the first-century CE author, Hero the Engineer. Composition at this middlebrow level is "literate but not literary, a written language designed primarily for conveying factual information" (1986:61). She observes, in this regard, that the Lukan prefaces do not contain the "more flowery, 'Alexandrian' vocabulary" of the prefaces found in Hellenistic Jewish literature (1986:60).

It is important, however, to extend this kind of analysis beyond the prefaces. It is noticeable, as Alexander has observed, that the implied author changes from septuagintal style into other styles throughout the narrative (also Plumacher 1972; 1974; 1977; 1979). Moreover, as a recent study of the Beelzebul episode in Luke has shown (Mack and Robbins 1989:185–91), the author uses a strategy for developing rhetorical topics by adding sayings, fables, examples, analogies, and exhortations that exhibits a rather advanced level of writing. A similar strategy is at work in the well-known travel narrative in Luke which, through the addition of sayings and apophthegms, creates ten chapters of material as Jesus travels to Jerusalem. Also, the implied author exhibits a significantly competent rhetorical approach to defense speeches (Veltman 1975; Long 1983; Neyrey 1984) and sea voyages (Robbins 1978) in Acts.

What social location, then, does the implied author exhibit in the arena of technology? The implied author produces written accounts of previous events from a social perspective cordial to the production of tents (Acts 18:1–3), aware of the activities of silversmiths (Acts 19:23–24), and interested in the value of books written by people who practice magical arts (Acts 19:19). There is a lack of interest in the production of the raw materials themselves, like the leather produced through the slaughter and skinning of sheep and goats, though the tanning of skins is in view with the mention of Simon the Tanner (Acts 10:32). The process of mining silver and bringing it to the city is not in view. But the plight of silversmiths significantly occupies the narrator as the narratee is told how certain patterns of buying and not buying influence their livelihood (Acts 19:23–41). As mentioned above, the narrator also refers to the specific value of books produced for magic arts as fifty thousand pieces of silver (Acts 19:19). Moreover, members of the Christian movement make friends with a woman named Lydia, a seller of purple goods, and receive hospitality from her (Acts 16:14). The point is that artisans performing their crafts and sellers of goods produced by artisans are significantly in view as a result of the social location of the thought of the implied author. Though technically skillful with writing and highly aware of administrative technology, the implied author does not locate his thought among the elite, who look with disdain upon the artisan class (see Hock 1980); neither is his thought located among the daily workers in the mines, fields, vineyards, or hillside grazing sheep and goats. Rather, the thought of the implied author is located near the artisan class, aware of the dynamics of life at this level of society, comfortable with working with one's hands at this level of production, and interested in friendship with sellers of goods and buyers of books that contain information about the practices of groups about which one may have only the most basic information.

4.5 Socialization and Personality

If an exploration of technology within the thought of the implied author suggests significant association with artisan workers in cities in the eastern Mediterranean, perhaps analysis of socialization and personality can give us even clearer definition. The inscribed author claims to be an insider to the story and has "followed all things closely for some time past" (Luke 1:3). As an insider, the inscribed author seeks to communicate with a person who has been informed (*kathēchēthēs*) but who, in the inscribed author's terms, needs accurate, secure (*asphaleia*) knowledge. It is not clear why the inscribed reader needs this information about the Christian movement. The inscribed author simply says that "inasmuch as" others have compiled a narrative, it "seemed good" for him also to write an orderly account and to make it available to the one whom he addresses as "most excellent Theophilus." The pretense, real or fictive, is that this true information is a gift. The implied reader is left to wonder why. Is the implied reader to suppose that Theophilus already is a patron of this writer, that this patron is wavering in his support or expressing uncertainty because someone has suggested that the movement is politically or otherwise problematic? Or is the implied reader to see in this prologue competition with other Christians who present a theologically or politically different story of Christianity? The social location of the thought of the implied author contains an upward-looking stance but also a competitive stance toward Christians who have produced narratives of some sort about Jesus and/or early Christians. In any case, the social posture of the inscribed author is to evoke a friend or patron who has in the past, is currently, or will be expected in the future to reciprocate in some manner for the honor bestowed by the dedication of this work and the gift of this information.

The lack of certainty concerning whether Theophilus is a genuine patron requires that we interpret the prologues with great caution (Robbins 1979). But whether the relation to Theophilus is fictive or real, the inscribed author knows the kind of social location experienced by a friend writing for a friend or a client writing for a patron. If writing as a friend to a friend, he evokes a status for himself among those with social rank in Mediterranean society. If writing as a client to a patron, he issues a fictive or real challenge for patronage present or future.

If the inscribed author knows about such social locations and has the resources to adopt the persona of one of these in a written document, then we have uncovered an important aspect of the social location of the thought of the implied author. A social location is "a structural term describing a position in a social system" (Rohrbaugh 1987:114). Our inscribed author is in a social location that allows time and materials for writing and for adopting a persona either of a friend of social rank writing to another friend of social rank, or of client to patron. The length of the two documents testifies to this, since, whatever the location is, it has sustained itself long enough to produce two volumes of the work.

The narrator in Luke and Acts addresses Theophilus as "most excellent," analogously to Josephus' address to Epaphroditus (*Life* 430; *AgApion* 1.1). Thus the person producing Luke–Acts does not have the inscribed author adopt a position of equality with the one whom he addresses, as Plutarch does to Socius and Polycrates (see *Theseus* 1.3; *Demosthenes* 1.3; *Dion* 1.3), but a subordinate position, as Josephus does to his patron Epaphroditus. It surely is informative that the inscribed author of Luke–Acts has used the same form of address in the prologues that subordinates use for their Roman superiors in the stories in Acts.

Outside the prologues, a tribune displays the use of the honorific appellation "most excellent" in a letter to the governor (Acts 23:26), a spokesman for the high priest, Tertullus addresses the governor in the same manner (Acts 24:2), and Paul addresses the governor Festus in this manner in a formal trial before the king (Acts 24:24). From the narrator's point of view, subordinates address superiors in the Roman hierarchy as "most excellent," and Paul does not adopt this subordinate position before the governors except in a formal trial setting when the king is present (Acts 26:2, 7, 19; cf. Acts 25:8, 10, 11).

In contrast to all of this, people in Luke–Acts do not use forms of honorific address when they speak to subordinates, and political leaders of high rank do not use honorific appellations when they address each other. Thus, Paul addresses the crewmen on the ship that is taking him to Rome as "men" (*andres*; Acts 27:10, 21), and local Jewish leaders in Rome who come to him as "men, brothers" (*andres adelphoi*; Acts 27:17). In turn, the Jewish leaders use no special form of address when speaking to Paul (Acts 28:21). Also, the governor Felix uses no honorific form of address when he speaks to Paul, whom he perceives to be below him in social and political rank (Acts 23:35; 24:22, 25; 25:5, 9, 12); and neither the governor Festus nor King Agrippa employ honorific appellations when they talk to each other (Acts 25:14–22, 31–32) or to Paul (Acts 26:1, 24, 28).

These data suggest that our inscribed author addresses Theophilus in a mode associated with a person who is willingly or unwillingly in a subordinate position to a person of rank in Roman society. We know this form of address was used for a procurator of the equestrian order from the time of the emperor Septimius Severus on (after 193 CE). As the equivalent of the Latin *optimus*, it is attested to in first-century documents in reference to any official (Fitzmyer 1981:300). It is likely we are getting an important look into the social location of the thought of the implied author when we see this data.

There is a possibility, as mentioned at the outset, that the address to Theophilus is fictive, that there is no real individual person to whom Luke and Acts are addressed. In this case, one or more unseen patrons, matrons, or associates are supporting the production of these documents by providing daily sustenance, shelter, freedom from labor, and the economic ability to acquire materials and time. The prologue to Acts, which refers to the first volume, implies that the support continues for a significant amount of time. But the challenge to Theophilus somehow facilitates the production of the documents. The inclusion of "most excellent" suggests a social location where one or more persons either seek to communicate with people who possess some prestige in Roman society or seek the image of communicating with such people. The inscribed author is adopting a stance subordinate to the one with whom he wishes to communicate. Two possibilities, therefore, already can be excluded—the inscribed author does not evoke a social location which communicates downward to people with lower social ranking, and it is not considered wise to communicate as though there were equality in social rank. The social location of the thought of the implied author suggests it is advantageous to adopt a stance of respect that evokes a social location slightly below but in communication with people who have higher status in the social structure. Thus, although the thought of the implied author is near the artisan class, and holds no disdain for artisan labor, there is a social posture of communicating upwards in the social order rather than downward to artisans or peasants.

4.6 Culture

Culture is a humanly constructed arena of artistic, literary, historical, and aesthetic competencies. Since writing itself constitutes a basic cultural product, when we examine the conception of reading and writing in Luke–Acts, we gain a further definition of the location of the thought in the two volumes. Let us begin in the arena of the characters.

In the social location of the Jerusalem temple, a male named Zechariah, a member of the social class of priests, with a defined status in the division of Abijah, was fulfilling his role of burning incense when an angel of the Lord addressed him about his social role as husband (Luke 1:5–17). In the domain of culture, special interest arises when the angel speaks to him in poetic verse (1:14–17). This is not the poetic verse of Homer, Greek tragedy, or Greek lyric poetry, but poetry in the style of Septuagint Greek. Six months later, when the angel Gabriel speaks to Mary, a virgin betrothed to a man named Joseph, a member of the royal family of David, this angel speaks in a similar septuagintal style of poetic verse (1:32–33, 35). When Mary visits Elizabeth, the now pregnant wife of the priest Zechariah, Mary speaks in even lengthier septuagintal-styled poetic verse (1:46–55). Then, after Elizabeth gives birth to John, Zechariah, the priestly father of John, first writes the name of John on a tablet, then produces extended prophetic speech in the style of septuagintal verse (1:67–79). Zechariah's ability to speak in this manner and to write reminds us that he comes from a priestly family that nurtures at least basic educational skills. After an angel of the Lord speaks in short septuagintal-styled verse to shepherds in the field (2:14), a righteous and devout man named Simeon also speaks in this stylized manner as he blesses God (2:29–32) and speaks to Mary about her son (2:34–35).

A very interesting social location begins to exhibit itself. The implied reader observes that the father of John, the mother of Jesus, the righteous and devout man Simeon, and angels of the Lord, including Gabriel, display a social location within Jewish culture that gives them the competence to produce poetic verse that imitates Septuagint Greek. And the implied reader sees that the father of John can write at least basic information on a tablet.

After the first two chapters the status of poetic verse styled according to the Septuagint verse changes. Prior to chapter 3, the poetic verse is produced either by heavenly beings or humans upon whom the Holy

Spirit has come (Mary—2:35; Zechariah—1:67; Simeon—2:27). This speech is characterized as prophetic (1:67; 2:26), and the impression is that it is being composed in the setting of oral performance rather than being quoted from a written document. In the ideology of the implied author, then, the poetic verse is "divine, spirit-inspired, prophetic speech" (which the inscribed author has now written). After Luke 1–2 and throughout Acts, all the poetic speech is said to be from a written document, and this speech occurs in two intratextual arenas. First, the narrator quotes septuagintal verse "written in a book of words of Isaiah the prophet" in Luke 3:4–6 and Acts 8:32–33. The words have the style of septuagintal poetic verse, like the poetic verse that was performed orally in Luke 1–2. With these quotations, the narratee sees that the narrator can find and read passages from Isaiah. Second, a large number of characters quote written poetic verse. After Jesus' response to his mother in the temple at twelve years of age (2:49), he responds to all three temptations by the devil by quoting scripture (4:4, 8, 12). But the devil also can quote from these written materials (4:10–11). In a Jewish cultural environment, Jesus has skillfully defeated the devil, since he quoted each time from the Torah (Deut 9:9; 8:3; 6:16), while the devil quoted only from the Writings (Ps. 91:11–12). But the narrator does not tell the narratee this, and we can not know for certain that the implied author is aware of it. At this point, the implied reader knows that Jesus has the ability to recite verses of written scripture orally, but the implied reader cannot be absolutely sure, yet, that Jesus can read these verses from a written document. Perhaps, Jesus simply has heard them so often that he can reproduce them orally.

When Jesus goes to the synagogue at Nazareth on the sabbath, he opens the book of Isaiah, finds a specific passage, and reads the passage with rhetorical grace (4:16–22). The implied reader will notice that this is the same book from which the narrator quoted in 3:4–6, but this reader will not yet know that the narrator will quote again from this book in Acts 8:32–33. Jesus, then, like the narrator, has access to a book of Isaiah's words. We never see Jesus carry this book, but he has access to it in the Nazareth synagogue. Like the narrator and the implied author, Jesus has the competence to find a specific passage in this book. When Jesus continues by telling about the days of Elijah and Elisha (4:24–27), the implied reader probably concludes that Jesus reads about these things in some other book that tells about Elijah and Elisha. But no one indicates where these stories could be found.

Jesus' social location, then, appears to be somewhat different from that of Zechariah, Mary, and Simeon, since he is a reader and oral performer of scripture, while they were oral performers of spirit-inspired poetic verse which no one claims was written before our implied author scripted it. Therefore, Jesus, as presented in Luke–Acts, is located within the social sphere of reading culture. This view of Jesus' social location is further supported by his quotation from the book of Psalms in Luke 20:17, 42–44, his specific reference to the passage in the Torah about the bush (Luke 20:37), and his interpretation of the things concerning himself "beginning with Moses and all the prophets" (Luke 24:27). Jesus, then, occupies a social location of reading literacy within Jewish culture. He has a reading knowledge of the Torah, the prophet Isaiah, and the Psalms.

In Acts, the implied reader sees Peter, John, Stephen, and James orally reciting passages from the Jewish writings, but only the Ethiopian eunuch is portrayed as possessing a book (Isaiah) and reading it. In fact, it surely is instructive about the social location of Luke–Acts that every major character quotes (often lengthy passages) verbatim from the Jewish scriptures very soon after being introduced to the implied reader (Peter—Acts 1:20; 2:16–21, 25–28, 34–35; 3:22–23; 4:11; other apostles— 4:25–26; Stephen—7:3, 26–28, 32–34, 35, 37, 40, 42–43, 48–50; James— Acts 15:15–18). In his inaugural speech (Acts 13:33, 33–35, 41, 47) and likewise at the end of his career (28:25–27) Paul quotes extensively from the Jewish writings. But for Paul there is more.

In Athens Paul quotes from both Epimenides and Aratus' *Phaenomena* (Acts 17:28). Culturally Paul is thus exhibited in a social location that reaches beyond Jewish writing into Greek poetry. It is possible that Peter and the apostles also have some ability in the sphere of Greek sayings, since Acts 5:29 may be a saying associated with Socrates (Pervo 1987:169).

Every competence the characters exhibit to the implied reader reveals an aspect of the competence of the implied author. Thus, the implied author is not limited to septuagintal poetic verse, but also has competence, though perhaps quite limited, with Greek poetry. To these things, however, we must add the implied author's competence in the prologues to Luke and Acts, the defense speeches of Paul in Acts, the sea voyage narratives, and the kind of historical biography and novelistic monograph the implied reader sees in Luke and Acts. Thus, the implied author occupies a social location within Jewish culture which is not limited to knowledge of the Septuagint. There is no attempt, however, to write a dactylic hexameter line of Homer or a poetic line of tragedy, and there are no references to these written works alongside written Jewish scripture.

What does this mean in terms of social location? Perhaps we can get a clearer view if we compare Luke–Acts with the *Infancy Gospel of Thomas*. On three different occasions in *Infancy Thomas*, teachers agree to educate Jesus, that is, to teach him "letters." The first two times Jesus resists the presupposition that proper knowledge and behavior comes through learning how to read and write (*InThom* 6:2–6; 14:1–3). The third time (15:1–2) he takes a book lying on the reading desk and, without reading any of the letters in it, opens his mouth and by the Holy Spirit teaches the law to people who are standing by. To understand this we must know that Infancy Thomas is rejecting the concept that "all knowledge" can be taught through letters, that is "Greek letters." The teachers try to teach Jesus the Greek alphabet, which is the basis of paideia—the education that makes people truly learned. In contrast to the portrayal in Luke, the Infancy Gospel of Thomas exhibits a social location that depicts Jesus refusing to learn from people who teach reading and writing. Along with this social location, the author of Infancy Thomas presents no quotations from scripture in the entire document. For reasons beyond the scope of this study, the social location of the Infancy Gospel of Thomas reflects a position against people who teach reading and writing in Greek. In contrast, Luke presents Jesus as a person comfortable with and trained in written scripture, and both the Gospel and Acts exhibit a high facility with scripture written in Greek language.

Also, Paul can quote brief lines from some ancient Greek poets (Acts 17:28) and produce articulate speeches that exhibit knowledge and skill. But in one of the speeches Paul makes it clear that he is an urban Jew who received a proper education under a tutor named Gamaliel (Acts 22:3). Thus, his learning came from Jewish culture, and this learning gives him competence even with some Greek poetry.

With this analysis of reading and writing culture in Luke–Acts, we see an interest in presenting Jesus and his followers as "lettered," but it is a literacy based on Jewish culture. The thought of the implied author, therefore, is emphatically bicultural: grounded in Jewish culture but competent in Greco-Roman culture. This biculturality also produces problems for this kind of Christianity. Festus recognizes Paul's "great learning" (ta polla grammata), but fears that his pursuit of truth is turning him mad (Acts 26:24). However, the high priestly family of Jerusalem perceives Peter and John to be uneducated and ungifted men (Acts 4:13). People in the narrative, then, can label the competencies of its characters as "unlettered" or "lettered," and they may describe the people themselves as "ungifted" or "mad."

4.7 Foreign Affairs

Once we see the attempt of the implied author to communicate upward from a bicultural location, our investigation of foreign affairs produces interesting results. In truth there are few foreign affairs in view in Luke–Acts. There are references to Roman emperors in two historical synchronisms: Caesar Augustus decreed that the inhabited world should be counted (Luke 2:1); and John began baptizing in the fifteenth year of the reign of Tiberius Caesar (Luke 3:1). In addition, the Emperor Claudius is known to have commanded all Jews to leave Rome (Acts 18:2).

Since the reign and decrees of the Caesars are essentially foreign to the history of Syria, Judea, Galilee, Iturea, Trachonitis, and Abilene, the thought of the implied author is located where the decrees of the emperors are perceived to be foreign history.

But what is the meaning of foreign? The first people who appear to be foreign are the Samaritans who will not welcome Jesus (9:52). Yet soon after, Jesus presents a Samaritan as a model neighbor (10:29-37). And later, when Jesus heals ten lepers it is the Samaritan, who is called a foreigner (17:18), who appropriately gives praise to God for his cleansing. Then in Acts 8:1-24, the people of Samaria, at one point called the "nation" of Samaria (8:9), respond positively to the preaching among them.

The people in Acts 2 who are gathered together begin to speak in their own native languages: Parthians, Medes, Elamites; people from Mesopotamia, Judea, Cappadocia, Pontus, Asia, Phrygia, Pamphylia, Egypt, parts of Libya belonging to Cyrene, Rome, and Cretans and Arabians. When these "foreigners" join Christianity, the Christian community begins to be constituted by foreigners. Next, the church is "scattered" throughout many regions. People in Athens call Paul a "babbler" and "preacher of foreign deities" (17:28).

It depends on where a person is located as to whether he or she is a foreigner, and the thought in Luke–Acts appears to exhibit a location of "inverted" foreignness. Christians appear to be the primary foreigners. In other words, the affairs recounted in Luke–Acts are the true foreign affairs. The thought of the implied author is located in a bicultural environment that has brought a self-consciousness of foreignness among people established in cities throughout the eastern Mediterranean. But the implied author has a solution to the anxiety this foreign identity produces. The "foreign" affairs of Christians must be narrated to people above them in the social order. In other words, some kind of advantage is to be obtained by admitting that the affairs of the Christian community are foreign events to established people in Roman society and by arguing that it is important for them to have a well-ordered, detailed account of these foreign affairs. Thus, the implied author is located socially in a position where he wants the foreign affairs that lie within his biculturality to find an accepted place within the affairs of Rome.

4.8 Belief Systems and Ideologies

The basic ideology of Luke–Acts appears to be the belief that God has ordained a place for the "foreign affairs" of Christianity within the affairs of the Roman Empire. This aspect of Luke–Acts regularly has been pursued under the rubric of an apologia for Christianity that shows that Christians are not guilty of illegal activity under Roman law (see Walasky 1983). The ideology of Luke–Acts, however, moves much beyond this goal.

The implied author wishes to show that God has "cleansed" a widely divergent and mixed group of peoples within a movement inaugurated by Jesus of Nazareth. The word "cleansed" challenges the purity system of Judaism at its center. As Elliott shows in this volume, Luke–Acts replaces the centric ideology of the temple with the distribution ideology of the household. One of the major aspects of this change is a transformation of the purity system of Judaism (Douglas 1966; Malina 1981:122–52; Neyrey 1988b).

Luke–Acts replicates the distributive economic approach within the realm of purity. As food is distributed to people of every social rank, so every social rank and ethnically divergent person may be "cleansed by God" through baptism into the Christian movement. The key verse occurs in Acts 10:15: "What God has cleansed, you must not call common." This ideology is exhibited through the cleansing of lepers, which includes Samaritans and Namaan the Syrian (Luke 4:27; 5:12, 13; 7:22; 17:14, 17). Also it emerges in a discussion with Pharisees, where Jesus tells them that God has made not only the outside but also the inside, and therefore giving for alms those things which are within will cleanse everything for them (Luke 11:40–1). This change of purity systems coheres with the ideology that God has cleansed a wide variety mixed together (Acts 11:9), which includes Gentiles whose hearts God cleanses by faith (Acts 15:9). Purity, then, is to be found within the mixed and diverse social and ethnic groups in the Christian movement. God's cleansing activity is exhibited in the devoutness (Luke 2:25; Acts 2:5; 3:12; 8:2; 10:2, 7; 17:23; 22:12) and righteousness or innocence (Luke 1:6, 17; 2:25; 5:32; 12:57; 14:14; 15:17; 18:9; 20:20; 23:47, 50; Acts 3:14; 4:19; 7:52; 10:22; 22:14; 24:15) of people associated with Christianity. When disagreements arise between Jews and Christians over precise practices, the implied author suggests that these disagreements are simply a matter of inconsistency within some people's thinking about how God has cleansed the diversity that lies within Judaism itself, and now within Christianity, throughout the Roman Empire.

Thus, the thought of the implied author is located in a social environment that accepts its foreignness and mixedness as blessed by God. This confidence in God's action reflects a social location in which Christians consider themselves equal to Pharisees and able to challenge them to be hospitable in their homes and generous in almsgiving. In addition, it gives these Christians confidence with the leaders of Roman society, which leads us to our last section.

4.9 Political-Military-Legal System

According to Carney, during the time of the Roman Empire, the political-military-legal system stood in a close symbiotic relationship with socio-economic affairs, affecting almost everything everywhere in the system (Carney 1975:235–79; cf. Andreski 1968). It is widely recognized that a political-military-legal system is extensively in view in Luke–Acts. Some have argued that the primary purpose of Luke–Acts was to show that no Christian had ever been found guilty of a crime against the Roman legal system. More recently, Philip Esler has argued that Luke–Acts legitimizes Christianity by exhibiting favorable relationships between early Christian leaders and Roman officials (Esler 1987).

On the one hand, we must remind ourselves of those parts of the political-military-legal system that are outside the boundaries of what is in view to the implied author. While Luke–Acts contains many references to Roman emperors, only three are referred to by name (Caesar Augustus—Luke 2:1; Tiberius Caesar—Luke 3:1; Claudius—Acts 18:2). Moreover, there is no scene in Luke–Acts where a Roman emperor is present. Paul is taken to Rome so he can appeal directly to Caesar, but such an appeal is never shown to the reader nor referred to as accomplished. In fact, there is such a social separation from the environment of the emperor that references to a specific emperor are absent except in the two synchronisms at the beginning of Luke and the reference to Claudius' edict against Jews in Rome. References to certain decrees and laws imply the presence of the emperor as a symbol of supreme political and legal power.

In contrast to the absence of emperors themselves, a number of upper-level representatives of the emperor's domain appear in Luke–Acts. The narrator depicts a majority of these people as holding a favorable attitude toward Christians (Esler 1987:202). Thus, Lysias, the Roman tribune in Jerusalem, goes to great lengths to protect Paul from the Jews in Acts 21–23; Sergius Paulus, the proconsul of Cyprus, converts to Christian belief (Acts 13:6–12); and Asiarchs in Ephesus, who are priests of the imperial cult, are described as friends of Paul (Acts 19:31). Most of the people at the level of prefect, proconsul, or king will take no legal action against individual Christians, but most exhibit some social distance from Christianity. Thus, Pontius Pilate declares Jesus innocent, but his social location is clearly distant from the activity of Jesus and his followers. Likewise Gallio, the Roman proconsul of Achaea, dismisses the case of the Corinthian Jews against Paul, and his reason is that this is a matter of dispute over Jewish words and names (Acts 18:12–17). In other words, people at the highest levels of the political-military-legal system are located socially at a distance from the Christian movement.

The number of centurions mentioned in Luke–Acts, and their favorable relation to Jesus and the later apostles, is quite a different matter. It would appear that Luke–Acts is produced in a social location where a number of centurions are members of the Christian community. The centurion of Capernaum has a favorable experience with Jesus (Luke 7:1–

10); the centurion at the foot of the cross "glorifies God," probably indicating a personal stance within Christian belief (Luke 23:47; see Esler
1987:202); the first gentile convert is the centurion Cornelius, along with
his entire household (Acts 10:1–11:18); and Julius, the centurion in charge
of Paul during the voyage to Rome, is especially kind to Paul, allowing
friends to visit him (Acts 27:3) and saving him from being thrown over-
board by the ship's crew (Acts 27:42–43). Luke–Acts is located in an environment where centurions are among the members of the community,
not simply outsiders looking in.

What, then, is the social relation of Christianity to the political-
military-legal system in the thought of the implied author? It implies
that representatives from this arena of the social system are fully constituted members of the Christian movement alongside the other representatives of diversity within it. Likewise the political-military-legal
system has an established practice of protecting, or at least attempting
to protect, Christians. Thus, in the ideology of the implied author, there
is every reason why members of the political-military-legal system can
feel at home within Christianity and every reason why Christianity
should be considered to have a comfortable place within the Roman
political-military-legal system.

Yet there is a deep uneasiness within this "at homeness." Throughout Luke–Acts, the political-military-legal system protects or attempts to
protect Christians. But in the end there is a social location of imprisonment within the system. On the one hand, Paul is a Roman citizen (Acts
22:27–28), he is free to move about openly and unhindered (Acts 28:31),
and he is able to meet with local Jewish leaders (Acts 28:17–23). Yet, a
soldier must guard him (Acts 28:16), much as there are representatives
of the political-military-legal system keeping an eye on the affairs of this
"foreign people" throughout the narrative. Paul, like the Christian movement, has a rightful home within the Roman Empire; yet his home, and
he himself, is continually guarded. The attentive guarding protects the
members of the movement, but it also imprisons them socially. Thus,
in this social location, the thought of the implied author hovers between
being at home, enjoying the hospitality and benefits of Roman society,
and being in prison, always guarded by people both inside and outside
the movement.

5.0 CONCLUSION

Many interpreters have claimed knowledge either about the author
of Luke–Acts or about the community in which he lived. Other interpreters have denied that the interpreter can know anything about either

the author or his community. There is, however, another way to ask the question. What can we know about the social location of the thought of the implied author?

The goal of this chapter has been to create a model for exploring systematically the social location of the implied author of a document written in Mediterranean society during the time of the Roman Empire and to make an initial application of the model to the study of Luke–Acts. As a result of our sortie through the arenas of the social system identified by Thomas Carney, a picture has begun to emerge. The implied author produces previous events as a written product, and this production of events is observable in virtually every arena of the narrative functions of the text. Major characters, the narrator, and the inscribed author produce previous events as a social product for their audiences. While most people in Mediterranean culture produced previous events as a social product, only certain people produced them in written form. The inscribed author refers to both written and oral production of previous events as a resource, the raw material if you will, for this production of an ordered account. The implied author produces previous events as a means of establishing and maintaining sets of relationships among various kinds of Christians, Jews, and Romans who encounter one another and exchange values, goods, beliefs, and challenges.

The thought of the previous events that constitute Luke–Acts occurs in a geographical space extending from Ethiopia and Cyrenaica east to Elam and west to Rome. The resources within this space are ships for travel and islands for protection and hospitality on the Great Sea, fish and boats for travel on lake Gennesareth, and houses for hospitality in ports, cities, and towns on the mainland and on islands. The differentiated people in view in this space are wealthy and powerful Jews, wealthy and powerful Romans, and afflicted men and women. Thus, the thought of the implied author is located in the midst of the activities of adult Jews and Romans who have certain kinds of power in cities and villages throughout the Mediterranean world from Rome to Jerusalem.

Within this space and among these people, the thought of the implied author exhibits technology in four spheres: administration, sea travel, writing, and crafts. The arena of socialization reveals an upward-looking use of technology toward Roman officials with political power. Jewish officials, however, are considered equal in social status and rank. Wealthy Pharisees are singled out as people who regularly offer hospitality to Christians sharing the social location of thought with the implied author, yet those Pharisees are accused of often not fulfilling aspects of social action valued by the Christians who receive hospitality from them. Christians in this social location of thought pride themselves on offering healing to afflicted people (see Pilch's chapter) and food to beggars, lame, maimed, blind, and those not allowed to stay in the city overnight (see Rohrbaugh's chapter). In this social location, Christians argue for distribution of wealth to the poor, but they do not argue the case for allowing the poor to become landowners or householders (see Oakman's chapter; Oakman 1986). In other words, the thought is located socially within cities and villages, not out in the countryside.

The primary culture exhibited by the social location is written literature and cultivated speech. The implied author knows substantial portions of Isaiah and the Psalms, as well as other scriptures. In addition, the implied author can produce short lines of Greek poetry, though there is no attempt to produce a hexameter verse from Homer or a poetic line from Greek tragedy. Rather, the implied author produces poetic verse out of the culture of Judaism. In other words, the cultural achievement represented by Luke–Acts reflects a Jewish sphere of society using the Greek language, the lingua franca of the Mediterranean world.

The arena of foreign affairs gives us additional insight into the social location of the thought of the implied author of Luke–Acts. Roman emperors, and thus foreign affairs are in view for the implied author. But the presence of Roman affairs has created a view that the affairs of Israelites, Jews, and Christians are "foreign" to the dominant population in the Mediterranean world. Thus, the thought of the implied author is located socially in a place where it seems advantageous, and perhaps necessary, to tell "these foreign affairs" to people slightly higher in social rank who read Greek and appreciate a people who strive to be devout, righteous, and lettered.

In the arena of belief systems and ideologies, the thought of the implied author appears to challenge the dominant Jewish purity system at its center. The thought in Luke–Acts celebrates diversity and claims that God has "cleansed" it. In this way, the thought of the implied author claims to be an authentic part of the heterogeneous population of the Roman Empire. Part of this diversity includes the presence of political-military-legal personnel within the Christian movement. Thus, it is quite acceptable in this social location to sell one's coat and buy a sword (Luke 22:36). Yet the sword is not to be used carelessly or with undue aggression (Luke 22:49–51). Nevertheless, life at this social location is uneasy. Members of the political-military-legal system both protect Christians and imprison them. Accepting a position of subordination, Christians speak with politeness and care upwards to those who dominate the system. Yet, bolstered by God's sanctioning of their diversity and by their ideology of "at homeness" in the Roman Empire, they not only tell their story to those above but engage in vigorous and continued confrontation with those from whom they claim their Jewish heritage and those with whom they enjoy the benefits of Greco-Roman culture.

12 RITUALS OF STATUS TRANSFORMATION IN LUKE–ACTS: THE CASE OF JESUS THE PROPHET

Mark McVann

0.0 INTRODUCTION

Weddings are occasions of great importance. During them, a woman and a man publicly enter into a new social relationship; they have crossed a line that cannot be crossed again. With that crossing, they assume a new identity with new rights and obligations. No matter what the future holds, neither of them can ever be "single" in the sense the word had before they married. A fundamental life boundary has been crossed, and its mark on personal and communal experience is virtually indelible. The wedding, which is a ritual of status transformation or "boundary crossing," signals to the members of the group that this man and woman have validly assumed the new role of *married* man and woman.

Weddings, baptisms, graduations, and ordinations are familiar examples of rituals of status transformation in our society. We all have felt the power and solemnity they express. They have a peculiar ability to move us, and at the same time, to tell us who we are. Rituals help us build and sustain our identities: Catholic, Protestant, or Jewish; married, divorced or widowed; professor, doctor, or lawyer. They assign us a location in cultural space, and designate a status for us which the members of our society recognize as proper to us. They help us make sense of society, and help society make sense of us. How do they work?

To understand rituals we must recognize that human beings live in culture. Unlike animals, we do not live directly in nature, but in nature and human society. Culture mediates society and nature to us; it interprets and shapes our attitudes toward them. Culture thus provides for us the means to interpret our experience and understand our place in the world. Therefore, meaning—how to live and what living is about—is established for us through the intricate and complex interlocking systems of nature and culture (Geertz 1973:3–30). One of the fundamental building blocks of culture is ritual. It serves the purpose of ordering, i.e., drawing boundaries around both natural and social spaces, and identifying them as good or bad, inside or outside, clean or unclean, high or low. In short, rituals construct and maintain a cosmos, an ordered universe.

Students of culture historically have concentrated on the analysis of ceremony, ritual, and related aspects of culture. These provide "blueprints" or maps of a culture, that is, highly visible displays of a culture's view of the world and society. They symbolize the ideal order of the world, and help structure identity within that order. Hence, our understanding of ritual presumes knowledge of the chapter on "symbolic universe" and its suggestions about the perceived order of the world. Rituals are concerned primarily with the boundary lines drawn within a society, and conditions which permit crossing of those lines. So if we would understand how people come to know about their symbolic universe and how this socializes their behavior, we need a special scenario, which is ritual analysis.

1.0 RITUAL AND CEREMONY DISTINGUISHED

This chapter deals with rituals of status transformation. The next chapter examines ceremonies. The two must be read together, for rituals and ceremonies together explain the way people assume and then function according to the roles and statuses of the symbolic world into which they are socialized. Rituals and ceremonies are not the same thing, and so we pause to distinguish them in a brief, meaningful way.

In the course of routine daily living, individuals take special time, either to pause from routine or to intensify aspects of it. When the pause occurs irregularly, or as a break in the routine, it is called *ritual*. When the pause happens predictably it is a *ceremony*. These pauses, moreover, are under the care of specific people. Those who preside over or direct ritual pauses, the irregular breaks, are *professionals*, such as physicians, judges, and clergy. Those who preside over or direct *ceremonies*, on the other hand, are *officials*, such as the father or mother presiding at a meal, a priest conducting a temple sacrifice, or a politician officiating at a Fourth of July picnic. *Rituals* function in terms of status transformation. People might change roles: those who have been excluded from aspects of societal life—for example, criminals, the sick, sinners—can be brought back into the life of society by means of rituals which signal their status reversal, from prisoner to free citizen, ill to healthy, guilty to forgiven. People might, moreover, take on new and better roles by means of rituals which signal their status elevation. For instance, people are declared trained professionals or educated men and women by graduation from professional schools or universities. Citizens become the "Honorable So and So" by inauguration as mayor, judge, senator.

Ceremonies, as distinguished from rituals, function in terms of confirmation of values and structures in the institutions of a society. Institutions are patterned arrangements of sets of (a) rights and obligations called roles, (b) of relationships among roles called statuses, and (c) of successive statuses or status sequences which are generally well-recognized and are regularly at work in a given society. Institutions encompass kinship, politics, education, religion, and economics (see the essay by Elliott on the institutions of Temple and Household).

Ceremonies confirm the social institutions that structure life shared in common. They confirm the respective statuses of persons in those institutions, even as they effectively demonstrate solidarity among all those who gather together and give shape to the them. Birthdays and anniversaries, for example, affirm the social roles of mother, father, child, priest, or king. The feasts of Passover and Purim celebrate the existence of the people of Israel and the holiness of God's temple respectively.

The following chart may help to highlight the distinguishing characteristics of rituals and ceremonies:

Ritual	Ceremony
1. frequency:	1. frequency:
irregular pauses	regular pauses
2. calendar:	2. calendar:
unpredictable,	predictable,
when needed	planned
3. time focus:	3. time focus:
present-to-future	past-to-present
4. presided over by:	4. presided over by:
professionals	officials
5. purpose:	5. purpose:
status reversal;	confirmation of
status transformation	roles and statuses
in institutions	

2.0 RITUAL: DEFINITION AND OVERVIEW

Our introductory remarks noted that rituals, unlike ceremonies, are concerned with status transformation and passage from one role or status to another. People may move horizontally up or down the social scale, or laterally from inside to outside. Ritual transformation of status may occur either voluntarily (e.g., marriage), or involuntarily (e.g., trial and execution). In either case, the movement from one status to another is presided over by persons qualified to supervise the transition and certify its legitimacy. We call such persons "professionals" or ritual elders.

Rituals constitute a highly significant aspect of life in society. While forms vary, all rituals mark off as peak events critical transitional moments in life, such as birth, adulthood, marriage, ordination, death and the like. These and other transitions in life are nearly always and everywhere surrounded with complexes of symbols. Rituals provide the participants with the means of understanding the way the world is perceived by their social group and a way of participating in its patterns.

Thus, ritual is a symbolic form of expression which mediates the cultural core values and attitudes that structure and sustain a society. As such, ritual is a mode of education which socializes its participants how to be fit for life in their varying statuses. We can see, then, that ritual, even if it dramatizes status change and transformation, has as one of its main functions the maintenance of the *status quo*. A given ritual may entail a change of status for participating individuals (e.g., marriage), but it also serves to emphasize the permanency of one or another of society's basic institutions (e.g., kinship). It is a means whereby a society marshals its authority to assure continuity for the values and attitudes embedded in its institutions. Nevertheless, we note that maintaining the *status quo* is not the only, or necessarily, the most significant function of rituals. The encounter with life's mysteries, which gives rituals their focus and power, prevents them from being merely instruments to enforce conformity to a society's standards of acceptable behavior.

The model employed in this analysis of ritual comes from the writings of the symbolic anthropologist Victor Turner. He points out that ritual is characterized by a three-step process involving (a) separation from, (b) marginality towards, and (c) reincorporation into society. This *process*, moreover, involves *elements* which help effect passage to the new role and status. We will take up in turn each of these aspects of ritual.

2.1 Ritual Elements

Among the elements of a status transformation ritual, Turner lists (a) the initiands, who undergo the change of role and status, (b) the ritual elders, who preside over the ritual, and (c) the symbols (or *sacra*) of the world, which the initiands learn during the ritual.

Initiands. These are the people who individually or as a group experience the status transformation ritual and so acquire new roles and statuses in their society.

Ritual Elders. Ritual elders are the persons officially charged with conducting the ritual. They see to the strict enclosure of the initiands and supervise their activity. They socialize them as to the mysteries of life in their culture by exhibiting and explaining to them, or coaxing them to think about, the sacred ritual symbols (*sacra*) of their group.

Thus, the elders are "limit breakers" or "boundary jumpers." Unlike other people, they are licensed to deal with initiands who are in the dangerous and ambiguous state of liminality. They are immune to the powers harmful to those outside the process because they have been appointed to conduct the ritual and have themselves been transformed by it (Turner 1967:97). For example, doctors deal with diseased persons, ministers with sinners, and police with criminals. Additionally, they may function as models for the initiands, because they are the "professionals" who embody the core values of their society. As such, they bear the authority of society to command and control.

In order to accomplish the transformation of the initiands, the elders may beat them, withhold food and sleep, taunt and insult them, strip them of clothing, and take other measures to humiliate and disorient them (Turner 1967:235–236). They see to it that the preconceived ideas about society, status, and relationships, in short, about life itself, are wiped out. In the space cleared by this demolition, the elders instill new ideas, assumptions, and understandings that the initiands will need to function effectively when they assume their new roles at the aggregation rite.

Ritual Symbols. The ritual symbols (*sacra*), which play a crucial role in the initiation ritual, take various shapes. Frequently they are masks or other such items in which aspects of familiar things appear, but combined in such a way as to make them seem bizarre. At key points they are brought out and exhibited to the initiands as a part of their instruction in the basic facts of their culture.

> The communication of *sacra* involves three processes, though these should not be regarded as in a series but as in parallel. First, the culture is reduced into recognizable components or factors; second, these components are recombined into fantastic or monstrous patterns and shapes; third, they are recombined once more in ways that make sense with regard to the new state or status that the neophytes will enter. . . . Thus, the communication of *sacra* both teaches the neophytes how to think about their cultural milieu and gives them ultimate standards of reference. At the same time, knowledge of them is believed to change the neophytes' nature, that is, to transform them from one kind of human being into another (Turner 1967:106 and 108).

Secret societies, for example, carefully hide from outsiders their "sacred objects," such as skulls, rings, books, and candles. Yet they are displayed to initiands with comments about their significance either at stages during the ritual or at the formal induction at its formal conclusion.

The ritual symbols may include stories or narratives which shape the way initiands learn to perceive the cosmos. Again, Turner helps us understand this phenomena:

> Initiands [in African secret societies] are . . . taught the main outlines of theogony of their societies or cults, usually with reference to the *sacra* exhibited. Great importance is attached to keeping secret the nature of the *sacra* exhibited (Turner 1967:103).

Ritual symbols, then, are sacred because they are objects "out of the ordinary." They provide a focus for the initiands during their liminality, and ensure that they concentrate on the values and attitudes of their society which are concentrated symbolically and highlighted in them.

In cultures where an initiand undergoes the rite of passage in solitude, ritual symbols representing the tribe frequently accompany the initiand to the place of isolation. During the ordeal of initiation, these objects help initiands to fix their minds on their rootedness in their people and their obligations to them (Peterson 1987:76).

2.2 Ritual Process

The prime analogy for the ritual process described in this section is that of the status transformation from childhood to adulthood in societies where such rites of passage are heavily ritualized (e.g., American Plains Indians' vision quests or African circumcision rites). Regardless of the specific status transformation or the particular ritualizing society, the fundamental stages in any rite of passage remain largely the same: separation, liminality-*communitas*, and aggregation. They may not, however, be equally articulated or important in every ritual.

2.2.1 Separation. Individuals undergoing status transformation rituals tend to experience separation in three ways: separation of people, place, and time.

Separation of People. Participants in a rite of passage are separated from the ordinary rhythm of the group's life. For example, young men or women who have come of age must be prepared to assume the responsibilities of adults such as marriage, childbearing, and parenting. When the proper time arrives (usually at, or soon after, puberty), they are separated from the village either as a group or individually and are removed to a place reserved for their ritual initiation into adulthood. At the point of ritual separation, the initiands and the place of initiation become "off limits" to all the villagers except the elders who will preside over the ritual (Turner 1967:97).

Separation of Place. It is important to remove the initiands to a place separated from the locus of ordinary life because the experience into which they will enter is very much "out of the ordinary." The place chosen for the rite may be difficult of access, a space to which tribal or clan traditions have been tied for generations, in other words, a sacred space. For example, mountains, deserts, and forests, which tradition identifies as locations of special revelation or habitats of spirits and gods, are ideal sites for such rituals (Turner 1967:223–26).

Separation of Time. Although rituals may have precise "fixed" or calendar times when they begin and end, the participants in a ritual are thought to be removed from the normal flow of time. They leave "secular" time, and enter into a sacred "timelessness." During the ritual, time is broken up or distributed in new or unfamiliar ways. The usual times for eating, sleeping, working, and learning are altered, and sometimes reversed. There may be long periods with no eating or sleeping (e.g., fasting, vigils), long periods of forced activity (e.g., singing, dancing) or inactivity (e.g., prayer, silence, immobility) (Turner 1967:238–39; Peterson 1987:75).

2.2.2 Liminality-Communitas. Liminality, the negative side of the ritual process, describes the state into which the initiands are brought by virtue of their separation from the everyday, familiar world. It is their "threshold" period (*limen* = "threshold"). During the liminal period, initiands may become disoriented, having been cut off from the persons, points of reference, and activities which shaped their previous way of living. In a sense they "disappear" from view, or "die." They are required to abandon their previous habits, ideas, and understandings about their personal identities and relations with others in their society. Because they are "lost" from culture during the time their status is ritually recreated, any status they had is lost as well. Their identity before the rite (e.g., as children) is no longer operative, but they have not yet attained a new role and status (e.g., as adults). Therefore, they are perceived as dangerous or as pollution to those outside the ritual process because the initiands exist in limbo, a realm where they are "in between," always a dangerous place.

> The attributes of liminality or of liminal *personae* are necessarily ambiguous since these persons elude or slip through the network of classifications that normally locate states and positions assigned and arraigned by law, custom, convention, and ceremony . . . Liminal entities, such as neophytes in initiation rites, demonstrate that as liminal beings they have no status. Their behavior is normally passive or humble. It is as though they are being ground down or reduced to a uniform condition to be fashioned anew and endowed with additional powers to enable them to enable them to cope with their new station in life (Turner 1969:95).

The participants' segregation from the rest of society for the duration of the rite, coupled with their subjection to the ritual elders, highlights the idea that they are brought into contact with powerful forces mediated to them by the elders. These forces are unleashed with the express purpose of shaping, even infusing, the identity proper to the station in life they will assume at the conclusion of the ritual. Their old roles as children are wholly inadequate for responsible adulthood. Hence, the old role and status must be rooted out, and a completely new one impressed permanently upon them. That is to say, a radical transformation of the initiands is thought to be accomplished by the experience of undergoing the ritual (Turner 1967:102).

Communitas, the positive side of the ritual process, cannot be considered apart from liminality, as the two are inseparably linked to form the heart of the ritual process. Communitas sharply emphasizes "an essential and generic human bond, without which there could no [status differentiating] society" (Turner 1969: 97). He continues: ". . . the bonds of communitas [formed among initiands undergoing a rite of passage] are anti-structural in that they are undifferentiated [and] egalitarian . . ." (Turner 1974:46).

Communitas thus refers to the initiands' recognition of their fundamental bondedness in the institution into which they are being initiated. The familiar expectations others had of them, and they had of themselves, emphasize differences in status between adults and children, men and women, superiors and inferiors, etc. These differing levels of status obscure the humanity common to all people. In the liminal period, nearly all such distinctions among the initiands disappear, and stress is placed on equality and unity. Since equality and unity are not obvious in everyday life, and can even threaten the structures of the established society, liminal entities, like ritual initiands, are marked off and isolated from the rest of society. Liminality, therefore, suspends routine and represses status differences. Communitas, the focus on common humanity, can then emerge into the foreground, and an "all for one and one for all" spirit often develops among the initiands in a rite of passage.

2.2.3 Ritual Confrontation. Certain status transformation rituals require some form of mock battle or hostile confrontation as a final step in the initiand's achievement and public recognition of the new status. In some instances there is real violence, in others, only playful and harmless insults. In others, however, there is a controlled and highly focused expression of hostility and tension such as occurs in a challenge-riposte situation. The initiand is tested to see whether the skills of the new role have been learned or to apprise whether the initiand is faithful to the charge. This would be especially true of rituals which effect the rite of passage of a warrior or prophet (see Girard 1977:98, 119, 274–308; Turner 1967:38–47; 1969:100–102).

2.2.4 Aggregation. The ritual process completed, the initiands return to society with new roles and statuses, and new rights and obligations. By virtue of the ritual, the larger society acknowledges that the initiands now have the capacities requisite for fulfilling their new roles within it. Their status in the community has been redefined. Now that the sacred liminal time has passed, initiands are no longer regarded as threatening or dangerous. In fact, after the ritual, they become useful again to society as they take up the roles for which the ritual has prepared them (Turner 1967:251–60).

Those, however, who have been initiated into particular roles such as shamans, prophets, or priests, undergo only a partial aggregation. While they provide indispensable services to their societies, they remain partially on its margins since they are thought to retain access to powers or forces which make them dangerous. They are "holy," and their holiness is often characterized by its distinction from the ordinary or "secular" (Heschel 1969:3–26; Turner 1969:128).

We have, then, a model of status transformation rituals. If we would understand the way people and their society are socialized as to the various roles and statuses in the institutions which structure their cosmos, we need such a scenario for reading and observing. The model is necessarily abstract, as it is meant to apply to a wide variety of status transformation rituals, but we have chosen to use it to read the specific narrative wherein the status of Jesus was transformed from that of a private person to that of public prophet.

3.0 THE MODEL APPLIED: THE PROPHETIC ROLE OF JESUS

Luke 3:1–4:30 marks a narrative and a ritual transition. According to 2:42, Jesus is a twelve-year-old child, who "grows in wisdom, age, and grace." In 3:1, he is still but a private person, but by 4:14 he has become a public figure with a new, clearly defined role and status. According to the narrative, Jesus, now thirty years old, begins his career of preaching in the synagogues of Galilee. A dramatic change has taken place: Jesus has been transformed from private person to public preacher. It is our hypothesis that Luke 3:1–4:30 should be understood as a ritual process which narrates the transformation of Jesus from private person at Nazareth to public prophet in Israel.

In terms of the model outlined above, we shall attend both to the elements of the ritual and the stages of the ritual process:

Ritual Elements	Ritual Process
initiand: Jesus	separation
new role: prophet	liminality
elder: John the Baptizer	communitas
symbols: river, desert, mountain,	confrontation
temple, scripture, etc.	aggregation

3.1 Ritual Elements in Luke 3:1–4:30

3.1.1 Jesus, the Initiand, and His New Role. In Luke 3:1–4:30, Jesus is presented as an initiand who takes on the role of prophet. Luke presumes his readers have some knowledge of what a prophet is, which he shares with other New Testament writers who label Jesus a prophet. For example, in John 6:14, the crowds acclaim Jesus a prophet at the multiplication of loaves; in Mark 6:15 and 8:28, when people see and hear about Jesus, they conclude that he is "Elijah, or John the Baptizer, or one of the prophets." In Luke, moreover, on the occasion of the raising of the widow's son the crowds acclaim Jesus as a prophet (7:16); and Cleopas, walking to Emmaus, summed up Jesus' identity as "a prophet mighty in word and deed" (24:19). Later, Acts 3:22–23 and 7:37 speak of a tradition rooted in Deut 18:15–18 that God would raise up a prophet like Moses. Luke regards this prophecy fulfilled in Jesus. The Gospels of John and Mark, however, do not tell us what is meant by "prophet" or when Jesus assumed that role. Luke 3:1–4:30 fills the gap for us by narrating the ritual of status transformation of Jesus from private person to public prophet.

Yet what constitutes the role of "prophet"? We are advised to abide by the emic description of a prophet which Luke provides for his readers. He first informs us about the role of prophet in his initial descriptions of John, who is clearly acclaimed a prophet. At the annunciation of his birth, John is called a holy figure (1:14–17); he will be separated from pollution, such as fermentation in wine (1:15); and he is acclaimed powerful in virtue of the Spirit given him (1:17, 41–44). As a prophet, then, he is "holy" because he is set apart from pollution, and "powerful" against sin by virtue of his possession of the Spirit.

Luke's description of John's behavior in 3:1–20 leaves no doubt that John fulfills his role: (a) he remains "holy" or separate, apart from society at the Jordan, and (b) he acts aggressively against sin. As prophet, John must penetrate the disguises of evil, which masquerades as good in this world. He must fearlessly identify and condemn all evil in his presence, especially evil disguised as good. Beyond Luke 1–3, Luke continues to cast John in the traditional role of Old Testament prophet, "a prophet and more than a prophet" (Luke 7:26). And Luke has a particular prophet in mind as John's model, namely, Elijah. In terms of clothing, John's dress recalls that of the great prophet (see 2 Kings 1:8). John, moreover, will be "in the spirit and power of Elijah" (1:17).

Prophets, moreover, spoke oracles of warning and judgment against sin (e.g., Jer 3:6–18). This pattern is replicated in John the Baptizer's powerful prophetic speech (Luke 3:11ff). His preaching against sin is even cited as the cause of his death (see Mark 6:18). Prophets, then, called sinners to repentance; they came to turn the hearts of children to their parents (Luke 1:17), and to make straight the way of the Lord (Luke 3:4). Prophets also spoke of revelations from God, a new word of grace or judgment, or both. John the prophet, then, is a man completely dedicated to God's business: holy, separate, all-seeing, faithful to God's covenant, and powerful in word.

This brief overview of the role and identity of the prophet hardly exhausts all its nuances, but it does provide an adequate summary of Luke's views. Furthermore, on the level of the narrative, Luke has intentionally presented a series of elaborate parallels in chapters 1–2 between the annunciations and births of John and Jesus. One function of these parallels would seem to be the association of John and Jesus, not merely as kin, but as prophets. The detailed description of John prepares the reader for the role which Jesus will later fill. Although Luke insists on Jesus' superiority to John, he likewise shows that they are both prophets.

Prophetic power will characterize Jesus as well. As Cleopas reported, Jesus was "a prophet mighty in word and deed" (24:19). In terms of mighty deeds, prophets like Elijah and Elisha cured lepers (2 Kings 5), raised the dead (1 Kings 17:17–24), and multiplied food (2 Kings 4). Comparable acts of power are attributed to Jesus, thus clarifying the complex role of prophet which he assumes (lepers cured, 5:12–16; dead raised, 7:11–17; food multiplied, 9:10–17). In fact, these mighty deeds serve precisely as the prophet's credentials and so legitimate his status (Acts 2:22). And Jesus was powerful in word as well, as his many oracles of judgment indicate (Luke 11:37–54; 13:1–5; 19:45–48). Mighty deeds and words, therefore, form a large part of the emic conceptual ground for Luke's presentation of Jesus as prophet.

In chapters 1–3, then, Luke provides in John the Baptizer an explicit model of prophet for Jesus the initiand. Yet despite the high status accorded Jesus in the infancy narrative (1:32–35; 2:11), he is not yet a prophet. He must be initiated into that role. He is not yet a public person and no one in the narrative so far has taken him as such. The transition from private person to public prophet must be narrated and legitimated. For this reason, Luke tells us that Jesus associated himself with John at the Jordan. Thus Luke establishes a link between Jesus and John to show that the mantle of prophecy is passed to Jesus in a valid ritual process.

3.1.2 John the Baptizer as Ritual Elder. In accord with our model, John the Baptizer functions as the ritual elder who introduces Jesus to the rite of passage. On the surface level of the story, this may not seem obvious. According to Luke, John is abruptly removed from the scene in 3:18–20 and imprisoned. We do not hear of John again until the prophetic career of Jesus has been firmly established and underway for some time (7:18–24). Evidently Luke has special reasons for handling the traditional material in this fashion (Matt 3:13–16; Mark 1:9). Viewed, however, from the perspective of ritual, Luke's narrative suggests that John has already fulfilled a specific role, namely, that of ritual elder who initiates Jesus' transition into the role of prophet. It is on 3:1–22 that we focus our attention now.

In terms of the model, the ritual elder knows the values of his culture and serves as a pedagogue to the initiand. He may also embody the new role and model it for the initiand. John is undoubtedly a prophet, and in Jesus' words, "the greatest of the prophets" (7:26). In Luke's narrative, the stories of Jesus and the Baptizer are frequently presented as parallel (Brown 1977:250–53). Although many functions have been suggested for this parallelism, one would seem to be the patterning of the role of prophet, first by John, then by Jesus. This is likely when one considers that Jesus in turn models the pattern of the prophetic role which the apostles will assume in Acts.

Let us focus more closely on aspects of "prophet" which John models for the initiand who comes to him. John's performance at the Jordan contained six elements of prophetic activity which Jesus will imitate. Luke thus informs his readers of the new role of Jesus by modelling it according to Jesus' own description of John as "greatest of the prophets."

1. John, a preacher of repentance, was holy and sinless, that is, wholly the servant of God.

2. He acted aggressively against sinners (3:7–9, 17).

3. John saw through the masquerade of evil which hides its true nature. He read the hearts of those approached: "Brood of vipers . . ." (3:7). It belongs to prophets to pierce through false exteriors and discern true natures, even as Jesus does with his revelations of "hypocrisy."

4. He called for justice and the righting of wrongs (3:11–14).

5. He preached repentance, that is, the change from being God's enemy to his servant.

6. Because of aggressive behavior in dealing with sinners, a prophet invites conflict and rejection. John was himself imprisoned and killed for his prophetic castigation of Herod's sinfulness (see Mark 6:17–28).

The historical facts concerning John's actual relationship with Jesus escape us. But Luke's narrative presents John as Jesus' ritual elder: an exemplary prophet and model to be followed. Luke's story implies that Jesus, having studied John, learned the role into which he is initiated, as the following comparison suggests.

John the Baptizer	Jesus the Prophet
1. holy figure (1:15–17)	Son of God (4:3, 9)
2. conflict with sinners (3:19–20)	conflict with evil (4:3–13)
3. discerns disguised evil (3:7–8)	discerns evil hidden in the tests (4:3–13)

4. proclaims justice (3:10–14)	proclaims justice (4:18–19)
5. preaches repentance (1:17; 3:3, 8)	preaches repentance (5:32; 13:3, 5)
6. faces rejection (7:31–33)	faces rejection (4:21–30)

Paul Hollenbach has made a strong case that Jesus was originally a disciple of John, hearing, observing, and learning from him. If this indeed was the historical situation, Jesus was no mere passerby that day at the Jordan, but had an association with John of some duration.

It must be pointed out, however, that Jesus is not present at the Jordan in the same capacity as others who seek out John. When John the prophet addresses the "multitudes," he knows they are sinners, and so issues harsh challenges to them. John is the ritual elder in their status transformation from sinners to righteous. These words are not addressed to Jesus, who is with John for quite another purpose.

Luke tells us that John recognizes Jesus' holiness and endorses his candidacy for the role of prophet. He speaks glowingly of him: "The one who comes after me is greater than I, the thong of whose sandal I am not worthy to untie" (Luke 3:16). This statement excludes Jesus from the multitudes to whom John preaches repentance, suggesting instead that John serves in another capacity in regard to Jesus. He acts as the ritual elder for Jesus, who is a candidate for initiation into the role of prophet. Jesus is with John, but not as just another person undergoing a purification rite. John models for Jesus the new role of prophet and endorses his candidacy for it.

3.1.3 Ritual Symbols. The symbols in this narrative represent basic elements of the symbolic universe into which the initiand seeks admission as a member in full standing. In 3:1–4:30, however, there are quite different sets of symbols; and to keep them straight, we must follow closely the plot line narrated. The narrative in 3:1–4:30 may be divided into three acts: Act I — John and Jesus at the Jordan (3:1–22); Act II — Jesus in the wilderness (4:1–13, with the genealogy in 3:23–38 as the narrator's lengthy aside), Act III — Jesus' reentry into society (4:14–30). In keeping with these narrative distinctions, let us consider the major symbols in the first two acts of the drama.

Act I (Luke 3:1–22). The principal symbols displayed in Act I are as follows: prophet (John the Baptizer), Jordan River, Spirit (Dove) and Voice from heaven:

Prophet. We stressed earlier John's role as representative of the prophetic tradition. He is not only preacher to the crowds, but tutor for Jesus and the embodiment of the great heritage of Israel's prophets, whose dedication to God was total and uncompromising. As such, he represents the authority of that tradition over both those who, like the crowds, come to hear his preaching and accept his baptism, as well as those who, like Jesus, would seek admission to the status of prophet.

Jordan River. In our perspective, it functions principally as a boundary symbol. That is, the Jordan represents the final reach or extent of culture. West of the Jordan is the world of humanity and culture — specifically the society of God's holy people, Israel. East of the Jordan is wilderness, a place of promise and renewal, but also an unclean place of madness and starvation, tests and demons.

Spirit and Voice. The Spirit and the Voice from heaven are ancient symbols which Luke's readers recognize as manifestations of the divine. They constitute God's intervention into human affairs, and signal that a dramatic change in those affairs is about to be effected (e.g., Deut 4:33; Pss 18:14; 68:34; Ezek 1:24). They suggest as well a scene of commissioning into a new role.

In sum, in the ritual context of baptism-investiture, this cluster of symbols informs the reader that the criteria for the transfer of prophetic power and authority from John to Jesus is firmly within the established tradition of Israel's prophets and has been divinely ordained.

Act II (Luke 4:1–13). Another cluster of symbols appears in Act II, the ritual combat described in 4:1–13. They are: a novice prophet, the devil, settings such as desert, mountain, temple, and scripture.

The Novice Prophet. At the baptism, Jesus is invested with the status of a prophet, a man of God. Yet as a novice prophet, he must demonstrate that he has learned well his lessons of what as prophet is. Jesus, no longer John, is now the prophet of God in Israel. During the ritual confrontation, moreover, Jesus demonstrates that he is worthy to bear the titles of God's Son and prophet; that is, he is totally loyal to God's affairs and able to function worthily.

The Devil. The devil is associated with bringing people to ruin. Famous examples of this include the serpent in Gen 3:1–13 and the tester in Job 1:6–12. The devil, then, symbolizes a traditional element of Jewish religious culture which represents a threat to God's people and a testing of their fidelity to God. He embodies the opposite of holiness and fidelity to God.

As was the case with evil in the New Testament world, the evils which come to Jesus are likewise in disguise, (see 2 Cor 11:3,14–15). The devil makes a proposal about bread, and at another time quotes scripture, things normally considered good. Yet under both is hidden the devil's poison. But just as John demonstrated (3:7–9), Jesus has learned to unmask hidden evil. And so he rejects even disguised evil in order to be God's Holy One and to speak for God as his prophet.

Settings: Desert, Mountain, Temple. Although we will consider these settings in greater detail below, it is important to point out that each of the settings represents a locus of encounter with God in Israel's history. God led the people through the desert (Exod 13:21–22), manifested himself to them on a mountain (Exod 19:16–20), and dwelt in the temple on Mount Zion (e.g., Pss 11:4; 100). It is appropriate, therefore, that each scene in the ritual confrontation between Jesus and the devil takes place in settings which recall adventures in Israel's experience where uncompromising loyalty to God is demanded, and, indeed, proves essential to escape destruction.

Scripture and Moses. For Luke and his world, scripture means the word of God, and so God's will and the canon of loyalty to him. Moses is the founder of Israel and father of the prophetic tradition; he symbolizes the stark opposite of everything the devil represents. The devil stands for chaos and ruin; scripture and Moses, for blessing and prosperity. It is not accidental that Jesus' three quotations from scripture during his confrontation with the devil are from Deuteronomy. Deuteronomy, the last of the books of Moses, contains his discourses on the necessity of loyalty to God and the consequences of disobedience (e.g., Deut 7:12–15; 28:1–69).

Deuteronomy, moreover, illustrates what prophets are all about. Moses exposes and confronts Israel's apostasies, and simultaneously pleads its cause (e.g., Deut 9; see Exod 32:30–34). Deuteronomy provides the archetype for the subsequent prophetic tradition (Deut 18:15). Thus, in the citation of Moses' words, the narrative presents Jesus in continuity and solidarity with Moses and the word of God during his confrontation with the devil.

In the second part of Luke's work, he pursues this identification of Jesus with Moses in connection with the identity of Jesus as the "prophet like Moses" (Acts 3:21–23). Moses serves, moreover, as an example of a rejected prophet in Acts 7:27, 35, 39, 51–53 (Karris 1985:18–20). Thus, Luke is quite conscious of Moses as type and model, a point which is important in the testing episode.

Specific verses of scripture occur in each of Jesus' testings: first testing: Deut 8:3; second testing: Deut 6:13; and third testing: Ps 91:11–12 and Deut 6:16. Quotations from the scripture during the exchange between Jesus and the devil are important because in his career as prophet, Jesus will herald God's word. It behooves him to know it (Luke 4:18–19/Isa 61:1–2). The Son of man will suffer "as it is written" (18:31–33), and Jesus must know the cost and risk of his loyalty to God. He will confront people in the synagogue who also profess knowledge of God's word, but are hypocrites and deceivers. Jesus must know when God's word is perverted or misunderstood (for example, false meanings of sabbath observance, 13:14–16; see also 6:41–42; 12:54–59). As authentic spokesman, Jesus must know the heart of God's word, the greatest commandment (10:27). In short, Jesus' quoting scripture at critical junctures demonstrates that he is schooled in God's word, knowledge of which is essential for a prophet.

The shocking device of having the devil quote scripture to the prophet (4:10–11) is one of the ways in which a basic component of the prophets' values, God's word, is combined with alien elements to enable the initiand to test whether he sees it clearly as God wishes. Jesus uses scripture to expose the devil's seductions, and so affirms that he alone knows God's word and is loyal to God. He does not serve God merely with his lips. The devil, therefore, distorts and perverts God's word; God's prophet understands it correctly and is loyal to its Speaker. This cluster of symbols in the context of the ritual confrontation between Jesus and the devil demonstrates that the transfer of prophetic power and authority from John to Jesus has been successfully accomplished.

3.2 Ritual Process in Luke 3:1–4:30

3.2.1 Separation. As the model suggests, we must attend to three types of separation: separation of people, separation of place, and separation of time.

Separation of People. Luke narrates several separations of people. First, large numbers of people separate themselves from their villages to go to John at the Jordan. Luke tells how "crowds" (3:7, 10) flocked to John for baptism, among whom he mentions tax collectors and soldiers (3:12, 14). These sinners, then, have entered into a liminal state by separating themselves from their ordinary social world to come to a prophet for repentance. They seek a status transformation from sin to purity. Among them is Jesus of Nazareth.

Separated from his family at Nazareth when he leaves for the Jordan, Jesus joins the crowds in their liminal state. Both he and they have temporarily abandoned their old statuses. Members of the crowds will return washed of sin to their homes to resume their old statuses. But Jesus is further separated from the crowds by the events which take place at the river. His baptism-theophany (3:22) sharply marks this second and highly dramatic separation. The first separation, from home to the Jordan, is initiated by Jesus and indicates his piety. The second separation, initiated by God, decisively indicates that Jesus is a different kind of man than the others being baptized. The reader thus recognizes that the descent of the Spirit and the voice of God function as the moment of investiture when Jesus' new identity is revealed.

A third separation, also initiated by God (4:1), occurs when Jesus abandons all human company and travels alone into the desert. "Jesus, full of the Holy Spirit, returned from the Jordan and was led by the Spirit for forty days in the wilderness, tempted by the devil" (4:1–2). Jesus' baptism, a revelation and investiture, results in a deeper liminality by his going into the wilderness. Thus, Jesus' process of becoming a prophet includes various separations (from Nazareth and the crowds at the Jordan), and culminates with his isolation in the wilderness. Here he completes his ritual initiation into the role of prophet.

Separation of Place. It is important to note spatial settings in Jesus' movement through the ritual:

—from Nazareth, place of established culture

—to the semi-wild Jordan area, farthest reach of culture

—to the desert beyond the Jordan, entirely outside culture

Jesus' progressive separation of place parallels and reinforces his separation from people.

Place	Role
Nazareth	private person
Jordan	commissioned: novice prophet
Wilderness	tested: confirmed prophet

The liminal wilderness is isolated from any traces of culture. It is a setting of intense ambiguity imbued with risk and threat, but also with promise of power and transformation (Fitzmyer 1981:514; Horsley 1985:456–58).

The wilderness evokes the memory of Israel wandering homeless and tested by God before entering the land as God's chosen people. From a ritual perspective, the narratives of Israel's period of trial in the desert describe the leadership role of Moses, the ritual elder, who was commissioned to transform the status of a rabble of escaped slaves into that of God's covenant people. Moses and Israel did not successfully achieve that ritual passage; for in Exodus and Numbers we read that the people did not heed Moses, and much is made of the punishment they received for their disobedience (e.g., Exod 32). Indeed, a whole generation died in the desert for its rebelliousness (Deut 1:35); and for the same reason, Moses himself did not live to enter the promised land (Num 20:12).

Luke's readers, doubtless familiar with the story of Moses and Israel, would understand that the wilderness is a place where loyalty to God and transformation of status are tested. Success is never a sure thing; witness that both Moses and Israel failed in their loyalty to God. Will Jesus, the new prophet, also be found wanting and repeat that failure?

Separation of Time. During "fixed" or calendar time, time marches on steadily. During rituals, time may be either stretched or compressed or both. For Jewish and Gentile readers, Luke clarifies just when John's preaching career began ("In the fifteenth year," 3:1–2). His obvious sensitivity to historical time has earned him a reputation as an historian (Fitzmyer 1981:14–18). Although Luke notes the general calendar time when John preached at the Jordan (3:1–2), he does not tell us exactly when Jesus went out to John or how long he stayed.

Luke is interested in another kind of time as well, the altered time experienced in ritual. According to Luke's narrative, the reader sees that the testing of Jesus takes place during an altered time precisely because the investiture-testing narrative is interrupted by Luke's insertion of the genealogy (3:23–38). The straightforward passage of historical time is ruptured in order to link Jesus with salvation time, i.e., salvation history. In Luke's genealogy, time is compressed (very few generations from Jesus to Adam) yet also stretched (from creation to new creation). Readers thus understand that Jesus' ritual confrontation with the devil, which follows immediately, has significant implications for salvation history because it has been placed in that context by Luke's ordering of the material (Neyrey 1985:166–172).

When the narrative resumes in 4:1–2, the mention of "forty days" further signals that the testing of Jesus occurs in the symbolically charged time-frame of ritual. Luke's mention of "forty" days resonates with numerous Old Testament references to forty days or years as times of preparation, waiting, or testing (e.g., Gen 7:4, 12, 17; Exod 24:18; 34:38; 1 Kgs 18:8). The single most important cluster of Old Testament references for this narrative, however, is concerned with the sojourn of Moses and Israel in the desert. Israel's forty years were a time of testing to see if it would rely exclusively on God and whether its transformation to the status of God's holy people would be effective (see Deut 8:2, 4; 9:9, 25). Additionally, Moses spent forty days on the mountain in preparation for the climax of his prophetic career, the mediation of God's law to Israel (Exod 34:28). So too, Jesus, who was designated "beloved son" at the Jordan, now undergoes a forty-day period which climaxes in a ritual testing of his preparation for a public career as God's loyal prophet and holy man.

Finally, time is highly compressed during the testing itself. At one point, for example, Jesus sees "all the kingdoms of the world *in a moment of time*" (4:5), and he is instantaneously transferred from wilderness to mountain to temple.

In sum, Jesus' separations, first from home and then from all other people, climax in the wilderness. This series of separations parallels the separations of Moses and Israel from Egypt, and they occur for the same purpose: to transform their status as people set apart and to test their loyalty to God. These objectives are accomplished by casting the "time of the test" into the "time" of ritual, i.e., the time when stakes are high, balances precarious, and when the decisions taken shake the world and reverberate throughout history. Therefore, the symbolically ambiguous wilderness combines with symbol-laden, ritual time to provide the perfect setting for tests of profound consequences.

3.2.2 Liminality-Communitas. We recall that *liminality* refers to the initiands' ambiguous status due to their placement outside cultural boundaries, and *communitas* refers to recognition of the generic human bond among society's members. The altered state of liminality affords initiands the opportunity to acquire knowledge of the new world they are entering.

Just as we divided our consideration of ritual symbols in Acts I and II of the narrative, so we repeat that procedure here, and consider the way the narrative demonstrates Jesus' experience of liminality-*communitas* distinctly in each act.

Act I (Luke 3:1–22). This segment of the status transformation ritual comprises Jesus' sojourn and experience at the Jordan. At that point in the narrative, Jesus' status is unclear, i.e., liminal. While we know from the infancy narrative and from John's prophecy (3:16–17) that Jesus is no sinner, we do not know what his status has been between ages twelve (2:42) and thirty (3:23), nor what future role he will assume. The investiture-testing narrative shows us that he will accomplish a mission by assuming the culturally specific, "high profile" role of prophet. Like all initiands in rituals of status transformation, Jesus' liminal or low status is reflected in his role as a disciple of John. He learns from John, and tradition indicates he accepted a ritual washing from him as well. Both of these actions suggest his low status as learner and recipient of services from others.

We also assume here that during the time at the Jordan, Jesus enjoyed *communitas* with John and the other people who came to John for baptismal cleansing from sin. That Jesus would have experienced *communitas* with John should come as no surprise. Luke narrated that they were kin; he repeatedly told his readers how intimately connected John and Jesus were even before their births (e.g., 1:44). He parallels their blood kinship with a religious one to highlight their bondedness as "spiritual brothers." Their meeting at the Jordan is a reunion of two men whom the reader already knows to linked by blood and by a common divine intervention (1:13–22, 26–37).

Nor should we be surprised by the claim that Jesus experienced *communitas* with the sinners who presented themselves to John for baptism. After all, it is with just such people as these that Jesus will share intimate relationships throughout the rest of the Gospel (5:8, 27–28; 7:36–50; 19:1–10; 23:39–43; 24:47). Indeed, according to some, his *communitas* with and concern for sinners will emerge as a major criticism of Jesus, for it threatens the divinely established and approved order of the world (6:20–23; 7:34; 11:14–20, 40–42; 14:1–24; 15:1–2; 19:47–48; 20:45–21:4; 22:2, 27). *Communitas* with sinners, once learned, will be a hallmark of Jesus' behavior throughout the Gospel.

Turner's comments about the power of liminality-*communitas* to effect a radical change of consciousness may be applied to Act I of the drama of Jesus becoming a prophet:

> The knowledge obtained in the liminal period is thought to change the inmost nature of the neophyte, impressing him, as a seal impresses wax, with the characteristics of his new state. It is not a mere acquisition of knowledge, but a change in being. His apparent passivity is revealed as an ab-

sorption of powers which will become active after his social status has been redefined (Turner 1967:102).

Act II (*Luke 4:1–13*). During this segment of his status transformation ritual, Jesus the novice prophet triumphs over the devil in a ritual testing of his role as prophet. This phase of the narrative also contains the ritual element of liminality-*communitas*. As readers see Jesus confronted by evil, they wonder whether Jesus has really inherited the mantle of prophecy passed to him by John and whether he is a loyal prophet of God. Therefore, Jesus' status during the tests, like during his time at the Jordan, remains ambiguous or liminal. This is dramatized in the mocking attitude of the devil: "If you are the Son of God" (4:3, 9).

These three tests are the only instances in the Gospel where the devil adopts a defiant or challenging stance towards Jesus. Jesus' authentic prophetic status is demonstrated during the tests; and after 4:13, neither the devil nor his minions can resist his will or question his authority (4:33–35, 41; 8:26–33; 9:37–43; 11:14–20). But during the tests, the devil taunts him and moves him from place to place; and Jesus allows himself to be so taunted and moved. He makes no attempt to escape from, punish, or destroy the devil (but see 10:17; 11:21). Most significantly, he does not object to the fact that he is being tested (see 11:4; 22:39–46). Indeed, by submitting to the tests he acknowledges their legitimacy as a component of the transformation of his status.

In regard to this type of role testing, Turner notes:

> [He acts in this way] due to obedience to the authority of tradition in the liminal situation—a type of situation in which there is no room for secular compromise, evasion, manipulation, casuistry, and maneuver in the field of custom, rule, and norm. . . . A normal man acts abnormally because he is obedient to . . . tradition, not out of disobedience to it. He does not evade but fulfills his duties as a citizen (Turner 1967:100).

In other words, Luke shows that Jesus endures a full-scale ritual liminality: physical isolation in the symbolically ambiguous wilderness, the vulnerability of forty days of starvation, and testing of his status as prophet. In any setting other than the status transformation ritual, Jesus' acquiescence to this treatment would be regarded as shameful by his society. But here it is acceptable, because it is done out of obedience to the Spirit of God which led him there. How unlike his subsequent aggressive confrontations with and easy dismissals of Satan and his demons, which is, of course, the normal behavior of prophets.

We noted Jesus' *communitas* with John and the penitents at the Jordan in 3:1–33; so also *communitas* is manifested in 4:1–13. Several of the tests begin with a taunt from the devil: "If you are the son of God" Readers might question: What is the real meaning of all that they have learned about Jesus in the infancy narrative and the scene at the Jordan? The answer is found in Jesus' response to the tests. Like authentic prophets before him, Jesus' faithfulness to God must be unreserved and total, which is the essence of the prophetic tradition. This fidelity constitutes the basis of his solidarity with (a) Moses, the tradition's founder, (b) Elijah, symbol of its greatness (Luke 4:26; 7:12, 15; see 1 Kgs 17:9, 23; Luke 9:30, 42; see 1 Kgs 19:4–8; Luke 22:43, 45; see 1 Kgs 19:5–8), and (c) John the Baptizer, the prophetic tradition's most recent glory. Luke demonstrates that by his faithfulness during the tests, Jesus belongs in the ranks of Israel's authentic prophets. He shares their identity and their fate. And his bondedness to the prophetic role will last his whole life long. He has ritual *communitas* with other prophetic figures of his tradition.

3.2.3 Ritual Confrontation: Jesus' Tests. The testing of Jesus in 4:1–13 is best understood as the narrative defense of the legitimacy of his new role. It should be read in terms of the liminal state of the status transformation ritual wherein Jesus proves to have the capacity for his new role in terms of his skills and loyalty.

The First Test Setting: As we noted above, the wilderness setting is sacred and liminal space in Israelite tradition. *Dialogue:* Jesus the initiand fasted a ritual fast of forty days, and he was hungry. He abstained from food, which suggests his separation from former patterns, which is part of the process of transformation. Jesus' hunger here suggests that the old person has been starved out of him, and so there is a radical break with his former private person. But what of the new? When the devil tempts Jesus to turn stones into bread and eat, Jesus reveals his transformed status: "It is written, 'Man shall not live by bread alone' " (4:4). His hunger cannot be satisfied on any natural plane, and certainly by nothing he can or will do for himself.

To the private person at Nazareth, it would have been wise to relieve hunger with bread. But the narrative suggests that eating, precisely because it is suggested by the devil, will mean that Jesus is less than totally reliant on God. This is no passing encounter between Jesus and the devil, but a genuine challenge-riposte episode (negative honor challenge), well known to people whose world is structured in terms of honor and shame. It belongs, moreover, for evil to disguise itself as good. A prophet surely must be able to penetrate disguises and unmask deceit. Seeing through the challenge to turn stones to bread, Jesus the prophet discerns hidden evil and succeeds in his first testing.

Therefore, Jesus proved to be totally dedicated to God. He will wait for God to give him his daily bread in due time. Thus, like the prophets before him, Jesus demonstrates the essential prophetic value of fidelity to God which supersedes even basic physical necessities. God, not bread, is the source and sustenance of life (see Jer 29:10–13; Amos 6:6).

The Second Test Setting: The setting dramatically shifts as the devil takes Jesus "up" from the wilderness to a place higher, presumably a mountain top (4:5). Although mountains are positively associated with

Moses, theophany, and covenant, they also convey strongly negative associations, which would be in keeping with the thrust of this test. As one commentator noted: "literary convention associates the height of mountains with human pride and arrogance. . . . Applied to humans, height is negative; high mountains remind the poet of human self-exaltation" (Cohn 1980:32–33). Since the notions of authority and exaltation are combined with height, we are probably correct here to envision this test as occurring on a mountain.

Dialogue: The devil now offers Jesus "authority" and "glory," which presumably include the vast wealth of all the kingdoms of the world. This test intensifies what was implicit in the previous one: whether to be God's client and depend on God-as-patron exclusively for glory and authority or whether to be the devil's client and so receive these as his patronage. Here again, Jesus is tested on the fundamental issue: will he be loyal and faithful to God alone? The test asks Jesus to serve a false god, but Jesus knows that "No man can serve two masters; for either he will hate the one and love the other, or he will be devoted to the one and despise the other. You cannot serve God and mammon" (16:13).

A prophet is characterized above all by complete fidelity to God. And Jesus makes clear that such is his loyalty: "It is written, 'You shall worship the Lord your God, and him only shall you serve' " (4:7). Jesus cites the very heart of the prophetic tradition, originally spoken by Moses (see also 10:27), in his absolute rejection of serving any but God.

The Third Test Setting: The setting of this testing—the temple in Jerusalem, the Holy City—is not accidental. "The temple is on earth, but because Yahweh dwells in it, it is one and the same with heaven" (Keel 1985:174). This new setting has radical implications for Jesus' identity and career. The devil suggests to Jesus that a prophet need not suffer or die, since God's own messengers will protect him (4:11). The devil insinuates that Jesus can avoid death, an exclusively divine attribute. But Jesus knows better. He will suffer a prophet's rejection and death in Jerusalem, not as punishment for sin, but precisely in fidelity to God (9:22; 18:31–33). This demonstrates his solidarity with the prophets who suffer rejection, even death in Jerusalem, for their unyielding fidelity to God (see 6:23; 9:22; 13:33–34; 18:31–34). Jesus' *communitas* with the prophets who came before him will be manifested again in the transfiguration (9:28–31) where he, Moses, and Elijah, will speak of his impending exodus in Jerusalem, the city that murders its prophets (13:34). Jerusalem, then, is the climactic setting for the definitive testing of a prophet: loyalty to God even unto death.

Dialogue: Characteristically, the devil presents evil under the guise of good. He cites Ps 91, a holy prayer prayed by pious people, to suggest that those totally dedicated to God will not experience suffering and death. But in this he hides evil (usurping God's power over death) under the guise of good (scripture), much the way evil is hidden in the first two tests. Jesus, who knows not only the true meaning of God's word, but also how to unmask disguised evil, sees through the ploy. He correctly unmasks the devil's suggestion as an invitation to "tempt the Lord your God." Failure to discern this disguised evil would immediately disqualify Jesus as a candidate for prophethood, since the test implies that man, not God, controls life and death (Deut 30:15–20; Jer 21:8; Hos 13:14). Jesus' mastery of the role of a prophet, both in unmasking evil and in loyalty to God, is demonstrated. As a true prophet, he will leave his destiny in God's hands.

In summary, the three testings illustrate that Jesus indeed has the capacity to function in his new role and that he has demonstrated unwavering loyalty to God:

1. God provides for us, not we for ourselves (e.g., Isa 49);

2. God alone is to be worshipped (e.g., Jer 2:1–35);

3. God alone controls life and death, not humanity (e.g., Isa 46:9; 48:11–13).

Thus, at the end of his testings, Jesus has demonstrated the loyalty to God which is the hallmark of authentic prophets.

3.2.4 Aggregation. Luke narrates Jesus' aggregation in 4:14–15: "And Jesus returned in the power of the Spirit into Galilee, a report concerning him went out through all the surrounding country. And he taught in their synagogues, being glorified by all." He returns after undergoing a radical change of role and status as a result of his status transformation ritual. When we compare the public Jesus who returns to Galilee with the private person who went out to John the Baptizer, we can grasp the full extent of the change in role Luke has just narrated:

From chaos to order. Jesus is back in the orderly world of villages and synagogues after a novitiate with John and a confrontation with chaos in the wilderness.

From student to teacher. Jesus is no longer the docile child of 2:51, nor John's follower, nor the novice prophet of the ritual confrontation in the desert. Instead of listening, he speaks: "He taught in their synagogues" (4:15). During his test in the wilderness, Jesus began to quote scripture as a demonstration of his knowledge of God's word and his fidelity to God. And at his inaugural public appearance in Nazareth, he reads the scripture and teaches its true meaning. He speaks, moreover, as a legitimate prophet because "The Spirit of the Lord is upon me." And he has the authority to speak a mighty word, "to preach good news . . . to proclaim release . . . to proclaim the acceptable year" (4:18–19).

From follower to leader. Starting out as a disciple of the Baptizer, Jesus announces his own legitimation as an anointed prophet, "Today this scripture has been fulfilled in your hearing" (4:21).

From private to public person. Beginning as a person with no public role or special standing (3:22b), Jesus now claims the honor due a prophet (4:18–21, 23–24). He now takes a public role in society: he reads scripture, proclaims the fulfillment of God's word, and interprets Israel's past (the examples of Elijah and Elisha, 4:25–27).

From passivity to power. From one who passively experienced the events at the Jordan and defended his new status in his ritual combat with the devil, Jesus now goes about "in the power of the Spirit" (4:15). He takes bold steps to assert his new role and status (4:18–21, 23–24). Hardly a passive victim, he can escape from his enemies (4:30) without loss of honor. He is aggregated back into society, but clearly as one capable of exercising his new role with great skill, power, and authority.

3.2.5 Living the New Role: Jesus the Prophet. Aggregated back into the society of Galilee, Jesus now possesses the skills or powers requisite for the exercise of his new role. Jesus has ritually demonstrated expertise in what constitutes a prophet, an expertise needed immediately upon his aggregation, as the following list indicates.

Prophetic Spirit. Like the prophets before him, Jesus is guided in his public career by God's Spirit. During the ritual of status change, the Spirit descended on him at the Jordan theophany (3:22), then led him into the desert (4:1). When aggregated back into society, Jesus begins his new role "in the power of the Spirit" (4:14) and legitimates his new role and status because of it: "The Spirit of the Lord is upon me" (4:18).

Prophet vs. Devil. In the wilderness, Jesus demonstrated his skill in battling successfully against God's enemy, the devil. After his aggregation, Jesus the prophet tours the countryside, healing the sick and casting out demons. All these activities, but especially the last, represent the prophet's efforts to rid the people of impurities and pollutions which exclude them from God's holy presence. As is shown in Pilch's chapter on illness and healing, disease in Luke's world was thought to be caused by the attack of an evil spirit (see Luke 13:16). Jesus' successful confrontations with the devil confirm him as the Mighty One who combats the Evil One in all his ploys and attacks (3:16; 11:21). Jesus, the Holy One of God, has mastered the devil in the desert and carries that mastery over evil with him wherever his prophetic mission takes him (10:17; 11:14–23).

Prophet and the World's Two Kingdoms. In 3:1–4:13, Jesus demonstrates that he knows that the world is divided into two kingdoms, God's and Satan's. When his loyalty was tested, Jesus betrayed no compromise, ambiguity, or indecision about which kingdom he belonged. This dualistic perspective structures his subsequent work, as he preaches to the crowds that they cannot serve two masters (16:13). He himself understands the simple fact that there are good and bad trees (6:43–45). Good and evil are mutually exclusive. The response he inspired in his career as prophet also left no grey areas: one was either for him or against him (11:23).

Prophetic Faithfulness. From John the Baptizer, Jesus learned the principles as well as the concrete meaning of holiness, faithfulness, and singleheartedness. In the wilderness he exercised these virtues learned from John in combination with the authority with which he was invested at the baptism-theophany. Jesus chooses God in all things, relies on him completely, and rejects evil completely. In this he demonstrates to the reader that it is undoubtedly his role to act as the prophet who heralds the kingdom of God (8:1; 17:20–21).

Prophetic Powers. From the time of his aggregation and throughout his career, Jesus publicly reveals his possession of the powers of the prophet:

- penetration of disguises: recognition of lack of faith (e.g., 4:23–27) and hypocrisy (e.g., 6:6–11)

- mastery over demons (e.g., 4:33–37; 7:21; 8:26–33; 37–43; 11:14–20)

- comfort of the afflicted (7:48–50), affliction of the comfortable (11:37–52; 20:45–47)

- revelation of hidden things (8:8–15; 10:17–20; 21:5–34)

- ability to read hearts and minds (5:22; 6:8; 11:17).

There is no doubt that Jesus, upon aggregation, functions clearly and successfully in his new role like one of the prophets of old (9:8).

Prophets and Rejection. Like his mentor before him, Jesus is schooled in conflict and learns that God's prophets have always been attacked by evil (13:34–35). In the wilderness, Jesus observes that in his world evil attacks good. His ability to withstand assault is a skill he will need as his enemies relentlessly pursue him in synagogues (4:16–30), at banquets (7:36–50), on journeys (13:31–33), and into the temple itself (20:1–8, 27–39). The religious authorities, who also held the Baptizer in contempt (7:29–30; 20:1–8), see Jesus as another renegade and outsider, and they are zealous in their persecution of him (6:7; 22:1–6). Jesus experiences conflict even with his own followers (9:51–56). Yet he is ever the faithful, loyal servant of God.

Prophets and Liminality. John the Baptizer lived on the margins of society in the wilderness of the Jordan region. Unlike John, Jesus' activity centers in villages, towns, and cities. But both, by virtue of their prophetic vocation, are men set apart, "out of the ordinary." Luke gives no indication that he married, retained strong kinship ties, practiced a trade, or had a permanent home: he had no place to lay his head. (9:58). On the contrary, his kin group was his disciples (8:19–21), and together they were often on the road, an important theme in Luke (see "the travel narrative," 9:51–19:28). Jesus, the wandering prophet and preacher was very much in his society, but not of it in any ordinary or conventional sense.

Luke portrays Jesus as a "limit breaker" who preached to and shared table with other people on the edges of Jewish society. In this sense, he was never fully aggregated back into Jewish life because his very role dictated that he remain on the edges as a physician to the sick and sinners (5:30–32). As prophet, he remained always in a liminal state, in the world, but not of it.

In conclusion, we see that at his aggregation into the world of Nazareth and Galilee, Jesus truly lived the role that he has assumed. His actions demonstrate that his status transformation into the role of a prophet has been successful. He now acts as a "prophet mighty in word and deed," as he bursts upon his society with a new identity, role, power, and authority. But the readers of Luke's Gospel need clear knowledge about the legitimacy of Jesus' proclamations, teachings, and actions. That knowledge is imparted plentifully to them in the course of reading of Jesus' status transformation ritual in Luke 3:1–4:30, which passage is foundational for the rest of Luke's narrative.

4.0 RITUALS IN LUKE–ACTS: FURTHER DATA

Many passages in Luke–Acts are listed below where ritual analysis offers an adequate scenario for understanding Luke's narrative. This essay on the transformation of Jesus from private person to public prophet is but one example of the wise use of that scenario for interpretation. A curious or diligent reader might find in the following examples worthy passages for further reading and understanding.

1. *Birth* Luke 1:57; 2:6

2. *Circumcision* Luke 1:59; 2:27

3. *Baptism* Luke 3:3–7, 21–22; Acts 2:38–41; 8:11–13, 26–39; 10:44–48; 16:13–15; 18:8; 19:2–5

4. *Consecration* Luke 2:27; Acts 2:34–36

5. *Exorcism* Luke 4:33–35, 40–41; 8:26–37; 9:37–43; Acts 5:16; 8:7–8

6. *Healing* Luke 4:38–39; 5:12–15, 18–25; 6:6–10; 7:2–10; 8:43–48 13:10–13; 14:1–4; Acts 3:1–8; 5:16; 8:7–8; 9:32–34; 14:3–18

7. *Forensic trials* Luke 22:63–71; 23:1–25; Acts 4:5–21; 5:17–24 18:12–16; 23:1–10; 24:1–23; 26:1–32

8. *Exaltation* Luke 9:28–40; 24:1–12; Acts 1:1–9

5.0 CONCLUSION

What have we learned by using ritual analysis that we might otherwise not have known? Ritual analysis helps the reader of Luke–Acts to establish an adequate scenario for assessing status changes and transformations. With a general knowledge of the way such rituals work, the considerate reader can perceive more accurately the elements of ritual and their processes and thereby understand the details of the narrative.

Ritual analysis benefits the reader in two ways. First, it focuses attention on narrative movements and key events in the text that are sometimes overlooked and misunderstood by historical methods of biblical interpretation. Seeing the narrative's dynamic in terms of ritual analysis, readers learn to recognize persons, events, things, etc. in their symbolic and functional roles in a rite of passage. Second, it offers a sense of coherence. Readers gain a sense of the large canvas of the narrative. They learn how the pieces all fit together and what significance is intended in the narration of an individual event. Ritual analysis, therefore, offers one more scenario for understanding the narrative of Luke–Acts.

This study concentrated on one specific status transformation ritual, 3:1–4:30. This passage and the process it narrates have considerable impact on the way the rest of the Gospel is understood. While commentators point out that 3:1–4:30 functions as "preparation for the public ministry" (Fitzmyer 1981:449, 506), ritual analysis sharpens that general insight by attending to the change of status that Jesus' achieved at the Jordan and in the wilderness, and by narrating how it was effected, for in 3:1–4:30, Luke took specific care to establish the legitimacy of Jesus' public activity. The question is asked constantly in the Gospel: "By what authority do you do these things?" And it behooved the evangelist to inform us adequately at the beginning of the narrative about the change in role and status of Jesus from private resident of Nazareth to public prophet of God.

No essay in this volume stands alone, least of all this chapter on ritual analysis. There must necessarily be an extended conversation among all the reading scenarios presented here for a truly comprehensive understanding of Luke–Acts. In particular we note how the essay by Malina and Neyrey on conflict and the presentation there of labelling and deviance theory can be supplemented by a detailed knowledge of status transformation rituals for a more adequate understanding of the forensic trials in Luke–Acts. They stated that forensic trials are status degradation rituals; and the model of ritual in this chapter can serve as a detailed scenario for understanding the trials of Jesus (Luke 22–23) and those of Peter (Acts 4–5) and Paul (Acts 21–26). Furthermore, Pilch's chapter on illness and healing should be in conversation with ritual materials, for all lapses into illness and all recoveries into healing are themselves status transformations.

In addition to them, we suggest that ritual analysis be read specifically in conjunction with Neyrey's essay on ceremonies in Luke–Acts. These two chapters necessarily complement each other in terms of an adequate understanding of rites. The concern of ritual processes for cultural boundaries and what is "out of the ordinary," liminal, and so forth, would lead a reader to the thorough study of the way cultures order and classify their world, which was the focus of the chapter on Luke's symbolic universe. Furthermore, this type of analysis draws heavily on the chapter on first-century personality and its arguments about ascribed status and roles. The testing of Jesus in 4:1–13 can quite profitably be understood further in terms of negative honor challenges.

An adequate reading of 3:1–4:30 requires many scenarios. Thus, ritual analysis does not force the text into an ideological mold which predetermines its meaning, nor stands in tension with other scenarios, but works in conjunction with them for a full and adequate understanding of Luke–Acts. Ritual analysis corroborates other studies found in this volume and is confirmed by their presentations as well. All this suggests that understanding ritual is an integral element of a full and rich understanding of Luke–Acts.

13

CEREMONIES IN LUKE–ACTS:
THE CASE OF MEALS AND TABLE FELLOWSHIP

Jerome H. Neyrey

0.0 INTRODUCTION

In the previous chapter we examined *rituals* and rites of passage. This chapter takes up ritual's counterpart, *ceremony*. Just as ritual was illustrated by attention to the status transformation of Jesus from private figure to public prophet, so this study of *ceremony* will focus on Luke's narrative of Jesus' meals and table-fellowship as an ideal illustration of what ceremonies are and how they should be perceived.

The meals and table-fellowship enjoyed by Jesus and his disciples are a major focus of recent studies of Luke–Acts. One commentator quipped that Jesus was killed because of the way he ate (Karris 1985:70). There is, moreover, considerable attention paid in Luke–Acts to the foods consumed at meals and the etiquette proper to them. Although it is not complete, the following collection of data indicates that Luke was highly attentive to issues of food, meals, table-fellowship and table etiquette (Karris 1985:49–52):

Eating, Meals, and Table-fellowship in Luke–Acts:

1. *Eating*: Luke 4:2; 5:30–33; 6:1–5; 7:33–34; 7:36; 8:55; 9:13; 10:7–8; 12:19–22, 29, 45; 13:26; 14:1, 15; 15:16, 23; 17:8, 27–28; 22:8, 11, 15–16, 30; 24:43; Acts 9:9; 10:13–14; 11:7; 23:12, 21

2. *Meals*: Luke 14:12, 16–17, 24; 22:14–38; 24:28–34; Acts 1:4; 10:41

3. *Commensality*: Luke 4:25; 7:36–50; 9:11–17; 15:1–2, 25–32; 19:5–7; Acts 10:28; 11:1–10

4. *Breaking of Bread*: Luke 22:19; 24:35; Acts 2:42, 46; 20:7, 11; 27:35

5. *Foods*: Luke 10:7–8; 12:23, 42; Acts 10:9–16; 11:6–10; 15:20, 29; 21:25

6. *Table Etiquette*: 14:7–11, 12–14; 22:24–27

7. *Hospitality*: Luke 4:39; 5:29; 10:38; Acts 16:14–15, 34; 18:7; 28:7, 14

A thorough study of Luke–Acts, then, must examine the material on meals, foods, and table-fellowship, a topic for which the social sciences are particularly helpful. Although everybody eats meals daily, meals and table-fellowship are highly complex social events. Any full, in-depth understanding of them will require an adequate scenario for perceiving them.

Some anthropologists speak of food as a "code" which communicates a multi-layered message:

> If food is treated as a code, the message it encodes will be found in the pattern of social relations being expressed. The message is about different degrees of hierarchy, inclusion and exclusion, boundaries and transactions across the boundaries. . . . Food categories encode social events (Douglas 1975:249).

Therefore, for a reader or observer to understand what is encoded in a meal, a variety of social-science perspectives on the many aspects of foods, meals, and table-fellowship are necessary. Meals tell us about patterns of social relations, about social ranking, about group solidarity, and about economic transactions. An adequate scenario for understanding the "code" of a meal, consequently, will not be simple. The model for gaining an adequate reading scenario contains five parts: meals must be examined (a) as ceremony, (b) as mirrors of social systems, (c) in terms of body symbolism, (d) in terms of reciprocity, and (e) in terms of social relations.

1.0 MEALS AS CEREMONIES

We recall at this point the introductory remarks about rituals and ceremonies. Meals are not *rituals*, rites of status change and transformation. Rather they are *ceremonies*, which:

(a) are predictable and occur regularly, and

(b) are determined, called for, and presided over by officials, and

(c) function to confirm roles and statuses within the chief institutions of a given group.

We are alerted, then, to inquire of a given meal whether it occurs daily, weekly (e.g., sabbath) or annually (e.g., Passover). About a specific meal we ask whether it is presided over by the head of the household, a priest, a governor, or king. It is important to know in which social institution a meal is celebrated, whether in the family or a fictive-family group (e.g., Pharisee haburah meal), or in a temple or civic center.

From this overview of meal-as-ceremony, we learn to ask the following questions which surface clues about the meaning of this particular ceremony: when was it eaten, by whom and in whose company, who presided over it, in which social institution did it take place? For example, in the context of first-century social roles, a daily meal confirms the basic family unit and bolsters the respective roles of father as provider and mother as nourisher. A Passover meal confirms membership in the covenant people of Israel, even as it bolsters the role of the head of the clan who presides at the meal (Exod 12:3–4, 26–27). A Pharisee haburah meal confirms membership in the brotherhood of those who share Pharisaic ideology. Because of their important position in Israelite society, scribes expect to be seated "in the places of honor at feasts" (Luke 20:46), thus confirming their role.

Ceremonies, moreover, do not focus on the crossing of lines and boundaries that define and structure a group, because that is the function of rituals. Nor are ceremonies concerned with status reversal or transformation. Rather they bolster the boundaries defining a group or institution, even as they confirm established roles and statuses within the group. Unlike rituals, which are concerned with the perimeter, ceremonies focus on the inside, the inward dimension of a social body and its structure. They attend, not to change, but to stability; they are concerned, not with newness, but with continuity. Meals-as-ceremonies replicate the group's basic social system, its values, lines, classifications, and its symbolic world.

2.0 MEALS AND PURITY SYSTEM

This part of the model requires cross-reference to another chapter in this book, "The Symbolic Universe of Luke–Acts." Inasmuch as meal-as-ceremony affirms the values and structures of a particular group or institution, we can use the insights of that other chapter to learn what values and structures meals affirm in the Jewish world of Jesus and his early disciples as described by Luke. We noted there that people tend to structure their world by classifying persons, places, and things and thus impose some order on what otherwise seems to be chaos. A system of classifications expresses order and gives clues to a group's symbolic universe. This is especially true of the classifications surrounding meals, for as it has been observed, "In no society are people permitted to eat everything, everywhere, with everyone, and in all situations" (Cohen 1968:508). Who may eat what, with whom and when? And how can we know this?

Since meals in Luke–Acts replicate the elaborate system of classifications found in Luke's world, we should pay attention to his clues about four basic maps of the New Testament cosmos: maps of persons, things, places, and times.

2.1 Map of Persons

Pharisees illustrate perfectly the principle that people basically eat with others with whom they share values (e.g., haburah meal). Hence, the Pharisees criticize Jesus, who claims to teach a way of holiness, for eating with tax collectors and sinners, because shared table-fellowship implies that Jesus shares their world, not God's world of holiness. Moreover, one would not expect Jews, God's holy people, to eat with Gentiles, just as Christians, who partake of the table of the Lord, cannot also eat at the table of demons (1 Cor 10:20–21).

Even when likes eat with likes, one would expect in a strongly structured cosmos such as the first-century Jewish world that there be some sort of map of persons even at the meal, viz., some order of who sits where (see 1 QSa 2.11–17). Seating arrangements signal and replicate one's role and status in a group. As regards roles, we speak of the "head" table at a banquet. We expect there to be a leader of the feast, a diakonos, who presides over the meal and seats guests, pours wine, leads the conversation, etc. (Collins 1984:32–33). As regards seating positions and status, the "right hand" of the host is traditionally the place of honor (see Luke 20:42; Acts 2:33). Luke acknowledges that there are "places of honor" at a feast reserved for high-ranking people (Luke 14:7–11; 20:46). There are, of course, distinctions of status symbolized by who sits and who serves. Recall the remark of Jesus: "Which is the greater, one who sits at table, or one who serves? Is it not the one who sits at table?" (Luke 22:27). Recall also the parable in which the master says to his servants, "Prepare supper for me, and gird yourself and serve me, till I eat and drink; and afterward you shall eat and drink" (Luke 17:7–10).

Greco-Roman and Jewish meals owe much of their structure to the classical form of the symposium. At such meals there were elaborate maps of persons. Roles were clearly specified: a host, a chief guest, and other guests (Steele 1984:382–89). The places taken by the participants in this meal reflect their status, with the chief guest closest to the host and the other guests arranged in some declining order of status (see John 13:23–25).

It could happen that not all the participants at a meal ate the same food or were served the same amount (Pervo 1985:311–13). Some hosts might rank their guests by different quantities and qualities of food and drink. It is argued that just such differences in foods consumed by people of differing social status occurred at the Christian meal in Corinth (1 Cor 11:21, 33).

At a sacrificial meal, for example, it matters who were eligible to receive portions of the meat sacrificed, itself a rare item in the diet of the ancients. The following citation from the rules of a Greek religious association, the Iobachoi, indicates who has a right to a portion of the meat even as it lists those people in some hierarchical order, viz., a map of persons:

> And when portions are distributed, let them be taken by the priest, the vice-priest, archibakchos, treasurer, boukolikos, Dionysos, Kore, Palaimon, Aphrodite, and Proteurythmos; and let these names be apportioned by lot among the members (Smith 1980:162).

A map of persons, then, gives us clues about the roles and statuses of participants at a meal: who sits and who waits on table, what specific actions one performs during the meal, who sits close or far from the host, what and how much food one eats, and when one eats, either first or last.

2.2 Map of Things

In terms of the classification of foods, certain foods can be proscribed and others are prescribed. Examples of this abound; Pythagoreans eschewed meat and ate legumes. Jews had an elaborate code of foods, which included: (1) foods automatically declared "unclean" (Lev 11:1–47; Deut 14:3–21; see Douglas 1966:41–57); (2) foods which needed to be prepared in a certain way; and (3) foods made "clean" in virtue of the tithes paid on them.

This concern with clean/unclean foods extended even to the dishes used in their preparation and consumption. As we learn from Matt 23:25–26 and Mark 7:4, there were Pharisaic rules concerning the porosity of vessels and rules concerning washing of them (Neusner 1976:486–95).

Even the talk at table is a thing to be mapped. Certain talk is appropriate and even required at meals, such as the benedictions over the cups at a meal, the Exodus haggadah at Passover meals and the Hallel psalms. At Greco-Roman symposia some questions and topics are appropriate and others are not (Smith 1987:620–23). At family meals, one would expect the conversation to be supportive of family ideals and traditions, not divisive or critical. Meals shared by philosophical groups such as the Epicureans regulated conversation so that it promoted the group's ideas of "pleasure" and "fellowship" (Smith 1980:56–68). Conversation, therefore, is one of the things that was regularly mapped.

In line with this concern with table talk, it should be noted how in the biblical tradition bread is a common symbol of wisdom and instruction, viz., words or talk. Lady Wisdom serves a banquet and feeds her guests (Prov 9:1–6), symbolizing how she instructs them and feeds them with the words of truth. The food which God provides to Israel is God's word (Feeley-Harnick 1981:71–106). In this vein Paul describes his initial teaching at Corinth as "milk, not solid food" (1 Cor 3:1); Jesus' "bread" which comes down from heaven is often understood as his words or teaching (John 6:63). And by the same token, the "leaven" of the Pharisees is their bad doctrine (Matt 16:6–12). Food and bread, then, symbolize words and instruction. Inasmuch as specific foods are appropriate for specific people at specific meals, so specific words, topics or doctrines are appropriate at those specific meals. And like foods and vessels, talk can be classified as good or bad.

2.3 Map of Places

The perception of an ordered universe is replicated in the spatial arrangement of persons and things at a meal and in regard to the place where one eats, such a dining room or a temple precinct. A Pharisee, for example, would be concerned about the place where he ate to ensure that the proper diet was prepared in a proper way and served on proper utensils. Conversely Jesus' celebrated multiplication of the loaves ostensibly flouted the perception of a specific place of meals. A "desert place" is unsuitable for eating because it would preclude concern for: (a) proper foods which were correctly tithed and properly prepared, (b) proper persons with whom one might eat, and (c) proper water etc. for purification rites. A "desert place," a chaotic place which admits none of the principles of an ordered cosmos, cannot in any sense meet the requirements of proper place for meals.

Even at a proper meal, there would also be concern over the seating arrangement of those eating, a ranking in terms of some value or honor system. This correlates with the previously mentioned map of persons and their appropriate place at a meal. For example, Jesus commented when he saw people *choosing the places of honor*: "When you are invited . . . do not sit down in a place of honor, lest a more eminent man than you be invited by him; and he who invited you both will come and say to you, 'Give place to this man,' and you will begin with shame to take the lowest place" (Luke 14:8–9). The anecdote concedes the principle that there are high and low places at a table which correspond to one's honor ranking. Sitting at the right hand, of course, is the most honored place (see Ps 110:1).

2.4 Map of Times

Although there would be considerable flexibility about the times for ordinary meals, other meals reflect a serious concern over proper time

Passover is not eaten just any day, but once a year on a day fixed by the calendar, which might be done according to lunar or solar computation. There was, for example, considerable dispute among temple Jews, Samaritans, and Qumran folk over matters of calendar. Christians themselves disputed over the date of Easter (e.g., the Quartodeciman controversy). Such concern with calendars directly affects when ceremonial meals are to be eaten. Comparably, the sabbath meal was celebrated once a week, and considerable attention came to be focused on the precise time when the sabbath began. Even in the course of a meal, there might be an elaborate time arrangement in which dishes are served in a fixed sequence, "from soup to nuts" (Jeremias 1966:41–62; Douglas 1975:257–260).

The following text illustrates the sequence of foods and rituals at a festive Jewish meal; although dated several centuries after the period we are examining, it nevertheless reflects traditions much earlier in practice, and for that reason it is typical of the phenomenon we are describing.

> What is the order of the meal? The guests enter [the house] and sit on benches, and on chairs until all have entered. They all enter and they [servants] give them water for their hands. Each one washes one hand. They [servants] mix for them the cup; each one says the benediction for himself. They [servants] bring them the appetizers; each one says the benediction for himself. They [guests] go up [to the dining room] and they recline, for they [servants] give them [water] for their hands; although they have [already] washed one hand, they [now] wash both hands. They [servants] mix for them the cup; although they have said the benediction over the first [cup] they say a benediction [also] over the second. They [servants] bring them the dessert; although they said a benediction over the first one, they [now] say a benediction over the second, and one says the benediction for all of them. He who comes after the third course has no right to enter (t. Ber. 4,8; Bahr 1970:182)

This text provides a typical example of the various maps governing meals which we are examining. As regards postures, the participants start seated and finish reclining. The meal itself has three distinct courses: appetizers, the main meal, and finally dessert—a pattern common to Greco-Roman as well as Jewish meals. There are appropriate benedictions to be said over the first, then the second cup of wine. A distinction is made between the two washings of hands: the meal begins with a washing of only one hand before the hors d'oeuvres and is punctuated later with a second washing of both hands before the main course. Although wine is drunk during the meal, the true drinking comes in the second part of the ceremony, the symposium itself.

This analysis of a classification system, then, indicates maps of persons, things, places, and times which structure not only the symbolic world but are specifically replicated in a meal ceremony. In sum:

Specific folk :: *Specific* foods :: *Specific* talk

where "specific" refers to the group-specific maps whereby certain people imposes value and order on their distinctive cosmos. Meals, then, are a potential source of information about a group's symbolic universe. In summary, an inquirer into a symbolic analysis of meals should regularly ask the following questions to get a sense of the maps encoded in a particular meal:

(a) Who: who eats with whom; who sits where; who performs what action; who presides over the meal;

(b) What: what one eats (and does not eat); how it is grown and prepared; what utensils are used; what talk is appropriate;

(c) When: when one eats (daily, weekly, annually); when one eats which course during a meal;

(d) Where: where one eats; where one sits; in which institution, family or temple (Booth 1986:192–93).

3.0 MEALS AND BODY SYMBOLISM

Just as the ceremonial meal symbolizes the social system of a group, there is another symbol of that same social system, the physical human body. The basic insight is: the individual physical body replicates the value, structure, and order of the social body.

3.1 Body as Microcosm

Anthropologists offer us a further model for assessing this material in the remarks on the relationship of the physical and social body. We are all familiar with the classical comparisons of the social body-politic with a physical human body (1 Cor 12). From her own studies, Mary Douglas takes up this comparison in a more thorough way. The human body is a replica of the social body, a symbol and microcosm of it: "The body is a model which can stand for any bounded system. Its boundaries can represent any boundaries which are threatened or precarious" (Douglas 1966:115). "The physical experience of body . . . sustains a particular view of society" (Douglas 1982a:65).

There is, then, a map of the body, which replicates the classificatory maps of society just discussed. The same norms which govern the "purity" of the social body are applicable to the physical body as well.

Just as the social body draws boundary lines around itself, restricts admission (e.g., visas, passports), expels foreign or unclean objects, guards its gates and entrances, so this tendency to order, classify, and locate is replicated in the physical body. Physical bodies tend to be concerned with (a) their boundaries or surfaces (skin, clothing) and (b) the bodily entrances and exits on that surface (mouth, eyes, ears, genitals). Just as guards are stationed at territorial boarders or city gates, so the physical body would tend to be on guard about what may enter (food) or leave the physical body (spittle, menses, semen, urine). This means that in a given culture with a strong system of maps and with high "purity" concerns, we would expect there to be clear rules for the map of the body concerning: (1) boundaries, (2) structure, and (3) margins.

3.2 Bodily Boundaries

As society is ordered and guarded, so is the physical body. The boundary of the physical body is its skin, and by synecdoche clothing, which replicates that boundary. Since clothing denotes gender classification, women should wear women's clothing and men men's (Deut 22:5). Certain clothing, moreover, indicates social location, such as priestly garments (Exod 28), which must be made of one kind of stuff, not a mixture of wool and linen (Lev 19:19). Observant Jews, moreover, wear clothing which tells of their concern to keep the law, i.e., phylacteries (Matt 23:5). Certain clothing, moreover, is required at certain meals: one recalls the person cast out of the wedding feast because he was not wearing the appropriate costume, a wedding garment (Matt 21:11–14). The servant who waits on table is told to "gird yourself" (Luke 17:8), indicating distinctive clothing or dress appropriate to a table server (see Luke 12:37). Nudity—the absence of clothing—removes the classification system and blurs the map and all lines on it. Nudity, then, suggests chaos, and so is a pollution and shame (see Gen 3:10–11; Ezek 16:39).

The true boundary of the body, its skin, is punctuated by certain orifices which are gateways to the body's interior, just as walled cities have gates, and countries have ports of entry or customs crosspoints. These orifices are the object of great scrutiny; for, since they are the gates to the interior, they must screen out what does not belong and guard against a pollutant entering within. The guarded orifices tend to be the eyes, mouth, ears, and genitals. The mouth is guarded against unclean foods entering into the body, which can pollute that pure body (Acts 10:14).

As regards the sexual orifices, we find rules for intermarriage which prescribe who may cross the sexual orifice and marry whom. There are rules prohibiting exogamus marriages (Neh 13:23–28; 1 Cor 7:39; 2 Cor 6:14–7:1), as well as rules within Israel regulating who may marry whom:

> The priestly, Levitic and Israelitish stocks may intermarry; impaired priestly stocks, proselyte and freedman stocks may intermarry; the proselyte, freedman, bastard, Nathin, sketuki, and asufi stocks may intermarry (m. Kid. 4.1).

It follows that where classification systems are strong and purity concerns are high, there will be considerably more attention given to bodily surfaces and orifices than to bodily interior. Our concern here is with the oral orifice for eating and speaking.

3.3 Bodily Structure

In a well-regulated society, where maps and classifications are clear, there will be a corresponding replication of this in the physical body. A hierarchy of social roles is mirrored in the hierarchy of bodily organs: eyes over hands, head over feet (1 Cor 12); right is preferred to left; higher is preferred to lower. Just as there is a structural hierarchy of bodily parts, there is a corresponding concern to supervise the parts of the body which are in dangerous contact with the outside world. Hands, feet, eyes, which are the external provinces of the body, are singled out for special scrutiny (Mark 9:42–48).

3.4 Bodily Margins

Since lines should be clear and things, persons, places, and times should be *fully* in their *right* place, there should not be too much or too little. "Too much" means that something spills over into other areas where it does not belong; "too little" suggests that something is incompletely in its place or unsettled in it. This is based on the perception that "wholeness" is related to "holiness." What is "marginal," then, is the focus of great concern, for it is not wholly one thing or another. With respect to the body, "too much" is polluting, as in the case of a hermaphrodite who is both male and female. In this vein effeminate males and masculine females are "too much," being both male and female (Murphy-O'Connor 1980:482–500).

Bodies might have "too little" and be un-whole and unclean. Eunuchs, those with damaged testicles, and those without a penis are deficient in what it means to be male (see *t.* Meg. 2:7). According to Lev 21:16–20, the lame, the blind, the deaf, and others with physical defects are lacking in wholeness. Lacking bodily wholeness, they are deficient in holiness; these may not be priests or bring offerings into the holy temple. This is relevant when we look at the people whom Jesus recommends to be invited to a banquet, viz., people who suffer from being bodily "too little" (Luke 14:13).

Concerning margins of the body, considerable attention is given to what crosses boundaries or margins. Hence attention might be focused on a woman's menses, which exit from her sexual orifice, just as there might be concern over men's semen and the effect of sexual intercourse on the purity of a priest or warrior. Leprosy, or at least skin diseases (Pilch 1981:108–13), are concerned with what is flaking off the body's surface, that is, what has become marginal to the body. One would expect comparable attention to be given to tears, spittle, vomit, etc. Apropos of meals, one would expect concern with what comes out of a mouth (speech) as well as what goes into a mouth (food).

As regards the orifices in the surface of the body, meals suggest that we pay particular attention to the mouth. It is through the mouth that food enters the body, and so the mouth will tend to be governed so that it admits prescribed, but not proscribed food (1 Cor 8; 10). But the mouth is also the orifice from which emanates speech, and so it is doubly scrutinized. Certain speech is prescribed for certain meals: toasts are appropriate at banquets and weddings. The Hallel psalms should be sung at Passover (Mark 14:26). Yet other speech might be inappropriate and so proscribed.

Other bodily parts must come into play during a meal, and so are the object of regulation and mapping. Since no utensils are used for eating, the right hand, which transfers food to the mouth, becomes the object of specific washing rituals (Mark 7:1–4). Occasionally there are specific postures to be assumed at a meal: although Passover was supposed to be eaten standing, with one's loins girt and with a staff in hand, it came to be celebrated reclining at table in Greco-Roman fashion. At formal meals reclining was the appropriate posture, while sitting seems to have sufficed for ordinary meals.

Although we probably can never know the full range of bodily maneuvers appropriate to a first-century Jewish meal, there surely must have been codes of etiquette for meals. We have some rules of decorum which proscribe unseemly behavior of guests at meals (Smith 1980:253–72; Pervo 1984:314). On a positive side, however, Luke 7:44–46 hints at good practices which accompany certain meals, such as:

(a) washing the feet of a guest upon "entering the house,"

(b) greeting the guest with a kiss,

(c) anointing the head of the guest with oil.

Washing, kissing, and anointing pertain to feet, face and head. The mouth and hands, then, are not the only bodily parts that receive attention and regulation.

4.0 MEALS AND RECIPROCITY

People are constantly making contracts with one another, whether familial, economic, or political. Contracts imply some notion of reciprocity (see essays by Moxnes and Elliott), some understanding of the back-and-forth social movement between two individuals, two groups, or two parties. Theories of contracts and exchange which are appropriate to the type of society found in the first century describe three forms of reciprocity:

(a) *generalized* reciprocity: disinterested concern for the other party,

(b) *balanced* reciprocity: mutuality in a balanced and symmetrical way,

(c) *negative* reciprocity: pure self-interest to the disadvantage of the other party (Malina 1986a:98–106).

Meals and table-fellowship are often contracts and exchanges, so it is important to investigate this aspect further.

Generalized Reciprocity. This type of reciprocity refers to interactions which focus immediately on the interests of another party, and so are considered "altruistic" because they are other-directed. Assistance, whether it be financial, material or influential, is given without specification of a return obligation in terms of time, quantity or quality. The expectation of returned assistance, however, is always implied, but left indefinite and open-ended. Common forms of generalized reciprocity include hospitality, gifts, and various types of assistance given to kin and friends especially. The clearest examples of this would be the nurture and support parents give their children.

Balanced Reciprocity. This type of reciprocity refers to interaction in which the concerns of both parties engaging in some social transaction are addressed. If generalized reciprocity looks to the benefit of the other, balanced reciprocity describes a symmetrical concern for equivalent benefit for both parties. This entails a balanced exchange, a quid-pro-quo, a tit-for-tat movement. Common forms of interaction that have the structure of balanced reciprocity include buying and selling of goods and services, payment of fees for education, payment to professionals for service rendered, trade agreements, and barter. Balanced reciprocity keeps score in terms of time, quantity, and quality of goods exchanged.

Negative Reciprocity. This type of reciprocity refers to interactions which focus immediately on the social interest of the self or one's extended self, family or group. If generalized reciprocity is altruistic, negative reciprocity is self-centered or egocentric. Negative reciprocity refers to a movement in which one party tries to get something from another without reciprocating at all, and so getting something for nothing or with impunity. Common forms of this interaction include cheating, theft, robbery, overcharging, and various sorts of appropriation or seizure of another's goods. Capitalism is basically negative reciprocity, maximizing one's profits at the expense of others.

Generalized reciprocity tends to describe the interactions among family members or members of one's clan or fictive family. Balanced reciprocity seems to be the norm for relations with neighbors with whom one trades. Negative reciprocity would hardly be practiced on members of one's family or village, but rather on those perceived as outsiders, strangers, or enemies. The type of reciprocity practiced, then, would tend to express a type of relationship and would define "who is my neighbor?" or "who are my brothers and sisters?" Because meals are ceremonies which confirm values and structures in institutions, especially the institutions of kinship/family or politics, they would tend to be understood either in terms of generalized and balanced reciprocity.

5.0 MEALS AND PATRONAGE

Patronage has been dealt with extensively in this volume in the chapter by Halvor Moxnes. The following summary might help to refresh one's memory about patronage and patron-client relations. In general, in societies with weak central governments where there is little direct contact between rulers and citizenry, patronage becomes the system whereby goods and services are mediated.

In the first century, peasants valued "self-sufficiency" as a prime value (*autarcheia*, 1 Tim 6:6; 2 Cor 9:8), illustrated by the injunction "Owe no one anything . . ." (Rom 13:8). To be avoided at all costs was indebtedness of every sort. But, of course, the world does not work perfectly and people find themselves in need. To satisfy these needs, they make contracts with those who have resources and influence; that is, they seek patrons who desire clients.

Such contracts are asymmetrical, yet for them to occur implies that the exchange is mutually beneficial for both parties, both the patron and the client. There is some sort of balance in the relationship. Obviously, the client obtains the desired resources, such as use of oxen for ploughing, a bride price for his daughter, loans of money or seed for sowing, etc. In turn the patron receives things highly valued in that world. We recall from the chapter on honor and shame that people in the New Testament world greatly prized respect, reputation, and honor. A patron who made gifts of food, money, resources and influence would be praised by the client; his name would be magnified; he would be acclaimed "worthy" (Luke 7:4). And he would be considered as a "benefactor," a highly commendable label. The patron, moreover, would gain a client who owed him loyalty and faithfulness.

Patron-client relations, however, might require the services of an intermediary, a broker. Clients might perceive the gulf between them and the patron as so great that they could never dare to approach the patron themselves. The services of a mediator are needed, as in the case of the centurion who uses the mediating services of "elders" to petition Jesus for some benefaction (Luke 7:1–10). Ordinarily in the Gospels Jesus is proclaimed as the broker of God's benefaction, the purveyor of salvation, food, healing, revelation, and other gifts. In fact, Luke would suggest that Jesus is the unique and necessary broker of all God's gifts (Acts 4:1–12; 13:36–37), including the Holy Spirit (see Acts 2:33).

So as we turn to Luke–Acts, we pay special attention to patronage as the model for understanding the relationship of God to the covenant people of Israel. Such a model would go a long way toward understanding the dynamics encoded in the Our Father, how the followers of Jesus both acclaim the honorable name of God and petition this same God for "daily" bread – an asymmetrical patron-client exchange. And Luke has much to say about the role of Jesus, the broker. Jesus, the founder of a faction, starts and sustains the group he gathers around himself precisely by meals or distribution of food. Since patron-client relations are a form of reciprocity, if the patron distributes food, then one might ask what he gets in return? what is expected of those who receive? Patron-client relations, then, are an indispensable scenario for understanding the full meaning of the social relations in Luke–Acts, especially those that deal with food and meals.

6.0 THE MODEL APPLIED

We now turn to Luke–Acts with a complex model of what goes into understanding a meal. It is our hope that examining meals and table-fellowship in terms of the five aspects of the model developed above will provide an adequate scenario for understanding the meals which Luke records that Jesus and his disciples ate.

6.1 Meals as Ceremonies

The many meals in Luke–Acts fulfil the definition of *ceremony* in ways that shed fresh light on their content and function. Ceremonies are predictable events which occur regularly, such as sabbath meals (Luke 14:1), Passover meals (Luke 22:7–8, 13, 15), and Christian meals on the first day of the week (Acts 20:7). They are presided over by officials, such as leading Pharisees (7:36; 11:37; 14:1), Jesus himself (22:13–37; 24:27–34; Acts 1:4; 10:41), and the apostles (Acts 2:42; 20:7–11). They confirm institutions and roles/statuses within those institutions: Pharisees would claim the role of teacher (Rabbi) and the status of models to be imitated by demonstrating how one eats in the correct manner (Luke 11:37). Jesus reinforces his role as leader of a faction and demonstrates his status by gathering and presiding at meals (Luke 22:13–37; Acts 10:41). The leaders of the Jerusalem church, either "the Twelve" or those newly delegated by them, are charged with distributing food to the Hebrew and Hellenist widows (Acts 6:1–6). Paul confirms his leadership by preaching and then breaking bread (Acts 20:7–11).

The context of the meals, therefore, indicates that the Pharisee who presides claims for himself a position of leadership and the correct knowledge for the haburah. Jesus too not only signals a form of kinship with those with whom he ate, but also indicates his role as their leader (see esp. Luke 22:14–37). Group identity is affirmed; roles of leader and disciple are confirmed; status is confirmed.

Ceremonies strengthen group identity, values, and structures. For example, the Passover supper was eaten by Jesus and his apostles, a clearly defined group with whom Jesus continued to eat after his resurrection (Acts 1:4; 10:41). The references to "breaking of the bread" in Acts (4:42, 46; 20:7, 11) refer to a specific group who has believed in Jesus, who accepts the teaching of the apostles, and who gathers for fellowship (koinōnia) and prayers together. This is called commensality, and it affirms the solidarity of the new group which formed around the apostles. Conversely, the refusal of the elder brother to go and eat the meal which honored his reprobate younger brother illustrates the principle in reverse: he declared that he had nothing in common with his lesser sibling who dishonored his father and himself (15:25–32). In this case commensality is denied.

Unlike the refusal of the elder brother to share a feast with his shameful sibling, there is another type of non-consumption which is basically a ceremony, namely fasting. When group members abstain from eating, this can signal the shared support of commonly held values. There are fast days in the liturgical calendar, such as the day of Atonement; fasting might accompany the mourning ceremonies for dead heroes such as Saul and Jonathan (1 Sam 31:13; 2 Sam 1:12); and there might be public fasts in times of political crisis (Ezra 8:21–33; 1 Macc 3:47; 2 Macc 13:12).

Luke frequently notes people fasting to signal that they are holy and observant people (Luke 2:37; 18:12; Acts 27:9). In other contexts, fasting in conjunction with prayer is the group ceremony on which occasion new leaders emerge (Acts 13:2–3) or in which confirmation of group membership occurs (Acts 14:23). Yet in Luke 5:33–35, Jesus refuses to fast, which distinguishes him and his disciples from the disciples of John and those of the Pharisees. And so, refusal to fast ceremonially affirms group boundaries and distinguishes contending parties in disputes (Malina 1986a:200–202)

6.2 Meals and Purity Systems

We noted in the chapter on the symbolic world of Luke that he both shared a common symbolic world with first-century Jews, and disagreed with it on many points. This double aspect is found also in the way meals are treated as symbols of that symbolic world. At times Luke confirms the accepted order pertaining to meals, but at other times he reports that it is upset.

6.2.1 The System Confirmed (Douglas-Isherwood 1979:115–118). One meal in particular illustrates this important principle of redundancy about specific group :: specific foods :: specific talk. Of all the synoptic Gospels, Luke alone narrates that at the Passover meal Jesus spoke at great length to his apostles (see also John 13–17). In the course of that meal, Jesus confirmed basic aspects of his ordered universe.

Map of Persons. A specific group is recognized, "He sat at table, and the apostles with him" (22:14). No crowds, no folk of lesser allegiance, only special and specific people. The expectation is that the people at this meal are strongly bonded together, so that their shared food symbolizes this unity (koinōnia/commensality). Jesus, however, signals that a pollutant is present at this table, even his mortal enemy, "Behold the hand of him who betrays me is with me on the table" (22:21). This disturbing exception to a "specific group" only proves the rule.

Even here, there is some attempt to rank the persons at the meal. Jesus is clearly the chief person at the meal: he calls it into being (22:7–13), begins it (22:14–15), determines the course of foods eaten and drunk (22:17–20), and presides over the conversation (22:21–37). The issue of ranking among his disciples surfaces in the course of the meal, "A dispute arose among them, which of them was to be regarded as the greatest" (22:24). Although the disciples are told not to understand "greatness" as secular rulers are great, nevertheless some principles of ranking are enunciated: "Let the greatest among you become as the youngest, and the leader as one who serves" (22:26). There will be a leader and a person of greater honor among them; this is confirmed when Peter is singled out for special affirmation as leader who will "strengthen your brethren" (22:32; see Neyrey 1985:28–35). Jesus' Last Supper/Passover meal, then, illustrates a map of persons: who eats with whom (Jesus and apostles), who should not be there (the disloyal disciple), and who ranks highest (Peter).

One important question which is raised in this context would be the gender of those who ate together according to Luke–Acts. From the clues given in the text, it would appear that Jesus' table companions were men. Moreover, from our knowledge of the concept of honor and shame in this culture, it is easy to imagine that the meals described in Luke's Gospel belong to men's space, not female space (see Luke 10:40); and so it would indeed be extraordinary if men and women ate together at these public meals. But these suggestions have to be tested by a more thorough reading of Luke–Acts and other Christian writings.

Map of Things. They ate specific foods. In Luke's version they ate "this Passover meal," which entailed among other things specific cups of wine (22:17, 20) and unleavened bread (22:19). Beside foods appropriate to the feast, other specific foods are reported to have been eaten, specifically Christian foods, viz., the Eucharist (22:19–20).

They talked specific talk, at least Jesus talked. It has been commonly noted that Luke cast the Passover meal in the literary form of a Farewell Address (Neyrey 1985:6–48), even a symposium. By this, Luke gathered statements attributed to Jesus elsewhere and placed them here for solemn emphasis as Jesus' final words to his disciples about himself and their relationship to him. Farewell speeches tend to have characteristic and predictable elements, such as (a) prediction of death, (b) predictions about the future, (c) bequeathal of a legacy, (d) exhortation to a specific virtue, and (e) commission of a successor. All of these items are of specific interest to Jesus and the apostles:

(a) Jesus predicts his death (22:15–16, 18, 19–20);

(b) he predicts crises for his disciples: for Judas (22:21), for Peter (22:31–32), for all of them (22:35–36);

(c) he bequeaths a legacy: the Eucharist (22:19–20);

(d) he exhorts them to specific virtues of service (22:24–27) and mutual support (22:31–32);

(e) he commissions the apostles as patriarchs to guide his disciples (22:28–30), and in particular he singles out Peter for special leadership in the group (22:32).

The group is thus strengthened by their specific gathering together to eat specific Christian foods and to talk specific Christian talk. Other meals which exhibit comparable features would include Luke 24:13–32; Acts 2:42 and 10:41.

Maps of Time and Place. The Passover meal, moreover, illustrates the relevance of the maps which people construct to make their world intelligible. A map of time is evident: the feast of Unleavened Bread and Passover. A map of place seems indicated, since they ate inside the city, in a room appropriately prepared for this festal occasion (22:10–13).

Turning from the Passover meal to other meals described in Luke–Acts, we note that many scholars have pointed out that three of Jesus' meals reflect the symposium form. At least on a literary level, this would indicate various maps of persons and things. For example, (a) the *host* always seems to be a Pharisee (Luke 7:36; 11:37; 14:1). (b) While Jesus is the *chief guest*, other *guests* are noted: scribes and Pharisees (7:49); scribes, lawyers, and Pharisees (11:37–54); and lawyers and Pharisees (14:3). (c) Implied by this is some sort of seating arrangement. (d) These three eating occasions, moreover, indicate a meal, which is followed by a conversational symposium. Appropriate to his role as chief guest, Jesus either occasions the topic by his actions (11:38; 14:2–4) or directly asks the leading question (7:40). On each occasion, Jesus then takes the lead and delivers a wise discourse (de Meeus 1961; Steele 1984). The symposium form, then, serves as a map which gives us clues about Jesus' meals with the Pharisees.

6.2.2 The System Turned Upside Down. Even as meals celebrate group cohesion and identity, Luke tells a story about Jesus which indicates that in many ways he turned his world upside down. From Luke–Acts, we would discern new maps being drawn by Jesus and his disciples which challenge and rearrange the maps implicit in their culture.

New Maps of Persons. Meals are ostensibly eaten among specific group members, but Jesus develops a strategy of eating across the board. He dines with Pharisees, who would be classified by his culture as holy, separated people (Luke 7:36–50; 11:37–44; 14:1–7). Yet he breaks the rules by eating with people regarded as sinners and outsiders (5:29–32; 15:1–2; 19:5–7). He boasts of the public criticism of him as the one who "came eating and drinking" but of whom some charge, "Behold a glutton and a drunkard, a friend of tax collectors and sinners" (7:33). Jesus could claim to be following the pattern of a saintly prophet who shared the table of a foreign woman in a foreign land (4:25–26). But he gives mixed signals in regards to the map of persons; he is upsetting the accepted norms.

Jesus' selection of table companions is no mere lapse of regard for the customs of his day but a formal strategy. Although likes should eat with likes, by eating with sinners and foreigners Jesus formally signals that God extends an inclusive invitation to non-observant and sinful outsiders for covenant membership and for status as forgiven persons. This is demonstrated in part by the parable of the great feast where the messengers went not to the houses of the elite but to those of the non-elite, even the despised outsiders, whom they invited to the banquet (14:21–23). The most striking example of the Lukan ideology of an inclusive meal comes in Acts 10 through the explanation to Peter of the foods which God lowered from heaven for him to eat. Peter protested that Jews do not eat unclean things: "I have never eaten anything that is common or unclean" (Acts 10:14). But the vision of the foods is really about the people with whom Peter should break bread, as Peter explains to Cornelius: "You yourselves know how unlawful it is for a Jew to associate with or to visit any one of another nation; but God has shown me that I should not call any man common or unclean" (Acts 10:28). The meals of Jesus and his disciples, then, suggest a new map of people who belong in God's inclusive covenant.

As ceremonies, meals are expected to reinforce the roles and statuses of members of the group, thus confirming the map of persons which indicates rank and status. This is evident in the saying in Luke 17:7–10 about expecting people to live up to their rights and duties. Jesus comments on how improbable it is to expect a householder to say to his hired servants "Come in and sit at table." That would obscure the roles of head of the household and of servant. Rather, the householder correctly says, "Prepare supper for me, and gird yourself and serve me, till I eat and drink, and afterward you shall eat and drink" (17:8). The meal described there would ceremoniously confirm the proper roles of master and servant. In keeping with this, one might consider the decision in Acts 6:1–6 where the apostles declare, "It is not right that we should give up preaching the word of God to serve tables." Whatever else this text communicates, it reflects a heightened sense of the higher role and status of the apostles ("preach the word of God") over against those who could serve table. On this point, see Luke 10:38–42.

Yet in the Lukan story of a world upside down we find meals used as occasions to reverse roles and statuses. The first mention of this occurs in Luke 12:35–37, where to undergird how important it is to be ready for the coming of the Son of man, the hearers are told to "be like men who are waiting for their master to come home from the marriage feast" (12:35). Their status as servants will increase to that of "blessed," which is dramatized by a radical reversal of roles upon the master's arrival: "He (the master) will gird himself and have them sit at table, and he will come and serve them" (12:37). Servants become masters and masters become servants!

In many ways, one's culture sends one unmistakable clues concerning the role and status of its members (see the chapter on honor and shame). In Jesus' world there was considerable jockeying for status among the non-elite. For example Pharisees would claim to know and practice Torah more perfectly than others, thus promoting their status. Other claims to status might come more informally by taking a particular place at a meal, since the actual spatial arrangement of a dining area served as a map of role and status. "Marking how they (those invited to the Pharisee's house) chose the places of honor" (Luke 14:7), Jesus criticized this strategy and urged that one take the lowest place and assume the lowest status in the group. The point is not that "lowest" is per se better than "highest," but that by role reversal and status substitution, one could succeed in the game of advancement, for the host will come to the person in the last place and say, "Friend come up higher." And so "you will be honored in the presence of all who sit at table with you" (14:11). This reverses the rules of the day: to get honor one forgoes honor; to rise higher one goes lower.

Questions of role and status also pertain to those whom one invites to a dinner or a banquet (Luke 14:12–14). A formal meal is envisioned, to which one would naturally invite one's social peers (recall *balanced reciprocity*). Jesus, however, says that one should *not* invite "friends, brothers, kinsmen, or rich neighbors," but rather "the poor, the maimed, the lame, the blind" (14:13). In terms of status, these people are clearly peasants or worse. According to Lev 21:16–20, such people have negative status, for they are prohibited from worship in the temple and so may not partake of the sacrificial table of the Holy Lord (Malina 1981:137;

Karris 1985:61–62). Yet they are God's chosen guests. God would have the wealthy, elite members of the Lukan church invite them to full membership and equal status with them.

Finally, at the Passover meal, Jesus deals with roles and statuses at meals. After finding out that there was a "least" brother at the table (e.g., Judas the traitor, 22:21–23), the disciples then disputed about who was the "greatest" (22:24). Jesus, of course, turned their world upside down by contrasting their role and status with that of known, honorable and great figures ("kings . . . lords"). The role and status of the apostles must be like that of their master, itself a shocking idea: the servants are like the master and the master is like the servants. The analogy of a meal is used: "Which is the greater, one who sits at table, or one who serves?" Obviously the one who sits at table enjoys the higher status. But Jesus inverts that by saying, "I am among you as one who serves" (22:27), reversing his role and setting an example for them. Although many passages reflect the old map of persons being maintained, nevertheless Luke portrays Jesus establishing new maps of persons, including the excluded and reversing the status of the lowly.

New Maps of Places. The feeding of the 5000 people in Luke 9:12–17 offers some further indications of a formal strategy concerning new maps of places. Although the stated cite is Bethsaida (Luke 9:10), the countryside around it is the real locus for this feeding: 5000 people are gathered into one place, a thing impossible in a small city of that region. The space, then, is the countryside, unregulated, chaotic space, and so presumably unclean space. At least it is hardly the space for a ceremony like a meal. For example, out there one would not expect to find water for the proper washing rites. The people gathered are a mixed lot: some were "in need of healing," and so unclean; and Luke describes them as "a crowd," which admits varying degrees of faithfulness to the law and so varying degrees of holiness. Food is brought to Jesus, "five loaves and two fish." Nothing is said about whether this is kosher food, whether the tithes have been paid on it, or whether it has been properly prepared. Nothing, then, seems right according to the cultural rules for meals: no concern whatsoever is had for who is eating with whom, where, how or what is eaten. Yet that is precisely Luke's point: Jesus' table-fellowship turns the world upside down for he welcomes anyone, especially sinners and the unclean, to eat with him anywhere and at anytime.

New Map of Things. Jewish dietary laws proscribe certain foods from being eaten, thus creating a specific map of things. Precisely on this point, Jesus himself created a new map, an anti-map of things. All foods are clean and may be eaten! For example, when his disciples are sent out to preach, they are expected to be housed and fed by those who receive their message, which in itself is a sort of *balanced reciprocity.*

Group solidarity is thus signaled by commensality. What is striking is the injunction to the missionaries that they "eat and drink what they (the hosts) provide" (Luke 10:7) and "eat what is set before you" (10:8). No concern is to be given to whether foods are clean or unclean, for such distinctions function to separate peoples. Jesus signals an inclusive sense of mission by breaking down distinguishing food concerns.

A reader thus conditioned will easily see the confirmation of Jesus' remark in Acts 10–11 where Peter and Cornelius are brought together.

A Cornelius' *dream* and the summons of Peter (10:1–8)

B Peter's dream of *all foods clean* (10:9–16)

C Peter's vision and the reception of Cornelius' men (10:17–23)

B′ Peter's declaration of *all peoples clean* (10:24–29)

A′ Cornelius recounts his *dream* about Peter (10:30–33)

Two themes, *food* and *people*, are carefully woven together; in fact the theme of clean and unclean foods symbolizes the issue of clean and unclean people.

Peter's first vision occurs in the context of food, "He became hungry and desired something to eat" (10:10). Peter saw in his dream a great sheet descending from heaven, the premier holy place, which surprisingly contained "all kinds of animals and reptiles and birds of the air" (10:12). The issue is food, for Peter is commanded to eat, "Rise, Peter; kill and eat" (10:13). Peter's reaction signals that among the food descending from heaven are things easily perceived as unclean and so proscribed: "No, Lord; for I have never eaten anything that is common or unclean" (10:14). But the heavenly voice commands a second time, "What God has cleansed, you must not call common" (10:15), which must be taken as a divine erasing of the previous map of clean and unclean foods (see Mark 7:19 and 1 Cor 10:26). Furthermore, the importance of this upsetting of old maps is symbolized by the fact that this vision and conversation happened "three times" (10:16). It is then rehearsed in detail in Acts 11:2–10 precisely in response to some disciples who found it profoundly disturbing.

Yet even as we see old maps erased and replaced by new maps, there is another occasion where certain old maps are brought back into force, but not for the purpose of separating insiders from outsiders, which was the function of Jewish dietary restrictions. The occasion is the great council in Acts 15 where the church debated the demand of some, "Unless you are circumcised according to the custom of Moses, you cannot be saved" (15:1). Circumcision here is a code word for "the law of Moses" in its entirety (15:4). The council unanimously rejects this demand, first Peter (15:7–11), then Barnabas and Paul (15:12), and finally James (15:13–

19). No, it is agreed, the law of Moses is not necessary for salvation. Yet a problem remains, which has to do with commensality and the foods eaten at meals by Jewish and Gentile Christians.

Surveying 1 Cor 8 and 10, Gal 2:11–12 and Rom 14, we have ample evidence that Christian unity was constantly threatened by problems of table-fellowship, specifically in terms of what foods diverse peoples ate at the common meals. While the issue might involve vegetarians eating with carnivores (Rom 14:2), the more common problem seems to have been between Gentile Christians and Jewish Christians, for whom the prohibitions against eating blood remained strong (Feeley-Harnick 1981:64–67) and for whom foods sacrificed to idols would be an abomination.

In service of a *common table* where no one's diet would offend another, the council in Acts 15 revives an old map of things which may not be eaten. James sends a letter to the Gentiles which proscribes certain foods: "Abstain from the pollutions of idols . . . and from what is strangled and from blood" (15:20, 29; 21:25). These newly proscribed foods are not intended to separate and divide peoples, as were the Jewish dietary regulations. On the contrary, to ensure commensality and thus to effect shared identity as Christians among those of Jewish and Gentile background, dietary restrictions are re-introduced. This does not cancel the abrogation in Acts 10–11 of the distinction between clean and unclean foods; rather it ensures that there will be an inclusive community by facilitating a common table. Here food proscriptions promote commensality, not division and separation.

6.3 Meals and Body

The physical body can serve as a symbol of the social body. Control exercised in structuring the social body (or its lack) will be replicated in the control of the individual physical body (or its lack). This perspective helps us understand the intense controversy between the Pharisees and Jesus over meals and table-fellowship. The Pharisees, who were not priests, sought to practice the high standards of temple purity required of priests in daily lives lived apart and distant from the Jerusalem temple. As one scholar puts it,

> The Pharisees held that even outside the temple, in one's own home, the law of ritual purity were to be followed in the only circumstances in which they might apply, namely, at the table. Therefore, one must eat secular food (ordinary, everyday meals) in a state of ritual purity *as if one were a temple priest* (Neusner 1973:83).

The reader is reminded of the symbolic temple arrangements discussed in the chapter on Luke's symbolic world. Zealous for the perfect keeping of the law and the maps which resulted from that value,

Pharisees gave special attention to their meals as ceremonies in which the temple laws of ritual purity were paramount.

Speaking of the pre–70 Pharisees, Jacob Neusner summarized what can be know about Pharisees, their concern for purity rules, and meals:

> The Houses' rulings pertaining either immediately or ultimately to table-fellowship involve preparation of food, ritual purity relating directly to food or indirectly to the need to keep food ritually clean, and agricultural rules concerning the proper growing, tithing, and preparation of agricultural produce for table use. The agricultural laws relate to producing or preparing food for consumption, assuring either that tithes and offerings have been set aside as the law requires, or that conditions for the nurture of crops have conformed to biblical taboos. Of the 341 individual Houses' legal pericopae, no fewer than 229, approximately 67 per cent of the whole, directly or indirectly concern table-fellowship . . . The Houses' laws of ritual cleanness apply in the main to the ritual cleanness of foods, and of people, dishes, and implements involved in its preparation. Pharisaic laws regarding sabbath and festivals, moreover, involve in large measure the preparation and preservation of good (Neusner 1973:86).

In terms of a model of the physical body, this translates into intense concern with the surface of the physical body, in particular with its orifices, especially the mouth. All food is destined to enter the body through the mouth, which is the equivalent of a gate for the social body, the city. As social boundaries are intensely guarded, so physical boundaries enjoy the same concern.

This attention to surfaces, moreover, is replicated in concern over the porosity of dishes from which food is consumed and over the washing of the surface of the hands which convey food to the mouth. Surfaces and orifices, then, are the chief bodily concerns of Pharisees. This same concern extends as well to those with who one eats. Unclean people eating unclean foods in an unclean manner likewise threaten the surface, the boundary or the orifices of observant Pharisees. The body, then, must be carefully guarded: the mouth must be regulated so that only clean foods, tithed, properly prepared, served in appropriate vessels, and eaten in clean company enter the physical body by means of hands ritually washed.

Hence it is no surprise in the Gospels that Pharisees engage in controversy with Jesus, who appears to disregard and even flout such concern. Their concern with the mouth for eating is illustrated in numerous ways in Luke. For example, they object to Jesus' eating with sinners (Luke 5:29; 15:1–2; see 19:5–7). They take him to task for not fasting at appropriate times (Luke 5:33–35; see Malina 1986a:185–204). They criticize his unkosher eating of grain on the sabbath (Luke 6:1–5), and express astonishment that "he did not first wash (his hands) before dinner" (Luke 11:38; see Mark 7:1–4).

Jesus, moreover, appears unconcerned with bodily surfaces and bodily orifices (Neyrey 1986b:107–9), especially as these pertain to meals and table-fellowship. Jesus eats with sinners; he tells his followers to eat whatever foods are served them; he defends their eating on the sabbath grain not ritually prepared. As we saw apropos of Acts 10–11, Jesus' disciples reject dietary restrictions, both in terms of what foods can be eaten and with whom they may be eaten. Evidently there is little concern for guarding the orifice of the mouth or bodily surfaces.

Pharisaic-Christian controversy over meals and bodily control is no minor matter in first-century culture. Because it is a veritable microcosm of the larger social and political macrocosm, it invites a reader to develop a proper reading scenario for understanding it. Attention to the way the physical body is constrained or not replicates societal attempts to order and structure the social world in certain ways. And so, observation of eating behavior should be seen vis-à-vis patterns of social structures and order. In the case of the Pharisees, their table concerns and behavior replicate basic values and structures in Israel (Neyrey 1986b:118–19). Like Israel and especially its temple, they are a people "set apart" and "holy," that is, separated from non-Jews and non-observant Jews. Their bodily concern with mouth (and hands) replicates social concerns among priests and others for God's holiness and orderliness, especially as this is embodied in the central symbol, the temple. Just as walls and courts separate outsiders from insiders and organize even the insiders into proper roles and statuses, so concern with the mouth (and hands) separates Pharisees from un-observant Jews, and affirms their role and status as teachers of the way of Torah. In short, Pharisees' table behavior embodies and confirms their view of a distinctive Israel and its temple, even as it affirms their particular role and status in Israel. Meals, after all, are ceremonies.

Jesus and his disciples, on the other hand, turn that world upside down. By eating with sinners, Jesus blurs the lines separating observant and non-observant Jews, and signals non-approval of the core value of "separateness." By eating on the sabbath grain not ritually prepared or tithed, Jesus devalues the system of Laws which structures the Temple. By eating foods previously judged unclean, the disciples explicitly reject the fundamental axiom that Israel is a unique people "set apart" by God from all others (Acts 10:28). All this is symbolized by the non-guarding of the mouth in these eating ceremonies. On an ideological level, Jesus and disciples clearly reject the value of "separateness" and the classification system which follows, because they celebrate porous social boundaries which welcome clean and unclean, Jew and Gentile into God's covenant family. On a bodily level, this porosity is symbolized by a rejection of control of the mouth as regards what is eaten and with whom it is eaten. Weak social control indicated by an inclusive mission is replicated in weak bodily control of the mouth by eating any food with anyone, anywhere and at any time.

A map of the physical body, then, is necessary for a complete and accurate understanding of meals. Whether or not the body, its surfaces and orifices are guarded can tell the astute observer much about the culture and its players. In particular we learn to appreciate why controversies between Jesus and the Pharisees focused on meals and foods. And this suggested how we might imagine the values and structures of the social body which were being argued at the same time. A microcosm can be an easy way to study the macrocosm.

6.4 Meals and Reciprocity

Generalized Reciprocity. Jesus' example in Luke 11:11–12 of petitioning in prayer illustrates how in a kinship group a parent is expected to show altruistic regard to children in terms of the food given them: "What father among you, if his son asks for a fish, will instead give him a serpent; or if he asks for an egg, will give him a scorpion?" The parable about the great banquet offers another example. The giver of the banquet sends his servants out with the command, "Go out quickly . . . and bring in the poor and maimed and blind and lame" (Luke 14:21). Even when they are brought in and there is still room at the banquet, the servants are sent once more, "Go out to the highways and hedges, and compel people to come in, that my house may be filled" (14:23). God's messianic banquet, moreover, would be an apt illustration of divine, generalized reciprocity in regard to meals. The fault of the "Fool," who planned to hoard the extraordinary good harvest in bigger barns so that he might "take his ease, eat, drink and be merry," exemplifies his failure to show generalized reciprocity to his tenants and neighbors by sharing this God-given boon of extra food. God, then, shows *generalized reciprocity* to humankind by gift of food, which should serve as a model for the members of Luke's church to do likewise.

Balanced Reciprocity. For many economic and social reasons, invitations to meals, be they wedding feasts, festive meals or fellowship meals, are normally considered under the rubric of balanced reciprocity. I invite you, you invite me. This would imply that such invitations are given to those who *could* reciprocate, that is, among social equals. The rule is illustrated when Jesus breaks it by enjoining: "When you give a dinner or a banquet, do *not* invite your friends or your brothers or your kinsmen or your rich neighbors, lest they also invite you in return, and you be repaid" (Luke 14:12). A person of meager means must decline an invitation from a wealthy person to dine because this would put the poor man at an enormous financial obligation to reciprocate with a rich, comparable meal for the wealthy person. But Jesus abolishes the expected balanced reciprocity when he continues, "You will be blessed, *because they cannot repay you*. You will be repaid at the resurrection of the just" (14:14b-15). God will balance the scales.

If one looks at several of the meals which Jesus shares in Luke's gospel, there seems to be a clear element of balanced reciprocity implied. In 5:27 and 19:5-7 Jesus is offered hospitality in a home. In both cases he has just benefited the inviter in some way, so that the hospitality shown Jesus balances the benefaction which Jesus showed to them: (a) after curing Simon's mother-in-law, the household feeds Jesus; (b) after honoring Zacchaeus, the forgiven tax collector feeds Jesus. Even Jesus promises a meal to his disciples ("eat and drink at my table in my kingdom," 22:30) as a response which reciprocates their loyalty to him ("you are those who have continued with me in my trials," 22:28). And Jesus' mission instructions indicate that those who proclaim the gospel are expected to be shown hospitality by the people who accept it (10:2-9), which should be seen as balanced reciprocity. See also Acts 28:7-10.

Negative Reciprocity. One would not expect negative reciprocity in any way to characterize meals in Luke-Acts, yet an example from Luke's gospel might argue otherwise. Although a Pharisee named Simon "asked him (Jesus) to eat with him," ostensibly a sign of shared ideals and respect, this host provided none of the expected signs of etiquette and hospitality, "I entered your house, you gave me no water for feet . . . you gave me no kiss . . . you did not anoint my head with oil" (7:44-45). The meal, then, was an insult to Jesus; on this occasion the Pharisee seemed to dishonor Jesus by shabby treatment of him, an example of negative reciprocity. The same principle is illustrated in 11:37-44; a Pharisee "asked him to dine with him," but insulted his guest by being "astonished that he did not first wash before dinner." Jesus might have received food, but was threatened with loss of honor and standing by his host's criticism (see 14:1-6).

7.0 CONCLUSION

This chapter set out to examine what anthropologists define as ceremonies. It is intended to be read as the complement of the study of rituals by McVann. It is our hope that the description of ceremony in both chapters might give readers insights with which to understand other ceremonies in Luke-Acts, such as marriages, feasts, the paying of taxes, and sundry temple appearances.

A specific ceremony became the focus of this chapter, the common phenomenon in Luke-Acts of meals and table-fellowship. Examining this one ceremony from the perspective of the social sciences, we learned that meals and table-fellowship are highly complex social events and so an adequate scenario for uncoding them was necessarily complex. An abstract knowledge of ceremonies in general would not be sufficient. What was needed was a fuller sense of the way meals and table-fellowship serve as symbols of both macro social systems and micro body control. And the scenario is not complete until one grasps the economics involved, the type of reciprocity expected of meals. Nor is the scenario complete until one learns of the social relations reflected in meals.

In a sense, our attempt to develop a scenario for understanding meals shows how many models are needed and how they replicate one another. This chapter presumes further knowledge of many other models developed in this volume: (a) the symbolic world of Luke, (b) notions of countryside, land and food production, (c) understanding of the institutions of family and politics, (d) concepts of patron-client, and finally (e) understanding of the honor-shame code. Clearly the description of the meal in Luke 14:15–24 would be incomplete without hearkening to the essay on the city by Rohrbaugh, where the parable of the Great Supper was extensively treated. As a result, there is a considerable sense of coherence in all these essay and a welcome sense of agreement. In many ways, we learn of what anthropologists describe as "redundance" in social patterns, the repetition of certain values and patterns of behavior in many areas of a culture. The reader of Luke, then, is not burdened with this complex model or scenario, but gains a welcome sense of thoroughness and coherence by so complete a perspective.

BIBLIOGRAPHY

Works Consulted

Aalders, G. J. D.
    1979   "The Hellenistic Concept of the Enviousness of Fate." Pp. 1–8
                in M. J. Vermaseren (ed.), *Studies in Hellenistic Religions*.
                Leiden: E. J. Brill
Abercrombie, N.
    1980   *Class, Structure and Knowledge: Problems in the Sociology of
                Knowledge*. New York: New York University Press
Abu-Hilal, Ahmad
    1982   "Arab and North-American Social Attitudes: Some Cross-
                Cultural Comparisons," *Mankind* 22:193–207
Alexander, Linda
    1982   "Illness Maintenance and the New American Sick Role." Pp.
                351–67 in N. J. Chrisman and T. W. Maretzki (eds.), *Clini-
                cally Applied Anthropology: Apologists in Health Science
                Settings*. Dordrecht: D. Reidel Publishing Co.
Alexander, Loveday
    1986   "Luke's Preface in the Context of Greek Preface-Writing,"
                NovT 28:48–74
American Psychiatric Association
    1980   *Diagnostic and Statistical Manual of Mental Disorders*, 3d ed.
                Washington, D.C.: American Psychiatric Association
Andreski, S.
    1968   *Military Organization and Society*. Berkeley, CA: University of
                California Press
Applebaum, S.
    1977   "Judea as a Roman Province: the Countryside as a Political
                and Economic Factor." Pp. 35–396 in *ANRW* 2.8

Aune, David E.
1987   The New Testament in Its Literary Environment. Philadelphia:
              Westminster Press
Bachmann, Michael
1980   Jerusalem und der Tempel. Die geographisch-theologischen
              Elemente in der lukanischen Sicht des jüdischen Kultzen-
              trums. BWANT 109. Stuttgart: W. Kohlhammer
Bahr, Gordon J.
1970   "The Seder of Passover and the Eucharistic Words," NovT
              12:181–202
Bailey, Kenneth E.
1976   Poet and Peasant. Grand Rapids, MI: Eerdmans
1980   Through Peasant Eyes: A Literary Cultural Approach to the
              Parables of Luke. Grand Rapids, MI: Eerdmans
Baltzer, Klaus
1965   "The Meaning of the Temple in the Lukan Writings," HTR
              58:263–77
Bammel, Ernst
1970   The Trial of Jesus. London: SCM
Barr, David L.
1987   New Testament Story: An Introduction. Belmont, CA: Wads-
              worth Publishing Company
Barr, James
1988   " 'Abba' Isn't 'Daddy,' " JTS 39:28–47
Barraclough, Geoffrey
1978   Main Trends in History. New York: Holmes and Meier Pub-
              lishers, Inc.
Bassler, Jouette
1979   Divine Impartiality. Paul and a Theological Axiom. Chico,
              CA: Scholars Press
Beare. F. W.
1981   The Gospel According to Matthew. New York: Harper & Row
Becker, Howard S.
1963   Outsiders. Studies in the Sociology of Deviance. New York:
              Free Press
Belo, Fernando
1981   A Materialist Reading of the Gospel of Mark. Maryknoll, NY:
              Orbis Books
Berger, Peter and Thomas Luckmann
1966   The Social Construction of Reality. Garden City, NY:
              Doubleday
Berkman, Lisa F.
1981   "Physical Health and the Social Environment: A Social Epi-
              demiological Perspective." Pp. 51–75 in L. Eisenberg and
              A. Kleinman (eds.), The Relevance of Social Science for
              Medicine. Dordrecht: D. Reidel Publishing Company
Berman, Ronald
1987   How Television Sees Its Audience: A Look At The Looking
              Glass. Newbury Park, CA: Sage Publications
Beteille, Andre
1969   Social Inequality. Baltimore: Penguin
Blanton, R. E.
1976   "Anthropological Study of Cities," ARA 5:249–64

Blinzler, Joseph
1959   The Trial of Jesus: The Jewish and Roman Proceeding against
        Jesus Christ Described and Assessed from the Oldest Ac-
        count. Westminster, MD: Newman
Blok, A.
1969   "Variations in Patronage," Sociologische Gids 16:365–78
Bloome, David and Judith Green
1984   "Directions in the Sociolinguistic Study of Reading." Pp.
        395–421 in P. David Pearson (ed.), Handbook of Reading
        Research. New York: Longman
Boehm, Christopher
1984   Blood Revenge: The Anthropology of Feuding in Montenegro
        and Other Tribal Societies. Lawrence, KS: University of
        Kansas Press
Boissevain, Jeremy
1974   Friends of Friends: Networks, Manipulators and Coalitions.
        New York: St. Martin's Press
1982/83 "Seasonal Variations on Some Mediterranean Themes,"
        Ethnologia Europaea 13:6–12
Booth, Roger P.
1986   Jesus and the Laws of Purity. Tradition History and Legal His-
        tory in Mark 7. Sheffield: JSOT Press
Borg, Marcus. J.
1984   Conflict, Holiness and Politics in the Teaching of Jesus. Lew-
        iston, NY: Edwin Mellen Press
Borhek, James T. and Richard F. Curtis
1975   A Sociology of Belief. New York: John Wiley
Bossmann, David
1979   "Ezra's Marriage Reform: Israel Redefined," BTB 9:32–38
Bourdieu, Pierre
1966   "The Sentiment of Honour in Kabyle Society." Pp. 191–241 in
        J. G. Peristiany (ed.), Honour and Shame: The Values of
        Mediterranean Society. Chicago: University of Chicago
        Press
Bowen, Murray
1978   Family Therapy and Clinical Practice. New York: Jason
        Aronson
Brandes, Stanley
1987   "Reflection on Honor and Shame in the Mediterranean." Pp.
        121–34 in David D. Gilmore (ed.), Honor and Shame and
        the Unity of the Mediterranean (American Anthropologi-
        cal Association special publication No. 22). Washington:
        American Anthropological Association
Braudel, Fernand
1972   The Mediterranean and the Mediterranean World in the Age
        of Philip II, vol. 1. New York: Harper & Row
1981   The Structures of Everyday Life. New York: Harper & Row
Brawley, Robert L.
1987   Luke–Acts and the Jews. Conflict, Apology, and Conciliation.
        Atlanta: Scholars Press
Bregman, L.
1987   "Baptism as Death and Birth: A Psychological Interpretation
        of Its Imagery," JRS 1:27–42

Brodie, Thomas L.
1979   "A New Temple and A New Law: The Unity and Chronicler-
            based Nature of Luke 1:1–4:22a," *JSNT* 5:21–45
Broshi, Magen
1986   "The Diet of Palestine in the Roman Period–Introductory
            Notes," *The Israel Museum Journal* 5:41–56
Brown, John Pairman
1976   "Techniques of Imperial Control: Background of Gospel
            Events." Pp. 73–83 in Norman Gottwald and Antoinette
            Wire (eds.), *The Bible and Liberation: Political and Social
            Hermeneutics. A Radical Religion Reader*. Berkeley, CA:
            The Community for Religious Research and Communication
Brown, Peter
1971   "The Rise and Function of the Holy Man in Late Antiquity,"
            JRelS 61:80–101. Reprinted, pp. 103–52 in *Society and the
            Holy in Late Antiquity*. London: Faber and Faber, 1982
Brown, Raymond E.
1971   "Jesus and Elisha," *Perspective* 12:85–104
1977   *The Birth of the Messiah*. Garden City, NY: Doubleday
1988   "The Burial of Jesus (Mark 15:42–47)," *CBQ* 50:233–45
Buchanan, George W.
1963   "The Role of Purity in the Structure of the Essene Sect,"
            ResQ 4:397–406
Bultmann, Rudolf
1963   *History of the Synoptic Tradition*. Oxford: Basil Blackwell
Burke, Peter
1980   *Sociology and History*. London: George Allen and Unwin
Cadbury, Henry
1937   "Rebuttal, A Submerged Motif in the Gospels." Pp. 99–108 in
            R. P. Casey and Silva Lake (eds.), *Quantulacumque*. Lon-
            don: Christophers
1958   *The Making of Luke–Acts*. 2d ed. London: SPCK
Callan, Terrence
1987   "Competition and Boasting: Toward a Psychological Portrait of
            Paul," *JRS* 13:27–51
Caplan, Arthur L., H. Tristram Engelhardt, Jr., James J. McCartney
1981   *Concepts of Health and Disease: Interdisciplinary Perspective*.
            Reading, MA: Addison-Wesley
Capra, Fritjof
1983   *The Turning Point*. New York: Bantam
Carney, Thomas F.
1975   *The Shape of the Past: Models and Antiquity*. Lawrence, KS:
            Coronado Press
Casalengo, Alberto
1984   *Gesu e il tempio: studio redazionale di Luca-Atti*. Brescia:
            Morcelliana
Cassell, E. J.
1976   "Illness and Disease," *Hastings Center Report* 6:27–37
Cassidy, Richard
1983   *Political Issues in Luke–Acts*. Maryknoll, NY: Orbis Books
Casson, Ronald W.
1983   "Schemata in Cognitive Anthropology," *ARA* 12:429–62

Catchpole, R. R.
1971   *The Trial of Jesus*. Leiden: E. J. Brill
Chrisman, Noel J. and T. W. Maretzki
1982   *Clinically Applied Anthropology: Apologists in Health Science Settings*. Dordrecht: D. Reidel Publishing Co.
Cicourel, Aaron V.
1985   "Text and Discourse," *ARA* 14:159–85
Clements, R. E.
1967   *Abraham and David*. Naperville IL: Alec R. Allenson
Cohen, Shaye J. D.
1979   *Josephus in Galilee and Rome*. Leiden: E. J. Brill
Cohen, Yehudi A.
1968   "Food: II. Consumption Patterns." Pp. 508–13 in David Sills (ed.), *International Encyclopedia of the Social Sciences*, volume 5. New York: Macmillan/Free Press
Cohn, Robert L.
1980   *The Shape of Sacred Space*. Chico, CA: Scholars Press
Collins, John
1986   "Central Place Theory is Dead: Long Live the Central Place." Pp. 37–40 in Eric Grant (ed.), *Central Places, Archaeology and History*. Sheffield: Department of Archaeology and Prehistory, University of Sheffield
Collins, John N.
1984   "Diakonia as an Authoritative Capacity in Sacred Affairs and as the Model of Ministry," *Compass Theology Review* 18:29–34
Conn, H. M.
1985   "Lucan Perspectives and the City," *Missiology: An International Review* 13:409–28
Cook, Michael J.
1978   "Jesus and the Pharisees–The Problem as It Stands Today," *JES* 15:441–60
Corrigan, G. M.
1986   "Paul's Shame for the Gospel," *BTB* 16:23–27
Coser, Lewis A.
1956   *The Functions of Social Conflict*. New York: Free Press
1968   "Conflict, Social Aspects. " *International Encyclopedia of the Social Sciences*. 15:232–36. New York: Macmillan and Free Press
Crossan, John D.
1973   *In Parables: The Challenge of the Historical Jesus*. New York: Harper & Row
Cuisenier, Jean
1975   *Économie et parenté: leurs affinités de structure dans le domaine turc et dans le domaine arabe*. Paris/La Haye: Mouton
Dabrowski, E.
1968   "The Trial of Jesus in Recent Research," *SE* 4:21–27
Dahl, Nils A.
1976   "The Story of Abraham in Luke–Acts." Pp. 66–86 in his *Jesus in the Memory of the Early Church*. Minneapolis: Augsburg

Danby, Herbert
1919   "The Bearing of the Rabbinical Criminal Code on the Jewish
            Trial Narratives of the Gospel," *JTS* 21:151–76
Danker, Frederick W.
1982   *Benefactor: Epigraphic Study of a Graeco-Roman and New
            Testament Semantic Field.* St. Louis: Clayton Publishing
            House
1987   *Luke.* Proclamation Commentaries. 2d revised and enlarged
            edition. Philadelphia: Fortress Press
1988   *Jesus and the New Age. A Commentary on St. Luke's Gospel.*
            2d revised and expanded edition. Philadelphia: Fortress
            Press
Davis, Fred
1961   "Deviance Disavowal: The Management of Strained Interaction
            by the Visibly Handicapped," *SP* 9:120–32
Davis, John
1987   "Family and State in the Mediterranean." Pp. 22–34 in David
            D. Gilmore (ed.), *Honor and Shame and the Unity of the
            Mediterranean* (American Anthropological Association
            special publication No. 22). Washington: American An-
            thropological Association
De Beaugrande, Robert
1980   *Text, Discourse and Process: Toward a Multidisciplinary
            Science of Texts.* Advances in Discourse Processes, vol. 4.
            Norwood, NJ: Ablex Publishing Company
De Beaugrande, Robert and Wolfgang Dressler
1981   *Introduction to Text Linguistics.* London and New York:
            Longman
Delaney, Carol
1986   "The Meaning of Paternity and the Virgin Birth Debate," *Man*
            21:494–513
1987   "Seeds of Honor, Fields of Shame." Pp. 35–48 in David D.
            Gilmore (ed.), *Honor and Shame and the Unity of the
            Mediterranean* (American Anthropological Association
            special publication No. 22). Washington: American An-
            thropological Association
Delcor, M.
1969   "Repas Culturels Esséniens et Thérapeutes, Thaiases et Habu-
            roth," *RevQ* 6:401–25
de Meeus, X.
1961   "Composition de Lc. XIV et Genre Symposiaque," *ETL*
            37:847–70
Detweiler, Robert (ed.)
1985   *Reader Response Approaches to Biblical and Secular Texts*
            Semeia 31. Decatur, GA: Scholars Press
Donahue, John R.
1973   *Are You the Christ?* Missoula, MT: Scholars Press
Douglas, Mary
1966   *Purity and Danger: An Analysis of Concepts of Pollution and
            Taboo.* London: Routledge & Kegan Paul
1968   "Pollution." *International Encyclopedia of the Social
            Sciences.* 12.336–42. New York: Macmillan and Free Press

1975   "Deciphering a Meal." Pp. 249–275 in *Implicit Meanings.*
        London: Routledge & Kegan Paul
1982a   *Natural Symbols.* New York: Pantheon
1982b   "Food as a System of Communication." Pp. 82–124 in *In the
        Active Voice.* London: Routledge & Kegan Paul
Douglas, Mary and Baron Isherwood
1979   *The World of Goods.* New York: Basic Books, Inc.
Duby, Georges and Philippe Braunstein
1988   "The Emergence of the Individual." Pp. 507–630 in Georges
        Duby (ed.), *A History of Private Life: II. Revelations of the
        Medieval World.* Cambridge: Belknap Press
Dumont, Louis
1970   *Homo Hierarchicus.* Chicago: University of Chicago Press
Dunn, James D. G.
1983   "The Incident at Antioch (Gal 2:11–18)," *JSNT* 18:3–57
Dupont, Jacques
1968   *Les tentations de Christ du désert.* Bruges: Desclée de Brouwer
1980   "Le Magnificat comme discours sur Dieu," *NRT* 102:321–43
Edwards, O. C.
1981   *Luke's Story of Jesus.* Philadelphia: Fortress Press
Eisenberg, Leon, and Arthur Kleinman
1981   *The Relevance of Social Science for Medicine.* Dordrecht: D.
        Reidel Publishing Company
Eisenberg, Leon
1977   "Disease and Illness: Distinctions between Professional and
        Popular Ideas of Sickness," *Culture, Medicine and Psy-
        chiatry* 1:9–23
Eisenstadt, S. N. and L. Roniger
1980   "Patron-Client Relations as a Model of Structuring Social Ex-
        change," *Comparative Studies in Society and History*
        22:42–77
1984   *Patrons, Clients and Friends: Interpersonal Relations and the
        Structure of Trust in Society.* Cambridge: Cambridge Uni-
        versity Press
Elliott, John H.
1981   *A Home for the Homeless: A Sociological Exegesis of I Peter,
        Its Situation and Strategy.* Philadelphia: Fortress Press
1986   *Social-Scientific Criticism of the New Testament and Its So-
        cial World. Semeia* 35
1987   "Patronage and Clientism in Early Christianity," *Forum*
        3/4:39–48
Ellis, E. E.
1974   *The Gospel of Luke.* 2d ed. London: Oliphants
Englehardt, H. Tristram, Jr.
1981   "The Concepts of Health and Disease." Pp. 30–45 in Arthur
        L. Caplan, H. Tristram Englehardt, Jr., James J. McCartney
        (eds.), *Concepts of Health and Disease: Interdisciplinary
        Perspectives.* Reading, MA: Addison-Wesley
1986   "The Social Meanings of Illness," *Second Opinion* 1:26–39
Esler, Philip F.
1987   *Community and Gospel in Luke–Acts.* Cambridge: Cambridge
        University Press

Evans, C. A.
1987   "Luke's Use of the Elijah/Elisha Narratives and the Ethic of
            Election," *JBL* 106:75–83
Fabrega, Horacio
1974   *Disease and Social Behavior: An Interdiscplinary Perspective.*
            Cambridge: MIT Press
Farb, Peter and Armelagos
1980   *Consuming Passions: The Anthropology of Eating.* Boston:
            Houghton Mifflin Company
Feeley–Harnik, Gillian
1981   *The Lord's Table.* Philadelphia: University of Pennsylvania
            Press
Fennelly, James M.
1983   "The Jerusalem Community and Kashrut Shatnes," SBLASP
            1983:273–88
Fensham, F. C.
1967   "The Good and Evil Eye in the Sermon on the Mount," *Neot*
            1:51–58
Finley, M. I.
1969   "The Silent Women of Rome." Pp. 129–42 in his *Aspects of*
            Antiquity: Discoveries and Controversies. New York: Vik-
            ing Press
1977   "The Ancient City: From Fustel de Coulanges to Max Weber
            and Beyond," *Comparative Studies in Society and History*
            19:305–27
Fischer, B.
1985   *Workshop on Shame.* Baltimore: The Resource Group
Fishman, Joshua A.
1971   *Sociolinguistics: A Brief Introduction.* Rowley, MA: Newbury
            House Publishers
Fitzmyer, Joseph A.
1981–85   *The Gospel According to Luke.* 2 vols. Garden City, NY:
            Doubleday
Fitzpatrick, Ray
1984   "Lay Concepts of Illness." Pp. 11–31 in Ray Fitzpatrick, John
            Hinton, Stanton Newman, Graham Scambler, and James
            Thompson (eds.), *The Experience of Illness.* London and
            New York: Tavistock Publishers
Forbes, Christopher
1986   "Comparison, Self–Praise, and Irony: Paul's Boasting and the
            Conventions of Hellenistic Rhetoric," *NTS* 32:1–30
Forkman, Göran
1972   *The Limits of Religious Community.* Lund: Studentlitteratur
Foster, George M.
1961   "The Dyadic Contract: A Model for the Social Structure of a
            Mexican Peasant Village," *American Anthropologist*
            63:1173–92
1967   "The Image of Limited Good." Pp. 300–323 in J. Potter, M.
            Diaz, and G. Foster (eds.), *Peasant Society: A Reader.* Bos-
            ton: Little, Brown and Company
1976   "Disease Etiologies in Non–Western Medical Systems," *Ameri-*
            can Anthropologist 78:773–82

Fowler, Roger
1981   *Literature as Social Discourse*. Bloomington: Indiana University Press

Freedman, Robert L.
1981   *Human Food Uses: A Cross-Cultural, Comprehensive Annotated Bibliography*. Westport, CT: Greenwood Press

Freyne, Sean
1980   *Galilee from Alexander the Great to Hadrian: 323 B.C.E. to 135 C.E.* University of Notre Dame Center for the Study of Judaism and Christianity in Antiquity 5. South Bend, IN: Univerity of Notre Dame Press

Frick, F. S.
1977   *The City in Ancient Israel*. Missoula, MT: Scholars Press

Fuchs, Esther
1982   "Status and Role of Female Heroines in the Biblical Narrative," *Mankind Quarterly* 23:149–60

Funk, Robert W.
1966   *Language, Hermeneutic and Word of God*. New York: Harper & Row

Füssel, Kano
1987   *Drei Tage mit Jesus im Tempel. Einführung in die materalistiche Lektüra der Bibel*. Münster: Editio Liberacion

Fustel de Colanges, N. D.
1976   *The Ancient City*. Garden City, NY: Doubleday

Gaines, Atwood D.
1982   "Knowledge and Practice: Anthropological Ideas and Psychiatric Service." Pp. 243–73 in N. J. Chrisman and T. W. Maretzki (eds.), *Clinically Applied Anthropology: Apologists in Health Science Settings*. Dordrecht: D. Reidel Publishing Company

Garfinkel, Harold
1956   "Conditions of Successful Degradation Ceremonies," *AJS* 61:420–24
1967   *Studies in Ethnomethodology*. Englewood Cliffs, NJ: Prentice-Hall

Garrett, Susan R.
1989   *The Demise of the Devil: Magic and the Demonic in Luke's Writings*. Minneapolis: Augsburg/Fortress Press

Gaventa, Beverly R.
1986   *From Darkness to Light: Aspects of Conversion in the New Testament*. Philadelphia: Fortress Press

Geertz, Clifford
1973   *The Interpretation of Cultures*. New York: Basic Books
1976   " 'From the Native's Point of View': On the Nature of Anthropological Understanding." Pp. 221–37 in Keith H. Basso and Henry A. Selby (eds.), *Meaning and Anthropology*. Albuquerque: University of New Mexico Press

Gellner, E.
1977   "Patrons and Clients." Pp. 1–6 in E. Gellner and J. Waterbury (eds.), *Patrons and Clients in Mediterranean Societies*. London: Duckworth

Gellner, E. and J. Waterbury
1977   Patrons and Clients in Mediterranean Societies. London:
            Duckworth
Gerhardsson, B.
1966   The Testing of God's Son. Lund: Gleerup
Ghosh, Amitav
1983   "The Relations of Envy in an Egyptian Village," Ethnology
            32:211–23
Giblin, Charles Homer
1985   The Destruction of Jerusalem According to Luke's Gospel.
            Rome: Biblical Institute Press
Gil, Moshe
1970   "Land Ownership in Palestine under Roman Rule," Revue
            Internationale des Droits de l'Antiquité 17:11–53
Gilmore, David D.
1982   "Anthropology of the Mediterranean Area," ARA 11:175–205
1987   Honor and Shame and the Unity of the Mediterranean
            (American Anthropological Association special publica-
            tion No. 22). Washington: American Anthropological
            Association
Gilsenan, M.
1977   "Against Patron-Client Relations." Pp. 167–84 in E. Gellner
            and J. Waterbury (eds.), Patrons and Clients in Mediterra-
            nean Societies. London: Duckworth
Giovannini, Maureen J.
1987   "Female Chastity Codes in the Circum-Mediterranean: Com-
            parative Perspectives." Pp. 61–74 in David D. Gilmore
            (ed.), Honor and Shame and the Unity of the Mediterra-
            nean (American Anthropological Association special pub-
            lication No. 22). Washington: American Anthropological
            Association
Girard, R.
1977   Violence and the Sacred. Baltimore: Johns Hopkins Press
Goffman, Irving
1963   Stigma: Notes on the Management of Spoiled Identity. Engle-
            wood Cliffs, NJ: Prentice-Hall
Good, Byron and Mary Jo DelVecchio Good
1981   "The Meaning of Symptoms: A Cultural Hermeneutic Model
            of Clinical Practice." Pp. 165–196 in L. Eisenberg and A.
            Kleinman, (eds.), The Relevance of Social Science for
            Medicine. Dordrecht: D. Reidel Publishing Company
Goodman, Martin
1983   State and Society in Roman Galilee, A. D. 132–312. Totowa,
            NJ: Rowman & Allanheld
Goody, Jack
1982   Cooking, Cuisine and Class. A Study in Comparative Sociol-
            ogy. Cambridge: Cambridge University Press
Gottwald, Norman K.
1985   The Hebrew Bible: A Socio-Literary Introduction. Philadel-
            phia: Fortress Press
Grant, Robert M.
1980   "Dietary Laws Among Pythagoreans, Jews and Christians,"
            HTR 73:299–310

Hall, Edward T.
1959   The Silent Language. Garden City, NY: Doubleday
1976   Beyond Culture. Garden City, NY: Doubleday
1983   The Dance of Life: The Other Dimensions of Time. Garden
              City, NY: Doubleday
Halliday, Michael A. K.
1978   Language as Social Semiotic: The Social Interpretation of
              Language and Meaning. Baltimore: University Park Press
Hamilton, Neill Q.
1964   "Temple Cleansing and Temple Bank," JBL 83:365–72
Hammond, Mason
1972   The City in the Ancient World. Cambridge: Harvard Univer-
              sity Press

Harris, Marvin
1985   The Sacred Cow and the Abominable Pig. Riddles in Food
              and Culture. New York: Simon and Schuster, Inc.
Harste, J., C. Burke and V. Woodward
1982   "Children's Language and World: Initial Encounters With
              Print." Pp. 105–31 in J. Langer and M. Smith-Burke (eds.),
              Reader Meets Author: Bridging the Gap—A Psycholinguis-
              tic and Sociolinguistic Perspective. Newark, DE: Interna-
              tional Reading Association

Harvey, A. E.
1976   Jesus on Trial. Altanta: John Knox Press
Havener, Ivan
1987   Q: The Sayings of Jesus. Wilmington, DE: Michael Glazier
              Inc.
Haviland, S. E. and H. H. Clark
1974   "What's New? Acquiring New Information as a Process in
              Comprehension," Journal of Verbal Learning and Verbal
              Behavior 13:512–21

Hay, David M.
1973   Glory at the Right Hand: Psalm 110 in Early Christianity.
              Nashville: Abingdon Press
Heichelheim, F. M.
1959   "Roman Syria." Vol. 4, pp. 121–258 in T. Frank (ed.), An Eco-
              nomic Survey of Ancient Rome. Paterson, NJ: Pageant Books

Hemer, Colin J.
1986   "Medicine in the New Testament World." Pp. 43–83 in Ber-
              nard Palmer (ed.), Medicine and the Bible. Exeter: Pater-
              noster Press
Heschel, Abraham
1969   The Prophets: An Introduction. New York: Harper & Row
Hobsbawm, Eric
1981   Bandits. Rev. ed. New York: Pantheon
Hock, Ronald F.
1980   The Social Context of Paul's Ministry: Tentmaking and
              Apostleship. Philadelphia: Fortress Press
Hollenbach, Paul
1979   "Social Acts of John the Baptizer's Preaching Mission in the
              Context of Palestinian Judaism." Pp. 850–75 in ANRW 19.2
1982a   "Jesus, Demoniacs, and Public Authorities: A Socio-historical
              Study," JAAR 49:567–88

1982b   "The Conversion of Jesus: From Jesus the Baptizer to Jesus the Healer." Pp. 196–219 in *ANRW* 25.1

1985   "Liberating Jesus for Social Involvement," *BTB* 15:151–57

Horsley, Richard A.

1985   "Like One of the Prophets of Old: Two Types of Popular Prophets at the Time of Jesus," *CBQ* 47:435–63

1987   *Jesus and the Spiral of Violence: Popular Jewish Resistance in Roman Palestine.* San Francisco: Harper & Row

Horsley, Richard A., and J. S. Hanson

1985   *Bandits, Prophets, and Messiahs at the Time of Jesus.* San Francisco: Harper & Row

House, Colin

1983   "Defilement by Association: Some Insights from the Usage of *Koinos/Koinoō* in Acts 10 and 11," *AUSS* 21:143–53

Houtart, Francois

1980   *Religion et modes de production precapitalistes.* Brussels: Université de Bruxelles

Hull, John M.

1974   *Hellenistic Magic and the Synoptic Tradition.* Naperville: Alec R. Allenson

Isenberg, Sheldon and Dennis E. Owen

1977   "Bodies, Natural and Contrived: The Work of Mary Douglas," *RelSRev* 3:1–17

Iser, Wolfgang

1972   "The Reading Process: A Phenomenological Approach," *New Literary History* 3:279–89

Jackson, F. J. Foakes and Kirsopp Lake

1979   *The Beginnings of Christianity: The Acts of the Apostles.* Vol. 2. *Prolegonmena II: Criticism.* Reprint ed. Grand Rapids, MI: Baker Book House

Jeremias, Joachim

1955   *The Parables of Jesus.* New York: Scribners

1968   *The Eucharistic Words of Jesus,* 3d ed. Philadelphia: Fortress Press

1969   *Jerusalem in the Time of Jesus.* Philadelphia: Fortress Press

Jervell, Jacob

1972   *Luke and the People of God.* Minneapolis: Augsburg

Johnson, Allen W.

1978   *Quantification in Cultural Anthropology: An Introduction to Research Design.* Palo Alto: Stanford University Press

Johnson, Luke T.

1977   *The Literary Function of Possessions in Luke–Acts.* Missoula, MT: Scholars Press

1983   "James 3:13–4:10 and the *topos peri phthonou*" *NovT* 25:327–47

Jones, A. H. M.

1928   "The Urbanization of Palestine." *Yale Classical Studies* 1:105–68

1971   *The Cities of the Eastern Roman Provinces.* London: Oxford University Press

1974   *The Roman Economy.* Totowa, NJ: Rowan and Littlefield

Jones, C. P.

1978   *The Roman World of Dio Chrysostom.* Cambridge: Harvard University Press

Juel, Donald
    1977   Messiah and Temple. Missoula, MT: Scholars Press
Kampen. N.
    1981   Image and Status: Roman Working Women in Ostia. Berlin:
                Mann
Karris, Robert J.
    1978   "Poor and Rich: The Lukan Sitz im Leben." Pp. 112–25 in
                C. H. Talbert (ed.), Perspectives on Luke–Acts. Danville,
                VA: Association of Baptist Professors of Religion
    1985   Luke: Artist and Theologian. New York: Paulist Press
Kaufman, Gershen
    1974   "The Meaning of Shame: Toward a Self-Affirming Identity,"
                Journal of Counseling Psychology 21:568–74
    1980   Shame: The Power of Caring. Cambridge: Schenkman
Kautsky, John
    1982   The Politics of Aristocratic Empires. Chapel Hill, NC: Univer-
                sity of North Carolina Press
Keel, O.
    1985   The Symbolism of the Biblical World: Ancient Near Eastern
                Iconography and the Book of Psalms. New York: Crossroad
Kelber, Werner
    1976   The Passion in Mark. Philadelphia: Fortress Press
Kilgallen, John J.
    1985   "John the Baptist, the Sinful Woman, and the Pharisee," JBL
                104:675–79
Kim, Chan-Hie
    1975   "The Papyrus Invitation," JBL 94:391–402
King, Karen
    1987   "Kingdom in the Gospel of Thomas," Forum 3:48–97
Kippenberg, Hans
    1978   Religion und Klassenbildung in Antike Judaëa. Göttingen:
                Vandenhoeck & Ruprecht
Kirk, J. A.
    1972   "The Messianic Role of Jesus and the Temptation Narrative: A
                Contemporary Perspective," EvQ 44:11–29, 91–102
Klausner, Joseph
    1925   Jesus of Nazareth. New York: Macmillan
Kleinman, Arthur
    1980   Patients and Healers in the Context of Culture. Berkeley, CA:
                University of California Press
Kluckholm, F. R., and F. L. Strodtbeck
    1961   Variations in Value Orientations. New York: Harper & Row
Kodell, Jerome
    1987   "Luke and the Children: The Beginning and End of the Great
                Interpolation (Luke 9:46–56; 18:9–23)," CBQ 49:415–30
Koenig, John
    1985   New Testament Hospitality: Partnership with Strangers as
                Promise and Mission. Philadelphia: Fortress Press
Kuhn, Karl Georg
    1957   "The Lord's Supper and the Communal Meal at Qumran."
                Pp. 65–93 in Krister Stendahl (ed.), The Scrolls and the
                New Testament. New York: Harper & Brothers

Kurtz, E.
1981   Shame and Guilt: Characteristics of the Dependency Cycle
            (An Historical Perspective for Professionals). Center City,
            MN: Hazelden
Kurz, William
1985   "Luke 22:14-28 and Greco-Roman and Biblical Farewell Ad-
            dresses," JBL 104:251-68
Lampard, Eric E.
1965   "Historical Aspects of Urbanization." Pp. 519-54 in Philip M.
            Hauser and Leo F. Scnore (eds.), The Study of Urbaniza-
            tion. New York: John Wiley & Sons
Lampl, Paul
1968   Cities and Planning in the Ancient Near East. New York:
            George Braziller
Lapidus, I. M.
1986   "Cities and Societies: A Comparative Study of the Emergence
            of Urban Civilization in Mesopotamia and Greece," Jour-
            nal of Urban History 12:257-93
Laszlo, Ervin
1972   The Systems View of the World. New York: George Braziller
Lattimore, Richmond
1959   Hesiod: The Works and Days, Theogony, The Shield of Hera-
            kles. Ann Arbor, MI: The University of Michigan Press
Lee, Bernard J.
1988   The Galilean Jewishness of Jesus: Retrieving the Jewish Ori-
            gins of Christianity. New York: Paulist Press
Leeds, Anthony
1979   "Forms of Urban Integration: Social Urbanization in Compara-
            tive Perspective," Urban Anthropology 8:227-47
1980   "Towns and Villages in Society: Hierarchies of Order and
            Cause." Pp. 6-33 in Thomas W. Collins (ed.), Cities in a
            Larger Context. Athens, GA: University of Georgia Press
Lenski, George
1966   Power and Privilege: A Theory of Social Stratification. New
            York: McGraw-Hill
Lenski, Gerhard and Jean Lenski
1974   Human Societies: An Introduction to Macrosociology. 2d. ed.
            New York: McGraw-Hill
Lévy-Strauss, Claude
1969   The Raw and the Cooked. Chicago: University of Chicago
            Press
Lewellen, Ted C.
1983   Political Anthropology: An Introduction. South Hadley, MA:
            Bergin and Harvey, Inc.
Lohfink, Gerhard
1984   Jesus and Community: The Social Dimension of Christian
            Faith. Philadelphia: Fortress Press
Lohse, Eduard
1971   "Synedrion." Pp. 860-71 in G. Friedrich (ed.), TDNT vol. 7.
            Grand Rapids, MI: Eerdmans
Long, William R.
1983   "The Paulusbild in the Trial of Paul in Acts." SBLASP
            1983:87-105

Lord, Albert R.
1960   The Singer of Tales. New York: Atheneum
Lull, David J.
1986   "The Servant-Benefactor as a Model of Greatness (Luke 22:24–30)," NovT 28:289–30
Lutz, Catherine and Geoffrey M. White
1986   "The Anthropology of Emotions," ARA 15:405–36
McCorkle, Lloyd and Richard Korn
1954   "Resocialization Within Walls," The Annals of the American Academy of Political and Social Science 293:88–98
McGoldrick, Monica, John K. Pearce, and Joseph Giordano
1982   Ethnicity and Family Therapy. New York/London: The Guilford Press
Mack, Burton L. and Vernon K. Robbins
1988   Patterns of Persuasion in the Gospels. Sonoma, CA: Polebridge Press
Mackintosh, Douglas R.
1978   Systems of Health Care. Boulder, CO: Westview Press
MacMullen, Ramsey
1966   Enemies of the Roman Order: Treason, Unrest, and Alienation in the Empire. Cambridge: Harvard University Press
1974   Roman Social Relations: 50 B.C. to A.D. 284. New Haven, CT: Yale University Press

McVann, Mark
1988a   "Markan Ecclesiology: An Anthropological Experiment," Listening: Journal of Religion and Culture 23:95–105
1988b   "The Passion in Mark: Transformation Ritual," BTB 18:96–101

Malherbe, Abraham J.
1983   Social Aspects of Early Christianity. 2d ed. Philadelphia: Fortress Press

Malina, Bruce J.
1978a   "Freedom:A Theological Inquiry into the Dimensions of a Symbol," BTB 8:62–76
1978b   "The Social World Implied in the Letters of the Christian Bishop (Named Ignatius of Antioch)." SBLASP 1978:71–119
1979   "The Individual and the Community – Personality in the Social World of Early Christianity," BTB 9:126–38
1980   "What is Prayer?" TBT 18:214–20
1981   The New Testament World: Insights from Cultural Anthropology. Atlanta: John Knox Press
1982   "The Social Sciences and Biblical Interpretation," Int 37:229–242; reprinted pp. 11–25 in Norman K. Gottwald (ed.), The Bible and Liberation, Maryknoll, NY: Orbis Books
1983   "Why Interpret the Bible with the Social Sciences," ABQ 2:119–33
1984   "Jesus as a Charismatic Leader," BTB 14:55–62
1985   "Review of The First Urban Christians: The Social World of the Apostle Paul," JBL 104:346–49
1986a   Christian Origins and Cultural Anthropology. Atlanta: John Knox Press
1986b   " 'Religion' in the World of Paul," BTB 16:92–101

1986c   "Normative Dissonance and Christian Origins," Pp. 35–59 in
               John H. Elliott (ed.), Social-scientific Criticism of the New
               Testament and Its Social World. Semeia 35
1988a   "Patron and Client: The Analogy Behind Synoptic Theology,"
               Forum 4:2–32
1988b   "Mark 7:1–23: A Conflict Approach," Forum 4/3:3–30
1989   "Christ and Time: Swiss or Mediterranean," CBQ 51:1–31
Malina, Bruce J. and Jerome H. Neyrey
1988   Calling Jesus Names. Sonoma, CA: Polebridge Press
Mannheim, Karl
1968   Ideology and Utopia: An Introduction to the Sociology of
               Knowledge. New York: Harcourt and Brace
Marshall, I. H.
1970   Luke: Historian and Theologian. Exeter: Paternoster
1978   The Gospel of Luke: A Commentary on the Greek Text. Grand
               Rapids, MI: Eerdmans
Marshall, Peter
1983   "A Metaphor of Social Shame: thriambeuein in 2 Cor. 2:14,"
               NovT 25:303–17
Martin, Josef
1931   Symposion. Die Geschichte einer Literarischen Form. Pader-
               born: F. Schoenigh
Matera, Frank J.
1988   "The Death of Jesus According to Luke: A Question of
               Sources," CBQ 47:469–85
Mauss, Marcel
1967   The Gift. The Forms and Functions of Exchange in Archaic
               Societies. New York: Norton
Mayer, Anton
1983   Der zenzierte Jesus: Soziologie des Neuen Testaments. Olten:
               Walter Verlag
Meeks, Wayne A.
1983   The First Urban Christians: The Social World of the Apostle
               Paul. New Haven, CT: Yale University Press
Merton, R. K.
1968   Social Theory and Social Structure. New York: Free Press
Meyer, Bonnie J. F. and G. Elizabeth Rice
1984   "The Structure of Text." Pp. 319–51 in P. David Pearson (ed.),
               Handbook of Reading Research. New York: Longman
Millar, Fergus
1977   The Emperor in the Roman World (31 BC–AD 317). London:
               Duckworth
Mitchell, J. C.
1969   "The Concept and Use of Social Networks." Pp. 1–50 in J. C.
               Mitchell, Social Networks in Urban Situations. Man-
               chester: Manchester University Press
Moessner, D. P.
1982   "Jesus and the 'Wilderness Generation': The Death of the
               Prophet like Moses According to Luke." SBLASP 1982:
               319–40
1983   "Luke 9:1–50: Luke's Preview of the Journey of the Prophet
               like Moses of Deuteronomy," JBL 102:575–605

Moore, Stephen D.
1988   "Stories of Reading: Doing Gospel Criticism as/with a
            'Reader.' " SBLASP 1988: 141–59

Mottu, Henry
1974   "The Pharisee and the Tax Collector: Sartian Notions as Ap-
            plied to the Reading of Scripture," USQR 29:195–213

Moulton, James H. and George Milligan
1974   The Vocabulary of the Greek Testament. Grand Rapids, MI:
            Eerdmans

Moxnes, Halvor
1986   "Meals and the New Community in Luke." SEA 51:158–67
1987   "The Economy in the Gospel of Luke in Light of Social An-
            thropology." Pp. 1–35 in Halvor Moxnes (ed.), Economy in
            the New Testament. Urkristendommen: Prosjektshefte 2.
            Oslo: Universitetet i Oslo
1988   The Economy of the Kingdom: Social Conflict and Economic
            Interaction in Luke's Gospel. Philadelphia: Fortress Press

Mumford, Louis
1961   The City in History: Its Origins, Its Transformations, and Its
            Prospects. New York: Harcourt and Brace

Murdock, George Peter
1980   Theories of Illness: A World Survey. Pittsburgh: University of
            Pittsburgh Press

Murphy-O'Connor, Jerome
1978   "Freedom or Ghetto (I Cor. VIII 1–13; X 23–XI 4)," RB
            85:543–74
1980   "Sex and Logic in 1 Corinthians 11:2–16," CBQ 42:482–500
1984   "The Corinth that Saint Paul Saw," Biblical Archeologist
            47:147–59

Nader, Laura and Harry Todd
1978   The Disputing Process—Law in Ten Societies. New York: Co-
            lumbia University Press

Neusner, Jacob
1973   The Idea of Purity in Ancient Judaism. Leiden: E. J. Brill
1975   "The Idea of Purity in Ancient Judaism," JAAR 43:15–26
1976   " 'First Cleanse the Inside' The 'Halakhic' Background of a
            Controversy Saying," NTS 22:486–95
1978   "History and Purity in First–Century Judaism," HR 18:1–17
1979   "Map Without Territory: Mishnah's System of Sacrifices and
            Sanctuary," HR 19:103–27
1982   "Two Pictures of the Pharisees: Philosophical Circle or Eating
            Club," ATR 64:525–38

Neyrey, Jerome H.
1981   "John III—A Debate of Johannine Epistemology and Christol-
            ogy," NovT 23:115–27
1984   "The Forensic Defense Speech and Paul's Trial Speeches in
            Acts 22–26: Form and Function." Pp. 210–24 in C. H. Tal-
            bert (ed.), Luke–Acts. New Perspectives from the Society of
            Biblical Literature Seminar. New York: Crossroad
1985   The Passion According to Luke. New York: Paulist Press
1986a   "Body Language in 1 Corinthians: The Use of Anthropologi-
            cal Models for Understanding Paul and His Opponents."

Pp. 129–70 in John H. Elliott (ed.), *Social-Scientific Criticism of the New Testament and Its Social World.* Semeia 35

1986b   "The Idea of Purity in Mark." Pp. 91–128 in John H. Elliott (ed.), *Social-Scientific Criticism of the New Testament and Its Social World.* Semeia 35

1987   "Jesus the Judge: Forensic Process in John 8,21–59," *Biblica* 68:509–41

1988a   "Bewitched in Galatia: Paul and Cultural Anthropology," *CBQ* 50:72–100

1988b   "Symbolism in Mark 7," *Forum* 4/3:63–92

Nida, Eugene A.

1975   *Componential Analysis of Meaning: An Introduction to Semantic Structures.* The Hague/New York: Mouton

Nolland, John

1979   "Classical and Rabbinical Parallels to 'Physician, Heal Yourself' (Lk. IV 23)," *NovT* 21:193–209

Oakman, Douglas E.

1986   *Jesus and the Economic Questions of His Day.* Lewiston, NY: The Edwin Mellen Press

Ogbu, John U.

1981   "Origins of Human Competence: A Cultural-Ecological Perspective," *Child Development* 52:413–29

Ohnuki-Tierney, Emiko

1981   *Illness and Healing Among the Sakhalin Ainu: A Symbolic Interpretation.* Cambridge: Cambridge University Press

1984   *Illness and Culture in Contemporary Japan: An Anthropological View.* Cambridge: Cambridge University Press

Ong, Walter J.

1982   *Orality and Literacy: Technologizing of the Word.* New York: Methuen

Papajohn, John and John Speigel

1975   *Transactions in Families.* San Francisco: Jossey-Bass Publications

Patai, Raphael

1983   *The Arab Mind.* Rev. ed. New York: Charles Scribner's Sons

Pepitone, Albert and Harry C. Triandis

1987   "On the Universality of Social Psychological Theories," *Journal of Cross-Cultural Psychology* 18:471–98

Perrin, Norman

1967   *Rediscovering the Teaching of Jesus.* New York: Harper & Row

Pervo, Richard I.

1985   "Wisdom and Power: Petronius' *Satyricon* and the Social World of Early Christianity," *ATR* 67:307–28

1987   *Profit with Delight: The Literary Genre of the Acts of the Apostles.* Philadelphia: Fortress Press

Petersen, Norman R.

1978   *Literary Criticism for New Testament Critics.* Philadelphia: Fortress Press

1985   *Rediscovering Paul: Philemon and the Sociology of Paul's Narrative World.* Philadelphia: Fortress Press

Peterson, T. V.

1987   "Initiation Rite as Riddle," *JRS* 1:73–84

Pfifferling, John-Henry
1981   "A Cultural Prescription for Medicocentrism." Pp. 197–222 in
               L. Eisenberg and A. Kleinman (eds.), *The Relevance of
               Social Science for Medicine*. Dordrecht: D. Reidel Publish-
               ing Company
Pfuhl, Erdwin H.
1980   *The Deviance Process*. New York: van Nostrand
Pilch, John J.
1981   "Biblical Leprosy and Body Symbolism," *BTB* 11:119–33
1985   "Healing in Mark: A Social Science Analysis," *BTB* 15:142–50
1986   "The Health Care System in Matthew: A Social Science An-
               alysis," *BTB* 16:102–106
1988a   "Interpreting Scripture: The Social Science Method," *TBT*
               26:13–19
1988b   "Understanding Biblical Healing: Selecting the Appropriate
               Model," *BTB* 18:60–66
Pilisuk, Mark and Susan Hiller Parks
1986   *The Healing Web: Social Networks and Human Survival*.
               Hanover, NH: University Press of New England
Pitt–Rivers, Julian
1977   *The Fate of Shechem or the Politics of Sex: Essays in the An-
               thropology of the Mediterranean*. Cambridge: Cambridge
               University Press
Plumacher, E.
1972   *Lukas als hellenistischer Schriftsteller: Studien zur Apostelge-
               schichte*. Göttingen: Vandenhoeck & Ruprecht
1974   "Lukas als griechischer Historiker." Pp. 235–64 in G. Wissowa
               (ed.), *Paulys Realencyclopädie der classischen Altertums-
               wissenschaft*. Sup. 14
1977   "Wirklichkeitserfahrung und Geschichtsschreibung bei
               Lukas," *ZNW* 68:2–22
1979   "Die Apostelgeschichte als historische Monographie." Pp.
               457–66 in J. Kremer (ed.), *Les Actes des Apôtres*. BETL
               48. Louvain: Louvain University Press
Plummer, A.
1922   *A Critical and Exegetical Commentary of the Gospel Accord-
               ing to St. Luke*. International Critical Commentary, 5th ed.
               New York: Scribner's Sons
Pokorný, P.
1974   "The Temptation Stories and Their Intention," *NTS* 20:115– 27
Polanyi, Karl, Conrad Arensberg, and Harry Pearson
1957   *Trade and Market in the Early Empires*. Glencoe, IL: Free Press
Polhemus, Ted
1978   *The Body Reader. Social Aspects of the Human Body*. New
               York: Pantheon
Porterfield, A.
1987   "Shamanism: A Psychosocial Definition," *JAAR* 60:721–39
Press, Irwin
1982   "Witch Doctor's Legacy: Some Anthropological Implications
               for the Practice of Clinical Medicine." Pp. 179–88 in N. J.
               Chrisman and T. W. Maretzki (eds.), *Clinically Applied
               Anthropology: Apologists in Health Science Settings*. Dor-
               drecht: D. Reidel Publishing Company

Prochaska, James
1979   Systems of Psychotherapy: A Transtheoretical Analysis.
              Homewood, IL: Dorsey Press
Räisänen, Heikki
1986   "Paul's Theological Difficulties with the Law." Pp. 3–24 in
              The Torah and Christ: Essays in German and English on
              the Problem of the Law in Early Christianity. Helsinki:
              The Finnish Exegetical Society
Rajak, Tessa
1983   Josephus: The Historian and His Society. London: Duckworth
Rappaport, Uriel
1976   "Josephus Ben Matitiahu [Flavius]: Remarks on His Personal-
              ity and Deeds," Ha-Umah 15:89–95 (Hebrew)
Redfield, R. and M. Singer
1954   "The Cultural Role of Cities," Economic Development and
              Cultural Change 3:30–46
Resseguie, J. L.
1982   "Point of View in the Central Section of Luke," JETS 25:41–47
Richard, Earl
1983   "Luke-Writer, Theologian, Historian: Research and Orientation
              of the 1970s," BTB 13:3–15
1984   "The Divine Purpose: The Jews and the Gentile Mission (Acts
              15)." Pp. 188–209 in C. H. Talbert (ed.), Luke–Acts: New
              Perspectives from the Society of Biblical Literature. New
              York: Crossroad
Rinsley, Donald B.
1982   Borderline and Other Self Disorders: A Developmental and
              Object-Relations Perspective. New York: Jason Aronson, Inc.
Robbins, Vernon K.
1978   "By Land and By Sea: The We-Passages and Ancient Sea Voy-
              ages." Pp. 215–42 in Charles H. Talbert (ed.), Perspectives
              on Luke–Acts. Macon, GA: Mercer University Press
1979   "Prefaces in Greco-Roman Biography and Luke–Acts," PRS
              6:94–108
1984   Jesus the Teacher: A Socio-Rhetorical Interpretation of Mark.
              Philadelphia: Fortress Press
1987   "The Woman who Touched Jesus' Garment: Socio-Rhetorical
              Analysis of the Synoptic Accounts," NTS 33:502–15
Rogers, Joseph and M. D. Buffalo
1974   "Fighting Back: Nine Modes of Adaptation to a Deviant
              Label," SP 22:101–18
Rogerson, J. W.
1984   Anthropology and the Old Testament. Sheffield: JSOT Press
Rohrbaugh, Richard L.
1978   The Biblical Interpreter. An Agrarian Bible in an Industrial
              Age. Philadelphia: Fortress Press
1984   "Methodological Considerations in the Debate over the Social
              Class Status of Early Christians," JAAR 52:519–46
1987a   " 'Social Location of Thought' as a Heuristic Construct in
              New Testament Study," JSNT 30:103–119
1987b   "Muddles and Models," Forum 3:23–34
Rostagno, Sergio
1976   "The Bible: Is an Interclass Reading Legitimate?" Pp. 19–25

in *The Bible and Liberation—Political and Social Hermeneutics*. Berkeley, CA: Community for Religious Research and Education

Rostovtzeff, Michael
    1957   *The Social and Economic History of the Roman Empire*. 2 vols. 2d. ed. Oxford: Clarendon Press

Ste. Croix, G. E. M. de.
    1981   *The Class Struggle in the Ancient Greek World*. Ithaca, NY: Cornell University Press

Saadawi, Nawal El
    1982   *The Hidden Face of Eve: Women in the Arab World*. Boston: Beacon Press

Sack, Robert David
    1986   *Human Territoriality: Its Theory and History*. Cambridge: Cambridge University Press

Sahlins, Marshall D.
    1965   "On the Sociology of Primitive Exchange." Pp. 139–236 in Michael Banton (ed.), *The Relevance of Models for Social Anthropology*. Association of Social Anthropologists Monographs 1. London: Tavistock
    1976   *Culture and Practical Reason*. Chicago: University of Chicago Press

Saller, R. P.
    1982   *Personal Patronage under the Early Empire*. Cambridge: Cambridge University Press

Sanders, E. P.
    1983   "Jesus and the Sinners," *JSNT* 19:5–36

Sanders, E. P. (ed.)
    1980   *Jewish and Christian Self-Definition. Volume One: The Shaping of Christianity in the Second and Third Centuries*. Philadelphia: Fortress Press

Sanders, Irwin
    1977   *Rural Sociology*. Englewood Cliffs, NJ: Prentice-Hall

Sanders, J. A.
    1975   "From Isaiah 61 to Luke 4." Pp. 247–71 in J. Neusner (ed.), *Christianity, Judaism and Other Graeco-Roman Cults: Studies for Morton Smith at Sixty*. Part 1. New Testament. Leiden: E. J. Brill

Sanford, A. J. and S. C. Garrod
    1981   *Understanding Written Language: Explorations of Comprehension Beyond the Sentence*. New York: John Wiley and Sons

Scarborough, John
    1982   "Beans, Pythagoreans, Taboos and Ancient Dietetics," *Classical World* 75:355–58

Schaberg, Jane
    1987   *The Illegitimacy of Jesus. A Feminist Theological Interpretation of the Infancy Narratives*. San Francisco: Harper & Row

Scheff, Thomas J.
    1968   "Negotiating Reality: Notes on Power in the Assessment of Responsibility," *SP* 16:1–17

Schiffman, Lawrence H.
    1979   "Communal Meals at Qumran," *RevQ* 10:45–56

Schmidt, Steffen, James Scott, Carl Landé and Laura Guasti
1977   Friends, Followers and Factions. A Reader in Political Clien-
              telism. Berkeley, CA: University of California Press
Schneider, Jane and Peter Schneider
1976   Culture and Political Economy in Western Sicily. New York:
              Academic Press
Schottroff, Luise
1987   "Das Gleichnis vom grossen Gastmahl in der Logienquelle,"
              EvT 47:192–211
Schottroff, Luise and Wolfgang Stegemann
1986   Jesus and the Hope of the Poor. Maryknoll, NY: Orbis Books
Schur, Edwin M.
1971   Labeling Deviant Behavior. Its Sociological Implications. New
              York: Harper & Row
1980   The Politics of Deviance: Stigma Contests and the Uses of
              Power. Englewood Cliffs, NJ: Prentice-Hall
Schurmann, H.
1969   Das Lukasevangelium. Freiberg: Herder
Scott, B. B.
1986   " 'Essaying the Rock': The Authenticity of the Jesus Parable
              Tradition," Forum 2/1:3–53
Scott, James C.
1977   The Moral Economy of the Peasant: Rebellion Subsistence in
              Southeast Asia. New Haven, CT: Yale University Press
Scroggs, Robin
1986   "Sociology and the New Testament," Listening: Journal of Re-
              ligion and Culture 21:138–47
Seccombe, D. P.
1980   Possessions and the Poor in Luke–Acts. Linz: Studien zum
              Neuen Testament und seiner Umwelt
Segal, Alan
1986   "Romans 7 and Jewish Dietary Law," Sciences Religieuses/
              Studies in Religion 15:361–74
Selby, Henry
1974   Zapotec Deviance: The Convergence of Folk and Modern Soci-
              ology. Austin, TX: University of Texas Press
Senior, Donald
1975   The Passion Narrative According to Matthew. A Redactional
              Study. Leuven: University Press
Sherwin–White, A. N.
1963   Roman Law and Roman Society in the New Testament. Ox-
              ford: Oxford University Press
Silverman, S.
1977   "Patronage as Myth." Pp. 7–20 in E. Gellner and J. Waterbury
              (eds.), Patrons and Clients in Mediterranean Societies.
              London: Duckworth
Simon, Marcel
1967   Jewish Sects at the Time of Jesus. Philadelphia: Fortress Press
1970   "The Apostolic Decree and Its Setting in the Ancient
              Church," BJRL 52:437–60
Simonds, A. P.
1978   Karl Mannheim's Sociology of Knowledge. Oxford: Clarendon

Sjoberg, Gideon
1960   The Preindustrial City. New York: Macmillan
Smith, Dennis E.
1980   Social Obligation in the Context of Communal Meals. Unpub-
            lished Th.D. thesis: Harvard University
1987   "Table Fellowship as a Literary Motif in the Gospel of Luke,"
            JBL 106:613–38
Smith, Jonathan Z.
1978   Map Is Not Territory. Leiden: E. J. Brill
Snow, David A., Louis A. Zurcher Jr., and Sheldon Ekland–Olson
1980   "Social Networks and Social Movements: A Microstructural
            Approach to Differential Recruitment," ASR 45:787–801
Soler, Jean
1979   "The Dietary Prohibitions of the Hebrews," New York Review
            of Books June 14:24–30. Reprinted pp. 126–38 in Robert
            Forster and Orest Ranum (eds.), Food and Drink in His-
            tory. Baltimore: Johns Hopkins University Press
Sorokin, Pitirim, Carl Zimmerman, and Charles Galpin
1930–1932 Systematic Source Book in Rural Sociology. 3 vols. Minneap-
            olis: University of Minnesota Press
Staley, Jeffrey Lloyd
1988   The Print's First Kiss: A Rhetorical Investigation of the Im-
            plied Reader in the Fourth Gospel. SBLDS 82. Atlanta:
            Scholars Press
Stannard, David E.
1980   Shrinking History: On Freud and the Failure of Psychohistory.
            New York: Oxford University Press
Steele, E. Springs
1984   "Luke 11:37–54 – A Modified Hellenistic Symposium?" JBL
            103:379–94
Stein, S.
1957   "The Influence of Symposia Literature on the Literary Form
            of the Pesah Haggadah," JJS 8:13–44
Stendahl, Krister
1963   "The Apostle Paul and the Introspective Conscience of the
            West," HTR 56:199–215
Stoops, R. F.
1986   "Patronage in the Acts of Peter," Semeia 38:91–100
Strack, Hermann L. and Paul Billerbeck
1961   "Die altjudische Privatwohltätigkeit"; "Die altjudische Liebes-
            werke." Pp. 536–58 and 559–610 in Kommentar zum
            Neuen Testament aus Talmud und Midrasch. Vol. 4/1. 3d
            ed. Munich: Beck
Sykes, Gresham and David Matza
1957   "Techniques of Neutralization: A Theory of Delinquency,"
            ASR 22:664–70
Talbert, Charles H.
1974   Literary Patterns, Theological Themes, and the Genre of
            Luke–Acts. Missoula, MT: Scholars Press
1977   What Is a Gospel? The Genre of the Canonical Gospels.
            Philadelphia: Fortress Press
1984a   Reading Luke: A Literary and Theological Commentary on the
            Third Gospel. New York: Crossroad

1984b   "Promise and Fulfillment in Lukan Theology." Pp. 91–103 in
Luke–Acts. New Perspectives from the Society of Biblical
Literature Seminar. New York: Crossroad

Tannehill, Robert C.
1986   The Narrative Unity of Luke–Acts: A Literary Interpretation.
Philadelphia: Fortress Press

Taylor, A. B.
1960   "Decision in the Desert: The Temptation of Jesus in the Light
of Deuteronomy," Int 14:300–309

Thackeray, H. St. John
1929   Josephus: The Man and the Historian. New York: Jewish Insti-
tute of Religion

Theissen, Gerd
1976   "Die Tempelweissagung Jesu: Prophetie im Spannungsfeld
von Stadt und Land," TZ 32:144–58
1978   The Sociology of Early Palestinian Christianity. Philadelphia:
Fortress Press
1987   Psychological Aspects of Pauline Theology. Philadelphia: Fortress Press

Tiede, David L.
1980   Prophecy and History in Luke–Acts. Philadelphia: Fortress Press

Todd, Emmanuel
1985   The Explanation of Ideology: Family Structures and Social
Systems. Oxford: Basil Blackwell

Turner, Ralph
1972   "Deviance Avowal as Neutralization of Commitment," SP
19:307–21

Turner, Victor
1962   Chihamba, the White Spirit. Rhodes-Livingston Papers 33.
Manchester: Manchester University Press
1967   The Forest of Symbols: Aspects of Ndembu Ritual. Ithaca:
Cornell University Press
1969   The Ritual Process: Structure and Anti-Structure. Ithaca: Cornell University Press
1974   Dramas, Fields, and Metaphors: Symbolic Action in Human
Society. Ithaca: Cornell University Press
1979   Process, Performance, and Pilgrimage: A Study in Comparative Symbology. New Dehli: Concept

Tyson, J. B.
1983   "Acts 6:1–7 and Dietary Regulations in Early Christianity,"
PRS 10:145–61

Vanhoye, Albert
1986   "Personnalité de Paul et exégèse paulinienne." Pp. 3–15 in
Albert Vanhoye (ed.), L'apôtre Paul: Personnalité, style et
conception du ministère. Leuven: Leuven University/-
Peeters

van Unnik, W. C.
1980   "Solitude and Community in the New Testament." Pp. 241–47
in his Sparsa Collecta II. NovTSup 30. Leiden: E. J. Brill

Veltman, Fred
1978   "The Defense Speeches of Paul in Acts." Pp. 243–56 in
Charles H. Talbert (ed.), Perspectives on Luke–Acts. Dan-
ville, VA: Association of Baptist Professors of Religion

Walaskay, Peter W.
1975   "The Trial and Death of Jesus in the Gospel of Luke," *JBL*
               94:81–93
1983   *"And So We Came to Rome": The Political Perspective of St.
               Luke.* Cambridge: Cambridge University Press
Walcott, Peter
1978   *Envy and the Greeks: A Study of Human Behavior.* Warmin-
               ster: Ares and J. Phillips Waterbury
1977   "An Attempt to Put Patrons and Clients in Their Place." Pp.
               329–42 in E. Gellner and J. Waterbury (eds.), *Patrons and
               Clients in Mediterranean Societies.* London: Duckworth
Waterbury, J.
1977   "An Attempt to Put Patrons and Clients in Their Place." Pp.
               329–42 in E. Gellner and J. Waterbury (eds.), *Patrons and
               Clients in Mediterranean Societies.* London: Duckworth
Weber, Max
1976   *The Agrarian Sociology of Ancient Civilizations.* Atlantic
               Highlands, NJ: Humanities Press
Weidman, Hazel Hitson
1982   "Research Strategies, Structural Alterations and Clinically Ap-
               plied Anrhopology." Pp. 201–41 in N. J. Chrisman and T.
               W. Maretzki (eds.), *Clinically Applied Anthropology:
               Apologists in Health Science Settings.* Dordrecht: D. Rei-
               del Publishing Company
Weinert, Francis D.
1981   "The Meaning of the Temple in Luke–Acts," *BTB* 11:85–89
1982   "Luke, the Temple and Jesus' Saying about Jerusalem's Aban-
               doned House," *CBQ* 44:68–76
Whitfield, Charles L.
1987   *Healing the Child Within.* Pompano Beach, FL: Health Com-
               munications Inc.
Wikan, Unni
1984   "Shame and Honor: A Contestable Pair," *Man* 19:635–52
Williams, Robin M. Jr.
1970   *American Society: A Sociological Interpretation.* 3d ed. New
               York: Knopf
Wilson, Christine
1979   "Food–Custom and Nurture: An Annotated Bibliography on
               Socio–cultural and Biocultural Aspects of Nutrition,"
               Journal of Nutrition Education 11 no. 4 Supplement 1:211–
               64
Wirth, Louis
1938   "Urbanism as a Way of Life," *AJS* 44:1–24
1951   "The Urban Society and Civilization," *American Journal of
               Oriental Studies* 45:743–55
Wolf, E. R.
1966   *Peasants.* Englewood Cliffs, NJ: Prentice-Hall.
Wolff, Janet
1981   *The Social Production of Art.* New York: St. Martin's Press
Worsley, Peter
1982   "Non-Western Medical Systems," *ARA* 11:315–48
Young, Allan
1982   "The Anthropology of Illness and Sickness," *ARA* 11:257–85

INDEX OF TOPICS

INDEX OF MODERN AUTHORS

INDEX OF SCRIPTURE PASSAGES